CONTEMPORARY EDUCATIONAL ISSUES

. . .

THE CANADIAN MOSAIC

Second Edition

CONTEMPORARY EDUCATIONAL ISSUES

•

THE CANADIAN MOSAIC

Second Edition

■

Edited by

Leonard L. Stewin
University of Alberta

and

Stewart J.H. McCann
University College of Cape Breton

▲

Copp Clark Pitman Ltd.
A Longman Company
Toronto

Any request for photocopying, recording, taping, or for storing on information and retrieval systems of any part of this book shall be directed in writing to the Canadian Reprography Collective, 214 King Street West, Suite 312, Toronto, Ontario, M5H 3S6.

ISBN: 0-7730-5284-4

Executive Editor: Jeff Miller
Editing: Maral Bablanian, Pamela Erlichman
Design: Gary Beelik
Typesetting: Andrea Weiler
Printing and binding: Edwards Brothers Incorporated

Canadian Cataloguing in Publication Data
Main entry under title:
Contemporary educational issues: the Canadian mosaic

2nd ed.
Includes bibliographic references.

ISBN 0-7730-5284-4
1. Education–Canada. I. Stewin, Leonard L.
II. McCann, Stewart J.H.

LA412.C65 1993   370'.971   C92-095790-0

Copp Clark Pitman Ltd.
2775 Matheson Blvd. East
Mississauga, Ontario
L4W 4P7

Associated companies:
Longman Group Ltd., London
Longman Inc., New York
Longman Cheshire Pty., Melbourne
Longman Paul Pty., Auckland

Printed and bound in the United States of America

2   3   4   5   5284-4   97   96   95   94

Contents

...

Contents

Contents

ACKNOWLEDGEMENTS

Many individuals have contributed to the successful completion of this book. We would like to thank, first of all, the contributors who made this volume possible.

We would also like to thank every person at Copp Clark Pitman who participated in the various stages of the publication process to bring this work to fruition. In particular, we would like to thank Jeff Miller, Barbara Tessman, Pamela Erlichman, and our editor, Maral Bablanian, for her commitment to the project, her attention to detail, and her gentle prodding to keep the book on schedule.

Stewart McCann would like to thank Margaret MacLeod for carrying out several word processing tasks with efficiency and good humour. He is also thankful for the other forms of support provided by the University College of Cape Breton. Finally, he would like to thank Patricia, his wife, for her continued support, understanding, and patience throughout the course of this project.

Leonard Stewin would like to extend his thanks and appreciation to Casey Boodt for his assistance with the preliminary overviews and the ongoing tasks associated with the compiling and organization of this volume. He is also appreciative of the continuing support of the University of Alberta. Last, but not least, he would like to thank his wife, Carol Chandler, for her never ending encouragement, support, and caring.

L. L. S.
S. J. H. M.
December, 1992

INTRODUCTION

The impetus for the first edition of this book grew from the challenge of developing a senior undergraduate educational issues course at the University of Alberta that was to have an interdisciplinary flavour and a firm focus on the Canadian educational milieu. In our opinion, a suitable text did not exist. During the fifteen years prior to the publication of the first edition, perhaps a half dozen books had been published that purportedly dwelled on Canadian educational issues. We found, however, that for our purposes, the material was outdated, or the coverage was too limited in scope, or there was not a clear enough emphasis on Canadian concerns. We felt the need for a substantial book of original readings comprising the Canadian educational issues that were surfacing most often in professional journals, conferences, and symposia as well as those issues that were attracting a great deal of popular attention in newspapers, magazine articles, radio talk shows, and television documentaries.

The second edition, as the first edition, is especially intended for a senior undergraduate audience. We feel that it can be most profitably employed in educational psychology courses, foundations courses, sociology of education courses, Canadian studies courses, and interdisciplinary courses where the principal intent is to survey and discuss the most common, current, and pressing issues facing educators in Canada today and, in particular, facing those who are soon to enter the teaching field. The book may also prove to be beneficial as a convenient resource for in-service and professional development wherein practitioners may examine some of the contemporary issues under one cover.

Before discussing the structure of the current edition, a few words are in order about how the issues and the authors were selected for the first edition. Through a multifaceted process including perusal of tables of content in relevant journals, examination of pertinent indexes of educational publication directories, general attention to popular media content that seemed to pertain to educational issues in a Canadian context, and varieties of editorial brainstorming, we managed to develop a rather broad list of issues we felt could be of importance to the project. Subsequently, some issues were pooled, some were subdivided, and some were made more specific. Some issues were rejected because their importance was on the wane, others were dropped because they were too localized, and many were discarded, not because they were unimportant educational issues, but because they were not deemed to be sufficiently "Canadian." Eventually, the issues were categorized under general themes, and these groups became the sections of the first edition.

By searching the indexes of various directories and abstracting services, by surveying the contents of more recent educational periodicals, and by appealing through academic grapevines, we managed to locate potential authors who ostensibly could produce papers related to most of the issues left on our still rather lengthy short list. Each of the potential authors had to meet two fundamental criteria: each had to be an experienced author with prior publication in the area concerned with our selected topic, and each had to be affiliated with a Canadian institution of higher education. In our initial contact with possible contributors, we provided a brief overview of the aim and structure of our book and asked the targeted author if he or she would be interested in producing an article on some aspect of an issue we had selected based on our needs and our knowledge of his or her interest area. We also specifically instructed potential writers to direct their efforts toward a fourth-year university audience and to feel free to bring in more general content than might ordinarily be allowed in most academic journals. The response to our requests for contributions was overwhelmingly positive, and we were enthusiastically encouraged to proceed.

The articles chosen for the first edition were written from a range of perspectives and traditions reflective of the multiplicity of backgrounds and disciplines spanned by the authors. We provided only minimal orchestration for the contributors and relied on their proven competence and expertise to produce chapters that discussed the topics in whatever fashions they felt might be appropriate. The authors spoke for themselves; occasional alterations were made in form but not in content.

We made no claim for an exhaustive selection of issues for the first edition but the ones chosen do appear to have comprised the more dominant issues of the day that had fundamentally Canadian implications, or at least implications that could be tailored for the Canadian context. No single volume can cover everything, but we did want the scope of the issues to be rather broad and diverse since the book was primarily intended for undergraduate courses where the main goal is the survey and discussion of contemporary problems and issues facing Canadian education.

The structure of the first edition evolved as we developed the list of suitable topics and as we received papers from our authors. The final order of sections in the first edition emerged somewhere in midstream, and the most appropriate sequence of papers within a section often only became apparent once all of the submissions for a section had been examined. In some cases, perhaps, arguments could have been made for alternative organization, but we believe we produced a rational and satisfying structure for the contributions that were included.

Essentially, the aims, editorial procedures, and structure of the first edition have been maintained in the production of the second edition. Fifteen popular and still timely chapters from the first edition were selected for the second edition, and the authors were given the opportunity to revise their contributions in light of recent developments. In some cases the revisions were very extensive, while in others the revisions were minor. In addition, fourteen new chapters have been produced by authors who did not appear in the first edition.

Continuing the theme of the first edition, several contributors to the second edition demonstrate how the Charter of Rights and Freedoms has prompted a reevaluation of a host of educational practices in Canada. Clearly, the full impact of this major constitutional change remains to be seen. In line with this theme, authors in Section 1 of our new volume deal specifically with human rights in Canadian education, discussing teacher and pupil rights and the courts; legal rights, duties, and responsibilities of classroom teachers; emerging issues in human rights education; and minority education rights.

Canada is a complex multicultural society and our fondness for the preservation of ethnic pluralism has created special problems for Canadian schooling systems. In Section 2, the authors examine issues arising from our ethnic diversity, such as the implications of ethnicity for teaching, the special attention that must be given to Native education, and the issues of prejudice and discrimination.

There is a growing consensus that the school must play a more active role in responding to a variety of social problems and issues that result from rapid changes and transitions occurring in our social fabric. In Section 3, the authors address the changing relationship between the school and the family; the emerging crisis in preschool education; the changing status of women and the attendant gender issues in education; and issues arising from the faltering of our traditional ways to inculcate values, our confusion of values, morals, and rules, and the implications for values education. The chapters of Section 4 are concerned with sex education in the schools, the role of the educator in coping with substance abuse, literacy issues, the dropout problem, and controversies surrounding censorship in Canadian schools.

Changing legislation regarding human rights has made us even more acutely aware of our educational responsibilities to not only the "typical" child but also the "exceptional" child. Over the past twenty years, we have become increasingly conscious of the desirability of affording all children appropriate educational opportunities regardless of their academic aptitude and their special needs. The Charter of Rights and Freedoms has spurred this movement. We appear to be more willing to modify our educational programs and criteria to accommodate differing student potentials. The authors in Section 5 discuss a number of educational and legal issues involving students at both ends of the spectrum.

Alterations resulting from human rights legislation, the implications of increasing ethnic diversity, the school's expanded role in relation to social problems and issues, and broadened services for exceptional children will, of necessity, lead to changes in teacher training and curriculum development in Canada. The authors in Section 6 examine many of the issues facing those involved in teacher education and curriculum development and suggest possible directions for the future.

The entire book is essentially about change. The problems and issues discussed by our authors largely result from changes—changes in human rights policy and legislation, in information and transportation technology, in demographics and family patterns, in values, in the status of women, in economic conditions, and in the balance of power. Education at all levels is undergoing a process of evaluation and redirection. The authors in Section 7 continue this theme of change by examining current developments that may have a marked influence on the future of education in Canada in the 1990s and in the twenty-first century. Discussed in this section are educational issues hinging on advances in computer technology, issues centred on teaching French as a second language, the pros and cons of using national standardized testing to reach educational decisions, and the profound nature of the whole language debate.

From the list of contributors that appears at the back of the current edition it is apparent that we have drawn on a wealth of knowledge, expertise, and experience. The second edition was written by some outstanding academics with current positions in government, universities, and colleges throughout the country.

HUMAN RIGHTS IN CANADIAN EDUCATION

...

Since 1982 the Canadian Charter of Rights and Freedoms has served as a potent catalyst for the evaluation of human rights in various facets of our educational system. The contributors in this section examine several issues resulting from the impact on the rights and responsibilities of educators and students of this renovation of our legal structure.

Magsino traces the transformations in teachers' and students' rights and obligations that have taken place as a result of Supreme Court decisions in the United States. Drawing parallels between Canada and the United States, he concludes that a similar transitional process has been set in motion by our Charter. He points out that, even though few cases have been heard or are pending, to ensure the protection of individual rights and freedoms, future court decisions will undoubtedly have repercussions on educational practices. Magsino argues that the Charter will result in changes in policy and procedure in Canadian education even though federal courts have traditionally been reluctant to interfere with the administration of our educational system.

Ray, in discussing some emerging issues in human rights education, stresses the responsibility of the schools to foster critical examination of human rights and their violations, and to encourage the development of ways in which conflicts over human rights may be resolved. He emphasizes the promotion of human rights through developmental education, peace education, global education, and through the understanding and support of all minorities who are limited in the extent to which they can effect their own destiny.

Eberlein provides a discussion of the rights, duties, and responsibilities of the classroom teacher, particularly in regard to discipline, classroom management, unintentional torts or negligence, and affirmative duty to act. Since there is clearly a lack of teacher training centred legal ramifications that might arise from teacher practices, this chapter, as an overview of legal and ethical concerns for the teacher, serves as a valuable springboard for future investigations of issues pertaining to the teacher's own position. The emphasis is on common sense, communication skills, and preplanning strategies in order to prevent situations with negative retroactive legal consequences. A code of ethics for teachers is also proposed.

The question of minority education rights is part of a larger issue concerning human rights. Burgess discusses the experience of Treaty Indians, Roman Catholics in some provinces, and Quebec Protestants within a historical context to demonstrate the weakness of constitutional protection for these groups. The issue of minority language rights is then explored with reference to Quebec and the evolution of section 23 of the Charter of Rights and Freedoms.

TEACHER AND PUPIL RIGHTS AND THE COURTS:
AN EXPLORATION OF STABILITY AND CHANGE

...

Romulo F. Magsino

THE LAW AND SOCIAL CHANGE

There is a recurrent controversy in legal history between those who believe that law should essentially follow clearly formulated social sentiment and those who believe that the law should create new social norms. In his pioneering study in the late 1950s, Friedmann concluded that the latter had emerged triumphant. He also noted that there is a variety of ways by which the law could foster social change. A determined "individual or small minority group may initiate and pursue a legal change in the face of governmental or parliamentary lethargy and an indifferent public opinion" (Friedmann, 1964, p. 25).

The United States, from the 1950s onward, provides a clear example of a society where a non-elected legal elite employed the law to bring about social and institutional changes in the country. Consisting of nine politically independent jurists, the U.S. Supreme Court penned, with profound potential for wide-ranging changes, major constitutional doctrines related in particular to equality in race relations, administration of criminal justice, the operation of the political process, and school law. Whatever the extent of changes, what is known as the Warren Court (after the chief justice, Earl Warren) opened the door for extensive societal reform through its constitutional decisions. The present Court, dominated by justices with conservative leanings, has frequently shown judicial restraint and deferred to the legislative wisdom of elected representatives (Davis, 1991; Lamb & Halpern, 1991; Rice, 1987). However, it has demonstrated how the law could be used to initiate new directions for society.

The reformist approach to American law attracted committed adherents among Canadian legal scholars. One prominent sympathizer was former professor of law, Pierre Trudeau. He attributed Canada's serious political and cultural problems to inadequacies in our fundamental law and to lack of action in correcting these legal flaws (Milne, 1982). As prime minister, he pushed the idea of renovating the country's legal structure and, in 1982, succeeded in patriating the Canadian Constitution with an entrenched Charter of Rights and Freedoms. The long-term changes that will occur following the new Constitution and the Charter are a matter of speculation. One thing is certain, however. Trudeau's constitutional success has opened up possibilities for liberal or reformist justices to act, using the Charter, as agents of societal change.

The functions of the Canadian federal courts have largely been the same as those of the U.S. Supreme Court. They can define the meaning of constitutional rights provisions and resolve all questions related to the constitutional protection of individual rights. Yet, in contrast with their American counterparts, Canadian federal courts have shied away in the past from breaking paths toward new societal policies. Legal scholars ascribe this at least in part to the absence of constitutionally guaranteed individual rights. But, as Sedler (1984) put it,

> With the entrenchment of individual rights in Canada by the promulgation of the charter, the structures of constitutional governance established by the Canadian and United States constitutions have moved more into congruence. In Canada, as in the United States, there are now constitutional limitations on the exercise of governmental power designed to protect individual rights and, under the constitutional systems of both nations, the courts can provide relief against governmental action that they find to be violative of those provisions. (p. 1202)

Indeed, section 24 of the Charter specifically invites anyone, whose rights or freedoms have been infringed or denied, to apply for remedy to a court of competent jurisdiction. Canadians have responded to this invitation and massive litigation has given the courts much opportunity to interpret the vaguely worded provisions of the Charter. However, it remains a matter of debate whether legal restraint or legal reformism will eventually predominate.

• • •

THE COURTS AND CHANGING ENTITLEMENTS IN EDUCATION: THE AMERICAN EXAMPLE

Teachers' Rights

The role that courts play in altering societal perceptions and relationships shows in the U.S. Supreme Court's decisions affecting the rights of teachers. There is no question that, prior to the 1950s, it was common practice to regulate wide-ranging aspects of teachers' lives in a way that would appear offensive today. As absurd as it might seem, American female teachers in the nineteenth century were required, among other things, "not to fall in love," "to abstain from dancing," and "to consider themselves willing servants of the [school] board and the townspeople" (Schimmel & Fischer, 1974, p. 262).

Such requirements were part of regulations that educational systems have used to govern teachers' grooming, sexual conduct, non-curricular speech, and other behaviours. Local school boards derived their power to establish requirements and to discipline teachers from state legislation that either proscribed specific conduct or delegated broad regulatory and disciplinary authority to school boards. This power was reinforced by a legal doctrine that public employment was a privilege to which the state could attach certain conditions. These conditions could be used to restrict the employee's freedoms and rights, subject only to the ill-defined limitation that such conditions be reasonable.

Fortunately, teachers at public institutions finally started to receive increased protection against interferences by school boards and school officials in their professional and personal lives. In a 1967 case, the U.S. Supreme Court explicitly discredited the doctrine of public employment as privilege. In its ruling, the Court rejected, as an Appeals Court in the same case had done, the doctrine that public employment (which may be denied altogether) may be subjected to any condition, regardless of how unreasonable such condition might be (*Keyishian v. Board of Regents*, 1967). This ruling has placed teachers on an equal footing with all public employees protected against unconstitutional conditions. Subsequently, teachers have won cases involving freedom of speech in the classroom, freedom of speech outside the classroom, personal sexual activities, personal appearance, and membership in controversial organizations.

There are, however, cases that teachers have lost involving similar issues. Although courts have strongly supported the right of teachers to express their beliefs freely in the schools, they have curtailed this right when certain state interests, such as the communication of fundamental values and the preservation of order in the schools, are involved. Still the burden of proof lies with school boards that are dismissing teachers, in light of the Court's conclusion in the *Pickering v. Board of Education* case: "A teacher's exercise of his right to speak on issues of public importance may not furnish the basis for his dismissal from public employment (p. 573)." Teachers' personal conduct and appearance have not always drawn support from the courts either. Particularly because of the strong influence that teachers exercise over their pupils at the elementary and even secondary levels, courts have tended to balance educational consideration against teachers' liberty. Still, Fischer and Schimmel (1982) have concluded that to dismiss teachers' liberty, it must be demonstrated that their private activity affects their ability to teach. They also found that, "As long as his competence as a teacher is not affected, most courts hold that his private acts are his own business" (p. 135). This is quite a departure from an earlier era when women teachers were required not to get engaged or secretly married.

Student Rights

Not too long ago, legal critics could complain that students were being treated worse than hardened criminals. While the latter had been enjoying due process rights (such as being informed of charges, having legal counsel, defending one-self at a fair hearing, etc.), students could be instantly suspended or expelled by school officials.

This differential treatment of students was inevitably intertwined with their status as children. Until recently, children were regarded as chattels of the family or wards of the state, with no recognized political power and few legal rights. To some degree, their situation was improved by the "child-saving" movement in the late 1800s and early 1900s. This movement secured legislation designed to protect children (e.g., laws regulating child labour or penalizing parents for abuse of their young) and to establish institutions for their education or reform (e.g., laws establishing compulsory schooling or juvenile court systems). Yet, as Platt (1969) found, the movement so assumed the "natural" dependence and incompetence of the young that the institutions it helped establish were charac-terized by paternalism and use of force.

To what degree American schools were influenced by the assumptions of the "child-saving" movement is uncertain. What is obvious, however, is that in con-trast with students' lack of rights or power, decision makers were permitted enormous discretion in enforcing established norms. Whether deriving from the common law doctrine of *in loco parentis*, which allowed educators as parental sur-rogates to determine students' conduct, or from state laws that delegated power to governmental bodies like school boards, school control over students was generally accepted. This acceptance was reinforced by judicial deference to edu-cational authority as, in case after case, the courts upheld action or policies by educators (Berkman, 1970).

The landmark case paving the way for the recognition of the rights of young people in the United States is *In re Gault* handed down by the Supreme Court in 1967. The Court ruled that a fifteen-year-old boy who had been committed by a juvenile court judge to an industrial school without observing due process requirements was unfairly treated. Young people like Gault, the Court declared, have the constitutional right to notice of charges, to counsel, to the privilege against self-incrimination, and to a hearing. Decisively it stated: "Neither the Fourteenth Amendment nor the Bill of Rights is for adults alone" (*In re Gault*, 1967, p. 13).

Subsequently, the Court decided in *Tinker v. Des Moines* (1969) that children are persons under the U.S. Constitution, "possessed of fundamental rights which the state must respect." It held that students are entitled to freedom of expression of their views, unless schools can show valid constitutional reasons to regulate such freedom. Then, in 1975, the Court applied the *Gault* pronouncement to the school situation. In *Goss v. Lopez* (1975) it ruled that schools are required to set up hearing procedures before students can be suspended. Such procedures should minimally include notification of the charges, presentation of evidence if the students request it, and the opportunity to argue their side of the conflict. *Wood v. Strickland* (1975) showed the Court's seriousness when it held school officials liable for damages (by fine and/or imprisonment) if they maliciously abridged the civil rights of students.

Ten years after the *Goss* and *Wood* decisions, the Court seemingly executed a turnaround when it decided *New Jersey v. T.L.O.* (1985). The Court ruled that a school official's search of a student's purse, based on a report that the student had been smoking, was not a violation of the student's constitutional rights. The Court differentiated between searches in non-school situations, which ordinarily would require probable cause to believe that a crime or violation of the law had been committed, and searches in school situations where legality simply requires reasonableness. However, to conclude, based on this decision, that the Court had turned around to deny students' constitutional right to privacy is erroneous. Here, the issue was simply the standard to be used in safeguarding this right. For the Court, the constitutional validity of the young's right to privacy was not contentious at all. Nonetheless, the Court's signal about the limited nature of students' rights was a real one. In *Bethel School District v. Fraser* (1986), the Court ruled in favour of the school board that penalized a student for an obscene and sexually suggestive nominating speech. Noting that although adults may not be prohibited in the use of an offensive form of expression in making what may be considered a political point, it denied the same latitude with respect to public school children. In *Hazelwood School District v. Kuhlmeier* (1988), the Court sustained the case of a principal who deleted two pages from an issue of a student newspaper because of their inappropriate content related to pregnancy, sexual activity, and birth control. It declared that schools need not tolerate student speech inconsistent with their basic educational mission.

It appears that, for the American courts, students' rights do not coincide with adult rights, and neither do teachers' rights with those of adults in general. Still, their status has been transformed from what it was barely twenty or thirty years ago. It is difficult to imagine this successful transformation had the American Supreme Court not led the way.

• • •

TEACHER AND STUDENT RIGHTS IN CANADA: EXPLORING PRESENT REALITIES

The issue of teachers' academic and civil rights has not seen much litigation in Canada. Why this is so awaits a socio-historical study that has yet to be initiated. A possible explanation emerges, however, when we consider the analogous situation of students. Sweezy (1969) critically observed that student cases seldom reached the courts due to the immense discretionary power wielded by school authorities; to a lack of precedents because lawyers, uncertain of litigation in this area, tended to settle out of court or to refuse handling school regulation disputes; and, more importantly, to a doubt that students could invoke constitutional rights to support their cause. These factors might equally have discouraged teachers from pursuing academic and civil rights grievances.

Academic and Civil Rights of Teachers

As McCurdy (1968) observed, there are very few statutory provisions in Canada that distinguish the teacher from any other citizen, professional or otherwise, in the full exercise of academic and civil rights. In the absence of relevant distinctions, he advised teachers to assume and exercise such rights for themselves. Still, we could doubt that teachers would have found it easy to follow this advice. The common law tradition, which defines the school board-teacher relationship as a master-servant or employer-employee relationship, where the latter party could be discharged if he or she turned out to be unfit, could be dissociated only with great difficulty from teachers' perceptions of their academic and civil liberties. This tradition has been reinforced by legislation passed by provincial governments exercising their constitutional powers over educational matters. This legislation—generally called the "Education Act" or "School Act"—establishes departments of education and school boards with wide-ranging authority. When we relate such authority to the fact that most educational legislation in Canada

allowed summary dismissals of teachers for cause or for such reasons as gross misconduct, inefficiency, immorality, insubordination, and the like, we can understand teachers' hesitation to test the limits of their academic and civil rights.
Add, on top of all this, the generally conservative tone of Canadian communities
and the lack of civil rights guarantees in this country in the past, and we end up
with a psychologically insurmountable barrier against the pursuit of academic
and civil rights cases by teachers.

This is not to say that teachers have had no protection against governmental
agencies employing them. Appropriate legislation has specified procedures to
validate and formalize school board-teacher contracts and relationships
(McCurdy, 1968). These procedures serve to prevent capricious and malicious
actions by school boards. Thus, teachers facing the prospect of termination from
service have been entitled to notice and reasons for dismissal, and to inquiry by
an investigating committee or a board of reference.

The courts have, consistently over the years, upheld sections of laws protecting educators. For example, in an early case, a Saskatchewan court insisted that
the right to proper notice of termination is obligatory and that a teacher's being
eligible for superannuation is no reason to act otherwise (*Metcalfe v. Board*,
1938). More recently, a British Columbia court ruled in favour of two teachers
who were suspended without pay for not appearing before a school board's
meeting to determine their involvement in staff problems in their school. The
board, the court held, did not follow the procedures laid down in the relevant
legislation (*Johnson v. Board*, 1979). In Alberta, a court that ruled in favour of a
superintendent dismissed summarily declared that his school board was bound
to act fairly and was under a duty to afford the superintendent a hearing
(*McCarthy v. Calgary R.C.*, 1979).

Finally, the role of teacher organizations in protecting their members against
school boards has to be noted. As Nediger (1981) pointed out, teacher organizations, using collective bargaining as a powerful weapon, have brought about significant changes not only to school board-teacher relationships but also to the
process of decision making on educational policies. Increasingly, school boards
have had to contend with guidelines established by the bargaining process. Insofar
as these guidelines are mutually agreed upon by the board and the organization
representing the teachers and insofar as the process is provided for in existing legislation, the courts may be expected to enforce such guidelines. Thus, in *Syrette v.
Transcona-Springfield S.D. No. 12* (1976) a Manitoba court decided in favour of a
teacher dismissed in contravention of a collective bargaining agreement, then in
force, that disallowed termination of any teacher's contract during the year.

Yet in spite of fairly heavy litigation pitting school boards against teachers, academic and civil rights cases seldom reached Canadian courts before the arrival of the Charter. One related case has been recorded, however. This involved the right of a teacher to speak out publicly against her teachers' union. Urged to engage in an illegal walkout by the union, she wrote two letters to a local newspaper editor, both critical of the conduct of the meeting that resulted in the walkout. When the union's professional committee found her guilty of unbecoming conduct and recommended a reprimand, she went to the court to quash the decision. The court ruled in her favour (*Re Busche and Nova Scotia Teachers' Union*, 1975).

One exception to the general passivity in civil rights litigation before the Charter period involved the right of teachers to conduct their personal lives as they see fit. A substantial segment in several provinces, Catholic school systems appear to be insisting on their right to determine the qualifications of their teachers in the face of increasing libertarianism in Canadian society. This insistence received support from the court in *Re Essex County Roman Catholic Separate School Board and Porter* (1977) involving two teachers discharged for having entered into civil marriages. When a board of reference ordered their reinstatement, the school board contested the order before the courts and finally received vindication from the Ontario Court of Appeal. Justice Zuber stated categorically, "If a school board can dismiss for cause, then, in the case of a denominational school, cause must include denominational cause." However, Newfoundland courts in similar cases denied the notion of "denominational cause." In *Re Stack and the R.C. School Board for St. John's* (1979), the court referred the case of a divorced Catholic teacher back to the arbitration board that had, in an earlier ruling, accepted the school board contention that it had the constitutional right to hire and fire for denominational reasons. The court ruled that the arbitration board had the duty, not simply to accept the school board contention, but to make a determination of the validity of the dismissal as mandated by the province's Collective Bargaining Act. Subsequently, in *Re R.C. School Board for Conception Bay North and Barron-Babb* (1986), involving a Catholic teacher who married an Anglican in an Anglican ceremony, the court found that the school board had dismissed her on the basis of an invalid by-law and in violation of an existing collective bargaining agreement between the school board and the Newfoundland Teachers' Association.

The landmark judgment on denominational teachers' rights is *Caldwell v. Stuart* (1984) in British Columbia. A catholic teacher on a yearly contract, Caldwell was terminated after marrying a divorced Methodist in the latter's church ceremony. In the federal Supreme Court she contended that the school board action violated the non-discrimination clause (section 8) in the British Columbia Human Rights Code. The Canadian Supreme Court declined, however, to support her contention. The Court, examining the Code's section 22 (exempting non-profit religious organizations that operate primarily for the welfare of its members), reasoned as follows:

> The purpose of the section is to preserve for the Catholic members of this and other groups the right to the continuance of denominational schools. This, because of the nature of the schools, means the right to preserve the religious basis of the schools and in so doing to engage teachers who by religion and by the acceptance of the Church's rules are competent to teach within the requirements of the school. This involves and justifies a policy of preferring Roman Catholic teachers who accept and practise the teachings of the Church. In my opinion . . . the dismissal of Mrs. Caldwell may not be considered as a contravention of the Code and the appeal must fail. (p. 21)

Further support for the curtailment of teachers' rights for denominational reasons has come about. In *Walsh v. The Roman Catholic School Board for St. John's* (1988), involving a Catholic teacher who left the Church and married a Seventh Day Adventist, the Newfoundland Appeal Court found section 29 a decisive tool in preserving the denominational right. It established that "Among the rights existing at Confederation was the right conferred upon a denominational Board of Education to appoint and dismiss teachers. . . . It is evident that it must encompass the right to hire and dismiss teachers for denominational cause (p. 25–26)." Thereafter, it stated: "Where a conflict exists, s.29 of the Charter clearly required the scale to be tipped in favour of the general (denominational) right" (p. 28). In *Casagrande v. Hinton* (1987), involving a Catholic teacher fired for pregnancies outside of marriage, her dismissal was sustained by the court on the basis of a constitutional right granted to Roman Catholic boards by s.17 of the *Alberta Act, 1905*, that is "expressly protected by s.29 of the Charter and overrides individual rights to s.15." Further, s.29 was held by the court to override the protection to individuals afforded by Alberta's *Individual's Rights Protection Act*. It is worth noting that public school teachers' lifestyle may be curtailed similarly. In British Columbia the court sustained penalty for both a female teacher and her teacher husband when her photo in the nude, taken by him, was published in a men's magazine (*Shewan v. Abbotsford School Division*, 1987).

With the Charter, the country has seen increased litigation involving teachers. Perhaps the most interesting issue centres on free expression in the classroom.

R. v. Keegstra (1990) involved a former Eckville, Alberta teacher and mayor who for several years taught that the holocaust was a hoax and that there is an international Jewish conspiracy to control the world. He was formally charged under s.319(2) of the Criminal Code prohibiting wilful promotion of hatred against an identifiable group. In court he argued that the Code infringed his freedom of speech through the general prohibition and his right to be presumed innocent through the Code's requirement that one may escape penalty only if one can establish the truth of his or her statement. The Supreme Court agreed that the requirement violated Keegstra's free speech. However, it is a justifiable limitation of free expression to prevent the dissemination of hate propaganda. Equally, the requirement violated his right to be presumed innocent; again, however, it is a permissible means of excusing truthful statements without undermining the objective of preventing harm caused by the intentional promotion of hatred (*R v. Keegstra*, 1990). Nonetheless, the Court ordered a new trial because of a defect in jury selection. The second trial proceeded, and Keegstra was convicted and fined $3000 for wilfully promoting hated against an identifiable group, the Jews ("Keegstra fined . . . ", 1992).

The teacher's right to free expression in the classroom is also implicated in the ongoing case of *Malcolm Ross v. The Board of School Trustees District No. 15* (1990) in which the teacher has been alleged to have made anti-Jewish and racist statements and written tracts antagonistic to the Jews. His contemplated appeal could still reach the Supreme Court in due course.

Several Charter cases lodged by teachers have not been successful. Thus an Ontario teacher who was transferred to a separate school system has been determined to have no right to move back to the public system despite an appeal to the freedom and equality rights provisions of the Charter (*Board for the City of York v. OSSTF*, 1990). Equally ineffective was an appeal for a probationary teacher refused re-hiring allegedly because of the Board's disapproval of religious materials he used in class (*Morin v. Prince Edward Island*, 1989). Further, the court was not convinced by a probationary teacher's appeal that her right was violated when not afforded the same procedures normally given to permanent teachers facing termination from employment (*Blue v. Board of Education of Antigonish District*, 1990).

Student Rights

The interrelationship between students and educational authorities is defined by both legislation and common law, which has been articulated by the courts in the course of time. Legislation, such as education, school, and school attendance acts, specifies student entitlements against educational systems. With respect to such legislation affecting students, the role of the courts has been to interpret contentious provisions brought to their attention through litigation. Pre-Charter litigation was concentrated on students' rights to attend school, to transportation, and to reasonable care and protection in school or while engaged in school-sponsored activities. Interesting litigation also occurred concerning the right of children to refuse or receive religious instruction in schools (Canadian Teachers' Federation, 1981).

Apart from interpreting provisions in educational statutes, courts have also been asked to rule on cases involving student conduct that can be resolved by use of common law principles. In Canada, the common law concept of *in loco parentis* underlies much current practice related to the control of students. Basically, this concept involves a delegation of parental authority to teachers and includes both the power to suspend or expel from school and the authority to administer corporal punishment. Combined with the necessity for maintaining order in and about the school, *in loco parentis* has justified an educational authority's power to control the conduct of pupils, limited only by the restraints that the law and the courts place upon it. Generally, courts do not interfere with this power unless the reasonableness of the power exercised is questioned. It is in this regard, however, that most litigations occur (Bargen, 1961).

The pre-Charter period saw little litigation on the civil rights of students. This does not mean that no contentious incidents involving students' attempts to exercise their claimed rights denied by school authorities arose, though litigation did not materialize (Mackay, 1983). Legal scholars criticized educational authorities for proscribing student styles of dress and grooming and for banning high school political clubs (Kerr, 1971; Sweezy, 1969), but they were insufficient to stimulate pre-Charter litigation.

At least four relevant pre-Charter cases may be noted, however. In Quebec a case involved three students who were expelled by school commissioners for dealing in drugs at school. The expulsion was decided by the commissioners in the absence of the students who were not informed of the details of the charges or given the opportunity to defend themselves. Judge Vallerand of the Superior Court of Quebec overturned the commissioner's action which, he believed, violated the rules of natural justice ("Expulsion of students," 1980). Whether, in this judgment, Judge Vallerand was influenced by the due process cases in the United States is an interesting question. The second (unreported) case related to a student's right to wear blue jeans and a T-shirt in school. Predictably, the court held that the principal, who banned the wearing of such attire, was acting within his authority (*Choukalas v. St. Albert Separate School Board and Potheridge,* 1962). The third case, *Ward v. Board of Blaine Lake School Unit No. 57* (1971), involved an eleven-year-old boy suspended for refusing to cut his hair in accordance with a school board resolution defining the maximum hair length for male students. When the boy and his mother appealed to nullify the resolution and the suspension, the court employed the common law to confirm the board's authority to pass the resolution and the principal's power to suspend the pupil for defying the resolution. This ruling did not remain unnoticed, however. In a critical article, Hunter (1972) sought to demonstrate that the court on the one hand focussed erroneously on a general provision in the relevant provincial education law stating that: "Subject to the other provisions of this Act, [the board may] . . . exercise a general supervision and control over the schools of a unit" (p. 479). On the other hand, it set aside conveniently the pertinent provision of the same act that specifically provided for procedures and valid reasons for expulsion. Hunter observed that the courts lent assistance to the increasing encroachment by the educational system on what would have been considered an individual and family decision.

The fourth case, in British Columbia, seems to indicate greater concern for just treatment of young people. In this case, a thirteen-year-old girl was suspended from October until the end of the academic year for smoking marijuana. The suspension was based on the school board's discipline policy, which allowed a school to suspend a pupil immediately for using narcotics for up to the remainder of the school year or for a minimum of five school months. The court, ruling in favour of the girl, declared the policy invalid. It pointed out that the policy's minimum of five-month suspension and the absence of "due warning" requirements did not conform to the province's School Act and its regulations, which require kind and judicious discipline as well as the use of procedural fairness in disciplining students (Anderson, 1985).

Clearly, pre-Charter cases moved in the direction of greater rights for young people in school. Strong, decisive signal has not been given, however, because until now, the Canadian Supreme Court has not ruled on any case directly involving students' Charter rights. A number, though, have been dealt with by the lower courts and the courts of appeal in various provinces. The most prominent of these cases are those involving the religious freedom of students. In *Zylberberg v. Sudbury Board of Education* (1988), a number of students challenged the provincial regulation requiring schools to hold religious exercises. The Court of Appeal in Ontario ruled that such a regulation, even when students may be exempted, violates constitutional guarantees of freedom of conscience and religion. In British Columbia a similar regulation was challenged in *Russow and Lambert v. Attorney General of British Columbia* (1985). In its short decision, the B.C. Court had no difficulty in accepting without reservation the views of the majority in the Ontario Court of Appeal case. Again in Ontario, the Corporation of the Canadian Civil Liberties Association (CCCLA) challenged the Elgin County School Board's religious education curriculum. It contended that the regulations and the curriculum violated the Charter and asked for an order to prevent the board from offering the curriculum. At the Ontario Court of Appeal, the earlier ruling of the Divisional Court, which dismissed CCCLA's claims, was reversed. The court declared that the Ontario regulations and the curriculum of religious education denied the rights and freedoms assured by the Charter (*CCCLA v. Ontario*, 1990).

Aside from the religious prayer and instruction cases, students' litigation against school boards has not been successful. Students who have challenged dress codes (*Devereux v. Lambton County R.C. Board*, 1988) or school regulations against smoking (*Mazerolle v. School District No. 7*, 1987) have lost their cases. In *R. v. J.M.G.* (1986), a student who was charged with possession of marijuana argued that his rights against unreasonable search and seizure and to be informed of his rights upon detention had been violated. However, the court rejected his claim. It emphasized the principal's obligation to maintain order and discipline, the reasonableness of the grounds for the search and seizure, and the inadvisability of securing authorization for every search or seizure of illegal material in educational institutions.

• • •

RIGHTS IN EDUCATION: REFORM IN THE OFFING?

Canadian courts have not made it their habit to interfere in the administrative affairs of educational systems. In general, they have seen fit to intrude only when these systems show lack of conformity to statutory or constitutional provisions. This judicial restraint, together with the absence of definitive declarations guaranteeing civil rights for Canadians, may partially account for a generally dim view, in the past, of teachers' and students' rights.

The Charter of Rights and Freedoms may be seen as an attempt to change that view. The declaration in section 2 guaranteeing fundamental freedoms of conscience and religion, belief and expression (including freedom of the press), peaceful assembly, and association may provide teachers and students a greater measure of autonomy in varied areas of school life. Intent on testing the boundaries of their newly declared entitlements, teachers feeling constraints in the school system may initiate action related to assigning controversial, "objection-able" materials for home study or projects; discussing and expressing their posi-tions on sensitive topics like creationism versus evolution, sex, and abortion; publicly criticizing school policies; including "objectionable" books in class-room resource centres or in libraries; and the like. Moreover, despite the unclear status of the right to privacy in Canada, teachers also may appeal (perhaps in conjunction with section 2) to section 7 of the Charter concerning their right to the personal conduct of their lives.

Students may equally see the Charter as the basis of new rights and freedoms for them in the classroom. As Bergen (1984) has pointed out, a substantial number of Charter provisions may relate to the liberties and protection of young people in the school. Sections 2 (fundamental freedoms), 7 (life, liberty, and security of person), 8 (unreasonable search and seizure), 9 (arbitrary detention), 10 (rights of persons arrested or detained), 11 (rights of persons charged with offenses), 12 (cruel and unusual treatment or punishment), 15 (equal protection and benefit without discrimination on the basis, for example, of age), and 28 (preservation and enhancement of the multicultural heritage of Canadians), are likely to attract, and have attracted, test cases.

The fact remains, however, that there is no infallible way to predict how Canadian courts will interpret relevant Charter provisions where teachers' and students' rights are at issue. Because Charter provisions are couched in general terms, their application to specific situations requires interpretation by the courts, notably the federal Supreme Court. The last two decades has provided us with some information, incomplete but significant no doubt, about how the courts will use the Charter and about its impact on society. Analysis of such information is needed if only to allay the fears of Charter critics or to moderate the expectations of its advocates. Critics warned, on the one hand, about the demise of parliamentary democracy and the loss of institutional authority resulting from the predominance of the judiciary and its imposition of judicial decisions on societal institutions. Advocates, on the other hand, trumpeted a new regime characterized by individual enjoyment of liberty and justice wrested from majoritarian domination and institutional control.

The first wave of Charter-related cases tended to confirm the fears of its crit-ics. These cases ominously signalled judicial confidence in its possession of unquestionable authority to review legislation in its role involving substantive interpretation of Charter provisions. Thus, in *Hunter v. Southam Inc.* (1986), the Supreme Court, in defining what constituted unreasonable search and seizure, referred to the judiciary as the guardian of the Constitution and to the Charter as capable (through judicial interpretation) of growth and development over time to meet new social, political, and historical realities often unimagined by its framers. In *Reference re Section 94(2) of the B.C. Motor Vehicle Act* (1985), the Court transcended the traditional procedure-oriented conception of fundamental justice by reading into it the substantive interests of life, liberty, and security of the person, some examples of which are the rights enumerated in sections 8 to 14 of the Charter. And, despite its apparent lack of intent to question legislative wisdom, the Court in *R. v. Oakes* (1986) established, pursuant to section 1, a set of criteria for legislative review that inevitably involves judicial questioning of the wisdom of legislation under consideration.

However, the subsequent wave of cases has exhibited the contrary tendency toward moderation. In Russell's estimation, only eight out of thirty-two cases decided between early 1986 to the end of January 1988 (when it struck down as illegal the country's abortion law in *Regina v. Morgentaler*) were successful in arguing their Charter claims. This success rate of twenty-five percent is clearly much more modest than the sixty percent success rate for the first wave of cases (Russell, 1989). Basically confirming Russell's findings, Petter and Monahan (1988) point to the emergence of conservative alliances in the Court that refrained from requiring the government to demonstrate its "pressing and sub-stantial interest" in a challenged legislation for it to withstand judicial scrutiny. They also showed wariness in pressing the Court's commitment to the liberal interpretation of the Charter as a "living tree" that could be shaped by the Court as it deems fit. This tendency of restraint remained in succeeding terms (1987–89) as the Court, in striking down pieces of legislation, left it open for legislators to replace them with constitutionally justifiable ones. Still, as MacKay and Pothier (1990) observed, some judges continue to assert their activist or quasi-legislative role with success on behalf of threatened or disad-vantaged groups. Thus, they note that in *Andrews v. Law Society of British Columbia*, the Court ruled that the Society's regulation requiring lawyers to be Canadian citizens discriminates against non-citizens and violates section 15. Again, in *Ford v. A.-G. of Quebec*, the Court found that the Quebec legislation prohibiting the use of any language other than French on commercial signs dis-criminates in having a harsher effect on non-francophones than on francophones. Notwithstanding some reformist decisions by the Supreme Court, its recogni-tion of the limits on its power is clear. In a recent case involving the issue of parental benefits for fathers, the Court declared that judges have limited powers to extend social benefits or to prescribe replacements for discriminatory laws. As Chief Justice A. Lamer (*Schachter v. Canada*, 1992) pointed out, "parliament and provincial legislatures are much better equipped to assess the whole picture in formulating solutions in cases such as these" (p. 48). Agreeing with Justice Lamer, Justice G. LaForest added: "The courts are not in the business of rewriting legislation."

The Court's deference to legislatures in socio-economic matters may be expected in educational matters too. Undoubtedly, judges would not wish to act as superintendents or school board members for the nation. But they are not likely to hesitate in imposing their views when educational decision makers adopt or implement unreasonable policies. Thus educators must continue to evaluate existing policies and arrangements to justify, modify, or replace them in conformity with acceptable standards. The shock and apprehension that followed judicial intervention in education in the United States need not be experienced in this country.

● ● ●

REFERENCES

Bargen, P. (1961). *The legal status of the Canadian public school pupil.* Toronto: Macmillan.

Bergen, J. (1984). Rethink your treatment of students. *Canadian School Executive, 3,* 13–15.

Berkman, R. (1970). Students in court: Free speech and the functions of schooling in America. *Harvard Educational Review, 40,* 567–577.

Bethel School District v. Fraser, 478 U.S. 675 (1986).

Blue v. Board of Education of Antigonish District, 95 N.S.R. (2d) 118 (1990).

Board of Education for the City of York v. Ontario Secondary School Teachers' Federation (1990). In *School Law Commentary,* case file 5-4-1.

CCCLA v. Ontario, 71 O.R. (2d) 341 (1990).

Caldwell and Stuart, 15 D.L.R. (4th) 1 (1984) at 21.

Canadian Teachers' Federation. (1981). *Schools, teachers, and the courts* (4th draft). Ottawa: Author.

Casagrande v. Hinton, 41 Alberta, L.R. (2d) 349 (1987).

Choukalas v. St. Albert Separate School Board and Petheridge, 1 August 1962 (unreported).

Davis, D. (1991). *Original intent.* Buffalo, NY: Prometheus Books.

Devereaux v. Lambton County R.C. Separate School Board (1988). Doc. No. RE 154/88 Ontario High Court.

Fischer, L., & Schimmel, D. (1982). *The rights of students and teachers.* New York: Harper and Row.

Friedmann, W. (1964). *Law in a changing society* (abridged ed.). Harmondsworth: Penguin Books.

Goss v. Lopez, 419 U.S. 565 (1975).

Hazelwood School District v. Kuhlmeier, 484 U.S. 260 (1988).

Hunter, W. (1972). Case comment–School board regulation relating to dress and grooming. *Saskatchewan Law Review, 36,* 479.

Hunter v. Southam Inc., 11 D.L.R. (4th) 200 (1986).

In re Gault, 387 U.S. 1 at 13 (1967).

Johnston v. Board of School Trustees (Langley), 12 B.C.L.R. (1979).

Keegstra fined $3000. (1992, July 11). *Winnipeg Free Press,* p. A16.

Kerr, R. (1971). Commentary of constitutional law–Political rights and high school political clubs. *Canadian Bar Review, 50,* 347–352.

Keyishian v. Board of Regents, 385 U.S. 589 (1967).

Lamb, C. C., & Halpern, S. (1991). *The burger court.* Urbana, IL: University of Illinois Press.

MacKay, A.W. (1983, June). *The Canadian Charter of Rights and Freedoms: Implications for students.* Paper presented at the National Educational Policy Conference in Vancouver, B.C.

MacKay, A.W., & Pothier, D. (1990). *Developments in constitutional law: The 1988–89 term,* 1 S.C.L.R. (2d) 81.

Malcolm Ross v. The Board of School Trustees District No. 15, 105 N.B.R. (2d) 34 (1990).

Mazerolle v. School District No. 7, 83 N.B.R. (2d) 389 (1987).

McCarthy v. Calgary R.C. Separate School District No. 1 Board of Trustees 4 W.W.R. 725 (1979).

McCurdy, S.G. (1968). *Legal status of the Canadian teacher* (pp. 68–95, 150). Toronto: Macmillan.

Metcalfe v. Board of Trustees of Moose Jaw District No. 1 2 D.L.R. 726 (1938).

Milne, D. (1982). *The new Canadian constitution.* Toronto: James Lorimer.

Morin v. Prince Edward Island, 78 Nfld. & P.E.I. R. 308 (1989).

Nediger, W. G. (1981). *The impact of collective bargaining on financial gains and management rights in Canadian education.* Paper presented at the CSSE Annual Conference.

New Jersey v. T.L.O., 105 St. Ct. 733 (1985).

Petter, A., & Monahan, P. (1988). *Developments in constitutional law: The 1986–87 term,* 10 S.C.L.R. 61.

Pickering v. Board of Education, 391 U.S. 563 at 573.

Platt, A. (1969). *The child savers.* Chicago: University of Chicago Press.

R. v. J.M.G., 33 D.L.R. (4th) 277 (1986).

R. v. Keegstra, 3 C.S.C.R. 697 (1990).

R. v. Oakes, 26 D.L.R. (4th) 200 (1986).

Re Busche and Nova Scotia Teachers' Union, 62 D.L.R. (3d) N.S. 330 (1975).

Re Essex County Roman Catholic Separate School Board and Porter, 89 D. L. R. (3d) 445 at 447 (1977).

Re Roman Catholic School Board for Conception Bay North and Barron-Babb, 59 Nfld and P.E.I. R 129 (1986).

Ref. Re Section 94(2) of the Motor Vehicle Act, 24 D.L.R. (4th) 536 (1985).

Rice, A. (1987). *The Warren Court.* Millwood, NY: Associated Faculty Press.

Russell, P. (1989). The Supreme Court and the Charter: A question of legitimacy. In D. Shugarman & R. Whitaker (Eds.), *Federalism and political community.* Peterborough, ON: Broadview Press.

Russow and Lambert v. Attorney-General of B.C., 35 B.C.L.R. (2d) 29 (1985).

Schacter v. Canada. Unpublished Supreme Court decision, 1992 July 9. Speaking for the majority, Lamer at 48.

Schacter v. Canada. Joining the majority, LaForest at 2.

Schimmel, D., & Fischer, L. (1974). On the Cutting Edge of the Law. *School Review, 82,* 262.

Sedler, R. A. (1984). Constitutional protection of individual rights in Canada: The impact of the new Canadian Charter of Rights and Freedoms. *Notre Dame Law Review, 59,* 1191 at 1202.

Shewan v. Abbotsford School Division, 47 D.L.R. (4th) 106 (1987).

Stack and Roman Catholic School Board for St. John's, 99 D.L.R. (3d) 278 (1979).

Sweezy, F. (1969). Free speech and the student's right to govern his personal appearance. *Osgoode Hall Law Journal, 7,* 297–299.

Syrette v. Transcona-Springfield S. D. No. 12, 67 D.L.R. (3d) 568 (1976).

Taylor v. Board of School Trustees of School District No. 35. In J. Anderson, Board's pupil suspension policy declared invalid. *The Canadian School Executive,* (1985, February), 22.

Tinker v. Des Moines Independent Community School District, 393 U.S. 503 at 511 (1969).

Vallerand, Judge C. (1980, June 5). Expulsion of students went beyond routine discipline. *The Montreal Gazette*, p. 15.

Walsh et al. v. Newfoundland (Treasury Board) et al. 71 Nfld & P.E.I. R.21 (1988) at 25–26; 28.

Ward and Board of Blaine Lake School Unit No. 57, 20 D.L.R. (3d) 651 (1971).

Wood v. Strickland, 420 U.S. 308 (1975).

Zylberberg v. Sudbury Board of Education (Director), 65 O.R. (2d) 641 (1988).

Legal and Ethical Issues for Classroom Teachers

...

Larry Eberlein

Teachers are confronted daily with a wide range of decisions to be made—each with some legal and/or ethical component. Most of these decisions directly involve students, a teacher's primary responsibility. Many involve commonplace questions such as the equity of homework assignments or the enforcement of class disciplinary rules. These are ethical issues (e.g., fairness or beneficence) that need consideration in the decision-making process, but have very few legal implications about the decision itself because physical constraint or punishment is not usually involved. These decisions are routinely and rapidly made. However, other problems demand more time and have legal as well as ethical implications. For example, when teaching undergraduate education majors, I have often posed the following fictional ethical and legal dilemma for class consideration. While out of the ordinary, this type of dilemma is repeatedly being reported in Canada's local newspapers.

Judy Frith was an attractive 15-year-old student at Pearson Junior High School. She was quite popular with her classmates and well accepted by the other teaching staff. Although not at the top of her class, she had been on the honour roll the previous two years. She had no record of difficulties or problem behaviour in school; her only previous contact with the school counsellor had been about her courses and scheduling concerns.

On Thursday afternoon, she came to see Janice Waite, her history teacher and part-time guidance counsellor, in a panic. She said she couldn't come back to school the next day and didn't know what to do.

After a brief attempt to calm Judy down, Janice attempted to discover the basis of the problem. Judy replied truthfully that she couldn't go back to her English class again because she was afraid of Mr. Foster, her English teacher.

When pressed, Judy said that Mr. Foster had been paying a lot of attention to her in the last few weeks and on a couple of occasions had fondled her breasts. This had upset Judy to the point that she didn't know what to do. She wanted to talk to someone about it, but was afraid to tell her parents. When she tried to say something to her friends about it, they laughed at her. When asked why, she replied, "They just don't take Mr. Foster very seriously, he does that to all the girls!"

What should the teacher do in this situation? What are Ms. Waite's ethical and legal responsibilities to Judy, her parents, the other girls in Mr. Foster's class, the school in general, and also specifically to Mr. Foster? Students do have rights. When individual teachers infringe on these rights, they are taken to court and Mr. Foster could well find himself before the bench. Mr. Foster could be charged under the Criminal Code or sued in civil court by Judy and her parents. Although few teachers concern themselves with issues of legal responsibility, teachers need to be aware that they can be held legally accountable for their activities in the classroom or when involved in school activities (Eberlein, 1988b). Teachers have ethical responsibilities as well.

Since deciding what action to take in Mr. Foster's case involves both legal and ethical issues, it would be helpful to consider some of the general legal issues of concern to a teacher and then the moral or ethical principles that need consideration. Please note that this is an artificial distinction since every legal issue raised has ethical implications; the reverse is also frequently true. Of particular concern will be a teacher's authority to act and the problems encountered when a teacher intentionally interferes with a student's freedom. This usually happens in disciplinary and classroom management situations. Also of concern will be the unintentional torts or wrongs done to students through carelessness or negligence, a problem that occurs when a teacher causes an accident though lack of due care. In conjunction with this I will also consider a teacher's affirmative duty to act, such as in playground supervision or in a medical emergency. Finally, in looking at the ethical implications of a teacher's action, I will propose a new code of ethics for teachers. In looking at these issues, my goal is to heighten the reader's awareness and sensitivity to potentially difficult areas. If a problem can be prevented, everyone is a winner.

. . .

LEGAL ISSUES

Teachers' Authority

Teachers have a solid basis for their authority to act in the classroom, particularly in disciplinary situations. There are three basic sources of this authority for control of student behaviour: the common law doctrine of *in loco parentis*, provincial school acts, and the Canadian Criminal Code.

IN LOCO PARENTIS

This is a legal concept that gains its definition from the common law. It refers to a person who has been put in a situation of a lawful parent by assuming the obligations incidental to the parental relationship, but without the formalities of a legal adoption. It embodies both the idea of an assumption of parental rights and the discharge of parental duties (*Niewiadomski v. U.S.*, 1947). In usage it commonly refers to parental surrogates during a child's minority years. These include step-parents, foster parents, or the relationship of master-apprentice (*Powys v. Mansfield*, 1836; *Shtitz v. C.N.R.*, 1927). When applied to education, the concept defines in a limited and ambiguous way, the relationship between student and teacher (Hammes, 1982).

Traditionally, when a parent delegated authority over a child to school personnel, the parent could restrict the actions of school officials and withdraw the authority at any time. Today, most public school personnel will listen to parental requests regarding their children and may even solicit their help. In actual fact the school has the final say and parental restrictions do not have to be honoured (*Baker v. Owen*, 1975).

When discussing corporal punishment, writers (Gee & Sperry, 1978; Spitalli, 1976) and the courts (*R. v. Trynchy*, 1970) assume the *in loco parentis* doctrine gives educational personnel the right to discipline and control. Hawkins (1976) asks what happens when the teacher believes in striking a child but the parent does not. Under the *in loco parentis* doctrine, no striking would be permitted. Yet no court has refused permission to teachers for reasonable control and discipline, including reasonable corporal punishment. The doctrine does, however, restrict the degree of authority to something less than the latitude or discretion allowed a parent. This means that the teacher does not have the same authority as a parent to exercise lay judgment when dealing with treatment of injury or disease. *Guerrieri v. Tyson* (1942) involved two teachers who immersed a child's infected finger in scalding water against the child's will. The court held the teachers liable for damages since the doctrine did not extend beyond the question of discipline.

PROVINCIAL SCHOOL ACTS

The real authority of school personnel stems from provincial legislation rather than from the common law doctrine of *in loco parentis*. For example, Section 368 of the pre-1970 School Act in Alberta required a certificated teacher to "maintain proper order and discipline." This section was eliminated in newer revisions but is probably covered in Section 65 of the revised act that authorizes a Board of Trustees to "make rules for the administration, management and operation of schools" and also to "settle disputes between a parent or child and a teacher or other Board employee." Section 146 permits teachers and principals to suspend pupils and the board to expel them. Section 167 makes parents, as well as students, responsible for intentional or negligent damage to school property. It should be clear from reading these few sections that parents cannot restrict rights of school personnel by simply saying, "You can't suspend my child!" These rights to take action come from statutory authority and not from the delegation of parental authority. Similar statutes exist in all provinces (Bargen, 1961). It is for this reason that a large group of North American legal scholars, attempting to codify the common law in this regard, concluded that teachers are public officers and do not act as delegates of the parents (Restatement of the Law, 1977). When public officers are in charge of the education or training of a child, they have a privilege to use force or impose reasonable confinement unrestricted by a parents' prohibitions or wishes. Teachers act for the government or school board in carrying out public policy.

CANADIAN CRIMINAL CODE

Although under challenge by the Law Reform Commission of Canada, two sections of this federal law still provide a degree of legal authority to school personnel, particularly in matters of corporal punishment. In principle, all violence is against the law. Section 43 exempts teachers, but is modified by Section 26 which denies the exception when excess is used.

> 43. Every schoolteacher, parent or person standing in the place of a parent is justified in using force by way of correction toward a pupil or child, as the case may be, who is under his care, if the force does not exceed what is reasonable under the circumstances.

26.   Every one who is authorized by law to use force is criminally responsible for any excess thereof according to the nature and quality of the act
that constitutes the excess.

These provisions, and their earlier antecedents, have been long used as the
basis of the claim of privilege that is made by school officials in Canada when
dealing with issues of assault and false imprisonment, and especially the use of
corporal punishment, discussed later. The 1984 Law Reform Commission recognizes that there are cases where nothing short of physical force may be necessary
to prevent a student from destroying school property or disrupting class.
However, these are recognized as emergency situations when the use of force can
be justified as a "necessity." All other situations should exclude the use of force.
I believe that this exemption should be removed (Eberlein, 1986b) and agree
with Wilson (1980) that a more appropriate response to discipline problems lies
in better professional training for teachers. Student teachers need to anticipate
and resolve problems in the classroom without resorting to violence.

Intentional Interference with Students

Like all people in our society, children and students are legally protected from
the wrongful conduct of others, including parents and teachers. The recent public attention given to child abuse situations is but one illustration. Through
regimentation and discipline, the freedom of students at school is more controlled than in most homes. This control often involves intentional interference
with the student, including physical punishment and restriction on freedom of
movement. The most obvious affirmative acts that would raise questions had
they occurred in other than a school setting are assault and false imprisonment;
when unreasonable, these actions have legal consequences. As Barnes (1977)
points out: "Assault may be committed by the application of unreasonable force,
by improperly searching the person of a child, or by improperly subjecting a
child to punishment such as standing in the corner. Unlawful detention of a
child after school may constitute . . . false imprisonment" (p. 209).

In addition to the acts mentioned above, there are often other forms of physical contact between teacher and students. These range from a well-intentioned
pat on the behind or an arm around a student to gross physical or sexual abuse,
such as that exhibited by Mr. Foster. Some contact may be welcomed and
acceptable in the lower grades only to become unwanted and problematic in
junior or senior high. Teachers should keep in mind that any *unwanted physical*

touching constitutes an assault. Unless justified by consent or permitted by a teacher's legal authority referred to earlier, this action could lead to a civil lawsuit or criminal charge. In such cases, the teacher's certificate is also often suspended or revoked. Teachers' associations are often recommending that to prevent any misunderstanding, *no touching* of a student ever take place.

Another intentional wrong that teachers need to consider is defamation—especially when they are writing or speaking about their students. Defamation is a false statement that would cause a person to be shunned, avoided, or discredited (Williams, 1976). Truth is one defense against such an action, but most teachers would find it difficult to show the truthfulness of rumours they repeat. More generally, when teachers are acting within the scope of their employment, they are protected by the doctrine of qualified privilege. This would protect them, for example, when discussing a student with the principal or counsellor.

Finally, a fairly recent addition to the legal responsibilities now recognized by courts is discussed by Linden (1977). This is the intentional infliction of mental suffering, as in a practical joke. This liability has usually been imposed when there has been extreme and outrageous conduct, even when no malice was intended. Needless to say teachers should not become involved in the hazing incidents or practical jokes that often occur in schools.

INFORMED CONSENT

With the exception of approving criminal activity (e.g., Judy cannot consent to Mr. Foster's sexual touching), people can consent to the intentional interference with their personal interests. Obvious examples are riding in an elevator or going to sporting events where one would expect to be bumped by the crowds. Hockey players agree to be checked according to the rules of the game and thus give consent to what would otherwise be an assault. But consent, to be valid, must be real consent, voluntarily given by one who understands the nature and consequences of the activity involved. Thus the hockey player does not consent to a game where players are to be hit over the head with a hockey stick. Also the Grade 1 student cannot give consent to an emergency appendectomy no matter how necessary.

This issue is of greatest importance in behaviour modification programs often used in conjunction with classroom management procedures (Eberlein, 1986a). Although teachers can use reasonable time-out or other punishment techniques as a one-time disciplinary control measure, to be safe, teachers should obtain the consent of both child and parent before using the techniques on an ongoing basis. Lack of information can lead to unexpected results. A recent Alberta case

(*Edmonton Journal*, 1992), while not going to court, has involved the parents, school officials, school board, Alberta social services, and the Psychologists Association of Alberta in an uproar over the limited use of a padded isolation room for disciplinary control. The teacher was quoted as saying, "It's totally ludicrous. This is a totally innocent situation. This kind of thing happens every day in schools. It's just another form of punishment." The school board later approved the continued use of the room.

If not related to discipline, consent is essential. The consent should be in writing, should specify the nature of the program, contain a description of the purpose, risks, and effects of the plan, and contain a statement of the right of the child and/or the parent to terminate consent at any time.

The age of consent presents real problems and there are differences of opinion among Canadian legal authorities about the appropriate age. For example, Linden (1977) suggests that "young children cannot give a valid consent; their parents must do so on their behalf" (p. 56). Klar (personal communication, January 4, 1979) suggests that the law is not this clear. While agreeing that young children cannot consent, older children do regularly consent in a variety of situations in schools. Teachers regularly control or restrict a child's behaviour and other students have physical contact in the course of play activity. Klar suggests that minors probably have a greater power to consent or not consent than has been often recognized. He also suggests that there are limits to which parents may consent on behalf of the child, when physical acts to which the child objects are involved.

An allied area is the *misuse* of consent forms. For example, in preparation for a field trip, teachers may request a slip from home to absolve the school and teacher for any accidents or injuries that might occur during the trip. Such a permission slip is of little value other than as an acknowledgement that parents know a child is going on the trip and the probable recognition that the trip itself would not be dangerous. Should an accident occur and the teacher's behaviour be found to be negligent, however, damages would be assessed against both the teacher and the school. A parent cannot waive a child's rights and cannot authorize a teacher to use less than the degree of care that any reasonable person would have used in that situation.

CORPORAL PUNISHMENT AS A FORM OF DISCIPLINE

There are legal implications that flow from classroom management practices and thus, teachers are subject to the general prescriptions of the law, although many disputes may be handled in the school or at the school board level. In the usual case, to the extent teachers act with legitimate consent or legal authority and stay within the bounds of reasonableness, they are protected by the law from charges of wrongful conduct. Linden (1977) cites the privilege that furnishes this defence to charges of intentional interference with a student's rights:

> Although most of the cases deal with the alleged misdeeds of police officers during the course of making arrests, this privilege is also available to parents, school teachers, shipmasters, and others who forcibly discipline children or crew members under their control. Minor assaults, batteries, and detentions for disciplinary purposes are excused, if they are reasonable, but not if any excessive force is employed. (p. 73)

The main problem in discipline cases is corporal punishment. In the past when criminal charges have been laid in disciplinary situations it has usually been because some type of corporal punishment had been carried too far. In light of the current focus on child abuse, some writers fear even a limited continuation of the present sanctioning of corporal punishment by Parliament will create a societal norm conducive to physical abuse of children (Robertsaw, 1980). This is one of the reasons for the decline in the use of the strap for disciplinary control.

Although the United States has accepted the view that corporal punishment is not prohibited by the Constitutional prohibition against cruel and unusual punishment, the Law Reform Commission of Canada thinks our situation is different. The Commission points out (1984, p. 57) that there is no similar history in Canada that would so limit the application of section 12 of the Canadian Charter of Rights and Freedoms. The Commission's view is that the right to security of the person (section 7) and the right to equal protection (section 15, 1) will protect children from assault by teachers.

On the civil side, the two principal reasons why lawsuits are presently brought against a teacher and the school are either physical assault or teacher negligence, an unintentional tort to be considered later. When force is used, the main question is what is reasonable under the circumstances. Internal school procedures handle all but a few such incidents and these few tend to be only the most severe cases that are turned over to the legal authorities and the Crown prosecutor.

In a criminal case only the school teacher would be charged, while in a civil lawsuit the school board would also be named as a defendant. In the event of a judgment, the school board's insurance would pay and only in an exceptional case would the board attempt to recover the damages from the teacher. While thus protected from paying monetary damages, the teacher may be seriously affected by the publicity and the psychological trauma associated with a trial and the lengthy pre-trial procedures. In the exceptional case where the damages exceed funds available from insurance or the school board (usually an action for negligence where a student is paralyzed for life), the teacher could be required to pay. Also if the teacher's actions were contrary to school rules, the board can recover compensation from the teacher (Barnes, 1977).

THE COURTS AND IMPROPER DISCIPLINE

In the past, many of the cases involving excessive corporal punishment have been tried in the criminal courts, usually at the instigation of a parent. A civil lawsuit for damages is available, however, and the required proof of wrongdoing is easier to establish. For example, in *Andrews v. Hopkins* (1932) a father and his eleven-year-old daughter recovered civil damages for assault when the teacher negligently struck the girl's breast while strapping the hands. An opposite result was reached in *Murdock v. Richards* (1954) when both the school board and the teacher were found not responsible for an alleged assault. After a full trial the judge found the facts did not prove unreasonable and excessive force. Win or lose, the teacher was still obliged to defend the lawsuit.

Bargen (1961) details many legal situations that affect the school pupil and includes a discussion on discipline. He concludes that courts must ask three questions when considering a discipline case:

> 1. Was the teacher acting within the scope of his legal authority? This question involves the statutory authority of the teacher as well as his authority *in loco parentis*.
> 2. Was there cause for punishment? In answering this question the Courts have indicated their reluctance to set aside a teacher's judgment.
> 3. Was the punishment reasonable under the circumstances? This question generally constitutes the heart of any litigation and must be answered on the basis of precedent and common law. (p. 117)

It is usually this last question upon which reported decisions focus. One American line of decisions held that a teacher was responsible only when a pupil received permanent injury, or punishment was inflicted with malice, hate, illwill, anger, or for revenge. The Nova Scotia Supreme Court rejected this extreme view in *R. v. Gaul* (1904). The court concluded that a teacher who inflicts unreasonably severe chastisement upon a pupil is criminally responsible under the Criminal Code for the excess of force used, although the punishment resulted in no permanent injury and was inflicted without malice. Other Canadian courts have tended to follow this Nova Scotia decision. In *Campeau v. R.* (1951) the Quebec Court of King's Bench approved this rule and held a teacher guilty of assault upon three children who attended the school in which he was teaching. The evidence showed that the defendant had punished an eight-year-old by taking his arm by the wrist and striking the back of his hand several times on the corner of the teacher's desk. The judges agreed that this was unreasonable.

THE COURTS AND NON-TEACHING PERSONNEL

It is less clear whether non-teachers can use force in disciplinary situations. In *Prendergast v. Masterson* (1917) a U.S. Court held a superintendent was not a teacher and thus was not privileged. The court decided in this case that the law considers the teacher to be the:

> One who for the time being is *in loco parentis* to the pupil; who, by reason of his frequent and close association with the pupil, has an opportunity to know about the traits which distinguish him from other pupils; and who, therefore, can reasonably be expected to more intelligently judge the pupil's conduct than he otherwise could, and more justly measure the punishment he deserves, if any. (p. 247)

By contrast, two recent Canadian criminal cases accepted the defence offered in the Criminal Code although the Code does not spell out who besides teachers should stand in the place of a parent. A Saskatchewan court held that a vice-principal was able to punish three pupils who shouted names at him on their way home from school (*R. v. Haberstock*, 1970). In *R. v. Trynchy* (1970) a Yukon magistrate's court extended the right of discipline or control to a school bus driver. On several occasions the driver had warned the students to behave. He was charged with assault after he had stopped the bus and picked up a seven-year-old who had been running in the aisles and hitting other students. The driver asked the boy if he was going to "smarten up" and upon receiving an "O.K." dropped him in a seat, the boy's head possibly hitting the side of the bus. The court found that when a parent sends a child to school via public transportation, the parent has given over the teaching and discipline of the child to the educational system. This extends to the bus driver charged with the safe transportation of the children. The court concluded that although the driver could have used other means of discipline, the corrective force used was in fact not unreasonable under the circumstances.

The Unintentional Tort or Negligence

The most important field of tort liability today is negligence since this field controls our behaviour on a day-to-day basis. Negligence law compensates victims of accidents whose injuries result from someone else's faulty behaviour. Society imposes a standard of care or conduct—an expectation of certain behaviour—on all of its members. Some who have special training are held to a higher standard (but the usual test is what would a reasonable person have done under these circumstances). Negligence can be either misbehaviour or lack of appropriate behaviour. Linden (1977) points out that the Supreme Court of Canada has defined negligence thus: "Negligence consists in the doing of some act which a person of ordinary care and skill would not do under the circumstances, or omitting to do some act which a person of ordinary care and skill would do under the circumstances" (p. 91).

The most common example of misbehaviour is an automobile accident. A driver is going too fast for the road conditions and skids into another car. This is an illustration of an unintentional *act*; the behaviour of the driver caused the accident. In a school setting, if a teacher accidently hurts a child while conducting a science experiment, the teacher can be held responsible. When an accident happens as a result of a teacher's negligence, the school board and the teacher are financially responsible. The behaviour can become the basis of a civil lawsuit.

The more common experience of negligence in schools, however, comes from incidents in the school gym involving students who are not properly trained and/or who are inadequately supervised in using the equipment. We will consider student physical well-being in more detail later. It is sufficient here to say that both action and inaction can be cause for concern to teachers.

A less usual type of negligence in education is malpractice, a topic discussed by Newell (1978). The basis of the malpractice lawsuits against teachers is for failing to meet their professional obligations in the classroom. The logic of these claims against school boards and teachers follows from the concept of *in loco parentis*, discussed earlier. The teacher is acting for the benefit of the child while under the teacher's supervision. When the teacher is negligent in the role of substitute parent and irreparable damage occurs, Newell argues the teacher could be held responsible for damages. This reasoning is hard for many to accept and, to date, none of the courts in which these suits have been filed (all in the United States) has been persuaded that teachers have this high a duty (Collingsworth, 1982). Over the years courts have been adding constraints that regulate teacher behaviour. However, judges have not been ready to establish academic guidelines similar to these behavioural guidelines. At the present time a student has no recourse against a teacher who negligently denies him the benefits of a proper education.

LEGAL PROOF REQUIRED

To receive damages, an injured student and his or her parent (the plaintiff) must sue the responsible parties and prove four major factors:

1. *Legal Duty.* There has to be a legal duty of care between the plaintiff and defendant. Such is true between drivers of cars or between a teacher and a student, or between the school and the student body. In these cases, the question is not so much whether a duty exists, but the extent of that duty. On the other hand, there is no such duty between a person who is drowning and a person who is merely walking by, even though attracted by the calls of the drowning person. Should the observer attempt to save the other, however, a duty of care then comes into play.

2. *Standard of Care.* There has to be a failure to meet this duty. The law requires a minimum level of performance regardless of capability but does not expect perfect behaviour. The reasonable person may be guilty of an error in judgment and under such circumstances there still may be no breach of the duty. The reasonable person test also considers, however, the education, experience, and qualifications of a professional person, such as a teacher.

3. *Damages.* An injury or loss must occur. If there is no damage, there would be little point in commencing a lawsuit. The court tries to restore the plaintiff, as nearly as possible with money damages, to the position prior to the negligent act. The real question thus relates to the extent of loss that has occurred. Physical loss, such as destruction of an automobile, or medical bills and actual loss of wages during hospitalization can be quantified. On the other hand, some kinds of damages such as pain and suffering are hard to demonstrate and little or no compensation may be awarded.

4. *Causation.* There must be a causal relationship between the damage to the plaintiff and the wrongful act of the defendant. The plaintiff must convince the judge that the loss was foreseeable by a reasonable person. If the accident would not have occurred had not the defendant been negligent, then his behaviour is the cause of the injury. Sometimes the defendant is also held responsible for unexpected events that follow from the accident that should have been foreseen, such as observers becoming ill from watching a classmate receiving a serious injury.

Despite the presence of a duty, a breach of duty and resulting damage, a plaintiff's claim can still be defeated because of his or her own conduct. Consider a mature high school football player. If he is negligent with regard to his own safety during the game such as by violating a rule designed to insure player safety, he may be denied the protection of the law in whole or in part. Again since he voluntarily assumes the risk of being hurt during the game, he may not be able to recover damages if the risk is one that he could reasonably have foreseen. This is similar to the idea of informed consent discussed earlier.

These elements apply to any action for negligence and teachers should keep them in mind as they think about their duty to the students entrusted to their care. For example, the duty implied by the doctrine of *in loco parentis* requires teachers to take action supportive of the student's physical well-being, but at the same time to recognize their limitation to provide direct assistance.

Student Physical Well-being

There are four main areas where the school has a duty of care. These include provision of: safe transportation to and from school and school activities; a safe building and grounds; safe equipment for use of students; and adequate supervision. Although the individual teacher is most concerned about the last area, there is a responsibility for teachers to report unsafe conditions to the principal when they cannot alleviate the situation on their own.

SUPERVISION

Teachers daily encounter situations that demand immediate decisions and immediate actions to preserve the physical well-being of students under their control. In each case, what is the extent of the teacher's legal responsibility toward the student? Elementary school teachers are often faced with issues of hall, gym, or playground injuries, students becoming ill in class, or with parental requests to medicate their child, often with regular doses of life-sustaining medication. Secondary school science, physical education, and vocational class instructors have special responsibilities in dealing with potential class, gym, and shop injuries or accidents. In addition, all teachers have a responsibility when they expect homework or out of school activity:

> When an instructor has reason to believe that a student will work or play with instruments or materials off the premises which relate to his schoolwork and which might cause harm to himself or to others, the instructor must advise the student clearly of all potential dangers and of the precautions necessary to prevent injuries. (Hagenau, 1980, p. 217)

Teachers have a special obligation to supervise dangerous situations and have on occasion been held legally responsible for improper or inadequate supervision when students have been injured. In most of these cases, the teacher has been found negligent for not preventing the accident. For example, in Prince George, B.C., a physical education instructor was found responsible because there had been a previous similar accident involving a different student. The court in that case said:

> Once one youngster had become hurt, would not a prudent father want to know how and why his child had become hurt in order to avoid the same kind of risk to another child. The teacher should have foreseen further trouble . . . he should have guarded against that further trouble. (Cited in ASTA, 1980, p. 16)

Teachers are responsible for a student's physical well-being on school grounds and during school hours. For example, when a teacher sees a larger child assaulting a smaller child, the teacher has an affirmative duty to intervene. It is less clear whether this responsibility extends to after-school activities when no school sponsorship is involved. However, if students regularly use the school facilities with the implied consent of the school authorities, liability may occur.

When school sponsorship occurs outside the school, the teachers' duty to supervise continues. For example, both the school and teachers were found liable for damages when an accident occurred during the taking of class pictures in a public park on a Saturday. A high school senior wanted to be photographed on his motorcycle, but was careless and injured another student. The teachers knew he was performing stunts on his motorcycle and should have foreseen the danger to others; they thus failed to properly supervise the school outing (Hagenau, 1980).

In addition, there may be serious problems when the school does not provide adequate transportation for out of school activities. In such cases teachers should not get involved in supplemental or unofficial transportation schemes. A common example is a field trip where cars are used. It is clear that teachers should not use their own personal vehicles for such activities. It is less clear what happens when teachers request students to make their own travel arrangements. Parents are usually responsible when they transport their own or other children to school-sponsored activities. However, if a teacher or school arranges for this type of transportation, the teacher and school also may be held responsible for a subsequent accident (Hagenau, 1980).

PARENTAL REQUESTS FOR MEDICAL TREATMENT

There is an increasing call upon teachers to administer either prescription medication (such as Ritalin or insulin) or non-prescription medication (such as
aspirin) during school hours. Both the Alberta School Trustees Association
(ASTA) and the Alberta Teachers' Association agree that teachers, unless medically competent, should not administer such medication. When facing such
requests the ASTA points out to teachers and principals: "Regardless of the
nature of the medication school personnel should refrain from acceding to such
requests. Suffice to say, the necessity for and the means of administering medication are not knowledge and skills ordinarily possessed by most school personnel" (1980, p. 5).

Nevertheless there is a duty to respond to a parental request for care while the
student is in school. The teacher is obligated to identify such students and
supervise the appropriate use of medication as would a reasonable and prudent
parent in like circumstances. Most students requiring continuing use of medication (including insulin shots) learn to take or give the medication to themselves.
Thus it might be appropriate for a teacher to provide safe storage for a drug, to
remind a student when to take the drug or ascertain if it has been taken, and to
provide a secure environment and the time during which the student can take
the drug required.

One area that has raised considerable concern is the school health care of allergic children. Elaborate procedures have been developed in some schools for the
emergency care of such children when minutes will make the difference between
life and death. Ekstrand (1982) suggests the following components to a supplemental educational program for staff:

1. *Knowledge of Allergens.* Preparation of lists of common allergens that should
   be recognizable to all personnel.
2. *Identification of Allergic Pupils.* The maintenance of lists of allergic pupils
   for the purpose of screening against school events and schedules that might
   cause allergic reaction.
3. *Recognition of Allergic Reaction in Pupils.* The conduct of in-service meetings to
   assist teachers in the early recognition of pupils undergoing allergic reaction.
4. *Limitation of Materials of Allergic Nature.* The maintenance of appropriate
   purchasing procedures for all school and classroom materials.
5. *Environmental Controls.* The maintenance of procedures regarding temperature and humidity control, air purification, cleaning routines, and insecti-
   cide/pesticide spraying.

CONSENT TO MEDICAL TREATMENT

From time to time teachers will be faced with injuries from accidents that demand immediate attention beyond first aid. Teachers taking an injured child to a doctor or emergency room may well have trouble obtaining medical treatment because of the issue of the consent needed to obtain such treatment, both from the hospital as well as the doctor. Consent has been one of the more troublesome questions facing doctors in recent years and only in a medical emergency involving life and death will the doctor intervene without it. There is some trend toward giving children under the age of eighteen the right to consent to treatment where their own physical well-being is at stake. For example, some writers believe that even a young child could consent to the setting of a broken leg (Picard, 1978). Even so, it is now the policy of most doctors and emergency rooms not to perform any intrusive therapy with a minor child without the appropriate consent.

This requirement makes it difficult to treat a student when no parent is immediately available, either because of work or due to being out-of-town. In addition to school personnel, neither neighbours nor friends may give valid consent—only a legal guardian may do so. This practice puts the teacher (or other school personnel) in a very difficult position. While the teacher has responsibility for the welfare of the child and does have parental authority in dealing with disciplinary situations, this authority does not extend to providing medical treatment. In the event a teacher or principal finds a child in need of medical attention, first aid should be provided where appropriate. The following three recommendations of the ASTA (1980, p. 8) should then be followed:

1. School personnel, unless medically competent, should not administer medication to students.
2. When required, staff should provide emergency transport of students to a medical practitioner or hospital.
3. The teacher or other staff member should stay with the student until: (a) competent medical assistance is secured; or (b) the parents or legal guardians arrive; or (c) the staff member is relieved by other board-authorized personnel.

Since no school personnel can grant consent to the doctor or hospital to treat the student involved, this means that the teacher usually will have to stay with the student until the parent or guardian arrives. The medical staff is unlikely to treat such a non-life threatening situation or baby-sit the student and the teacher is left with this responsibility. Teachers have a duty of care for the

physical well-being of their students. At times this obligation could be oner-
ous if the full support of the other school staff is not available.

• • •

ETHICAL ISSUES

As professionals, teachers need to understand the moral aspects of teaching and
beware of how to make ethical decisions relating to their profession and the welfare of their students. Most provincial teachers' associations require teachers to
follow a Professional Code of Conduct that offers little ethical guidance. Like
most professional groups, teachers are bound by statements about behavioural
expectations rather than guided by a systematic ethical code based on articulated moral principles (Eberlein, 1988d).

Some have argued that ethics is the responsibility of management, not of the
teaching profession (Libermann, 1988). It is true that teacher groups are often in
a conflict of interest position when dealing with certain ethical dilemmas. Often
management is as well. What would be useful is a new code of ethics for teachers
based on moral principles with some guidance in the ethical decision-making
process (Eberlein, 1987; 1988c). I have developed one such possibility utilizing
four principles, based on the work of the Canadian Psychological Association
(CPA, 1986; Eberlein, 1988a; 1990; 1991). Although ethical decision making is
the primary responsibility of the individual teacher, support for the process is
needed from colleagues, management, and the professional associations.

Principle I: Respect for the Dignity of Persons

In all contacts with students, teachers should accept as fundamental the principle of respect for the dignity of their students. This is the belief that each student should be treated as a person or an end in himself or herself, not as an
object or a means to an end. Teachers should acknowledge that all students are
entitled to have their innate worth as human beings appreciated and that this
worth is not enhanced or reduced by any individual differences. Although
teachers have a responsibility to respect the dignity of all persons, they always
have a greater responsibility to their students, who are in a more vulnerable
position, than to persons indirectly involved (school boards and other teachers,
parents, and the general public).

The concept of moral rights is an essential component of respect for the dignity
of persons. Rights to privacy, self-determination, and autonomy are of particular

importance, including the right of students to provide informed consent to activities that involve them. As vulnerabilities increase (at younger ages), the power of persons to control their environment or their lives decreases. The younger the child, the greater the teacher's responsibility to establish safeguards to protect that student's rights.

This principle also includes the concept of equal justice. All students are entitled to benefit equally from the knowledge and contributions of the teaching profession.

Principle II: Responsible Caring

A basic ethical expectation of any profession is that a practitioner be competent and involved in activities that are not harmful to members of society. Teachers must be concerned about the welfare of any student, family, or group with whom they have a relationship as a teacher. Their greatest responsibility is to protect the welfare of those directly involved in their activities (usually the student); their responsibility to school boards, parents, and the general public is therefore secondary.

Because students are seldom "asked" for their consent to take part in many school activities, there is a greater urgency for responsible caring by teachers to protect the welfare of students under their control. This principle would lead teachers to consider the potential harm and benefits involved in their proposed activities, to predict the likelihood of the risks or benefits occurring, and to choose activities where the potential benefits outweigh any potential harm. In the process, teachers need to use pedagogical methods that minimize harm and maximize benefits and to take responsibility for correcting any harmful effects that have occurred as a result of their activities.

This calls for a self-awareness on the part of the teacher and a recognition that incompetent action is, by definition, unethical. Competent teachers continue to expand and update their knowledge and engage in self-reflection to see how their own values and social position affect their teaching activities. These teachers are concerned about both short-term and long-term physical and psychological factors in their students. These include self-worth, fear, humiliation, and interpersonal trust, as well as physical safety, comfort, and freedom from injury.

Responsible caring recognizes the ability of individuals, families, and groups to care for themselves, and each other. However, teachers do recognize that as vulnerabilities increase or as power to control one's own life decreases, they have an increasing responsibility to protect the well-being of the student, family, or group involved.

Principle III: Integrity in Relationships

Relationships formed by teachers with students, families, and other staff members embody explicit and implicit mutual expectations of integrity. These include fairness, impartiality, straightforwardness, avoidance of deception, avoidance of conflicts of interest, and the provision of accurate information.

As these values exist within the context of the first two principles (Respect for the Dignity of Persons and Responsible Caring), there will be circumstances in which honesty and straightforwardness will need to be tempered. At times, full disclosure may not be needed or desired and, in some circumstances, it may be a risk to the dignity or well-being of others, especially those in more vulnerable positions.

Professional integrity and teaching accountability imply a responsibility for teachers to maintain competence in their respective fields and require that teachers actively rely on, and be guided by their professional community and its guidelines and requirements.

Principle IV: Responsibility to Society

Teaching exists as a profession within the context of society. Teachers have responsibilities to the society in which they live and work and to the welfare of all human beings in those societies. Teachers are expected to use their knowledge in the development of social structure and policies that will be used for beneficial purposes—purposes that support and reflect the first three principles.

Teachers acknowledge that many social structures have evolved slowly over time in response to human need, are valued by society, and are primarily beneficial. Teachers convey respect for these social structures and avoid unwarranted or unnecessary disruptions. Suggestions for, and action toward, change or enhancement of such social structures are carried out only through an educational process that seeks to achieve a consensus within society through democratic means.

On the other hand, some social structures ignore or oppose the principles of respect for the dignity of the person, responsible caring, and integrity in relationships. In extreme cases, it would be irresponsible for teachers to work within these social structures and not be critical of them. They would be advocates for change to occur as quickly as possible.

Teachers as a whole need to be self-reflective about the role of education and their own role in society, and about the ways in which they might be contributing to or detracting from beneficial societal changes. Teachers need to engage in even-tempered observation and interpretation of social structure and policies, their effects, and their process of change. Individual teachers must decide for themselves the most appropriate and beneficial use of their time and talents in helping to meet this collective responsibility.

. . .

APPLICATION OF ETHICAL
PRINCIPLES TO CASE STUDY

There is no single answer to the type of dilemma presented at the beginning of this paper. A review of the legal responsibilities does not provide a definitive answer. Child abuse statutes may or may not require reporting this case to welfare authorities. When discussing this dilemma, students almost always think that some form of action must be taken by Ms. Waite, but there is usually a wide diversity of proposed solutions. In every case, the student's foremost goal is to protect Judy and the other students in Mr. Foster's class (Eberlein, 1988d). Focussing on the four ethical principles, Judy Frith's dignity and right to autonomy, privacy, confidentiality, self-determination, and freedom from harassment are relevant issues. Because Mr. Foster also has similar rights, responsible caring would consider that public knowledge of the charge could destroy Mr. Foster's teaching career and have a lasting impact on him and his family. Even if Judy's story is not proved, Mr. Foster's life would continue under a cloud. Fairness implies an honest consideration of alternatives; due process implies a chance to be heard. The impact on other students and school personnel needs consideration.

An issue of some importance is Judy's family's right to know and be involved in what has happened to her and to have input into the decision process. Society has given parents general control over the upbringing and education of their children, even when parental wishes conflict with the children's desires (Henniger, 1987).

With these thoughts in mind, what can Ms. Waite do? Students have suggested the following possible alternatives (Eberlein, 1990, 1991):

1. Counsel and support Judy but take no further action.
2. Move Judy to another English class.
3. Quietly observe Mr. Foster's behaviour.
4. Call in other students to verify Mr. Foster's behaviour.
5. Discuss the matter with Mr. Foster.
6. File a complaint with the teacher's association.
7. Refer the matter to Mr. Foster's principal.
8. Call Judy's parents, even against her wishes, and let them decide.
9. Call the child welfare authorities or police.

Although several alternatives appear to be ethical, none will fully meet the competing demands of the case. Ms. Waite may want to consult and discuss the issues with others but ultimately, she will have to make a decision on which alternative (or combination of alternatives) to choose. In the process, she may well find another choice of action that is more acceptable than those listed.

• • •

CONCLUSION

In the preceding pages we have discussed only a few of the many legal rights, duties, and ethical responsibilities encountered daily by teachers. There are other important issues that have not been discussed because of lack of space or because they have been covered elsewhere. Some of these issues have seen extensive development in the U.S. and are of relevance to teachers. For example, behaviour modification programs are extremely important in education and have serious and complex social and legal implications (Eberlein, 1986a; *Edmonton Journal*, 1992). When behavioural programs are experimental in nature or when there are risks to the child, special care must be used to gain the informed consent discussed above. Reward contingencies or a token economy do not raise the same concerns as long as the child is not denied rights or privileges generally provided the rest of the students.

Another important contemporary issue is the teacher's role in child abuse, incest, and family violence (Eberlein & Swindlehurst, 1979). In some provinces teachers are by law placed on the *front line* and legally expected to report suspected cases to the authorities, perhaps even by-passing the principal. One can argue this was true in the Judy Frith case.

Privacy issues in Canada may follow the American lead. In the past few years the U.S. Congress has become sensitive to the public school's invasion of a family's privacy. The Family Educational Rights and Privacy Act of 1974 requires parental consent to many teaching and counselling situations including testing and behavioural modification experiments (Ziskind, 1975). And what of a student's right to privacy or to be secure against unreasonable searches? For years many courts in the U.S. have recognized that students and their school lockers or dorm rooms, are not to be searched by school authorities without permission (Stevens, 1980). Will there be similar issues in Canada arising under the new Charter of Rights and Freedoms?

The discussion in this paper is general and should not be considered legal advice. Decisions ultimately are made by the courts when the law is applied to a specific factual situation. At times, decisions may seem to be inconsistent.

However, it is not the law that changes as much as its application to a new and different set of facts. Teachers should not be intimidated by what has been discussed. Almost all legal and ethical conflicts can be avoided by the use of common sense. Schools should anticipate possible dangerous situations and provide teachers with a plan of action for common emergencies, such as is done for fire drills. Teachers should act in a reasonable way in their daily contact with students. If there is active communication with parents about what is happening in school, small difficulties will not become major problems with the potential for lawsuits. Common sense and good will can avert most of the problems discussed in this paper.

· · ·

REFERENCES

Alberta School Trustees Association. (1980). *Medication treatment of students: A dilemma for school systems*. Edmonton: ASTA.

Andrews v. Hopkins, 3 D.L.R. 459 (N.S.S.C.) (1932).

Baker v. Owen, 395 F. Supp. 294 (M.D.N.C.), affd mem., 423 U.S. 907 (1975).

Bargen, P. F. (1961). *The legal status of the Canadian public school pupils*. Toronto: Macmillan.

Barnes, J. (1977). Tort liability of school boards to pupils. In L. Klar (Ed.), *Studies in Canadian Tort Law*. Toronto: Butterworths.

Campeau v. R., 14 C.R. 202 (Que.K.B.) (1951).

Canadian Psychological Association, Committee on Ethics. (1986). Code of ethics. *Highlights, 8*(1), 6E–12E.

Collingsworth, T. P. (1982). Applying negligence doctrine to the teaching profession. *Journal of Law and Education, 11*, 479–505.

Eberlein, L. (1986a). *Behaviour modification in the classroom: Part II—Legal and ethical issues*. Unpublished manuscript. Department of Educational Psychology, University of Alberta, Edmonton.

Eberlein, L. (1986b). Corporal punishment to be banned in Canada? Proposed changes to the Criminal Code. *The Canadian School Executive, 6*(6), 15–17.

Eberlein, L. (1987). Introducing ethics to beginning psychologists: A problem-solving approach. *Professional Psychology: Research and Practice, 18*, 353–360.

Eberlein, L. (1988a). *Canadian teachers: Legal and ethical concerns*. Edmonton: University of Alberta.

Eberlein, L. (1988b). Judicial intervention in school administration. *The Canadian School Executive, 8*(5), 3–10.

Eberlein, L. (1988c). The new CPA Code of Ethics for Canadian psychologists: An education and training perspective. *Canadian Psychology, 29*, 206–212.

Eberlein, L. (1988d). Psychologists vs. teachers: Code of ethics in conflict? *Matrix: The Counselling Psychology Newsletter, 1*(1), 6–7.

Eberlein, L. (1990). Ethical decision making for teachers. *Clearing House, 63*(3), 125–129.

Eberlein, L. (1991). Ethical decision making for teachers. In F. Schultz (Ed.), *Education 91/92*. Guilford, CT: Dashkin.

Eberlein, L., & Swindlehurst, B. (1979). Child abuse, the law and the counsellor. *The School Guidance Worker, 345*, 37–42.

Edmonton Journal. (1992, June). Board examines "time-out" cubicle school punishment (June 1, p. A7); Isolation cubicle under scrutiny (June 4, p. A6); Schools told they can use padded rooms (June 11, p. A7).

Ekstrand, R. E. (1982, May-June). Doctor, do you make (school) house calls? *Children Today*, 2–5.

Gee, E. G., & Sperry, D. J. (1978). *Educational law and the public school: A compendium.* Boston: Allyn and Bacon.

Guerrieri v. Tyson, 147 Pa. Super. 239, 24 A.2d 468 (1942).

Hagenau, W. P. (1980). Penumbras of care beyond the schoolhouse gate. *Journal of Law and Education, 9*, 217.

Hammes, R. R. (1982). In Loco Parentis: Considerations in teacher/student relationships. *Clearing House, 56*, 8–11.

Hawkins, V. J. (1976). The negativism of corporal punishment. *Clearing House, 49*, 226–233.

Henniger, M. L. (1987). Parental rights and responsibilities in the educational process. *Clearing House, 60*, 226–229.

Law Reform Commission. (1984). *Assault.* Working Paper 38. Ottawa: Law Reform Commission of Canada.

Libermann, M. (1988). Professional ethics in public education: An autopsy. *Phi Delta Kappan, 70*, 159–160.

Linden, A. M. (1977). *Canadian Tort Law.* Toronto: Butterworths.

Murdock v. Richards, 1 D.L.R. 766 (N.S.S.C.) (1954).

Newell, R. C. (1978). Teacher malpractice. *Case and Comment, 83*(4), 3–10.

Niewiadomski v. U.S., 159 F.2d 683 (6th Cir. 1974).

Picard, E. (1978). *Legal liability of doctors and hospitals in Canada.* Toronto: Carswell.

Powys v. Mansfield, 6 Sim 528, 58 E.R. 692 (1836).

Prendergast v. Masterson, 196 S.W. 246 (Cr. Civil Appeals, Texas, 1917).

R. v. Gaul, 8 C.C.C. 178 (N.S.S.C.) (1904).

R. v. Haberstock, 1 C.C.C.(2d) 433 (Sask C.A.) (1970).

R. v. Trynchy, C.R.N.S. 95 (Y. Magis. Ct.) (1970).

Restatement of the law: Torts 2nd. (1977). St. Paul, MN: American Law Institute.

Robertshaw, C. (1980). *Outline of key legislative issues relating to child abuse.* Discussion paper prepared for Social Services Division. Ottawa: Department of National Health and Welfare.

Shtitz v. C.N.R., 1 D.L.R. 951 (Sask. C.A.) (1927).

Spitalli, S., Jr. (1978). Corporal punishment. *Clearing House, 49*, 418–420.

Stevens, R. E. (1980). Invasion of student privacy. *Journal of Law and Education, 9*, 343–351.

Williams, J. S. (1976). *The law of defamation in Canada.* Toronto: Butterworths.

Wilson, F. C. (1980). *A look at corporal punishment and some implication of its use.* Toronto: Ontario Ministry of Community and Social Services.

Ziskind, M. A. (1975). Protecting the privacy of school children and their families through the Family Educational Rights and Privacy Act of 1974. *Journal of Family Law, 14*, 255–279.

EMERGING ISSUES IN HUMAN RIGHTS EDUCATION

...

Douglas   Ray

his chapter examines the definition, scope, method of, and resources for human rights education in Canada. The debate about the validity of human rights education is reviewed from the perspective of four current philosophies underlying curricular decisions. Some legal issues are examined, including traditional human rights protections and cases that have emerged as a result of appeals based on the Canadian Charter of Rights and Freedoms. Since the standards or arguments that are respected elsewhere in the world influence Canadian thinking, the chapter concludes with a look at certain international issues that are relevant to the Canadian scene. The conclusion identifies some current research about human rights.

This chapter reflects school data from a 1984 survey of human rights education conducted in eight provinces and the territories, subsequent curricular changes, and pertinent information from influential Canadian and international authors. The content of human rights education is identified, but there are notes on justifications, limitations, and methodology, and the interdisciplinary nature of resources is stressed.

Human rights education, as it has emerged in Canadian society, has a political and legal impetus deriving from the constitutional debates, several court cases based on the Charter of Rights and Freedoms, and recent discussions of the roles of the federal or provincial human rights commissions. One aspect of human rights education is to promote awareness of these key legislative and jurisdictional issues (Webking, 1984).

Ministries of education, school boards, faculties of education, and teachers' federations evince a "school based" interest in human rights issues and how they may be discussed most effectively. They expect discussion of international events, problems, and approaches to result in comparisons and evaluation. They do not rely exclusively upon international, federal, or provincial documents.

Teachers see the age or maturity of pupils to be vital in determining strategy and selecting appropriate examples (Brown, 1988). Young children are rarely taught human rights as a subject, but teachers try to ensure that it is reflected in most school or social activities (e.g., it is *wrong* to discriminate on the basis of sex, race, or disability). This kind of lesson is conveyed in games and other school-controlled activities, as well as in the formal curriculum. Although this "atmosphere approach" is continued into secondary schools, at this level specific subjects introduce issues calculated to involve and transform the students' perceptions (Kehoe, 1980).

Teachers are advised to use pedagogical strategies to select appropriate examples rather than use ephemeral trivia (Whitehead, 1988), to involve students in meaningful appraisals of events (Kehoe, 1983), to move beyond an exchange of opinions to mastery of expert advice on public policy (Webking, 1984), and to introduce particular themes at the most effective moment (Torney-Purta, 1982). Consequently, pre-service and in-service programs for teachers are vital to the success of human rights education (Kidd & Ray, 1983). Although Ray's (1984b) Canadian survey revealed that many teachers were interested in training courses reflecting human rights, few had such opportunities. Only Nova Scotia has human rights as a theoretical requirement in teacher education, and only some faculties elsewhere offered optional courses. Still other faculties contain aspects of human rights in other courses.

In universities and community colleges, many disciplines offer a specialized approach to human rights education: women's studies, the rights of the accused and convicted, workers' compensation, and the right to work. The interests of the teachers in their own political and economic environment—such as academic freedom and tenure—may result in these topics being discussed as case studies of vocational rights.

This chapter emphasizes schools because they can most effectively communicate public policy to the population, and because none of the 1984 interviews revealed opposition or indifference to human rights education in the schools. In fact, most curriculum directors believe that their official programs promote awareness and respect for various rights, with some attention to challenges to rights in Canada or elsewhere. Protection of rights is considered to be vital civic behaviour in a democracy (Berger, 1981), and such ideas have to be promoted. The most serious threats or infringements of human rights in Canada need to be examined.

Documents that list and define human rights are drawn upon as appropriate to the age of the pupils and the purposes of a particular subject. The most important international sources are the Universal Declaration of Human Rights (1948) and subsequent United Nations declarations and covenants. Certain historical documents such as the Magna Carta, the American Constitution and Bill of Rights, and speeches such as "The Four Freedoms" are still vital. Canadian documents like the Charter of Rights and Freedoms, provincial charters and codes, and certain legislation are drawn upon for many classes. Several teachers employ sacred books and great literature for discussing human rights because legal documents are not usually comprehensible in the original wording.

Within Canada, certain events violated or denied rights to particular persons (Berger, 1981; Poonwassie, 1992). Canadians differ on remedies for these violations. One of the most important aspects of human rights education is the discussion of means for resolution of such differences of opinion. Many Canadians hold views about fairness or justice that do not correspond with the law. There are various processes by which citizens are able to change the law, and it is possible that they will receive official support for their efforts to win remedies. Human rights education, particularly in higher education, may even advise citizens how to participate effectively in selected struggles for rights: for women, children, the aged, language groups, ethnic or racial minorities, particular occupations, or the disabled (Gifford, 1988).

• • •

DOUBTS CONCERNING EFFECTIVE INSTITUTIONALIZATION OF HUMAN RIGHTS

The school curriculum can transform what children know with considerable speed. What they value and how they act are not so easily changed (Urman, 1980). Perhaps it is just as well. For over forty years most educators have been reluctant to impose beliefs upon their students, hoping that providing knowledge and skills for addressing problems would promote independent thinking and resistance to facile ideologies. "Brainwashing" and "indoctrination" seemed repulsive to the liberal educator. Several "value neutral" systems of exploring issues rather than imposing solutions were devised by liberal educators (Harmin et al., 1973; Kohlberg, 1975).

But were these retreats from clearly defended and publicly perceived principles justified? Could the schools *lead* rather than merely respond to society? These questions were posed and answered convincingly by several giants of educational thought, most of whom agreed that teachers (and education as a whole) should affirm and reflect a consistent set of moral principles (Counts, 1969; Faure et al., 1972; Lauwerys, 1968). It is this positive affirmation that gives denominational schooling its special cachet. Perhaps unfortunately, public schools are often defined in negative terms by detractors who claim that, without religious instruction, they lack any moral conviction (Bergen, 1990). Supporters of public schooling take the opposite tack and propose that understanding, appreciation, or toleration are vital for Canadian society (McLeod, 1989). Early attempts at publicly financed education (by Strachan and Ryerson, for example) were often efforts to impose the educator's own religious convictions, but eventually a broader perspective emerged.

Human rights offer a means to make more rational the diversified public, denominational, linguistic, and ideologically based schools of Canada. If constraints were placed upon private schools (probably coupled with grants to induce them to conform), their curriculum and perhaps their teacher selection would fall under public scrutiny (Shapiro, 1984). The most divisive aspects of their activities would be curtailed, but not necessarily their capacity to appeal to different interests (Committee on Tolerance and Understanding, 1984). The possibility that individual teachers abuse their roles within public schools remains: periodic episodes underline the danger to children, to society, and to the reputation of professional education.

The challenge is how to devise and operate a system of education that is flexible, responsive, and responsible; it is not acceptable to maintain complex security checks of all that transpires within individual classrooms (Committee on Tolerance and Understanding, 1984). Proposals assume the participation of pupils, professionals, parents, and the interested public. Human rights education would likely serve only as a framework within which diversity would be variously justified and promoted.

Not all Canadians are convinced that human rights are best promoted by government intervention (Ray, 1983). To some, the periodic election of governments at the local, provincial, or federal level is the best protection—and almost the only one required. An alert and aroused electorate will "turf the rascals out" if they threaten traditional rights.[1] According to conservative interpretations of promoting rights, autocratic authorities, or bureaucratic bunglers (such as advocates of only politically correct works) are a bigger threat to freedom than many direct challenges to it. By this reasoning, human rights commissions restrict the right of managers to run their businesses; equal rights or minimum wage regulations undermine competitiveness, prosperity, and, in the long run, jobs. Similarly, traditional parliamentarians argue that ordinary legislation is more appropriate than entrenched constitutions and codes that, over time, lose their congruence to the emerging situations (Romanow, 1982–83). The most obvious example of this viewpoint has been the continuing reluctance of most provincial governments to entrench official language rights.

Although these debates among theorists and parliamentarians may not reflect the typical views of the public, this subject needs more systematic investigation.

. . .

WHO KNOWS WHAT IS BEST FOR THE CHILD?

Some balance must be found among the conflicting claims that the best interests of the child lie in:

1. the freedom to develop, unrestrained by conventions;
2. firm but loving guidance from the family;
3. professional management of learning situations; and/or
4. respect for eternal truths devised through the ages.

Recent Canadian and international experience includes some indication why a balance among these ideals is appropriate. The period from the mid-1960s to 1975 saw progressivism and a brief flirtation with the "freedom promotes growth and responsibility" thesis, with mixed results. Few schools were able to demonstrate that effective, let alone maximum, learning was ensured when there was great freedom and diversity. More attention to *demonstrating* what was learned would have helped, but the era encouraged or permitted behaviour that saddened and alarmed traditionalists. Perhaps the ideals of schools like Summerhill were unrealistically high. At any rate, the risk of perceived failure led educational systems to tighten controls, reduce the proportion of optional courses in secondary and higher education, add examinations, and require more attention to the basics (Allison, 1984; Hersom, 1980). Although this official recentralization dismisses the argument for more personal autonomy by the learner, there remains a degree of selection among a range of course alternatives and some freedom of study and evaluation modes. "The best interests of the child" are officially upheld, except for very mature students, it is likely to be identified and exercised on behalf of pupils by a parent or professional educator.

The family has traditionally been the official safeguard for the child's best interests (Magsino, 1991). In fact, The Universal Declaration of Human Rights (1948, Article 26,3) proposes that "parents have a prior right to choose the kind of education that shall be given to their children." A Quebec case (*Chabot v. Les Commissaires d'Écoles de Lamorandière*) and two Ontario cases (*Zylberg et al. v. The*

Director of Education of the Sudbury Board of Education and Essex County) ruled that parents had the right to prevent religious exercises from being imposed upon their child. Chabot (in MacKay, 1984) cited a natural law principle of "the authority of the father to guide and govern the education of his child" (p. 65).

This is not the same as controlling, providing, or censoring of course. Censoring particular subjects or sources of information, or avoiding particular teachers may be extreme forms of parental choice, which for most situations are not practical because of restricted educational resources. Imperfect though existing opportunities may be, they are usually worthy of students' time and effort and pose no threat to the "full development of their human potential."

Neglect of children, or making choices that restrict educational opportunities, is not the worst offence committed by some parents. The Badgley et al. (1984) study reveals that an alarming number of families offer more dangers than protection in sexual offences: "it appears that about three in four victims are girls and that one in four is a boy. . . . a large number of victims were very young children" (p. 519). A great many of these incidents happened in the home, and the offenders were family members or trusted friends of the family. Children of single-parent families were often particularly vulnerable. Religious boarding schools were shocked to learn that similar incidents marred their reputations.

Physical abuse within the family is no longer tolerated. "A man's home is his castle," but even within that castle wife and children are theoretically protected by the possibility of legal action against abusers. Court procedures are available to remove children from families that pose dangers to their safety, development, and emotional health. Increasingly, the school plays a role in alerting authorities to risks of this kind, a very vital extension of human rights education (MacKay, 1984). Never before have teachers been named so explicitly as protectors of the child's best interests. It goes far beyond the professional or academic respect that had traditionally led parents to defer on many issues.

Conversely, the right of the school authorities, especially of the principal and teachers, to manage all aspects of the learning process has now been effectively challenged by parents and other members of the community. The law still gives professionals the authority to maintain discipline and teach without interference by the community (MacKay, 1984), but *realpolitik* has made it necessary to listen to the parents and the community (Magsino, 1991). Students in jeans or unorthodox haircuts are no longer automatically presumed to challenge the system, so they are usually tolerated. This aspect of principals' authority, although still on the books, is eroding through disuse and through a natural reluctance to engage in political or legal arguments related to relatively minor aspects of school responsibility (MacKay, 1984).

The fourth justification of particular educational practices—"eternal truths" or "timeless traditions"—varies according to the group being considered. In Canada this has necessarily promoted compromise as various groups sent their children to the same schools. It is not easy to insist that the traditions of Ireland, Italy, Iran, India, Israel, and Indiana be simultaneously observed. Social relationships among the students become one means of questioning long established ways. It may even be that particular traditions are illegal in Canada (Fairweather, 1987). The growing diversity of the Canadian population has made it less possible to insist on exclusively British traditions in any province, and even an officially French Quebec proves to be elusive (Majhanovich & Ray, 1991). The definition of official language may become more flexible so that other languages have more possible applications.

Canada has officially embraced multiculturalism for the federal jurisdiction, and many provinces have accepted a similar stance. The administration of multiculturalism requires viable ethnic or cultural groups to devise educational programs to which the government can lend support rather than ongoing state sponsorship for any particular group (even those buttressed by aboriginal status or "founding nations" credentials, which have assured funding from various sources). Although groups may be assured that their language will be taught where appropriate and their culture will be included in the social studies programs, no group will be able to exclude other languages or cultures from the curriculum. No single language or culture will be able to assimilate and dominate all others (Mallea, 1984). Although these interpretations of the meaning of various provincial legislation and regulations may not be upheld in every judicial decision, they seem to be the current mode. For example, the language policy proclaimed in 1984 for the Northwest Territories assures the rights of English, French, and six native languages. These types of policy go some distance in ensuring the group rights of the populations concerned. More aspects of human rights may in time become a significant part of education.

• • •

LEGAL ISSUES

The courts have always been important in interpreting grey areas of legislation and practice, such as defining the rights of parents, students, and teachers within the context of education, even before human rights codes and the Charter of Rights and Freedoms (Enns, 1963; McCurdy, 1968). Decisions have

an influence far beyond the particular criminal or civil cases that are actually lit-
igated, for each ruling is taken as a general guide for other similar situations.
Teachers' federations, trustees' associations, faculties of education, and sometimes other groups such as religious organizations ensure that judicial findings
of particular importance have a wide audience. Recent findings often reveal
human rights to be a vital part of school management and teachers' personal
rights.

The test of fairness is a recent example. Basically, it requires that the process
used to arrive at a decision that is of great importance to an individual must
have been *fair*: for example, information could not be suppressed or protected
from reasonable challenge, there must have been opportunity to seek advice and
to weigh consequences, the plaintiff cannot also act as the judge, etc. The test
does not ensure that decisions will be reversed, only that unfair procedures will
be struck down, in effect guaranteeing a new trial or an automatic appeal
(MacKay, 1984). Schools must provide appeal procedures for minor student
infractions or leave themselves vulnerable to the charge of unfairness (Bergen,
1982). Until recently, when the courts have ruled on teachers' or principals
supervisory decisions, they have endorsed the right of the authority to decide,
rather than the correctness of particular actions. For important matters, there
has always been the protection of the appeal to the school board and even to the
minister of education.

The test also applies to disputes involving teachers and their boards. For
example, no tenured teacher could be disciplined or dismissed for an unsubstan-
tiated complaint. The appeal board might also rule that the case was properly
proven but that the penalty was inappropriate.

Schools were once operated on authoritarian lines. Teachers had authority *in
loco parentis* in almost every situation as it arose. If they proved unnecessarily
brutal, they could be charged with assault, but such legal actions were seldom
successful (MacKay, 1984). Their relationships with students were occasionally
exploitive, but only in extreme cases were there likely to be challenges. The
schools operated very much like the traditional family, where secrets were seldom revealed. This is changing: students may successfully assert their rights
against physical abuse, sexual harassment, psychological intimidation, and discrimination (Dickinson & MacKay, 1984).

Many such disputes are heard by professional boards with quasi-judicial
standing, which make neither criminal nor civil judgments. In some important
criminal or civil cases (like rape, narcotics, assault, etc.), quasi-judicial boards
may determine separately the professional consequences for a teacher (i.e., loss of

job, removal of certificate, etc.) (McCurdy, 1968). Teachers are among the few Canadians who are thereby subject to double jeopardy—they can be punished twice for the same offence.[2]

A noteworthy example came in Alberta where the professional decisions (by the board) to fire James Keegstra and (by the Minister) to revoke his teaching certificate preceded the decision to lay criminal charges of promoting hatred against a particular group of persons (MacKay, 1984). More commonly, the professional decisions follow the disposition of a criminal charge or lawsuit and will be influenced by the outcome of that trial. It would be unusual to dismiss or decertify a teacher who had received an absolute discharge or a court's verdict of not guilty.

The personal life of a teacher is subject to an unusual degree of public scrutiny and potential official interference. Education acts invariably require teachers to lead respectable lives, and denominational school boards may legally require teachers to follow sectarian requirements (MacKay, 1984). Interpretations vary, but teachers have lost their jobs for living with persons who were not close relatives or legal spouses, whether such persons were of the same or opposite sex (MacKay, 1984). So far as is known, teachers no longer lose their jobs for refusing sexual favours to board members or senior administrators (MacKay, 1984).

Another interpretation of teachers' personal freedom is illustrated by the case of Joanne Young, who participated in demonstrations at nuclear installations, Litton Industries, and city halls. In 1984 she was fired. She claimed that the nature of her political convictions was the reason for the principal's denials of leave to demonstrate and her ultimate dismissal. She also claimed that a higher duty than to her pupils required her to protest against the military-industrial establishment. An arbitrator who heard her appeal against suspension rejected her claim (Hunter, 1984). Other ways must be found by teachers who wish to be participants in political activities.

• • •

INTERNATIONAL ISSUES

No country can ignore events or ideas just because they occur beyond its borders. Most Canadians probably feel a sense of shame that Canada declined requests to help threatened Jewish populations of Europe before and during World War II (Abella & Troper, 1982). They have been subsequently more generous with respect to refugees from Hungary, Uganda, Vietnam, Nicaragua, and El Salvador. Most Canadians feel that merely offering sanctuary to survivors of a military, political, social, or economic catastrophe is inadequate, so they regularly support various efforts to avert such events. Because military intervention may be required, Canadian peacekeepers or observers frequently have been posted abroad, particularly for United Nations actions. "Intervention" may be much less obvious, such as in the diplomatic disapproval and sanctions to protest racism or other forms of discrimination in Zimbabwe and South Africa or military oppression in the USSR or Iran. Financial assistance and various forms of technical aid are available in selected cases, and these forms of assistance can promote a degree of reform. Global citizenship is realistic for Canadian schools if the government assumes obligations for UN activities.

Systematic programs to reduce racism and other forms of discrimination by the United Nations, or the United States, Britain, France, Canada, and various other nations, raise vital academic, judicial, and political issues. Because few topics are more compelling in the field of human rights education, these are mentioned in appropriate courses, discussed in current affairs, become the focal points of school projects, and occasionally influence career decisions. In several cases, the formal analyses have been supplemented and even supplanted by artistic interpretations, as novelists, musicians, painters, choreographers and cinematographers tackled the great issues. However, the artistic approach is sometimes faced with a new test—that of political correctness. For example, the terminology used for a particular group should be what is now preferred, not what was once used. Huckleberry Finn should no longer refer to his friend as "Nigger Jim."

Relief of the distress of famine, earthquake, flood, etc., is another potential objective of human rights education. It may focus upon Ethiopia, El Salvador, or Myanmar. The critical aspect of this type of education is that it should not be restricted to bandaids for consequences when the international behaviour of governments, the private sector, non-governmental organizations, and many individuals may be exacerbating the situation. Education that starts with human rights can quickly branch into development education, peace education, or global education. It is equally likely that educational programs that start with one of these other themes also address human rights very quickly. The categories blur and most educators address as many of them as appropriate to their audience and the particular discipline.

Canadians preoccupied with jurisdiction may be surprised to learn that all the provinces and the federal government have agreed to surrender to international agencies a degree of sovereignty in human rights. The authority for this intervention is most explicit in the optional protocol to the *International Covenant on Civil and Political Rights* (1966), which became binding for Canada a decade later. The implication was that victims of human rights violations in Canada could bring their cases to the attention of an international committee set up by the United Nations, which could investigate and propose remedies. A grievance against Canada has already been received and disposed of, although the response by Canada may prove to be less than satisfactory.[3]

. . .

RECENT RESEARCH AND ITS IMPLICATIONS

Social and educational research in Canada dispels mistaken views about the fundamental and even-handed justice of Canadian society. Translating research findings quickly into effective political or social reforms has proven to be discouraging. For example, there can be no doubt that women are disadvantaged in Canadian society (see table 1).

The explanations for why women have been or should be financially disadvantaged have been challenged: women are not usually working to gain luxuries; they do not needlessly interrupt their participation in the work force; they do not court or receive special advantages because of their sex; they do not lack qualifications.

To dispel such myths, human rights education must be directed at a very large slice of Canadian society. The immediate solutions to the problems lie in the hands of business owners and governments, both often arguing that a competitive advantage can best be maintained by holding the line on current salaries. A preoccupation with inflation leads to general cutbacks in education and hiring, making it very difficult for women to achieve educational, economic, or social equality.

TABLE I
Average Employment Income of Population 15 Years and over, 1985

Occupation	Female	Male	Female income as a percentage of male income
Managerial	21 328	37 939	56.2%
Clerical	12 746	18 147	70.2%
Processing/Machining	23 193	43 805	53.1%
Transport	11 087	22 113	50.1%

Source: *1986 Census of Canada*, unpublished data, Ottawa: Minister of Supply and Services Canada, 1989.

TABLE 2
Graduate Degrees by Field of Study, 1988

Field of study	Total	Female
Agriculture/Biological Sciences	1114	452
Education	3213	1931
Engineering/Applied Sciences	1919	219
Fine and Applied Arts	363	211
Health Professions	1137	692
Humanities	2491	1360
Mathematics/Physical Sciences	1625	338
Social Sciences	6787	2820

Source: *Education in Canada, A Statistical Review for 1988*, Ottawa: Minister of Supply and Services Canada, 1990.

The issue of qualifications has some relevance. Research has shown that women are discouraged from taking high school courses in mathematics and sciences, which of course denies them entry into several high prestige, high income professions (Collis, 1987; Mura et al., 1987). This is too simple an explanation of the disadvantaged position of women in the labour force, however, for women *with qualifications* are still by-passed. Recognizing this historical discrimination, some authorities are undertaking affirmative action programs.[4] The implication for human rights education seems to be that women should not be channelled into traditional female courses (see table 2) and occupations; women should be encouraged to compete in traditional male occupations; and there should be attempts to compensate for the effects of class discrimination with special remedial programs wherever necessary.

Multiculturalism masks a host of oppressions. Disadvantages are faced by several "other minority groups," such as Native Canadians, racially, religiously, and linguistically distinguishable cultural minorities, persons with disabilities, and sometimes those defined by geography, occupation, or economic status. Elliott (1971) defined minorities not in terms of their numbers—which for women constitute slightly more than half the population—but for their capacity to affect their own destiny.

Native persons, whether Indian, Inuit, or Metis, have long endured systematic deprivation. At one time, Indians were denied status as citizens. Now they are often denied the dignity of jobs, the capacity to direct the education of their own children, or the right to make business decisions independently. They appear to provoke particular vigilance on the part of police and judicial authorities. Their despair is reflected in low self-esteem, alcoholism and family violence (Douglas, 1987).

No doubt many Canadians consider that the disadvantaged are the authors of their own misfortunes. They believe that persistence, pluck, talent, and virtue will inevitably triumph. The other explanation is that those born with the silver spoon in their mouths will seldom use it to feed others. Neither stereotype is entirely true. The implication for human rights education seems to be that a two-pronged approach is justified. For each disadvantaged group, a focussed, systematic educational program should be mounted to deal with that group's typical shortcomings for participation: upgrading of general education or specific skills, devising human relations skill training, building self-esteem. These affirmative action programs are envisaged as an important means of lessening discrimination (Canada Act, 1981, 15). It is important to remember, however, that *individuals* within a group may not be best served by group programs (Wolfgang, 1984).

The second part of the strategy must address the education of other Canadians, particularly those who are in positions to decide how minorities will be treated in the community group. If citizens, employers, and policy makers continue to shun and demean minorities, if they avoid their role in offering a chance to prove competence, disadvantage will continue in Canada (Ray, 1984a).

· · ·

NOTES

1. The confidence in the protection of an aroused electorate is reflected in section 33 of the Canadian Charter of Rights and Freedoms, which ensures that legislation enacted notwithstanding, violation of the Charter can stand for only five years, thereby giving the electorate a guaranteed opportunity to vote on that government's record.

2. It should be noted that suspension, dismissal or suspension of certificate may be regarded as non-punitive but as protection for the students and society against incompetence or other hazards.

3. Sandra Lovelace, born a Malacite Indian, married a white man and thereby lost her Indian status as then stipulated in the Indian Act. Subsequent to her divorce, she sought to re-establish her Indian status, which could then only be accomplished by marriage to an Indian. This discrimination was an injustice that was apparently beyond remedy in Canada, but when requested by the United Nations Human Rights Committee to find a solution, a new initiative was taken federally (see Surma, 1982). As a result, the Indian Act no longer strips women of their Indian status if they marry non-Indians. The status of those who previously lost their legal claim to Indian rights is now determined by band councils.

4. In 1984, Saskatchewan identified women, Native persons, and persons with disabilities for affirmative action programs. In 1985, the University of Western Ontario strengthened its "equal opportunity" policies to "affirmative action," expecting to increase the proportion of women hired.

• • •

REFERENCES

Abella, I., & Troper, H. (1982). *None is too many. Canada and the Jews of Europe 1933–1948*. Toronto: Lester and Orpen Dennys.

Allison, D. (Ed.). (1984). *The yellow papers: The recentralization of Canadian education*. London, ON: Faculty of Education, University of Western Ontario.

Badgley, R. F., Allard, H. A., McCormick, N., Proudfoot, P. M., Fortin, D., Ogilvie, D., Rae-Grant, Q., Gélinas, P. M., Pépin, L., Sutherland, S. (1984). *Sexual offences against children*. Ottawa: Minister of Supply and Services.

Bergen, J. J. (1982). Should schools provide appeal procedures for disciplined students? *Challenge in Education Administration, 21*(2), 17–24.

Bergen, J. J. (1990). The emergence and expansion of private schools in Canada. In Y. L. Jack Lam (Ed.), *The Canadian public education system: Issues and prospects*. Calgary, AB: Detselig Enterprises.

Berger, T. R. (1981). *Fragile freedoms: Human rights and dissent in Canada*. Toronto: Clarke Irwin.

Brown, J. (1988). Individual development for peace education: A prosocial approach. In D. Ray (Ed.), *Peace education: Canadian and international perspectives*. London, ON: Third Eye.

Collis, B. (1987). Adolescent females and computers: Real and perceived barriers. In J. S. Gaskell & A. T. McLaren (Eds.), *Women and education: A Canadian perspective*. Calgary, AB: Detselig Enterprises.

Committee on Tolerance and Understanding. (1984). *Final Report to the Minister of Education for Alberta* (The Ghitter Report). Edmonton: Ministry of Education.

Counts, G. S. (1969). Should the teacher always be neutral? *Phi Delta Kappan*, (Dec.), 186–89.

Douglas, V. R. (1987). The education of urban native children: The Sacred Circle Project. In J. Barman, Y. Hébert, & D. McCaskill (Eds.), *Indian education in Canada*. (Vol. 2). Vancouver: University of British Columbia Press.

Dickinson, G. M., & MacKay, A. W. (1989). *Rights, freedoms and the education system in Canada: Cases and materials*. Toronto: Montgomery Publications.

Elliott, J. L. (Ed.). (1971). *Minority Canadians: Immigrant groups*. Scarborough, ON: Prentice-Hall.

Enns, F. (1963). *The legal status of the Canadian school board*. Toronto: Macmillan.

Fairweather, G. (1987). The constitution and multiculturalism: A closer look at section 27. *Multiculturalism, 11*(1), 15–20.

Faure, E., Herrera, F., Kaddoura, A-R., Lopes, H., Petrovsky, A. V., Rahnema, M., Ward, F. C. (1972). *Learning to be: The world of education today and tomorrow*. Paris: UNESCO.

Gifford, C. G. (1988). Peace, social awareness and political participation in Canadian adult education. In D. Ray (Ed.), *Peace education: Canadian and international perspectives*. London, ON: Third Eye.

Harmin, M., Kirschenbaum, H., & Simon, S. B. (1973). *Clarifying values through subject matter*. Toronto: Holt Rinehart and Winston.

Hersom, N. (1980). The British Columbia core curriculum: A case study in recentralization. In R. Farquhar & I. Housego (Eds.), *Canadian and comparative educational administration*. Vancouver: University of British Columbia, Centre for Continuing Education.

Hunter, I. A. (1984). *In the Matter of an Arbitration between: Huron County Board of Education and the Ontario Secondary School Teachers' Federation and Mrs. Joanne Young*. London.

Kehoe, J. (1980). An examination of alternative approaches to teaching the Universal Declaration of Human Rights. *International Journal of Political Education, 3,* 193–204.

Kehoe, J. (1983). Strategies for human rights education. In D. Ray & V. D'Oyley (Eds.), *Human rights in Canadian education*. Dubuque, IA: Kendall Hunt.

Kohlberg, L. (1975). The cognitive-developmental approach to moral education. *Phi Delta Kappan*, (June), 670–677.

Lauwerys, J. (Ed.). (1968). *Ideals and ideologies*. London, UK: Evans Brothers.

MacKay, A. W. (1984). *Education law in Canada*. Toronto: Emond Montgomery.

Magsino, R. (1991). The family: Parents' and children's rights. In R. Ghosh & D. Ray (Eds.). *Social change and education in Canada* (2nd ed.). Toronto: Harcourt Brace Jovanovich.

Majhanovich, S., & Ray, D. (1991). Official and heritage languages in Canada: How policies translate into practice. In R. Ghosh & D. Ray (Eds.), *Social change and education in Canada* (2nd ed.). Toronto: Harcourt Brace Jovanovich.

Mallea, J. R. (1984). Introduction: Cultural diversity and Canadian education. In J. R. Mallea & J. C. Young (Eds.), *Cultural diversity and Canadian education issues and innovations*. Ottawa: Carleton University Press.

McCurdy, S. G. (1968). *The legal status of the Canadian school teacher*. Toronto: Macmillan.

McLeod, K. A. (1989). Exploring citizenship education: Education for citizenship. In K. A. McLeod (Ed.), *Canada and citizenship education*. Toronto, ON: Canadian Education Association.

Mura, R., Kimball, M., & Cloutier, R. (1987). Girls and science programs: Two steps forward, one step back. In J. S. Gaskell & A.

T. McLaren (Eds.), *Women and education: A Canadian perspective*. Calgary, AB: Detselig Enterprises.

Poonwassie, D. H. (1992). Aboriginal populations and equal rights in education: An introduction. In D. Ray & D. H. Poonwassie (Eds.), *Education and cultural differences: New perspectives*. New York: Garland.

Ray, D. (1983). Human rights in Canadian education. In D. Ray & V. D'Oyley (Eds.), *Human rights in Canadian education*. Dubuque, IA: Kendall Hunt.

Ray, D. (1984a). Human rights and multiculturalism: Education and cultural minorities in Canadian schooling. In M. Conley (Ed.), *Teaching human rights*. Wolfville, NS: Acadia University Centre.

Ray, D. (1984b). *Teaching human rights in Canada*. A report to the Secretary of State and the Council of Ministers.

Romanow, R. (1982–83). Reworking the miracle: The Constitutional Accord of 1981. *Queen's Law Journal,* 8(1–2), 74–98.

Shapiro, B. (1984). *The Report of the Commission on Private Schools in Ontario*. Toronto: Office of the Commission.

Torney-Purta, J. (1982). Socialization and human rights research: Implications for teachers. In M. Stimmann & J. Torney-Purta (Eds.), *International human rights, society and the schools*. Washington: National Council for the Social Studies.

Urman, L. (1989). The American school in the political socialization process. *Review of Educational Research, 50,* 99–119.

Webking, E. (1984). Using the Charter of Rights and Freedoms as a tool for teaching civics. In M. W. Conley (Ed.), *Teaching human rights*. Wolfville, NS: Acadia University Centre.

Whitehead, R. (1988). Current events for a broader context. In D. Ray (Ed.), *Peace education: Canadian and international perspectives*. London, ON: Third Eye.

Wolfgang, A. (1984). Intercultural counselling: The state of the art. In R. J. Samuda, J. W. Berry, & M. Laferriere (Eds.), *Multiculturalism in Canada: Social and educational perspectives*. Toronto: Allyn and Bacon.

MINORITY EDUCATION RIGHTS:

SOME CURRENT ISSUES

...

Donald A. Burgess

The needs and wishes of minority groups in Canada, as elsewhere in the world, have assumed an increased importance in recent years. As part of what is known as the human rights movement, the treatment (or, unfortunately, the mistreatment) of racial, ethnic, religious, and linguistic minorities in all six inhabited continents tend on occasion to dominate world affairs. Some would go so far as to claim that the manner in which a nation or state treats its minorities is an indicator of that country's level of maturity and civilization. Others, in contrast, point to the increasingly strident demands from minority groups for special treatment and describe this phenomenon as the tyranny of minorities. Whatever one's personal views of the matter, the fact is that minorities exist; and given the ease and rapidity of modern communications, the treatment of minority groups can quickly become headline news throughout the globe. With the possible exception of Japan, few countries are so homogeneous that they do not include racial, ethnic, linguistic, or religious minorities somewhere in their territory. Canada is no different in this regard—it is a nation peopled by minorities. With one or two noted exceptions to be discussed below, little attention was paid in the past to the needs of minority groups. Today, the situation is very different: some of these groups have rights that are well entrenched in law, other groups do not, and still others are the subject of continuing constitutional negotiations.

The purpose of this chapter is not to examine the rights of all minorities in Canada (that subject would require a whole book in itself!), but rather to look at specific minority rights particularly as these apply to education. This topic has gained in importance in the past ten years in part because of the implementation of the 1982 Canadian Charter of Rights and Freedoms that, *inter alia*, granted certain education rights to the English and French linguistic minorities. A major element that complicates the issue is the ongoing interaction between federal and provincial fields of jurisdiction. Although education in Canada is a provincial responsibility, minority rights are often a matter of direct federal concern or at least are subject to interpretation by federal institutions, such as the Supreme Court. The potential therefore exists for genuine disagreements as to the actual meaning and implementation of education rights for minority groups. The result is that minority education rights in Canada are not static but are in a state of evolution. And, because of the decentralized structure of education in Canada, changes tend to come about province by province rather than nationally. It is therefore difficult to speak of minority education rights in Canada without undertaking a study of each province. The bulk of this chapter will be focussed on the recently acquired minority language education rights in the Charter; but, in order to provide some context and a point of departure, this will be preceded with a brief overview of minority education rights inherited from the past. The basis for discussion will be the legal framework rather than a chronological survey.

• • •

MINORITY EDUCATION RIGHTS AT CONFEDERATION

It is a characteristic of most governments that they are opposed to the idea of the devolution of powers: the more power they cede to others, the less they will have for themselves. This is especially true of totalitarian states where respect for diversity and for individual rights tends to be weak. It is also true of governments in some unitary states who fear that any dispersement of powers to the regions might result in the balkanization of the nation state. It is considerably less true in states where there is a federated system, because this form of governance implies a sharing of powers and the acceptance thereby of a certain degree of diversity. Canada, of course, came into being as a confederation of different colonies and territories and it was clear from the beginning that there would be diversity and even the entrenchment of diversity in the constitutional documents. The provincial systems of education and the existence of two official languages are perhaps the prime examples of this entrenched diversity. It has been suggested, however, that at the time of Confederation, most minority groups in Canada were neither numerous enough nor powerful enough to obtain special rights. While this broad statement may have been generally true, it was also

true that many minorities simply wanted to integrate themselves into the mainstream of society as quickly as possible and that the last thing they wanted was
for their children to be treated differently from the majority. Three minority
groups, however, were afforded special treatment: Treaty Indians, Roman
Catholics in some provinces, and Protestants in Quebec. Examining each of
these groups shows that the motivation, status, influence, and the rights of each
group were very different.

Treaty Indians

An interesting feature of the British Royal Proclamation of 1763 was that it
recognized Indian sovereignty on Indian territories in Canada. Some treaties
were subsequently "negotiated" between the British Crown and aboriginal leaders, establishing Indian reserves where the Crown assumed responsibility for
providing schools and teachers. However, at the time of Confederation, there
were still sizeable tracts of land where Indian sovereignty had not been extin-
guished. It was mainly for these reasons that section 91 of the Constitution Act
of 1867 (formerly known as the British North America Act) granted the
Government of Canada the exclusive right to make laws for "Indians, and Lands
reserved for Indians." This paternalistic view was elaborated further in the
Indian Act of 1876 that not only legally defined who was qualified as an
Indian[1] but also made Indians virtual wards of the federal government. The
story of federal provisions for native education, to say the least, has not been a
happy one. Some would say that it has been nothing short of shameful (Henley
& Young, 1990). Generally speaking, the Indian Act permits the federal government either to provide schooling directly or to contract out this responsibility to provincial governments or to local school districts. The actual situation,
then, may vary considerably not only between provinces but within provinces.

Contrary to most arrangements for minority education in Canada, the responsibility for management and control of native education was strongly centralized through the federal government. Although the original motives for this
arrangement might have been praiseworthy at the time, it was the federal
politicians and federal civil servants who were entrusted with deciding what was
best for native education. Whether the aboriginal peoples of Canada have bene-
fitted from or been victimized by these various arrangements is at best debat-
able. What is now becoming evident is that aboriginal peoples in general are
demanding a return of their original sovereignty. An important part of this
movement includes responsibility for the management and control of their own

education systems. Only in this manner, they argue, can they promote their own distinctive cultures and avoid assimilation. But once the question of political control has been determined, a major problem facing aboriginal educators is the dissonance of educating children to live in two very different cultures: the native culture on the one hand, and the ubiquitous and pervasive modern North American culture on the other. Is it possible to preserve one and yet to participate in the other? Or is it necessary to isolate one from the other? These and similar questions are not unique to aboriginal peoples; to a greater or lesser extent, the same basic questions apply to all minority groups.

Catholic School Rights

If it is true that native peoples in 1867 did not have much power, then the same cannot be said for the Roman Catholic church. The Church had been present in Canada since the beginning of European settlement and had been an important element of the original colonizing mission to New France. Furthermore, the Church was able to preserve its power base after the Conquest primarily because the Quebec Act of 1774 in effect offered the Church official status in return for persuading the French Canadians to stay out of the American revolutionary war. The result was that the Catholic church was a force to be reckoned with, especially in what became known as Lower Canada (Quebec), where the Church had a virtual monopoly on the religious beliefs of the French-speaking majority. On the other hand, in Upper Canada (Ontario) and in the maritime colonies of British North America, the Catholic church was considerably less powerful and tended to be equated either with recent Irish immigrants or with those inhabitants who spoke French.

The development of public schooling in Upper and Lower Canada during the first half of the nineteenth century was largely composed of a search for a satisfactory accommodation between those who supported a common school system on the one hand, and the Catholic church on the other. The predominantly English-language governments of the day tended to support the development of a common school system, open to all children, regardless of religious beliefs. The Church, however, was opposed to the notion of common schooling because it feared that this would lead to loss of control and to assimilation—not an unfounded fear in the light of the recommendations in Lord Durham's report. The power of the Catholic church, particularly in Lower Canada where its members formed a clear majority, was such that it could in effect veto any arrangements for public schooling that did not provide adequate provision for education under the control of Church authorities (Magsino, 1986).

The solution in Upper Canada led in 1841 to the establishment of separate schools for those professing a religious faith different from that of the majority. Although this right applied to both Catholics and Protestants, in practice, the vast majority of separate schools were Catholic. The schooling rights of the religious minority were subsequently consolidated in the Separate Schools Act of 1863 which was the legislation in force at the time of Confederation, and thus became entrenched by section 93 of the Canada Constitution Act, 1867. In the years between Confederation and the 1980s, it became clear that the Separate Schools Act did not always provide the type of protection that the Catholic minority in Ontario would have wished. First of all, it did not protect French as the language of instruction in separate schools; the now infamous Regulation 17, adopted in 1912, severely curtailed and in many cases actually prohibited the use of French as a language of instruction. The constitution protected denominational rights, said the courts, not language rights. Secondly, it became clear that separate schools would not be publicly funded beyond the elementary grades. Although Catholic taxpayers were required to pay taxes for the support of public high schools, they were not permitted to establish their own separate high schools nor to offer secondary level courses in separate elementary schools. Again, according to the courts, the pre-Confederation law permitting separate schooling applied only to elementary grades for the reason that separate secondary schools did not exist in law in Upper Canada at the time of the union.

In practice, then, the constitutional protection afforded to the Catholic minority in Ontario was limited. It protected denominational rights at the elementary school level, but it offered no protection for those who wanted instruction in French, and it failed to provide public funding for separate high schools. In recent years, it is important to stress that the situation concerning schooling for the Catholic minority in Ontario, French and English, has improved considerably. The Education Act was revised in 1968 to permit the use of French as a language of instruction in all subjects and in 1986 Ontario passed Bill 30 which extended full public funding to separate secondary schools.

The situation regarding Catholic minorities in the other provinces is dependent on whether or not denominational school rights existed, in law, at the time that a particular province entered Confederation (Bezeau, 1989). Four provinces (New Brunswick, Nova Scotia, P.E.I., and British Columbia) did not have denominational school rights in law at the time these provinces entered Confederation, so there is no constitutional protection for the Catholic minorities in those four provinces. Saskatchewan and Alberta, on the other hand, had denominational schools when they were formed from the Northwest Territories in 1905 and, as a result, there are separate school districts for denominational minorities in both provinces. Manitoba is a special case because it was neither a colony nor a province when it entered Confederation in 1870, and it had no laws concerning education, denominational or otherwise. Initially, the French Catholic population in Manitoba was about the same size as the English Protestant, with the result that the first school legislation enacted in 1871 provided for both Catholic and Protestant school districts. By 1890, however, the population had become predominantly English speaking, and the Manitoba government decided to abolish the denominational system and to replace it with a secular school system. This action led to what become known as the Manitoba School Question and to a major political crisis in Canada (Clark, 1968). The eventual outcome was in the form of a political rather than a constitutional settlement, known as the "Laurier-Greenway compromise" that permitted the teaching of religion after normal school hours, but which in practice highlighted the weakness of the protection afforded to the Catholic minority in Manitoba. Finally, in Newfoundland there is a denominational system of schooling that at one time recognized as many as seven different religious groupings (Anglican, United Church, Salvation Army, Presbyterian, Roman Catholic, Pentecostal, and Seventh Day Adventists) each with its own system of schools. At the present time, the first four denominations listed above have amalgamated to form an integrated system which, together with the separate Catholic system, results in two large school networks together with two relatively small school boards for the Pentecostal Assemblies and Seventh Day Adventists. The situation in Newfoundland highlights some of the advantages and disadvantages involved in the organization of public schooling along denominational lines. Such a system provides respect for diversity, for deeply held religious beliefs, and for the rights of parents to choose the type of schooling that they want for their children. The disadvantages include the increased costs associated with operating several different networks, especially administrative, transportation and construction costs, and the problem of what do with non-Christians and others who do not belong to the recognized denominations.

The status of the education rights of Catholic minorities in Canada varies considerably from province to province. In some provinces there is full constitutional protection for denominational minority school rights; in others there are no denominational school rights; and in yet others, minority school rights have been either severely curtailed or only grudgingly and reluctantly provided. In these circumstances it is not unreasonable to question whether this difference in treatment is not in itself discriminatory. Section 15 of the Charter of Rights and

Freedoms, the Equality clause, speaks of "the right to the equal protection and equal benefit of the law without discrimination and, in particular, without discrimination based on race, national or ethnic origin, colour, religion, sex, age, or mental or physical disability." Is it right that denominational minorities are protected in some provinces but not in others? Is it right that history and the constitution dictate that some religions have rights whereas others do not? Should the laws of the land discriminate positively in favour of some groups solely because they were once an important element in our heritage and tradition?

Protestant School Rights

At the time of Confederation, and with only one exception, Protestants formed or were soon to become a majority in all provinces. In Quebec, the majority was Catholic, giving the Protestant groups there some reason to be concerned for their school rights. But, unlike the Catholic minorities in the other provinces, the Protestants in Quebec were relatively powerful. While they accepted that education would become a provincial responsibility at Confederation, and thus controlled by the French majority, they wanted to be absolutely certain that adequate safeguards would be written into the constitution so as to protect their Protestant school rights. As this minority also happened to be English speaking, it was perhaps taken for granted that the protection of a Protestant education system would also serve to protect the English language.

A system of public schooling based on religious differences had slowly been evolving in Quebec from the beginning of the nineteenth century. At the time of Confederation in 1867, there already existed in law a system of confessional school boards (that is, school boards for Protestants and school boards for Catholics) in the two urban areas of Montreal and Quebec City. Outside these two cities, in the so-called rural areas of the province, there was a system of common school boards, legally non-denominational and open to all, but with an important provision, known as the right of dissent. This provision allowed any number of the religious minority (Protestant or Catholic) to withdraw their children from the common school and establish a denominational school to be managed exclusively by trustees of that same religion. In practice, when this right of dissent was activated by Protestants, the common school by default became a school "for Catholics." Conversely, if the right of dissent was activated by a Catholic minority, as happened in a few districts, then the common school became a school "for Protestants." Thus the province ended up with a *de facto* dual denominational system of school boards, even though many of the schools in the rural areas were *de jure* common. Both the French-speaking Catholic majority and the English-speaking Protestant minority were relatively happy with this arrangement, for it permitted each group to manage its own school system, without interference from the other (Henchey & Burgess, 1987; Magnuson, 1980). As a result, the Protestant minority in Quebec has never been prevented from establishing secondary schools and has always been funded on the same basis as the Catholic majority. In comparison to the structure in some other provinces, where there is a public system for the majority and a separate system for the minority, in Quebec it is more accurate to speak of two parallel systems, different in size, but operating under the same set of rules.

It is often assumed, both in Quebec and elsewhere, that this dual denominational arrangement also protected the French and English languages, as virtually all the Catholics were French speaking and nearly all the Protestants were English speaking. But, even as the original denominational school system was being established in the 1840s, there already existed in Quebec a group of immigrants who were neither French Catholic nor English Protestant. These were the English-speaking Catholics from Ireland fleeing the ravages of the potato famines. "Between 1825, when the first reasonably complete records were kept, and 1845, at least 450 000 Irish landed in Canada, by far the largest migration from any country" (MacKay, 1990, p. 13). While many of these moved on to Upper Canada and to the United States, a considerable number settled in Lower Canada, particularly in Montreal where at one time the Irish formed a quarter of the city's population, and where they found at least the religion to their liking. But these immigrants had to struggle to obtain schooling to their liking. The English-language schools of the Protestants were, of course, off limits for religious reasons. And the problem with the Catholic schools, at least initially, was that they were conducted only in French. The Irish community eventually established Catholic schools where the instruction was in English, but always under the ultimate control of the French-language Catholic majority. The result has been that the English-speaking Catholics in Quebec have never had the opportunity to manage and control their system of schools as have the English Protestants. This problem was later to be compounded with the arrival of immigrant groups who were neither Catholic nor Protestant. When Jewish immigrants, for example, began to settle in Montreal, they experienced major problems fitting into the dual denominational system based on Christian faiths. "As non-Christians before a Christian school system, their attempt to find educational relief precipitated a host of financial and legal problems. . . . At the same time the Jewish educational challenge served to expose a flawed public school system that was more private than public, more

restrictive than open and unbefitting an increasingly pluralistic society"
(Magnuson, 1980, p. 84).

It is important to emphasize that the Constitution Act of 1867 says very little
about language rights. The only reference is Section 133 that requires the
Parliament of Canada and the Legislature of Quebec to enact laws in both
English and French and to recognize the use of both languages in the legislatures and the courts. Section 93 on education, however, says nothing at all about
language: the words "English" and "French" do not appear (see Appendix A for
the wording of s.93 of the Constitution Act of 1867). As far as the English
minority in Quebec was concerned, constitutional protection was reserved only
for those who were Protestant. But this denominational protection has proven
insufficient to protect English as the language of instruction, even for those who
are Protestant. And neither was the French-language majority at all certain that
a Catholic school system was adequate protection for the French language. As a
result, the Quebec government in 1974 (Bill 22) and in 1977 (Bill 101) passed
language legislation that, *inter alia*, restricted access to English-language
instruction in all public schools, both Catholic and Protestant. In 1974, access
was limited to those students who could demonstrate "sufficient knowledge" of
English. But, when the meaning of this phrase proved to be imprecise and difficult to implement in practice, the law was replaced in 1977 by Bill 101,
Quebec's Charter of the French Language, whereby only the children of those
who had received elementary schooling in English in Quebec could have access
to English-language schools. The intent of this legislation was to require all
immigrants, English-speaking immigrants and others, to receive instruction in
French. As a result, the number of English schools (Catholic and Protestant) has
declined dramatically in the past fifteen years and, contrary to what might be
expected, an increasing proportion of Protestant schools are operating as French
schools.

As has been demonstrated, a system of schooling based on denominational differences does not always serve to protect minority interests. In Quebec, for
example, there is a tendency to regard all non-Catholics as Protestants. In fact,
in 1903, the provincial government passed a law declaring that, for educational
purposes at least, all Jews were to be regarded as Protestant! Although this law
was later declared unconstitutional, it illustrates some of the problems associated with dual denominational systems of education. Who can qualify, for
example, as a Protestant? All those who are non-Catholic, or only those who
profess non-Catholic Christianity? Who is eligible to vote in Protestant school
board elections or to serve as trustees? Can Catholics have access to Protestant

schools? Can Protestants have access to Catholic schools? And what is the legal status of those such as Hindus, Moslems, Humanists, Agnostics, and Atheists who are neither Protestant nor Catholic? If all non-Catholics must attend Protestant schools, then isn't the Protestant school really a public school?

Denominational Minority Rights

The constitutional arrangements of 1867 were designed to protect denominational minorities. According to at least one observer: "These original guarantees proved woefully inadequate right from the start. In many provinces, French Catholic schools were denied all public support from the tax base [and] French was prohibited as a language of school instruction and administration" (Magnet, 1986, p. 106). As the first part of this chapter has demonstrated, the constitutional protection afforded to denominational minorities, especially to Catholic minorities, was only partially successful. Nevertheless, denominational systems of schooling continue to exist in a number of provinces and the separate (Catholic) school systems that do exist are now relatively healthy. As has been demonstrated, however, these denominational guarantees did not prove successful for the protection of minority languages nor, it seems, for the protection of the majority language in Quebec.

> In 1987, the Fathers of Confederation did not see fit to provide explicitly for protection of language rights in the schools. There were sociological reasons for taking this approach: at that time, education was still largely under the control of the Catholic and Protestant clergy. . . . It was therefore believed that if denominational rights were protected, the language of the schools would also be preserved. Nevertheless, the courts held that language and religion were not legally identical, and that only religion enjoyed the protection granted by section 93. (Foucher, 1985, p. 2)

We now know that the Fathers of Confederation succeeded in preserving a denominational system of education in some provinces but that they utterly failed to find the right constitutional formula for the protection of linguistic minorities. This lacuna was an important element of the negotiations leading up to the 1982 constitutional arrangements and continues to be a major bone of contention in the 1992 rounds of negotiations. It is a matter of some irony that it is the province where these denominational rights were perhaps the strongest, namely Quebec, that is now most anxious to change its denominational school system for a system based on language (Burgess, 1992).

• • •

LANGUAGE MINORITIES IN CANADA

Addressing Minority Rights

At the same time as Quebec was considering the enactment of language legislation in order to protect French, the Federal government established a Royal Commission on Bilingualism and Biculturalism (1963), whose mandate primarily was to enquire into the status of the French language and culture across Canada. The various reports of this Commission, known as the B & B Commission, served to highlight not only the critical state of the French language in use by the rapidly shrinking French-language minorities in Canada, but also the depressed state of the French language even in Quebec. The Commission called for nothing less than "a new charter for the official languages of Canada, a charter based on the concept of equal partnership."[2] In Book II (Education) of its Report (1968), the B & B Commission developed the link between language and culture, and between these two elements and schooling. It went on to propose a series of measures to entrench the right of minority language communities to obtain instruction in their own language and in their own schools.

The work of the commission led to developments on two major fronts. The first was the enactment in 1969 of the Official Languages Act and the establishment of the Office of the Commissioner of Official Languages, which laid the foundation for a number of programs including initiatives in minority-language education and in second-language instruction. As a direct result of these initiatives, a number of provinces began to liberalize their approach to French-language instruction. Ontario, for example, amended its Education Act to permit the teaching of elementary grades and of secondary subjects in French. French immersion programs were expanded in a number of provinces and enrolments increased. The other major development was at the constitutional level. In 1969 the Federal government first proposed that individuals be granted the right in a Charter to choose to have either English or French as their main language of instruction.[3] The intention at this stage was to entrench individual freedom of choice in language of instruction, and not to grant special rights to minority language groups.

This viewpoint began to change, however, especially in the light of developments in Quebec. First, freedom of choice would continue to permit all who wished, including immigrants and French Québécois, to enrol in English schools in that Province. Second, freedom of choice for individuals was seen as contrary to the interests of those wishing to protect or to promote the language of linguistic groups who perceived themselves as under threat. In the case of Quebec, it was the French majority that felt itself under threat within the North American context. In the case of French minorities in the other provinces, the situation was quite different. For them, freedom of choice implied the uncontrolled access by the English-speaking majority to the schools of the minority which, in turn, could result in bilingual schools and a watering down of the French program. The increased interest in French schooling by the majority could in fact lead to the eventual assimilation of the minority.

By the time of the St. Andrews Conference in 1977, it was clear that the ground had shifted from freedom of choice in language of instruction to the protection of minority group rights within the provincial context. It is perhaps not simply coincidence that this was the same year that the Quebec government passed Bill 101. After numerous and significant changes in the wording (Foucher, 1985), section 23 of the Canadian Charter of Rights and Freedoms entitled "Minority Language Education Rights" came into force in 1982 as part of the Constitution Act of 1982 (see Appendix B for the full wording of this section).

Minority Language Education Rights in the Charter [4]

The general purpose of section 23 of the Charter is to provide the official language minorities of Canada with education rights equivalent to those of the majority. The major limits are: that these rights apply only to citizens of Canada (and not immediately to immigrants); that the rights are claimed by the parents on behalf of their children; and that these rights will apply only where the numbers in a province so warrant. [5] "We may conclude that section 23 seeks not only to ensure the survival but also the vitality of official language minorities through an educational framework which will stop assimilation. It recognizes the fundamental role education plays in this process" (Martel, 1991, p. 18). And, given the similarities in wording between section 23(1)(b) of the Charter (the so-called "Canada" clause) and the so-called "Quebec" clause of Bill 101 (limiting access to English-language instruction to parents who had been educated in English in Quebec), we may also conclude that "the drafters of the Constitution Act 1982 were aware of Bill 101 and its restrictive requirement and intended section 23 to remedy this perceived defect" (Bezeau, 1989, p 108). Indeed, it is reasonable to state that the overall purpose of section 23 is remedial in nature, that is: "It was designed to remedy an existing problem in Canada, and hence to alter the status quo" (Mahé, 1990, p. 14).

The remedial nature of section 23 was clearly acknowledged by the Supreme Court in 1984 and reported again in 1990 in the following statement:

> The special provisions of s. 23 of the Charter make it a unique set of con-
> stitutional provisions, quite peculiar to Canada. This set of constitutional
> provisions was not enacted by the framers in a vacuum. When it was
> adopted, the framers knew, and clearly had in mind the regimes governing
> the anglophone and francophone linguistic minorities in various provinces
> in Canada so far as the language of instruction was concerned. They also
> had in mind the history of these regimes, both earlier ones such as
> Regulation 17, which for a time limited instruction in French in the sepa-
> rate schools of Ontario . . . as well as more recent ones such as Bill 101 and
> the legislation which preceded it in Quebec. Rightly or wrongly—and it is
> not for the courts to decide—the framers of the Constitution manifestly
> regarded as inadequate some—and perhaps all—of the regimes in force at
> the time the Charter was enacted, and their intention was to remedy the
> perceived defects of these regimes by uniform corrective measures, namely
> those contained in s. 23 of the Charter, which were at the same time given
> the status of a constitutional guarantee. (Mahé, 1990, p. 15)

Section 23, then, is a major new element in the Canadian educational scene. Not only does it provide guarantees of education rights for the official linguistic minorities across the country, but it suggests that these be implemented by means of "uniform corrective measures." This means that as far as the two offi-cial linguistic minorities are concerned, the provinces no longer have exclusive jurisdiction in the field of education[6]—that they are required to provide minor-ity language education services and facilities as specified in the Charter and as interpreted by the Supreme Court (Sussel & Manley-Casimir, 1986). In addi-tion, the constitutional protection previously afforded to denominational schooling by means of section 93 continues to apply. This protection is, in fact, strengthened by section 29 of the Charter which establishes that denomina-tional rights are to prevail over any other provision of the Charter, including language rights (Foucher, 1985). As a result, it appears as if certain francophone Catholics outside of Quebec and anglophone Protestants within Quebec enjoy double protection. And, if anglophone Catholics in Quebec enjoy section 23 protection in addition to section 93 denominational protection, then the possi-bility exists for a multiplication of the school systems that is even more divisive than it is already (Burgess, 1991: Foucher, 1985).

Historically, section 23 was designed to respond to the overall objective of ensuring the vitality of the official language minorities in Canada (Martel,

1991). This was to be accomplished through three complementary paths: correction of an historical situation of assimilation experienced by French-language minorities; correction of the excesses of Bill 101 on the English language minority in Quebec; and implementation of effective instructional and management systems for official language minorities across Canada. What is the situation after ten years of experience with this section of the Charter? Does the English minority feel any more secure in Quebec? And what has been the experience of the French minorities in the other provinces?

Minority Language Rights: Some Current Issues

When the Canadian Charter of Rights and Freedoms came into force on 17 April 1982, it was anticipated by many that section 23 would quickly lead to major changes in the provision of education services to minority linguistic communities. The record, however, is very irregular. As two interested observers have put it: "linguistic minorities, at worst, are being neglected with their constitutional rights denied and, at best, are being treated inconsistently across the country" (Hurlbert and Hurlbert, 1989, p. 148). Part of the problem lies in the fact that the provision of educational services is a responsibility that belongs to the provinces. As a result, the ten provinces and the two territories have different social and cultural agendas, different minority language populations, different priorities, and different educational regimes. In some provinces, minority rights are not granted generously or automatically, but must be contested and won in the courts. The number of court cases on section 23 issues is now numerous enough that there is insufficient space to cover them all here.[7] However, two cases that reached the Supreme Court are of particular importance.

The first case concerned the question of who was eligible to receive minority language instruction in Quebec (*Attorney-General of Quebec v. Quebec Association of Protestant School Boards*, 1984). According to Quebec's Charter of the French Language (Bill 101), the only children (other than temporary residents and special cases) eligible to receive instruction in English were those whose mother or father had themselves received elementary instruction in English in Quebec. According to section 23 of the Charter of Rights and Freedoms, however, the right to receive minority language instruction belongs to those who had received elementary instruction in English anywhere in Canada. The judgment of the court was that limiting access to those with elementary schooling received in Quebec was not a reasonable limit that could be demonstrably justified in a free and democratic society; that section 23 was, in fact, specifically designed to remedy this element of Bill 101; and that Quebec was the only province where minority language rights were regressing. As a result, the Quebec clause in Bill 101 (not the whole of Bill 101) was struck down in favour of the Canada clause of the Charter, thus permitting children from elsewhere in Canada to have access to English schools in Quebec. This ruling also demonstrated that the Charter had precedence over provincial legislation (even legislation that had been enacted prior to the coming into force of the Charter), and that the education rights enshrined in section 23(1)(b) cannot be unreasonably restricted and must be applied equitably across Canada.

The second significant judgment was the unanimous decision of the Supreme Court in the case of *Mahé v. Alberta* (15 March 1990). At issue here were the rights of a relatively small group of francophone parents in Edmonton, Alberta, who claimed that their rights under section 23 of the Charter were not being respected by the education legislation of the province. In particular, they argued that section 23 should guarantee them the right, in Edmonton, to the "management and control" of a minority-language school. The main issues in this case concerned whether there were sufficient numbers to warrant the provision of minority language instruction; and the degree, if any, of "management and control" of a French-language school that might be accorded to minority parents.

In outlining the general objectives of section 23, Chief Justice Brian Dickson stated:

> The general purpose of s. 23 of the Charter is to preserve and promote the two official languages of Canada, and their respective cultures, by ensuring that each language flourishes, as far as possible, in provinces where it is not spoken by the majority of the population. . . . Section 23 is also designed to correct, on a national scale, the progressive erosion of minority official language groups and to give effect to the concept of the "equal partnership" of the two official language groups in the context of education. (Mahé, 1990, p. 3)

In terms of "where numbers warrant" the Court indicated that the calculation should not be limited by existing school district boundaries, and may, if necessary, be extended to the province as a whole. Where numbers are minimal, suggested the Court, it may be necessary to provide transportation for students, or perhaps to provide boarding, in order to meet the requirements of section 23. The Court also specified that the relevant figure was not the existing demand, but the number of persons that will in the end benefit from the services offered. The Court concluded that the best way to interpret the "where numbers warrant" provision was by means of a sliding scale: at one end would be the example of a solitary, isolated minority language student where there is little that a government can be expected to do; whereas at the other end of the scale would be the example of a relatively large number of minority language students enrolled in minority language schools controlled by minority language school boards. In the case of the French-language parents in Edmonton, with 242 eligible students, the Court recommended the establishment of guaranteed elementary and secondary schooling, controlled and managed by minority parents, but stopped short of ordering the establishment of an independent school board (Burgess, 1991). In terms of management and control, the Chief Justice stated:

> In my view, it is essential . . . that, where the numbers warrant, minority language parents possess a measure of management and control over the educational facilities in which their children are taught. Such management and control is vital to ensure that their language and culture flourish. . . . Furthermore, as the historical context in which s. 23 was enacted suggests, minority language groups cannot always rely upon the majority to take account of all their linguistic and cultural concerns. . . . If s. 23 is to remedy past injustices and ensure that they are not repeated in the future, it is important that minority language groups have a measure of control over the minority language facilities and instruction. (Mahé, 1990, pp. 22–23)

Where the numbers did not warrant the establishment of an independent school board but were sufficient for a school, the Court recommended that the minority should have exclusive control over those aspects of education that related to language and culture, including such items as the expenditure of funds, the appointment and direction of those responsible for administration, the establishment of programs of instruction, the recruitment and assignment of teachers, and the making of agreements for the provision of minority educational services. The Court went on to state that the specific form of minority education did not have to be identical to that provided for the majority, and that, whereas funding on a per student basis must be at least equivalent to that provided for the majority, special circumstances may dictate that funding for minority schooling may need to be proportionally greater than that provided for majority schooling. In other words, the linguistic minorities in Canada must be provided with the public funds to operate minority schools and must also be permitted to manage those funds themselves as well as to control the pedagogical programs in the schools.

• • •

CONCLUSION

In the few section 23 cases that have come before it, the Supreme Court of Canada has addressed the matter of minority language school rights in what can only be described as a broad and liberal manner. As a result, the historical protection afforded to Catholic and Protestant minorities in section 93 of the 1867 Constitution Act is now considerably enhanced by the protection afforded to the French and English linguistic minorities by section 23 of the Charter. Both sections carry the force of constitutional guarantees and, according to the Supreme Court in the Mahé decision, there is no conflict between the denominational guarantees of s. 93 and the linguistic guarantees of s. 23. In fact, it can be argued that s. 23 guarantees appear to be stronger than s. 93 guarantees. This is so because s. 93 protects certain denominational aspects of schooling in only some of the provinces, whereas s. 23 applies to all the provinces and territories and protects all those aspects of schooling concerned with the preservation of a language and culture, and not just denominational rights (Burgess, 1991). The Supreme Court has thus indicated the manner in which the different provinces can implement their Charter obligations to their respective linguistic minorities. Some provinces have moved quickly and others are still in process of studying the situation. But, even if the application of these obligations is still problematic in some jurisdictions, at least the principle of school governance by linguistic minorities has been accepted by the courts.

As indicated earlier, however, the official linguistic minorities are not the only minorities in Canada. Canada, in fact, is full of minorities, whether based on race, national or ethnic origin, colour, religion, sexual preference, age, or mental or physical disability. As Judge Thomas Berger has pointed out: "Some minorities wish to integrate, some even to assimilate, and they fear that cultural distinctions will be used to exclude them from equal opportunities in political, social, and economic life. Others seek to defend and protect such distinctions, fearing that their erasure will lead to assimilation and the surrender of their identity" (Berger, 1986, pp. 97–98).

The issues that are raised by the existence of minorities are not always easy to answer, and they are not always the same. Neither is it clear that entrenching minority rights in constitutional documents has always led to equity and survival, as the history of section 93 has demonstrated. On the other hand, the absence of legal rights can lead to the tyranny of the majority, as has happened all too often in the past. Even a benevolent and well-intentioned majority cannot always know what is appropriate for a minority. The question then arises as to whether *all* minorities, whatever their origin, status, or persuasion, should be granted specific legal rights. To some extent, the rights of all are protected in the Charter by virtue of section 15 on equality before and under the law. But, to go further and to specifically entrench all minority group rights in a constitutional document can lead only to confusion and disorder. Where does one draw the line? Which groups qualify for inclusion and which do not? Are there some groups that qualify because they are special cases? Do some groups deserve special consideration in order to correct historical injustices? Does not the inclusion of just one group, however, not imply reverse discrimination against all the others?

Although the issue of minority rights is a relatively new one in terms of human history, it already poses what can only be described as a classic dilemma. The extent to which this dilemma is solved, peacefully and without conflict, will be a test of human wisdom and ingenuity. As a nation officially committed to multiculturalism, and with some first-hand knowledge of the problems associated with pluralism, diversity, and the treatment of minority groups, Canada is in a unique position to make a major contribution to the resolution of this human rights problem.

· · ·

APPENDIX A

Constitution Act 1867

SECTION 93
In and for each Province the Legislature may exclusively make Laws in relation to Education, subject and according to the following Provisions:

(1)   Nothing in any such Law shall prejudicially affect any Right or Privilege with respect to Denominational Schools which any Class of Persons have by Law in the Province at the Union;

(2)   All the Powers, Privileges, and Duties at the Union by Law conferred and imposed in Upper Canada on the Separate Schools and School Trustees of the Queen's Roman Catholic Subjects shall be and the same are hereby extended to the Dissentient Schools of the Queen's Protestant and Roman Catholic Subjects in Quebec;

(3)   Where in any Province a System of Separate or Dissentient Schools exists by Law at the Union or is thereafter established by the Legislature of the Province, an Appeal shall lie to the Governor General in Council from any Act or Decision of any Provincial Authority affecting any Right or Privilege of the Protestant or Roman Catholic Minority of the Queen's Subjects in relation to Education;

(4)   In case any such Provincial Law as from Time to Time seems to the Governor General in Council requisite for the due Execution of the Provisions of this Section is not duly executed by the proper Provincial Authority in that Behalf, then and in every such Case, and as far only as the Circumstances of each Case require, the Parliament of Canada may make remedial Laws for the due Execution of the Provisions of this Section and of any Decisions of the Governor General in Council under this Section.

• • •

APPENDIX B

Canada Constitution Act 1982
Charter of Rights and Freedoms

SECTION 23:
MINORITY LANGUAGE EDUCATION RIGHTS

Language of instruction

23.(1)   Citizens of Canada

(a)   whose first language learned and still understood is that of the English or French linguistic minority population of the province in which they reside, or

(b)   who have received their primary school instruction in Canada in English or French and reside in a province where the language in which they received that instruction is the language of the English or French linguistic minority population of that province, have the right to have their children receive primary and secondary school instruction in that language in that province.

Continuity of language instruction

(2)   Citizens of Canada of whom any child has received or is receiving primary or secondary school instruction in English or French in Canada, have the right to have all their children receive primary and secondary school instruction in the same language.

Application where numbers warrant

(3)   The right of citizens of Canada under subsections (1) and (2) to have their children receive primary and secondary school instruction in the language of the English or French linguistic minority population of a province

(a)   applies wherever in the province the number of children of citizens who have such a right is sufficient to warrant the provision to them out of public funds of minority language instruction; and

(b)   includes, where the number of those children so warrants, the right to have them receive that instruction in minority language educational facilities provided out of public funds.

• • •

APPENDIX C

Constitution Act 1982

SECTION 59

(1)   Paragraph 23(1)(a) shall come into force in respect of Quebec on a day to be fixed by proclamation issued by the Queen or the Governor General under the Great Seal of Canada.

(2)   A proclamation under subsection (1) shall be issued only where authorized by the legislative assembly or government of Quebec.

(3)   This section may be repealed on the day paragraph 23(1)(a) comes into force in respect of Quebec and this Act amended and renumbered, consequentially upon the repeal of this section, by proclamation issued by the Queen or the Governor General under the Great Seal of Canada.

• • •

NOTES

1.   The term "Indian" is more or less synonymous with the term "Aboriginal." According to the Constitution Act of 1982 the term "aboriginal peoples of Canada" now includes Indians, Metis, and Inuit.

2.   For an account of the status of the two official languages in Canada see the various annual reports on Official Languages issued by the Department of the Secretary of State of Canada.

3.   In Quebec, in the same year, the Legislature had passed Bill 63 (an act to promote the French language in Quebec) that for the first time in Quebec law provided parents with freedom of choice

in language of instruction. This law was withdrawn when Bill 22 was passed in 1974.

4. Before examining these new constitutional minority rights in detail, it is important to call attention to three features of the Charter that are often misunderstood. First, even though the province of Quebec was not a signatory to the Constitution Act of 1982, the constitution is a national document and thus the Charter applies in Quebec as it does in the other provinces. Second, the infamous "notwithstanding" clause (section 33 of the Charter) that enables a legislature to exempt itself from the application of certain clauses of the Charter, does not apply to section 23 on minority language education rights. As a result, all provinces including Quebec are subject to section 23 of the Charter. Third, the term "minority language" in the Charter applies only to the official languages of Canada, that is to English and French; and the word "minority" in this context refers to the English or French minority in the province as a whole rather than to a minority in a specific school district or geographic area. Consequently, minority language education rights in the Charter apply only to

the English minority in Quebec and to French minorities in other provinces.

5. There is a further limitation in Quebec to the effect that section 23(1)(a) of the Charter, concerning the criterion of mother tongue eligibility, does not apply until such time as it is specifically authorized by the National Assembly or government of Quebec (Section 59 of the Constitution Act 1982). The wording of section 59 is shown in Appendix C.

6. This restriction on the right of the Quebec National Assembly to legislate in the field of language and education was one of the reasons why Quebec refused to sign the constitutional accord of 5 November 1981.

7. The legal situation in each province with reference to section 23 rights is covered in Martel, A. (1991). *Official language minority education rights in Canada: From instruction to management*. Ottawa: Office of the Commissioner of Official Languages. Another useful source is: Foucher, Pierre (1985). *Constitutional language rights of official-language minorities in Canada*. Ottawa: Canadian Law Information Council. Recent legal and educational developments in each province are described in the Annual Reports of the Commissioner of Official Languages.

• • •

REFERENCES

Attorney General of Quebec v. Quebec Association of Protestant School Boards, 10 DLR (4d), 321 (SCC) (1984).

Berger, T. R. (1985). Towards the regime of tolerance. In M. E. Manley-Casimir & T. A. Sussel (Eds.), *Courts in the classrooms: Education and the Charter of Rights and Freedoms* (pp. 95–104). Calgary: Detselig.

Bezeau, L. M. (1989). *Educational administration for Canadian teachers*. Toronto: Copp Clark Pitman.

Burgess, D. A. (1991). Denominational and linguistic guarantees in the Canadian constitution: Implications for Quebec education. *McGill Journal of Education, 26,* 175–188.

Burgess, D. A. (1992). Minority education rights in Quebec: Recent legislative issues. In W. F. Foster (Ed.), *Education and law: A plea for partnership: Proceedings of the Inaugural Conference of the Canadian Association for the Practical Study of Law in Education* (pp. 265–275). Welland, ON: Soleil Publishing.

Clark, L. (Ed.). (1968). *The Manitoba school question: Majority rule or minority rights?* Toronto: Copp Clark.

Commissioner of Official Languages. (1991). *Annual Report 1990*. Ottawa: Supply and Services Canada.

Commissioner of Official Languages. (1992). *Annual Report 1991*. Ottawa: Supply and Services Canada.

Dickinson, G. M., & MacKay, A. W. (1989). *Rights, freedoms and the education system in Canada: Cases and materials*. Toronto: Montgomery Publications.

Foucher, P. (1985). *Constitutional language rights of official-language minorities in Canada*. Ottawa: Canadian Law Information Council.

Henchey, N., & Burgess, D. A. (1987). *Between past and future: Quebec education in transition*. Calgary: Detselig.

Henley, D., & Young, J. (1990). Indian education in Canada: Contemporary issues. In Y. L. J. Lam (Ed.), *Canadian public education system: Issues and prospects* (pp. 193–214). Calgary: Detselig.

Hurlbert, E. L., & Hurlbert, M. A. (1989). *School law under the Charter of Rights and Freedoms*. Calgary: University of Calgary.

Lam, Y. L. J. (Ed.). (1990). *Canadian public education system: Issues and prospects*. Calgary: Detselig.

MacKay, D. (1990). *Flight from famine: The coming of the Irish to Canada*. Toronto: McClelland and Stewart.

Magnet, J. E. (1986). A new deal in minority language education. In M. E. Manley-Casimir & T. A. Sussel (Eds.), *Courts in the classrooms: Education and the Charter of Rights and Freedoms* (pp. 105–114). Calgary: Detselig.

Magnuson, R. (1980). *A brief history of Quebec education: From New France to parti québécois*. Montreal: Harvest House.

Magnuson, R. (1992). *Education in New France*. Montreal: McGill-Queen's University Press.

Magsino, R. (1986). Denominational rights in education. In M. E. Manley-Casimir & T. A. Sussel (Eds.), *Courts in the classrooms: Education and the Charter of Rights and Freedoms* (pp. 77–94). Calgary: Detselig.

Mahé v. Alberta. (March 15, 1990). Ottawa: Supreme Court of Canada.

Manley-Casimir, M. E., & Sussel, T. A. (Eds.). (1986). *Courts in the classrooms: Education and the Charter of Rights and Freedoms*. Calgary: Detselig.

Martel, A. (1991). *Official language minority education rights in Canada: From instruction to management*. Ottawa: Commissioner of Official Languages.

Royal Commission of Inquiry on Bilingualism and Biculturalism. (1968). *Book II: Education*. Ottawa: Queen's Printer.

Secretary of State. (1992). *Official languages: Annual report 1990–1991*. Ottawa: Supply and Services Canada.

Sussel, T.A., & Manley-Casimir, M.E. (1986). The Supreme Court of Canada as a "national school board": The Charter and educational change. In M.E. Manley-Casimir & T.A. Sussel (Eds.), *Courts in the classroom: Education and the Charter of Rights and Freedoms*. Calgary: Detselig.

IMPLICATIONS OF ETHNIC DIVERSITY

...

Canada is a land of ethnic diversity where people are encouraged to retain ties with their past rather than forfeit their traditions to a cultural melting pot. This emphasis on the preservation of heritage results in a number of special and complex problems and issues for Canadian educators and educational institutions. The articles in this section reflect, at least in part, problems posed by our insistence on weaving a multicultural social fabric.

Friesen traces the history of Canada's multicultural challenge and outlines current criticisms of multicultural policy. He then discusses various approaches to multicultural education and articulates a set of principles, derived from a variety of sources, for teaching with the ethnic factor in mind.

Urion discusses changing issues in the schooling of Native people in Canada. The historical background of educational policies for dealing with aboriginal people is outlined and the effects of the policy discussions of the 1960s are described. Urion also discusses the burgeoning academic literature on Native issues, which is being formulated from a variety of perspectives.

Young focusses on the role of schools in dealing with the issues of prejudice and discrimination. He identifies several factors he believes are relevant for developing the attitudes and behaviours necessary for a tolerant multicultural society: the development of a suitable knowledge base for a multicultural curriculum, the opportunity for positive emotional experiences with ethnicity, the opportunity for adequate cognitive and moral development, the purging of prejudice from our language, and the modifying of the pedagogy of instruction. He also attempts to delineate the teacher's role in developing students who are committed to a multicultural reality for Canada.

IMPLICATIONS OF ETHNICITY FOR TEACHING

...

John W. Friesen

The emphasis on ethnic studies as a field of study is scarcely two decades old in Canada, hardly long enough to establish an academic discipline. Still, the production of related research studies and the teaching of appropriate subject matter in schools and universities has burgeoned. In 1989, the Canadian Ethnic Studies Association held its twentieth anniversary celebration by hosting a conference at The University of Calgary with the appropriately valuative theme, "Canadian Ethnic Studies: The State of the Art." The organizers planned for the celebration of an interdisciplinary approach to the theme and the conference paper reflected this. Represented in the sessions were the perspectives of anthropology, sociology, history, geography, psychology, history, education, and folklore. Included in the various conference discussions were such concepts as: multiculturalism, intercultural education, minority studies, cross-cultural studies, culturally unique studies, biculturalism, and so on. In evaluating the event, analysts worried that while the field of ethnic studies is still in its early growth stages, its future will largely be dependent upon a wide variety of interrelated factors, i.e., changing ideological currents and fashions in academia; changing public opinions on immigration, multiculturalism, and ethnic relations; government funding; and the availability of jobs in universities. An element of consolation was evident in the fact that ethnic themes and concerns have been integrated into a variety of disciplines and subject matters, and it is hard to tell exactly how effective this arrangement will be. As conferences continue to feature a high degree of interdisciplinary interaction and a cross-fertilization of ideas, there is every reason to believe that the thrust of ethnic studies will be sizable in the future (Burnet & Palmer, 1990).

An encouraging note is that Canadian ethnic studies is developing an increasingly stronger base through the formulation of appropriate national and provincial legislation that is sometimes also translated into policy. Until recently many observers were content to stress that Canada is an ethnically diverse or multicultural country in the sense that it is made up of many cultures. Beyond that, few are ready to take seriously the implications of such an arrangement for effective functioning as a nation (McAndrew, 1991). The evidence would suggest that this is both an ongoing as well as a future concern for Canada.

Strictly speaking, "ethnicity" refers to "an involuntary group of people who share the same culture, or descendants of such people who identify themselves and/or are identified by others as belonging to the same involuntary group" (Isajiw, 1985, p. 16). One could say that the operational word for ethnic studies is "inter-culturalism" in the sense that the term conveys some form of interplay or interaction among the various sectors of a multicultural reality. It has even been suggested that the more popular rendition of this reality, namely "multiculturalism" is a purely Canadian invention (Cummins & Danesi, 1990), and is supplemented by a series of national accomplishments in this area. These include what might be called a very generous immigration policy (compared to other countries), Canada being the first country to pass a national multiculturalism act (in 1988), and the first to establish a federal Department of Multiculturalism and Citizenship.

The announcement of a formal policy of multiculturalism in Canada in 1971 received quick endorsement from a variety of national sectors but for different reasons. Many saw it as a societal acceptance of ethnicity, both as a reality and as a field of study. Ethnic leaders saw it as an opportunity to vindicate their heritage cultures without having to merge into one of the "founding nations." In addition, they hoped for sponsorship of cherished cultural maintenance programs through government funding. Without that they had no hopes of promoting their cultural heritage (Li, 1988). Politicians from all major parties supported the policy, and subsequent criticism has been directed to the shortcomings of implementation rather than the basic concept (Ray, 1990).

• • •

THE SOCIAL REALITY

The establishment of relevant policy is itself a commendable act, but even the best laws cannot guarantee their fulfillment on the street. For example, when the Canadian Charter of Rights and Freedoms was passed a few years ago, many believed that racism and intolerance were now outlawed in Canada. In reality the Charter has made little difference on either count, and even its goal of encouraging national unity has been "fragile and often threatened by intolerance" (Trudeau, 1990, p. 336). The bottom line is that the implementation of the spirit and letter of the Charter are dependent upon the will and spirit of the people (Ray, 1985). The Charter does not have authority to override other laws that violate human rights. This is because the Charter, like much other "human interest" legislation is interpretive and does not confer rights. It is intended only as suggesting behaviour that is consistent with "the preservation and enhancement of the multicultural heritage of Canada" (Leal, 1983, p. 25). The Charter prohibits racial discrimination in law but it cannot require governments (nor citizens) to promote racial or cultural equality. It is, at best, indicative of a long range social goal or ideology (Matas, 1991).

The roots of Canada's cultural pluralism are at least three centuries old, dating to the "founding of the nation" by the two dominant incoming European groups—English and French. Aboriginal peoples would naturally take issue with the dating of the nation to that time, and in light of constitutional talks currently underway across the land, their interpretation is increasingly heard. Perhaps in the near future, all talk about the relatively recent origins of this nation will be amended by the Aboriginal correction of written history.

Clearly the most significant period of immigration in Canada, at least in terms of numbers, occurred between 1896 and 1914. During that time, because of the massive influx of peoples from so many different cultural backgrounds, ethnicity in Canada came to be. Contrary to what this somewhat generous attitude might imply on the part of Canadians, the truth of the matter is that we were, at best, reluctant hosts to incoming groups. Throughout this period of immigration, Anglo-conformity was the predominant ideology, based on the philosophy of the dominant culture. It was expected that newcomers would adopt the values and institutions of Anglophone Canadian society. There was virtually no thought given to the possibility that WASP values might not be the apex of civilization which all citizens should strive for (Palmer, 1984).

The intrigue of Canada's massive immigration period arises from the fact that while people of many different cultural backgrounds were being lured here, little consideration was given to the matter of their adjustment to Canadian life. The "brains" behind the immigration move, was of course, Clifford Sifton, Minister of the Interior from 1896 to 1905. Sifton viewed immigration as a business proposition and a long-term investment for the country, and his actions showed the extent to which a single individual can influence national policy (Friesen, 1984). Sifton was clearly a businessman, not a social scientist. He believed that settlers from many different countries in the world should be encouraged to immigrate, settle on the prairies, and thus ensure maximum national productivity. His goal was to get the job done as quickly as possible, with as many people as possible. Thus he simplified federal legislation to promote homesteading, freed many of the encumbered lands, and conducted large-scale promotion of immigration in the United States and overseas (Hall, 1977).

The ethnic factor was pronounced in the immigration period supervised by Clifford Sifton. At this time the British Empire was at its height and the concomitant immigration policies reflected this. In fact, a preferential list for potential immigrants was drawn up featuring Anglo-British and Americans at the top. Next came northern and western Europeans as the most desirable, followed by central and eastern Europeans who had a slight edge over Jews and southern Europeans. These groups were followed in the pecking order by "strange" groups such as Mennonites, Hutterites, and Doukhobors, with no thought as to the possible cultural and philosophical differences among them. Last were the "Asian hordes," including the Chinese, Japanese, East Indians, and Blacks (Palmer, 1984). This "official" attitude undoubtedly set the tone for the reception these groups were later to enjoy or endure at the hands of their future neighbours.

If it was not enough to act with discrimination in group selection with regard to immigration, the Canadian past also reeks with evidence of misleading advertising in order to lure immigrants to a land of plenty. The West was advertised as the land of opportunity, a land virtually flowing with milk and honey, where anyone exerting only minimal effort would grow rich. As one government pamphlet put it: "It is no Utopian dream to look forward and see the endless plains thickly populated with millions to whom Western Canada has given happy homes, larger opportunities in life, and the assurance of a prosperous future" (Francis, 1989, p. 109). It is plausible that a correlation may be drawn between the later disillusionment that many of the "less desirable" groups felt and the treatment they received in their invitation to make Canada their home (Fleras & Elliott, 1992).

• • •

ETHNICITY AS A NATIONAL CHALLENGE

Although most political leaders in English-speaking Canada have accepted and supported the desirability of Canada's ethnic diversity, the Canadian public has sometimes been slow in endorsing the policy. Legitimate questions that arise in this regard have to do with the possibility of formulating a workable pluralist society, e.g., what possible effect will the encouragement of pluralism have on the vertical mosaic in which socio-economic class lines coincide with ethnic lines? How can one hope to establish government policies that are mutually compatible with a myriad of subcultural goals and lifestyles? Finally, there is the question of how much the encouragement of ethnic group solidarity threatens the freedom of individuals who are members of such groups (Palmer, 1984). For example, when the Commission on Biculturalism and Bilingualism was set up in 1969, its purpose was to develop a policy that would represent Canada's pluralist make-up. Of the six linguistic and cultural regions in Canada identified by sociologist Leo Driedger, only one, the province of New Brunswick, could be described as being both *bicultural* and *bilingual*. The other five regions comprise a mixture of varying characteristics, for example, the Northlands (multilingual and multicultural), Quebec (Francophone and multicultural), the Atlantic provinces, (Anglophone and Anglocultural), Upper Canada (Anglophone and multicultural), and the West (multicultural and Anglophone) (Driedger, 1989).

The report of the Commission on Biculturalism and Bilingualism was quickly undermined by the formulation of a federal policy on multiculturalism on 8 October 1971. While retaining the concept of two official languages, the new policy was designed to more closely represent the reality of cultural pluralism in Canada. In essence the policy guaranteed every ethnic group the right to preserve and develop its own culture and values in the Canadian context—with government support (Friesen, 1985). At this point, the nation was committed to the impossible; attempting to build a kaleidoscopic culture featuring a flexible solidarity of sorts, complete with unity in the midst of diversity. The props for that magic act are apparently still being developed behind the curtain.

The development of multicultural policy or "playing to the ethnics" in Canada has been the target of critics from its inception. Four major criticisms may be mentioned (Friesen, 1992). The first suggests that honouring ethnicity to the extent of supporting or even financing cultural differences in the Canadian lifestyle is a hindrance to national unity. This position implies an "either-or" situation, which rarely works in any situation of diversity, and makes the familiar error of believing that uniformity creates unity. Second, is the complaint that multiculturalism is a "sop to the ethnics," and mainly offers them platitudes and little bits of money to finance aspects of their cultural maintenance programs such as heritage language schools. It is, in essence, a simple way of buying votes. It may be true that multiculturalism is fraught with a degree of political opportunism, but if its programs have even limited success in helping to bridge the gap of understanding between newcomers and established citizens, it may still have merit. Perhaps a strengthening of these programs rather than dismantling them would bode better for the nation.

A third criticism of multiculturalism is that it magnifies human differences and builds unnecessary walls between individuals and between groups. After all, we are all more nearly alike than different. Multiculturalism is accused of trying to enshrine pluralism in Canadian society along with its correlates of individualism, relativism, and freedom, which will assist in the development of a "visionless co-existence" for Canadians (Bibby, 1990). Wood (1980) has argued that the promulgation of ethnicity or multiculturalism does threaten democracy, and well it should. Too much togetherness can be as harmful to a society as too much separateness. The education process in a democracy values above all else the development of reasoning abilities, wisdom, and morality in the individual. This requires the free and open participation of the full membership of a given society that will of itself also produce a degree of disagreement and diversity. Therein may be the exact measure of enrichment through creativity that a society needs for growth.

The fourth criticism originates with the Charter groups of English and French who disagree with elevating the status of any immigrant group to that of their own. The Anglophone population has had cultural and political control in various regions of the country for so long they naturally object to any kind of equality-awarding policy that might simultaneously lessen their own power base. The French community in Quebec also opposes the concept of multiculturalism and worries about any possible political or cultural reduction of their status. They claim that the multicultural policy distorts the historical and political realities of the nation because Canada has only two main cultures as well as two official languages. In fact, the Government of Quebec prefers the word, "inter-cultural" as opposed to "multicultural" in its documentation on the grounds that the latter implies equal status of *all* cultures in Canada. What is interesting about this position is that it is offset by rather generous decrees on multicultural matters by the Quebec government. A stronger plea is put forth by other groups in the province, for example, the Protestant school board in Montreal. Their recommendations for the provincial Department of Education insist that efforts should be made: (1) to ensure the maintenance and development of cultural communities other than French in Quebec; (2) to sensitize citizens to the enrichment by the other cultural communities; and (3) to promote the integration of non-Francophones into Quebec society (Zinman, 1988).

Aboriginal peoples also have serious questions about the whole business of cultural pluralism, starting with the notion of "founding nations." They have found little comfort in knowing that none of the documentation pertaining to that concept, nor the related legislation pertaining to multiculturalism offers any recognition of Aboriginal existence or of their rights as First Nations.

In reality there can be a great gulf between multicultural policy and practice. Originally the problem of synthesizing the two entities developed when incoming groups objected to being assimilated into the mainstream. The bloc settlements that immigrant groups were encouraged to establish in the West at the turn of this century, further hindered the social interaction necessary to unified nation-building. Each of the groups occupying bloc settlements developed their own institutions, and maintained their own separate lifestyles quite apart from the rest of the country. In some instances their neighbours resented their isolation and treated them with suspicion. The bloc settlements developed neighbourhood "walls" and inadvertently fostered exclusivity, thereby contributing to the racism that developed in that period and persisted in modified form in the decades which followed (Friesen & Verigin, 1989).

Incidents of racism in Canadian history are easily documented, (McKague, 1991), even though there are those who claim that racism has virtually been eliminated. In essence there are two theories of racism in Canada, particularly with regard to immigration policy and practice. One theory holds that racism has disappeared, while the others see racism persisting in changed form (Taylor, 1991). Brown (1991) argues that racism and discrimination cease only when the victims of these practices, alone or in solidarity with others, muster the power to force the aggressor to stop. Until this happens, the option is dialogue between aggressor and victim with the latter creating sufficient pressure on the power of the dominant group so that it decides that the dialogue is either in its best interest, or at least superior to the alternative. Appeals to government as a means of combatting racism are ineffective since the ultimate resolution of their situation is found in political organization and political action. This will require community support or at least some measure of tolerance on the part of dominant society. Generally speaking, "white ethnics" or Anglophones are by no means a natural support group. As one observer put it, "Indeed it would undoubtedly be easier to muster support for Canadian seals than Canadian racial minorities" (Buchignani, 1991, p. 204).

As the twentieth century has unfolded, there is evidence that at least one social institution has picked up more than its share of responsibilities in seeking to resolve social ills such as racism. This overworked institution is the school. Schools have continually undertaken an increasingly heavy workload, ranging from becoming a glorified babysitting agency to dealing with a myriad of other social "obligations" such as the provision of driver education, consumer education, family life and sex education, and substance abuse education. All of this is to be accomplished while effectively carrying out the traditional mandate of instilling the three "Rs" (Friesen & Boberg, 1990). Naturally, when the subject of multicultural education came up, with its attending challenges of combatting discrimination and racism, the public made a "quick trip to the school to lengthen the school day" (Friesen, 1987, vii).

• • •

THE ROLE OF SCHOOLING

Historically, Canadian schools and teachers were employed as agents of cultural imperialism in an effort to stamp out the cultural heritage of immigrant students and to assimilate them into the Canadian way of life. Until the entrenchment of appreciation for cultural diversity inherent in the passing of the multicultural policy in 1971, no one raised an eyebrow in regard to this missionary orientation of the various provincial school systems. In light of recent developments across the land, many modern educated teachers, who have been raised on the values of tolerance and cultural pluralism, find the actions of past school officials and educators "downright bigoted" (Mazurek & Kach, 1990, p. 133).

Today's "enlightened" multiculturalism has not come easily. In addition to convincing the public about the value of cultural equity, educators have had to work hard in developing relevant, workable school structures as well as functional classroom methodologies. Gibson (1976) was probably the first to delineate or categorize initial school thrusts into multiculturalism starting with the "education of the culturally different" approach. Probably representative of the bulk of early multicultural efforts some twenty years ago, this approach was concerned with equalizing learning conditions for minorities so they "could catch up to the rest of society." The implication was that any shortfall in ability or achievement was in the court of minority students and they would have to make it up.

A second approach concentrated on teaching about cultural differences in an effort to promote tolerance. This was a reversal of the school's traditional stance that promulgated the concept that cultural differences of any kind were inferior to the counterpart beliefs and practices in dominant society, and demanded dramatic changes in school policy and practice. Needless to say these were not necessarily forthcoming in such vital areas as teacher training and classroom methodology (Henley & Young, 1981). Further research also indicates that without appropriate meaningful field experience, teaching *about* the value of cultural differences essentially has little effect (Kehoe, 1984).

Gibson's third identified approach shows a little more promise. Its central focus is to educate for cultural pluralism with the primary objective of maintaining and extending ethnic and cultural diversity within society. A tall order for the school to fulfill, its promoters see cultural equity as a multi-institutional obligation that cannot singly be fulfilled by the school. According to this view, meaningful multiculturalism cannot be achieved unless the other players in the field, particularly the community, are viewed as equal partners to the extent of positive involvement in and commitment to the day-to-day issues in the school (Duncan, 1987). A multicultural education program that does not address the topics of power, agenda-setting, and decision-making cannot correctly read the problem. Its capacity to solve problems, therefore, is aborted (Fleras & Elliott, 1992). Hard-hitting multicultural education implies trying to affect changes in public attitudes even to the extent of allowing or, better still, encouraging, the development of corollary substructures such as culturally inspired private schools or heritage language schools. Naturally, such "generosity" has been met with a great deal of resistance in some public sectors, with opponents arguing that pluralism in schooling eventually damages national unity.

Fourth, there is the approach of educating children for "biculturalism," which focusses on the idea that learners should be taught how to function effectively in two different cultural worlds—their heritage or minority culture, and that of dominant society. A fundamental concern of this concept, however, is the assumption that the acquisition of competencies in a second culture can be achieved and maintained (Young, 1979). A concern is that this approach may lead to marginality or cultural schizophrenia. This challenge arises out of the need for the school to strike an appropriate balance between the educational goals of each ethnic community on the one hand, and the educational goals of the larger society on the other (Mallea, 1984). A feasible resolution of the dilemma emanates from the Native world where biculturalism is sometimes defined in terms of the individual adhering to their Native beliefs while, at the same time, adjusting to a technological age on their own terms. The hope is to retain the core of traditional Indian ways and selectively add the best in the dominant society (Snow, 1977). This would provide the individual with a single but solid cultural base with an orientation to allow for change on a personally selective basis.

A recent player on the multicultural court is "antiracist" education, which purports to be a hard-hitting replacement for disillusioned multiculturalists to adopt.

A commitment to antiracist education represents a logical alternative to short-comings within multicultural education (i.e., its refusal to confront minority grievances and aspirations). Criticism also stems from an unwillingness to restructure the education system in a manner that is likely to improve the lives and life-chances of minority students. Besides, much of what passes for multicultural education is simply a magnification of ethnic foods, festivals, finery and folklore, which, in the final analysis is shallow and peripheral in terms of effecting attitudinal changes. It studiously avoids the racism and racial discrimination inherent within the school system and in society generally (Fleras & Elliott, 1992).

A difficulty with the antiracist approach to education is its inherent militancy or missionary zeal. Its mandate is not so much to instruct as it is to initiate specific changes. Its stated goal is to change institutional organizational policies and practices that have a discriminatory impact, and to change individual behaviours and attitudes that reinforce racism. The primary thrust is on behaviour and practice instead of on perceptions and attitudes (Tator, 1987/88). In the topology of good teaching, the shaping of behaviour as an objective implies "training," rather than "teaching"; the difference being in "teaching someone to do so-and-so," versus "teaching someone that so-and-so is the case" (Green, 1972). By the first of these expressions the teacher clearly means to focus on the formation of behaviour and by the second to focus on the transmission of knowledge. We may train a young tree to grow a certain way, but, hopefully, not human minds. We may teach persons to perform certain operations or exercises that have the consequence of strengthening their muscles, but we do not speak of "teaching" the muscles. The distinction between teaching and training turns upon the degree to which the behaviour aimed at in teaching or training is a manifestation of intelligence. Intelligence is a property that belongs to the behaviour of individuals, and not to their muscles or other organs. The dependent variable between teaching and training has to do with the degree of intelligence displayed in the behaviour we are seeking to shape (Green, 1972). Since the objectives of antiracist education more closely resemble the activity of training, the question must be raised, how is antiracist education different from its antecedent or the traditional forms of "teaching" such as behaviour modification or indoctrination?

• • •

TEACHERS AND STUDENTS

Does a teacher with some knowledge of ethnic lore and cultural diversity teach differently than other teachers? Hopefully, the answer is affirmative, even though an exact science of multicultural teaching has yet to be developed. Any discussion of cultural diversity as it affects schooling runs the risk of stereotyping and suggests an overdependence on generalizations. Consider the furor over learning styles research a decade ago when it was "discovered" that Native American children, for example, "learned differently." No one following that path took note of the great diversity of culture and socio-economic status within the various Native communities (Baruth & Manning, 1992), and much of the early research in the area was poorly conceived and biased (Piwowar, 1990). Besides, even such cherished educational clichés as "educating for enhanced self-esteem" can be problematic when one considers that there are cultural variations in the way that such an objective is operationalized in a particular cultural setting. However, if short-cuts are the primary target of hurried educators, little will stop them from jumping onto the "band wagon of the quick fix" in seeking to resolve a particular educational challenge.

Two decades of wrestling with the intrigue of ethnicity in the school has resulted in the explication of a multiplicity of relevant principles from a variety of sources. To illustrate:

1. Multicultural education should reflect and respect the historical and sociological realities of ethnicity in all curricula (*Multicultural education journal*, 1991). Students should be encouraged to accept themselves in terms of their total individual identity—physically, emotionally, and culturally. Teachers should present alternative explanations for normative behaviour in the classroom in order to provide students with an opportunity to expand their own perspectives (Friesen, 1985).

2. If teachers are to have equally positive expectations for students of all cultural backgrounds, they must first understand the cultural differences that often exist in the integrated (multicultural) classroom (Bennett, 1990).

3. Students should be given the opportunity to display a positive feeling of self-esteem by becoming aware of the characteristics of their own individual cultures. They should be encouraged to learn about and to appreciate the unique contributions of their own cultures. Each student should be assisted in realizing that they are worthy of making a unique contribution to society (Tiedt & Tiedt, 1991).

4. Teachers may have extra homework to do in assessing their attitudes towards their own heritage and make-up before they set out to help their students to disentangle theirs. Unresolved personal cultural baggage can have dysfunctional effects on the teaching-learning process when culturally affected behaviours come into play (Friesen, 1983).

5. An effective multicultural education program should address and stand against racism in all forms, and in all situations (Baruth & Manning, 1992).

When the ethnic factor is accounted for in teaching, another source of input about students becomes available to the teacher. While this new source of knowledge will initially demand additional homework, it will simultaneously provide the teacher with a fuller working knowledge of the learner. In the context of everything we know about effective education, this is as it should be, because a better equipped teacher is a more effective teacher. Thus the guidelines for teaching with the ethnic factor in mind, while they require an additional element of specialized knowledge on the part of the professional teacher, coincide with the principles of good teaching practice in any context.

$\bullet\bullet\bullet$

REFERENCES

Abruscato, J. (1985). *Introduction to teaching and the study of education*. Englewood Cliffs, NJ: Prentice-Hall.

Baruth, L.G., & Manning, M.L. (1992). *Multicultural education of children and adolescents*. Neeham Heights, MA: Allyn and Bacon.

Bennett, C.I. (1990). *Comprehensive multicultural education: Theory and practice* (2nd ed.). Boston: Allyn and Bacon.

Bibby, R. W. (1990). *Mosaic madness: The potential and poverty of Canadian life*. Toronto: Stoddart.

Brown, R. (1991). Overcoming sexism and racism—How? In O. McKague (Ed.), *Racism in Canada* (pp. 163–177). Saskatoon: Fifth House.

Buchignani, N. (1991). Some comments on the elimination of racism in Canada. In O. McKague (Ed.), *Racism in Canada* (pp. 199–205). Saskatoon: Fifth House.

Burnet, J., & Palmer, H. (1990). State of the art. *Canadian Ethnic Studies, 22*(l), 1–7.

Cummins, J., & Danesi, M. (Eds.). (1990). *Heritage languages: The development and denial of Canada's linguistic resources*. Toronto: Garamond Press.

Driedger, L. (1989). *The ethnic factor: Identity in diversity*. Toronto: McGraw-Hill.

Duncan, C. (1987). The multicultural community and the school. In R. Arora & C. Duncan (Eds.), *Multicultural education: Towards good practice* (pp. 200–212). London: Routledge & Kegan Paul.

Francis, R.D. (1989). *Images of the west: Responses of the Canadian prairies*. Saskatoon: Western Producer Prairie Books.

Friesen, J.W. (1983). *Schools with a purpose*. Calgary: Detselig.

Friesen, J.W. (1984). Factors affecting minority education: A rural perspective. In R.J. Samuda, J.W. Berry, & M. Laferrière (Eds.), *Multiculturalism in Canada: Social and educational perspectives* (pp. 282–291). Toronto: Allyn and Bacon.

Friesen, J.W. (1985). *When cultures clash: Case studies in multiculturalism*. Calgary: Detselig.

Friesen, J.W. (1987). *Reforming the schools—for teachers.* Lanham, MD: University Press of America.

Friesen, J.W. (1992). *Multiculturalism in Canada: Hope or hoax?* Edmonton: Alberta Teachers' Association.

Friesen, J.W., & Boberg, A.L. (1990). *Introduction to teaching: A socio-cultural approach.* Dubuque, IA: Kendall Hunt.

Friesen, J.W., & Verigin, M.M. (1989). *The community Doukhobors: A people in transition.* Ottawa: Borealis Press.

Gibson, M. (1976). Approaches to multicultural education in the US: Some concepts and assumptions. *Anthropology and Education, 7*(4), 7–18.

Green, T.F. (1972). The modes of teaching. In J.M. Rich (Ed.), *Readings in the philosophy of education* (2nd ed.) (pp. 263–274). Belmont, CA: Wadsworth.

Hall, D.J. (1977). Clifford Sifton: Immigration and settlement policy, 1896–1905. In H. Palmer (Ed.), *The settlement of the west* (pp. 60–77). Calgary: Comprint Publishing.

Henley, R., & Young, J. (1981). Multicultural education: Contemporary variations on a historical theme. *The History and Social Science Teacher, 17*(1), 7–16.

Isajiw, W.W. (1985). Definitions of ethnicity. In R.M. Bienvenue & J.E. Goldstein (Eds.), *Ethnicity and ethnic relations in Canada: A book of readings* (pp. 5–17). Toronto: Butterworths.

Kehoe, J. (1984). *A handbook for enhancing the multicultural climate of the school.* Vancouver: Wedge Publications.

Leal, H.A. (1983). Multiculturalism and the Charter of Rights and Freedoms. *Multiculturalism, 8*(1), 24–28.

Li, P.S. (1988). *Ethnic inequality in a class society.* Toronto: Thompson.

Madaus, G.F., Kellaghan, T., & Schwab, R.L. (1989). *Teach them well: An introduction to education.* New York: Harper and Row.

Mallea, J.R. (1984). Introduction: Cultural diversity and Canadian education. In J.R. Mallea & J.C. Young (Eds.), *Cultural diversity and Canadian education: Issues and innovations.* Ottawa: Carleton University Press, 1–19.

Martin, R.E., Jr., Wood, G.H., & Stevens, E.W., Jr. (1988). *An introduction to teaching: A question of commitment.* Boston: Allyn and Bacon.

Matas, D. (April, 1991). The Charter and racism. *Currents: Readings in Race Relations, 7*(1), 14–15.

Mazurek, K., & Kach, N. (1990). Multiculturalism, society and education. In E.B. Titley (Ed.), *Canadian education: Historical themes and contemporary issues* (pp. 133–160). Calgary: Detselig.

McAndrew, M. (1990). Ethnicity, multiculturalism, and multicultural education in Canada. In R. Ghosh & D. Ray (Eds.), *Social change and education in Canada* (2nd ed.) (pp. 130–141). Toronto: Harcourt Brace Jovanovich.

McKague, O. (1991). *Racism in Canada.* Saskatoon: Fifth House.

Multicultural Education Journal. Edmonton: Multicultural Education Council, The Alberta Teachers' Association.

Ornstein, A.C. (1990). *Strategies for effective teaching.* New York: Harper and Row.

Palmer, H. (1984). Reluctant hosts: Anglo-Canadian views of multiculturalism in the twentieth century. In J.R. Mallea & J.C. Young (Eds.), *Cultural diversity and Canadian education: Issues and innovations* (pp. 21–40). Ottawa: Carleton University Press.

Piwowar, E.A. (1990). *Towards a model for culturally compatible Native education.* Unpublished master's thesis, University of Calgary, Calgary, AB.

Ray, D. (1985). Human rights and multicultural perspectives in Canada. *Multiculturalism, 9*(1), 10–12.

Ray, D. (1990). Multiculturalism in a bilingual context: A current review. In Y.L.J.

Lam (Ed.), *Canadian public education system: Issues and prospects* (pp. 47–63). Calgary: Detselig.

Sadker, M., & Sadker, D.M. (1991). *Teachers, schools, and society* (2nd ed.). New York: McGraw-Hill.

Snow, Chief John. (1977). *These mountains are our sacred places: The story of the Stoney Indians*. Toronto: Samuel Stevens.

Tator, C. (1987/88). Anti-racist education. *Currents*, 4(4), 8–9.

Tiedt, P.L., & Iris, M. (1990). *Multicultural teaching: A handbook of activities, information, and resources* (3rd ed.). Boston: Allyn and Bacon.

Trudeau, P.E. (1990). The values of a Just Society. In T.S. Axworthy & P.E. Trudeau (Eds.), *Towards a Just Society* (pp. 357–385). Markham, ON: Penguin.

Wood, D. (1980). Multiculturalism: Appreciating our diversity. *Accord*, November/December, 7.

Young, J. (1979). Education in a multicultural society: What sort of education? *Canadian Journal of Education*, 4(3), 5–21.

Zinman, R. (1988). *A multicultural/multiracial approach to education in the schools of the Protestant school board of greater Montreal*. Montreal: Report of the Task Force on Multicultural Education, The Protestant School Board of Montreal.

FIRST NATIONS SCHOOLING IN CANADA:

A REVIEW OF CHANGING ISSUES

...

Carl Urion

uring the past few years dramatic changes have taken place in the relationship between the First Nations of Canada and the federal government, from armed confrontation during the summer of 1990 in Quebec, to negotiation of constitutional recognition of the inherent right to aboriginal self-government. Less publicly visible changes have been taking place since the 1960s in the field of Native education, and these may be as important as the more widely publicized changes. Many of the changes have come about because both Native and non-Native people have agreed that straightforward principles of justice and equity have been violated in times past and that it is time to remedy that situation. The principles are clear and understandable; the issues are complex. The complexity arises, in part, in defining just who is a Native person, in accounting for the diversity of the aboriginal population, and in trying to understand the history of relations between Natives and others in Canada.

Almost a million aboriginal people live in Canada, and the country's aboriginal population is increasing faster than other Canadian groups (Hagey, Larocque, & McBride, 1989). These people of Canada's First Nations constitute a diverse group. The languages and cultural histories of Canada's aboriginal people are as different from each other as those of Europe and Asia. Before contact with Europeans, their economies included agriculture, trade, whaling, fishing, and hunting and gathering. Indigenous political organization ranged from confederations of distinct nations to chieftainships and band organization. Some regions of Canada had highly stratified societies with hereditary noble classes, commoners, and slaves, whereas in other regions, societies were egalitarian, and a range of social organizations existed between those extremes (Dickason, 1992).

It is not surprising that such diverse backgrounds have produced at least as much contemporary diversity among Canadian aboriginal people as there is in the rest of Canadian society in terms of lifestyle, aspirations, and attitude. Canada's one million Native people are even diverse in terms of legal status: the peculiar way that Canada has defined its responsibilities under law and treaty has created a bewildering list of aboriginal legal statuses that vary by region and bear only tangential relationship to common logic, heredity, or community histories (Chartrand, 1991).

There is diversity in patterns of residence. Though they constitute only 3.6 percent of the total Canadian population (Hagey et al., 1989), in several large regions in Canada, Natives constitute a majority or near majority. Many Native people live in rural areas, but large Native populations live in all Canada's major cities (McDonald, 1991; Secretary of State, 1991).

Despite this diversity, Native people have much in common. One important area of common experience has been with schools. Though some individuals and even whole communities have had remarkably good experiences in schools, for most of this century the relationship between the Canadian educational establishment and aboriginal people has been disastrous. The educational picture for Native people has changed substantially during the past twenty-five years, but it appears that educationists still have difficulty defining the basic issues involved in what must rank as one of the worst failures in the complex history of Canada's school systems.

This history is not peculiar to Canada. Its central characteristics are shared by countries such as Australia, New Zealand, Japan, India, and most of the other countries of the Americas where large immigrant populations have overwhelmed and marginalized indigenous populations. Indigenous people themselves and several of the national governments of those other countries recognize that the current situation is one of crisis (see for example, Cahape & Howley, 1992). In almost all areas where indigenous people have survived, during this century schools appear to have been vehicles for social control, containment, and assimilation of indigenous people rather than for individual achievement and mobility. National governments have made concerted efforts since the 1960s to work with indigenous people to change this situation, but problems persist in the definition of issues and objectives. It is impossible to understand the current situation without looking at the 120-year history of policy that created it.

• • •

THE HISTORICAL BACKGROUND OF CANADIAN NATIVE EDUCATIONAL POLICY

Most of the problems in aboriginal education in Canada this century have their origins in the government policies of the nineteenth century, that were articulated and put into effect as Europe and eastern North America accelerated industrialization. The economic and military interdependence that had characterized Indian-White relations in North America came to an end in the early nineteenth century when the economy of eastern North America changed rapidly with an unprecedented demand for land for westward expansion (Patterson, 1973).

Educational policies for dealing with aboriginal people were developed in Canada between the 1830s and the time of Canadian confederation. These policies appear to have been justified with reference to at least three currents of thought: the past experiences of church missionary groups with Indians; the requirements of British and international law in dealing with indigenous groups; and a social philosophy argued by the academicians and educationists of the day that assumed not only that aboriginal people were inferior in evolutionary terms, but that such inferiority would lead to their inevitable disappearance as distinct groups.

Between the 1870s and the end of the nineteenth century, a well-rationalized system of residential schools and day schools for Indians became part of that policy: funded by the federal government, the missionary bureaucracies of a select group of Christian churches, primarily Roman Catholic, Anglican, and Methodist, were commissioned to provide education to Indian people. A modified curriculum that focussed on agricultural and domestic skills and included a significant component of religious instruction and religious discipline was taught both in day schools on Indian reserves and in residential schools where young people were kept separate from their communities and families.

We now deal with the legacy of educational issues from that period of repression that continued into the early 1960s. During that period, people who were recognized as Indian by the federal government were not considered to be citizens of Canada and had virtually no effective political rights. Their mobility was restricted by a pass system similar to that adopted later in South Africa. Local administrators of federal policies held almost inconceivable power over Indian people, and it appears that many of those administrators exercised that power in arbitrary and self-serving ways. The government and churches not only discouraged the practice of Native religion, they managed to bring legal sanction against the practice of traditional ceremonies: Indians who participated in the West Coast potlatch or in the "dancing" of the Plains and Woodlands cultures were jailed and fined. The schools to which most Indian people had access had been set up following an explicitly stated policy to eradicate Indian culture by changing the children and adolescents who were students in the schools. The students were often sent to schools at long distances from their families, and there was usually little contact between the students and their parents or other kinfolk. Many alumni of those schools recall that their cultures, families, and elders were unremittingly ridiculed. In many of the schools, speaking an indigenous language was prohibited (Bull, 1991).

Many Indian communities appear to have made an initial accommodation to life on reserves during the 1880s, succeeding in farming ventures—and in some cases, such as the Brantford Institute in Ontario (Daniels, 1973) and Joseph Dion's school in Alberta (Dion, 1979), establishing their own schools. The period between the early 1920s and the early 1960s seems to have been particularly bleak. While educational opportunities were rapidly increasing for most other Canadians, proportionally few Native people finished school or went beyond grade school. Very few Native people entered post-secondary education, especially in Western Canada.

A majority of First Nations people were not recognized by the federal government as Indians, but in a society where legal definition of status and social identification as Native were only arbitrarily distinguished, there was not much difference in effect between "status" or "Treaty" Indians and other Natives. Inuit people were in an unusual position, not recognized as "Indian" under terms of federal statutes for Natives, but nonetheless administered by the same federal department and living under the same general sets of restrictions and opportunities.

One of the most remarkable aspects of this nineteenth-century model was its longevity. Much educational change took place in other sectors of Canadian society in the early part of this century and again in the 1930s, but aboriginal education retained its nineteenth-century colonial characteristics until after World War II when the federal government began taking more administrative interest in curricular and instructional matters. By the 1960s, some churches still operated residential facilities connected to schools, but the federal government became administratively responsible for curriculum and instruction and increasingly referred to provincial governments to promote a program of school integration.

Native people had always reacted strongly to the policies of containment and social control followed by Canadian governments but had limited opportunity for publicly articulating that reaction. Native political groups that were organized geographically along lines dictated by treaty area, by provincial and territorial boundaries, or by aboriginal status had developed during the 1920s and 1930s. Much of the credit for the decade of change in policy that began in the early 1960s must be given to First Nations veterans of World War II and the Korean War who returned from military service to find social conditions for First Nations people intolerable, and who joined those organizations or their own First Nations governments to work for change. An example of the courage this struggle demanded is the experience of the group led by John Tootoosis (Sluman, 1984), that tried to travel from Saskatchewan to Ottawa to appear before a Senate committee on Indian conditions and were apprehended and jailed because they had left their small reserves without permission of the local Indian agent.

. . .

THE EFFECTS THE POLICY DISCUSSIONS OF THE 1960s

The 1960s brought, for the first time, widespread public awareness of the miserable state of Canadian Native education. The public discussion set the stage for the policy changes of the early 1970s. A few social scientists began investigations of Native conditions, attempting to find theoretical models that would explain how such a system could have been tolerated for so long. In academic and public discussion they raised the ideological and moral issues that were involved in the attempt to maintain social control through schooling. First Nations spokespersons and organizations were included in a tumultuous and sometimes acrimonious public discussion of the need for change, and federal and provincial governments made several attempts at rapid remediation.

Provincial governments had developed an interest in Native education in the early 1960s, even before the federal government began large-scale integration. The western provinces established uniquely structured large school jurisdictions, particularly for the northern parts of each province where the majority of the students were Native.

By the end of the 1960s the federal government had a new policy proposal ready that would see the end of federal responsibility for Indians and the end of special status and reserves. It was designed to integrate Indian people once and for all into "mainstream" society. The government's White Paper brought a strong and immediate negative response from Native organizations and individuals who pointed out that the objectives of the policy were not new. That

Native response brought the federal government to a position of negotiation for educational change rather than administration of education by government fiat; by 1972 that negotiation had resulted in the statement of a fundamental principle, articulated initially by the National Indian Brotherhood (1972) and then stated as federal government policy, that Indian education should be locally controlled by Indians.

If the administrative implications of the new policy could be characterized as local Indian control of Indian schools, the characterization of the curriculum was that it had to be "bilingual and bicultural" in order to be "culturally relevant." First Nations teachers would be needed for First Nations schools, but the number of aboriginal people with teaching certificates was small, probably fewer than fifteen in each western province, and fewer than forty in either Ontario or Quebec. By the mid-1970s federally funded university-based special programs had been established in every region of Canada, several of them in or near Native communities, to provide teacher education for First Nations teaching candidates.

Law and education were the first fields of academic post-secondary study with programs especially designed for Native students, and they began a pattern of almost exponential increase in Native participation in post-secondary education. For example, in 1960 only sixty registered Indians were attending post-secondary institutions in all of Canada. Ten years later there were 432, but by the mid-1970s there were more than 2000. By the mid-1980s, 5800 Indians were attending Canadian universities, with another 11 170 in other post-secondary institutions, and by 1990 the total registered Indian post-secondary enrolment had grown to 21 300 (INAC, 1991, p. 39).

These figures reflect only aboriginal people identified as Indian by the federal government. It is difficult to find accurate data for the large group of aboriginal people who do not have federal status as Indians but are in fact of aboriginal ancestry; until the 1991 census data have been analyzed, estimates about that large group are tentative. It is safe to say, however, that there has been a similar dramatic increase in indicators of educational success.

Demographic data that reflect educational participation and completion for Indian people at the K–12 level are similarly impressive since the early 1960s when only 3.4 percent of Canadian Indians who lived on reserves completed high school by attending twelve consecutive years of school. That figure grew to around sixteen percent in the mid-1970s, and by 1990 was forty-seven percent (INAC, 1991, p. 36). The indicators are even more favourable for Native people who live away from reservations, but they are still not as favourable as for the Canadian population as a whole (McDonald, 1991).

It may appear at first that these improvements are the result of the policy that dictated local control of schools and a relevant, bilingual, and bicultural curriculum, but except in rare local circumstances that does not appear to have been the case. Schools on Indian reserves have indeed moved toward local control: by 1975, fifty-three schools on reserves were operated by Indian bands, and by 1990, there were 312 band-operated schools on reserves. Fewer than nine percent of the on-reserve school population now attend schools operated by the federal government, and more than forty-four percent attend band-operated schools. On the other hand, the largest group (more than forty-seven percent) of K–12 students who live on Indian reserves attend provincially operated schools (INAC, 1991, pp. 40-41). When the aboriginal students who live off-reserve—and who constitute the majority of Native people—are included, it is clear that between eighty percent and ninety percent of Canada's total aboriginal population attend provincially operated schools, and few of those schools provide for aboriginal culture or for Native participation in school governance or administration. Furthermore, the growing consensus is that band-operated schools have been just that: schools operated by bands, but controlled in fact by the federal government, adhering to a curriculum derived from provincial schools.

Given the remarkable changes reflected by selected educational demographic data, it is tempting to assume that continuing improvement in Native education will eventually bring about social change. In 1988, the Assembly of First Nations completed a comprehensive review of research findings and demographic measures and called for further political and educational change. Unfortunately, the broad picture that can be drawn from other demographic data indicates that the situation of aboriginal people in Canada is still of crisis proportions, and that problems exist even in the areas where positive changes have occurred. For example, a still common pattern of experience with schools requires some explanation: individual student performance as indicated by standard measures may be average to excellent in a band-operated school, but when students transfer to a provincial school where they are in a minority, a common outcome is failure and dropping out (Wilson, 1992). Moreover, staying in school and attending university has not meant equality in Canadian society: the median income for First Nations people who complete university degrees is almost one-third less than that of the comparable group in the general population, and the rate of unemployment for university-educated aboriginals is almost double that of their non-Native peers (Armstrong, Kennedy, & Oberle, 1990).

The larger economic and social picture is still one that Canada cannot sustain. The differences between aboriginal people, on and off reserve, and the Canadian population as a whole are still such that virtually all indicators of social distress—unemployment, underemployment, infant mortality, indices of crowded housing, suicide rates, life expectancy, and income level, for example—indicate that there is a social reality for Native people as a group that is quite different from that of other Canadians (Hagey et al., 1989).

• • •

THE ISSUES AS SEEN BY EDUCATIONISTS

Educationists' arguments have been based predominantly on the observation of cultural differences between aboriginals and others. During that long period of social control and repression through residential schools, educators justified their efforts at educating Indians by referring imprecisely to nineteenth-century doctrines of social evolution or to religious dogma. Toward the end of that period, after World War II, the educators' academic arguments were couched in terms of differences that produced a cultural deficit: the idea was that aboriginal cultures, as diverse as they were, did not include reinforcement of the cognitive operations and skills that were required in school or in "modern" society. That is generally the implicit argument in the major academic report of the mid-1960s commissioned by the federal government, the Hawthorn Report (1966-1967).

Since the mid-1960s a huge academic literature about Native education has emerged and an overwhelming majority of it explains Natives' poor school performance in terms of the cognitive or behavioural consequences of cultural difference. When educators involved in Black education in the United States criticized the "deficit" model as a form of institutional racism, educationists began using the less pejorative term "cultural difference," but used generally the same arguments as those of the deficit model, adding to it the ideological proviso of cultural relativism: cultures were different, but none was better than another. What educators were supposed to do was to teach from the perspective of the Native culture. It was out of such arguments that the promotion of bilingual and bicultural education grew: Indian children should be educated in the language they know, the Native language, and the curriculum should be based on things familiar to the students; instructional methods should be based on the protocols and communicative etiquettes of the students' own communities, along with instruction in the "majority society's" norms and values. That appeared to fit well with First Nations' fairly consistent statement that their differences—from each other and from Eurocanadian society—should be taken into account in the schooling of their children. A large literature about language of instruction, addressing bilingual education, focusses as much on Native-language retention as on instruction in the mother tongue of the student.

A major critique of those models, put forward by Hedley in 1976 and 1977, looked at the underlying assumptions of the models. He said that the theory of the connection between economic and social conditions on the one hand, and people's values and cognitive patterns on the other, was too simplistic and mechanical and that the model was still based on the idea that eventual assimilation of Indians into the dominant society was inevitable. He pointed out that this model of acculturation, on which almost all the academic literature and the new educational policy had been built, did not work.

The education literature continues to focus predominantly on differences. A fairly large but ambiguous corpus has been generated about Native children's self-image or self-concept. There is a significant literature about Native-specific cognitive styles and learning styles: Native children are said to be more visually than verbally oriented, though their culture is "orally" based, as opposed to being "literacy" based. There is a much smaller literature on differences in numeracy and cognitive functions associated with numeracy skills. There is even some literature about brain hemisphere dominance, which may seem unimportant except that it is taken seriously by many who argue that Native children are "right-brained" while schools communicate with and reward "left-brained" thinkers.

An increasingly vocal current in phenomenological research and critical theory in education is focussed on aboriginal people. It is claimed that participatory research with Native people will give them the conceptual tools to recognize the specific terms of their continued oppression and will lead to recognition of both their right to re-create the terms in which they articulate their social histories and the terms of their empowerment. The ideological premises of that tradition are obvious. It is incredible that there has been very little research or literature about prejudice and racism in Canadian society and how to deal with it in schools.

A new current has emerged in the academic literature. Its research agenda seems to be more specifically focussed. Many of the researchers and leading spokespersons are First Nations people who have completed postgraduate degrees in education and are now engaged in research or post-secondary teaching. Perhaps its first characteristic, however, is that though there is an attempt to use First Nations precepts in the framing of issues, the tradition is not exclusive to First Nations researchers. In this tradition, cultural differences are noted, but culture is not the domain where behaviour (or school success or failure) is explained, nor is it assumed that culture determines cognitive patterns. In other words, the tradition discards the doctrine of cultural determinism that was implicit in so much explanation of the past. Intractable boundaries around "cultures" or the people who were thought to represent them have no place in the tradition.

The focus is on the complementarity of multiple cultural, or traditional ways, on common "human" attributes and values, and on ways of expressing differences so that they are understandable in context and not considered to be the determiners of behaviour. Cultures are not objectified and defined, but the researchers appeal to epistemological premises from First Nations cultures to articulate the research questions and to specify research design. This has produced studies such as Swampy (1981) about the stability of traditional gender role identification through decades of schooling; the paramount importance of interpersonal respect in post-secondary education (TeHennepe, 1992); a redefinition of basic educational issues in "traditional" terms (Hampton, 1988; Weber-Pillwax, 1992); a survey of personal and social effects of abuse as a result of the residential school system (Cariboo Tribal Council, 1991); explanations of discourse systems of traditional narrative (Cruickshank, 1990; Lightning, 1992); the publication of some of those narratives themselves (Ahenakew & Wolfart, 1991); the development of curriculum materials about substance abuse (Zaharia, 1992); and the complementarity of oral tradition with the acquisition of literacy (Archibald, 1990).

This tradition represents one of the most positive of all the changes since the 1960s. In its assumptions of First Nations theory as direction of the enterprise of schooling, it is a bolder step toward First Nations control than even the constitutional agreement. In its openness and accessibility to all and in its contribution to general theory in education, it demonstrates that the relationship between First Nations and other Canadians is not a zero-sum proposition, but that gains by Canada's First Nations contribute to a common good.

• • •

REFERENCES

Ahenekew, F., & Wolfart, H.C. (Eds. & Trans.). *Kohkomaniawak otacimowiniwawa: Our grandmothers' lives as told in their own words*. Saskatoon, SK: Fifth House.

Archibald, J. (1990). Coyote's story about orality and literacy. *Canadian Journal of Native Education, 17*(2), 66–81.

Armstrong, R., Kennedy, J., & Oberle, P.R. (1990). *University education and economic well-being: Indian achievement and prospects.* Ottawa: Quantitative Analysis and Socio-Demographic Research, Finance and Professional Services, Indian and Northern Affairs Canada.

Assembly of First Nations. (1988). *Tradition and change in education: Towards a vision of our future* (3 vols.). Ottawa: Author.

Bull, L.R. (1991). Indian residential schooling: The Native perspective. *Canadian Journal of Native Education, 18*(Supplement), 1–64.

Cahape, P., & Howley, C.B. (Eds.). (1992). *Indian nations at risk: Listening to the people* (Summaries of Papers Commissioned by the Indian Nations at Risk Task Force of the U.S. Department of Education). Charleston, WV: ERIC Clearinghouse on Rural Education and Small Schools, Appalachia Educational Laboratory.

Cariboo Tribal Council. (1991). Faith misplaced: Lasting effects of abuse in a First Nations community. *Canadian Journal of Native Education, 18,* 161–198.

Chartrand, P.L.A.H. (1991). "Terms of division": Problems of "outside naming" for aboriginal people in Canada. *Journal of Indigenous Studies, 2*(2), 1–22.

Cruickshank, J. (1990). *Life lived like a story: Life stories of three Yukon Native elders.* Lincoln, NE: University of Nebraska Press.

Daniels, E.R. (1973). *The legal context of Indian education in Canada.* Unpublished doctoral dissertation, University of Alberta.

Dickason, O.P. (1992). *Canada's first nations: A history of founding peoples from earliest times.* Toronto: McClelland and Stewart.

Dion, J. (1979). *My tribe, the Cree.* Calgary: Glenbow Museum.

Hagey, N.J., Larocque, G., & McBride, C. (1989). *Highlights of aboriginal conditions 1981–2001* (vols. 1–3, Working Paper Series 89). Ottawa: Quantitative Analysis and Socio-demographic Research, Finance and Professional Services, Indian and Northern Affairs Canada.

Hampton, E. (1988). *Toward a redefinition of American Indian/Alaska Native education.* Unpublished doctoral dissertation, Harvard Graduate School of Education, Cambridge, MA.

Hawthorn, H.B. (1966–1967). *A survey of the contemporary Indians of Canada: A report on economic, political, and educational needs and policies.* Ottawa: Indian Affairs Branch.

Hedley, M. (1976–1977). Acculturation studies of North American Indians: A critique of the underlying framework and its implications. *Indian-Ed, 3*(3) and 4(1,2,3).

Indian and Northern Affairs Canada. (1991). *Basic departmental data.* Ottawa: Quantitative Analysis and Socio-demographic Research, Finance and Professional Services, Indian and Northern Affairs Canada.

Lightning, W. (1992, in press). Compassionate mind. *Canadian Journal of Native Education, 19*(2).

McDonald, R.J. (1991). Canada's off-reserve aboriginal population. *Canadian Social Trends,* Winter, 2–7.

National Indian Brotherhood. (1972). *Indian control of Indian education.* Ottawa: Author.

Patterson, E.P. (1973). *The Canadian Indian: A history since 1500.* Toronto: Collier-Macmillan Canada.

Secretary of State of Canada. (1991). *Canada's off-reserve aboriginal population: A statistical overview* (Cat. No. S2-220/1991). Ottawa: Social Trends Analysis Directorate, Department of the Secretary of State.

Sluman, N. (1984). *John Tootoosis.* (J. Goodwill, Transcriber). Winnipeg: Pemmican Publications.

Swampy, G.M. (1981). *The role of Native women in a Plains Cree society.* Unpublished master's project report, University of Alberta, Edmonton, AB.

TeHennepe, S. (1992). *Issues of respect.* Unpublished master's project report, Simon Fraser University, Vancouver, BC.

Weber-Pillwax, C. (1992). *Whose vision? Whose reality?* Unpublished master's thesis, University of Alberta, Edmonton, AB.

Wilson, P. (1992). Trauma in transition. *Canadian Journal of Native Education, 19,* 46–56.

Zaharia, F. (Ed.). (1992). *First Nations freedom: A curriculum of choice (alcohol, drugs, and substance abuse prevention) K–8.* Vancouver, BC: Mokakit, First Nations House of Learning, University of British Columbia.

PREJUDICE AND DISCRIMINATION:
CAN SCHOOLS MAKE A DIFFERENCE?

...

John   Rowland   Young

That Canada is a multicultural society is as banal as it is true. Although it was not until 1971 that the federal government announced a policy of "multiculturalism within a bilingual framework," we have been culturally heterogeneous for centuries. According to Burnet (1984), "Even before contacts with Europeans the 250 000 to 300 000 inhabitants of what is now Canada constituted about 50 societies, belonging to a dozen linguistic groups. Some of the societies were nomadic bands of hunters and gatherers; others were highly structured chiefdoms of fishers and cultivators of the soil" (p. 18).

Whether multiculturalism is possible is dependent upon at least two major factors: the desire of minority ethnic groups to retain their linguistic and cultural identities, and the commitment of the majority groups to provide cultural and structural support in all its forms for this retention of diversity. Although the federal government, in its desire to implement the policy of multiculturalism, instituted six programs designed to promote the language and cultural development of "the other ethnic groups," the policy's actual realization is in the hands of average Canadians. Canadians, individually and collectively, must be committed to multiculturalism as a goal and be aware of what is required to encourage it.

In the light of recent developments in Canada, such as the Keegstra affair, one has to ask how successful we have been in breaking down discriminatory attitudes and behaviours and in providing structural support for all ethnic groups in our society. Seldom a week goes by that we are not exposed by the media to examples of violence against some member of a visible ethnic group. Before the goals of multiculturalism—tolerance of all ethnic groups and the full participation of all groups in society—can be achieved, changes must occur not just in people's attitudes towards themselves and others, but also in the reward structure so that all individuals and groups can expect to participate in society and be rewarded accordingly. This paper will not focus on institutions generally, but will deal with the role of schools in attitude development and change, and as structural and cultural reproducers. Let us look first at the role of schools in attitude development and change.

For our purposes, we will define attitude, as does Berry (1984), to include "the affective, cognitive, and behavioural characteristics of individuals" (p. 104). We can further assume that attitudes are learned and, consequently, have the possibility of being changed. The specific attitude with which we are concerned is prejudice: a negative and inflexible attitude based in part on incomplete or inaccurate information. Translated into behaviour, this prejudicial attitude is manifested as discrimination, which can be sexist and ageist as well as racist.

Does racial prejudice exist in Canada? In order to answer such a question, it is important to determine what one can use as a reliable measure of prejudice. If one uses media headlines, one could reach the conclusion that there is extensive prejudice and discrimination: "Study shows racism growing in Calgary"; "Racism in article denied"; "Admitting racism first step in cure"; "'Keegstras everywhere, says race council report." Do we reach the conclusion that deep-rooted prejudicial attitudes are rampant in society? Or is this simply the media's way of attracting reader attention?

A danger confronting sociologists is to assume that prejudice varies in magnitude directly to the number of reported acts of violent racist attacks. There may be no relationship between the cases reported and those actually committed. An approach more favoured by sociologists is the sampling of a population for attitudes of prejudice. Using this procedure, we find the various conclusions somewhat confusing. So much depends on how prejudice is defined and from what part of Canada the sample is drawn. A generally accepted conclusion comes from Berry, Kalin, and Taylor's classic study of multiculturalism (1976), which argued that, although there is not a great deal of explicit racism or overt bigotry, "there is some evidence that race is an issue and is being employed by Canadians in their acceptance or rejection of groups of people" (p. 127).

From the various approaches discussed, it seems obvious that a degree of prejudice does exist in Canada and that its actual measurement is not that important if it is sufficient to influence behaviour to the extent that the goals of a multicultural society are adversely affected. Also, if teachers are going to do anything about prejudice and discrimination within schools, they are going to have to step back from the frenzy of headlines and look for solutions in rational solitude. Solutions will not come from hysteria or self-condemnation by the majority group. Prejudicial attitudes and discrimination are not the sole prerogative of the majority group. As Jean Burnet (1984) says,

> if we are to understand one another, we must forego the pleasure of regarding some ethnic groups as more virtuous than others and look instead in a detached way at the kinds of things people—all people—do in various situations—nothing is so devastatingly egalitarian as detachment. (p. 27)

When looking at the nature of prejudice and discrimination from an educational perspective, one must examine not only attitudes at the individual level, but also the role the educational system plays in fostering and perpetuating inequality in its very rewards structure. According to Patel (1980), prejudice and discrimination must be seen "as a form of stratification built into the structure of society; the roots of this division are located in the structure of the division of labour and in the organization of political power" (p. 14). Specifically, prejudice and discrimination are not understood simply as the ideas that one group has about others, but are also the outcome of inequalities within institutions, like schools.

If the school can both harbour and perpetuate prejudice and discrimination, how can a teacher work most effectively towards the goals of multiculturalism? First, we can not assume that teachers should accept full responsibility for changing societal values about multiculturalism and eradicating prejudice and discrimination. Attitudes are the outcome of the influences of all social institutions, including school, family, mass media, government and, increasingly important, the peer group. Secondly, teachers and schools cannot accept total responsibility for the lack of mobility of some students into certain areas of the economy. Inequality of educational opportunity is the outcome of many processes at work in society. However, teachers do have a responsibility to see that all students are rewarded for their talent and motivation regardless of social factors such as class, race, and ethnicity.

What is it, then, that teachers can reasonably be expected to do about prejudice and discrimination? The findings of sociopsychological research indicate that no single practice in education will be sufficient to combat prejudice because of the multidimensional nature of attitude change. According to Ijaz (1984),

> Cognitive and perceptual principles of categorisation may combine with effects of socialisation, personality variables, and emotional and affective

factors to produce prejudicial ethnic attitudes. . . . A truly successful educational program for attitudinal change in youngsters has to combine a variety of approaches, intellectual and factual, emotional and affective. (p. 135)

What will such a multifaceted approach look like? If teachers are committed to developing the attitudes and behaviours necessary for functional multiculturalism, they must be concerned with five specific areas: the knowledge base of the curriculum; positive experiences of ethnicity; cognitive and moral development; purging the language of prejudice; and modifying the pedagogy of instruction.

• • •

KNOWLEDGE BASE OF THE CURRICULUM

There has been an increasing trend in the provinces to establish a curriculum reflecting an appreciation and an understanding of all ethnic groups, not just the two so-called founding nations. All attempts have not been successful. Werner and associates (1977) analysed various ways in which ethnic groups have been treated within different curricula during the 1970s and have identified six approaches, none of which seem desirable. The study maintains that minority ethnic groups are frequently treated as marginal Canadians, as contributors to the dominant society, as beneficiaries of the dominant society, as minority groups seen as problems, as ethnic groups seen within a hierarchy of cultures, and, finally, as a "museum" of minorities' differences. These approaches are problematic in that they do not promote the goal of multicultural education; that of being tolerant and understanding, where all groups are seen as beneficiaries of and contributors to all societal outcomes. These approaches do not show the minority groups as active participants in the life of the country. The knowledge base is often not factually accurate, and ethnic groups are often singled out by focussing on their uniqueness as opposed to the many similarities between all ethnic groups.

What would be the basis of a suitable knowledge base for a multicultural curriculum? The information presented must be balanced and factual. Stereotyping must be avoided. It is important that a factual information base be not just accurate in terms of what is presented but that it include a balanced presentation, without the exclusion of cases that might be embarrassing (such as the treatment of Japanese-Canadians during World War II or the wholesale slaughter of the Boethuk Indians in Newfoundland).

Two other factors must be considered in a multicultural curriculum. When cultural diversity is discussed, it can be interpreted by students as simple quaintness if its sources are not discussed and understood. Perhaps most importantly, information must be presented on the commonality of the human situation or the similarities of basic human values. At the level of basic needs and values, Canadians, regardless of their ethnic background, have more in common than is often presented in multicultural curricula.

These curriculum requirements appear to be minimal but necessary for developing the attitudes and values associated with multicultural outcomes.

• • •

POSITIVE EXPERIENCES WITH ETHNIC DIVERSITY

Prejudice is not modified by the presentation of information alone, however accurate it may be. Students must have positive experiences with ethnic diversity. Students must be given opportunities for personal association or identification with members of other ethnic groups. Numerous Canadian studies have confirmed the importance of affective relations with members of other ethnic groups in changing attitudes towards these groups. Kalin (1984) concludes that:

> Experience with ethnic diversity is likely to reduce the excesses of bigotry (emotional intensity and inflexibility) and instead promote tolerance (respect, acceptance, and fair treatment of others) and flexibility (ability to suspend stereotypes and ethnic preferences) when dealing with individual persons. This goal is most likely to be achieved through individualized contact with other members of other ethnic groups. (p. 124)

Teachers must take every opportunity to encourage all students to interact as freely as possible without the restrictions that streaming and grouping place on students. For example, in some situations, students who do not speak English as a first language are placed in a stream with students of poor academic achievement. Consequently, they do not interact with all students in the system. Ethnic ghettos are often created within school systems that limit the possibility of the formation of multi-ethnic friendship groups. Where schools attract students who are from a similar ethnic background, it is imperative that students be exposed to other cultures.

• • •

COGNITIVE AND MORAL DEVELOPMENT

This approach is based on the assumption that to solve moral problems, such as prejudice and discrimination, a student must be given experiences in developing capacities of reasoning and cognition. An example of this approach is the model supplied by the Association for Values Education and Research (AVER, 1978).

The AVER model is based on the assumption that a morally autonomous or morally responsible individual must bring to bear upon any moral problem a number of abilities and dispositions. The AVER Prejudice Unit (1974) attempts to make the student conscious of prejudice and discrimination so that she or he can recognize "irrationality, inconsistency, injustice and lack of human-heartedness." The AVER unit encourages the student to make judgments about ethnic minorities. Basically, the student has his or her consciousness raised and is encouraged to see the importance of justifying the values he or she holds. This is done by increasing the student's ability to distinguish between mere descriptive claims and value claims, to evaluate moral arguments, to determine the role of authority, and to understand the consequences of one's actions as they affect others. In a study of the effects of the use of this procedure, the results suggest that "the Prejudice Unit is an effective condition for improving senior secondary students' ethnic tolerance and normative reasoning ability, [and] changes in tolerance and reasoning produced . . . are reasonably stable over time" (p. 18).

This requirement of a multicultural program is based on the assumption that teachers must accept the responsibility for developing cognitive abilities of students and providing them with opportunities to make mature moral judgments in the areas of prejudice and discrimination. This must become one of the objectives of all teachers.

• • •

PURGING OUR LANGUAGE OF PREJUDICE

The negative consequences of ethnic stereotyping and its relation to prejudice has been previously discussed. Related to this is the relationship of language to the development of prejudice. It seems reasonable to accept that the very socialization of an individual's consciousness and her or his personality are to a degree determined by language. Values and attitudes are, to some extent, the outcomes of the language that an individual experiences in gaining access to culture and society. Thus, the language we use in understanding our world shapes how we relate to that world. According to Luckman (1975), "Language evidently plays a central part in the processes of social objectivation and social transmission of such thought, value, and attitude configurations as have a relevance and validity that goes beyond individual experience" (p. 20).

Language itself can be responsible for conditioning the attitudes that students accept about members of other ethnic or racial groups or those singled out on the basis of age or gender. Words like "Wop," "Paki," and "Dago" are obviously demeaning when applied to specific ethnic groups. But there are less obvious words that serve the same function of influencing the attitudes of students about members of minority groups. Words that are common to our vocabulary can change our attitudes when they are used in certain contexts. Moore (1976) shows how words like defend, conquest, victory, and massacre, which are common in our history books, shape our understanding of groups of people. Specifically,

> Eurocentrism is also apparent in the usage of "victory" and "massacre" to describe the battles between Native Americans and whites. *Victory* is defined in the dictionary as "a success or triumph over an enemy in battle or war; the decisive defeat of an opponent." *Conquest* denotes the "taking over of control by the victor, and the obedience of the conquered." *Massacre* is defined as "the unnecessary, indiscriminate killing of a number of human beings, as in barbarous warfare or persecution, or for revenge or plunder." *Defend* is described as "to ward off attack from; guard against assault or injury; to strive to keep safe by resisting attack." (p. 11)

These seemingly innocuous words become value-laden when we talk about Western European immigrants being "victorious" in defending themselves against an Indian "massacre." Another common term used to describe certain ethnic groups is "culturally deprived." This is problematic, since no group can be said to be *deprived* of culture if by culture we mean language, dress, norms, and values. The term itself is probably meant to refer to a cultural difference between two groups, but the word deprived connotes the inferior status of one culture. It consequently serves the function of condemning, demeaning, and detracting from the acceptance of differences between groups.

What teachers must realize is the power of words to negatively condition attitudes. Prejudice can be the unanticipated outcome of the indiscriminate use of certain words that are ideologically and politically loaded. We cannot change the language, but we can change our usage of it. This will not entail avoiding certain terminology, but encouraging students to look at the effect of the language we use on attitudes and perceptions.

. . .

MODIFYING THE PEDAGOGY OF INSTRUCTION

Up to this point, emphasis has been placed on changes that can be made to the content of the classroom curriculum. Changes will also have to be made in the pedagogy or the process of transmission of the curriculum. Morgan (1975) develops two models of pedagogy, which she labels the *psychometric model* and the *epistemological model*. These two models differ significantly in their assumptions about and treatment of students in educational settings. The psychometric model is the one most frequently found in schools today. It is based on the following assumptions.

1. The child is regarded as an *object*, more particularly, as a *deficit system* whose passivity is a necessary condition for being initiated into public thought forms.

2. The child is regarded as "having" *intelligence* in the sense of a specific property that can be measured by objective tests.

3. The world of knowledge is regarded by those who adopt the psycho-metric model as composed of pre-existing theoretical forms into which the child must be initiated.

4. The pre-existence of such forms and the possession of such by the educator legitimizes a highly *didactic* form of pedagogy.

5. As a possessor of such theoretical forms, the educator assumes the role of societal surrogate one of whose main roles is to assess the growing congruence of the child's thought forms with the pre-existing standards.

6. *Educational development* consists of growing rationality as the child moves away from the concreteness of her or his immediate world towards the increasingly abstract theoretical forms.

7. *Educational achievement* consists in progressing towards increasingly specialized and highly discipline-bound subject matter and is measured in terms of objective evaluative criteria such as behavioural objectives. (p. 126)

In this model, the student is someone who "has education done to them." Morgan contrasts these features with those of the epistemological model, which has the following characteristics.

1. The child is regarded primarily as a *subject*, that is, as a being who is actively involved in constructing and arranging her or his knowledge of the world in terms of personally relevant interpretational schemata.

2.   The main property that the child is thought to possess and that is most relevant to the educational setting is the non-quantifiable property of *curiosity*.

3.   Following the leads of Piaget and Bruner, the world of knowledge is regarded as composed of thought forms that are in a constant process of construction and that are dialectically related to the development of individual subjects interacting with socially approved and socially distributed knowledge.

4.   Emphasizing the constructive aspect of human knowledge and placing value on intellectual initiative legitimizes a pedagogy that is highly *interaction oriented*.

5.   As a similarly constructive, growing subject, the educator assumes the role of social model in the process of knowledge construction, one of the main responsibilities of which is the heuristic channeling of the pre-existing curiosity of each individual student.

6.   *Successful pedagogy* consists not in the measuring of the achievement level of the students but in the ability of the teacher to apprehend and recreate the intentionality and subjective reality of the students so as to provide greater individual stimulation.

7.   Although *educational achievement* is measured in distance from the starting point to present level of development, this is a highly individualized measure. The child is essentially treated as a self-regulative being insofar as she or he controls the sequence and pace of the experience. In many cases, the child controls the content of the experience as well, insofar as his or her interests and desires are often the crucial curriculum determinants in the setting. (p. 126)

In this model the students would be active in their education and responsible for its outcomes. The epistemological model would be the better model to foster the development of positive attitudes and values associated with a multicultural program. Students would be held responsible for their intellectual and moral growth. It seems to follow that this pedagogy would be less authoritarian and would encourage the acceptance of differences between individuals, the enhancement of self-esteem, the development of critical thinking, the understanding of the consequences of holding certain beliefs and attitudes, and the desire to engage in activities leading to social justice. This model of pedagogy, combined with the four previously discussed conditions of the multicultural classroom could provide a sound basis for the desired educational outcomes of tolerance and understanding.

What role does education play in either creating structural inequalities or bringing about their demise? One is made constantly aware of a recurrent theme in Canadian education, namely that of equality of educational opportunity. The principle of equality of opportunity has been an important part of the general liberal ideology that has influenced the development of public education in the past one hundred years. The guiding principle has been the assumption that education would provide equal opportunities for all individuals to achieve, through the use of their abilities and motivation, whatever position in society they desire. The assumption is that every child should have the opportunity to make fullest use of his or her potential and that the means to achieve this would be the educational system. Although education would not completely eliminate inequality, the argument goes, talent found among children of minority ethnic groups would be encouraged, and the unfair advantages open to the majority group would be reduced. Education would be a means of assuring that children would end up in a position in society commensurate with their abilities and motivation and not merely with their socio-economic status or place of birth.

However, when one looks past this ideology to see what really happens, one finds a very close and persistent relationship between the adult occupational hierarchy and the type or level of education gained by the children of those adults. This is often quite independent of the child's ability and motivation. Those adults who have had their experiences and characteristics recognized and rewarded by the educational system have been allocated higher positions in the occupational hierarchy; in turn, these adults can pass these experiences on to their children, assuring that the latter will be allocated like positions through the educational qualifications they gain. If we relate this to ethnicity, we find that, in a country such as Canada, the hierarchial occupational structure corresponds to the ethnic background of its citizens. Certain ethnic groups are more successful in using the educational system than are others. What results is a hierarchy of ethnic groups. Consequently, ethnic and racial inequalities are by and large reproduced in the next generation by the educational system. This is the structural basis of discrimination discussed earlier.

We have seen that schools have successfully forged clear linkages between educational attainment and the occupational structure. It is clear that faith in the ideal that the educational system can be the means to bring about equality in society is misplaced. Schools have not been successful as vehicles of mobility for children of certain ethnic groups or as agents for social change. Schools reproduce the inequalities that already exist in society, and later the credentials awarded by schools are used to justify an individual's success, or lack thereof, in the social hierarchy. Schools, indirectly if not directly, legitimize inequalities. Contrary to the goal, professed by those who control schools, of using education as a means of restructuring society by rewarding individuals according to talent and motivation rather than according to characteristics ascribed at birth, schools are themselves directly shaped by the realities of the broader society. Consequently, the goal of social change, which schools often profess, becomes the reality of social control.

It is not just the structural factors outside of schools that have a profound effect on what schools actually do. The hidden curriculum and educators' assumptions about educability and future achievement exert a significant influence on the different values taught to students. Moreover, inequalities and their stratifying outcomes are built into the very structures of schools themselves. Streaming and tracking are two such structures. Raymond Breton (1970) showed that academic stratification (streaming) is considerably more important in influencing students' aspirations to higher education than is their measured ability and that this streaming is often directly related to the child's ethnic background.

Children from minority groups differ from children of the majority group not only in their levels of educational attainment and in their rates of educational participation but also in the kinds of education they receive. In that subjects are stratified into a hierarchical structure, children of certain ethnic groups may be exposed to different kinds of pressures and expectations, which create different aspirations and lead to allocation to occupations that are differentially rewarded.

The educational system is not just an innocent bystander when it comes to the creation of inequalities in society. According to Jaenen (1972):

> If we accept the view that Canada is a multi-ethnic and polycultural society, then it would seem to follow that the public school systems of the nation ought to reflect this cultural pluralism. Such a conclusion would seem to impose itself if for no other reason than publicly supported school systems should serve all and reflect the educational objectives of the entire community. The tendency in all public or state school systems, however, is towards uniformity and centralization. Uniformity and centralization, whether defended on grounds of administrative efficiency, in the name of equality, or on grounds of scholarly attainment of stated common objectives, discourage educational recognition of cultural pluralism. Thus, one may declare that it is possible for public schooling, equated in the popular mind with education, to retard the development of a unique and significant culture in Canada, to downgrade what is genuinely and authentically Canadian in our lifestyle, and to depreciate the moral, relevant, and innovative aspects of public schooling. (p. 199)

We have attempted to look "through" what educationalists in Canada say they are doing and better see the reality of educational outcomes. This may have led to a fairly pessimistic conclusion. But it does not mean that teachers are totally helpless. Changes in teacher training, curriculum, and pedagogic practices may be required and useful if for no other reason than providing a more humane and stimulating environment for students who spend the better part of each day for twelve years or more within these institutions.

If teachers accept the difficult task of making the suggested changes in the curriculum, pedagogy, language of education, and in their understanding of the cognitive, affective, and moral possibilities of education, then prejudical attitudes and discrimination, which threaten the existence of our multicultural society, can be reduced. Teachers must not just teach about multiculturalism. They must realize the instrumental role they play in creating structures of inequality through the practices common in many schools.

This goal is no less controversial than it would be difficult to obtain. However, if we accept that the inequalities that exist in Canada are costly in both an economic and social sense, inimical to our sense of social justice, and destructive of the realization of multiculturalism, then we may wish to do something about them. And here is where teachers can play their part. It seems reasonable to assume that schools could teach the norms of distributive justice and the principles of equality. Rather than teaching loyalty and commitment to the status quo, schools could teach sincere questioning and critical analysis. Rather than accepting the role of allocator of credentials that reduce students to products, schools could foster knowledge and skills that would lead students to see themselves as producers of reality. By creating a truly multicultural school system, as has been outlined, our students will leave schools strong, capable, and committed to a multicultural reality for Canada. The challenge is great, but can we ask for anything less of our schools?

• • •

REFERENCES

Association for Values Education and Research. (1974). *Final report of a study of moral education in Surrey, B.C.* (Report no. 6). Vancouver: University of British Columbia.

Association for Values Education and Research. (1978). *Evaluation of the AVER prejudice unit in a senior secondary school.* (Report no. 7). Vancouver: University of British Columbia.

Berry, J.W. (1984). Multiculturalism attitudes and education. In R.J. Samuda, J.W. Berry, & M. Laferrière (Eds.), *Multiculturalism in Canada: Social and educational perspectives.* Toronto: Allyn and Bacon.

Berry, J., Kalin, R., & Taylor, D.M. (1976). *Multiculturalism and ethnic attitudes in Canada*. Ottawa.

Breton, R. (1970). Academic stratification in secondary schools and the educational plans of students. *Canadian Review of Sociology and Anthropology, 7*, 1.

Burnet, J. (1984). Myths and multiculturalism. In R.J. Samuda, J.W. Berry, and M. Laferrière (Eds.), *Multiculturalism in Canada: Social and educational perspectives*. Toronto: Allyn and Bacon.

Ijaz, M.A. (1984). Ethnic attitude change: A multidimensional approach. In R.J. Samuda, J.W. Berry, & M. Laferrière (Eds.), *Multiculturalism in Canada: Social and educational perspectives*. Toronto: Allyn and Bacon.

Jaenen, C.J. (1972). Cultural diversity and education. In N. Byrne & J. Quarter (Eds.), *Must school fail?* Toronto: McClelland and Stewart.

Kalin, R.K. (1984). The development of ethnic attitudes. In R.J. Samuda, J.W. Berry, & M. Laferrière (Eds.), *Multiculturalism in Canada: Social and educational perspectives*. Toronto: Allyn and Bacon.

Luckman, T. (1975). *The sociology of language*. Indianapolis: Bobbs-Merrill.

Moore, R.B. (1976). *Racism in the English language*. New York: Racism and Sexism Resource Center.

Morgan, K. (1975). Socialization, social models, and the open education movement: Some philosophical considerations. In D. Nyberg (Ed.), *The philosophy of open education*. London: Routledge and Kegan Paul.

Patel, D. (1980). *Dealing with interracial conflict policy alternatives*. Montreal: Institute for Research on Public Policy.

Werner, W., Connors, B., Aoki, T., & Dahli, J. (1977). *Whose culture? Whose heritage?* Edmonton: University of Alberta.

CHANGING FAMILY AND GENDER ISSUES

...

Canadian educational systems are reverberating to the largely unpredictable and cumulative impacts of the concurrent forces that are reshaping our institutions and our social conscience. These forces include the disintegration of the extended family, the faltering of the nuclear family unit, the rightfully enhanced role of women in our society, and the waning influence of traditional purveyors of values. The issues dealt with in this section result, at least in part, from these forces.

Friesen contends that, although the family and the school have often been perceived as being in "partnership" regarding the education of children, this has not always been the case and it is at best an uneasy but essential partnership. He notes that, with the growing resurgence in family-related research, there is mounting evidence that the family exerts the most powerful influence on the developing child's educational expectations, verbal skills, affective relationships, discipline, and beliefs, and consequently, on his or her academic performance. Friesen develops this theme, purporting that parents should assume a greater role in the education of the child by developing a stronger, "co-operative partnership" between the home and the school.

Pence examines the "new reality" wherein increasing numbers of preschool children are experiencing peer socialization and institutionalization external to the family at a very young age. Pence outlines the history of family and school life, the nature of our current state of social and institutional transition, and discusses the issues that face us in this area as individuals, as educators, and as a society planning for the future.

The changing role of women in society and the impact of the women's movement within education has challenged many of the assumptions about educational scholarship. Focussing on the three most common ways that the feminist "critique" has been formulated, Gaskell provides a historical account of how these critiques have shaped, and are shaping, educational practices. Gaskell astutely points out, however, that while each critique has provided some insight into how schools work, the net result has only served to extenuate the tension, by focussing solely on the difference between women and men. To emphasize only the difference, however, is to see this difference as a weapon, as an edge that one may have over another. When this occurs, the diversity that is also present when we notice a difference becomes obscured. It is this recognition of diversity in difference, that "an emphasis on difference leaves us with various versions of knowledge and justice and educational practices," that Gaskell feels we should use to facilitate communication within the educational setting. Scholarship along these lines Gaskell concludes, forces us to challenge and rethink our "standards of excellence, measures of achievement, criteria for knowledge and forms of governance," and allows us to "contribute to some of the most difficult and persistent concerns in our ongoing dialogue about education."

The concept of the school system as a major agent for the inculcation of values inevitably leads to conflict in a complex society. Whose values should the school system reflect? What values should be taught? Which group's values should be paramount? Such questions may force intense pressure onto the educational system and onto the educators within that system. Hague surveys contemporary Canadian values education. Some ways in which values education has been carried out, especially traditional indoctrination, the Values Clarification approach, and Kohlberg's Cognitive Developmental approach to moral education, are criticized by Hague for their subjectivism and narrow understanding of personality. The new Character Education approach is examined as a potential solution to the present need for values and moral education.

FAMILY AND SCHOOL:
AN ESSENTIAL PARTNERSHP

• • •

John D. Friesen

R eaction in the 1970s and 1980s to intrapsychic and individualistic explanations of human growth and development has brought into sharp focus the impact of environmental influences, particularly those of the family and school, on the developing child. A wide range of studies has been undertaken in the last fifteen years, to determine the influence of the family on the child's intellectual, emotional, and career development, as well as his or her school achievement. It is now generally accepted in the research literature that the family is the most powerful and optimal context for the developing child and that it has a significant influence on the child's academic performance (Anderson, 1980).

This article consists of three parts. The first part traces the historical relationship between the school and the family as partners in the educational process. The second section examines the research regarding the family's influence on the cognitive, academic, and career development of the child, and the third part will consider applications of child development research on educational theory and practice.

• • •

THE RELATIONSHIP BETWEEN
FAMILY AND SCHOOL

Historically, as Cremin (1976) has shown in his work on the history of education, many seventeenth- and eighteenth-century families taught their own children to read, write, and count. Education occurred primarily in the home and church, and the family functioned as the transmitter of moral, psychosocial, cultural, and legal information (Radcliffe, 1979).

During the first half of the nineteenth century, the public school increasingly took on the major responsibility for educating the child. This shift in educational responsibility from the home to the school has led, in extreme cases, to parents being bluntly told by teachers not to "interfere" in the education of their children. Many things contributed to this shift in responsibility. Among these were the difficulty families had in finding the personal and financial resources to educate their children on their own and the greater efficiency of appointing teachers to perform teaching tasks for the whole community. Teachers were appointed to carry out educational responsibilities as society moved from an agrarian to an industrial society and role differentiation became more formal.

Along with societal changes, the early political and educational philosophers also promoted the movement of education from the home to the school. For example, Horace Mann (1957) in his famous report on the teaching of reading, spelling, and composition, did not once make mention of the family as a place where some of this instruction might take place. Similarily, Dewey (1966), although he was aware of the danger of school education becoming abstract and bookish, was also of the opinion that the school served as a special educational institution in "advanced" society, and he associated "participant education" with "low grade society" (Varene, 1981). Dewey did not recognize the importance of families in the intellectual and cognitive development of children and the contributions parents potentially make to the educative process. Similarly, Parsons (1955), although he recognized its expressive qualities, reinforced the view that the family was losing its overall usefulness. He took the position that families in advanced societies would become "factories which produce human personalities," and that education would occur outside the home in schools and factories.

The view that parents are unimportant as educators of their children was not only held by leading educational and political philosophers of the past, but is also held by many teachers today. In a recent study designed to assist learning- and behaviour-disabled Grade 3 children, an intervention strategy designed to involve parents actively in helping a child to read was vigorously opposed by some school staff (Friesen & Der, 1984). It was assumed by some teachers that teaching reading was the role of the school, and that parents could not be trusted to read to their children. This illustration is not uncommon, for often parents tell stories of meetings with teachers who complained that parents should not have tried to teach their children to read and that, by doing so, they had created problems for the child. The overall attitude of many teachers is "leave the educating to us."

It is the thesis of this paper that parents should assume an important role in a child's education, and that a co-operative partnership between the home and school needs to be promoted. In the following section, research data will be presented to illustrate ways in which families influence the academic and cognitive development of their children. Because there is a large body of literature in this area, I have been selective in my coverage of the topic. The reader may refer to several comprehensive reviews of the literature (Anderson, 1984), which provide extensive references and research designs of significant studies dealing with the impact of the family on school performance.

• • •

PARENT PARTICIPATION IN SCHOOLING

In the last ten to twenty years, there has been growing pressure for parent participation in schools. Such participation has taken many forms, such as parental involvement in instruction of aides, volunteers, and tutors; education to improve parental skills and knowledge; community-school movements; and, finally, parent-school consultative committees.

However, many of the programs involving parents in educational endeavours have not been well received by professional educators. For example, in a recent study on parent-school consultative committees in British Columbia, it was revealed that only sixteen percent of school boards in that province have a policy and provide backup support for parent-school committees (B.C. Council for the Family, 1980). Many boards indicated that they had no policies of their own nor any interest in the concept of a district-wide policy to establish parent-school committees.

In contrast to such resistant attitudes toward parent involvement in education, a number of empirical studies concerned with parental participation in the child's education show that parental contacts initiated by the school staff are effective in increasing attendance of chronically absent students, reducing talking in the classroom, increasing the rate of completion of homework, raising the level of performance on daily math assignments, and reducing disruptive/aggressive student behaviour. Similarly, children asked to read to their parents gained in reading skills, compared with children in a control group. Several large-scale community projects, including Home Start and Parent-Child Development Centres, reveal that parental involvement has positive consequences for the child and parent; however, the results of these investigations are not consistent, and thus not conclusive (Hess & Holloway, 1984).

Family Variables and Achievement

A wide range of family variables is associated with school achievement. While it is difficult to summarize the many studies that have investigated these relationships, Hess and Holloway (1984) have identified five general categories and obtained considerable research evidence addressing these variables.

1. Parental educational expectations. Boocock (1972) maintains that high-achieving children come from families that have high expectations for them. Empirical studies on the relation between parents' expectations and academic performance generally support this contention (Seginer, 1983). Children's school performance is associated with the parents' own achievement orientation, their press for their children's achievement, their aspirations for their child's educational and occupational achievement, and their emphasis on school work generally.

2. Parental verbal interaction with children. Numerous studies have shown the strength of the link between aspects of the verbal environment of the home and achievement in school (Hess & Holloway, 1984). The findings show that school achievement is related to how much the parent reads to the child, the amount of verbal interaction in the family, the children's participation in interaction at meals, and parental playing and talking with children.

3. Parental affective relationships with children. A series of research reports show that parental warmth facilitates performance in school. Representative studies reveal that school achievement is related to parental warmth and avoidance of restriction and punishment and is negatively correlated to maternal rejection.

4. Parental discipline. Although research in this area is hampered by definitional problems, the available data show a consistent association between modes of parental discipline and children's achievement. School achievement is positively correlated to authoritative parental control as opposed to permissiveness and autocratic control, the use of physical punishment and discouragement, as well as to the degree of fit between authority structures at home and at school. Hess and Holloway (1984) point out that the findings in this area have been impressive, and they encourage more careful theoretical analysis of the data.

5. Parental beliefs and attributions. The effects of parental beliefs on child-rearing behaviour and children's school achievement is becoming increasingly clear as research evidence accumulates. Preliminary studies reveal

that parental knowledge of developmental norms is associated with competence in child rearing. Parental beliefs also seem to influence children's self-concepts and expectations for school performance as well as their problem-solving behaviour.

Family Effects on Reading

The family's role in promoting interest and skill in reading has been widely studied. Hess and Holloway (1984) identify five general areas of family functioning that have a positive effect on school achievement. These areas include:

1. The value placed on literacy, which involves the amount of reading parents do, the quality of their reading material, and their interest and involvement in reading.
2. The press-for-achievement dimension includes such indicators as parental expectations, involvement in attempting to teach their children to read, interest in having the children watch educational TV programs such as "Sesame Street," and the possession of books and records. All these factors are positively related to reading achievement.
3. The availability of reading and writing materials for preschool and elementary school children tends to produce more competent readers. Good readers are frequently taken to the library by their parents.
4. The tendency of parents to read to their children is also related to the children's reading interest and performance. This finding was also present when the parents did not speak English but encouraged their children to read aloud to them. In these cases, parental involvement and interest was motivational rather than instructional.
5. Parent-child interactions influenced both language development and competence in literacy skills. Research findings on the impact of the family on reading performance clearly establish the importance of family involvement in the school.

Family Influence on
Vocational Development

In their comprehensive review of the influence of the family on vocational development, Schulenberg, Vondracek, and Crouter (1984) identify four family factors that influence vocational development. These factors are socio-economic status; family process variables such as socialization patterns, child-rearing practices, and interpersonal relationships and communication patterns; family interaction patterns such as acceptance and rejection, dominance and submission, and emotional/rational and assertive/non-assertive behaviour; and, finally, family structure and organization (i.e., family size, birth order, sibling spacing, and single parenthood).

Family Functioning and Conduct Problems in Children

Hetherington and Martin (1986) in a review of family interactions and child misconduct assert that all major psychological theories on the origins of conduct problems in children consider parent and family functioning as key etiological factors. This perspective is based on substantive evidence showing correlations between several types of familial dysfunction and childhood conduct problems. Furthermore, high rates of antisocial personality disorders, substance abuse, and depression have been consistently found in the parents of boys referred to clinics for antisocial or aggressive behaviour. In regard to the impact of parenting behaviour on conduct disorders, a comprehensive review of the literature by Loeber and Stouthamer-Loeber (1986) found that four of the strongest correlates to severe conduct problems in children were poor parental supervision, lack of parental involvement in their child's activities, harsh or abusive forms of discipline, and inconsistent child rearing.

Although much less significant, there is also some evidence that family problems are associated with less severe conduct problems such as oppositional, non-compliant, negative, and defiant behaviours. As a means of reducing the behaviour problems of these children, teaching parents to become more involved in their children's behaviour and to consistently use non-corporal methods of punishment has been found to be effective.

Family Influence on School Dropout Rates

There is growing body of evidence, including that of Ainley, Foreman and Sheret (1991) that family socio-economic factors are consistently associated with school retention. The association is strongest with the social aspects of the family background rather than the economic factors. Family wealth itself does not strengthen school attendance. However, parental encouragement and education are strongly linked to retention rates.

Numerous studies such as Williams (1987) in Australia reveal that a higher proportion of students of non-English-speaking backgrounds than students of English-speaking, Australian-born backgrounds completed year 12 at a secondary school. This situation may result from higher levels of aspiration among young people of certain ethnic backgrounds and possibly stronger parental encouragement in those groups to continue formal study.

Family Environments and IQ

The degree to which family environments influence cognitive competence as measured by IQ tests has been much debated. The studies of this relationship generally reveal a moderate to high positive correlation between measures of home environment and IQ. Even when the IQ of the parents is controlled for, this correlation, although smaller, continues to exist as is demonstrated by Luster and Dubow (1992). However, further longitudinal studies are needed to determine if this influence is diminished over time as the child reaches adulthood. There is some evidence that the greatest family influence on IQ occurs in the early childhood years and this influence is reduced during adolescence.

Other Related Studies

While this paper does not purport to provide an exhaustive survey of the literature on the theme of family influence on school achievement, I will nevertheless briefly identify several other areas of enquiry that can be pursued more fully by the reader. They are presented below as areas of potential research activity that show considerable promise.

1. The influence of parents in shaping cognitive skills like perception, memory, cognitive scanning, and selective attention.
2. The effects of maternal communication styles on mental rehearsal in the child.
3. Parental encouragement of children's use of memory strategies.
4. Parental influences on motivational processes such as attempting challenging tasks and working intensively and persistently.
5. Parental influence on the children's moral development.
6. The impact of the parents' cognitive style on the children's performance.
7. The role of parents in facilitating children's language development through knowledge of syntax, vocabulary, and communication skills and by monitoring the children's comprehension.

8. The effects of divorce, poverty, employment, illness, number of children, marital harmony, and support networks on the child's cognitive growth and school achievement.

• • •

APPLICATIONS TO THEORY AND PRACTICE

As the above review of the child development literature suggests, during the last twenty years we have entered a new era of family-related research that demonstrates the role of the family as educator and the importance of establishing vital relationships between the home and the school. While some of the data remain somewhat inconsistent and obscure, the fundamental finding that families play an important role in the education of children is supported.

Professional educators must now rethink their practices in the light of current data that points to the family as an important agent of socialization. One of the obvious indications of this research activity is the need of the school and the family to develop a partnership in the educational enterprise. Education is a joint activity of the home and school.

Before outlining the nature of the partnership, I want to make more explicit some of the assumptions and views that have guided my analysis. The first proposition is that children are shaped by their interaction with the contexts in which they find themselves. According to this formulation, as Bronfenbrenner (1979) states, "learning and development are facilitated by the participation of the developing person in progressively more complex patterns of reciprocal activity with someone with whom that person has developed a strong and enduring emotional attachment" (p. 60). This viewpoint holds that the individual is embedded in and interacts with ever more expanding and complex contexts. The second proposition, as Hess and Holloway (1984) point out, is that in many ways the school and family cannot fully control the cognitive activities of the child that involve remembering, perceiving, forming categories, making associations, and deriving generalizations, for all of these are linked to the biological and anatomical characteristics of the species. The third is that agents of socialization affect the outcomes of basic mental operations by controlling the content or raw materials of experience that children use in developing their mental worlds. School and family may restrict, enlarge, and generally select the material that is to be learned by the child, and thereby give personal and cultural meaning to the knowledge the child acquires, making some of it important and valued and some irrelevant.

Agents of socialization may also influence the child's use of certain cognitive strategies and perceptual mechanisms involved in selecting information, filtering out other information, and using processes to scan the environment for stimulation. It is also generally agreed that these agents have a strong influence on personality development, including the formation of such characteristics as self-esteem, attributions of self, personal monitoring mechanisms, and the internalization of standards and values.

While the home and school are the childs' two most prominent agents of socialization, there are other agents, which may include the mass media (such as television), the peer group, and the community. Where a mismatch exists between the values and information offered a child, her or his learning may be hampered, and inner confusion may result.

One of the characteristics of contemporary society is the existence of great cultural variation in ethnic, religious, political, and economic background. In our multicultural Canadian society, families hold disparate values and beliefs regarding child-rearing practices, the goals of education, and the meaning of human existence. It is very difficult for the school to acknowledge and affirm the wide diversity of opinion and belief that exists among school children. Consequently, schools have a tendency to deny the influence of all home environments, as educators try to equalize educational opportunities for all children. But the school and family are not independent and separate organizations. One cannot disregard the influence of one upon the other. They are part of one system and organization; each influences the other.

In the light of a growing body of literature dealing with the ecology of human development, educators in the future should recognize more fully that schools are built on the educational structures developed in the home. One way of acknowledging the important influence of the home on the child's school performance is for teachers to become well acquainted with families, including their cultures, beliefs, patterns of socialization, and educational purposes and goals. The curriculum needs to be developed with a recognition of the importance of the family. Educational policies need to integrate this information into educational practices through practical administrative and instructional linkages.

In order to utilize more fully the potential resources of the family, schools will need to become more aware of the contribution the family makes to the educational process. In this regard, Hayward (1979) suggests: "There are two kinds of knowledge required by the schools to fulfill their role, knowledge about the nature of human mental development and knowledge about the families of the particular children attending each school" (p. 185). By obtaining such information, it will be possible for teachers to develop a keen interest and respect for the family and its traditions, culture, and belief system. Schools and families have a reciprocal relationship that requires the development of a partnership in which co-operation, trust, and mutual understanding exist.

Occasionally, families do not possess the necessary resources to influence their children positively, and families sometimes develop dysfunctional patterns of interaction. When this occurs, the school must go beyond offering programs such as parent education, remedial work, or special education for needy children. While these programs have considerable value, they are all school-based, and fail to involve the families directly.

A program, recently implemented by the author and a colleague, went beyond the school but continued to maintain a close link with it and actively involved families with children who had learning and behaviour disorders (Friesen & Der, 1984). In this program, perceptions of a child's learning problems were shared between the school and the family. The parents' thoughts and suggestions were welcomed, rapport was developed, and school and home interventions were planned. Where dysfunctional family patterns existed, the family was helped to make beneficial changes in such areas as family structure, communication patterns, and child-rearing. The results of the study indicated that, not only did the reading scores of the children in the experiment improve more rapidly than those of the children in the control group, but also the parents indicated that, as a result of the program, their children appeared more co-operative, engaged in less frequent fighting, and were generally less disruptive at home.

• • •

SUMMARY

This paper has reviewed the literature and current practices having to do with the relationship between the family and the school as the institutions jointly responsible for educating children. The first section dealt with some historical developments, such as societal changes and philosophical perspectives, that have had a profound influence on educational policies and practice. The second section considered the empirical research studies that have examined the influence of the home on children's school performance. The data from the investigations have provided compelling evidence in support of the view that the family influences school achievement by fostering the child's cognitive development, communication skills, reading competence, and motivation. The third section described some practical ways in which the school could establish a more meaningful relationship with the home. The theoretical underpinning of this paper is an ecological systems perspective that views the child as an active participant interacting with a variety of contexts. The most important of these contexts are the home and the school.

• • •

REFERENCES

Ainley, J., Foreman, J., & Sheret, M. (1991). High school factors that influence students to remain in school. *Journal of Educational Psychology, 85*(2), 69–81.

Anderson, C.W. (1980). Parent-child relationships: A context for reciprocal developmental influence. *The Counselling Psychologist, 9*, 35–44.

Boocock, S.P. (1972). *An introduction to the sociology of learning.* Boston: Houghton Mifflin.

British Columbia Council for the Family. (1980). *Parent-school committees in BC: An Overview.* Victoria: Queen's Printer.

Bronfenbrenner, U. (1979). *The ecology of human development: Experiments by nature and design.* Cambridge: Harvard University Press.

Cremin, L.A. (1976). *Public education.* New York: Basic Books.

Dewey, J. (1966). *Democracy and education.* New York: Free Press.

Friesen, J.D., & Der, D. (1984). The outcomes of three models of counselling and consulting. *International Journal for the Advancement of Counselling, 7*, 67–75.

Hayward, B. (1979). The family and education. In D. Radcliffe (Ed.), *The family and socialization of children* (p. 185). Ottawa: SSHRC.

Hess, R.D., & Holloway, S.D. (1984). Family and school as educational institutions. In R.D. Parke (Ed.), *Review of Child Development Research.* Chicago: University of Chicago Press.

Hetherington, E.M., & Martin, B. (1986). Family interaction. In H.S. Quoy & J.S. Werry (Eds.), *Psychopathological disorders of childhood* (3rd ed.) (pp. 332–390). New York: Wiley.

Loeber, R., & Stouthamer-Loeber, M. (1986). Family factors as correlates and predictors of juvenile conduct problems and delinquency. In M. Lonny & N. Morns (Eds.), *Crime and Justice* (Vol. 7, pp. 29–149). Chicago: University of Chicago Press.

Luster, T., & Dubow, E. (1992). Home environment and maternal intelligence as predictors of verbal intelligence: A comparison of preschool and school-age children. *Merrill Palmer Quarterly, 38*(2), 151–176.

Mann, H. (1957). *The republic and the school.* New York: Teachers College Press.

Parsons, T. (1955). The American family: Its relations to personality and social structure. In T. Parsons & R.F. Bales (Eds.), *Family socialization and interaction process.* Glencoe, IL: Free Falls.

Radcliffe, D. (1979). The family and socialization of children: An overview of the discussion. In D. Radcliffe (Ed.), *The family and socialization of children.* Ottawa: SSHRC.

Schulenberg, J.E., Vondracek, F.W., & Crouter, A.C. (1984). The influence of the family on vocational development. *Journal of Marriage and the Family, 46*, 129–43.

Seginer, R. (1983). Parents' educational expectations and children's academic achievements: A literature review. *Merrill Palmer Quarterly, 29*, 1–23.

Varenne, H. (1981). *Parental influences on child's education.* Paper presented at the meeting of the International Union of Family Organizations, Montreal.

Williams, T.H. (1987). Participation in education. *ACER Research Monograph 30.* Hawthorn, Victoria, Australia.

Day Care:

CHANGES IN THE ROLE OF THE FAMILY AND EARLY CHILDHOOD EDUCATION

...

Alan R. Pence

ew rites of passage are as significant and universal in Canadian life as a child's entry into school. Traditionally, this transition has represented the child's passage from the protective environment of home and family to a broadened social involvement in peer-oriented institutions. Such has been our tradition, but it is no longer our contemporary experience. This chapter will examine the nature of our traditions and of our new reality wherein an increasing number of preschool-aged children experience peer socialization and institution-alization outside the family at increasingly younger ages. The history of family and school life, the nature of our current state of social and institutional transition, and an examination of issues that face us as individuals, as teachers, and as a society in planning for the future will be explored in the following pages.

...

THE TRADITION

The "traditional" relationship between family and school life referred to above is not one that extends back over a number of centuries in European or North American societies. Indeed, in English-speaking Canada its development can be seen as an essential component of the "framing of the twentieth-century consensus," the roots of which are imbedded in the nineteenth century (Sutherland, 1976).

The traditional relationship between families and schools in Canadian society is based on a particular model of the family and a particular model of education. The familial model with which we are most familiar today, and with which we have strong ties of sentiment and moral sensibility, has been termed the Victorian model (Strickland, 1981). The rise of the Victorian model, with its characteristic strong differentiation of "spheres of influence," or specific roles, for men, women, and children, is closely associated with the rise of industrialization and urbanization in England and in English-speaking North America. The Victorian family model supplanted an earlier agrarian-based, domestically centred economic unit that had a less strictly defined conception of "separate spheres" of activity and purpose.

The Victorian model was based on a "father-breadwinner, mother-homemaker, child-dependent" ideal of family responsibilities. The home itself became the nest of family life, a "haven in a heartless world," to borrow Christopher Lasch's image (1977). It was seen as a fortress against the evils of the world.

One of the early challenges against the sanctity of the home, and the inviolability of the family gathered within, was the proposed system of compulsory, public schooling. The resistance of many communities and families to this "violation" of parental rights and responsibilities was strong. Yet, in the space of the nineteenth century, Canada passed from a system of private education for a few, to public education for the majority. "School had begun to rival the family as a determining influence of the formative years" (Gaffield, 1982, p. 69).

The line of demarcation between what one was "to give unto" schools and what was "of the family" came, over time, to settle around children six years of age. In a somewhat surprising fashion, both the family and the school ultimately came to honour and support the territorial integrity of the other. The North American "tradition" evolved into the paramountcy of *family* life for the preschool-aged child and the supremacy of *school* life for the child aged six, seven, or older. The line of demarcation became transformed over time, and most of society forgot that the boundary had ever been in dispute.

Public school teachers became some of the strongest defenders of the rightful province of parents (young children) versus that of schools (children six and older). One of the very earliest North American experiments to test the firmness of this evolving division was the infant school movement introduced from England to the United States and Canada in the 1820s. These preschool programs (and first day-care programs in North America) extended from Halifax throughout "all principal cities and towns of the Atlantic States" (Russell, 1829, p. 462). The reaction of one school board to their introduction was unequivocal:

> It is the decided opinion of every [primary school] instructress in the district who has had any experience on the subject, that it is better to receive

into the Primary Schools children that have had no instruction whatever, than those who have graduated with the highest honors of the Infant Seminaries. (Bigelow, 1820)

The infant schools had died out in North America, leaving hardly a trace, by 1840, but their meteoric rise and fall demonstrate the rapid spread and popular acceptance of the notion that young children belonged exclusively with the family but that they were to be claimed by the school system as they grew older.

At various periods in Canadian (and American) history, a bridge between the domain of home and that of school was introduced. One such bridge was the Froebelian kindergarten. James L. Hughes, a Toronto school inspector, was largely responsible for developing the first public school kindergarten in Canada in 1883. The Toronto school board employed Ada Marean as the first instructor. She later married Hughes, and the couple became the principal promoters of the kindergarten movement in Canada, linking up with similar proponents in the United States. The Canadian advocates of kindergartens were, as historian Neil Sutherland notes, divided into two camps. There were those who saw the kindergartens "primarily as an agency which used young children as agents to improve the family life of the poor," while "others directed their efforts to use Froebelian ideas to reform the whole school system" (Sutherland, 1976, p. 174). Both perspectives can be seen in preschool movements from the infant schools of the 1820s to the "head start" movements of the 1960s and 1970s (which impacted on Canadian preschool practice and theory as well as on U.S. developments).

Despite the considerable impact of various preschool movements on pedagogical practice and on community services, the overriding reality of preschool experience for the vast majority of North American children has been family life and family nurturance. More specifically, in the scheme of the Victorian family model, *mothers* have been the central caregivers of preschool children. In surveying the history of early childhood and preschools over the last 150 years, preschool and day-care movements have come and gone with varying degrees of impact and import, but the activity has taken place in the ever-present shadow of motherhood and the Victorian family model. This is beginning to change.

• • •

OLD AND NEW TRADITIONS: A SYSTEM IN FLUX

The contemporary movement of mothers out of the home and into the paid labour force is the most significant phenomenon in preschool child care in Canadian history. Insofar as mothers and their activities are a part of a number of interrelated social systems, a change in mothers' traditional roles and functions impacts on a great number of other social systems. There are few aspects of Canadian society that have not been affected by women's and, in particular, mothers' changing roles. Indeed, many see the increase in the number of women in the labour force as the most significant social revolution in the post-World War II period.

In 1951, the percentage of mothers who were a part of the paid labour force was approximately ten percent. In 1961, this figure had climbed to twenty percent and in 1971 rose to thirty percent. By 1988, the percentage of mothers in the paid labour force had risen to over forty percent. It is interesting to note that over the past fifteen years, the group of mothers who have moved most rapidly, on a proportional basis, into the labour force were women with children under three (Statistics Canada, 1991). These revolutionary changes in mothers' and families' lives have totally redefined the nature of child-care needs in Canada. In 1973, the newly formed Federal Office of Day Care Information in Ottawa noted that there were approximately 26 516 licensed day-care spaces available in Canada to service the needs of an estimated 543 000 children age birth to five years (a service-to-need ratio of 1:20). In 1982, the child-care need estimate for children age birth to six years was 950 000, and the available licensed spaces had risen to 108 677 (a service-to-need ratio of 1:11). By 1989, the numbers of children age birth to six years with mothers in the labour force had risen to 1 276 000, and the number of licensed spaces to 223 000 (a service to need ratio of 1:6) (National Day Care Information Centre, 1973; 1984; 1990).

It is apparent from the above that the licensed services model utilized in Canada has proved insufficient when faced with a greatly altered social model of need. The Victorian family service model is a limited-need model, insofar as the principal early childhood caregiving unit is defined as the family and, more specifically, as the mother. Services under such a model are needed only for the limited number of families who do not fit the "norm"—but the norm is no longer mother at home.

Funding for day care in Canada, since 1966, has been on a matched basis of fifty percent federal and fifty percent provincial funds through the Canada Assistance Plan (CAP). Parents eligible for subsidy assistance are described in the plan as: "Canadians who require social services to prevent, overcome, or alleviate the causes or effects of poverty or child neglect" (Department of National Health and Welfare, 1974). Clearly CAP legislation is reflective of day care as viewed from the Victorian family model, not present-day need. Given this discrepancy, many question whether CAP should continue to be the mechanism whereby day-care funding is generated. This call for child care to be seen and funded as a social need of the many, rather than the need of the welfare few, has led some to a review of the history of public education in Canada and the suggestion that such a universal program approach might serve as a model for the development of child-care services.

In the period 1984–88, the issue of child care moved to the forefront of the federal political agenda. In that four-year period, three major national reviews of child care were conducted: the first was a Task Force on Child Care appointed in 1984 by the short-lived Liberal government of John Turner; the second was a Federal–Provincial Committee composed of the Ministers Responsible for the Status of Women; and the third was a Parliamentary Special Committee on Child Care appointed by the then recently elected Conservative government of Brian Mulroney. The Task Force on Child Care and the Special Parliamentary Committee received the greatest amount of media attention and each produced a public report. The two reports represent opposing perspectives on the continuum of possible public policy.

The *Report of the Task Force on Child Care* (National Task Force on the Status of Women, 1986), envisioned a socially progressive, multi-billion dollar development of child-care services and parental-leave policies similar to that in existence in a number of European countries. The *Report of the Special Parliamentary Committee* (1987), on the other hand, envisioned a much greater emphasis on tax-related approaches and on "Sharing the Responsibility" (the title of their report) among governments, parents, employers, and child-care providers. Both the New Democratic Party and the Liberal Party members of the Special Parliamentary Committee developed dissenting reports.

The outcome of the Special Parliamentary Committee's work was the tabling of Bill C-144 in 1988. The bill was criticized by all sections of the child-care advocacy community and by "pro-family" and anti-child-care conservative groups as well. Given the large majority of Conservative members in Parliament, the bill passed easily and went to Senate, where it died in September 1988 when an election was called.

During the election in the fall of 1988, all three national parties called for the tabling of a new child-care bill. Following its election victory, the Conservative government noted throughout 1989, 1990, and 1991 that they would table new child-care legislation during this, their second term of office. However, such a commitment was not to be honoured. In February of 1992, the Minister for Health and Welfare, Benoit Bouchard, announced that the government would not proceed with child-care legislation. Framing the decision as an "either/or" proposition between expenditures on child poverty or on child care, the Minister noted, "I had to make a choice," and support for child care was not the winner (Allen, 1992).

With the government's announcement in February 1992, the policy issue of child care comes full circle to a status not unlike February 1986 when the first edition of this chapter was written. At that time, neither the *Report of the Task Force on Child Care* nor the Report of the Special Parliamentary Committee were publicly available. Bill C-144 had not yet been drafted, and there was a general air of hopeful expectancy throughout the child-care community. When this paper was written in the spring of 1992 there was again, despite the government's announcement, an air of expectancy: an election will be called within the year; the Conservative Party has now moved away from vague promises to a clear statement of non-support for child care; both the Liberals and the NDP are in the process of forging child-care positions; the database regarding the need for child-care services is much stronger than it was in 1986; and provinces are, in general, more supportive of progressive child-care policies than they were in 1986. Many believe that the stage is set for child care to again emerge as a high priority for government attention.

In the period between 1986 and 1992 a number of significant advances have been made in child care, including the following important research activities:

1. The Canadian National Child Care Study (CNCCS) surveyed 24 000 families in an effort to determine not only where children are cared for, but the relationship between employment variables, child-care use, and family characteristics (Lero et al., 1985).

2. The Caring For A Living Project (CFALP) surveyed child-care centre employees across the country and determined that child-care workers are somewhat better educated, but far worse paid, than the average female employee in Canada, and that child-care worker wages, when adjusted for inflation, have actually declined since 1984 (Karyo Communications, 1992).

3. Through a number of United States and Canadian studies the relationship between higher program quality and higher levels of staff training, staff support, and licensing regulations has been demonstrated (Doherty, 1990; Pence & Goelman, 1991).

There have also been significant advances organizationally and in the growth and strengthening of child-care associations. The following are some examples:

1. Arising out of a major 1982 Child Care Conference, The Canadian Day Care Advocacy Association (CDCAA) fought an effective battle against

Bill C-144 and continues to generate media attention in response to the Conservative government's 1992 "killing" of child-care legislation.

2. Since its establishment in 1983, the Canadian Child Day Care Federation (CCDCF) has emerged as a strong and capable national resource for professional and field interests in child day care.

3. At the provincial and territorial levels, provincial associations have demonstrated growing strength on behalf of child-care and early childhood education professionals. Examples include successful lobbying for government pay subsidies in both Manitoba and Nova Scotia.

And last, but not least, there have been a number of noteworthy government initiatives, for example:

1. Throughout the mid-1980s, Ontario assumed a leadership role in the development of improved child-care services. A Child Care Branch was established within government that led to initiatives such as the 1987 introduction of the "New Directions" policy. New Directions proposed strategies for the Ontario government to both improve the accessibility and quality of day-care services. For example, new school buildings were required to provide space for preschool-age children. More recently the NDP government in Ontario has initiated a new phase of child-care reform with the document *Child Care Reform in Ontario: Setting the Stage* (1992).

2. The Territorial Government of the Yukon engaged in a remarkable demonstration of public consultation and policy development in the period 1987 to 1989 culminating in the establishment of a new and progressive Child Care Act in 1989 and a 100 percent increase in funding in the two fiscal years 1987–88 and 1988–89.

3. The Province of Quebec has taken the lead in Canada in developing family policy. In response to a falling birthrate, Quebec established several pro-natalist policies. For example, the introduction of both tax breaks on family income and baby bonuses paid on the birth of first and subsequent children are designed to provide child-bearing incentives for Quebecers.

4. Introduced as part of the Federal government's Child Care Strategy in 1988, The Child Care Initiatives Fund (CCIF) will have spent approximately ninety million dollars on child-care demonstration and research projects over its seven year lifespan. Both the CNCCS and the CFALP were funded by CCIF.

Despite the significant advances that have been made, six critical social issues, are yet to be fully resolved.

1. Whose responsibility is the care and well-being of Canadian preschool children? Is it primarily individual, familial, or societal, and to what degree is it a shared responsibility?
2. Does caregiving responsibility, shared or singular, imply financial responsibility as well?
3. Developmentally, what are "optimal," affordable caregiving experiences and environments for preschool children of various ages?
4. To what degree is a definition of "optimal" dependent on child factors, family variables, and societal dimensions, and to what extent is "well-being" defined at an individual or some broader social level such as that of the family, ethnic community, or country?
5. To what degree do actual or potential conflicts exist among the various social levels noted above, and at what level should the decision-making power be placed?
6. Insofar as our changing socio-familial dynamics are in large part the result of changes in work force requirements, to what degree should employers be held accountable for and included in a redefined interactive system of responsiblities that would include families, communities, employers, and governments?

Also unresolved is the question of the role of schools in addressing the care and education needs of pre-elementary-age children. Ontario is the only province that has specifically defined a role for schools to play in the pre-kindergarten-age group. The system of junior kindergartens established in Ontario in the 1980s is currently under attack in some districts as the province attempts to emerge from the recession of the early 1990s. However, when utilizing a school-based model, it should not be forgotten that this apparently benign model experienced a somewhat turbulent early history as zealous supporters of the "one-best-system" approach imposed its common structure across a diversified human-scape of ethnic, religious, urban, and rural lifestyles. The relative tranquility of schoolyards today belies their history of social discord and confrontation.

The public school model, has, over time, addressed in its own unique way the six questions posed earlier. The relationships between children, institutions, parents, community, and the broader society have been spelled out, as have been financing and the pedagogical environment. Definitions of "optimal" are largely institutional decisions that have evolved over time, the "norm" is revered, and the role of employers has never been considered. Conflicts are de-emphasized by the ponderous logic of a professional bureaucracy, which cherishes the certainty of "tradition" in the same way that Tevye could set his life-clock by the traditions upheld in "Fiddler on the Roof."

In Canada's public school system there is a level of "certainty," bred by early victories and reinforced over time, that is both comforting and frightening. It is a uniform system designed to train children for the uniformity of adult work life. Its enforced uniformity exists in sharp contrast to the diversity of post-Victorian Canadian family life with its complexity of single-parent, blended, and one-and two-income families, as well as a host of ethnic traditions and values spread across a landscape of metropolitan centres and rural dispersion.

Children are born into diversity and uniqueness in Canada and, at age six, they enter normative uniformity. What should take place in the years in between?

A very different model from the downward extension of the institution of schools is a model of *planned* diversity. It is true that the existing state of preschool care in Canada is one of diversity: the great majority of children are not in licensed facilities. But the existing state is not one of *planned* diversity; rather, it is the result of an overflow of a limited welfare model. There exist problems of availability, affordability, and quality, which effectively limit parental choice.

One child-care option that has not been developed adequately in Canada is parent care. Existing benefit structures deny parents viable options to care for their own children (beyond a period of a few months) without endangering the family's financial well-being or parents' career advancement. Given the choice of the family's economic hardship, for possibly extended periods of time, or remaining home to care for a baby over the first years of his or her life, many parents opt for non-parental care. (Supporting this economic hardship theory are a number of studies that indicate a majority of two-income families would fall below the poverty line without the second income.) This first and most basic option of child care, through extended parental care, is built into the social systems of most European countries including Austria, Hungary, Sweden, and France, but it is not an available, affordable option for Canadian parents.

Extended benefits for parental care are but one component in an options-oriented model, which is totally underdeveloped in Canada at present. There are similar problems of affordability and availability in the non-parental care sector of child care in Canada as well but, added to the restricting elements of affordability and availability, are questions of quality. As noted earlier, the great majority of all day care provided in Canada is unlicensed, and one must be sceptical about the quality of care offered even in licensed spaces when Canadian experts such as Howard Clifford of the National Day Care Information Office could note that "Half of the 85 000 licensed day care centres in Canada are not fit to be open" (Clifford, 1979).

At present, the basic orientation that must guide Canadian parents seeking child-care arrangements is *caveat emptor*, let the buyer beware. Yet if we as a society have done little to prepare individuals to become "good" parents, we have done even less to provide them with the information and skills necessary to become effective consumers of child care (Pence & Goelman, 1986).

It is apparent that if we are to pursue a parental-option model of child care addressing the six questions posed earlier in new and creative ways, we must resolve very pressing questions of affordability, availability, and quality.

The issue of quality is one that must involve our training institutions, whichever basic model is developed: a downward extension of schooling or a broader parental-option plan. In all likelihood, certain regions of the country will place a greater emphasis on one approach over the other, but the end result will be a mixed model for the country as a whole. Early childhood education and child-care training programs at both college and university levels must present a broad introduction to the child and her or his developmental needs within a social-ecological structure. A definition of quality in early childhood programs cannot be limited to the intra-program elements of curriculum, play materials, and social interactions. Isolated learning, independent of family, peers, and cultural and neighbourhood groupings, is an inappropriate training orientation for working with a child of any age, but it is particularly inappropriate for the preschool-aged child given our historic respect for and demarcation of family responsibility for preschool-aged children.

Training for early childhood education and care must see the child as a learner in the broadest possible sense. Students must learn instructional and communication skills that *bridge* the ecological domains of school, family, neighbourhood, and culture rather than *block* that flow of systemic interaction through an over-emphasis on a particular domain or system in isolation.

Such a training imperative represents a serious challenge to many traditional educational programs. The "us/them" orientation between schools and families that characterizes far too many school systems in Canada today, cannot be allowed to dominate the preschool care system without doing great damage to our socio-historical traditions and to the development of our children.

In summary, the rite of passage that school entry represents in our society is shifting, the portico of that passage is in motion. The traditional roles and responsibilities that families and schools have assumed on either side of school entry are in a state of flux, with a variety of future scenarios possible. Decisions that we, as a society, make over the next five years will be critical to the future role of families, educational institutions, and society as a whole, and to our children's development as we approach the twenty-first century.

• • •

REFERENCES

Allen, G. (1992, March 16). Grown-up's choice. *Maclean's*, p. 23.

Bigelow, J. (1820). Minutes of the Boston Primary School Committee.

Clifford, H. (1979, October 23). Fifty percent of centres unfit, care seminars told. *Globe and Mail*.

Doherty, G. (1990). *Factors related to quality child care: A review of the literature*. Report prepared for the Child Care Branch, Ontario Ministry of Community and Social Services.

Gaffield, C. (1982). Schooling, the economy, and rural society in nineteenth-century Ontario. In J. Parr (Ed.), *Childhood and family in Canadian history*. Toronto: McClelland and Stewart.

Health and Welfare Canada. (1974). *Canada Assistance Plan*. Ottawa: Author.

Health and Welfare Canada, National Day Care Information Centre. (1973, 1984, 1990). *Status of day care in Canada*. Ottawa: Author.

Karyo Communications. (1992, May). *CDCAA, CCDCF, Caring for a Living Project*. Press Release.

Lasch, C. (1977). *Haven in a heartless world: The family besieged*. New York: Basic Books.

Lero, D., Pence, A., Brockman, L., & Goelman, H. (1985). *Where are the children? An ecological survey of families and their child care arrangements*. Research proposal to Health and Welfare Canada.

National Council on the Status of Women. (1986). *Report of the task force on child care*. Ottawa: Author.

Pence, A., & Goelman, H. (1986). *The puzzle of day care: Guide for parents and counsellors*. Toronto: University of Toronto Guidance Centre Press.

Pence, A., & Goelman, H. (1991). The relationship of regulation, training and motivation to quality of care in family day care. *Child and Youth Care Forum, 20*(2).

Russell, W. (1829). Intelligence. *American Journal of Education 4*, 462.

Special Committee on Child Care. (1987). *Report: Sharing the responsibility*. Ottawa: Queen's Printer.

Strickland, C. (1981). *Day care and public policy: An historical perspective*. Unpublished paper, Emory University, Atlanta, GA.

Sutherland, N. (1976). *Children in English-Canadian society: Framing the twentieth-century consensus*. Toronto: University of Toronto Press.

FEMINISM AND ITS IMPACT ON EDUCATIONAL SCHOLARSHIP IN CANADA

...

Jane Gaskell

ducation is often seen as a women's field. Most of those who work in schools are women. Most teachers are women. However, positions at the top of the educational hierarchy are overwhelmingly held by men. Principals, superintendents, and top ministry officials are almost always men, as are most educational researchers and commentators (Rees, 1990). This is quite congruent with the overall position of men and women in the Canadian labour force. Women working full time earn about sixty percent of what men earn. Men and women tend not to work in the same jobs: women predominate in secretarial jobs, in nursing, in particular segments of the sales and service sector. Men predominate in managerial jobs, as doctors, lawyers, electricians, and in particular segments of the manufacturing and sales sectors. And of course, women take primary responsibility for work in domestic settings. Gender is implicated in the organization of work in our society, and it is implicated in how education is organized. This has not gone unremarked by the women's movement. In this article I will look at how feminist thought has explored the meaning of male dominance in education and what the implications might be for educational policy and practice.

While feminist thought and practice is profoundly important for educators, it tends to get marginalized, treated as a problem of concern only for women, one that a few people specialize in, rather than one that everyone needs to know something about. This is unfortunate, because feminism raises issues that are thoroughly "mainstream"—about curriculum and culture and knowledge and language and morality, about the social location of educational thought and its implications for practice. All educators need to take account of how discussion about education has been dominated by men, and how it might be rethought as a discourse that takes into account the diverse experiences of men and women.

For our ideas about what is appropriate, even "natural" for males and females, for the public sphere and the private sphere, for women's work and men's work, have influenced the way educational issues have been framed and talked about and researched. Educational scholarship and research is shaped by "ordinary" knowledge (Lindblom & Cohen, 1979). Research and scholarship are embedded in ordinary understandings of what is important and just and true. The framing of the questions asked and the conclusions drawn from observations depend upon assumptions about how the world works. As these assumptions shift, so does scholarship. At the same time, scholarship has an impact on public discussion. It can challenge conventional wisdom, add documentation on educational problems, and raise to public awareness, discussions that are buried in staff rooms, parent-teacher interviews, and classroom interactions. Over the past twenty years, the women's movement has challenged many assumptions about how educational issues should be conceived, how the world works, and what is appropriate and natural for whom. Educational scholarship and research has reflected its influence, and, in taking up feminist issues, has had an influence on public policy.

Feminist critique and analysis has had no single face. Its forms have been shaped by the important intellectual currents of history and by the social and political commitments of its various proponents. It stands in the context of its times. There is no single feminist position, today or in the past. Here I will sketch in some different conceptions of what the women's movement has meant by providing an equal education for girls and women and try to draw out ways this has both reflected and constituted a critique of the dominant discourse in education. The positions I will sketch out (and of course oversimplify) are as follows:

1. *Eliminate the difference gender makes.* Make women more like men so that they can compete equally for rewards. This leads to, and grows from research that indicates women can do the things men do, and need not be—indeed should not be—relegated to a separate sphere. Research in this tradition emphasizes the role of nurture over nature and documents and critiques the different and unequal treatment that girls and women get in schools and in society. It embodies views of human nature, of family and school and the division of labour that stress individual opportunity and the possibilities of mobility.

2. *Value the difference women make.* In this version of feminist thought, the problem is not that women are different from men, but that they are valued so much less. Less importance is attached to what women do than to

what men do. Research and scholarship in this tradition document differences between men and women, stress their resilience, and critique the institutional structures that continue to exclude and devalue female characteristics and the people having them. This version of the feminist critique rethinks knowledge, curriculum, and school structures as reflections of male power, and is concerned less with individual mobility than with redressing the power balance between men and women, reason and emotion, reproductive and productive spheres.

3. *Learn to respect and work across difference, whatever it may be.* Feminists in this tradition point out that differences exist not just between men and women, but among and within groups of women and men. Research in this tradition extends the search for difference and its institutional treatment to include an awareness of how factors like social class, race, ethnicity, language, and sexual preference shape and subdivide gender categories. The critique raises questions about the nature of power and identity and their reflection and construction through curriculum and school structures. It borrows much from the postmodern emphasis on discourse, language and the relational nature of power and authority.

Now, we will examine in more detail each of these three areas of thought.

• • •

MAKING GIRLS MORE LIKE BOYS: "EQUAL RIGHTS" FEMINISM

Early feminists in Canada challenged women's outright exclusion from male spheres of activity, an exclusion that has been far from constant through western history, but that took on rigid and mythic dimensions during the Victorian era. As education was the route to many important occupations and spheres of knowledge, feminists argued for the right of any qualified woman to attend any program at any educational institution. In the late nineteenth century, Egerton Ryerson, true to Victorian ideals, tried to "raise standards" in Ontario schools by stopping local school boards from admitting girls to the elite grammar schools where they could study Latin. He argued that girls and boys were different, and that they needed different kinds of education for their different adult destinations and their different interests. Latin was just not appropriate for girls. But for local school boards, recruiting more girls mean recruiting more pupils, and therefore getting more money for their grammar schools. They fought the centre and won. In rural areas particularly, the main impetus for co-education was not a belief in sexual equality, but in financial stability.

The admission of women to higher education and professional training was a more difficult struggle. While women, many of them preparing to be teachers, attended secondary schools at a higher rate than men, admission to the normal schools was not granted without a fight, for the normal schools were to prepare educational leaders, and these were to be men. Universities were supposed to prepare men for their work in the public sphere. Women's entrance into the university was considered at best irrelevant, and more likely detrimental, to their future roles as wives and mothers. It was argued that entrance to university would damage women's fertility.

Rosalind Rosenberg (1982) has written about the period between about 1890 and 1920, when some of the first women entered the University of Chicago as students, then as scholars, and took on the issue of sexual equality. She notes that their work arose "in the shadow of Dr. Clarke." Dr. Clarke was a Victorian doctor who believed, drawing on Darwin and Spencer, that civilization meant increasing specialization and that males and females were becoming increasingly specialized organisms. Since bodies had a limited amount of energy, if women put their energy into studying at college, Clarke believed, they would have much less left for reproduction, and become sterile and hysterical (all of which he had case studies to prove). Moreover, women's brains had "different though excellent qualities" that were not up to the mental exertion of college. These beliefs were well rooted in the intellectual currents of the day, and hard to dislodge. To take them on meant taking on some of the fundamental assumptions about human nature and biology embedded in psychology, sociology, religion, and medicine.

But this did not deter women like Marion Talbot and Jesse Taft who were at the University of Chicago along with the much better known John Dewey, W.I. Thomas, and George Herbert Mead. These women started to ask whether the biological differences between men and women were as great as Clarke had thought. And they went on to ask whether women's social role was rooted in her biology, or in cultural conditioning. They ended up challenging not only the biologically based stereotypes that underpinned the Victorian ideology of separate spheres for men and women, but the models of human nature that existed at the time. They argued that women could be equal to men. Only outmoded and repressive cultural and social conditioning held them back.

This research was important not just "for women" but for our understanding of biology and society, of human nature and its formation. It grew out of the political energy of feminism at the time, and it drew on and contributed to new assumptions about human nature, learning, and knowledge that were developing at the university and in the society.

We skip ahead now to the 1970s and the second wave of feminism in Canada, marked particularly by the Royal Commission report on the Status of Women. The research and the political rhetoric in this report is still in the shadow of Dr. Clarke, in several ways. The child development literature of the 1960s looked at the process of sex role socialization as based in biological difference and Freudian processes of sexual identification. Learning "sex-appropriate" behaviours and traits in childhood was one of the prerequisites for adult mental health and smooth social functioning (Kagan, 1964; Parsons, 1942). Sex differences were important—boys should be clear they were boys and girls should be clear they were girls. Boys were strong, independent, and ambitious; girls were soft, kind, and nurturant. The process of schooling could contribute to the individual and the society by being clear about and reinforcing the differences.

It was not a completely natural phenomenon, for it could be messed up by parents and schools. If there was a problem, it concerned boys, not girls. Commentators were preoccupied with the trouble boys had with reading, blaming it on the "feminized" classroom (Sexton, 1969). Teachers were encouraged to use books that represented the world of little boys, in an attempt to cater to their needs in the classroom.

Feminists and researchers were arguing, on the other hand, that sex differences were not as large as had been believed, were not biologically based, but were based in stereotypical and restrictive expectations coming from society and should be eliminated. This view of child development was adopted in the Royal Commission report. The commission argues against "stereotypes" of women, which they maintain prevent women from achieving as much as men, in school, and in the society. There was a substantial research component to their argument. The Royal Commission lists thirty-four "studies prepared for the commission," and some of these involved original research. The commission also cites social science liberally throughout its text. There are frequent technical footnotes used to bolster points in the argument, documenting the way young children were inappropriately socialized into "sex roles" in the school and in the family. As Esther Greenglass wrote at the time,

> While attributes such as independence, aggressiveness and competitiveness are rewarded and encouraged in males because these are the characteristics perceived as essential for success in traditionally male-dominated fields, dependence, passivity, and compliance are rewarded in females. Hardly

those traits making for success . . . If male and female teachers think that
females are intellectually inferior to males . . . female students are less
likely to have original intellectual contribution to make, and they are less
likely to be logical. (1973, pp. 112–113)

Equality didn't just mean equal access to schooling, it meant equal treatment in
the curriculum, doing away with stereotypes in books and classroom processes.
The Royal Commission sponsored a study on sex-role imagery in the textbooks
used to teach reading, social studies, science, mathematics, and guidance courses
in Canadian schools. It concluded that "a woman's creative and intellectual
potential is either underplayed or ignored in the education of children from their
earliest years. The sex roles described in these textbooks provide few challenging
models for young girls, and they fail to create a sense of community between
men and women as fellow human beings." The many studies that followed, done
by ministries, teachers federations and academics, all confirmed their verdict.
These studies showed that women were underrepresented in school books, and
that when they were represented, they were stereotyped in less active and powerful roles. Little girls in elementary school texts played with dolls while their
brothers played baseball; mothers wore aprons and baked cookies, while fathers
drove off to work; adult women were princesses and witches, while men were
doctors and farmers (see for example Fischer and Cheyne, 1977).

The critique of sex role socialization also focussed on the more intangible
social relations of sex role stereotyping by teachers, parents and school practices
(Shack, 1976; Spinks, 1970)—practices such as having separate playground
line-ups for girls and boys, allocating different chores for boys and for girls,
and having girls and boys compete against each other. Teachers' expectations
about the capacities and interests of males and females were revealed to be
stereotyped (Eichler, 1979; Ricks & Pyke, 1973; Russell, 1979). Studies
showed that boys received more attention from teachers than girls. The result
was a well-documented assault on stereotyping in its various guises in the
school (Wilkinson & Marrett, 1985).

The research, in combination with political lobbying, had an effect. Publishers
and ministries of education across the country appointed advisory groups on sexism and began to issue guidelines for doing away with stereotyping in materials
and in classroom practices. The Ontario guidelines made statements such as:
"Illustrations of groups should include both females and males"; "Both males and
females should be shown indoors and outdoors, in the home and at their places of
work, with a wider range of occupational roles"; and "When indoors, not all

women need to wear an apron" (p. 4). In B.C. in 1974, the ministry of education, which had appointed a provincial advisory committee and a special advisor on sex discrimination, issued a directive "On the Equal Treatment of the Sexes: Guidelines for Educational Materials." And in 1976, the Quebec government published *L'École Sexiste C'est Quoi?* They all took the same tack. Alternative materials were developed and published. In 1976, the Ontario ministry of education published a resource guide entitled, *Sex-Role Stereotyping and Women's Studies,* "to assist educators in the ongoing task of developing a learning environment that is free from sex-role stereotyping of males and females and curriculum that accurately depicts the roles of women."

By the early 1980s there had been a dramatic change in the primary readers and in some school practices. Girls no longer had to take home economics while boys took industrial education and were less frequently officially segregated into separate playgrounds from the boys. Teachers had been exposed to discussions of sex discrimination, and separate staff rooms for male and female teachers became less common. The critique of stereotyping had caught on. The idea that biology did not mean destiny, that equality meant open access and equal treatment had been more or less accepted.

Research played a part in establishing the necessity for action. It documented conditions in schools and in families. It made public a discussion about what was in texts, what went on in classrooms, what teachers believed about gender. The research was shaped by a changing political climate, and it shaped this climate in turn. Biology as destiny and the notion of separate spheres fell into disrepute in most quarters. And at universities, women's studies programs and journals sprang up, and an institutional base for the development of feminist thought appeared.

• • •

REVALUING THE FEMALE

After a revival of feminism and a burst of state support in the 1970s, the issue of gender equity in schools died down as a matter of discussion in the public sphere, and the focus changed a bit. Instead of fighting the shadow of the Victorian Dr. Clarke, a more introspective and established feminist movement explored revaluing femininity and the female experience. Difference had been used to exclude women, so women had argued against the differences that were attributed to them. But now some feminists pointed out that denying difference and getting rid of stereotypes had led to a climate in which everyone was expected to achieve in a masculine image. Co-education meant male education for everyone. There had been no shift in the power of or value attributed to women; just a recognition that they should be treated like men.

But nurturance, sociability, and interdependence, feminists argued, can foster learning, are important in schools, and have been too often devalued by men. As Jeri Wine (1982) points out (compare this with Greenglass, above),

> the large literature on psychological sex differences is highly problematic from a feminist perspective because of its apparent demonstration of the inferiority of the female. In this work, the guiding assumptions are that any characteristic that males have more of than do females is an essential characteristic, a mark of superiority, while any characteristic that females have more of is a sign of weakness, of inferiority. Women's investment in the interpersonal realm has been consistently devalued in psychology, our connectedness with others seen as pathological dependency needs, nurturance and interpersonal sensitivity defined as weakness. (p. 70)

One of Wine's studies was of marijuana use among college students. She looked at how students interacted when they had smoked marijuana and when they had not. In all the groups studied, the only consistent difference the investigators could find was the difference between men and women. Women smiled more, and asked more questions in order to keep the conversation going.

These kinds of observations suggest that instead of centring our analysis on how we can get rid of sex roles, and make women more like men, we should pay more attention to the ways women are different from men, and value those ways. The world has depended on women's work. Women should not have to be like men to deserve equal respect and power. The world might well be a much better place if women and women's characteristics were valued seriously. As Finn and Miles (1982) put it, "female characteristics, concerns, and abilities marginalized in industrial society, are necessarily central to the building of new more fully human society. The holistic, collective, intuitive, co-operative, emotional, nurturing, democratic, integrated, internal, and natural are affirmed against the over-valuation of the competitive, analytical, rational, hierarchical, fragmented, external, and artificial" (p. 13).

This kind of analysis has a substantial history. The argument for separate spheres rather than equal rights characterized many struggles at the turn of the century. It fit well within the Victorian ideal of separate spheres. The Local Council of Women told the Royal Commission on Industrial Training and Technical Education in 1913, that women's work should be publicly recognized as worthy of study; they wanted its value and its scientific knowledge base acknowledged. "The Local Council of Women would like to see service in the home lifted to the same plane as the profession of nursing. The Council does not believe the home should continue to be the only place for which special training is not regarded as necessary." They saw that putting something in the curriculum was a way of publicly acknowledging its value (Danylewcyz et al., 1985; Stamp, 1977). They accepted as natural the division between men's and women's work and capacities, but they wanted recognition for women's contributions.

The more recent version of revaluing, recognizing, and incorporating the neglected "female" into education suggests a rethinking of education in a whole variety of ways. It involves a wholesale rewriting of the curriculum so that women's traditional concerns are included. In a frequently quoted address to a group of female college graduates in 1977, the poet Adrienne Rich said,

> What you can learn here (and I mean not only here but at any college or in any university) is how men have perceived and organized their experience, their history, their ideas about social relationships, good and evil, sickness and health, etc. When you read or hear about "great issues," "major texts," "the mainstream of western thought"; you are hearing about what men, above all white men, in their male subjectivity, have decided is important. (p. 232)

Mary O'Brien (1981) has felicitously dubbed this curriculum the "malestream." To add what women think is important into the educational process can mean a variety of changes, and many feminist scholars have discussed the implications for different areas of the curriculum. Jane Roland Martin (1985) makes a broad philosophical argument about how education must be reconceived to include women's work. She points out that those who debate the purposes of education have misconstrued the arguments of philosophers such as Rousseau and Plato by dismissing their discussions of the education of women as unimportant. The ideals they held out for men's education—the rational and productive ideals we now apply to the education of both sexes—omit, even while they depend upon, the existence of a different kind of education, one concerned with caring and reproduction in its broadest sense including the rearing of children. This education has been relegated to second-class status: Rousseau assigned it to Sophie; Plato assigned it to the lower classes. Both recognized its necessity, and how the education of the dominant group depended on it. Martin argues we must reincorporate the neglected and devalued "female" into the education we give everyone. We can no longer expect women alone to learn the three C's of caring, concern, and connection, and to do it for everyone.

Evelyn Fox Keller (1982, 1985) has made the argument in relation to science. She says that women tend to do and talk about science in different ways from men and that we need to change our ideas of how science should be represented and taught. In her biography of Barbara McClintock, who won the Nobel prize for corn genetics, she contrasts McClintock's "feeling for the organism," her "conversations" with nature, with male conceptions of science as domination and imposition. She argues that these ways of doing science have been denigrated by the scientific establishment, but that they must be revalued, re-examined, and recognized as an intrinsic part of the scientific process, and of science curriculum.

Gilligan (1982) makes similar arguments in relation to moral reasoning. Her research on adolescent girls in a private school in New York suggests that women tend to reason through moral dilemmas differently from boys, and that women's ways of working through moral problems have not been recognized in moral philosophy and moral education. Individualized arguments about justice, which underpin our legal system and our tests of moral reasoning, ignore the kind of contextualized reasoning and concern for community and commitment, termed "the ethic of care" by Gilligan. This ethic of care, she argues, should inform the practices of schooling and the content of social studies and values education.

Feminist scholarship challenges such basic assumptions as the relation of public and private (Elshtain, 1981), the ways to read a text (Silverman, 1985), and the nature of the economy (Cohen, 1982). In all cases, the argument is that if one starts from the way women understand it, things appear in a different light. The questions one asks are different; the ways one goes about looking for answers are different. Adding feminist perspectives, knowledge developed from, as Dorothy Smith (1974) puts it "the standpoint of women" means transforming the malestream, not just adding on women's knowledge.

It is not only the content of curriculum that is at issue. Feminists have charged that the organization of educational institutions and the ways knowledge is transmitted to students have a male bias because institutions have failed to incorporate the ways women prefer to organize and learn (Briskin, 1990). The notion of a distinctive feminist pedagogy arises from the experience of "consciousness raising" in the women's movement in the late 1960s. Consciousness raising involved small, leaderless groups of women coming together to share their life experience and to use it to discover what was common among them and how women's oppression was organized. It was a mode of learning that was enormously powerful and politically influential, and can be compared to Freire's (1970) "conscientization," which also combined political action and the active reconstruction of knowledge by learners.

"Feminist pedagogy" is based in a questioning of traditional authority relations between teacher and student, and a distrust of bureaucracy (Bowles & Klein, 1983; Gardner, Dean, & McKaig, 1989; Tancred-Sheriff, 1987). It eschews the separation of the public classroom from private experience, and of emotion from reason. Belenky and her co-authors (1986) outline a distinctive pattern through which women come to know. Their book is based on interviews with a diverse group of women about how they learn. The authors conclude by recommending a "yoghurt" classroom, emphasizing "connected knowing," rather than the dissemination of information in a traditional lecture format.

Finally, the emphasis on revaluing women's experience and work leads to a different analysis of connections between education and work. Instead of arguing that girls must be equally represented with boys in mathematics classes and industrial education and physics, feminists in this tradition emphasize the value of the jobs women have traditionally done, and call for more respect and higher wages for the work. Equal pay legislation stands as a recognition that the work women have done is underpaid in relation to the skills, education, and responsibility it entails. Day-care workers have been paid less than dog catchers; secretaries are paid less than male technicians with equal levels of skill. The problem, from this point of view, is not the representation of women in male spheres, but the undervaluing of female spheres.

This second version of feminist thought takes on not the biology lessons of Dr. Clarke, but ideas about the neutrality of central educational concepts like science, ethics, knowledge, curriculum, pedagogy, and labour markets. It points to the socially constructed and political nature of all of them, and to the ways in which male experience underlies their formation and discussion. The focus on the political location of curriculum and schooling is found in a great deal of sociology and educational thought. Its particular feminist forms link politics with research in a dialectical way. Political analysis leads to research, and the research both contributes to and develops the analysis. The research and the politics challenge assumptions in the schools and the academy, point to practical changes that should be made in schools and have implications for how we generally think about the educational process.

• • •

VALUING DIFFERENCE

A third version of feminist thought, the one most prevalent in its general outlines in the academy today, calls for more than allowing women access as long as they behave like men, and more than revaluing the female, as femaleness has been constructed in opposition to maleness. It calls for something like the celebration of difference and the renegotiation of power inequalities, wherever they are constructed. This critique adds to the previous two, contradicts some of the previous two, and is sometimes silent where the previous two were clear.

It takes its force from a critique of any simple "revaluing the female." For revaluing the female can glorify characteristics that women have developed in response to male domination, and can automatically denigrate male characteristics. It tends to biological dichotomies that feel restrictive, to women as well as to men. (This is sometimes labelled essentialism, referring to the "essential" nature of men and women.) And most importantly, it ignores the diversity of experiences that women and men have.

In the labour market, using the single category of "woman" to analyze economic disadvantage in relation to men, conceals an increasing differentiation in economic advantage among women. Construing all women as equally disadvantaged fails to highlight particular pockets of poverty, for example among single mothers, or among native women, and can be used to advantage already relatively privileged professional women. We need to pay attention to the increasing polarization in women's employment opportunities. And we need to adopt economic strategies that recognize differences among women and do not assume a communality of interest that will not exist under all conditions.

The most influential critique of the "revalue women" position has come from women of colour who point to the differences among women with different national, ethnic, and language backgrounds (Hooks, 1989; Trinh, 1989). The feminist movement often signals its origins with the publication of Betty Friedan's *Feminine Mystique*, a book that, as Hooks (1984) points out, actually referred to the plight of "a select group of college-educated, middle and upper class, married white women—housewives bored with leisure, with the home, with children, with buying products, who wanted more out of life." To define these women's experience as "women's" experience is to overgeneralize the experience of the powerful to others. It is exactly this problem that the feminist movement has been most concerned with, for men have done it to women.

Women's experience of mothering, women's experience of paid labour, women's experience of school, women's experience of books, of the law, of housing, of anything is hugely different depending on which women we are talking to or about. To universalize "women's experience" is tremendously risky and politically suspect because of what it eclipses. The point is not to define one "female" experience. The point rather is to see that gender relations have been relations of power, and that they need to be examined in whatever forms they take, and to be challenged and reformulated. The point is not to privilege the examination of gender over the examination of race, class, handicap, ethnicity, nationality and all the other factors that shape our lives. The point is to see that these things do not necessarily work the same way for men and women, and to look for gender relations as they co-exist with, influence, and interact with other relations of domination and exclusion.

Feminist scholarship has its value in pointing to difference, in validating difference, in criticizing the ways one side of a difference gets privileged through inequitable social relations. It respects the voices "on the margins." It is in this way that postmodern theory has been attractive to feminists, even while its masculine origins, its often apolitical and relativist stance, its treating of the world as merely text, its abstruse discourse and its bid for hegemony in the academic world have also made it suspect for many feminists. An emphasis on difference leaves us with various versions of knowledge and justice and educational practice. It is through the recognition of diversity that we see ourselves, understand our own location, politically and academically, situate ourselves. But islands of difference that cannot communicate with each other do not represent a world many feminists with political commitments to equality would advocate. The notion of conversation among those who are located differently is a worthier ideal, and the role of education is encouraging this conversation.

The school then should be inclusive, embrace differences among students, and represent this difference in the curriculum so it can be talked about. It must represent women's understandings of the world, but make sure no single version of the female or the male is taken as representative and normal. The concern becomes not stereotyping, but including traditional roles along with others in order to provoke discussion and understanding.

In history classrooms, this means including the study of women's work in First Nations families in Labrador as well as including the study of pioneer women in the prairies. In English classes, it means examining Audre Lorde's poetry and as well as Virginia Woolf's novels and essays. In art and in music, it means examining the ways the categories have been put together in different times and cultures and places, and examining the variety of expression that is possible. In short, it means adding diversity to what has been a curriculum based in the history and experience of white men.

This version of feminism places difference rather than commonality at the centre of feminism and of academic analysis. It emphasizes the shifting and local construction of identity, meaning and power. For "woman" is no fixed, unchanging category with a given meaning, and power. The meaning of gender, its organization and relation to material and symbolic power shifts and changes. Feminists with this kind of analysis would transform the curriculum and pedagogy to ensure that all people are able to give voice to their experience, to analyze and understand it, and to connect it to the experience of others. Scholarship in this tradition explores the changing discourse about men and women, the different ways in which people have understood experience in schools, and the ways in which teachers can negotiate a variety of discourses, and differences in privilege, to engage students in reflection (Bannerji et al., 1991; Giroux, 1991; Lather, 1991; Luke and Gore, 1992; Walkerdine, 1991).

. . .

CONCLUSION

The women's movement has addressed most aspects of education, asking for equal representation for female students and female educators, and in the process asking for a reshaping of the institution and of our thinking about the institution in some fairly fundamental ways. The women's movement has posed the challenge of rethinking standards of excellence, measures of achievement, criteria for knowledge and forms of governance. It has engaged and contributed to some of the most difficult and persistent concerns in our ongoing dialogue about education.

And feminism offers no simple answers. I have stressed different versions of feminist thought, not to rank one above the other, but to point to various ways in which the concerns of women have been addressed and to enter the dialogue among them. Each version has important insights into how schools work. Each is committed to change and rethinking education so that it benefits women. But there are important disagreements among the different traditions (see Hirsch and Keller, 1990 for a detailed discussion of this). The third version of feminism that I set out above begins to see the categories of male and female as a problem, because of the differences within them; while much of the importance of the first and second versions was to call attention to gender categories, and to say that woman is a category we need to use and pay attention to in our analysis. I continue to see the value of using male and female as ways of analyzing classrooms, if only to open up what goes on in schools and start a discussion. A recent ethnography of life in a multi-ethnic Grade 8 classroom in Vancouver provides a simple but important illustration of why gender still matters (Eyre, 1991). The interviewer asked the students about the use of language to insult girls:

Student: Oh, cow's a normal one, yeah. That's what guys call girls when they get mad at them . . . It doesn't bother me cause I don't really care you know. . . .
Interviewer: Do they call you anything else?
Student: Slut, tramp, pig, whore, bitch, stuff like that. I just tell them to shut up.

Or, on the segregated seating patterns that were obvious in a supposedly integrated classroom, one student claimed: "If you sit with the guys the girls would say you're boy crazy and all those things."

Gendered patterns of interaction are absolutely central to the students' experience of being in school. Differences are not treated with respect. There has been progress in a hundred years since Ryerson tried to stop girls from taking Latin, but the struggle is not won. The level of male violence and female poverty is still appallingly high. Our understanding of education cannot ignore the patterning of social and educational life along gendered lines.

· · ·

REFERENCES

Bannerji, H., Carty, L., Dehli, K., Held, S., & McKenna, K. (1991). *Unsettling relations: The university as a site of feminist struggle.* Toronto: Women's Press.

Belenky, M., McVicar Clinchy, B., Rule Goldberger, N., & Mattuck Tarule, J. (1986). *Women's ways of knowing: The development of self-voice and mind.* New York: Basic Books.

Bowles, M., & Klein, S. (1983). *Theories of women's studies.* London: RKP.

Briskin, L. (1990). *Feminist pedagogy: Teaching and learning liberation.* Ottawa: Canadian Research Institute for the Advancement of Women.

Cohen, M. (1982). The problem of studying economic man. In G. Finn & A. Miles (Eds.), *Feminism in Canada*. Montreal: Black Rose Books.

Danylewcyz, et al. (1985). L'Enseignement ménager et les "Home Economics" au Québec et en Ontario au début du 20e siècle: Une analyse comparée. In J.D. Wilson (Ed.), *An imperfect past: Education and society in Canadian history.* Vancouver: Centre for Curriculum & Instruction.

Eichler, M. (1979). Sex role attitudes of male and female teachers in Toronto. *Interchange, 10*(2), 2–14.

Elshtain, J. (1981). *Public man, private woman: Women in social and political thought.* Princeton, NJ: Princeton University Press.

Eyre, L. (1991). Gender relations in the classroom: A fresh look at coeducation. In J. Gaskell & A. McLaren (Eds.), *Women and education.* Calgary: Detselig.

Finn, G., & Miles, A. (1982). *Feminism in Canada: From pressure to politics.* Montreal: Black Rose Books.

Fisher, L., & Cheyne, J.A. (1977). *Sex roles: Biological and cultural interactions as found in social science research and Ontario educational media.* Toronto: Ontario Ministry of Education.

Friere, Paalo. (1970). *Pedagogy of the oppressed.* New York: Seabury Press.

Gardner, S., Dean, C., and McKaig, D. (1989). Responding to differences in the classroom: The politics of knowledge, class, and sexuality. *Sociology of Education, 62*(1), 64–74.

Gilligan, C. (1982). *In a different voice: Psychological theory and women's development.* Cambridge, MA: Harvard University Press.

Giroux, H. (1991). *Postmodernism, feminism and cultural politics: Redrawing educational boundaries.* Albany, NY: SUNY Press.

Greenglass, E. (1973). The psychology of women, on the high cost of achievement. In M. Stephenson (Ed.), *Women in Canada.* Toronto: New Press.

Hirsch, M., & Keller, E. F. (1990). *Conflicts in feminism.* New York: Routledge.

Hooks, B. (1984). *Feminist theory: From margin to centre.* Boston: South End Press.

Hooks, B. (1989). *Talking back: Thinking feminist, thinking black.* Boston: South End Press.

Kagan, J. (1964). Acquisition and significance of sex typing and sex role identity. In M.L. Hoffman & L.W. Hoffman (Eds.), *Child development research: Vol. 1* (pp. 137–167). New York: Russell Sage Foundation.

Keller, E.F. (1982). Feminism in science. In N. Keshcone, M. Rasaldo, & B. Galphi (Eds.), *Feminist theory: A critique of ideology.* Chicago: University of Chicago Press.

Keller, E.F. (1985). *A feeling for the organism.* San Francisco: W.H. Freeman.

Lather, P. (1991). *Getting smart.* New York: Routledge.

Lindblom, C., & Cohen, D. (1979). *Useable knowledge.* New Haven, CT: Yale University Press.

Luke, C., & Gore, J. (1992). *Feminism and critical pedagogy.* New York: Routledge.

Martin, J. (1985). *Reclaiming a conversation: The ideal of the educated woman.* New Haven, CT: Yale University Press.

O'Brien, M. (1981). *The politics of reproduction.* Boston: Routledge and Kegan Paul.

Parsons, T. (1942). Age and sex in the social structure of the U.S. *American Sociological Review, 7,* 604–612.

Rich, B. (1977). *Claiming an education: On lies, secrets and silence.* New York: W.W. Norton.

Ricks and Pyke, S. (1973). Teacher perceptions and attitudes that foster or maintain sex role differences. *Interchange, 4*(1), 26–33.

Rosenberg, R. (1982). *Beyond separate spheres: Intellectual roots of modern feminism.* New Haven, CT: Yale University Press.

Royal Commission on the Status of Women. (1970). *Status of women in Canada.* Ottawa: Information Canada.

Russell, S. (1979). Learning sex roles in the high school. *Interchange, 10*(2), 57–66.

Sexton, P. (1969). *The feminized male.* New York: Random House.

Shack, S. (1966). How equal is equal in education? *Quest, 3*(4), 14–15.

Silverman, K. (1985). *Subject of semantics.* New York: Oxford University Press.

Smith, D. (1974). Women's perspective as a radical critique of sociology. *Sociological Inquiry, 44*(1), 7–13.

Spinks, S. (1970). Sugar 'n spice. In S. Repo (Ed.), *This book is about schools.* New York: Oxford University Press.

Stamp, R. M. (1977). Teaching girls their God-given place in life. *Atlantis, 2*(2), 18–34.

Tancred-Sheriff, P. (1987). *A century of women in higher education: Canadian data and Australian comments.* Lecture at Macquarie University.

Trinh, M. (1989). *Woman/ Native/ other: Writing postcoloniality and feminism.* Bloomington: Indiana University Press.

Walkerdine, V. (1981). Sex, power & pedagogy. *Screen Education, 38,* 14–24.

Wilkinson, L.C., & Marrett, C.B. (1985). *Gender influences in classroom interaction.* Orlando, FL: Academic Press.

Wine, J. (1982). Gyrocentric values and feminist psychology. In G. Finn & A. Miles (Eds.), *Feminism in Canada.* Montreal: Black Rose Books.

Teaching Values in
Canadian Schools

...

William J. Hague

here is pressure on today's teacher from all sides: "Teach our children values; make them good." "Don't teach our children *your* values; teach them *my* values—the right ones." "Don't teach them any values at all; teach them how to think, and they will come to the right values on their own." "Leave the children alone, and let their intuitive goodness develop independently to choose whatever values they want." If the pulls on teachers come from all directions, they also come with a strong, sometimes strident, emotional intensity, for, with values, we are into something important—we are into the practical realm of how people behave, and sometimes we are even into morals, how people *ought* to behave. People have a great deal of personal and emotional investment in values education. It is evocative of discussion which, though never lacking in fervour, is sometimes lacking in conceptual depth. It is our purpose here to achieve some degree of conceptual depth without destroying the fervour. To do this, I will come at the issue of teaching values in Canadian schools from four perspectives:

1. What values are and what they are not.
2. The challenges we generally face when teaching values, and the special challenges of values education today.
3. Some of the ways in which values education has been conducted.
4. New directions we might take in Canada to meet today's needs.

...

WHAT VALUES ARE AND WHAT THEY ARE NOT

There is a big difference between a statement of fact and a value statement. "It is raining today," is a statement of fact. "I love rainy days," is a value statement; it gives an assessment. *Value* is a broad term for the concept we have of things or actions when we place a positive or negative weighting on them. Some of these value loadings are moral; some of them are not. Let me illustrate: fishing is just fishing until I say, "I like fishing." Now I have made a value statement; I have attached a positive valence to fishing. The same is true if I say, "The fishing is good in this lake; I catch a lot of fish." Now I am saying the lake is good for fishing, and that is why I value this lake. But if the lake is on private property, and the fish belong to someone else, I am now into the realm of morality; my fishing in this lake now touches on someone else's rights, and I must ask the value questions that are now moral judgments, "Is it right to fish in this lake?" and "Ought I to be fishing here?" I have moved from a statement of general value (the fishing is good here) to a moral value (the owner has a right to his or her private property) and that imposes a certain moral imperative on me— some way in which I *ought* to behave, if I wish to preserve that value.

The distinction between values in general and moral values is an important one to keep in mind when talking about values education—and when actually *doing* it. But there is another distinction that seems to become lost by the wayside when people are involved in values education, particularly when it touches on moral values. Values are not rules; values and rules are two quite different things. Values are conceptions of the desirable that lead us to choose from among various modes of behaviour. This simple little definition contains three elements that help in identifying a value. A value is: a "conception"—a concept, an idea, not just a feeling; "of the desirable"—not just a concept of a fact, but an emotion-charged concept of something as desirable; "that leads us to actually choose a particular behaviour"—a value is full and real only if it flows into action, sometimes even into a consistent lifestyle.

Values are the guides for choosing rules of behaviour. Our values lead to our behaviour. Particularly when we are making choices about moral behaviour, our values are there, whether we are conscious of them or not. They are like a foundation underlying the specific choices of behaviour, supporting and guiding us to make these choices. But frequently there is a large gap between this theoretical understanding of the relationship of values to action, and the practice of "values education" in our schools. Often what goes under the name of values education does not arrive at the conscious consideration of values themselves, but stays at the more superficial level of discussing rules, regulations, and ways of behaving. A classroom discussion that starts out with a school's rule prohibiting smoking is not "values education" if it stays with the specifics of rules or even the various ways students *feel* about the rules. It must dig deeper and bring into consciousness the values each student holds that cause those feelings and reactions to the rules—values such as respect for other people, health, and the freedom to choose for oneself.

All these deeper, enduring values are the real meat of values education. If we talk only about the rules of behaviour, we may be moralizing, but not really conducting values education since we are not reaching for the sources of that morality that are to be found in the enduring values underlying behaviour. Values are enduring, relatively stable things. Rules, on the other hand, are norms we derive from our values; they are specific, adaptable to the occasion, and constantly changing. As an example, look at the various rules about dress and clothing that people have made to express the value, "modesty." An Australian Aborigine's interpretation is very different from that of an Australian ladies' lawn bowling club. Today's interpretation of what is "modest" beachwear is very different from that of fifty years ago. We only have to flip through our grandparents' photo album to see that. So rules that interpret values vary from time to time and from place to place. The value itself goes on undisturbed by varying interpretations—even by erroneous interpretations. The key is that rules, if they are to be good rules, must truly reflect lasting values.

The image that best illustrates this relationship of rules to values is that of surface versus bedrock. It is up on the surface of the earth that all the activity takes place when human beings are searching for oil. But, to find oil that is deep below the surface, a seismic crew sends down soundings into the depths of the earth and "listens" for the responses that come back from the bedrock. The return message tells them something about the depth and configuration of the bedrock, providing some rules to guide decisions about where to drill. The activity on the surface is guided by rules that come from sounding the bedrock. The same is true with values and rules of behaviour. When we want some specific guidelines, some laws or rules, we should sound out the bedrock of our values, making our rules a conscious interpretation of our values (Hague, 1986).

In summary, values are concepts of the desirable that lead us to choose how we will act. Some values are moral values; some are not moral. It is important to distinguish values from rules of behaviour, so that education will not limit itself to discussing behaviour alone, but can deal with those deeper forces that influence behaviour—the values we hold.

• • •

THE CHALLENGES WE FACE IN VALUES EDUCATION

The first challenge thrown to a would-be value educator is: what values are you going to teach? If the world were unchanging, the answer would be relatively simple: "I will teach the rules of behaviour that were passed down to me from my elders; they were good enough for them, they are good enough for me, and they will be good enough for all time." If the world were static, that may be a satisfactory answer, and, indeed, those who try to create a static, unchanging society in a protected environment for their children do give this traditional command: teach unchanging, traditional values; guard our children from change of any kind. (By the way, have you noticed that, in presenting this approach, I have deliberately fudged the argument by using "values" and "rules" as though the words were interchangeable?)

But the real world in which most of us live is not static, not protected from the winds of change; it is in flux. Manners, mores, and even morals change. Political, economic, scientific, and military developments create new challenges to old ways of acting. Religious revelations that for some have been the authoritative guide for behaviour are challenged by a world with new insights, and to cling unquestioningly to an authority, even a religious authority, may blind us to possibilities of new insights into how one might be more fully human in a world in flux. Does one then respond to a changing world by saying "Everything is up for grabs; everything is relative; nobody knows what is valuable"? This was the response of some educators a few years ago, and it influenced some theorists to try to introduce a complete relativity into values education. At the present time a reactionary, conservative swing of the educational pendulum back to tradition is attempting to counter this relativity of values with a return to the indoctrination of "traditional values." It is my intention here to maintain that neither of these two extremes, neither relativity, nor indoctrination, is the answer. The answer hinges on the distinction between values and rules that we considered in the first section of this essay, and will be developed in the last section, after a brief overview of some of the ways values education has been approached in the last few years.

• • •

HOW THE CHALLENGE OF VALUE
EDUCATION HAS BEEN APPROACHED

The term *values education* has frequently been used interchangeably with *moral education*. As we have seen, they are not exactly the same thing, *values* being a broader term than *morals*. Some moral theories are not axiological; that is, they do not explicitly depend on values, but trace the origins of "oughtness" back to rights or obligations. But, as we will see, moral education theories with any depth ultimately get back to values.

Perhaps the two theories of moral/values education that have recently had the most influence on Canadian education are *values clarification*, as initiated by Raths, Harmin, and Simon (1956), and spelled out for school practice by Simon, Howe, and Kirschenbaum (1972), and the *cognitive-developmental* approach of Lawrence Kohlberg (1968, 1981). We should look at what these theories have to say, noting some of their similarities and some of their differences.

One similarity between values clarification and Kohlberg's approach is that each was conceived in an American context and tailored to meet North American philosophy and educational needs. Consequently, their powerful influence on Canadian values education was inevitable. North American society is pluralistic, and the diversity of views, educational approaches, and values prevails. There is no established church, for example, imposing dogmatic or moral unanimity on society. In fact, the United States is in the throes of a rather lengthy debate as to whether God should be in or out of the school curriculum. One cannot, in this context, presume, as might have been the case in other times and other places, to present a method of values education built upon a set of moral rules more or less generally accepted by society. That would be the traditional approach we discussed earlier in which the task of the values educator is to accept the rules of his or her society and pass them on unchanged to students who will accept them through the power of indoctrination as well as the rewards and punishments that follow good or bad behaviour.

Values Clarification

Raths, Harmin, and Simon, following John Dewey, deplored this "keeping dreary watch over ancient values" as not worthy of a citizen in a democracy. They proposed, as good Deweyites, that each individual should "clarify" his or her own values. Each person should, through education, be given the opportunity to explore values, freely select those they want to maintain, and proudly live by them. Raths, Harmin, and Simon, in their book, *Values and Teaching*, generated seven criteria for judging a value, and they created exercises in which students were guided in becoming conscious of their actual values. But, underlying the whole values clarification approach, was a philosophical premise of vast proportions that was destined to have profound repercussions on values education in the United States, and, in turn, in Canada, where in some provinces it was accepted as the theoretical framework of a value-based social studies curriculum. The important philosophical premise on which values clarification was built was that of value relativity. In a democracy envisioned as a society in which each person decided for himself or herself, there was no room for outside authority or even guidance in choosing one's own, individual values. A hierarchy of values was one's own, subjective choice, judged only by the extent to which one understood the options, freely chose, was proud of the choices, and lived by them. Judging the worth of one's values against some outside criteria, was destructive of the individual's inalienable freedom. The scene created by values clarification was a road without guideposts, each individual being left to his or her own subjective resources to discover and choose values.

Kohlberg and the Cognitive-Developmental Approach

Kohlberg also built a philosophy, a psychology, and a methodology of moral education suited to a pluralistic society. He deplored what he called the "bag of virtues" approach of traditional character education, claiming that teaching specific virtues had been shown by research (Hartshorne & May, 1928–30) to have little real effect on moral development, and, besides, people could not agree on which virtues should be taught, or, even more fundamentally, could not agree on what words like honesty, love, and kindness really meant.

Instead Kohlberg proposed a model for moral education based on a framework of six stages of moral development. Following Piaget (1948), Kohlberg discovered through his research, that moral development took the form of levels of reasoning, the higher levels taking one closer to the core of all morality—justice. The "just person" and the "just society" were the goals of Kohlberg's approach to moral education. Justice was the one yardstick by which all morality could be measured. In this way he claimed to have objective norms of moral development, and thus claimed he avoided the value subjectivity of some approaches, while, at the same time, not getting into the confusion of the "bag of virtues" presented by traditional character education.

For Kohlberg, moral education, far from inculcating a plethora of individual virtues, was to be aimed at improving the reasoning powers of individuals so that they would come to moral decisions that were just, not haphazardly or from egocentric ways of thinking, but from abstract reasoning that was universal. The educational technique to be used was to expose children, through classroom discussions of moral dilemmas, to reasoning that was just one stage above their own stage. They would be capable of understanding thinking just one stage above their own; they would be attracted to it, and ultimately incorporate that next higher stage as their own. A just society in the school would create just citizens for society. Lisa Kuhmerker (1991) in her book, *The Kohlberg Legacy for the Helping Professions*, has published one of the clearest, most practical guides to understanding Kohlberg, his theories, and his ideas of how moral education should be conducted. Tom Lickona's book (1985), *Raising Good Children*, is a down-to-earth, practical guide for teachers and parents that works within the parameters of Kohlberg's approach but is not bound to it slavishly.

Kohlberg's ideas, like values clarification, had a profound influence on values education in Canadian schools, synopsized all too often in his six neat stages of moral development, and popularized all too often in the many kits and programs that flowed out of the theory. A "Kohlberg bandwagon" developed, and many an harassed classroom teacher, called upon to do values education with little preparation, jumped on it without critiquing Kohlberg's research or considering the narrowing effect of bringing values education down to the confines of reasoning alone.

In Canada, a reaction developed to values clarification and Kohlberg, researched and popularized by such books as Kathleen Gow's *Yes Virginia, There is Right and Wrong*, (1980). Gow and others reacted on scholarly grounds to the weaknesses of research in the values education area, and, as the book's title implies, reacted, too, against the value subjectivity that they saw as rampant in values education in Canada. There is no point in reviewing here the objections of Gow and others; they have been amply documented. But it is important to point out that many of the horror stories these critics recount of how values education was conducted in the classrooms of Canada, were, in fact, in many cases, abuses of values education, perpetrated by individuals who did not understand the philosophy of the methodology they had adopted, or who, in their enthusiasm, got carried away into conducting moral education in a way that was itself immoral because it was hurtful to its students. Asking children, even in a game, to rank order their peers as to who deserves most to live, is not the way to teach worthwhile values or moral behaviour.

In summary, the challenges of values education have been approached from several directions. We have concentrated on only three of them here:

1. traditional values education aimed at preserving "tried and true" values by teaching and rewarding the expression of these values in "good" behaviour, or punishing "bad" behaviour;

2. values clarification, creating situations in which the students are called upon to examine the values they hold, and to make free, independent, and subjective choices of what values they want to continue to hold, and to live by; and

3. cognitive-developmental, incorporating the idea that individuals go through stages of moral reasoning development, the goal of moral education being to encourage better moral reasoning.

• • •

NEW DIRECTIONS IN VALUES EDUCATION

We began this essay by saying that values are important. Perhaps we can best begin this section by returning to that theme and developing from there some new directions that will have practical import for those who are engaged in values education in Canadian schools.

Values are important because they set direction in our lives; some values answer the question, "What is worthwhile?" Simple values may determine nothing more than that we prefer Coke to Pepsi. But if they are major values, they may determine what we give our lives to, and ultimately what gives our lives meaning. Each person has an "ultimate environment," the farthest horizons of one's personal world within which and in relation to which one makes meaning out of life. But life, if we reflect on it, is for most of us a vast circumference, and could for many be empty and confusing, bereft of landmarks, like the vacant horizon for a sailor in mid-ocean. Life landmarks are centres of value, guides to our navigation. Islands of value set in a landscape of ultimate horizons are something to which we can commit ourselves. In turn, we ourselves feel valued and sustained, because values give direction, security, and ultimately meaning to life. The noted Canadian moral philosopher, Charles Taylor (1991), speaks about "horizons of significance," those truly meaningful elements in a person's life that guide an individual toward moral objectivity as he or she searches for an authentic morality in an age of individualism.

But when we become values educators ourselves, we realize something new: the task of the values educator is not really to *teach* values in the sense of giving students something they never had before. Everyone has some values already. From the beginning, even a newborn baby values pleasure over pain; an elementary school child, asked what he or she likes best about school, will promptly answer, "recess." The values are already there implicitly even though its name is not spoken. If you ask a child, "Why do you like recess?" he or she may reply, "Because it's fun." Recess is the thing chosen. Fun is the *value* behind the choice of the thing. Children cannot always "clarify" their values by verbalizing them in abstract terms, but they surely act on them. The task of values education is to dig down to the values we have deep within each of us, to provoke the values

into consciousness, and to look at them, deciding which are real values by examining whether they actually influence action in our lives, and making decisions
on whether we want to keep those values or not, and in what *order* we keep
them.

I have highlighted the word "order" in the previous sentence because it brings
in a very important element about the way values work in specific situations.
When the school bell rings for dismissal, a mad dash for the door could result if
teachers did not impose some order. The same is true for values. We hold many,
many values. When a value discussion calls for reflection, a mad rush of values
competing to be the solution of the problem is not helpful. Instead we organize
our values into orderly but fluid systems. These are systems we construct
according to values that are more important and those that are less important in
our lives—usually called value hierarchies. Value hierarchies are nice, neat
structures we can make for ourselves and that can even help older children to
organize for themselves in the abstract. But if the moral or value problem is "for
real," we get a new rush of values competing not just against each other for a
place, but now being judged for their relevance and practicality in dealing with
a concrete situation. This may shake up the hierarchy of values we made in the
abstract situation of, for example, filling out the Rokeach Value Survey. Moral
judgment is then no longer simply recourse to a neat chart of values. It is
instead involvement in a system where the contingencies of real life take over.
Children will argue: if A is the case then I would do B, but if X is the case then
Y is the right way to go. The value chosen does not depend on what I *generally*
prefer, but what I prefer as a solution *in this situation*. If values relate in systems,
perhaps the term "hierarchy of values" may be too linear, limited, and constrict-
ing, not taking into account the complexities and relativities involved in considering not only the relationship of values in an abstract sense, but the values
we actually live by, and the contingencies that direct which of these will be
effective in a concrete situation.

Perhaps a better model is what has recently come to be called a "heterarchy".
A heterarchy is akin to networking. The word "heterarchy," like networking,
denotes the input by others who are neighbours. The "neighbours" in this case
are not just competing values, but the contingencies of the real situation for
applying values. It is visualized as a flat, circular model in place of the linear or
pyramidal model of a hierarchy. It also carries the notion of recursive communication, systems within systems. "Heterarchy" is a better word for what we are
naming here because it holds the connotation of process. It is not a structure but
a *process*. It is not a rigid structure designed predominantly for self-preservation

through conservation. It is instead a system in which relationship, communication, and feedback are predominant. This has important implications for value heterarchies. The process of making value judgments is not linear but recursive, circular, involving communication, feedback, and modification in the process of judgment. Input and feedback into this system are multiple. With more diverse and recursive feedback, the contingencies of value judgments are more readily taken into account. The question becomes: "Which value in what context?" A value heterarchy is not so much a structure as a truly systemic relationship reflective of relative behaviour choices that are dependent on time and context. There is much to be gained by thinking of value systems not as hierarchical but heterarchical. There is much to be gained, too, in thinking of values and moral education as a process which, in the context of real situations, calls on the student to communicate not only with fellow students and the teacher but to consciously participate in the systems within himself or herself. There, through personal reflection, the student will find values competing for relevance in a particular situation, and learn a fundamental lesson—this internal competition, this inner conflict, (though sometimes painful) is necessary and healthy. That is what values education gives students: an opportunity to raise values into consciousness and to choose the order that will give form and proportion to the way they influence the actions, and shape the meanings of their lives.

The concept of some kind of order is important in working out new ways of conducting values education. Since we already have values, then our first task in values education is to bring them into conscious awareness. This is the essence of the process of values education: getting in touch with the values we already have, and then making some deliberate, conscious choices of which values we want to keep, and which are most important to us. The first revelation that comes from this reflective approach is the realization that most of our values are good, and that we do not want to throw any of them out. But we do have to decide which comes first, which values supersede others. One can, for example, value both freedom and security. But if the situation arises in some concrete case, in which I have a choice of one or the other, which will I give up? Some people have given their lives for freedom; others (recruits to religious cults for example) have given their freedom to someone or some institution that promises them security. One must make decisions in specific cases as to which value shall prevail. That is how our values become clear to us.

But values come clear to us in another way: when they clash with the values of other people. That is why so much of values education takes place in the form of discussion of dilemmas. When our values clash with someone else's values, we are called upon to do two things: re-examine our own values, and put ourselves in the other person's shoes and try to see the problem from his or her point of view.

To pull a few themes together before we go on, values are important because they put meaning and direction in our lives, giving us a sense of personal continuity and worth. The task of values education is to bring into consciousness those values that are already there within us, directing our lives. Values education affords the opportunity of discovering what values we have, and the order in which we hold them. Most important, it forces us into making conscious choices of the values that direct our lives. Values education sounds below the surface of action for the depths of values that ultimately direct those actions.

This little recapitulation allows us to see that we have been coming at the whole task of values education in a way that is so typical of values educators—backwards! It is backwards because we have talked about doing something for our students before we have talked about doing it for ourselves. We have talked about students becoming conscious of their values, leaving out that essential step of the teacher first becoming conscious of his or her own values. There is an old saying: "values are not so much taught as caught." What we say in values education is frequently overshadowed by what we are and what we do. It is absolutely essential that the would-be values educator be working himself or herself on what their values are and how their personal values direct their lives. Techniques of values education fade into insignificance in the face of this imperative. As a teacher, clarifying my own values is necessary if I am to be able to respond to questions or demands from students to take a stand. It is imperative that I be aware of the direction in which my values are influencing the values and behaviour of others. Being conscious of my own values, and how they are distinct from but directive of the actions in my own life is a constant and perfect pedagogical reminder of the distinction made earlier between values and ways of behaving. The teacher's own reflection and the constant passing back and forth from the surface of actions down to the depths of value that guide those actions, will save many a values education class from being a mere discussion of rules, making it instead a real opportunity for deep value clarification.

At the beginning of this chapter I made the distinction between values in general and moral values in particular. Moral values are a subset of values in general. Only some values are moral values. So far I have let our discussion roam over the range of general values. I would like to conclude with a consideration of values education in the particular sense of moral education because there are some specific aspects of this that deserve to be looked at closely.

• • •

MORAL EDUCATION

The first new direction in moral education that should be explored is paradoxically, not new at all. It is, in fact, an ancient idea, taught by Aristotle and Aquinas, called "character education" or "virtue ethics." When values clarification was popular, character education was brushed off as undemocratic because it seemed doctrinaire. Criticizing the Hartshorne and May (1928-30) studies, Kohlberg also turned a generation of educators against a multiple-virtue approach. His influence was powerful and pervading—enough to cause a generation of educators to close an eye to the long tradition of character and virtue and invest instead in the promise of ways of measuring moral development by cognitive stages and teaching it with ready-made dilemmas. Aristotle and Aquinas were neglected. But the limitations of a less than holistic view of the child, and emphasis on the form of morals education over its content has recently led to disillusionment. Some voices such as those of MacIntyre (1984), Hauerwas (1981, 1985), and Meilander (1984) lamented that society was striving to subsist morally "after virtue." MacIntyre (1988) in particular continues to argue against a one-virtue, one-faculty approach, asking, "Whose justice? Which rationality?" Thus in the period we have just come through, in trying to narrow all morality down to the single virtue of justice, and in attempting to emphasize form over content to meet the needs of a pluralistic society, our conception of the human person is in danger of being limited. Character education is a counter-force, attempting to reach back to a broader, more realistic, and holistic view of the person than some brands of cognitive developmentalism proposed.

James Fowler (1986) sums up the transition from cognitive developmental thinking to an appreciation of broader concepts of personality when he says:

> Neither Piaget nor Kohlberg intends to provide a theory of ego or personality development. Both, therefore, have approached the task of identifying the forms of reason or logic characteristic of different "stages" in human thought without making a critically important distinction: They have not attended to the differences between constitutive knowing in which the identity or worth of the person is not directly at stake and constitutive knowing in which it is. This has meant that Kohlberg has avoided developing a theory of the moral self, of character, or of conscience. Strictly speaking, his stages describe a succession of integrated structures of moral logic. He has given very little attention to the fact that we "build" ourselves through choices and moral (self-defining) commitments. His theory,

for understandable theoretical and historical-practical reasons, has not explicated the dynamics of the inner dialogue in moral choice between actual and possible selves. (p. 22)

Clearly our current call is to return to a moral education that is holistic, that does not narrow our conception of the human person down to the cognitive, but sees moral development as part of self-development, development of the whole personality. There is now, as a result of this broader view in the post-Kohlbergian period, renewed interest in character education.

What is character education? It is the teaching and consistent practice of virtues "defined" by the lives of those who live them with all the moral force of the significant lived experience of both the individual and the community. Proponents of character education see the person not simply as a philosophical solver of dilemmas that come along from time to time in life, but as a whole person with pervading good habits of acting morally. Moral action in a particular situation comes more from what the person *is* than from what he or she *thinks* at the moment. The primary question of the character/value approach to morality then is not so much, "What shall I *do?*" as, "What shall I *be?*" It is not merely a fleeting matter of this or that moral dilemma, but a question of the self acting in a persistent manner.

These pervading habits of acting are called virtues (from the Latin word *virtus* meaning strength). A person with high moral character is a complex system of a multiple of virtues working in collaboration. This view of moral action, in keeping with the systemic concept of valuing discussed earlier, sees moral choice as a highly complex interaction of systems, including (with the rational) systems of feeling, emotion, self-concept, and sense of self in the perspective of one's own life story—sometimes called a narrative approach.

The Use of Narrative

Since moral education is more complex than simply being sharp enough to come up with a "higher stage" rational answer to a particular problem, its techniques are broader than solving hypothetical dilemmas. Techniques include real life stories that engage the whole child and the use of both positive and negative modelling. Proponents of character education such as Hauerwas (1981, 1985), use the words "narrative" or "story" a great deal. Story is used in two senses:

1. A personal narrative of one's own life that provides a sense of self, who I am, what I have been, and what I might be. If you wonder how important this is, observe a child's eager interest in old photo albums with pictures of

himself or herself as a baby. Listen to conversations. Frequently they consist of individuals vying for the opportunity to tell their story even if it is only the story of a fishing trip or a visit with the dentist. Even a small, personal story comes into perspective when put in the context of the story of society often called history. It is the story of my people—what we have been, and thus where I have come from. History tells me something important about what we can and even what we should be. There is a moral in it all. Witness the immense popularity of the public TV series on the Civil War. It was not just history; it was a moral narrative on human relationships enriched with all the strength and pathos of personal stories.

2. The second meaning of story is its usual sense of narrative or fiction. Simply put, it is a story about someone else, not me personally, as in the first meaning. It can however, reflect and implement the other sense. Someone else's story can have meaning for me; someone else (a hero or heroine) can be a model for me. More and more there is a growing call for the use of story in morals education. It is more than an old-fashioned teaching device used to get students' attention; it is, rather, reflective of the immense power that exists within story and myth (May, 1991) to stir the emotions, inspire identification, and flow into action. You can "follow" almost any story, but a really good story "grabs" you. Good stories have characters who personify strength, sometimes known as "heroic virtue," either by its presence or its tragic absence. One need not reach the moral, to make it an occasion for moral development. The hero has his or her own strength, and his or her own attractiveness to exemplify and lure one to goodness.

When we are talking about heroes, we are not talking about just "nice" people—"Dick and Jane" characters. Children do not need to find others "just like themselves." Character education means bringing the hero back into moral education. Children need to find heroes who are better than they. Not just better at baseball or basketball, but better in imaging what a human being ought to be. If as children, we learned to sense the gap between *what is* and *what is possible* and then went on to learn about the gap between *what is* and *what ought to be*, perhaps as adults we could acknowledge the gap between things as they are and what ought to be, and earnestly strive to close that gap first in ourselves and then in our society.

Nor will moral dilemmas substitute for real stories. Kilpatrick (1986, p. 183) states that, "no attempt is made to delineate character in a moral dilemma, whereas character is everything in the heroic story . . . Heinz (the subject of Kohlberg's most famous moral dilemma) is no Ulysses but a blank, a cipher . . . We have no interest in him, only in his case." What is implied in the traditional dilemma is that flesh and blood relationships, loyalties, and loves, are largely irrelevant to moral issues. One can skip the particulars, it seems, and go immediately to universal principles. Consequently, as Kilpatrick (p. 185) puts it, "we are forced to create the fiction that each child is a miniature Socrates, a moral philosopher in his own right." Perhaps he or she is if guided to be so, but as Johnston (1988) has pointed out, children are capable of at least two strategies of moral problem solving, one of justice reasoning, and one of caring through understanding. To neglect fuller understanding and teach only one way of thinking would be a mistake. Moral education goes on all the time, not just in the classrooms of those who purport to teach it, but also, for example, in the social studies classrooms with their timeless and world-encompassing moral dilemmas, and in English Literature classrooms where heroes and villains clash in moral struggles depicted by those masters of psychology—the great authors. If moral education, then, is widespread, it follows that all teachers (not just those deliberately trying to teach or counsel morals, are moral educators through exemplifying day-to-day, the values by which they live. Their character shows, and that teaches.

One danger of believing that moral educators should teach not just the form of moral reasoning but the content of moral judgment, is that this seems to open the way to all kinds of indoctrination, which is shunned by most Canadian schools. But indoctrination, no matter how much we denounce it, goes on inevitably, subtly, and unconsciously. Realizing one's role as a former of character, at the very least calls for a conscious teaching of values. This is healthier than its opposite—not even being aware of the values we do teach!

R. S. Peters (1969), the eminent British moral philosopher, has reminded us that the ultimate question of moral education is "How do children come to care?" How do we teach empathy, that kind of justice that means putting oneself in the other person's shoes, seeing the situation as they would see it, thinking as they would think, feeling as they would feel, or, more precisely, feeling as I would feel if I, myself, were in that situation.

That last phrase, "feeling as I would feel if I, myself, were in that situation," is a loaded statement. It carries two main themes of moral judgment making—the emotional component in moral judgment and the central role of experiencing authentic feelings in moral development. Too many theories of moral education have emphasized the cognitive, rational approach to moral judgments, giving the impression that the best moral judgments are made with cool logic alone, precluding all feeling and passion. This is a misleading way of looking at moral judgments, as though we could and should cut off our feelings about vital issues.

It is a whole human person that makes moral choices. Rather than try to avoid feelings as misleading us or clouding the issue, (which has been the view of some cognitivists), the task of the moral educator is to develop feelings, hone their edge, polish them like a mirror until they are authentic reflections of the world around, sensitive perceptions of how I would feel if I were in another person's dilemma. Emotions developed to high levels, can be sure guides to judgments about how one ought to behave. Again I have slipped in another phrase that is crucial—"emotions developed to high levels." Not just any emotion will do, but feelings that are empathic responses to a situation, in which I feel a sense of responsibility for myself and for others, founded on a sense of oneness between myself and others. Empathy, that response one has of feeling with and for another, is at the heart of higher level emotions. Or rather, it could be at the core of our responses if it did not get squashed by a world that does not really encourage authentic feeling.

Children feel deeply. But if we are not careful, they can grow up without being able to experience deep feeling. It seems strange to have to talk about actually experiencing real emotion. We live in a world full of intense emotion; the trouble is it usually comes to us in those neatly packaged containers that fill the spaces between advertisements on TV. In front of the TV set in a single evening, a child can witness a dozen deaths, and yet not be emotionally participant in any of them. So much of the "drama" is played out by cardboard-thin characters who can never really involve us because they are not real, and they work through their story line of violence in a pre-programmed system that is meant to raise the viewer's attention just before the commercial to keep you riveted to the screen. Commercialism can be absurd in its lack of sensitivity to other values. Is it not radically obscene to suddenly interrupt two men who are clobbering each other to death to remind us not to offend our neighbours with underarm perspiration? Such travesties of real emotional involvement contribute to the development of numb, non-participant persons, not necessarily bad persons, but glassy-eyed, bored, overstimulated but emotionally undernourished persons. Someone has said, "Our young people know the price of everything, and the value of nothing." If we have people confused about what is worthwhile, is it not because they have never been really participant in living, never really called forth to feel as another may feel? If their motto is, "Don't get involved," is their apathy not the result of a feeling of impotence because there are no value guidelines from without, and no sense of real moral choices from within that would make them feel like they belong on planet earth?

The challenge to the values educator, particularly the moral educator, is to let children feel the appropriate emotional responses to their own situations. Let them experience fear, disappointment, loneliness, confusion; they are all part of the human condition. They are all schooling for being able to feel for others too, to identify with others, to know their hurts as though they were one's own and to act morally to prevent those hurts to oneself and to others. This is justice, not just an abstraction calling for purely cognitive understanding. It is a passionate sense of justice that we are striving for—a justice, that people must "hunger and thirst after."

Moral education asks the teacher to accept the child's spontaneous expression, "It's not fair," and to challenge him or her to jump the gap between "It's not fair to me" and "It's not fair to you, or really to me either" because he or she has come to think and to feel; "My good must be your good or it is really no good at all." That is asking a lot; it is asking the child to move from lower levels of self-ishness to higher levels of empathy and altruism. It is asking the teachers to have made that movement themselves already before they can pass it on to others. Those ways of thinking and feeling that are lower and not reflected upon must, in the course of moral education, disintegrate, and be replaced by that which is higher, more an integrated part of the personality because it is felt deeply and reflected upon. It comes from the themes of one's own personal life story. That really is what moral education is all about.

If we accept the premises that people are at various levels of moral development; that moral judgment making involves the whole person and is neither just a logical exercise of pure reason nor an experience of capricious emotionality; that real values education (including moral education) means striving for deeper level values and not staying in the more superficial realm of rules and regulations, how then should we proceed with moral education? Not by the route of utter value subjectivity as in values clarification, leaving moral judgments up to the individual—any individual—regardless of his or her personal capacities to make those judgments. This is only pseudo-freedom, leaving each person the victim of one's own immaturity; not by the route of total indoctrination, for this takes away the individual's responsibility for his or her own value choices, imposes conformity, and provides at times what is only a pseudo-objectivity. Indoctrination can be a way of imposing one's own set of subjective judgments onto others; not by the route of over-simplification—either seeing moral judgment making as an exercise in rational thinking alone, or, on the other hand, as a totally emotional, irrational response of the passions. Neither approach is holistic, and that is what we are dealing with in moral judgments—whole, living, breathing, real human persons making judgments with all the data their senses can provide, all the reason their intelligence gives, and all the emotional maturity their level of development equips them with, deciding how they shall work out the course of their lives in the most caring way possible.

Kaplan (1991, pp. 530–531) gives a brief, interesting, and fairly accurate summary of how morality might be taught in the future. Looking at the present, too, he suggests a practical approach to moral education, using Kevin Ryan's "Five E's." They follow from the ideas we have looked at here, and could be implemented in today's Canadian classroom:

> *Example*: Teachers and parents are themselves role models. Models from history and literature can also teach values and morals by example.
> *Explanation*: Character education does not neglect reason. If rules are to be enforced, students deserve to know the reasons behind them.
> *Exhortation*: Children need encouragement to risk change and to persevere in a new moral direction.
> *Environment*: The classroom and the school must be environments where the individual and the community together can work out their ways of being moral.
> *Experience*: If values are the foundations of action, and if, as we have seen, morality is not just something to be discussed hypothetically ("What do I think?") but actually lived ("What kind of a person am I?" . . . "How do I usually act?), then the richest values and morals education will provide opportunities not just to talk, but to be and to act.

How then, do we teach people to care? First, of course by caring ourselves, but then by recognizing the power and vitality of the "informed heart," the whole person in real life, the emotions working in collaboration with what we call intellect. The human person is far from being a kind of moral computer that can be carefully programmed to come up with the "right" answer to any moral dilemma. Nor, on the other hand, should we encourage feeling that is merely whimsical, subjective, and uninformed. Secondly, by recognizing that all of us are at various levels of emotional development and need to be drawn from lower level to higher level functioning, the lower, more instinctual, unreflected ways give way to higher level reflected ways. The infant's egocentrism must, in the long run, give way to the reflective ability to put one's self in another person's shoes, to see the world as others see it. Childish conformity for the sake of "keeping out of trouble" must yield to a real concern that justice be done for others as well as for oneself. Adolescent rebellion and emotional distancing must give way to real involvement, care, and concern. Adult feelings of inferiority must be transposed into a healthy feeling of dissatisfaction with oneself, and a quest for the moral ideals of what one ought to be.

Moral education is that part of values education that especially teaches people to care. Of all the delicate and demanding tasks of the values educator, perhaps moral education is the most demanding and most delicate, but its course can be more surely guided by seeing the need for moral education to go beneath the surface of moral rules and find firm roots for moral behaviour in values that are truly humanizing.

· · ·

REFERENCES

Fowler, J. (1986). Faith and the structuring of meaning. In C. Dykstra & S. Parks (Eds.), *Faith development and Fowler*. Birmingham, AL: Religious Education Press.

Gow, K. (1980). *Yes, Virginia, there is right and wrong*. Toronto: Wiley & Sons.

Hague, W. (1986). *New perspectives on religious and moral development*. Edmonton: University of Alberta Publications Services.

Hartshorne, H., & May, M.A. (1928/30). *Studies in the nature of character: Vol. 1: Studies in deceit; Vol. 2: Studies in service and self-control; Vol. 3: Studies in organization of character*. New York: Macmillan.

Hauerwas, S. (1981). *A community of character*. Notre Dame, IN: University of Notre Dame Press.

Hauerwas, S. (1985). *Character and the Christian life*. San Antonio, TX: Trinity University Press.

Johnston, D.K. (1988). Adolescents' solutions to dilemmas in fables: Two moral orientations—two problem-solving strategies. In C. Gilligan, J. Ward, & J. Taylor (Eds.), *Mapping the moral domain*. Cambridge, MA: Harvard University Press.

Kaplan, P. (1991). *A child's odyssey*. St. Paul, MN: West Publishing.

Kilpatrick, W. (1986). Moral character, storytelling and virtue. In R. Knowles & G. McLean, *Psychological foundations of moral education and character development*. New York: University Press of America.

Kohlberg, L. (1968). Moral development. In *Encyclopedia of the social sciences, 10*, (pp. 483–494). New York: Macmillan.

Kohlberg, L. (1981). *The philosophy of moral development*. San Francisco: Harper & Row.

Kuhmerker, L. (1991). *The Kohlberg legacy for the helping professions*. Birmingham, AL: Religious Education Press.

Lickona, T. (1985). *Raising good children*. New York: Bantam.

MacIntyre, A. (1984). *After virtue*. Notre Dame, IN: University of Notre Dame Press.

MacIntyre, A. (1988). *Whose justice? Which rationality?* Notre Dame, IN: University of Notre Dame Press.

May, R. (1991). *The cry for myth*. New York: W.W. Norton.

Meilander, G. (1984). *The theory and practice of virtue*. Notre Dame, IN: University of Notre Dame Press.

Peters, R. (1969). *Ethics and education*. London: Allen & Unwin.

Piaget, J. (1948). *The moral judgment of the child*. Glencoe, IL: Free Press.

Raths, L., Harmin, M., & Simon, S. (1966). *Values and teaching*. Columbus, OH: Charles E. Merrill.

Simon, S., Howe, L., & Kirschenbaum, H. (1972). *Values clarification*. New York: Hart.

Taylor, C. (1991). *The malaise of modernity*. Concord, ON: Anansi Press.

SOCIAL PROBLEMS & ISSUES IN EDUCATION

. . .

Educational institutions are at the forefront of the fight against several threats to the health of our society. Several of these threats and the corresponding potential in educational defenses are discussed in the chapters in this section in the context of changing views of sex education, substance abuse, literacy, the school dropout phenomenon, and censorship in Canadian schools.

Herold and Hess review the history of sex education in Canada and discuss the objectives of sex education. They identify a number of issues pertinent to the inclusion of sex education in the curriculum and discuss popular misconceptions, the attitudes of students and of the general population, and the preparation of teachers to conduct sex education classes. They conclude by speculating on the prospects for sex education in Canadian schools.

Pagliaro explores the extent and the nature of substance abuse among Canadian youth and the implications for our society and our educational systems. The new danger of HIV infection and AIDS is also underlined. To Pagliaro, traditional educational programs for substance abuse have largely failed because of their restrictive focus and more effective models utilizing student peers and outside experts are needed.

Fagan discusses literacy as a social, economic, and educational issue. In describing the scope and the intricasies of literacy concepts, he addresses the present concern over literacy standards, school-age and adult literacy, and the implications for classroom teachers and literacy instructors.

Allison analyzes the dropout phenomenon to determine the extent, the cause, and the treatment of the problem. It is Allison's contention that the present poorly informed obsession with the dropout issue is masking serious weaknesses in our secondary education and that these educational deficiencies will not be solved by school restructuring or by forcing unwilling students to remain in the system.

Jenkinson discusses contemporary censorship in Canadian schools by responding to the following questions: What is censorship? What is the difference between censorship and selection? What are the causes of censorship? Who are the censors? What gets challenged? When does censorship occur? What forms does censorship take? Why do censors censor? The chapter also provides some practical suggestions for those who may be confronted with censorship attempts.

Sex Education in
Canadian Schools

...

Edward S. Herold

Gretchen C. Hess

*W*hile some may still believe that young people are better off not knowing the "facts of life," there are many tragic consequences of not properly informing young people.[1] Consider the following:

> At midnight on January 26, 1983, a 15-year-old Hamilton high school
> student who was alone in her bedroom gave birth. She lay in bed with the
> baby through the night and in the morning hid the child in a garbage bag.
> The mother of the teenager had no idea her daughter was pregnant. In
> court, the defense lawyer stated the girl had no knowledge of childbirth
> and did not know how her parents would react to the situation. (*Globe and
> Mail*, 9 August 1983)

Another example is that of a twenty-one-year-old university student who felt
that, because she received no sex education at home or at school, she suffered
unnecessary worry and anxiety about the physical changes she experienced during and after puberty. "My ignorance in the area of sexuality, until I reached the
university level, fills me with regret, shame, and a determination that my children will not be left in such an educational vacuum in this area."

In addition to the many personal stories such as the two just cited, there is no
denying some of the facts related to teenagers and their sexuality. With the fear
of contacting the HIV virus or AIDS becoming a reality for many Canadians,
inadequate knowledge about all aspects of sexuality and sexual behaviour can
actually threaten teenagers' lives. The numbers of teenagers who contract other
sexually transmitted diseases in addition to AIDS, who conceive unwanted children, or who suffer emotional trauma about issues connected with their sexuality, all serve to strengthen the argument for adequate sex education.

Sprinthall and Collins (1988) state another reason for endorsement:

> However, as the statistics point out, ignorance is neither blissful nor a barrier to sexual activity by adolescents. Nor is it a reality. No matter how much we as adults may feel about it, sexuality is present in every way in this society, both in healthy and unhealthy forms. Popular songs, movies, television, books, billboards—in short, almost every conceivable aspect of media constantly presents sex in almost every possible form. (p. 331)

Our youth today need some education to help them critically analyze and understand their sexuality and sexual behaviour amid society's bombardment of the topic.

Many different agencies and professional groups are involved in sex education, including religious institutions, the medical profession, social service agencies and birth control groups. Nevertheless, most formal sex education takes place in the school setting. During the 1970s and 1980s, many Canadian school systems began offering sex education courses. However, very few have developed comprehensive programs that teach physical, emotional, sociological, and psychological aspects of sexuality and sexual behaviours in such a way that Canadian youth can use the information and discussions to make informed choices in their own lives. As a result, we are still of the belief, even today, that most young people in Canada are not receiving adequate sex education.

• • •

HISTORY OF SEX EDUCATION IN CANADA

Until the 1960s, there were virtually no organized sex education programs in Canada. In those few cases where sex was discussed, little or no information was given other than vague references to the avoidance of temptation. However, beginning in the late 1960s, in response to the increased sexual activity among young people, and the accompanying increase in unplanned pregnancies, health professionals, educators, social workers, and parents co-operated to develop sex education programs.

In 1967, Ortho Pharmaceutical organized the first national conference on Family Life Education, which was attended by 3000 participants. In 1972, a conference on family planning was organized under the sponsorship of John Munro, then the national minister of health and welfare. In that same year, the Family Planning Division of the Department of National Health and Welfare was created. This division was instrumental in helping to establish new clinical and educational programs in family planning and sex education.

During the 1970s, some of the provinces developed policies and guidelines for the teaching of sex education. Although the implementation of sex education programs was left to individual school boards, simply having provincial approval facilitated school board involvement in these programs. Two of the earliest programs were developed by school boards in Calgary and London.

In 1977, a survey by the Canadian Education Association found that twenty-one percent of school districts in Canada had a family life education program. With the exception of puberty, few topics in sex education were introduced before high school. One of the main problems reported was that few of the teachers had received specific training to teach family life education.

A 1984 survey of school superintendents by the Planned Parenthood Federation of Canada found that fifty percent offered a family life education program (Notte, 1984). Whereas eighty-seven percent of urban districts had a program, only twenty-five percent of rural districts provided family life education. Of 125 family life co-ordinators surveyed, only twenty-six percent indicated their school board had a policy statement on family life education. Co-ordinators stressed the necessity of obtaining school board commitment to the program in order to push reluctant administrators to act and provide the needed resources and training for the teachers to do a good job. Only half of teachers surveyed indicated that they had taken courses to prepare them for teaching family life education. Many teachers said that more in-service training programs were needed to keep them up-to-date on specific topics and resources. Few teachers reported having experienced any opposition to their programs, and most indicated that parents provided overwhelming support.

During the 1980s, most provinces were leaving the responsibility for sex education to local school boards. Generally, the provinces provided only minimal support for these programs. A 1983 national health education study of 29 000 Canadian school children ages nine, twelve, and fifteen showed a considerable lack of sex education (King & Robertson, 1983).

In the 1990s more programs are being offered in schools across Canada, but sex education is not universal. In their survey of almost 4000 teenagers across Canada, Bibby and Posterski (1992) found that eighty-five percent reported that they had received some sex education. Most provinces organize sex education in health or guidance programs. In Quebec, however, sex education is included under moral and religious education. Ontario and New Brunswick provide extensive family planning programs funded by the province through local health units. Many of these programs also include sex education components. Manitoba's Department of Education offers a family life education curriculum for Grades 5,

7, and 9 to interested school boards only. A far greater number of urban than rural school boards choose to offer the program. Alberta appears to be the exception among the provinces. Sex education was first introduced in the form of a provincial curriculum as an optional unit in part of a course called "Health" in Grades 4 through 9 and "Career and Life Management (CALM)" in Grade 11. However, in 1989, the minister of education required all board operated schools to teach the sex education units. Parents maintained the right to exempt their children from the sex education classes. Currently, it is believed that all but about one and a half percent of the students in the province receive sex education.

. . .

COMMON QUESTIONS ABOUT SEX EDUCATION

Even as sex education gains wider acceptance across Canada, there is still some confusion, and sometimes controversy, about it. The next section of this chapter will focus on the answers to four questions that are commonly asked about sex education: (1) does teaching about sexuality increase sexual activity? (2) do parents support sex education? (3) do students support sex education? (4) what principles should be followed when teaching sex education?

Does Teaching About Sexuality Increase Sexual Activity?

One belief of some opponents of sex education is that sex education promotes promiscuity. The research evidence clearly does not support this belief. Instead, research has shown that sex education does not increase premarital sex but may increase the more responsible use of contraception among young people who are sexually active. For example, Zelnik and Kim (1982), in studying a large random sample of American teenagers, found that those with sex education were no more likely than those who had no sex education to engage in premarital intercourse. However, those whose sex education included birth control education were less likely to become pregnant because they were using contraception. Within Ontario, Orton and Rosenblatt (1980), found that adolescent pregnancy rates declined the most between 1975 and 1979 in districts with the most developed family planning and sex education programs. Meikle and his colleagues (1985) found that, among fifteen- to eighteen-year-old Calgary high school students, there was no significant difference in coital experience between those who had or did not have sex education, while among thirteen- and fourteen-year-old girls, fewer of those with sex education had experienced sexual intercourse. In a controlled experiment with 1100 students in Grades 9 and 11 in Quebec, Frappier (1983) found that those students who were given sex education were not more likely to engage in sexual intercourse. However, the sex education students did acquire more knowledge, and they showed a more responsible and less exploitative attitude towards sexuality.

Do Parents Approve of Sex Education?

In 1974, the Gallup Poll asked Canadians, "It has been suggested that a course in sex education be given to students in high school. Do you approve or disapprove?" seventy-three percent approved. Those who approved were asked, "Would you approve or disapprove if these courses discussed birth control?" eighty-nine percent approved. The strongest supporters were people from large communities and those who were younger and well educated. Nevertheless, a majority of people over the age of fifty approved of sex education.

A 1979 survey in Ontario found that ninety-one percent of adults said that the school should be involved in sex education (Livingstone & Hart, 1989). Over fifty percent said that sex education means more than the provision of medical or factual information on topics such as birth control and includes a fuller treatment of the social and emotional as well as the physical aspects of sex. In a 1980 survey of Calgary parents, Meikle and his colleagues (1985) found that eighty-one percent of parents agreed that schools should teach contraception. In 1980, in Prince Edward Island, ninety percent of parents agreed that birth control information should be included in family living courses (MacLeod, 1980). In 1982, sixty-nine percent of mothers in Wellington County, Ontario, agreed that schools should inform teenagers about the different methods of birth control; eighteen percent were undecided and only 1.3 percent disagreed (Marsman, 1982). Only two percent believed that providing teenagers with knowledge about contraception would lead to sexual experimentation. A 1984 Gallup survey for the Planned Parenthood Federation of Canada found that eighty-three percent of Canadians believed sex education should be taught in schools.

Indeed every survey of parents that has been done has found the great majority supporting sex education in the schools. This needs to be emphasized because opponents of sex education programs time and again will say parents are opposed to sex education, when what they are really saying is that a small vociferous minority of parents are opposed to sex education. As long as parents are informed about what is being taught and are involved in curriculum design and revision, most will support the school system. A good example of this occurred in Halton Country, Ontario, when the Renaissance Committee organized a parents' night

featuring the film "Sexuality and Communication." The opponents of sex education had spread so many rumours about the film that the curiosity of parents was
raised and several hundred attended the showing. When parents had the opportunity to view the film, their reaction was opposite to that predicted by the
Renaissance Committee. Most parents liked the film and wished they could have
seen such a film when they were in high school. Rather than remaining to listen
to a tirade against sex education, most parents streamed out of the meeting
(Herold, 1984). The opponents of sex education thrive in an atmosphere where
lack of knowledge about a program exists and consequently many false rumours
arise. The correct action is to provide adequate information to the community.

Further indication of parental support can be seen in the fact that when parents are given the opportunity to refuse permission for their child to take a sex
education course, very few do so. In many communities, parents have been so
involved in the process of program planning and curriculum review that they
have requested sex education for themselves.

Do Students Support Sex Education?

One concern of adults is the possibility of teaching sex education before the
young people are ready. However, young people have the opposite concern: that of
being taught too little material at a time when it is too late to be of much use to
them. In 1972, one of the authors (Herold) surveyed attitudes of Grades 10 and
12 students in Wellington County, Ontario, toward family life education
(Herold, Kopf, & de Carlo, 1974). Students were found to be overwhelmingly in
favour of more family life and sex education being offered in the schools. They
also preferred to have the sex education topics introduced earlier than they had
been. Over eighty percent said that, at least before the end of Grade 10, they
wanted to know about such topics as birth control methods, masturbation, and
sexual response. When we presented the statement "Teenagers are better off not
knowing about contraception," ninety percent disagreed. When asked if information on methods of contraception leads to experimentation, almost all disagreed.
The students believed that they should be provided with information about birth
control and they did not believe this information would encourage sexual activity.

What Principles Should be Followed?

For sex education programs to be accepted and supported by parents it is essential that some basic principles regarding the school's role in sex education be
established. The following are some fundamental principles that should be considered by all school boards before sex education programs are developed:

1. The primary responsibility for sex education rests with parents and the school's role is to support the parents' role.
2. School sex education programs should reflect both parental values and student needs.
3. Parents and educators should be partners in designing and implementing school sex education programs.
4. Parents who do not wish their children to be involved in sex education should have the opportunity to withdraw their children from these classes.
5. Wherever possible, sex educators should assist both parents and their children to communicate with one another.
6. Many young people do not want to become sexually involved and their views should be supported.
7. The sexual difficulties faced by young people are increased when they are not given adequate information.

...

OBJECTIVES OF SEX EDUCATION

When sex education courses were first introduced, the emphasis was on the negative pathological aspect of sexuality. Sex was never talked about in positive terms, but rather was viewed almost as a disease that had to be cured by repression. Masturbation, for example, was seen as a filthy habit resulting in various physical and psychological illnesses. The main objective of sex education was to stamp out as much of sexual thoughts and behaviour as possible by instilling in people a tremendous amount of sexual guilt. In more recent years, although the negative aspects of sexuality are still being taught, there is a trend toward examining its positive, life-enriching aspects.

Reducing Unwanted Pregnancy and Transmission of STDs

Of course, we need to be concerned with unwanted pregnancy and sexually transmitted diseases (STDs), and an important objective of sex education programs should be the development of sexual responsibility so that these problems will be reduced. But there is more to sex education than pregnancy and disease prevention. Today, most mental health professionals recognize that healthy sexual functioning is important to the well-being of individuals and of marital relationships. Most people consider a satisfying sex life to be important for their happiness.

Acquiring Accurate Information

What should be the goals of sex education? The first objective is to acquire accurate information. A good sex education program should provide students with basic facts about sexuality and clear up misconceptions. This factual presentation of information must include topics relevant to the teenagers in the courses. Too often "factual information" consists only of expositions about *vas deferens* and fallopian tubes and fails to cover the specific kinds of information important to teenagers; such as the fact that many birth control pills are ineffective when the woman is taking antibiotics or that twenty-five percent of all males experience some kind of temporary breast enlargement during pubescence.

An educator planning information to meet this objective must take into consideration the needs and desires of the specific group of adolescents who will be hearing the information and make adjustments accordingly. This point must be recognized. Teenagers vary greatly in physical and cognitive development as well as in their values, beliefs, and lifestyles. In one Grade 7 classroom the majority of the students might be sexually active, whereas in another Grade 7 classroom in another school, the majority might not engage in sexual intercourse for four or five years. Programs in sex education must reflect the specific interests and behaviours of the students involved.

Developing Self-awareness

A second objective is to develop greater self-awareness and understanding. When students acquire more information regarding sexuality, it enables them to develop greater insight into their own sexuality. This can lead to a reduction in anxieties about sexual development and help individuals better manage their sexual concerns. A female university student commented: "I feel I have learned to appreciate sex as natural and healthy behaviour and not as something dirty and not to be talked about. The course has given me a better understanding of myself in this area and has helped me to answer many of the questions I have had about sex."

Discussing Values

A third objective is to help students clarify their own values regarding sex so that they are less dependent on the standards of peers and are less likely to engage in sexual relations if they do not feel ready. This should result in more satisfactory and more informed decision making.

Most sex educators believe that it is irresponsible to separate the reproductive and physical aspects of sex from its broader context. A comprehensive sex education program provides "through coverage of the body's sexual anatomy and how it functions. It also examines the relationship of sexuality to the whole person—feelings, values, decisions—and to the society in which the person lives" (Kelly, 1992, p. 247).

The inclusion of values discussions in a sex education course is essential if students are going to use the information in their lives. Many educators think that parents will be uncomfortable with values being taught in schools. However, the experience of one of the authors (Hess) in teaching sex education showed otherwise. She found that parents supported and agreed on most values: values such as honesty, freedom, respecting others, being responsible, standing up for one's own beliefs, thoughtfully making decisions, having choices, concern for others, and family life. Bibby and Posterski's study (1992) shows that the vast majority of Canadians support these values. The Alberta Health and CALM curricula mandate teaches a similar list of values believed to be universally accepted across the province. Teachers can discuss, clarify, and indeed "teach" these values. And students can be encouraged to discuss the behaviours that reflect their values. When behaviours are discussed there is certainly more potential controversy, and teachers should be wary and certain to allow students to thoughtfully form their own beliefs.

Improving Communication Skills

A fourth objective is to improve communication skills. It is a myth that people are open in their discussions of sex. Despite the sexual revolution of the 1970s which is generally acknowledged as encouraging more freedom in the discussions about sex, most individuals remain fairly reticent in discussing their personal frustrations, concerns, and anxieties. Most of the openness is carried out in a superficial way, and sex education can provide the opportunity to discuss sex in a serious manner. However, it must be emphasized that many aspects of sex are personal and private. In promoting classroom discussion of sexual issues, it is essential that educators be aware of this and refrain from attempting to impose complete self-disclosure. Students should never feel forced to divulge matters that they believe are personal and that they do not want others to know about.

The development of open communication can only occur in a classroom setting where the teacher is a warm, accepting person who respects the opinions of the students. This point cannot be overemphasized. Communication cannot take place if students are reluctant to express their opinions because they fear being ridiculed by the teacher or other students. However, given a supportive atmosphere, students are highly enthusiastic about being able to discuss sexual topics in a serious manner. One student commented:

> I do feel more comfortable talking about sex. I think this is because now I realize I'm not the only dumb one and other people really don't know as much about it as they would like people to think they do. Also what I have learned in this course gives me more background to draw upon when discussing the topic.

Communication is important for several aspects of sexuality. A study in 1992 surveying high school students in Alberta found that some students did not use birth control when they were sexually active because they didn't know how to discuss it with their partners (Fehlauer, 1992). Communication problems about sexual issues are not limited to dating couples. Marriage counsellors report that many couples have great difficulty communicating. By developing the communication skills of our students, they will hopefully be better prepared to discuss all types of problems relating to sexuality with their long-term partners and spouses.

Increasing a Sense of Self-efficacy and Self-worth

Being more knowledgeable about sexual issues, having greater self-understanding, and being able to communicate more effectively can increase one's self-esteem. A very important objective of sex education is the fostering of positive feelings of self-worth. With greater self-confidence, teenagers may be more comfortable in saying "no" to sexual encounters or be better able to make thoughtful decisions about sexual actions. Hopefully, this will enable them to function more successfully in society.

Developing Tolerance and Understanding

Another objective of sex education is to develop tolerance for different beliefs and values. Certainly one of the goals of any educational program is to respect the opinions of others. Too often our society is divided into conflicting groups that try to impose their views on one another rather than accepting the differing views that exist. Sex education in schools is unlikely to change fundamental values regarding sexual behaviour. Students in sex education courses indicate that their basic values, behaviour and moral beliefs are not changed as a result of the course (King, Camp, & Downey, 1991). This is important to stress because of the fear some people have that talking about sex encourages students to engage in it. In actual fact, given a peer group environment that is usually supportive of premarital sex, the teacher can play an important role in providing support to the students who do not want to engage in premarital sex.

Finally, another goal of sex education should be to increase communication and closeness between parents and their children. Many students who take sex education courses indicate that it provides them with the opportunity to openly discuss sexual matters with their parents for the first time, and that this enables them to feel close to their parents.

• • •

TOPICS IN SEX EDUCATION

Two of the most controversial aspects of sex education concern teaching about choosing a sexual standard and birth control. Parents are understandably worried that a particular teacher might discuss these topics in ways that do not promote their values and beliefs. This section of the chapter focusses on the teaching of these two topics.

Choosing a Sexual Standard

Given the conflicting values about sex in our society, choosing a sexual standard is a serious and difficult matter. Yet this is a decision that every young person has to face. Ira Reiss (1967) has outlined four basic standards of sexual morality: abstinence, the double standard, permissiveness with affection, and permissiveness without affection.

1. The abstinence standard prohibits sexual intercourse before marriage for everyone.
2. The double standard prohibits sexual intercourse before marriage for women, but accepts it for men.
3. The permissiveness with affection standard permits sexual intercourse within a love relationship.
4. The permissiveness without affection standard allows for sexual intercourse outside of a love relationship.

THE ABSTINENCE CODE

Young people adhering to the abstinence code do not have to face the turmoil of going against religious and parental beliefs, since this code follows traditional religious and parental values. Sexual decision making is simplified in that one does not have to decide continually whether to engage or not to engage in sexual intercourse. Certainly one does not have to worry about pregnancy or sexually transmitted disease. The major cost of this code is that it might result in considerable sexual frustration as well as conflict if one's partner does not accept this code. If the code is transgressed, then considerable sexual guilt would result. Because of sexual repression, some people following this code may have difficulty adjusting to a sexual life later when they get married.

THE DOUBLE STANDARD

The so-called double standard is theoretically rewarding to males and exploitative of women. Obviously if the code were strictly applied, males would have a difficult time finding accessible sexual partners. Prostitutes would be about the only women available. Males accepting this code tend to categorize women into two types: sexual or bad and non-sexual or pure. This type of belief system could cause problems in a relationship when the male might have a difficult time adjusting to a sexually experienced woman whom he might perceive as being pure or non-sexual. Similarly, women might have a difficult time adjusting from being non-sexual to sexual.

THE PERMISSIVENESS WITH AFFECTION STANDARD

While allowing for sexual expression when in love, following the permissiveness with affection standard may cause problems in terms of defining when one is in love. Decision making is difficult because the person may be uncertain about whether he or she is ready to experience intercourse. Feelings of guilt can arise when the relationship with the sexual partner ends and a new relationship is started. One nineteen-year-old woman stated, "Previously I had rationalized my sexual activity through the expectation that my first sexual partner would be my only one. With a change of partners I had feelings of guilt in that this seemed like promiscuity."

THE PERMISSIVENESS WITHOUT AFFECTION CODE

Potentially offering the greatest sexual excitement and the least sexual frustration, the permissiveness without affection code often carries a penalty. One has to face the possibility of being labelled promiscuous, which might cause guilt feelings and lowered self-esteem. In addition to the possibility of unwanted pregnancy, there is also the greatly increased probability of contracting a sexually transmitted disease through casual sexual contacts.

MAKING A CHOICE

In summary, every sexual standard has its costs as well as its rewards. One of the responsibilities of sex educators should be to discuss the different sexual standards with young people and to point out the costs and benefits of each so that young people can be in a better position to make responsible decisions about their own sexual behaviour. Ultimately, the sexual standard young people choose will be affected by their own values regarding religious teachings, parental views, personal freedom, affection, and sexual pleasure.

Sex educators should be aware that many parents want them to emphasize traditional values, with the abstinence code being presented as the best one for young people. On the other hand, there is not a consensus among parents with respect to how the issue of sexual standards should be presented. When asked if an important objective of sex education should be to discourage premarital sex, only thirty-three percent of mothers in Wellington County, Ontario, agreed (Marsman, 1982). Furthermore, sixty-seven percent of the mothers agreed that sex education teachers should avoid preaching at youngsters. In a 1990 national survey, eighty percent of adult Canadians indicated that "sex before marriage is acceptable when people LOVE each other." In a comparison study in 1992, by the same researchers, eighty-seven percent of Canadian teenagers agreed with the statement (Bibby & Posterski, 1992).

Nevertheless, most people would agree that the majority, if not all, younger teenagers are not mature enough to handle the responsibilities involved in having sexual intercourse. Indeed, most recent studies suggest that about half of Canadian teenagers engage in sexual intercourse by the end of high school, either because they do not feel ready or for moral reasons (Herold, 1984). For this group, it is especially important that sex educators provide support for these values.

However, it should be emphasized again that teenagers vary considerably in their behaviour. A 1992 survey of a small rural community in Alberta found that behaviour differed greatly when the students in Grades 10, 11, and 12 were compared. Among the Grade 10 students, twenty-nine percent reported they had sexual intercourse by age fourteen, whereas only seven percent reported they were sexually active by fourteen among the students in Grade 12 (Fehlauer, 1992).

Also, educators need to stress the building of communication skills, to help these young people deal with the peer and partner pressures that might lead to early sexual involvement. This would include specific examples of how to say no to such pressure. Of course, there are other alternatives to sexual intercourse, such as petting or masturbation, and sex educators should be prepared to present these topics in a sensitive manner.

In providing guidance about sexual decision making, sex educators should encourage students to consider the following questions:

1. What is the view of your religion regarding premarital sex? Are you conforming with your religious ideals?
2. Are you taking your parents values into consideration? If your decision goes against parental values, how would you feel about acting contrary to them? How would you feel if your parents found out?
3. Will you feel guilty about your decision?
4. Are you being pressured by peers or your dating partner into sexual activity for which you are not ready?
5. Are you exploiting your partner or is your partner exploiting you?
6. Are you expecting too much from sex?
7. How important to you is having a sexual relationship and what does a sexual relationship mean to you?
8. Do you have trust in your dating partner and can you communicate honestly about your needs and concerns?
9. Are you prepared to use effective contraception?
10. If contraception should fail, how would you handle pregnancy?
11. Have you considered the possibility and consequences of contracting a sexually transmitted disease?

By encouraging students to answer the above questions honestly and thoroughly, teachers can promote thoughtful decision making among their students without pushing their own values and beliefs. Educators hope that students who have thought about and discussed their choice of sexual standard in the classroom will make better, and less impulsive, choices when confronted in more emotional and sexually arousing situations within their relationships.

Birth Control Education

Too often educators believe that birth control education consists only of a description of the different methods of birth control. This approach ignores the many other factors influencing birth control use, especially attitudes and values. What, then, should be included in the ideal birth control education program?

BASIC BIOLOGY

First, young people should know about the male and female reproductive systems, especially the menstrual cycle. Unfortunately, many adolescents have incorrect assumptions about the cycle of female fertility and attempt to use the old-fashioned rhythm method on a chance basis.

BIRTH CONTROL METHODS

Students need to know about the different methods of birth control and have a clear understanding of precisely how to use them. They should also be aware of the effectiveness rate and advantages and disadvantages of each method. However, educators must avoid presenting too much information and thereby overwhelming adolescents with factual detail. Given that there is no ideal contraceptive, young people need to be familiar with more than one method because they are likely to use several different methods throughout their lives. Attitudes about different methods should also be discussed because adolescents are unlikely to use methods that are "untried" or about which they feel uncomfortable.

Teachers and clinicians must be aware of their own biases in presenting the different methods of birth control. For example, consider how you would answer the following: Can the condom and/or foam be used effectively by adolescents? Are IUDs safe for young women to use? Do the benefits of the pill outweigh possible side effects? Educators and clinicians have differing opinions regarding these and other issues in birth control. It is essential that we be aware of these biases and how they can affect our teaching or counselling. Every method of birth control has its positive aspects and these should be stressed. The best method of birth control is one that will be used consistently by the individual.

Adolescents, especially the younger ones, often are not aware of how to obtain birth control services and of the procedures involved in obtaining them. Precise information should be provided about birth control services such as clinics, including their hours, location, and policies regarding confidentiality. This should also include detailed information about the procedures for internal examinations. Young women are particularly embarrassed about an internal pelvic examination, and it is important that teachers and clinicians carefully explain the procedures involved so that young people will be less fearful and therefore not avoid medical help out of embarrassment. Also, when physicians are conducting an internal exam, they should be aware of the awkwardness many teenagers experience and try to reduce feelings of embarrassment. When clinics provide birth control to young people they should make certain that written instructions are provided for the use of that method and include a description of side effects plus a telephone number to call in an emergency.

Too often we think we are making birth control available to teenagers by simply providing condoms for sale in pharmacies or by machines in washrooms. We only need remember the character in the movie, *The Summer of '42*, who went in the store to buy a condom and came out with sprinkles on his ice cream to understand just how intimidating it can be for teenagers to purchase birth control in public places.

TIMING OF BIRTH CONTROL INFORMATION

Birth control education should be presented at different grade levels throughout the junior high school and high school years. This would overcome the problem of forgotten information and, even more importantly, provide continual reinforcement of responsible sexuality. Too often sophisticated information about birth control is left until high school, which is too late for many of the students. The results of Fehlauer's study in Alberta in 1992, are not atypical of recent findings in many studies. Of the fifty-five percent of the students who were sexually active by the end of high school, ninety-three percent of them were active by the age of sixteen. Clearly, we can not afford to wait until high school to educate students about birth control. Furthermore, sexually active younger teenagers are less likely to use birth control than are older teenagers. Thus, it is important to begin formal birth control education programs during the early adolescent years.

EDUCATION FOR BOTH SEXES

Often educators assume that sexuality is the female's responsibility and typically female students receive more sex education than males. One study found that in Saskatchewan, eighty-three percent of females indicated that they had some sex education compared with only sixty-six percent of males. In particular, females were twice as likely as males to be taught about menstruation (Weston, 1980).

Adolescent males need to be educated about their sexual responsibilities. Here educators could work toward instilling feelings of respect toward the other person and, through values clarification exercises, support the value that it is wrong to use physical or emotional coercion to try to get one's partner to become involved sexually. A recent study by Fehlauer (1992) found that males and females reported feeling very different emotions about their first experience of sexual intercourse. Males were more likely to have felt "fulfilled," "mature," "stimulated," and "wonderful"; whereas females were more likely to have felt "worried," "anxious," "hurt," "afraid," and "guilty." A discussion of these gender differences could take place in relation to either the topic of choosing a sexual standard or birth control.

Males have an equal responsibility in birth control and should be knowledgeable about the different methods. It is sometimes more difficult to teach males than females because males are socialized to present the image of "knowing it all." Fortunately, there are audio-visual and other resource materials directed specifically at males that can help the teacher to overcome some of the difficulties involved in teaching and counselling males.

THE ROLE OF ROMANCE

It seems that many teenagers choose the double standard in many of their beliefs. Often it is acceptable among teenagers for a guy to try to convince the girl to have sex. But girls who plan ahead, and therefore have birth control available, are often considered to be "sluts" or "easy." Yet the females who spontaneously let sexual intercourse occur are considered "romantic and pure," even though they are the ones who are more likely to become pregnant. Both sexes need to understand the roles of romance and responsibility in their sexual activity.

APPLYING BIRTH CONTROL KNOWLEDGE

Educators are often asked "Why is it that so many sexually active young people know about birth control but don't use it?" The answer, of course, is that many factors influence birth control use. In order to have adequate sex education, these factors need to be addressed.

We need to make young people aware that, if they have sexual intercourse, there is a good possibility of pregnancy unless they take preventive action. Here statistics can be used to illustrate the large number of pregnancies occurring among adolescents. Also, we need to deal with local myths. Unfounded beliefs such as "I won't get pregnant if I do it only once" or "if I only have sex once in a while" or "if I do it standing up, since it's against gravity" are still popular among adolescents. In discussing perceived susceptibility we need to make young people aware of the necessity to plan ahead to use birth control. Adolescents seldom anticipate becoming sexually active and find it difficult to think rationally about birth control after they have become sexually aroused.

To increase the perceived seriousness of a pregnancy, we need to make adolescents aware of the costs of childbirth. Teenage mothers face many economic, psychological, and social problems. Also, their infants face greater health and social risks than infants born to older mothers. For those few teenagers who intentionally want to become pregnant, we need to pay attention to the emotional needs they are trying to satisfy through pregnancy. They must be shown that having a baby would more likely increase rather than decrease their emotional problems.

In any discussion of birth control, the psychological costs of using birth control need to be presented. Adolescents may be so overwhelmed by the emotional

costs of contraception at the time of intercourse that they put aside consideration of the long-term costs of a possible unwanted pregnancy. Or, sometimes,
the immediate fear of a parent finding a birth control device in one's room may
be greater than the distant fear of a possible pregnancy.

Underlying many of the costs involved in using contraception is sexual guilt.
Many young people cannot use contraception because it would make them feel
guilty about having sexual relations. We should encourage young people to
accept, as a rule, that they should never have intercourse without using contraception and, if they feel guilty, they should not be having sexual relations.

Educators can play an important role in providing a cue to action for responsible sexuality. One technique is to use a motivating film. In 1972, one of the
authors (Herold) produced the film, *It Couldn't Happen to Me*, which dealt with
the psychological costs of using contraception and made young people more
aware of the risk of pregnancy. The goal of the film was to encourage birth control use among the sexually active, while at the same time supporting the views
of those who did not want to have premarital sex. Indeed, adolescents who are
opposed to premarital sex have stated that their views have been strengthened as
a result of seeing the film.

SEX EDUCATION FOR PARENTS

Ideally sex education should not only be limited to teenagers. There should be
education for parents so that they will feel more comfortable discussing topics
such as birth control with their sons and daughters. It is easier for teenagers to
be responsible for their sexuality when their parents are able to provide positive
sex education. Programs at schools in the evenings where parents and adolescents could jointly discuss issues relating to sexuality might serve to bridge the
gap that sometimes exists between the generations.

PEER PRESSURE

Young people with high self-esteem are less likely to be pressured into having
sex when they do not want to and are more likely to use contraception if they
do engage in sexual intercourse. Teens with high self-esteem may also feel less
need to become pregnant in order to satisfy emotional needs. Thus, wherever
possible educators and counsellors should use strategies to raise the self-esteem
of adolescents.

Peer group influence could also be used to encourage responsible sexuality.
For example, Family Planning Services of the City of Toronto has sponsored the

development of a teenage drama group entitled STARR (Students Talking About Responsible Relationships). Through the use of dramatic role-playing, this theatre group presents important decision-making aspects of sexuality and birth control. By providing a role model, the actors help adolescents to feel comfortable about discussing contraception and related issues. To make the best use of techniques such as the drama group, it is essential that students have the opportunity to discuss their own feelings and reactions in a small group setting. In this way, their own peer group in the classroom can be used to reinforce the concept of responsible sexuality.

COMMUNICATION

Most young people find it difficult to communicate about sexuality and birth control. Sexually active couples who discuss contraception are more likely to use it. Therefore teachers should attempt to increase the communication skills of their students. Communication exercises designed to improve the sending, receiving, and interpretation of verbal and non-verbal messages should be incorporated into all sex education programs. We also need to develop contraceptive assertiveness so that a young person can tell the partner that intercourse definitely would not occur unless he or she were using effective contraception.

• • •

RECOMMENDATIONS TO IMPROVE SEX EDUCATION INSTRUCTION

In order to teach a comprehensive sex education program on such topics as choice of sexual standard, birth control, and other sensitive issues teachers need some extra help. The last section of this chapter discusses three needs that must be addressed in order to provide adequate sex education to Canadian youth: (1) the need for specific education of teachers, (2) the need for resources, and (3) the need for more research to determine if students have learned the information provided and are applying it in their lives.

The Need for Adequate Teacher Preparation
Sex education is one of the most difficult subjects to teach because there are so many conflicting attitudes and emotions surrounding the topic. Unfortunately, some administrators assume that any teacher, simply by being a man or woman,

is automatically qualified to teach sex education. The importance of adequate preparation for teachers of sex education is absolutely essential. A particular concern of one of the authors (Herold) is that inadequately prepared teachers are less able to distinguish between value statements and statements of fact and will often state value assertions that may not have factual validity. For example, there are still many people who believe that sexual behaviour rates among young people have not significantly changed over the past twenty years. There are others who believe that women do not enjoy sex and only do it to please males. The following student comments also illustrate the consequences of inadequate teacher preparation:

> While I was in Grade 5, the boys were sent to shovel snow off the outdoor rink and the girls were kept indoors to observe a film on menstruation. It was terribly confusing even when all the facts were laid down in front of me. I felt as though there was something wrong because the boys were not allowed to observe the movie. This increased my negative feelings about the topic of sexuality.
>
> Every year the school did its duty and showed "from girl to woman" and "boy to man" films. No teacher ever asked us what we thought of these films or if we had any questions. At the time, I remember that viewing these films was rather a stressful experience, particularly while we all waited for the film to roll. As I look back on this now I realize that our teachers were uncomfortable too, and that this may have been transmitted to us.

The other author (Hess) has also witnessed the correlation between teacher interest and preparation and student interest and knowledge. When teachers who have an interest in teaching sex education are given adequate preparation, support, and resources they are much better equipped to spur the interest of students. When students are motivated with a relevant and personal curriculum they are much more likely to retain the information and use it in their daily lives. In Alberta, where sex education is required by the provincial Department of Education, too many teachers without adequate preparation are required to teach the courses. When principals dictate that every teacher in a particular junior high has to teach Health, too often students spend the sixty minutes a week completing outdated worksheets.

There can be no doubt that a major problem in sex education all across Canada is the lack of adequately prepared teachers. Fortunately, many teachers

recognize this deficiency and are attending courses and workshops in sex education such as the University of Guelph's conference on human sexuality, that
brings together more than seven hundred teachers and clinicians from across
Canada each year in June. Many school boards offer in-service training for interested teachers. However, the preparation is often sporadic and insufficient in
both depth and breadth.

The Need for Resources

A related problem is the lack of adequate resource facilities. Very few school
boards have a full-time specialist in sex education. Because of this, the responsibility for developing curriculum on sex education or of providing guidance to
teachers is given to a consultant who is often busy with other responsibilities and
does not have the time to deal adequately with the sex education program. If
teachers are provided with comprehensive and current resources, even those who
are asked to teach sex education in addition to several other course preparations
may be able to provide much better programs. One of the strongest recommendations we can make for improving sex education programs is that funds and
personnel be made available at the provincial level as well as at local school board
levels for the development, implementation, and evaluation of such programs.

The Need for Research and Evaluation

Most surveys conducted in the 1980s designed to measure students' knowledge
about sexuality or contraception have found considerable gaps in their knowledge. A 1982 study found that North American children were the least well
informed about sexual concepts in a study of British, Swedish, and Australian
children aged five to fifteen (Wade & Cirese, 1991). A 1983 Canadian survey of
school children showed only thirty-five percent of Grade 7 students knew that
it was possible for a girl to get pregnant between the ages of twelve and fifteen.
Most thought pregnancy could not happen until after age sixteen. Only twenty-
two percent of Grade 10 students knew that usually there are no early symptoms of gonorrhea in females. Only forty-six percent knew that mothers who
smoke are more likely to have premature babies than those who do not smoke
(King & Robertson, 1983). A third study of high school students found that
despite the fact that sixty percent said they had sex education, the average score
on a fifty item test of sexual and contraceptive knowledge was less than half
(Wade & Cirese, 1991).

Even though the results of these studies are very distressing, there is some evidence, however meager, that the situation may be improving. If we can believe self-assessment, Bibby and Posterski reported in 1992, that nine out of ten Canadian teenagers maintain that they are "fairly knowledgeable" about birth control. Fehlauer's 1992 Alberta survey found that seventy percent of students used birth control during their initial experience of sexual intercourse, a far greater number than was expected after reviewing studies from the 1980s. Of those who used birth control, forty-seven percent used condoms. The students' self-reports may indeed be accurate. Statistics Canada data for the period 1975 to 1989 indicate that teenage pregnancies declined during those years from 53.4 per 1000 teenage girls to 44.1 (Bibby & Posterki, 1992).

Recent research surveys about the effect of AIDS on sexual behaviour are also somewhat encouraging. Among older adolescents one study found that although the AIDS scare has not influenced the frequency of sexual activity or the number of partners, it may have been responsible for the sharp rise in the use of condoms (Sebald, 1992). Canadian teens reported that eighty percent regard AIDS as "very serious," although the effect it has had on their behaviour is less clear (Bibby & Posterski, 1992).

A great deal more research needs to be done to determine the effects of sex education programs and to study the understanding teens have about sexuality and contraception. However, as Ginzberg (1988) believed, "The search for effective interventions is seriously compromised by the scarcity of knowledge about the determinants of individual adolescent behaviour." We fail to understand such common behaviours such as "why teens invent, then cling to, irrational or absurd beliefs concerning pregnancy; especially the near-universal fable 'it can never happen to me'" (Mitchell, 1992, p. 193). What past research has demonstrated is that sexuality is not the simple matter it was once thought to be, but rather is a highly complex area of life that is influenced by numerous factors. We need to understand all aspects of this complex set of behaviours and attitudes in order to plan better sex education programs.

• • •

PROSPECTS

What are the prospects for sex education? We personally believe that, despite some controversies, sex education programs in Canada will continue to develop and grow. We are optimistic because our children need and want the information and because most parents approve of sex education. Granted, there will be some difficulties. Nevertheless, parents in the 1990s are more willing to educate their children about sexual matters than parents of previous generations. As parents become more comfortable about providing sex education for their children, they will further increase their support of sex education programs in the schools. In time a comprehensive program of sexual education may be available to all Canadian youth.

• • •

NOTE

1. Portions of this article were originally published in E.S. Herold, *Sexual Behaviour of Canadian Young People* (Markham, ON: Fitzhenry and Whiteside, 1984). Permission to reprint these portions has been granted by Fitzhenry and Whiteside. The quotes by students are taken from various research studies conducted by Herold with Ontario university students.

• • •

REFERENCES

Bibby, R.W., & Posterski, D.C. (1992). *Teen trends: A nation in motion.* Toronto: Stoddart.

Fehlauer, E.E. (1992). *Attitudes, influences and expectations of adolescent dating behaviours: A survey of high school students.* Unpublished master's thesis, Department of Educational Psychology, University of Alberta.

Frappier, J. (1983). *Evaluation of a sex education program in high school.* Unpublished manuscript, University of Montreal.

Ginzberg, E., Berliner, H.S., & Ostrow, M. (1988). *Young people at risk: Is prevention possible?* London: Westview Press.

Herold, E.S. (1972). *It could happen to me.* [Film]. Magic Lantern Films.

Herold, E.S. (1984). *Sexual behaviour of Canadian young people.* Markham, ON: Fitzhenry and Whiteside.

Herold, E.S., Kopf, K.E., & de Carlo, M. (1974). Family life education: Student perspectives. *Canadian Journal of Public Health,* 65.

Kelly, G.M. (1992). *Sexuality today: The human perspective* (3rd ed.). Guildford, CN: Dushkin.

King, A., & Robertson, R. (1983). *Canadian health knowledge survey for ages 9, 12, and 15.* Kingston, ON: Queen's University.

King, B.M., Camp, C.J., & Downey, A.M. (1991). *Human sexuality today.* Englewood Cliffs, NJ: Prentice-Hall.

Livingstone, T., & Hart, L. (1979). *Survey of attitudes to Ontario schools.* Toronto: Ontario Institute for Studies in Education.

Macleod, M. A. (1980). *Opinion survey of the family planning and sex education needs in Prince Edward Island.* P.E.I. Department of Health.

Marsman, J. (1982). *Mother-child communication about sex.* Master's thesis, University of Guelph.

Meikle, S., Peitchinis, J.A., & Pearce, K. (1985). *Teenage sexuality.* San Diego: College-Hill.

Mitchell, J. (1992). *Adolescent struggle for self-hood and identity*. Calgary: Detselig.

Nolte, J. (1984). Sex education in Canadian classrooms. *Tellus, 5*(3), 13–16.

Orton, M.J., & Rosenblatt, E. (1980). *Adolescent birth planning needs: Ontario in the eighties*. Toronto: Planned Parenthood.

Reiss, I. (1967). *The social context of sexual permissiveness*. New York: Holt, Rinehart and Winston.

Sebald, H. (1992). *Adolescence: A social psychological analysis* (4th ed.). Englewood Cliffs, NJ: Prentice-Hall.

Sprinthall, N.A., & Collins, W.A. (1988). *Psychology: A developmental view* (2nd ed.). New York: Random House.

Wade, C., & Cirese, S. (1991). *Human sexuality* (2nd ed.). San Diego: Harcourt Brace Jovanovich.

Weston, M. (1980). *Youth health and lifestyle*. Report of work in progress submitted to Saskatchewan Health.

Zelnick, M., & Kim, Y. (1982). Sex education and its association with teenage sexual activity, pregnancy, and contraceptive use. *Family Planning Perspectives, 14*, 3.

Issues in Substance Abuse for Canadian Teachers

...

Louis A. Pagliaro

he use of substances of abuse is such a commonplace occurrence in Canadian society that it has come to be generally accepted as part of the normal phenomenon of human existence. Indeed, a party or celebration at which one or more substances of abuse are not being used would likely be considered an exception to adult social norms. Thus, it comes as no surprise that the Government of Canada has stated that "there is no doubt that there is a very real and substantial problem of alcohol and drug abuse in this country" (*A drug problem in Canada?*, 1988) and that "the widespread availability and use of drugs means that, whether we like it or not, all Canadians will probably come into some contact with the drug problem in one way or another" (*Straight facts*, 1985).

If there were few or no negative consequences associated with substance abuse, teachers, as well as psychologists and other health care providers, would find little professional interest in this topic. However, in Canada today, approximately one in four deaths is related to drug or substance abuse; ten to fifteen percent of the population are alcoholics; and the fetal alcohol syndrome is the most common preventable cause of mental retardation among Canadian children (Pagliaro, 1991). Substance abuse can, and does, affect all Canadians regardless of age, race, cultural or ethnic background, education, or socio-economic status.

The damage caused by substance abuse includes not only physical harm that is generally related to personal health (e.g., premature mortality), but also psychological and sociological harm that typically affect both the substance abuser

---

Classification Scheme for the Major Substances of Abuse*

Central Nervous System Depressants

Opiates (e.g., Codeine, Heroin, Meperidine, Morphine, Pentazocine)

Sedative-Hypnotics (Alcohol, Barbiturates, Benzodiazepines, Miscellaneous)

Volatile Solvents (e.g., Gasoline; Glue)

Central Nervous System Stimulants

Amphetamines

Caffeine

Cocaine

Nicotine (Tobacco)

Psychedelics

Lysergic Acid Diethylamide (LSD)

Mescaline (Peyote)

Phencyclidine (PCP)

Psilocybin (hallucinogenic mushrooms)

Tetrahydrocannabinol (THC) (Marijuana, Hashish, Hashish Oil)

* (Pagliaro, 1990; Pagliaro & Pagliaro, 1992a)

---

and those with whom he or she comes into contact with such as family members or victims of a drug related crime (Bland & Orn, 1986; Boyle & Offord, 1991; Boyle, et al., 1992; Hoberman & Garfinkel, 1988; Whyte, et al., 1987). For example, substance abuse has been associated with up to: seventy percent of criminal assaults; fifty percent of spousal abuse; seventy percent of child sexual abuse; fifty percent of traffic fatalities; seventy percent of drownings; forty percent of suicides; fifty percent of rapes; seventy percent of robberies; and eighty percent of murders (Pagliaro, 1991). Youth are the most frequent victims of substance abuse related violence and, perhaps not surprisingly, one of the three leading causes of death among adolescents is substance abuse related accidents. In addition to these serious sequelae, and of particular concern to educators, are the lesser known negative effects of substance abuse upon learning and memory.

This chapter will further explore the nature and extent of substance abuse among Canadian youth and the resultant implications for society in general and for the educational system in particular.

• • •

SUBSTANCE USE BY CANADIAN YOUTH

Figure 1 (Pagliaro, 1989) lists the five most frequently used substances of abuse in Canada and illustrates the percentage of the Canadian population who use or abuse these substances. A brief discussion of each of these five major substances of abuse follows.

FIGURE I

Drug Use in Canada (all age groups)

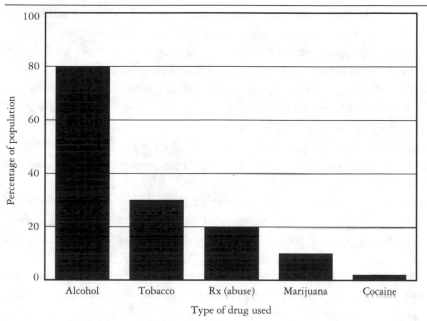

Alcohol

On average, approximately eighty percent of Canadians consume alcoholic beverages including beer, wine, and distilled spirits. Although the legal drinking age across most of Canada is nineteen years (eighteen years of age in Alberta, Manitoba, Prince Edward Island, and Quebec), over half the teenagers in Canada have consumed alcoholic beverages during the previous twelve month period. By the time these teenagers become seniors in high school, the percentage who consume alcoholic beverages is approximately equal to the adult percentage (*Alcohol in Canada*, 1989).

The major factors contributing to the high rate of teenagers who consume alcoholic beverages include: a desire to be more "adult-like"; peer pressure; risk taking behaviour; pharmacopsychologic effect of alcohol of decreasing social inhibitions, particularly in relation to sexual activity; ready availability of alcoholic beverages; and societal attitudes (i.e., alcohol is legal for adults and is a major part of many social gatherings and media advertisements).

The morbidity and mortality associated with alcohol use in Canada is significant. As noted previously, ten to fifteen percent of the population are alcoholics and the fetal alcohol syndrome is the most common preventable cause of mental retardation in Canada (Pagliaro, 1991). Some Canadians, however, appear to be at higher risk of developing problems of alcohol related morbidity and mortality. Educators should be aware of this fact in order that they might more readily recognize these problems and intervene appropriately. For example, fetal alcohol syndrome is more prevalent among Canadian native children than non-native children (Bray & Anderson, 1989). In fact, all alcohol-related problems appear to be significantly more prevalent among native peoples than other groups of Canadians (*Alcohol in Canada*, 1989).

Alcohol use has been implicated in over half of all fatal motor vehicle (including snowmobile) deaths for which youth are disproportionately over-represented (*Alcohol in Canada*, 1989; Rowe, et al., 1992). Surveys conducted at various locations across Canada tend to indicate that over thirty percent of Canadian youth in Grades 7 to 12 have experienced significant alcohol related problems including: aggressive behaviour; drinking before breakfast; blackouts; and weekend drinking sprees (Dunne & Schipperheijn, 1989; Faulkner & Slattery, 1990; Pagliaro, 1989) and this pattern appears to follow these youth into their college years (Kteily-Hawa, et al., 1990). Indeed, for those who have attended college or university and who later are identified as having substance abuse problems, the overwhelming majority can trace these problems back to their college or university years (Pagliaro, 1989). In addition, approximately ten percent of health care budgets, both provincially and nationally, are spent on alcohol related disease (e.g., heart disease, cancer, cirrhosis) and related sequelae (e.g., accidents, depression, suicide) and one in every ten deaths in Canada is related to alcohol use (Pagliaro, 1989).

Tobacco

Overall, approximately thirty-three percent of Canadians smoke tobacco, although this percentage is significantly higher (approximately forty percent) among French speaking Canadians. Tobacco, like alcohol, is a legal substance in Canada and is a major agricultural crop in Ontario where approximately

60 million kilograms of tobacco are produced annually ("Tobacco Road," 1991). The per capita consumption of tobacco declined steadily over the past two decades in light of increasing public warnings concerning the health risks associated with both primary and secondary (i.e., second-hand or side-stream) smoke, but has now appeared to have stabilized at approximately 1800 cigarettes annually per person fifteen years of age and older (Canadian tobacco consumption, 1992). In an effort to regain a larger portion of the domestic market, Canadian tobacco companies have increasingly focussed and directed advertisements toward youth.

Over half of Canadian school-aged youth have smoked tobacco at least once and the percentage of regular users increases, expectedly, with increasing age until the percentage observed in adults is reached during high school. An interesting demographic change in smoking behaviour among Canadian youth over the past decade has been the decrease in smoking among boys and a corresponding increase in smoking among girls (Boyle & Offord, 1986; Millar & Van Rensburg, 1983). The over fifty percent of both Native and Asian-immigrant youth who smoke tobacco remains significantly higher than the percentage observed in the general population (Millar & Van Rensburg, 1983).

Morbidity and mortality associated with tobacco smoke is significant and contributes to up to seventeen percent of all deaths in Canada. The majority of these deaths are related to lung cancer and various forms of chronic obstructive pulmonary disease (i.e., asthma, emphysema) that are observed both in people who smoke tobacco and in those who have been chronically exposed to side-stream (second-hand) tobacco smoke, either in the home or work environment.

Prescription drugs

Note that for this category of substances we are concerned with *abuse* only, not *use*, as in the other categories. For the purpose of this discussion, the prescription drugs included in this category have been limited to the abusable central nervous system stimulants (e.g., dextroamphetamine) and central nervous system depressants, for example diazepam (Valium), pentazocine (Talwin), and secobarbital (Seconal). Nationally, approximately twenty percent of Canadians abuse these substances. "Tranquilizers and sedatives rank second on the list of abused substances. Canadians are among the world's largest per capita users of licit [legal] psychoactive drugs" (*A drug problem in Canada?*, 1988). Demographically, the most frequent abusers are found among women and the elderly (*Licit and illicit*, 1989; Pagliaro & Pagliaro, 1992a).

Prescription drug abuse is one of the few categories in which percentage use or abuse among youth does not meet or exceed that noted in the general adult Canadian population. Approximately ten percent of Canadian youth abuse prescription drugs and these are roughly equally divided between abuse of the central nervous system stimulants and the central nervous system depressants.

Cannabis

Cannabis, in at least one of its forms (i.e., marijuana [plant form], hashish [resin form], hashish oil [extracted oil form]), is used by approximately ten percent of Canadians. "The most frequently used illicit drug is cannabis . . . Nine-and-a-half percent of Ontario residents reported using cannabis at least once a month in 1987" (*A drug problem in Canada?*, 1988). Use of cannabis by youth is, as one probably expects, significantly higher than that found among the general Canadian population. Although use varies from province to province and study to study, it is generally estimated that approximately twenty percent of Canadian teenagers have used marijuana within the previous year and ten percent within the previous month. Provincially, use is generally reported as being lowest among youth in Quebec (Deschesnes, 1992) and highest among youth in British Columbia.

Contrary to old, but well-ingrained erroneous beliefs, cannabis does not cause permanent brain injury or damage (as portrayed, for example, in the cult classic movie, "Reefer Madness"). However, four well-defined related toxicities have been identified and are particularly significant for youth. These include: respiratory disease; decreased ability to operate a motor vehicle; amotivational syndrome; and learning impairment.

RESPIRATORY DISEASE

A number of studies have documented the irritation (e.g., coughing, dry mouth, sore throat) that cannabis smoke causes to the respiratory tract and the negative effects that it has on pulmonary function including causing and exacerbating asthma, bronchitis, and emphysema (Kalant, et al., 1983). The severity of the respiratory disease appears to be clearly related to the smoking techniques employed by the cannabis smoker (i.e., inhaling deeply and holding the smoke in for several seconds). For this reason too, many researchers have noted the risk of cannabis smoke in relation to lung cancer and have also noted that overall, in terms of respiratory toxicity, smoking one marijuana "joint" is roughly equivalent to smoking a package of twenty tobacco cigarettes (Pagliaro, 1983; Pagliaro, 1988).

DECREASED ABILITY TO
OPERATE A MOTOR VEHICLE

The acute use of even moderate doses of cannabis produces a state of intoxication that is associated with a dose-related impairment in the ability to drive a motor vehicle or to operate other complex and hazardous machinery (Pagliaro, 1983; Pagliaro, 1988). This impairment is primarily related to the following effects of tetrahydrocannabinol (THC), the principle active abusable ingredient in cannabis: time-space distortion; impaired visual accommodation; decreased reflexes; and impaired short-term memory (*Licit and illicit*, 1989); which can be significantly exacerbated by concurrent alcohol consumption.

AMOTIVATIONAL SYNDROME

This psychological syndrome was originally associated with chronic barbiturate abuse in the 1950s, but since the 1970s it has been predominantly associated with chronic cannabis use, particularly by pre-adolescents (youth under twelve years of age) (Pagliaro, 1983; Schwartz, 1987). Typically, these youth lack the normal motivation and drive observed in other youth of their same age and background (excluding chronic cannabis users). They generally spend an inordinate amount of time alone, "stoned," listening to music, or watching television. These youth are often referred to by their peers as being "burned" or "burned out." Since they use cannabis to cope with the various problems that they have encountered in their lives, these youth have not developed the normal coping skills necessary to progress psychologically from childhood to adulthood (Pagliaro, 1983; Pagliaro 1988).

LEARNING IMPAIRMENT

Cannabis use significantly impairs short-term memory and hence the ability to learn (McConnell, 1988). This topic will be discussed in greater detail in a subsequent section of this chapter.

Cocaine

Cocaine has been used by approximately one to two percent of Canadians, however, this percentage is expected to increase significantly by the end of this decade (Pagliaro, 1992b). Currently, approximately five percent of Canadian youth have used cocaine. An increasing trend is for youth to administer cocaine by injection with the resultant risk of transmission of the human immunodeficiency virus (HIV) and subsequent development of the acquired immune deficiency syndrome (AIDS) (Pagliaro, et al., 1993). This change in pattern of use comes at a time when the transmission of HIV is increasing among intravenous drug users in Canada and poses one of the greatest risks of transmission among heterosexuals.

Cocaine use by women appears to be increasing at a faster rate than cocaine use by men (*Licit and illicit*, 1989) and is commonly associated with "exchanging" sexual favours for cocaine. Cocaine use by adolescents has also been associated with prostitution, particularly by girls but also by boys, in order to support the cost of cocaine use (Pagliaro, et al., 1993).

A NOTE ABOUT STATISTICS

It should be noted that the statistics presented concerning substance use among youth have referred to the entire population of youth in Canada. Regional differences (Smart, et al., 1991) and yearly fluctuations are to be expected. However, within this population there are subpopulations in which usage statistics are significantly higher than those reported, such as incarcerated youth (Miller, et al., 1989), Native youth (Lalinec-Michaud, et al., 1991), non-English/French speaking immigrant youth, and street youth (Smart & Adlaf, 1991). For example, a study of street youth in Toronto indicated that over ninety percent used both alcohol and illicit drugs (Smart & Adlaf, 1991; Warren, 1991). Although some studies or reports may indicate, sometimes for political reasons, that substance use within a particular youth group or within a particular geographical region within Canada has decreased from years past, no one can refute the fact that serious substance abuse causing harm to self or others is currently at an all time high.

Other substances such as solvents, inhalants, and psychedelics are also used by Canadian youth. For additional detailed information on the use of these substances and the specific substances discussed in this chapter, the reader is referred to the textbook by Pagliaro and Pagliaro (in press–c).

• • •

SUBSTANCE ABUSE AND LEARNING

Developmental Effects

Many different drugs can affect the physical prenatal development of the human central nervous system (CNS) and can, hence, subsequently affect learning. The greatest risk for these types of teratogenic substance effects is associated with maternal substance use during the first trimester of pregnancy (the first twelve weeks post fertilization). After this time period, the mother's substance use would have to be associated with direct neurotoxicity or physical trauma (e.g., a fall related to alcohol induced dizziness, syncope, or CNS depression) or anoxia (e.g., profound respiratory depression related to an opiate narcotic overdose) to cause CNS damage. It is currently estimated that over ten percent of all newborns in Canada have been exposed to substances of abuse while *in utero*. The two substances of abuse that appear to be both the most problematic in this regard and the most frequently consumed by pregnant women in Canada are alcohol and cocaine (Pagliaro, 1992a).

Alcohol use during pregnancy is associated with the development of the fetal alcohol syndrome with its characteristic physical and mental abnormalities, including varying degrees of mental retardation and a high incidence of attention deficit disorder with or without hyperactivity (Nanson & Hiscock, 1990). Specific cognitive processing related learning deficits have been clearly associated with the fetal alcohol syndrome. Those deficits that have been observed in school-aged children include deficits for sequential processing (short-term memory and encoding) (Coles, et al., 1991a; Pagliaro & Pagliaro, in press–a). Several researchers (e.g., Fried & Watkinson, 1988) have suggested that even light or moderate levels of alcohol exposure prenatally (i.e., less than that necessary to clearly be identified with the fetal alcohol syndrome) may significantly lower intelligence scores and hence affect subsequent learning.

Cocaine use during pregnancy increased steadily and dramatically during the 1980s, so that today, excluding alcohol, cocaine is the primary substance of compulsive use among pregnant women. When available, cocaine is generally consumed in the smokeable "crack" form. The consequences of maternal cocaine use during pregnancy, which resemble those noted with alcohol use in terms of subsequent learning disorders for the developing fetus, include mental retardation and attention deficit disorder (Elliott & Coker, 1991). However, with cocaine use, the associated attention deficit disorder is generally accompanied by hyperactivity (Pagliaro & Pagliaro, in press–a).

Intoxication

Intoxication by virtually any substance of abuse has the propensity to have significant negative effects upon learning. It is, therefore, not unusual for educators, after observing the behaviour of a youth, to label the behaviour a learning handicap (e.g., attention deficit hyperactivity disorder, behavioural disorder, learning disability, mental impairment) when in fact the youth actually suffers from a substance abuse disorder (Fox & Forbing, 1991).

Substance abuse can affect learning primarily by means of effects upon motivation, perception, attention, cognitive processing, and memory. As previously noted, use of both barbiturates and the cannabis preparations can result in an amotivational syndrome. The central nervous system stimulants (e.g., amphetamines, cocaine) and the psychedelics (e.g., LSD, mescaline, THC) can alter perception and decrease attention. The use of the central nervous system depressants for example, alcohol, benzodiazepines (e.g., Halcion, Valium), or opiates (Demerol, Talwin) can negatively affect cognitive processing and memory.

• • •

SUBSTANCE USE AND AIDS

Teachers in Canadian classrooms are increasingly being faced with and asked a number of difficult practical and policy questions in relation to HIV infection and AIDS. For example, at the elementary school level, "If a young child falls in the school playground and scrapes his or her knee so that it bleeds, does the teacher need to put on protective gloves before tending to the child's injury?" At the secondary school level, the question may involve policy, for example, "Should condom machines be placed in the student washrooms in junior and senior high schools?" The answer to these questions is not always simple and clear-cut. However, knowledge regarding HIV infection and AIDS will assist the teacher in making properly informed decisions regarding these and related issues.

The spread of HIV and AIDS poses an unprecedented threat to youth in Canada. This threat is to school-aged youth and, increasingly, to children born to teenage HIV infected mothers. Youth are reaching sexual maturation at a time of heightened sexual freedoms during which many types of difficulties abound, including a significant number of serious social (e.g., family dysfunction, homelessness), physical (e.g., physical and sexual abuse), psychological (e.g., emotional abuse), and economic (e.g., unemployment) problems. In addition, serious substance abuse among youth is at an all time high and is expected to remain so throughout the remainder of this decade largely in response to the problems just noted.

Substance use contributes to HIV infection and AIDS among youth in several different manners. Firstly substance use, particularly alcohol use and cocaine use, have commonly been associated with increased and more promiscuous sexual behaviour. This is a result, in the case of alcohol use, predominantly of decreasing social inhibitions and, in the case of cocaine use, of increasing sexual prostitution to "pay" for the cocaine use. In either case, the increase in sexual intercourse results in an increased risk of HIV infection. In addition, youth who are under the influence of substances of abuse are less likely to engage in safer sexual practices (e.g., use of condoms), thus further increasing the risk of HIV infection.

Currently, in Canada, intravenous drug users represent the fastest increasing AIDS population and are the primary source of transmission of the HIV infection to: women, by shared contaminated needles and syringes and unprotected sexual contact with infected intravenous drug users; heterosexuals, by unprotected sexual contact; and neonates, by *in utero* transmission or infection during delivery or breast feeding. In addition, infants and children may also be infected as a result of sexual abuse (Pagliaro, et al., 1993). Although intravenous substance use in Canada has been reported in children as young as eight years of age, the average age of starting intravenous drug use is approximately sixteen years of age (Pagliaro, et al., 1992). Thus, youth are at risk of contracting the HIV if they share needles or if they have sexual intercourse with another youth who shares needles. This is of particular concern in a population of youth who often engage in high risk behaviours without an appropriate perception of the degree of risk involved (Feldman, et al., 1986; Jonah & Dawson, 1987; Pagliaro, et al., 1993).

• • •

SUBSTANCE ABUSE EDUCATION PROGRAMS

Substance abuse education programs in schools have typically failed in their goal to reduce students' substance use by means of educating them to the dangers of use. There are two major reasons for this failure: poor preparation of teachers in terms of the topic of substance abuse; and lack of good correlation between knowledge regarding substance abuse and the behaviour of abuse.

Teacher Preparation

Traditionally, teachers have been ill prepared to teach the special topic of substance abuse, a topic that is often filled with emotional, moral, legal, and historical biases. This situation becomes particularly problematic when the teacher makes a statement such as "using LSD causes birth defects" or "marijuana use kills brain cells" that the students empirically know is incorrect. Students have been exposed, both literally and figuratively, to substances of abuse all of their lives. They have used substances; they have observed their parents, friends, and peers use substances; they have heard about substance use on news programs and television specials; they have been exposed to extensive alcohol and tobacco advertising intended to promote substance use; they have been exposed to media campaigns that discourage substance use (e.g., the "just say 'no'" advertisements and posters); and they have seen substance use represented in the popular entertainment media though rap songs and movies.

A better way to approach the issue of substance abuse education is to have "experts" with varying opinions and backgrounds come to schools and present various aspects of the topic of substance abuse to students as a basis for teacher-led discussion groups. These experts can include a reformed alcoholic from Alcoholics Anonymous, a member of the local RCMP narcotics unit, or a counsellor from the provincial alcohol and substance abuse commission/foundation. The "Values, Influences, and Peers" program of the Windsor Western Hospital Centre (Foster, 1988) is an example of the many types of educational approaches that have been implemented in various parts of the country with reported good success. The use of student peer support and discussion groups, such as those developed by the Alberta Alcohol and Drug Abuse Commission (Davis, 1987), can be used to augment and complement the use of experts from the community.

Knowledge and Substance Use

Typically, substance abuse educational programs have been predicated upon a knowledge-attitude-behaviour model that assumes a significant relationship among knowledge, attitudes, and behaviour. However, this model is a simplistic device that has not yielded fruitful results. Generally, in terms of substance use, the correlation between knowledge and behaviour is not very high. Thus, drug education courses that focus solely, or even primarily, on knowledge may succeed in making the students better informed, but may have no effect, or even a negative effect (e.g., experimentation with substances of abuse may increase), in terms of reducing substance use. Youth, in particular, are commonly identified as society's risk takers (Tonkin, 1987). Therefore, in their minds, sometimes the more risky an action is the more desirable it becomes. An educational program that details the risk associated with certain forms of substance use might actually inadvertently contribute to promoting the very behaviour it was trying to prevent.

Substance use is a complex phenomenon (see figure 2) and, as just noted, is not dependent solely, or even primarily, upon knowledge or lack thereof (Pagliaro & Pagliaro, in press–b). Figure 2 represents the substance abuse milieu and indicates that the outcome for an individual youth in terms of substance abuse (i.e., the unit coterie) is dependent upon the product of the interaction of

FIGURE 2

Mega Interactive Model of Substance Abuse Among Youth (MIMSAY)

Young Person Dimension

Physical Variables
age
gender
general health status (e.g.,
    robust vs frail)
genetic predisposition (e.g.,
    positive family history of
    substance abuse)[1]
physical impairment or
    handicap
race

Psychological Variables
aggressiveness
anxiety
attitudes
boredom
cognitive function
depression[1]
developmental level
fears and phobias
general mental health
impulse control
intelligence
loneliness
major life events or
    lifestyle changes (e.g.,
    failing grades at school)
personality disorders (e.g.,
    antisocial personality)[1]
physical abuse
psychological adjustment
risk taking behaviour[1]
self-esteem
sexual abuse[1]
stress
treatment experiences

Social Variables
culture
death of parent(s)
delinquency
divorce of parents
dysfunctional family
economic status (e.g., poverty)[1]
education
morals
ethnic background
gang membership[1]
homelessness
parental attitudes towards
    substance abuse
peer pressure[1]
religion
sexual orientation/preference
social competence
social stability
social support (e.g., family, school,
    and other social networks)

Time Dimension

Time Variables
historical period (e.g., 1960s vs 1990s)
length of time of substance use period
of user's life (e.g., school age
vs adolescence)

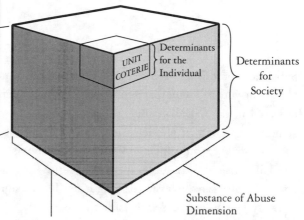

Societal Dimension

Societal Variables
attitudes toward pertinent factors
    (e.g., ageism, sexism, substance
    use and abuse)
cultures[1]
community structure
economy (e.g., availability of jobs)
educational systems
ethics
health care system
"Law of the Land" (e.g.,
    legal age for purchase
    of alcohol or tobacco)
media (e.g., movies,
    rock videos, rap songs)
religions
school system
social controls
social mores[1]
social programs
treatment availability (e.g., access, cost)
youth correctional/detention facilities

Substance of Abuse Dimension

Substance Variables
abuse liability
addiction potential
availability[1]
cost
amount used
    (e.g., individual dose,
    frequency)
interactions
legal status
pharmacokinetics
pharmacology[1]
toxicology

Pattern of Use Variables
non use
initial use
social use
habitual use
abuse
compulsive use

[1] Indicates factors that have been associated with the highest
incidence of substance abuse among youth.

four variable dimensions: 1. Young Person Dimension; 2. Societal Dimension; 3. Substance of Abuse Dimension; and 4. Time Dimension. As noted in figure 2, psychological variables, such as self-esteem; social variables, such as peer pressure; societal variables, such as rock videos; and substance variables, such as availability, all play important roles in mediating substance use among youth. This is another important reason to have experts and student peers talk to students about more than just the "facts."

$$\cdots$$

SUMMARY AND CONCLUSION

Substance abuse is an extensive and well-ingrained problem behaviour among Canadian youth. Usage patterns tend to follow, perhaps as expected, those observed in the Canadian adult population. The most commonly abused substances are those that are: legal (e.g., alcohol and tobacco); perceived to cause little harm (e.g., cannabis); and fashionable among youth peers (e.g., cocaine and LSD). Use of these substances would cause little concern for parents, teachers, and health care professionals were it not for the significant amounts of physical, psychological, and social harm that is clearly related to their use. A new additional danger associated with substance use by youth is that of HIV infection and AIDS. Traditional educational programs, which have been developed and implemented to deal with the issue of substance abuse among youth, have largely failed because of their restrictive focus. More effective educational models utilizing outside experts and student peers are suggested.

$$\cdots$$

REFERENCES

A drug problem in Canada? (1988). Ottawa: Minister of Supply and Services Canada (Cat. H39-127/1988).

Alcohol in Canada. (1989). Ottawa: Minister of Supply and Services Canada (Cat. H39-158/1989E).

Bland, R., & Orn, H. (1986). Family violence and psychiatric disorder. *Canadian Journal of Psychiatry, 31*, 129–137.

Boyle, M. H., & Offord, D. R. (1986). Smoking, drinking and use of illicit drugs among adolescents in Ontario: Prevalence, patterns of use and sociodemographic cor-

relates. *Canadian Medical Association Journal, 135*, 1113–1121.

Boyle, M. H., & Offord, D. R. (1991). Psychiatric disorder and substance use in adolescence. *Canadian Journal of Psychiatry, 36*, 699–705.

Boyle, M. H., Offord, D. R., Racine, Y. A., Szatmari, P., Fleming, J. E., & Links, P. S. (1992). Predicting substance use in late adolescence: Results from the Ontario child health study follow-up. *American Journal of Psychiatry, 149*, 761–767.

Bray, D. L., & Anderson, P. D. (1989).

Appraisal of the epidemiology of fetal alcohol syndrome among Canadian native peoples. *Canadian Journal of Public Health, 80,* 42–45.

Canadian tobacco consumption declining but doctor warns against complacency. (1992). *Canadian Medical Association Journal, 146,* 210.

Coles, C. D., Brown, R. T., Smith, I. E., Platzman, K. A., Erickson, S., & Falek, A. (1991). Effects of prenatal alcohol exposure at school age. I. Physical and cognitive development. *Neurotoxicology and Teratology, 13,* 357–367.

Davis, B. (1987). *Peer support: Teacher's resource.* Edmonton: Alberta Alcohol and Drug Abuse Commission.

Deschesnes, M. (1992). Substantial drop in drug use seen in west Quebec schools. *Action News, 3,* 3.

Drew, L. (1988). Acculturation stress and alcohol usage among Canadian Indians in Toronto. *Canadian Journal of Public Health, 79,* 115–118.

Dunne, F. J., & Schipperheijn, J. A. (1989). Alcohol and the young. *Alcohol & Alcoholism, 24,* 213–215.

Elliott, K. T., & Coker, D. R. (1991). Crack babies: Here they come, ready or not. *Journal of Instructional Psychology, 18,* 60–64.

Faulkner, R. A., & Slattery, C. M. (1990). The relationship of physical activity to alcohol consumption in youth, 15–16 years of age. *Canadian Journal of Public Health, 81,* 168–169.

Feldman, W., Hodgson, C., Corber, S., & Quinn, A. (1986). Health concerns and health-related behaviours of adolescents. *Canadian Medical Association Journal, 134,* 489–493.

Foster, R. (1988). Youth, alcohol and drugs: Truth and sober consequences. *Dimensions,* October, 25–26.

Fox, C. L., & Forbing, S. E. (1991). Overlapping symptoms of substance abuse and learning handicaps: Implications for educators. *Journal of Learning Disabilities, 24,* 24–31, 39.

Fried, P. A., & Watkinson, B. (1988). 12- and 24-month neurobehavioural follow-up of children prenatally exposed to marihuana, cigarettes and alcohol. *Neurotoxicology and Teratology, 10,* 305–313.

Hoberman, H. M., & Garfinkel, B. D. (1988). Completed suicide in youth. *Canadian Journal of Psychiatry, 33,* 494–504.

Jonah, B. A., & Dawson, N. E. (1987). Youth and risk: Age differences in risky driving, risk perception, and risk utility. *Alcohol, Drugs, and Driving, 3*(3–4), 13–29.

Kalant, O. J., Fehr, K. O., Arras, D., & Anglin, L. (1983). *Cannabis health risks: A comprehensive annotated bibliography (1844–1982).* Toronto: Addiction Research Foundation.

Kteily-Hawa, R., McIntyre, S., Russell, M., Martin, T., & Mitic, W. (1990). *Drinking patterns and alcohol-related problems: An assessment of first year students at Dalhousie University.* Halifax: Dalhousie University.

Lalinec-Michaud, M., Subak, M. E., Ghadirian, A. M., & Kovess, V. (1991). Substance misuse among native and rural high school students in Quebec. *The International Journal of the Addictions, 29,* 1003–1012.

Leung, A. K. (1986). Ethyl alcohol ingestion in children: A 15-year review. *Clinical Pediatrics, 25,* 617–619.

Licit and illicit drugs in Canada. (1989). Ottawa: Minister of Supply and Services Canada (Cat. H39-159/1989E).

Millar, W. J., & Van Rensburg, S. (1983). *Tobacco use among students in the Northwest Territories, 1982.* Ottawa: Minister of National Health and Welfare.

Miller, B. A., Downs, W. R., & Gondoli, D. M. (1989). Delinquency, childhood violence, and the development of alcoholism in women. *Crime & Delinquency, 35,* 94–108.

Nanson, J. L., & Hiscock, M. (1990). Attention deficits in children exposed to alcohol prenatally. *Alcoholism: Clinical and Experimental Research, 14,* 656–661.

Pagliaro, A. M. (1990). Addiction as disease: Death of a theory of drug abuse (abstract).

Proceedings of the Western Pharmacology Society, 33, 290.

Pagliaro, A. M., & Pagliaro, L. A. (in press–b). Drug and substance abuse among youth. In L. A. Pagliaro & A. M. Pagliaro (Eds.), *Problems in pediatric drug therapy* (3rd ed.). Hamilton: Drug Intelligence Publications.

Pagliaro, A. M., Pagliaro, L. A., Thauberger, P. C., Hewitt, D. S., & Reddon, R. R. (1992, May 28). *Knowledge, behaviours, and risk perception of intravenous drug users in relation to HIV infection and AIDS: The PIARG projects.* Poster presented at the Second Annual Conference of the Canadian Association for HIV Research, Vancouver, British Columbia.

Pagliaro, A. M., Pagliaro, L. A., Thauberger, P. C., Hewitt, D. S., & Reddon, R. R. (1993). Knowledge, behaviours, and risk perception of intravenous drug users in relation to HIV infection and AIDS: The PIARG projects. *Medical Psychotherapy: An International Journal.*

Pagliaro, L. A. (1983). Up in smoke? A brief overview of marijuana toxicity. *Kerygma, 41*, 1–4.

Pagliaro, L. A. (1988). Marijuana and hashish: What are the risks? *Let's Talk, 13* (June), 12–14.

Pagliaro, L. A. (1989, June 17). *An overview of drug and substance abuse in Canada.* Featured speaker at the New Brunswick Pharmaceutical Society Convention, Edmunston, New Brunswick.

Pagliaro, L. A. (1991). The straight dope: An introduction. *Psynopsis, 13*(2), 7.

Pagliaro, L. A. (1992a). The straight dope: Focus on learning–interpreting the inter-pretations. *Psynopsis, 14*(2), 7.

Pagliaro, L. A. (1992b). The straight dope: Predictions for 1992. *Psynopsis, 14*(1), 8.

Pagliaro, L. A., & Pagliaro, A. M. (1992a). The phenomenon of drug and substance abuse among the elderly, part I: An overview. *Journal of Pharmacy Technology, 8*, 65–73.

Pagliaro, L. A., & Pagliaro, A. M. (1992b). Sentenced to death? HIV infection and AIDS in prison–current and future con-cerns. *Canadian Journal of Criminology, 34*, 201–214.

Pagliaro, L. A., & Pagliaro, A. M. (in press–a). Human teratogens. In L. A. Pagliaro & A. M. Pagliaro (Eds.), *Problems in pediatric drug therapy* (3rd ed.). Hamilton: Drug Intelligence Publications.

Pagliaro, L. A., & Pagliaro, A. M. (in press–c). *Substance abuse among children and adolescents.* New York: John Wiley & Sons.

Rowe, B., Milner, R., Johnson, C., & Bota, G. (1992). Snowmobile-related deaths in Ontario: A 5-year review. *Canadian Medical Association Journal, 146*, 147–152.

Schwartz, R. H. (1987). Marijuana: An overview. *Pediatric Clinics of North America, 34*, 305–317.

Smart, R. G., & Adlaf, E. M. (1991). Substance use and problems among Toronto street youth. *British Journal of Addiction, 86*, 999–1010.

Smart, R. G., Adlaf, E. M., & Walsh, G. W. (1991). *The Ontario student drug use survey: Trends between 1977 and 1991.* Toronto: Addiction Research Foundation of Ontario.

Straight facts about drugs & drug abuse. (1985). Ottawa: Minister of Supply and Services Canada (Cat. H39-65/1984E).

Tobacco road. (1991, July 20). *The Edmonton Journal*, p. F8.

Tonkin, R. S. (1987). Adolescent risk-taking behavior. *Journal of Adolescent Health Care, 8*, 213–220.

Warren, R. (1991). Research update: Drugs, youth and the street. *Health Promotion, 30* (2), 17.

Whyte, K., Gallagher, T., Koch, G., Powell, D., Cote, J., Cairney, R., Lequire, S., & West, L. (1987). Crime & calamity: A pre-scribed urban nightmare. *Alberta Report, 14* (7), 38–39, 42–44.

LITERACY IN CANADA:

AN OVERVIEW OF THE ISSUES

• • •

William T. Fagan

*L*iteracy as an educational, a social, and an economic issue, has attained greater prominence in the past five years than at any point in our past history. During the 1950s, there was great concern, especially in the United States, over the advances of the Soviet Union in space exploration. The school system in the U.S. (and in Canada) came under attack for not producing students who could compete with the graduates of the school system in the Soviet Union. However, the focus was not just on literacy (reading, actually) but also on science and mathematics. Furthermore, the focus was on school-age children. Adults who had not attained expected levels of literacy while in school, were largely ignored, especially those who were functioning at the lower levels of literacy development.

Today, the emphasis on literacy in Canada moves back and forth between the school-age population and adults. It is unfortunate, however, that school-age literacy and adult literacy are often seen as two distinct issues. There is often little understanding of school-age literacy on the part of adult literacy workers, and of adult literacy by classroom teachers. In fact, both groups tend to have their own terminology; a "student" to a classroom teacher, is a "learner" to an adult literacy instructor. But, adults are grown-up children (Venezky, 1990). The school dropout of today is the adult illiterate of tomorrow; today's low achieving Grade 3 student is a future adult illiterate unless something intervenes to help that child become successful in his or her school work.

Literacy is a complex issue that has become almost as much emotional as educational. In this paper, I plan to address the following issues:

1. the present concern over literacy standards
2. a definition of literacy
3. school-age literacy
4. adult literacy
5. school-age/adult literacy connections, and
6. implications for classroom teachers/literacy instructors.

. . .

CONCERN OVER LITERACY STANDARDS

While rates vary according to the source of the data, it has been estimated that the dropout rate in Canadian schools is as high as thirty percent, with the result that the adult illiterate population is increasing by 30 000 each year (Mishra, 1987).

Two surveys of adult literacy standards have been published within the past five years (Southam Communications, 1987; Statistics Canada, 1990). The overall rate of adult literacy appears to be about twenty-five percent. This has led some public figures to conclude that illiteracy in Canada constitutes a crisis situation:

> Illiteracy is truly a national disease and a national crisis. It spreads across all groups in our society, regardless of age, economics, or region. It cripples individual[s] . . . for a lifetime—in a way sometimes just as deadly as a physical disability—and, in so doing, it also cripples the social development and economic productivity of our country. (Fairbairn, 1987, p. 597)

Until now, there has been no national measure of school-age literacy. In June 1990, the Council of Ministers of Education in Canada announced plans for the School Achievement Indicators Project, with the goal of assessing the reading and writing accomplishments of Canadian school children aged 13 and 16. At approximately the same time, the IEA International Literacy Study was initiated, designed to assess the reading comprehension of children in Grades 3 and 8 in thirty countries. The need for comparative data for both school-age students and adults appears to be increasing.

However, most people including educators, politicians, and the general public are often too quick to jump on statistics or the results of surveys when deciding how literate our nation is. Any measure is only as good as the definition on which it is based. If one person says that literacy is being able to read and find the main idea of a page-length article, another person might say that it is the ability to write a member of parliament and clearly outline a particular issue. One person might say it is synonymous with being able to identify your social insurance number, fill out an application form for a driver's licence, and read the label on prescription medicine. Then, if each person constructs a literacy test, their conclusions of who is literate will be like the results of the blind men who each tried to define an elephant by feeling different parts of its body. The Southam Literacy Survey, for example, measured the extent of literacy by one of two forms, one with ten items and one with fourteen items. If a person failed three of the ten items, he or she was declared illiterate. All of the items were supposedly "functional," or relevant to the lives of the people taking the test. Yet, one might argue that reading menus, long distance telephone bills, or plans for a meeting, are not relevant to the lives of all Canadians. Our understanding of literacy (our definition) guides our interpretation of survey or test results, and our plan of action for improving literacy standards. For this reason, it is essential that we are clear on how we understand literacy.

• • •

A DEFINITION OF LITERACY

The problem is not the lack of a definition, but of too many definitions with little common ground. Providing a definition of literacy may be likened to providing a definition of poverty or happiness. What these concepts mean is influenced by who possesses them, to what extent they enhance or interfere with a person's life, and by the motivation or desire to make one's situation more rewarding. One other point in providing a definition is to question who benefits from a particular definition. To use poverty as an example, people living in a particular region may define poverty in terms of a higher income cut-off point than the government since the goal of the former may be to obtain more funds, while the goal of the latter may be to reduce them.

Literacy is a global term in referring to various competencies with language. About twenty-five years ago, it was common to talk about reading, writing, phonics, and spelling as part of the school curriculum. These labels were then largely replaced with "language arts" which included all those aspects of language but focussed on how one related to the other. Literacy is an advancement on the term "language arts." Interestingly, the label "literacy" was first used to talk about language development (reading, writing, oral language) of young children (usually pre-schoolers) and the language competencies of adults. Now the term has become popularized and refers to language competencies at all age levels. It is now common to hear of teachers talk about their "literacy programs" or to find university courses dealing with such topics as "methodologies of literacy instruction" or "literacy process: theory and practice."

Literacy commonly refers to competencies in written language (reading and writing); however, it is sometimes used to refer to oral language competencies. Competencies in written language for instructional and learning purposes may be grouped as skills, knowledge, and strategies. A skill may be considered an ability to do something with language such as: sounding out words using letter-sound correspondences, dividing words into syllables, using a variety of words in writing to describe something, spelling words correctly, finding a main idea of a passage, or comparing two issues whether in reading or writing. The term "skill" is often used synonymously with knowledge, although knowledge can be extended to include background information to a story, the letters of the alphabet, a repertoire of words or vocabulary, punctuation marks, and occasions for their use.

Strategy, generally refers to a plan or course of action in accomplishing a goal via language. Knowing the answer to a question, for example, may be considered knowledge or skill, but knowing *how* to go about finding the best possible answer is a strategy. Skills and knowledge add to the individual's stock of information about language; strategies enable the individual to use this information effectively (how) under different conditions (when). An individual may know that there are different text genres (narrative, explanation, cause-effect, problem-solution, etc.) but unless the individual possesses strategies for how and when to use a particular genre, the knowledge may be considered static in the sense that his or her appropriate use of the genre will depend on feedback from another person as opposed to the individual being able to monitor its effective use. Literacy as competency in language (knowledge, skill, strategy) provides the learner with control over language use.

Literacy or language use in the classroom has been referred to as "vanilla literacy" (Venezky, 1990) because of its "blandness." School-age children frequently read stories prescribed by teachers (actually prescribed by authors or editors of commercial programs), answer questions or make predictions about the story content, complete worksheets or exercises, write in a set time period, and share their writing by reading aloud. The school often becomes its own world in terms of language use and this use only takes its meaning from a school context.

What about the child's language world outside of school? Rather than being devoid of written language, it is often alive and filled with it. Children read flyers, concert announcements, information on hockey or other sports cards, T.V. guides, slogans on t-shirts, notes from friends, and information on tapes or CDs; and they write notes for family members, engage in record keeping for their paper delivery, make posters, and keep score during games. Adults, of course, because of social and economic commitments, encounter even many more instances of written language in their lives than do children. Use of language to accomplish a task within one's environment via language is referred to as "functional literacy." From the examples above, it should be obvious that it is difficult to find functions of language common to everybody; literacy as use or function often varies considerably from one individual to another.

Finally, literacy does not occur in isolation. That is, an individual does not engage in literacy independent of other individuals. Certainly, there are times when a person goes to a quiet place and reads a book, or writes in a diary, but most often engaging in literacy is shared with or conducted in the presence of others. In school, children interact with each other and with the teacher on reading and writing tasks. The teacher may ask a question, a child responds, another child may add a point. Or a child may be unable to answer correctly (as judged by the teacher), and the question is then directed to another child. A study with low-literate adults showed that when they were in school, they believed that when a teacher directed another child to answer, this was done on purpose by the teacher to "show them up" (Fagan, 1990). As a result, they developed negative feelings about the teacher and about literacy.

For adults, literacy also occurs in social contexts. For example, a parent may read to a child; an adult may complete a form at the bank, read a notice at work, or write a letter requesting a response. Literacy may be considered a social or an interpersonal act and, as such involves emotion—excitement at having received a perfect score on a quiz, embarrassment at not knowing the answer to a question and having another child answer, or frustration at not being able to complete an application form for a job.

The control over language (skill, knowledge, strategy) and the ability to use it effectively to accomplish personal goals involving language to bring about change, and to feel good about the outcome is known as the power of language, or literacy as empowerment. In brief, literacy can be defined as language competence, its functional application involving social or interpersonal interaction, and empowerment.

• • •

LITERACY IN THE CLASSROOM

Accepting the above definition of literacy entails a number of responsibilities or decisions. One is the decision as to what constitutes a literacy curriculum. There has been much controversy over phonics versus "look-say" versus whole language, as approaches to literacy development. Such controversies often become red herrings and detract from the main issue, that of providing a well-rounded curriculum that includes competency and language use in a social atmosphere conducive to learning. Unless the literacy curriculum addresses all these aspects of literacy, it is not a complete curriculum. Assuming that it does, each component must be dealt with adequately.

Language Competency
(Skills, Knowledge, Strategies)

Over the course of twelve years of school, children should develop competency in various aspects of language (examples have been indicated earlier in this paper) so that by the end of Grade 12, or year of leaving school, they will have achieved a certain level. While a child in the third year of school should be able to understand and write simple stories, students in high school should be able to adopt the author's point of view, and recognize satire, including an appreciation of its intended impact on the reader. Young writers (Grades 1 and 2) who are grappling with the use of language, may "invent" spelling (that is, spell the word as they think it sounds) to continue recording their flow of thoughts. Such invented spelling should decrease over the years so that by junior high, except for unusual words, students should employ standard spelling in their writing. And, even before this level students should check for appropriate spellings in their writing if it is directed to an audience that expects correct spelling. By the time children reach the elementary or intermediate grades they should be able to recognize words independently through using various cues: sound-symbol correspondences (phonics), word structure, immediate context (prior and subsequent sentences), and use of the knowledge framework that supports the meaning of the passage.

Literacy as language competency should always be based in meaning so that when phonics is taught, for example, the children can immediately see how this knowledge allows them to identify words in a meaningful print situation. Phonics or any other knowledge or skill is never learned for its own sake but for the sake of developing control over language use. In the past, spelling was taught as remembering word lists, sometimes involving words that the student would never meet again. Unfortunately, the pendulum has swung to not requiring children to remember words at all. The issue is not one of remembering or not remembering, but of remembering words that are useful or functional for the child in meeting his or her writing needs, and in providing strategies for remembering words so that children can capitalize on visual and auditory cues in so doing. Words commonly misspelled in children's writing, commonly used words in the English language, spelling generalizations (for example, adding "s" to words ending with "y"), and personal choice words are all word candidates for correct spelling.

Language Use

Children must understand that reading and writing are used outside the classroom. In fact, they must do more than understand it; they must experience it. Children already experience reading and writing outside the classroom; what they do not often do is make the connection between what goes on in the classroom and what goes on outside. It is not uncommon for children to walk the hallways of the school that are lined with "language" in the form of posters, notices, and so on, and not be aware of these uses of literacy. Rather than having two distinct views of literacy—one for school, and one for elsewhere—they should understand literacy as an encompassing construct including all aspects of written language, regardless of where the language activities occur.

Social and Interpersonal Relations

Children's emotional reactions to literacy activities in the classroom are as significant in explaining literacy development as factors such as instructional techniques or home support. Research has shown that low-achieving children tend to be singled out in the classroom and feel isolated as victims of differential treatment (McDermott, 1977). Children who come to school possessing knowledge and skills valued by the school often find themselves in the teacher's favour and at an advantage in terms of classroom privileges and opportunities for learning. Low-ability groups, which are usually organized by the teacher in good faith in the belief that such groups will assist the children involved to better develop their literacy competency, sometimes have more negative than positive effects on these children. Research has indicated that teachers spend less instructional time and provide less effective help to low-ability groups than to high-achieving groups, even though the length of grouped time is the same for all (Brown, Palinscar, & Purcell, 1986). The teacher's attitude towards low-achieving children (that is, the teacher's agenda) is part of the school's "hidden curriculum."

The key to developing literacy in a social context is establishing "trusting relations" (McDermott, 1977) between teachers and students and among students themselves. Students must feel free to learn. They must be uninhibited by unnecessary demands, negative feedback, and differential treatment.

Evaluation

Evaluation is always a difficult task and there is often much disagreement as to what constitutes a valid evaluation. Some educators strongly oppose the use of standardized tests for measuring literacy development; they claim that such tests contain items irrelevant to the school curriculum and the students are unfairly compared to a particular norm group. Today, the use of "portfolios" or records (kept in folders) of literacy tasks that the students engaged in, is common. These, in turn, are criticized for being too general and not identifying a child's strengths and weaknesses in relation to others in the classroom.

In keeping with the definition of literacy given earlier, evaluation must embrace all aspects of literacy. While a standardized test tends to focus on measuring language components, portfolios may provide a better record of the variety of literacy use.

. . .

ADULT LITERACY

Literacy, of course, has the same definition for adults as for children. The difference is that adults no longer have the privilege of twelve years to learn how to read and write effectively; their lives are much more complex than are children's, and many more demands are placed on them. Furthermore, adults are mature, thinking individuals who have a variety of needs for furthering their literacy development and in most cases, can choose to enroll in a literacy program and can choose to withdraw.

A greater variety of adult literacy programs in increasing numbers are being set up across the country. Adults can participate in regular class situations, small groups, one-on-one tutoring, and computer projects, all of which may occur in a range of settings: community colleges, trades and technical institutions, school system evening programs, charitable organizations, public libraries, or in the home of the adult or the tutor.

Adults are faced with four general types of programs. One is a fairly structured group program with a set body of knowledge, skills, and strategies (often called adult basic education or ABE), designed so that it follows a sequence through to the completion of a high school certificate and then possibly to a trade or work-oriented program. A second type of program is a computer-based program that may have the same content and goals as the group structured program. The difference, of course, is that in this program, the adults work singly with a computer and may at times get help from an instructor who acts as a resource person. Another type of program is fairly flexible and is geared towards the adult learner's specific needs. This may be as narrowly defined as understanding a landlord-tenant agreement, or more broadly defined as wanting to help one's children with their schoolwork, or to be able to read to them, or to want to feel good about oneself. This kind of program usually occurs in a one-to-one tutoring situation. A fourth type of program is a work-related literacy program. The purpose is to enhance one's literacy skills for the job the person presently holds. Such programs are often run by businesses, industry, unions, or as a joint venture by these agencies.

While the first two types of programs have a strong focus on the language competence aspect of literacy, the next two tend to stress functionality of language or language use. But there must be a balance. As in the case of classroom literacy instruction, if an ABE program ignores functional literacy, the adult learners will develop a very restricted view of literacy and may not always transfer what is learned in class to reading and writing in other settings. Likewise, if functional literacy is too emphasized in the third and fourth types of program, the adult learners may acquire knowledge of such issues as tenants' rights, but may not be able to critically read a landlord-tenant agreement.

Empowerment

This aspect of literacy is more prominent in adult literacy than in school-age literacy. Empowerment or the acquisition of power involves bringing about change in one's personal, social, economic, or political conditions. This can mean succeeding in getting a rent deposit back from the landlord, or having city council clean up a garbage dump within view of one's house. A common misunderstanding regarding empowerment is not distinguishing it as a way of bringing about change, from one of bringing about change *via literacy (language)*. Protests, rallies, and hunger strikes can often engender change, but change via literacy entails competency in language control over language use. Too often adult literacy programs focus on empowerment without developing the language competence necessary to pressure or negotiate for change.

Schools are the key agencies for developing language competence and control. However, concern has been expressed that schools may be doing a disservice to low ability, low socio-economic status, and ethnically different children in terms of preparing them for literacy as empowerment (Delpit, 1988). The whole-language philosophy, for example, tends to accept children's language as is, without setting definite standards or language milestones. Consequently, it is possible that many children will leave school without the degree of language competency and control to present their case in an attempt to attain power. What should not be forgotten is that those holding the power are extremely skilled in language use and sometimes manipulate language for the very purpose of denying power to others. Unless the power-seeker is on an equal footing in terms of language competency with the power-holder, it is unlikely that he or she will attain any power not willingly dispensed by the power-holders.

. . .

CLASSROOM/ADULT LITERACY CONNECTIONS

School is an institution of society with a special mandate—to educate the young or to help them attain a level of academic competency (including literacy competency) through which they can further their goals as independent and responsible citizens. Teachers who complain that homes and parents do not do enough to foster children's literacy development must be reminded that parents do not have to have a certificate to educate their children; teachers do, and therefore teachers must understand that they have a greater responsibility for this task. A second common statement is that teachers only have children for five hours a day, compared to nineteen hours when the children are with the parents. What is overlooked is that for the five hours children spend with teachers, they are constantly involved in academic-type activities in a structured and relatively closed (classroom space) context. The time spent at home includes time for sleeping, eating, playing, and many other activities. A parent never has five hours a day to monitor a child's academic work.

While the mandate for literacy development rests with the classroom, competency in literacy is best acquired if it becomes a joint effort between home and school (Chall & Snow, 1988). Parents should be encouraged to read to their children often, discuss topics with them, buy them books, take them to public libraries, and volunteer to assist in the school or classroom. However, if parents do not or cannot engage in such literacy support activities, the child should not become the victim and schools must compensate for the lack of such experiences.

If literacy instruction is based on the definition presented earlier, then literacy inside and outside the classroom becomes a literacy continuum with many commonalities. When children acquire literacy competency—the ability to use literacy in various situations—they feel positive about their literacy experiences, and can use literacy to improve their lives. This potential is not confined to classrooms nor is it operable only in out-of-school contexts but in both. This potential is activated whenever children are faced with any context having literacy demands.

While adult literacy programs can never reach back into classrooms since adult learners never again will become children, the school can make efforts to reach beyond the classroom.

The literacy curriculum of the classroom must be expanded to include all aspects of the definition of literacy given above. In the case of functional literacy or literacy use, children should have occasions to read and write in relation to materials that are part of their world outside the classroom. An unfortunate practice is that commercial literacy programs provide facsimiles of many types of out-of-school literacy: a copy of a menu, a page from a T.V. guide, a hockey ticket, or a stop sign do not reflect real life. Not only do these items lack the "manipulative dimensions" that they possess in real life, but they occur within the context of a book, a context associated with the classroom and for the purpose of developing language competency, not for providing occasions for language use.

Reading for enjoyment transcends school and out-of-school. The priority and pleasure of reading cannot be instilled by regulating such an activity to the last twenty minutes or half hour on a Friday evening before school closes for the weekend. Reading for enjoyment means that children should select their own materials, in many cases bringing the materials from home. During recreational reading time, the teacher must set the model and not use this opportunity to catch up on marking or other tasks. Recreational reading is reading for enjoyment, and there should be no teacher accountability such as book reports (these could be part of other assignments or projects). Accountability of reading for enjoyment does not parallel this activity in out-of-school settings.

Literacy development in schools has been criticized as having little relevance for job or workplace literacy (Mikulecky, 1990). One reason for this is that literacy development in the classroom is mainly based on language competency where students read for relatively long periods of time and then answer questions or complete worksheets. Workplace literacy usually involves reading smaller segments of text at a time, and interacting with co-workers between reading and writing activities through talking and listening. Clarification often occurs during such interactions. A school activity that most parallels workplace reading is having children work on assignments or projects in small groups. Such assignments involve a search for material, whether in the library or elsewhere, accessing resource personnel, deciding how to structure the material for presentation, reading, writing, discussing, and assigning or taking responsibility in preparing the information. In a study that I conducted with low-literate adults and achieving and low-achieving children in Grades 3, 6, and 9, the one kind of classroom activity that they all enjoyed was small group assignments. However, the achieving students were more likely to engage in this kind of activity than were the low achievers—the ones who could benefit most (Fagan, 1989).

• • •

IMPLICATIONS

Classroom teachers and adult literacy instructors must have a clearly thought through definition of literacy to avoid acting in ad hoc, piecemeal, and at times contradictory fashions in their literacy practices.

A definition should guide the selection of the literacy curriculum, including goals, materials, and methodologies. It should determine the nature of testing or evaluation of literacy progress of stages of literacy development. It should serve as a screen or "sifter" during in-service programs or speaker presentations. Too often, teachers or adult literacy instructors are readily influenced by such sessions and often adopt ideas or purchase materials that are little more than "gimmicks," rather than items contributing to an integral and solid literacy curriculum.

While the whole-language movement has done much to make language development more meaningful for children and engenders a respect for each individual, it also, unfortunately, often leads to loosely structured learning situations that are more social than academic. There is no doubt that many children learn a lot in such situations, but these are usually, the bright, the motivated, and the prepared; that is those whose home backgrounds are conducive to academic success. These children who may be considered "at risk," while enjoying such situations often make little progress in their literacy development. These children at times need more structure and direct instruction to aid in their literacy development. In addition, for all children, one aspect of language competence necessitates structured and direct instruction, and that is strategy learning. A strategy, by definition, is a plan of action encompassing definite procedures that lead to a goal. Strategy development is more efficient and effective if strategies are developed systematically rather than expecting that children (or adults) will develop them through trial and error, or in a hit-and-miss fashion.

One other point about developing literacy competency is the necessity to distinguish instruction from practice. Many commercial materials (especially adult literacy materials) provide for the learner to work through a set of exercises, such as reading a passage and answering questions, which are then checked by a teacher or literacy instructor. These are practice-type situations in which the learner is actually testing what he or she knows. Instruction, on the other hand, is interactive and includes providing a rationale, an objective, engaging in various instructional behaviours (modelling, explaining, questioning, providing examples, etc.) and synthesis.

The social dimension of literacy development should not be overlooked. A study of adult illiterates showed that they identified the concern, the warmth, and caring of an instructor as the most significant aspect of a literacy program (Amoroso, 1986). While computers do have a particular function in literacy development, adult learners often prefer computers to other options, not because of their instructional value, but because computers are neutral in feelings and the learners are assured of not receiving negative feedback from an individual, an experience that still haunts many from their earlier school days.

Adult learners must be provided with a variety of literacy programs. Their needs must be considered and an attempt must be made to meet these needs. Adult learners are generally polite but sceptical. They will not usually question the relevance of various activities for literacy development. They will politely withdraw and become no-shows, a common problem in adult literacy programs. This is also becoming more common with school-age students, especially with junior high students in cities, who prefer to go to a video arcade rather than return to school after recess or lunch break. This kind of behaviour tends to precede dropping out of school altogether.

Since the lives of adult learners are often complicated by many factors (personal, family, economic, etc.) and since some are reticent and even scared about enrolling in a literacy program, there is a greater need for counselling services prior to and while they are enrolled in a program.

Literacy as empowerment must be seen as bringing about change in one's life through literacy and language. While social activism has a role in society, it does not constitute a literacy program unless there is a provision for the development of competency in language.

There must be more concerted effort by all literacy instructors (of children and adults) to develop a greater understanding of each other's roles and responsibilities. Joint conferences or seminars could be arranged. Adult learners could be invited to speak to pre-service teachers (those taking literacy courses), or part of a pre-service teacher's practicum could be completed in an adult literacy setting.

Finally, the walls of the classroom or adult literacy program should not be viewed as a barrier to language development. Literacy, as defined in this paper, knows no physical bounds. Literacy involves competency in language. It is the ability to function with or use language for different purposes, and to feel positive about one's literacy experiences. The only thing that distinguishes literacy activities within the classroom or adult literacy program and literacy activities outside, is that the contexts change and one or other aspects of literacy take on greater significance. However, in order to meet the different literacy demands and to acquire the flexibility needed to cope with a variety of literacy contexts, an individual must possess literacy in its broadest definition.

• • •

REFERENCES

Amoroso, H.C. (1986). Conversations with a new literate. *Journal of Reading, 29,* 484–488.

Brown, A.L., Palinscar, A.S., & Purcell, L. (1986). Poor readers: Teach, don't label. In U. Neisser (Ed.), *The school achievement of minority children* (pp. 105–143). Hillsdale, NJ: Lawrence Erlbaum.

Chall, J., & Snow, K. (1988). School influences on the reading development of low-income children. *The Harvard Education Letter, 4,* 1–4.

Delpit, L.D. (1988). The silenced dialogue: Power and pedagogy in educating other peoples' children. *Harvard Educational Review, 58,* 280–298.

Fagan, W.T. (1990). Socioaffective factors and literacy development. In S.P. Norris & L.M. Phillips (Eds.), *Foundations of literacy policy in Canada* (pp. 227–244). Calgary, AB: Detselig.

Fagan, W.T. (1989). Prisoners and non-institutional adult's perceptions of conditions affecting their learning. *Journal of Correctional Education, 40,* 152–158.

Fairbairn, J. (March 11, 1987). Illiteracy in Canada. *Senate Debates*, Ottawa.

Literacy in Canada: A research report. (1987). Ottawa, ON: Southam Communications.

McDermott, R.P. (1977). Social relations as contexts for learning in school. *Harvard Educational Review, 47,* 198–215.

Mikulecky, L. (1990). Literacy for what purpose? In R.L. Venezky, D.A. Wagner, & B.S. Ciliberti (Eds.), *Toward defining literacy* (pp. 24–34). Newark, DE: International Reading Association.

Mishra, M. (1987). Southam report shocks Canadians: Special report—literacy in Canada. *Worldlit, 78,* 1–3.

Statistics Canada. (1990). *Survey of literacy skills used in daily activities.* Ottawa, ON: Statistics Canada.

Venezky, R.L. (1990). Gathering up, looking ahead. In R.L. Venezky, D.A. Wagner, & B.S. Ciliberti (Eds.), *Toward defining literacy* (pp. 70–74). Newark, DE: International Reading Association.

THE PROBLEM WITH
SECONDARY SCHOOLS

...

Derek J. Allison

$\mathcal{I}$n a recent address to the Canadian School Boards' Association, federal
youth minister Pierre Cadieux declared "Our high school dropout rate
of approximately 30 per cent is one the highest in the industrial world." He
went on to claim that if this rate did not decrease, Canada could expect on the
order of one million new dropouts over the next ten years. "The waste of human
potential in terms of social and economic consequences is staggering" he continued, for dropouts will face a "foreclosed future" in the competitive, high-tech
employment market that awaits them ("Cap dropout flood," 1991). More
recently, New Brunswick premier Frank McKenna rehearsed a similar argument
during the course of what amounted to a wholesale condemnation of the
Canadian education system: "Although Canada spends a great deal on education," McKenna was reported as saying, "it has one of the highest drop-out
rates, shortest school years and lowest student scores in math and sciences"
("Lack of," 1992).

Such pronouncements, reiterated and embroidered by editorial writers, corporate spokespersons and critics across the country, demonstrate a growing concern
with what appears to be the scandalously large number of young people not completing high school. Although, as McKenna observed, many other faults can be
found with Canadian education, the dropout problem has been taken as providing clear and unambiguous evidence that something is seriously wrong with our
schools. At the same time, the symptom used to diagnose the illness seems to
point to an obvious cure: simply put, we need to find ways to ensure that more
students stay in school. This is certainly the view of the federal government, as

illustrated by statements by ministers such as Cadieux, by federally funded prime-time television advertisements, and by the wave of federally funded studies aimed at raising public and political consciousness of the dropout problem as a national issue. These activities are particularly noteworthy given that education falls under provincial jurisdiction.

Yet some provincial governments have been assiduously beating the dropout drum for some time. Perhaps the best illustration is provided by the 1987 *Ontario study of the relevance of education and the issue of dropouts* (Radwanski, 1987). As signalled by its title, this government commissioned inquiry treated dropouts as the central problem confronting Ontario schools. Since then, the Ontario Ministry of Education has launched an ambitious restructuring of Ontario secondary schools with the declared intent of reducing dropout rates. Other provinces have also embarked on dropout reduction initiatives. Quebec's 1992 budget, for example, allocated $42 million to a special dropout prevention fund ("Teachers hopeful," 1992). Indeed, the dropout issue appears as a concern not only across the breadth of the country, but at all levels of the educational hierarchy, with individual school boards and schools publicly adopting various innovative measures designed to combat—as the current jargon has it—high dropout rates. In Edmonton, for instance, school counsellors are spending time in shopping malls talking to truants and dropouts, inviting them into storefront counselling centres, and encouraging them to reconsider their decision ("Edmonton educators," 1992).

Are these efforts likely to cure the illness? Any answer to this question clearly depends on whether or not the initial diagnosis is correct. Is the dropout rate from Canadian secondary schools as serious a symptom as it appears to be? Where does the root of the illness lie? How might it best be treated?

This chapter explores these and related questions. The chapter begins with an overview of some of the complexities involved in estimating dropout rates; this is followed by an alternative interpretation of the dropout phenomenon, and a brief consideration of some implications for secondary schools and educational policy. The thesis of the chapter will be that while there are serious weaknesses in our system of secondary level education, these weaknesses are being masked and ignored by the current obsessive and ill-informed concern with dropouts. On this basis I will argue that evident shortcomings in our system of secondary *education* will not be remedied by restructuring secondary *schools*, or by trying to persuade, bribe, or force unwilling students to remain within their walls.

• • •

DEFINING DROPOUTS

One likely reason for the current pervasiveness and political popularity of the dropout issue is that the basic concern seems simple and the solution appears obvious: a dropout is obviously someone who leaves school prematurely, someone who literally "drops out," withdraws from, the program of formal schooling provided so as to ensure a solid and useful education for the young citizens of our society. It obviously seems to follow, therefore, that we need to find ways of keeping dropouts and potential dropouts in school. Given that our systems of universal secondary schooling have been created with the best of intentions at some considerable cost, then it is not unreasonable to imagine that "dropping out" would be interpreted as implying a certain ingratitude to society in general and to hard-working taxpayers in particular. This point often goes unvoiced, however, for it smacks of "blaming the victim"; instead, and as illustrated in the introduction, the dropout phenomenon is typically interpreted as providing clear evidence that our secondary schools are failing to meet both the needs of their students and the expectations of society. In order to solve the dropout problem, then, it seems obvious that we need to identify and fix whatever is wrong with our secondary schools.

It is not, however, the act of dropping out that fuels this argument, but the apparently large numbers of young people that do this: it is the dropout rate, rather than the dropout phenomenon *per se* that is of concern. If only a relative handful of young people left school early, then this would presumably be acceptable. Or would it? Much of the political rhetoric surrounding the issue often implicitly—sometimes explicitly—adopts a "zero-tolerance" attitude toward dropouts, on the apparent assumption that an ideal system of secondary schooling would retain each and every student in school until graduation. But could this be entertained as a serious policy objective, given the wide variation in individual ability, interests, aptitudes, circumstances, and aspirations within the student population? It does not seem to be expected under current compulsory attendance legislation, that allows students to leave school before they complete the secondary school curriculum. Although the details can be complex, some educational jurisdictions in North America and Europe permit students to legally leave school at age fifteen, others insist on age sixteen, but some allow students to leave as early as age fourteen. No Canadian province or American state forces students to remain enrolled until age eighteen, or until they satisfy full graduation requirements (Pauker, Desnoyers, & Pauker, 1988).

Thus, by making completion of the senior years of secondary school voluntary, current policies allow—some might argue invite—students to drop out, and in so doing imply the acceptance of a less than zero dropout rate. This returns us to the question of what might constitute an acceptable rate. Would one percent qualify? How about ten percent? Clearly there is no obvious answer to this intriguing question; yet there seems to be virtually universal agreement that a dropout rate of thirty percent is unacceptable.

A dropout rate of thirty percent appears to mean that thirty out of 100 students leave secondary school without completing the full program of studies. Or does it mean that thirty percent of students fail to acquire a secondary school graduation credential? Note that the first of these interpretations does not necessarily imply the second: a student who drops out can drop back in again, and then graduate. Nor does the second interpretation necessarily imply the first: a student could remain continuously enrolled in school, but fail to qualify for a graduation diploma. And how about students who wish to remain in school, but are "pushed-out" by personal or other circumstances; students who become pregnant, for example, or are taken seriously ill, or fall afoul of the law, or who must seek employment to help keep bread on the table at home? Should such students, many of whom may sincerely wish to improve their education, be counted as dropouts, or should they be more properly treated as unfortunate victims of a less than perfect society and economy?

Once we start to reflect on questions and problems such as these, it becomes clear that neither the basal notion of dropouts nor the derived construct of dropout rates are obvious or simple ideas. To the contrary, it turns out that these apparently straightforward and concrete concepts are notoriously complex and difficult to apply. This is perhaps most clearly illustrated by the fact there is no generally accepted definition of a dropout, and thus no agreed upon way of calculating dropout rates. In the first interim report of a federally funded study of the economic costs of dropouts, the Conference Board of Canada (1991) pointed out that each Canadian province "has developed its own definition(s), or is in the process of doing so" (p. 10). This last point is fascinating, for it appears that at the time the report was compiled (7 July 1991), five Canadian provinces had yet to adopt an official definition of a dropout, a strange state of affairs given the declared seriousness of the problem. Three of these five provinces had nonetheless adopted "informal or interim" definitions, a point that the Conference Board found reassuring. But regardless of the official or unofficial status of these definitions, the important point is that they are all different.

This variation is partly explained by the different curriculum structures and operational terms native to each province. Even so, some definitions are quite distinct from others. According to the Conference Board (1991), Newfoundland defines a dropout as "any student who ceases to attend school after an unexcused absence of 20 consecutive days or more during the school year," while Ontario defines the supposedly same phenomenon as "any student under the age of 21 who has not successfully completed the requirements for a secondary school diploma" (p. 10). Depending on how the marvellously malleable "unexcused absence" is interpreted by administrators—a point that could seriously affect the reliability of the final statistics—the Newfoundland definition could yield a considerably higher or lower dropout count than the Ontario one. But more importantly, there are clearly profound policy and philosophical differences between Newfoundland's focus on school attendance and the focus on secondary school completion in the Ontario definition. The "unofficial" Saskatchewan definition reported by the Conference Board introduces further complications by defining dropouts as "those who enter the school system and do not graduate from Grade 12 or any other program such as a leaving certificate program" (p. 10). This definition apparently allows Saskatchewan to count students who complete a non-Grade 12 course of study as secondary school graduates rather than dropouts, an option that is specifically denied in the Ontario definition, which requires the completion of the full thirty credit diploma program. Another interesting aspect of the Saskatchewan definition is the omission of any reference to age or to students, this latter term often being understood as meaning adolescents or young adults. Together with the reference to "those who enter the school system," these omissions imply that adults returning to secondary school would be counted as dropouts if they failed to complete their program of study.

There is no obvious reason to prefer any of these, or other definitions over competing conceptions: all have limitations, and each could be considered useful or useless depending on one's point of view and the arguments or policy conclusions one wished to advance. The broad point to be stressed is that there are considerable philosophical and operational variations in the ways in which dropouts are counted and dropout rates calculated. This obviously makes the comparison of dropout rates between jurisdictions a hazardous business. It also begs the question of how a reliable Canadian dropout rate might be arrived at, given the competing provincial definitions. The Conference Board (1991) solved this problem by adopting yet another definition, one that is used by the federal department of Employment and Immigration. Under this approach, "a dropout is a student who does not graduate from grade 12 four years after entering grade 9" (p. 9). This definition imposes far stricter conditions and assumptions than any of those adopted by the provinces: no allowances are made for drop-ins, push-outs, or for students who take more than the four lock-step years allowed for completion of the secondary school curriculum. The formula used by the Conference Board to calculate a national dropout rate introduced more inflexibility by factoring in the number of fourteen and eighteen year olds in the population, adjustments that assume all Grade 9 students will be fourteen years of age and ignore the effect of immigration within this age range.

How reasonable and reliable is the thirty percent dropout rate so blithely cited by politicians, corporate spokespersons and editorial writers? If alternate definitions and formulae were to be used, we could presumably produce a whole range of different but plausible dropout statistics: which of these would be "correct"? And if we accept that a zero dropout rate is likely as unattainable as a zero unemployment rate, then we might conceivably produce a dropout rate that could be considered acceptable. I do not want to press the point. My concern in these paragraphs has been to illustrate some of the problems associated with the apparently simple concept of dropouts, and to raise a few healthy doubts about the accuracy of the statistics that constitute the linchpin of much current argument. But these concerns also bring the usefulness of the basic concept under question.

Given the broad range of definitions in use, given the problems these raise for accurately calculating and comparing dropout rates, and given other technical problems, such as the many difficulties associated with collecting and collating reliable year-to-year enrolment data, it should be clear that dropout statistics constitute a less than trustworthy source of information about the performance of school systems. Indeed, because there is no standard definition of who should be counted as a dropout and because there are substantial differences in how schools are organized within different jurisdictions, dropout statistics are essentially useless when it comes to comparing the relative performance of different national and sub-national systems of education. Consequently, most reputable comparative analyses make use of other indicators of educational outcomes, such as the proportion of secondary school graduates in the adult population, or the proportion of appropriate population age cohorts, such as fourteen to seventeen year olds for example, enrolled in school. We must wonder, therefore, about the source and reliability of the information used by critics claiming that Canada's dropout rate is one of the highest in the industrial world. Such claims are particularly worrisome in the light of UNESCO statistics showing that Canada enrols a higher proportion of its secondary school age group than any other country except the Netherlands (National Center for Educational Statistics, 1990, Table 359). Viewed in this light Canadian secondary schools appear to be doing very well indeed.

· · ·

RECONCEPTUALIZING THE DROPOUT PROBLEM

From the brief review offered above, there are good practical reasons for abandoning the concepts of dropouts and dropout rates in favour of more sensible measures of educational outcomes. But regardless of how dropouts might be defined and dropout rates calculated and interpreted, the fundamental reality of the current situation cannot be denied: some young people, probably a disturbingly large number, are choosing to opt out of secondary school before completing the full program of studies. Why should this be? Why would anyone choose to voluntarily sentence himself or herself to what will likely be a bleak future of underemployment or unemployment? The politically popular answer to this perplexing question has two parts to it: first, that these young people do not fully understand the dire economic consequences of dropping out; and second, that secondary schools are not meeting their needs. The tenability of the first part of this answer depends heavily on how valuable a secondary school diploma is likely to be in future employment markets, a question I will return to at a later point. The second part of this answer is undoubtedly true: secondary schools are not meeting the educational needs of those who drop out. This appears to be the main reason why those who are not pushed out by life circumstances choose to leave. Moreover, the failure of secondary schools to provide an education that is valued by some of our young citizens is even more serious than implied by dropout statistics, however they may be calculated, for those deal only with students who physically remove themselves from school, ignoring the potentially substantial numbers of students who are mental dropouts: those who remain in school simply to serve their time but who are not seriously engaged in the educational activities provided.

The Failing Secondary School

The claim that contemporary secondary schools are failing to meet the educational needs of all young people is amply supported by research investigating the questions of who drops out and why. As Hahn (1987, as quoted by Kronick & Hargis, 1990, p. 62) observed, "dropping out is a problem not confined to a handful of minority students who couldn't learn." Although dropouts tend to have lower IQ than graduates, some very bright students also choose not to stay in school; while students from some minority groups tend to drop out more frequently than their peers from the socio-cultural mainstream, students from other minority groups drop out less frequently than mainstream students; students from lower socio-economic backgrounds tend to drop out more frequently than those from higher ones, but some children from rich, advantaged backgrounds also drop out; students with part-time jobs, especially if they work more than fifteen hours a week, are more likely to drop out, but some dropouts lack jobs and have no reasonable prospect of finding one; a greater proportion of dropouts come from single parent families where the parent in question did not complete high school, but children from two-parent, professional homes also drop out; and so it goes. The research shows that dropouts come from all levels and corners of society, and share no single determinative social, academic, or psychological profile (Ekstrom, Goertz, Pollack, & Rock, 1986; Kronick & Hargis, 1990; Natriello, 1987; Rumberger, 1983; Sullivan, 1988; Watson, 1974–75).

When dropouts are asked why they chose to leave school, however, one clearly dominant answer emerges: they are simply not willing to endure the schooling experience any longer. Watson's (n.d.) detailed study of Ontario dropouts in the mid-1970s found that most said they had left school because they had a job or a job offer, or they thought they could get a job, the prospect of working in the outside world being seen by these students as obviously preferable to staying in school. The next most frequently cited reasons all revealed dissatisfaction with the secondary schooling experience; "hated school" was the third most frequently given reason for dropping out; "failing anyway" the fourth; "dissatisfied with teachers" the sixth; "dissatisfied with courses" the eighth (pp. 271–72). Since then the situation has deteriorated further. Sullivan's (1988) more recent comparative survey of 700 Ontario dropouts found that forty-three percent cited school-related factors as the main reason why they left school, while only twenty-seven percent cited work-related reasons, the remaining twenty-three percent identifying push-out reasons such as problems at home, marriage, pregnancy and financial difficulties. The school-related reasons cited included "lack of interest/dislike/boredom" (twenty-four percent of the total responses) "problems with teachers" (seven percent), "discipline problems" (four percent), "courses offered" (four percent), and "poor grades" (four percent) (p. 34).

The Sullivan study also surveyed a matching sample of 700 non-dropouts. As might be expected, eighty-five percent of the non-dropouts declared that a good education is very important—but so did sixty-two percent of the dropouts. Even more startling perhaps, when response categories are collapsed there is virtually no difference between the ninety-nine percent of non-dropouts who considered a good education to be "very important" or "somewhat important" and the ninety-four percent of dropouts who expressed a similar view (p. 19). Dropouts, then, do not necessarily fail to appreciate the value of a good education: they just do not believe that secondary schools can provide them with this. But then not all those who stay in school believe this either. Only twenty-three percent of the non-dropouts in the Sullivan study rated the quality of the education they received as "excellent," fifty-eight percent rated it as "good," and the remaining thirty-nine percent as "only fair" or "poor" (p. 20).

The pattern sketched above is by no means restricted to Ontario. As Kronick and Hargis (1990) observed, "what appears continually in the literature is that the dropout reports 'School was not for me' as the main reason for leaving. Hence something in the very nature of the [secondary] school is operating to facilitate these youth in their leaving school" (p. 67). In Husen's (1979) words, "there is ample evidence to show that in highly industrialized countries . . . attitude towards schooling becomes increasingly negative as the students progress through the grades constituting compulsory schooling" (p. 13). The industrial nations, of course, are the only ones that have been able to afford systems of universal secondary education, systems which for the most part rely almost exclusively on mass secondary schooling, as is the case in Canada. But they are not working.

At least one key claim in the dropout argument is thus substantiated by the evidence: our secondary schools are not meeting the educational needs of all of their clients. But the problem is more chronic and widespread than current critics appear to recognize. Rather than providing a useful and valued education for all young people, contemporary systems of mass secondary schooling seem to be alienating many of those they were created to serve; and this is not just a Canadian phenomenon. To the contrary, it appears endemic to all nations that have placed their faith in systems of universal secondary schooling. Rather than behaving irrationally, dropouts, are, in effect, "voting with their feet": they are registering their dissatisfaction with contemporary secondary schools by walking out. So are the many thousands of other young people who, while they remain registered in school, are often absent from the classroom. On this point, Husen (1979) reports daily absenteeism rates on the order of thirty to thirty-five percent in North American and European big-city secondary schools. Moreover, it seems that many of those who stay in school and graduate are less than satisfied with the form and quality of the education they receive.

So, what can be done? As it is currently presented, the dropout argument assumes that secondary schools should be able to provide a useful education for most, if not all, of our youth. If, as seems clear, they are failing to do this, then, so the argument goes, we must somehow "fix" whatever is wrong with our secondary schools and redouble our efforts to keep dropouts and potential dropouts enrolled. It is imperative to do this, we are reminded, so that our youth will be able to find employment in the high-tech job market of the future, and thus ensure that Canada will remain competitive in an increasingly cut-throat global economy. There are at least three fallacies in this line of reasoning. The first is what I have previously called the fallacy of structural adequacy (Allison, 1984); the second is what my colleague James Sanders (1991) has termed the moralistic fallacy; and the third might be dubbed the fallacy of linear extrapolation.

The Fallacy of Structural Adequacy

The view that it is possible to provide a full range of educational opportunities through the sole vehicle of the secondary school represents a radical and recent redefinition of long-established expectations. Prior to the second world war, secondary schools throughout most of the world were structured, staffed, and operated as selective institutions of higher learning or vocational training. Entry was normally restricted to those who did well on competitive examinations; the program of studies was prescriptive and demanding, and graduation was dependent on success in final examinations. In addition to the broad goal of providing a higher level education to young people able to cope with the demanding curriculum, these "high" schools served society and the economy by training and selecting the few who would go on to become university graduates, professionals, highly skilled artisans and, we should not forget, future secondary (but not at that time elementary) school teachers. In such schools, a high "dropout" rate might well have been taken as evidence that the schools were doing their job well, rather than poorly.

By mid-century, most of the United States had begun to move toward a more inclusive form of secondary level education with the introduction of the credit-based comprehensive high school of the kind immortalized in Hollywood movies portraying small town, middle American life in those times, such as the James Stewart classic, *It's a Wonderful Life*. Some seventy-four percent of that nation's fourteen to seventeen year old population were enrolled in secondary schools in 1940, although only a little more than half of all seventeen year olds actually graduated (Tanner, 1972, Tables 2-1 & 2-2). Some western Canadian provinces were moving in a similar direction, but as far as all other educational jurisdictions were concerned, secondary schools continued to function as special-ized, essentially elite institutions dedicated to providing an advanced education for a select few, rather than a general education for all. Thus, as late as 1951 less than half of Canadian youth aged fourteen to seventeen were enrolled in school (Statistics Canada, 1978, Table 2). In Europe, Husen (1979, p. 27) estimates that before 1950 "less than twenty percent of the teenage cohort proceeded in full-time schooling beyond completion of mandatory schooling at 13 or 14." After mid-century, however, nations in the developed world began to commit themselves to providing free and equal access to secondary level education for all their young citizens. Two major alternatives were identified by policy makers faced with the problem of how to convert the new ideal of secondary education for all into reality: the differentiated model and the comprehensive model. The differentiated option retained the traditional academic secondary school and added new kinds of secondary level schools designed to provide general and vocational education for those unable to gain entry into or to survive the demanding academic curriculum of the traditional secondary school. The com-prehensive solution sought to modify and extend the secondary level curriculum to accommodate all students in the same school. Thus, while the differentiated model aimed at creating and operating a variety of different kinds of secondary schools, each intended to serve specialized educational needs and interests, the comprehensive model sought to create new non-selective, omni-capable schools similar to those pioneered in the United States.

The differentiated model was the preferred policy solution in many European countries, while the comprehensive model dominated in North America. Some educational authorities, such as the United Kingdom and Ontario, initially opted for the differentiated approach, and then changed policy horses mid-stream and adopted the comprehensive model. But regardless of which model was adopted, each embodied what now appears to have been an over-reliance on the process of schooling as the sole educational instrument. This is the fallacy of structural adequacy: the assumption that an entirely new and previously unat-tempted service can be provided by simply modifying or augmenting existing educational structures that were originally created to serve quite different needs.

There are essentially two reasons why the secondary school, in all its modern variants, has proved inadequate to the task of educating everyone. First, the tra-ditional secondary school has proved to be remarkably resistant to attempts to change it into a fully functional omni-capable educational institution. Although the modern comprehensive secondary schools in North America and the systems of differentiated secondary schools in countries such as Germany and Japan purport to provide a useful education for all young people, it appears that only some students gain any substantial benefit from the experience. To be fair, some of the new vocational and technical schools and programs have been reasonably successful, but as a general rule it is the more demanding, academically oriented schools and programs that are most valued by parents, employers, and those students who stay in school. Thus, the students who appear to benefit most from the new systems of universal secondary education are those who would likely have been candidates to attend the selective secondary schools of the past. Second, many of the other students attending the new schools find them oppressive and alienating, and the schooling experience meaningless. As reviewed earlier, the research evidence shows that most students drop out simply because they can't bear to endure the schooling experience any longer, while many of those that stay in school find the experience less than valuable.

To summarize, the assumption that secondary schools are capable of providing a useful and valuable education for all young people is a relatively recent idea, one that did not gain wide currency until the middle decades of this century. It is an assumption that appears to have been adopted by default as a result of a laudable desire to provide universal access to higher levels of education for young citizens in developed societies. Having committed themselves to providing a secondary level education for all their young citizens, the policy makers concerned appear to have automatically and uncritically assumed that this goal could be achieved by adapting or augmenting existing secondary schools, institutions which had, for the most part, evolved over previous centuries to perform a quite different, indeed quite opposite, function. Given the refractory nature of secondary schools—their apparent deeply rooted resistance to change—and given that the new policy was expected to be an immediate success, then it is not surprising that it has failed.

The Moralistic Fallacy

Can this policy be made to work if we persevere? Is it reasonable to expect that secondary schools can be changed so that they will be able to deliver a useful and valuable education to everyone? I think not: the collective experience of Western societies in attempting to achieve this goal over the past four decades or so implies that by themselves secondary schools will always be an inadequate vehicle for the creation of truly effective systems of universal secondary education. The full scope and range of the educational interests and individual abilities to be served is just too great. On one hand, secondary schools, or at least some of them, are still expected to deliver modern versions of their traditional, academically demanding curriculum for those students willing to submit to this regimen; on the other they are expected to provide alternate programs of study that both society at large and all other students will consider worthwhile and relevant. All past efforts to do this show that attempts to offer both of these kinds of programs in secondary schools, regardless of whether this is done in single, comprehensive institutions or a differentiated system of schools, will result in the less academic programs being judged as inferior by parents, employers, and the students themselves.

Educational policy makers thus face a no-win dilemma if they continue to pursue the goal of universal secondary education through secondary schooling. They can abandon the traditionally derived academic curriculum, the teaching of which has long been the specialized function of secondary schools, or they can abandon the students who are not willing or able to meet the demands of this form of education. The first option implies the adoption of a popularized curriculum that will appeal to the greatest number of student interests. But this will not satisfy all students, especially those who want an academically demanding education; nor will it satisfy social expectations and economic needs that demand a sufficiently challenging educational experience be provided for our "best and brightest" adolescents. Hence this option cannot reasonably be expected to produce a viable and acceptable system of universal secondary education. The second option appears politically unacceptable, as it implies a reversion to the selective schooling policies of the past.

The thrust of the dropout argument as it is currently being presented implies a continued commitment to trying to steer between the Scylla and Charybdis of these two irreconcilable and inherently unacceptable options, but with a swing toward the reconstitution of a more demanding secondary school curriculum. Contemporary critics seem to be arguing that we must somehow restructure secondary schools so that they will provide an improved, higher quality, more relevant education for all young people. As expressed by George Radwanski (1988) the premise here is that "all children, except those with specific and insuperable mental or physical handicaps can be brought to a common, necessary level of knowledge and skill through the application of appropriate pedagogical techniques" (p. 131).

For Radwanski and many others, the appropriate pedagogical techniques would consist of secondary schools offering a traditionally inspired common curriculum taught on mastery learning principles. But specifics aside, the recommended solution relies on somehow managing to change and recalibrate existing secondary schools. To adopt James Sanders' (1991) terminology, this idealistic reconstruction of the possible commits the moralistic fallacy wherein conceptions of what ought to be, are allowed to reconfigure the facts of the case. The brute fact of the matter is that while it is pleasant and politically expedient to believe that everyone, or almost everyone, has the scholastic potential and the motivation to master a modified version of the traditional secondary school curriculum, we know this is not so. Although our egalitarian social ideals make us want to believe that all, or virtually all, of our young citizens can master trigonometry, appreciate Shakespeare, apply economic theory, become orally fluent in a second language, and solve chemical equations, the ability to do any or all of these things is not equally distributed throughout the population. Still less do most young people recognize any intrinsic or instrumental reason for attempting to master such knowledge and skills.

The Fallacy of Linear Extrapolation

This brings us to the claim that young people need to stay in school if they wish to have any reasonable chance of finding a job. Of the three fallacies reviewed here, this is by far the most obvious in that it is based on a simple extension of past conditions into an imperfectly imagined future: because a secondary school diploma bestowed a competitive advantage in seeking a better paying job in past employment markets, it is assumed that this will continue to be the case in the future. Moreover, the full-fledged argument runs, the high-tech, increasingly competitive economy that is confidently expected to dominate employment opportunities in the future will ensure that a secondary school graduation diploma will be a necessary qualification for any worthwhile job.

These assumptions prompted the Conference Board of Canada (1992) study of *The economic cost of dropouts* mentioned earlier. Commissioned by the department of Employment and Immigration Canada, this ambitious econometric analysis concluded that high school dropouts cost the Canadian economy a cool four billion dollars a year (p. 128). This analysis utilized data collected over the last several decades to estimate the total amount of additional income that would have been earned by dropouts if they had remained in school until they graduated. The findings of this and similar studies, and any policy implications they may hold for the future—or for that matter the present—must necessarily rest on the assumption that relationships between employment, earnings, and level of schooling that were obtained in the past will extend into the future. Yet there are sound grounds for questioning both the tenability of this assumption, and thus the findings reported by the Conference Board.

An independent analysis recently reported by my colleague Jerry Paquette (1991), for instance, found a spectacular decline in the economic value of secondary schooling in Canada: while completing secondary school was associated with an average twenty-three percent increase in employment income in the 1980 census data, this advantage declined to only five percent in the 1985 data (p. 462). In other words, the relative difference between the earnings of secondary school graduates and dropouts appears to be declining. This decline may, of course, be only a temporary reversal brought about by current economic difficulties. There are good reasons to believe, however, that this is not the case; that the employment and economic advantages associated with secondary school completion will not apply in the future.

First there is the phenomenon of incremental credentialism: the more common a secondary school diploma becomes amongst job-seekers, the less utility it has in providing a competitive advantage. Inevitably, then, employers who are prepared to pay higher wages to attract more motivated workers will tend to prefer candidates with some kind of post-secondary educational credential. Rather than being a guaranteed passport to a secure economic future, a secondary school diploma thus becomes but one rung on an ever escalating ladder of formal qualifications. Second, there is the massive restructuring of the employment market that is being driven by potent technological advances that are transforming the world economy. Many of the middle status jobs for which employers were once willing to pay higher wages in order to secure better educated and motivated workers are rapidly disappearing as computers and automation transform business and industry. These are precisely the kinds of jobs, of course, that fuelled a demand for secondary school graduates in the past. But as human secretaries, accounting clerks, receptionists, telephone operators, bank tellers, middle managers, and so forth are increasingly replaced by intelligent machines and advanced computer applications, a secondary school diploma may well become economically worthless, except as a ticket to post-secondary training.

In this respect at least, the critics banging the dropout drum are correct when they claim that a secondary school education will be necessary to secure a worthwhile job in the future; but it will not, in itself, be sufficient. In the view of analysts such as Menzies (1989) the technological revolution now under way will result in a radical bifurcation of future employment markets. The high status, high paying jobs will demand advanced post-secondary training, and thus those who aspire to such positions must be willing and able to continue their formal education well beyond secondary school. Then there will be the "Mcjobs": service and retail industry work epitomized by the kind of employment currently offered by the McDonalds food chain. As many current secondary school students and dropouts know from personal experience, one does not need to complete secondary school in order to get and keep such a job. Indeed, many secondary school students already have a Mcjob, and if the only reasonable chance of finding markedly better employment will require extended schooling beyond the secondary level, why would they bother to stay in school?

. . .

CONCLUSION

As it turns out, then, dropping out of secondary school can be an entirely rational and sensible choice for young people who believe they do not have the ability or the motivation to continue their formal education to at least the community college level, and preferably as far as graduate school. The fact that so many students find secondary schools alienating places, and the education provided meaningless, makes the decision to dropout only more sensible.

What does this mean for educational policy? To paraphrase Hamlet, the first step is to recognize that the fault lies not in our schools, but in our system of education. As long as policy makers continue to commit the fallacy of structural adequacy, to assume that secondary schools can provide a sensible education for everyone, we will be unable to make any significant progress toward creating an adequate system of secondary level education. Contemporary critics are quite correct when they stress the desirability of encouraging young people to continue their education. Where they go wrong is in assuming that this must be done through secondary schools, and in assuming that this must be done for economic reasons.

The prime purpose of education is to enhance and extend the talents, knowledge and abilities of individuals so that they may lead more enjoyable and enriched lives, and in doing so enrich society. Pursuit of this objective will obviously yield economic benefits, but we would be wise not to let a preoccupation with economic competitiveness dictate educational policy. This is especially so given the huge and potentially terrifying social implications of the dualistic employment market being spawned by the technological revolution currently under way. How will people find meaning, joy, and satisfaction where only a few will qualify for highly rewarded and respected work, and the rest will have to subsist on Mcjobs or endure continual unemployment? How much worse will it be if we continue to attribute social status primarily on the basis of employment? And how much worse might it become if we bribe our children and youth to stay in school with empty promises? Under such circumstances, the provision of unlimited educational opportunities offering meaningful ways for all members of society to develop their individual talents and interests may offer the only alternative to social collapse or a descent into high-tech feudalism. Systems of mass secondary schooling will never be able to do this. The challenge, then, is to imagine, invent and create new forms and kinds of educational systems and processes that can.

Just what such systems may be like is not immediately evident, that is why policy makers who glimpse the future importance of truly universal education continue to cling to secondary schools as an obvious solution to the problem. But secondary schools are specialized educational institutions that can be sensibly expected to provide a reasonable range of different kinds of schooling; they cannot, by themselves, be expected to provide the full spectrum of rich and varied educational experiences that will be necessary in the near future that, indeed, are necessary today, if we are to provide useful and valued learning opportunities for everyone. What will be required is some form of multi-level, recursive network of formal and non-formal learning contexts that will allow and enable people to pursue their specific interests, develop their particular talents, and acquire needed skills. This does not imply that access to secondary schooling should therefore be limited. To the contrary, it is clearly sensible and desirable to allow and encourage free and unfettered access to secondary schooling for anyone—young or old—who wishes to freely submit themselves to this kind of formal education. But at the same time, those that do not choose to do so, those who find the secondary schooling experience alienating, uninteresting, or simply too challenging, should have equally free and unfettered access to alternate forms and kinds of education that will allow them to enhance their knowledge, to develop and extend their abilities, talents, and skills, and thus enrich their lives and the society to which they belong.

To simply say that everyone should be encouraged—or shamed, bribed or forced if some current policy makers have their way—to earn a secondary school graduation diploma will never achieve this broader end. Nor, is it morally defensible if we are seriously committed to providing equal educational opportunities for all.

. . .

REFERENCES

Allison, D. J. (1974, April). The limitations of secondary schooling and the problem of secondary education. *Teacher Education*, 18–35.

Cap dropout flood, youth minister tells trustees. (1991, July 9). *Toronto Star*, p. D2.

Conference Board of Canada. (1991, July). *The economic cost of dropouts*. (Phase 1 report prepared for the Youth Affairs Branch, Employment and Immigration Canada). Ottawa: Author.

Conference Board of Canada. (1992, March). *The economic cost of secondary school dropouts*. (Final report prepared for the Youth Affairs Branch, Employment and Immigration Canada). Ottawa: Author.

Edmonton educators take pitch to malls. (1992, April 21). *London Free Press*, p. C8.

Ekstrom, R. B., Goertz, M. E., Pollack, J. M., & Rock, D. A. (1986). Who drops out of high school and why? Findings from a national study. *Teachers College Record*, 87(3), 356–373.

Hahn, A. (1987). Reaching out to America's dropouts: What to do. *Phi Delta Kappan*, 256–263.

Husen, T. (1979). *The school in question: A comparative study of the school and its future in Western society*. Oxford: University Press.

Kronick, R. F., & Hargis, C. H. (1990). *Dropouts: Who drops out and why—and the recommended action*. Springfield, IL: Charles C. Thomas.

Lack of national school testing a threat to Canada, McKenna says. (1992, April 7). *Toronto Star*, p. A2.

Menzies, H. (1989). *Fastforward and out of control: How technology is changing your life*. Toronto: Macmillan.

National Center for Educational Statistics. (1991). *Digest of educational statistics 1990* (NCES No. 91-660). Washington, DC: US Department of Education, Office of Educational Research and Improvement.

Natriello, G. (Ed.). (1987). *School dropouts: Patterns and policies*. New York: Teachers College Press.

Paquette, J. (1991). Why should I stay in school? Quantizing private educational returns. *Journal of Educational Finance*, 16, 458–477.

Pauker, J. D., Desnoyers, J., & Pauker, R. (1988). *School attendance and non-attendance in Canada and the United States* (Contract no. 0640 ON04699). Toronto: Ontario Ministry of Education.

Radwanski, G. (1987). *Ontario study of the relevance of education and the issue of dropouts*. Toronto: Ontario Ministry of Education.

Rumberger, R. W. (1983). Dropping out of school: The influence of race, sex and family background. *American Educational Research Journal, 20*(2), 199–220.

Sanders, J. T. (1991). From ought to is: Radwanski and the moralistic fallacy. In D. J. Allison & J. Paquette (Eds.), *Reform and relevance in schooling: Dropouts, destreaming and the common curriculum* (pp. 19–27). Toronto: OISE Press.

Sullivan, M. (1988). *A comparative analysis of dropouts and non-dropouts in Ontario secondary schools* (Contract no. 1094 ON04527). Toronto: Ontario Ministry of Education.

Tanner, D. (1972). *Secondary education: Perspectives and prospects*. New York: Macmillan.

Teachers hopeful for dropout program. (1992, May 27). *London Free Press*, p. C6.

Watson, C. (1974–75). *Focus on dropouts*. Abridged version of the report on the "Ontario Secondary School Dropout Study, 1974–75" by C. Watson and S. McElroy conducted under contract to the Ontario Ministry of Education.

CENSORSHIP AND CANADIAN SCHOOLS

...

Dave Jenkinson

Dear [Teacher]

Please review the following pages of *Double-Dare O'Toole* by Constance C. Greene, i.e., pp. 14, 34, 52, 72, 73, 74, 81, 82, 102, 118, 129, & 130. I find this material extremely unsuitable for an elementary student.

Please advise me of your opinion and whether necessary steps will be taken to have this book removed from our elementary schools.

Thank you for your anticipated cooperation.

[A Concerned Mother]

The above communication, received by a Winnipeg teacher in 1990, is representative of the challenges Canadian teachers and school librarians face daily regarding the learning materials found in their classrooms and school libraries. Some parents, by questioning the contents of schools' books and other learning materials, are simply exercising their democratic right to be involved in their children's schooling; however, in other cases, their requests are acts of censorship.

...

WHAT IS CENSORSHIP?

The *ALA World Encyclopedia of Library and Information Science* (1986) defines censorship as: "An effort by a government, private organization, group or individual to prevent people from reading, seeing or hearing what may be considered as dangerous to government or harmful to the public morality" (p. 173). For the school setting, a reworked definition might more appropriately read:

"Censorship in schools is an effort by an individual or group to prevent students from reading, seeing, or hearing what may be considered as harmful to the students' morality." Two key words in the definition are "prevent" and "harmful." Censors believe that students' morality (i.e. their principles of right and wrong in conduct), will be somehow harmed if the students read, see, or hear an objected-to item.

What is the Difference Between Censorship and Selection?

A portion of a 1991 letter to the editor of *The Christian Family Advocate*, a quarterly Manitoba publication, illustrates the difficulty censors have in understanding the differences between selecting and censoring learning materials. A woman wrote, "The old tune of 'censorship' by parents needs to be focussed on the fact that censorship by [professionals] is called 'textbook selection.'" The censors' "argument" labelling teachers and school librarians as censors takes the following form: the censor rejects some learning materials; the teacher/librarian, in selecting learning materials, also rejects some; therefore, the teacher/librarian is a censor.

Some forty years ago, Asheim (1954) succinctly articulated the differences in behaviour between selectors and censors.

> The selector's approach is positive, while that of the censor is negative. . . . To the selector the important thing is to find reasons to keep the book. Given such a guiding principle, the selector looks for values, for virtues, for strengths, which will overshadow minor objections. For the censor, on the other hand, the important thing is to find reasons to reject the book. [A censor's] guiding principle leads [him or her] to seek out the objectionable features, the weaknesses, the possibilities for misinterpretation. . . . The selector says, if there is anything good in this book let us try to keep it; the censor says, if there is anything bad in this book, let us reject it. And since there is seldom a flawless work in any form, the censor's approach can destroy much that is worth saving. (pp. 95–96)

• • •

WHAT ARE THE SOURCES OF CENSORSHIP?

Teachers confront the dilemma of having to educate all while offending none. Kuhn (1992) explained the sources of censorship as residing in the differences in beliefs between the liberal left and conservative right.

> The motivation to censor comes from conflicting ideas and attitudes within a community. Typically, in Canada, this involves a confrontation

between the values of a liberal humanism, which is concerned with social and political freedom of action and expression, and evangelical fundamentalism, which is concerned that such expression be limited by appropriate social, moral and political constraints. (p. 24)

These differences, in turn, can find their expression within the school system. Macdonald (1984) suggested that competition between the "free marketplace of ideas" and "prescriptive" models of education forms the ideological base for censorship problems (p. 23). Adherents to the former position would posit that "schools are responsible for developing young minds in a climate where nothing is hidden" (pp. 21–22), and would argue that exposure to the marketplace of ideas is less harmful than insulation. "Prescriptive" model supporters, on the other hand, hold that schools are expected to transmit basic, traditional societal values by conveying to students only the best that is known and thought in the world. "The belief is that once students have learned these basic ideas they will be able to cope in a larger world" (p. 22).

Obviously, the "free marketplace of ideas" concept leaves little or no provision for the withdrawal of learning materials whereas the "prescriptive" model would allow resources to be removed from schools whenever it could be "demonstrated" that an item did not reflect "acceptable" community standards. Since all public schools operate somewhere along the continuum between the "free marketplace of ideas" and the "prescriptive" models, this lack of consensus means that censorship will remain an issue for teachers.

The last two decades have seen a great change in the locus of challenges to school materials. In the past, most censorship came from the conservative right, but, as Martin and Ford (1983) point out, in recent years, "no less militant have been groups from the centre and left who formerly might have been found among the opponents of censorship but now take issue against materials which they find offensive to their causes. Such groups have targeted materials alleged to lend aid and comfort to sexism and racism" (p. 4).

• • •

WHO ARE THE CENSORS?

Most complaints about school materials originate in the home. A Manitoba study found parents to be "the single most frequent source of complaints in school libraries with four of every ten complaints coming from a parent or guardian" (Jenkinson, 1986, p. 8). Although the American experience of organized, ongoing, pro-censorship lobbies has not yet become part of the Canadian scene, sometimes objecting parents will assume a corporate identity. Concerned Citizens for Bible-Centred Religious Education For Our Schools was a group formed to fight for the banning of Margaret Laurence's books from the Peterborough (Ontario) County Board of Education (Contenta, 1985). In 1987, Parents for Quality Curriculum (PFQC) came into being in Victoria County (Ontario) "to express concern about the perceived negative implications and anti-Christian slant in certain poetry, short stories, novels and plays that can be or are currently being taught to secondary school students in Fenelon Falls" (Hurst, 1989, p. 26). Parents in Winnipeg protesting the use of William Valgardson's *Gentle Sinners* as a Grade 11 English text adopted the name Parents for Quality Education (PFQE) and took the step of becoming legally incorporated (Jenkinson, in press). PFQE was also the name used by a Calgary group lobbying to have the *Impressions* reading series banned (Ross, 1990).

Censors from the religious right appear to be sharing their concerns via their publications. The 1991 summer issue of *The Christian Family Advocate* contained an article, "Caution: Elementary Literature," in which the writer discussed the Holt, Rinehart and Winston *Impressions* series. Among the criticisms directed at the books was that "unlike the old stories of evil, witchcraft appears good. Furthermore, the series features other religions with the exclusion or distortion of Christianity. The series also presents Satanic and Occult overtones" (p. 3). The article provided examples of the books' violent and witchcraft/occult content and concluded by asking, "How did such materials get into your schools? How can they be removed?" and urging, "It's a time for action, to purge our children's reading and curricula of content condemned by both educators and psychologists" (p. 4).

One of the Manitoba study's more surprising findings was the degree of involvement of in-school personnel in challenges to school library materials. "Though classroom teachers made up one-quarter of the remaining complainants, when the various within-education sources such as the school staff, administrators, and library workers were grouped together, they originated slightly more than half the challenges" (Jenkinson, 1986, p. 8).

· · ·

WHAT GETS CHALLENGED?

Schools contain two types of learning materials: classroom "texts" which students must view, listen to, or read; and materials housed in the school library that support the curriculum. In some instances, student use of specific library items may be required, but, in most cases, students will voluntarily select the library materials they borrow. Both required classroom texts and free-choice school library materials are censorship targets. It seems that, if any word in a piece of literature offends, then the entire work offends. "A suburban [Vancouver] school district banned *The Baby Project* by Sarah Ellis because it used—just once—the word f * * *" (McDowell, 1990, p. 29). *The Annick ABC*, by Roger Pare, was removed from a Red Deer school library because a parent complained "the reference 'N is for nudist eating noodles in Naples' is inappropriate for kindergarten students" (In Alberta, 1992, p. A8).

Particularly prone to challenge from the conservative right are materials containing "bad language" or "explicit sex." In the Manitoba study (Jenkinson, 1986), fiction charged with containing offending language included Harry Mazer's *The Last Mission* and Alice Childress' *A Hero Ain't Nothing But a Sandwich*. Judy Blume's *Forever* and Anne Holm's *I Am David* were just two of many titles considered to contain explicit sex. Non-fiction was not exempt, and the *Dictionary of American Slang* was restricted to teachers in a rural Grade 9 to 12 school because it contained "obscenities." Volumes 14 and 15 of *Childcraft Encyclopedia* were removed from a rural kindergarten to Grade 8 school as these volumes dealt with human reproduction, which, in the complainant's eyes, was "explicit sex."

In a "man-bites-dog" incident, a mother in Burnaby, BC complained that a sexual reference in the play *Macbeth* was censored from the standard Grade 11 school text (Out, 1983). An eleven-line passage, in Act II, Scene 2, wherein a porter comments that alcoholic beverages first stimulate sexual appetite and then deaden it, was deleted in a version of the play used Canada-wide. Her son apparently spotted the deletion while reading the play as a recorded version— with the passage intact—played alongside. The mother, demanding that her son be taught the complete version, argued, "Kids can't afford to be innocent in today's world. If you take the reality out of what they read, they will be left defenseless."

A commonly used censorship tactic is "snippet warfare" in which censors, having identified offending portions of a book, parade these out-of-context snippets before others, saying, "Look at the filthy, immoral books schools are using to teach your children!" The Winnipeg controversy over the use of William Valgardson's *Gentle Sinners* as a Grade 11 English text first came to wider attention when a mothers' group circulated a letter in which were enclosed excerpts taken from the book. A separate page contained ten passages of two to eleven lines in length lifted from the book's 213 pages. Excerpts labelled as "graphic pornography" included: "The dark outline of her nipples were round and firm and the nipples were like dark stones," and "While he watched, she took off her raincoat, then her white dress and underclothes and piled them neatly to one side. Naked, they rolled into the comforter."

The mother whose letter about *Double-Dare O'Toole* introduced this chapter was also engaging in a form of snippet warfare. Greene's 158 page book, identified by the publisher as suitable for Grades 4 and up, deals with an almost-twelve-year-old whose habit of accepting dares continually gets him into trouble. Egged on by his elder brother and an older classmate, sixth grader Fex O'Toole takes his first awkward, exploratory steps into the uncharted waters of boy-girl relationships.

If the teacher had explored the mother's ten cited pages, what "evidence" would have been found to support the parent's request for the book's removal? Some of the offending pages used variations of the expressions "getting any" and "making out," without either being explained. The term "French kiss" was repeated a number of times, while page 14 had Fex vainly looking for his brother's hidden *Playboy*. Apparently, "Concerned Mother" believed that students in Grades 4–6 should not be encountering these terms. Interestingly, if the mother had focussed on the book's theme, as opposed to the work's language, she may have discovered that Greene supports the position that elementary school children of opposite sexes should resist peer pressure and remain at the "friend" stage. When, for example, Fex's older and supposedly "experienced" brother asks, "You know how to French kiss?" (p. 73), Fex does not even recognize the term. Later, having looked it up in the dictionary and discovered its meaning, Fex's reaction is, "Gross. Really gross. Forget it. I'm not getting into any of that stuff" (p. 75). And he does not!

More recently, fiction and non-fiction books containing anything related to witchcraft, the occult, satanism, or New Age beliefs have been challenged. Fiction titles accused of containing witchcraft include Mercer Mayer's *Liza Lou and the Yeller Belly Swamp* and Alvin Schwartz's *Scary Stories to Tell in the Dark* (Jenkinson, 1986). In 1992, a Grade 5 teacher in Winnipeg withdrew Madeleine L'Engle's Newbery Medal book, *Wrinkle in Time*, from classroom study following parents' complaints that the book was "unChristian" and "too fanciful." On the first day of school in September 1991, parents from twenty-eight families of children attending Rosary Catholic School in Manning, Alberta "stormed their children's school, held the principal captive in his office and then cleaned the classrooms of allegedly satanic materials" (MacCallum, 1992, p. C2). The object of the parents' wrath was the *Impressions* series of language arts texts published by Holt, Rinehart and Winston. "After reading some incendiary brochures from the United States, the Christian fundamentalist parents who led the raid on the school had become convinced that the series represented the work of Satan."

Materials that appear to be beyond reproach still become censorship targets. Members of the Sechelt, BC area's IWA–Canada International Woodworkers of America local called on the local school board to pull Diane Leger-Haskell's *Maxine's Tree*, a fiction title aimed at readers aged four to seven, because the book was anti-logging (Collins, 1992). Timothy Findley's *The Wars* was challenged by an Ontario high school principal because it was a "downer" (Findley, 1983, p. 16). Hughes (1989) explains that "negativism, as a reason for censorship, can embrace such diverse subjects as teenage suicide, discussions of death, the confusion of growing up, and such issues as nuclear war, poverty, slavery, and the Holocaust" (p. 6).

Sometimes items that are not even school purchases become censorship subjects. Peterborough County Board of Education trustees asked the Ontario Public School Boards Association to seek to have the "Garbage Pail Kids," a popular series of bubble gum cards, withdrawn from the market. The five cards in a 25 cent package were described by the board as "most objectionable and contrary to the values taught in public schools" (Mayes, 1988, p. A4). To illustrate the point that the cards "unduly exploit violence and degradation of children," trustees cited "Upset Tommy and Sidney Kidney [who] emphasize vomiting and urination."

Targeted for censorship by the liberal left are the various "isms," such as racism and sexism. The Waterloo (Ontario) County Board of Education, one of Canada's largest school jurisdictions, banned William Shakespeare's *Merchant of Venice* from Grades 7 through 11 in response to parents' complaints that the teaching of the play in Grade 9 was leading to anti-Semitism (Bowen, 1986). The Chief of the Fort McMurray band in Alberta sought to have Laura Ingalls Wilder's *Little House on the Prairie* banned because he feared "children are being exposed to literature which reinforces negative stereotypes about native people" (O'Farrell, 1989, p.11). A mother in Kitchener, Ontario asked the Waterloo Board of Education to remove Mark Twain's *The Adventures of Huckleberry Finn* because she feared "the word [nigger] may be legitimized by classroom discussion of the book" (Kitchener, 1986, p. F1).

. . .

WHEN DOES CENSORSHIP OCCUR?

Much, if not most, censorship is largely invisible because it occurs "quietly" and unknown to the larger public. Some 150 school library items representing 111 different titles were challenged in Manitoba in a two-year period, but only three of these incidents were reported by the province's principal daily newspaper (Jenkinson, 1986, p. 12).

Between the time an author generates an idea for a book and that book is used by a student, there are at least three distinct periods when censorship can occur. They are: the creative/pre-publication period; the post-publication/pre-purchase phase; and the post-purchase period. Most visible censorship occurs in the last phase, that is, in the weeks and years following a book's publication and after it has been acquired by a school. Sometimes, challenges commence almost simultaneously with a book's appearance as was the case with Robert Munsch's *Giant, or Waiting for the Thursday Boat* which was initially banned by the Middlesex County Board in Ontario before being returned with the limitations that "because of the book's religious implications, it won't be in the primary curriculum and teachers won't be permitted to read it to children" ("Children's book," 1990, p. 19).

A book can also enjoy years of "peaceful" existence before suddenly being criticized. Described as a "mainstay in the Ontario school curriculum for decades" (Holden, 1988, p. A3), William Golding's 1954 novel *Lord of the Flies* was challenged in Toronto in 1988 because "there are racist undertones throughout the book. There's a bias against people who hunt, a whole bias in favour of Western civilization, against people of tribal cultures, for want of a better term" (Ip, 1988, p. A15). As well, in one passage, the term "niggers" was used. The publicity director of Faber and Faber, the book's publisher, expressed surprise at the racism charges, saying, it was the first time anybody had ever raised this to her knowledge (Reid, 1988). While the Toronto board did not accept its race relations committee's recommendation to withdraw *Lord of the Flies* from the curriculum, it did decide that "teachers will be given training next fall in the selection and use of novels." ("School board," 1988).

A title can be challenged repeatedly in the same jurisdiction or at varying times in different locales. The best known example of the first scenario is Margaret Laurence's *The Diviners*, which was twice heatedly debated as a teaching novel in Peterborough, Ontario. While appearing before a textbook review committee, a secondary school English department head said, "In 1976, standing approximately here, I little dreamed I would be standing here in 1985 defending the same book against the same charge to a similar committee" ("Laurence books," 1985, p. 48). One of the most frequently censored books in North America is Mark Twain's *The Adventures of Huckleberry Finn.* Challenged as a high school teaching text in Winnipeg in 1982 (Hill, 1982), and in Kitchener in 1986 (Teahen, 1986), the book's place on the list of approved novels taught in New Brunswick's high school English courses was questioned in 1992 ("N.B. Group," 1992).

Challenges to school materials, whether positively or negatively resolved, can create a lingering climate of self-censorship on the part of those in the education system charged with selecting materials and with those involved in the creative process—the authors and their editors and publishers. A librarian offered the opinion that "the ripple effect of one publicized complaint is enormous and probably results in multi cases of unofficial or unpublicized censorship" (Jenkinson, 1986, p. 13). Some evidence for this perspective is provided by Bruce (1990) who reported that, following a well publicized book-banning debate over a number of secondary school English texts, including Mordecai Richler's *The Apprenticeship of Duddy Kravitz*, the Essex County Board of Education issued a memo to its secondary schools indicating that textbook "selections which might evoke undue controversy should be avoided." The board's executive director asserted that this directive did not mean that the board was "getting into the business of banning books," but a secondary school English department head responded that the guidelines will affect "future textbook selections" (p. 14).

Certainly, members of the teaching profession who approach the material selection process with one eye focussed on potential censorship problems can, themselves, become censors. Armed with a mental checklist of "no-no"s, the selection-censor reads reviews to discover if materials contain any content that would disqualify them as purchases. A school administrator said his school had received no complaints in twenty-one years because "in my capacity as vice-principal, I try to ensure that books which would cause controversy are never placed in the library" (Jenkinson, 1986, p. 15). One result of this "preventative" approach was proffered by a teacher-librarian. "Our selection practices . . . tend to be on the conservative side. While not ignoring important issues such as abortion, etc., we tend to collect only the most innocuous types of controversial materials" (Jenkinson, 1986, p. 15).

Trade and educational publishers, who are not just in the business of publishing books, but also of selling them, are certainly aware of the self-censorship climate that seemingly pervades education, and some act accordingly. Author

Margaret Buffie recounts how she was asked to submit two stories for a text anthology and had both turned down. "They didn't say anything about literary value at all. One was turned down because it had an occult edge to it. The other was a humorous story about a young girl deciding to loan or sell her younger sister to a woman who had no children, and they [the publisher] felt that was undermining the family." From Buffie's perspective, the publisher was asking, "Is there anything in these stories that could offend anyone?" (Bildfell, 1992, p. 13).

Author Monica Hughes (1989) expressed concern about publishers' efforts to precensor. "I am afraid that publishing paranoia may lead to the pabluming of language in favour of the safe, the unrisky, the bland, the colourless, and to the sanitizing of Canadian history" (p. 5). Evidence for Hughes' concern is offered by John Trueman, a history professor and co-author of three school history texts, who stated he would not write a text today. "To say what you really believe historically would be very difficult now. There's a perception on the part of the ministries of education that the past is, or somehow should be, perfect. If you try and tell it like it really was, that will make any number of groups really upset. The textbook gets planned down to a kind of uniformly dull level so it doesn't offend anyone. It's rewriting history" (Bildfell, 1992, p. 13). Another history text author, Paul Bennet, also believes the nervousness of publishers results in texts that are "innocuous, lacking in any contentious interpretations, and quite homogenized." He cites the situation where, in a senior high text, "a gory documentary account of the scalping of Radisson was deleted, not because it was inaccurate, but because it might run afoul of [Ontario's] Circular 14 guidelines regarding positive portrayals of aboriginal peoples" (Bildfell, p. 13). In another example, a Canadian publishing firm apparently rejected an essay on the Fathers of Confederation because no women were present at the Charlottetown meetings in 1864 (McMurtry, 1989).

The above examples should not lead to the conclusion that all publishers always commit such acts of self-censorship in response to the demand for "political correctness." When Macmillan received a request to excerpt a piece of historical fiction—Jack Hodgin's *The Barclay Family Circus*—in a Grade 9 anthology "with permission to remove sex bias," the firm refused. Anne Nelles, rights and permissions manager, responded to the request, saying, "When an author is writing about a particular time in history, he must portray the language, the morals, and the customs of that time. For an editor to alter the author's words to conform to our standards now is dishonest" (Bildfell, 1992, p. 13).

Ministries of education can also become more directly involved in the censorship game. The contents of *Themes for All Times*, a Grade 12 anthology to be published by Jesperson Press, had been approved by Newfoundland's curriculum committee when two department employees objected to twelve stories. The short stories cited contained such phrases as "damn" or "hell" and the odd "for Christ's sake" (Sullivan, 1989, p. C3). When publishers, writers, and the Opposition protested the deletions, the Department of Education "whittled down its original stance to cutting two stories and editing four others."

As the Newfoundland situation demonstrated, when censorship attempts are exposed to the scrutiny of the larger public, an anti-censorship lobby often develops. While it was suggested earlier that censorship incidents can create a negative climate of self- or precensorship, positive outcomes can also occur. Henniger, a Peterborough trustee involved in the Margaret Laurence controversy, commented that one benefit was that "the community did, through the process of considering what books were suitable for students to read, develop new and, I would suggest more tolerant, community standards" (1988, p. 14).

· · ·

WHAT FORMS DO THE CENSORS' *PREVENTION* TAKE?

Obviously, the censor's most complete means of preventing the claimed harm from occurring would be to effect the total removal of offending items from the school setting. A two-year Manitoba study (Jenkinson, 1986) revealed that nearly sixty percent of the challenges to school libraries' contents resulted in the questioned materials being permanently taken off library shelves. Some of the discarded titles included Beatrice Culleton's *In Search of April Raintree*, Dennis Lee's *Garbage Delight*, Brian Doyle's *You Can Pick Me Up at Peggy's Cove*, and Alice Munro's *Lives of Girls and Women*.

Some censors propose what appears to be a less radical solution—the deletion of just the offensive portions. The Manitoba study identified cases of school-level expurgation, including the tearing out of the first chapter of Avery Corman's *Kramer vs. Kramer*, the removal of several pages from Norma Mazer's *Up in Seth's Room*, and the whiting-out of four-letter words in Stephen King's *Cujo*. In 1991 in Dartmouth, Nova Scotia, the father of a primary-level child complained that, in Sheree Fitch's *Sleeping Dragons All Around*, one of the eight dragons is called Beelzebub which "means 'prince of demons' and is one of several demonic names for the Devil himself." Having connected the book with the occult, the father then said, "In the Occult, in particular, the danger involved is Satanism. In this book, the Devil is portrayed in a harmless, innocent way. . . . One of the names of the Devil should not be allowed in Children's [*sic*] literature, portrayed in such a light manner." The father proposed "the book be pulled off the shelves of children's libraries and either the dragon be renamed [i.e. altered] or remove the book altogether."

A third means of "prevention" suggested by censors is to restrict the availability of the allegedly harmful material. In the Manitoba study (Jenkinson, 1986), some twenty percent of challenges were resolved in that manner. For instance, all of Paul Zindel's books were restricted to high school students in a rural Grade 4 to 12 school; Shel Silverstein's poetry book, *Where the Sidewalk Ends*, had restricted access in a rural kindergarten to Grade 6 school; a rural Grade 7 to 12 school kept the magazines *Chatelaine* and *Ms.* under the counter where they were "given out with discretion"; students in a rural Grade 7 to 9 school had to request Charles Darwin's *Origins of the Species*; and students in an urban Grade 7 to 9 school were required to ask for Richard Peck's *Are You in the House Alone?* More recently, Robert Munsch's *Giant, or Waiting for the Thursday Boat* was restricted to students in Grades 4 and up by the Middlesex County Board of Education (Vincent, 1990).

The restrictive approach has a certain initial appeal for it seemingly satisfies both the censor and the material's defender. By not being completely banned, the item remains in the school while still being unavailable to the student grouping that the censor believes it will harm. In practical terms, however, restricting access to materials can yield the same result as outright banning. Said one library worker, "In my school, anything regarding human sexuality is not to be on open [free access] shelves. I find storing them away an unrealistic option as young teenagers will not ask for these books" (Jenkinson, 1986, p. 11).

A fourth means of restriction is to "label" an item. The label is to function as a warning or caution so that potential users will be alerted to a material's "offensive" content. Forewarned, individuals can decide whether or not to proceed. Following the Fort Garry school division's decision to uphold the continued use of William Valgardson's *Gentle Sinners* as a Grade 11 English text, a trustee introduced a motion calling for the novel to include a warning to parents indicating that some readers have found it offensive. However, the motion was defeated 5–4 (Nikides, 1990). When Lynne Reid Banks' *The Indian in the Cupboard* was challenged in a Kamloops school district on the basis of its supposed negative portrayal of native people, the school board decided to tag the book with a disclaimer rather than withdraw it from the school district's libraries. The label would serve to alert the reader that the book contains "sensitive" material ("British author," 1992).

Though most of the censors' acts of "prevention" are related to the reading of printed materials, especially books, the "seeing" and "hearing" aspects are not totally ignored. The Manitoba Director of Renaissance International tried unsuccessfully to win support for the banning of Roman Polanski's film version of *Macbeth* on the grounds that it was too violent for high school students (MacKenzie, 1980). After the Waterloo Board of Education withdrew *The Merchant of Venice* from the curriculum, it subsequently announced that students from that district would not be permitted to attend the special student matinees of the play at Stratford (Hayes, 1989).

Because human beings can be both seen and heard, they also become censorship targets. Not just books, but their authors are now being banned from schools. Among Canadian authors for children and adolescents who have been "dis-invited" to speak at schools are award winners Margaret Buffie, Welwyn Wilton Katz, Kevin Major, Sandra Richmond, and Kathy Stinson. Sometimes an author is censored after being allowed into a school, as was the case with Sandy Frances Duncan who was asked not to mention one of her books during a day of scheduled readings in Labrador. "I was told *Listen to Me, Grace Kelly* was a fine book but it was unsuitable for the scheduled audiences. . . . Nobody would explain why it was unsuitable" (Collins, 1991, p. 27). Diana Wieler is wary of public readings since she was cautioned to keep it clean during a reading of *Bad Boy*, her 1989 novel that centres on a homosexual teenager. "I was warned twice not to say anything dirty. . . . It really made me angry because I've written about intimate matters and I would know what to read and what not to read publicly" (Quattrin, 1992, p. C25).

• • •

WHAT IS THE "HARM" CENSORS CLAIM WILL BEFALL STUDENTS?

In the Manitoba study, the most frequently cited reasons for objecting to materials were: immaturity of readers; profanity; and explicit sex (Jenkinson, 1986, p. 10). "Immaturity of readers" was the means objectors used to register their concern that an item's content was inappropriate for a certain age grouping while simultaneously suggesting that the item would possibly be acceptable if it were restricted to higher grades. Books dealing with sex education, such as Eric Johnson's *Love and Sex in Plain Language* or *The Teenage Body Book* by Kathy McCoy and Charles Wibbelsman were particularly susceptible to this form of complaint. Paul Zindel's *The Pigman* was challenged and its circulation restricted because of "profanity," and yet there is no profanity in the book. John, one of the work's two central characters, wants to swear but is persuaded by Lorraine to substitute "@#$%" for cuss words. As John says, "Now that isn't too bad an idea because @#$% leaves it to the imagination and most people have a worse imagination than I have." Obviously John was correct! The charge of explicit sex was directed at fiction titles such as Todd Strasser's *Angel Dust Blues* and Judy Blume's *Are You There God? It's Me, Margaret.*

A group of parents told the education committee of the Essex County Board of Education that they wanted Mordecai Richler's *The Apprenticeship of Duddy Kravitz* removed from high school reading lists because of "vulgarity, sexual expressions, and sexual innuendoes" ("Writers alarmed," 1990, p. C1). In Peterborough, a mother sought to have Margaret Laurence's *A Jest of God, The Stone Angel,* and *The Diviners* plus J.D. Salinger's *Catcher in the Rye* withdrawn as high school teaching materials. She said "she objects to the profanities and explicit sexual scenes they contain because she believes they harm children's minds" (Bird, 1985, p. 19). An aunt of an eight-year-old in Winnipeg described the language in Thomas Rockwell's *The Thief* as "pornographic garbage" (Roberts, 1984, p. 3).

The proffered reasons, such as immaturity of readers, profanity, and explicit sex, are, however, just the surface explanations for complaints. Deeper reasons are essentially twofold. The censor would argue that, at best, a school's owning materials with offensive content is equivalent to the school's condoning the behaviours contained within the items. Far worse, by using or circulating these materials, the school is endorsing this offensive content and is thereby encouraging children and youth to behave in the manners described in the items.

The censor's belief that the school's ownership and use of an item condone or encourage particular behaviours can be found in the wording of their complaints. When a nine-year-old girl brought home Willard Espy's *The Almanac of Words at Play*, a collection of rhymes, word games, and literary anomalies, and began reading some of the verses aloud, her parents complained to the North Shore Board of Education that the book "condones nudity, drinking and drugs, and attacks religion and other moral values" ("Immoral book," 1987). Junior secondary schools in a Vernon, BC school district removed Norma Klein's *Breaking Up* because a group of parents felt the book of fiction condoned teenage sex and homosexuality ("Book pulled," 1984). Three Winnipeg parents seeking a ban of William Valgardson's *Gentle Sinners* answered the question "What do you think might be the result of reading this work?" by saying, "Kids that may be prone to pornography could justify it by saying it's taught in school";

"School authorities validate pornography"; and "Students see this as an acceptable lifestyle when taught by schools" (Jenkinson, in press).

In a dispute lasting some four years, a mother in Prince George, BC, sought to have Wardell Pomeroy's *Boys and Sex* permanently removed from the school's library because she felt that it promotes promiscuity among teenagers ("Mother sues," 1987). A student in Sarnia, Ontario wanted Timothy Findley's *The Wars* dropped from her high school's curriculum because she believed "that studying the book pressures students into accepting homosexuality" ("Student calls," 1991, p. C5). A mother in Portage la Prairie, Manitoba said that studying Paul Zindel's *The Pigman* "prompted her son and daughter to become rebellious and irresponsible and she fears her youngest child will also be affected when she studies the novel in grade 9 next fall" (Cole, 1985, p. 12).

. . .

WHAT CAN YOU DO TO PREPARE YOURSELF FOR THE CENSOR?

Canada does not have a tradition of resolving educational issues in the courts. Thus, public discussion centres on media presentations and public meetings. Generally, decisions regarding disputes are made by school boards or provincial ministries in what is usually an emotionally charged atmosphere. Teachers and professional educators have little time to explicate ideologies to an audience that is concerned with the specific issue at hand. (Macdonald, 1984, p. 22)

Macdonald's comments suggest that preparations for censorship confrontations must begin long before the first complaint is received. Today's censorship climate has changed the question from "*Will* censorship happen to me?" to "*When* will it happen?" In just two years, one-quarter of Manitoba's schools received at least one challenge to school library material (Jenkinson, 1986).

A good beginning is to become aware of groups that oppose censorship. Amey's (1988b) suggestion, "to discover whether your local, state or provincial library organizations have committees concerned with the defense of intellectual freedom" (p. 20), is worth pursuing. Since 1985, the Book and Periodical Council has sponsored a "Freedom to Read Week" to focus local, regional, and national attention on aspects of intellectual freedom. The Council also produces a kit of activities for students, teachers, librarians, and booksellers.

Part of your advance preparation for the censor should include knowing precisely why, in educational terms, you are teaching what you are teaching. If you are an English teacher, you need to create a written rationale for each item in your literature program. Though first-year teachers are, for example, frequently limited to teaching the class texts that are already in a school, using that reason as a response will not likely satisfy a complainant. You must still prepare a rationale that you would be willing to share with anyone questioning your text choices.

Thinking through how you will respond to a complaint is also part of your advance planning. For instance, Cavanagh and Styles (1981b) suggest that "an alternative text procedure should be used whenever a parent objects to a son or daughter reading or studying a particular book. The right of parents to be directly involved in shaping the learning of their own children needs to be recognized and guaranteed in a way that does not discriminate against parents or their children" (p. 132). An example of such non-discriminatory behaviour can be found in the actions of the Winnipeg teacher involved in the William Valgardson *Gentle Sinners* incident. Upon receiving one parent's complaint, the teacher immediately made an alternative novel available to everyone in the class and utilized a set of assignments and summative evaluation that were equally applicable to either book (Jenkinson, in press).

Determine if your school jurisdiction has a document called a "selection policy." Normally consisting of two basic parts, the first section includes statements concerning who is responsible for selecting learning resources. In Manitoba, for example, the *Public Schools Act* assigns that legal responsibility to school boards. For practical purposes, however, most boards delegate learning material selection to the professional teaching staff. Statements of such delegation would be recorded in the selection policy. This first portion might also include the criteria and procedures utilized in selecting learning resources.

The selection policy's second section deals with the procedures the school jurisdiction uses when someone challenges a learning material. These procedures usually consist of three stages with the first being the informal reconsideration phase wherein the complainant meets with the teacher, and perhaps the principal, to discuss the complaint. Often matters are resolved at this point. Possibly the parent does not want his or her child to study a particular book and so an acceptable alternative is found. In other cases, the complainant, satisfied by the teacher's explanations, simply withdraws the complaint.

Many times, however, a satisfactory conclusion is not arrived at via this informal process, and the challenge moves to the formal reconsideration stage that usually requires complainants to provide the specifics of their complaints in writing, using a form provided by the school jurisdiction. The selection policy will detail the membership of a reconsideration committee, including the process of their selection and the procedures the committee will follow in responding to the complaint. The decision of the reconsideration committee is reported to the school board. Should the complainant not be satisfied with the committee's recommendation, the process moves to the third stage wherein the school board acts as a final appeal court.

School trustee Henniger (1988), in reviewing the procedures used to deal with challenges to Margaret Laurence's books in Peterborough County, said, "There does come a point at which the matter becomes a political one" (p. 14). The "point" in Henniger's statement is that time when a complaint, having been considered both informally and formally according to a board selection/reconsideration policy, reaches a school board acting in its capacity as the final arbiter of a challenged item's fate. According to Henniger, "Politicians are elected to interpret community standards and to make political decisions. If the electors do not like the decisions, they can turn out the trustee in the next election" (p. 14).

If your school jurisdiction lacks a selection policy, which Amey (1988a) describes as the "first line of defence against censorship" (p. 9), one needs to be developed. Guidance can be found in two most useful resources: Amey's article (1988a), "In defense of intellectual freedom," examines the fine collection policy developed by Vancouver's School District 39, while Manitoba Education and Training's document, *Selection of Learning Resources*, (1990) provides "guidelines for schools and school divisions/districts to develop their own selection policies" (p. iv).

Obviously, your first level of support in resisting a censorship attempt should come from your fellow teachers and administrators. Unfortunately, that assistance may not always be forthcoming, and, in some cases, you will find some within the school actively opposed to your stance. Davis (1989), in describing the censorship of a student publication in Toronto, observed that "with notable exceptions like teachers and administrators who have fought for *The Catcher in the Rye* and *The Diviners*, teachers do not have a good record as fighters for strong curriculum. It was a shock to me to see how few teachers supported my fight . . ." (p. 109). Recall, as well, that the Jenkinson (1986) study found that over half of the challenges to materials in Manitoba school libraries originated within the school. Rainey's survey (1989) of the censorship attitudes of school principals in Manitoba and British Columbia indicated that more than half of the principals felt that they "should have the authority to unilaterally remove materials from the school library" (p. 20).

Rainey (1987) posits a number of reasons for the lack of within-school support. "Administrators and teachers must be concerned with the smooth and efficient running of the school. Removing challenged materials may seem to be the quickest and easiest way to solve a problem without causing disruptions in the school and the community" (p. 28). As well, Rainey (1988) faults pre-service teacher education when he observes that "in Canada, there are no universities which deal in any depth with this issue [censorship] in teacher education courses. Indeed, aside from the limited topics taught in some English Education classes and in school librarianship, there appears to be little or no time spent on the problems of censorship" (p. 4). Rainey's survey (1989) of principals in Manitoba and British Columbia offered evidence supporting his last statement, for only eleven percent of principals surveyed had taken any courses at either the undergraduate or graduate level in which censorship was a topic of discussion (p. 19).

Another source of assistance is your teachers' union. The Saskatchewan Teachers' Federation, for example, adopted a formal intellectual freedom policy in 1990. The increase in censorship attempts may be causing teachers' unions to assume a more aggressive posture. When the Fort Garry school division decided to again re-evaluate William Valgardson's *Gentle Sinners*, the president of the area's teachers' union wrote the board, saying, in part:

> I wish the Board of Trustees to be aware that the Manitoba Teachers' Society is concerned about attacks on learning material by small pressure groups. It is also concerned about the apparent failure of Trustees to defend the rights of their schools and their teachers to academic freedom. It has reached a point where the Society is ready to go to court to defend the rights of teachers to academic freedom including the right to teach without harassment by small pressure groups who demand the right to make decisions for everyone else. (Jenkinson, in press)

Cavanagh and Styles (1981a) observed that "the politics of confrontation is now perceived by citizen groups as one of the few effective means by which government bodies can be forced to listen and change can be brought about in the schools" (p. 125). Arguing that those opposed to censorship need to band together, author Monica Hughes (1989) said, "I believe we can no longer take it for granted that our elected bodies will represent the interest of the silent majority. The silent majority must become aware of the increasing trend towards censorship and plan strategy to combat it. . . . I also believe that we need a national anti-censorship organization, such as The People for the American Way, in Canada" (p. 7). Although such an organization has yet to emerge, British Columbia has established an "Intellectual Freedom, Education and Defence Fund to help librarians, school principals, and others combat the growing threat of censorship. The fund . . . will be used to publish pamphlets, sponsor workshops, and provide speakers who can illustrate the ways of fighting literary repression" (McDowell, 1990, p. 29).

• • •

SOME FINAL WORDS

While generalist elementary teachers, English teachers in middle and senior years, and school librarians appear to be the principal recipients of challenges, teachers of other subject areas would be unwise to assume they will remain untouched by censorship. Some years ago, junior high science teachers in one Manitoba rural school division were confronted by a group of parents claiming that J.D. Hoyes' *Solids, Liquids, and Gases*, a supplementary science text, contained subliminal illustrations supporting abortion. One of the parents' complaints was that the book's full-colour cover photograph of a bubbling liquid-filled beaker included a "picture" of rats eating fetuses dumped on a garbage heap.

In 1991, a father in Dartmouth, Nova Scotia complained to the school board when his primary-level son played a game in gym class in which the "teacher was a Wizard, a male witch, with a magic wand." Seeing the teacher's actions as exposing children "to the tenets of Witchcraft," the father proposed that the board establish a policy requiring "all teachers, whether in gym or classroom, [to] refrain from using religious props (objects or names)." A Williams Lake, BC, mother did not want her Grade 1 daughter being taught yoga and threatened to pull her out of physical education class (Alexander, 1990). The teacher was utilizing Rachel Carr's yoga exercise book, *Be a Frog, a Bird or a Tree*, which the mother characterized as having potentially evil influences. One of the exercises was the stork, where one stands on one leg and stares straight ahead. According to the mother, this position is designed to create a trance state and, "in a trance children could end up with the devil speaking through them."

Though it may be another teacher in your school who is having to deal with a censorship challenge, it is your challenge as well. According to Bildfell (1992), despite his experiences with *Impressions*, David Booth, Professor of Education at the University of Toronto, and one of the series' editors, firmly believes most people, and most schools, are against censorship. "But you've got to fight back, and not give in, but explain, and clarify the situation, and be very strong in upholding your principles. If you give in to one complaint, you will give in to 300" (p. 14).

. . .

REFERENCES

ALA world encyclopedia of library and information services. (1986). Chicago: American Library Association.

Alexander, K. (1990). The devil and the stork position. *British Columbia Report, 2*(10), 51.

Amey, L. (1988a). In defense of intellectual freedom: What to include in a school library collection policy. *Emergency Librarian, 15*(4), 9–13.

Amey, L. (1988b). Pyramid power: The teacher-librarian and censorship. *Emergency Librarian, 16*(1), 15–20.

Asheim, L. (1954). The librarian's responsibility: Not censorship but selection. In F. Melcher (Ed.), *Freedom of book selection* (pp. 95–96). Chicago: American Library Association.

Bildfell, L. (1992). Class warfare. *Quill & Quire, 58*(4), 1, 13–14.

Bird, B. (1985, January 12). Township's action angers novelist Margaret Laurence. *Winnipeg Free Press*, p. 19.

Book pulled from school following sex complaint. (1984, October 11). *The Vancouver Sun*, p. B7.

Bowen, B. (1986, July 12). School board bans *Merchant of Venice* over anti-Semitism. *The Globe and Mail*, pp. A1, A2.

British author objects to proposal to label her novel offensive to some. (1992, March 14). *The Vancouver Sun*, p. A3.

Bruce, A. (1990). War of words. *Quill & Quire, 56*(12), 14.

Cavanagh, G., & Styles, K. (1981a). The many faces of censorship. *Canadian Library Journal, 38*(3), 123–125.

Cavanagh, G., & Styles, K. (1981b). Sanity in handling censorship issues. *Canadian Library Journal, 38*(3), 129–132.

Children's word book banned from schools. (1987, November 19). *The Globe and Mail*, p. A13.

Cole, B. (1985, June 5). Portage parent raps book used in school. *Winnipeg Free Press*, p. 12.

Collins, J. (1991). Suffer the little children. *Books in Canada, 20*(7), 25–27.

Collins, J. (1992). Controversy over *Maxine's Tree. CM, 20*(3), 134–135.

Contenta, S. (1985, March 3). 'Ban Margaret Laurence' group says she's too disgusting for schoolkids. *The Toronto Star*, pp. A1, A8.

Dafoe, C. (1992, February 21). Union calls children's book an insult to B.C. loggers. *The Globe and Mail*, p. C4.

Davis, B. (1989). Two dogs, *The Diviners* and teenage sex. *Our Schools/Our Selves, 2*(1), 101–115.

Findley, T. (1983). Censorship by every other name. *Indirections, 8*(4), 14–20.

Hayes, E. (1989). The Merchant of Venice: A moral dilemma. *Indirections, 14*(3), 29–32.

Henniger, I. (1988). The censorship wars in Peterborough. *Ontario Education, 20*(4), 10–14.

Hill, L. (1982, December 14). Huckleberry Finn expelled from Maples Collegiate. *Winnipeg Free Press*, p. 1.

Holden, A. (1988, July 1). Toronto board won't ban 'racist' *Lord of the Flies. The Toronto Star*, p. A3.

Hughes, M. (1989). Censorship and juvenile literature. *Alberta Learning Resources Journal, 9*(3), 5–8.

Hurst, A. (1989). Book banning goes down to defeat in Victoria County. *Education Today, 1*(1), 26–27.

"Immoral" book of verse under attack by parents. (1987, November 5). *The Toronto Star*, p. A2.

In Alberta B is for book, bad and ban. (1992, June 11). *Winnipeg Free Press*, p. A8.

Ip, G. (1988, June 24). *Lord of the Flies* is racist, school board panel says. *The Globe and Mail*, p. A15.

Jenkinson, D. (1986). Censorship iceberg. *Canadian Library Journal, 43*(1), 7–21.

Jenkinson, D. (1990). Censorship: The role of the reviewing journal. *CM, 18*(3), 100–102.

Jenkinson, D. (1991). Can I say that? The writer and censorship. *Dateline Arts, 4*(4), 6–9.

Jenkinson, D. (in press). Valgardson's *Gentle Sinners*: A book more sinned against than sinning. *CCL.*

Kitchener woman wants *Huckleberry Finn* banned. (1986, December 4). *Calgary Herald*, p. F1.

Kuhn, M.A. (1992). Censorship in Canadian schools: A double-edged sword for school librarians. *School Libraries in Canada, 12*(1), 23–27.

Laurence books given approval. (1985, April 11). *Winnipeg Free Press*, p. 48.

MacCallum, E. (1992, February 26). U.S. fundamentalists blamed for dispute. *The Globe and Mail*, p. C2.

Macdonald, J. (1984). The concept of censorship: Two ideological perspectives. *School Libraries in Canada, 4*(3), 21–24.

MacKenzie, Glen. (1980, September 19). School ban of *Macbeth* film urged. *Winnipeg Free Press*, p. 1.

Manitoba Education and Training. Instructional Resources Branch. School Library Media Program Curriculum Committee. (1990). *Selection of learning resources: Policies and procedures for Manitoba schools*. Winnipeg: The Crown.

Martin, R.G., & Ford, T.M. (1983). The threat of censorship. *The Canadian School Executive, 2*(7), 2–5.

Mayes, Alison. (1988, November 28). Trustees seeking ban on bubblegum cards. *The Globe and Mail*, p. A4.

McDowell, J. (1990). Battling the barbarians: B.C. librarians prepare to fight book banners. *British Columbia Report, 1*(39), 29.

McMurtry, J. (1989). Literature provides more than comfort. *The Canadian School Executive, 8*(9), 21–22.

Mother sues school board for right to enter library. (1987, April 16). *The Vancouver Sun*, p. A23.

N.B. group wants classics banned. (1992). *Quill & Quire, 58*(2), p. 35.

Nikides, G. (1990, April 15). Board backs book. *Winnipeg Free Press*, p. 2.

O'Farrell, E. (1989). Chief calls for book banning. *Windspeaker, 6*(50), 11.

Out, damned spot, out! Schools censor *Macbeth*. (1983, January 5). *Montreal Gazette*, p. B1.

Quattrin, L. (1992, February 24). Book censorship generates workshop. *Winnipeg Free Press*, p. C25.

Rainey, M. (1987). Handling censorship. *Reading-Canada-Lecture, 5*(1), 27–30.

Rainey, M. (1988). How to pre-empt censorship. *The Canadian School Executive, 7*(7), 3–8.

Rainey, M. (1989). A study of the role of school principals in the censorship of school library materials. *School Libraries in Canada, 10*(1), 16–24.

Reid, S. (1988, June 25). *Lord of the Flies* 'racism' surprises publisher, blacks. *The Toronto Star*, p. A8.

Roberts, D. (1984, April 6). Language in child's book worries aunt. *Winnipeg Free Press*, p. 1.

Ross, E. (1990, May 25). Province won't ban book series. *Calgary Herald*, p. B10.

School board rejects bid to ban novel. (1988, July 1). *The Globe and Mail*, p. A4.

Student calls for removal of Findley book. (1991, June 6). *The Globe and Mail*, p. C5.

Sullivan, J.M. (1989, July 1). Censorship cries heard as province changes textbooks. *The Globe and Mail*, p. C3.

Teahen, K. (1986, December 4). Mother would ban 'racist' Huck Finn. *The Globe and Mail*, p. A17.

Vincent, I. (1990, November 7). Book banned by Ontario school. *The Globe and Mail*, p. C1.

Writers alarmed at move to ban book. (1990, June 14). *The Globe and Mail*, p. C1.

EDUCATION FOR THE EXCEPTIONAL CHILD

...

The education of the exceptional child in Canada has received widespread and heightened attention during the past twenty years. We have become much more conscious of the need to provide equality of educational opportunity to all children regardless of their academic capacities. We have become more attuned to considering the needs of children who differ in their manner of coping with educational experiences and we have become more willing to modify school routines or programs in order to maximize each student's potential. The authors in this section address a number of educational and legal issues pertaining to pupils who are at both ends of the scholastic ability spectrum, from those who have mental and physical disabilities to those who may be defined as gifted.

Kysela, French, and Brenton-Haden provide an analysis of each province's legislative mandate for the provision of educational services for the handicapped, noting the permissive conditions that apply in some provinces and the mandatory conditions that exist in others. The implications of these provisions for the development and implementation of special education programs are noted and potential issues, concerns, and challenges in the field are identified.

Gall, in a similar vein, discusses major issues arising from the current provision of special education services for special needs students in Canada. Given the unique sociopolitical fabric of this nation, Gall argues that legislative reform is desirable and necessary so that greater federal co-ordination and financial support can be utilized to provide appropriate educational strategies for special needs children.

Wilgosh examines issues related to the integration of children with special needs into regular classrooms. The chapter offers some direction on teacher preparation for meeting the needs of children with special needs in regular classrooms, touching particularly on issues related to assessment of student needs, management of behaviour problems, and collaborative program planning and implementation.

The chapter by O'Neill and Norris reflects the growing recognition of the responsibility of educators to provide special programs to fulfil the psychological, educational, occupational, and social needs of gifted and talented students. After explaining definitions and identification procedures used in this area of special education, they discuss the goals, implementation, and operationalization of educational programs that are vital for the optimal development of the gifted student. To O'Neill and Norris, the challenge to schools and teachers is to become involved in initiating and continuing to support special programs for the gifted until such programs are a part of every school system in Canada, regardless of size.

LEGISLATION AND POLICY INVOLVING CHILDREN WITH SPECIAL NEEDS

...

G . M . Kysela

F . French

S . Brenton - Haden

INTRODUCTION

Educational matters traditionally have been left to provincial jurisdictions in Canada, particularly with respect to the issues of educational principles, policy, regulations, and specific service provisions. Even though the Bill of Rights passed in 1958 by the Diefenbaker government guaranteed specific rights to individuals within Canadian federal jurisdiction, specific provincial statutes or regulations were seldom challenged on the basis of equal opportunities or experiences. However, since that time, a number of legislative, litigative, and social factors have brought this disparity to the attention of lawmakers and the public.

These factors have been particularly focussed, in part, upon the educational experiences of those persons in our society with special needs or handicapping conditions such as mental handicaps, behavioural adjustment problems, and physical handicaps. During the past fifteen years, the Commission on Children with Emotional and Learning Disorders in Canada, Public Law 94-142 in the United States, the Warnock Commission in the United Kingdom, and more generally, the human rights movement in North America, have each provided either legislative or policy changes affecting the educational experiences of exceptional persons. In this chapter, we will focus on the impact of these developments upon the schooling of children with special needs.

It was increasingly recognized in the 1960s that children with special needs were experiencing de facto segregation and exclusion from normal schooling experiences because of the "special environment" institutions provided for their education. Although these provisions were made with the best intentions, under the assumption that similar special needs or handicapping conditions in some way resulted in similar educational needs, it was realized that neither the person with exceptionalities nor the other members of our communities were benefiting from this exclusionary process. That is, the child with special needs was completing school without the requisite competencies to function in our communities, and was often unable to read, write, compute, or perform the other academic and social skills presumably being taught in their segregated schools and institutions.

Respecting the conditions mentioned above, the definition of special needs adopted in this paper includes the following description: the educationally special child is thought of as any child who differs in her or his manner of coping with educational experiences to such an extent as to require support and/or modification of typical school routine, program, or practices in order for the child to have maximum opportunity for successful development.

This notion of special need and/or handicapping condition encompasses a wide variety of children with varying degrees and kinds of exceptionalities. The idea of the school routine requiring adjustment to suit the dynamic needs of each child with special needs (Kirk, 1979) provides an initial basis for the special educational requirements the school must meet. These children have many needs and strengths common to the majority of children as well as unique needs and strengths relative to their exceptionality. It is now generally accepted that both types of educational needs must be addressed by the educational system. Such an undertaking requires alterations in the typical functioning of the school related to the policy, legislation, and regulations affecting the provision of these educational experiences.

In attempting to meet the children's special needs, schools have extended services to these children through local special programs, integrated learning experiences, and more functional, community-oriented programs of study. In addition, the provinces and the country as a whole have gradually altered statutes of educational relevance in order to provide legislative and regulatory provisions to ensure that the child with special needs will be able to gain access to these special programs on a continuing basis. A major change, in this regard, occurred with the passage into law of the Canadian Constitution and its attendant Charter of Rights in 1982.

• • •

THE CANADIAN CONSTITUTION AND PROVINCIAL LEGISLATION

Educational Control

Schools in Canada are administered through local school boards under the legislative authority of the provincial government. There is no specific federal law outlining the provision of education to children. Under section 93 of the

Constitution Act, 1967, provincial legislatures are responsible for enacting legislation pertaining to education. Each provincial government develops its own legislation, regulations, policies, procedures, and guidelines concerning education. As noted by Dickinson and Mackay (1989), this practice had resulted in a wide array of legislative and procedural rules rendering the provision of education subject to wide-ranging interpretations on local as well as provincial levels. This variability of interpretation is particularly evident in the education of students who have special needs.

With a few exceptions, the federal government does not have direct authority regarding the provision of educational experiences to children as is the case in other nations such as the United States. Exceptions exist in the education of First Nations people through Indian and Northern Affairs, national defence, certain employment programs, health and welfare, and some indirect involvement in correctional services as outlined in the Young Offenders Act and the Criminal Code.

However, federal agencies and national organizations such as the Department of Health and Welfare, the Canadian Council for Exceptional Children and the Canadian Association for Community Living have provided task force reports, information, and recommendations to the provinces regarding provisions for children with special needs. As well, precedents from other nations such as the Education for All handicapped Children Act of 1975 by the US Congress and the 1978 Warnock Report in the United Kingdom have had a significant impact on legislation, policy, and practice.

With the passage in 1982 of the Canadian Charter of Rights and Freedoms by the Parliament of Canada, an enhanced opportunity to reflect upon the impact of provincial legislation and local school board policies was created. Although not pertaining exclusively to education for persons with special needs, the Charter does outline some basic rights to equality of opportunity for persons with mental or physical handicaps for all provinces and territories of Canada.

The section that has received the greatest attention relative to the rights of persons with exceptionalities has been section 15 of the Charter. Section 15 reads as follows:

> 1. Every individual is equal before and under the law and has the right to the equal protection and equal benefit of the law without discrimination based on race, national or ethnic origin, colour, religion, sex, age or mental or physical disability.
> 2. Subsection (1) does not preclude any law, program, or activity that has as its object the amelioration of conditions of disadvantaged individuals or

groups including those that are disadvantaged because of race, national or ethnic origin, colour, religion, sex, age or mental or physical disability.

While the Charter was proclaimed and implemented in 1982, some sections such as section 15 did not come into effect until April, 1985. The supposition was that each province would bring existing legislation to a level consistent with the specified rights for all persons by the 1985 deadline. Many provinces did review existing legislation and policy, which resulted in various directives addressing provincial interpretations of the intent of the Charter and the existing provincial legislative and procedural statements.

An ongoing debate has existed over the interpretation of the wording of section 15. For example, Dickinson and Mackay (1989) indicated that the wording of equality before and under the law and equal protection and benefit of the law may imply an intent to refer only to inequality arising out of the application of the law rather than a private action. This interpretation opens the issue of what constitutes a private action.

Indeed, just about every word and clause of section 15 is open to interpretation and debate. Furthermore, trial cases involving section 15 have appeared to address procedural rather than substantive issues in their rulings. For example, in a 1985 case involving a child with developmental delays and the Banff School District, the court refused to grant an order to compel the board to admit the child as a pupil. The child had been attending the Banff School District for six years when the school board decided that the child should be directed to a school in Calgary. The parents were not given a hearing by the board before its decision and subsequently took the matter to court seeking an order that the child attend school in Banff. The School Act in Alberta allows for discretion on the part of the board in deciding the placement of pupils and the court was not able to direct the board to exercise that discretion in a specific way. An order was granted, however, to compel a hearing in the case since procedural fairness required that the child's parents be given a hearing before the board made its initial decision regarding placement.

Before moving ahead to discuss the issue of mandatory and permissive legislation, the issue of whether education is seen as a right or a privilege requires comment.

Education: A Right or a Privilege?

Rights are protected by law while privileges are granted by persons in authority and power and can be withdrawn at the discretion of the grantor. This difference is a significant issue relative to children with special needs. If education is seen as a right, then it must be provided in an equitable manner to all persons, including those with special needs. It would follow that if education is a right, then each and every province would be required to provide for the education of all its citizens regardless of their needs. However, if it is a privilege, then provinces can continue within their legal mandate the control of education as permissive in the legislation and allow for exclusionary clauses regarding the education of all persons.

The nature of what constitutes an education also is one which is subject to some debate. For example, in reviewing several provincial school acts, it is informative to note that most provinces have Education or School Acts that constitute the legislation pertaining to the education of persons. The Nova Scotia Education Act does not use the word education. The term used in the Act is "the right to attend a school." In other words, education itself is defined in terms of the right to attend school, not in terms of what goes on in school.

Dickinson and Mackay (1989), who have reviewed this issue in much more depth, have argued that the Act in Nova Scotia as in most other provinces tends to imply a privilege not a right to an education. However, within the context of the entire Act, the right to attend a school can only be taken away by following procedures designed to protect the interest of those involved. As well, a later section in the Education Act of Nova Scotia indicates that "a school board shall make provision for the education and instruction of all pupils." Thus, the Act goes beyond defining education as attendance and addresses the term education as entitling students to the courses set out by the "Governor in Council as are included in the school program."

In order to gain a full understanding of the issue of right versus privilege, the Education Act also must be considered in terms of provincial human rights acts. Only two provincial human rights acts list education as a right, Quebec and Saskatchewan. Other provinces do not specifically mention education in their human rights acts.

Returning to the question of whether education is a right or a privilege brings home the concern that while the Canadian Charter indicates that every person "is equal before and under the law and has the right to the equal protection and equal benefit of the law," there is considerable room for interpretation for the implications of the Charter for persons with special needs. The fact that education is a provincial responsibility, that education is covered by provincial legislation, and that local school boards are ultimately responsible for the delivery of that education leaves much more room for interpretation and debate. Education should be a right, not a privilege. However, it would appear that with the exception of Saskatchewan, Quebec, and possibly Ontario, education is treated more as a privilege than a right. In the provinces of Saskatchewan, Quebec, and Ontario the argument that education is a right would seem easier to defend.

• • •

THE LOGIC OF MANDATORY LEGISLATION

Baldwin (1991), following a cross-Canada sample of provincial legislation, concluded that neither the Charter nor human rights legislation will sufficiently assist persons with special needs in advancing their cause of challenging the discretion of school authorities in the provision of educational programs and services. He states that "the present stance of the courts is clearly that statutory directives to reasonably accommodate special students meet constitutional guarantees."

Given the fact that education is a provincial responsibility and mandate, it follows that it is at the provincial level that legislation must be clear and direct regarding the provision of educational programs and services for all children, including those with special needs. Mandatory legislation requires all school boards to provide educational programs and services to all children regardless of their exceptionalities. Permissive legislation "permits" provision of special programs and services without requiring that local school boards supply such programs and services.

A third term that is important to note is that in certain provinces with permissive legislation, a "zero reject" policy exists that entails a process to prevent any child from being excluded from access to schooling.

In Canada, the following provinces have what might be termed mandatory legislation: Newfoundland, New Brunswick, Quebec, Ontario, Manitoba, Saskatchewan, and Alberta. Provinces and territories with clearly permissive legislation are Prince Edward Island, British Columbia, the Yukon, and the Northwest Territories.

Nova Scotia is somewhat unique in that it was the first province to introduce specific legislation directing school boards to be responsible for the instruction of students with special needs in 1973. However, a significant change took place in 1984 when the original clause concerning instruction for children with a physical or mental disability was changed to include two additional statements.

One of those statements is viewed as positive by advocates for the child with special needs in that it provides a mandate that school boards cannot simply place a child with special needs in the regular classroom without the necessary support programs and services. In other words, children cannot be "dumped" into the mainstream with the argument that they are receiving an education if no enhancements are provided to enable their meaningful learning.

The second change is viewed with more concern. A new clause, "capable of benefiting from such programs and services" was added. The implications of this statement are of concern since there is a suggestion that there may be some children who could be deemed not to be capable of benefiting from such programs and services. This decision could provide an exclusionary option for school districts. While there are many arguments against the use of such an exclusionary option, the effect has been to reduce the stringency of the original act.

However, such an effect may result in exclusion from special programs and services and not from school, since other aspects of the Nova Scotia legislation would make it difficult for a local school board to exclude a child from school. The matter is now one of debate and it is now questionable whether Nova Scotia really does have mandatory legislation with a zero reject policy.

While legislation in the provinces and territories has tended to focus on persons with a handicap, a few provinces have included the education of children described as gifted in their definition of the student with an exceptionality. Only Ontario has mandatory legislation that includes these children, while Saskatchewan has legislation that permits special programming for such students. Other provinces such as Quebec, Manitoba, and British Columbia have addressed the education of students thought to be gifted through existing sections of their education acts. The lack of mandatory legislation addressing the needs of these learners has had a significant impact on the provision of programs and services. In Nova Scotia, during the 1992 restraint on spending in education, one of the areas that became most vulnerable to curtailment and abandonment was the programs and services for students described as gifted. This example typifies the fears of parents and advocates with regard to the lack of legislation and policy enshrining the rights of persons with special needs to needed programs and services.

• • •

THE RIGHT TO APPEAL

Historically, appeal processes have been available to parents in the United States for many years. More recently, some provinces in Canada have established procedures intended to assist in the resolution of disagreements between parents and school jurisdictions regarding due process and student placement. Two of the more notable examples of appeal procedures exist in Ontario and Alberta.

However, procedures are in place in Nova Scotia, New Brunswick, Ontario, Saskatchewan, Alberta, and the Northwest Territories.

In the case of Ontario, parents or students who are not satisfied with the decision of the Special Education Identification Placement and Review Committee may request an initial review and discussion with the committee making the determination. After this process is complete, parents or students who are not satisfied may request referral to an Appeal Board established by the local school board. If the matter is still not resolved to the satisfaction of the parties, an appeal to a provincial tribunal is possible. The decision of the tribunal will be final and binding.

Appeal boards in Ontario may only deal with identification and placement issues and an ongoing debate exists over whether the provincial tribunal can make program changes. This limitation impacts an appeal hearing in that the choice may be one of selecting the more appropriate placement from existing resources rather than helping define what might be an appropriate program for the child.

Barnsley and French (1988), in reviewing the information that had emerged on the appeal process existing in Canada, particularly Ontario and Alberta, highlighted a number of issues. Several questions were raised: Who should bear the cost of an appeal? What would be the mandate and authority of the appeal body? Should appeals be local or provincial undertakings? Particular concern continues to exist with the content of the appeal in dealing with substantive and/or procedural matters as well as whether the principles of fundamental or natural justice have been followed in accordance with the intent of the Charter.

The principles of natural justice are intended to ensure that the appeals procedures are fair and just for both parties. To ensure access to fairness and justice, it is critical to establish an impartial review body to make recommendations and conduct a hearing independent of the parents, the school district, and provincial government or other agencies with a vested interest.

With regard to the nature of the appeal, whether procedural or substantive, a considerable debate continues. In general, appeals tend to focus on the assessed strengths and needs of the student, the procedures used and the qualifications of persons involved in the assessment, and the timely and meaningful involvement of the parents in the assessment and decision-making process. Substantive matters such as the nature of the program to be offered the child tend not to be appealable. As noted by Baldwin (1991), this type of failure to address substantive issues tends to provide parents with little authority to legally influence the programs their child will receive. On the other side of this issue are the arguments addressing reasonable responses to needs and the difficulties school boards face in meeting an ever-widening set of needs on the part of their consumers. It would seem that a reasonable compromise should exist between the two poles of procedural and substantive issues.

• • •

POLICY DEVELOPMENT AND SERVICE DELIVERY ISSUES

In the introduction to this chapter, several major issues were identified that form the basic premise of the provision of special education services to students in Canadian schools. Such premises as the right to life experiences commensurate both with that of their peers and with social standards usually form the basis for mandatory legislation. The presence of such legislation makes possible associated policies and regulations that specifically endorse *and* ensure educational programs for students with special needs. In this section, the philosophical issues associated with these policies will be briefly examined. Following this, a description of these major policy areas and a service delivery model are outlined describing the steps necessary to provide for the integration of students with special needs within our schools and communities. The final area to be discussed includes new directions identified through these policy areas and the service provision model, and challenges to education for children with special needs.

• • •

PHILOSOPHICAL BASIS FOR POLICY DEVELOPMENT

The Charter of Rights and Freedoms and mandatory provincial legislation helped educators focus upon the provision of services to *all* children. However, the problem issues discussed under provincial legislation have existed for some time. In attempts to solve these problems, advocacy groups, provincial government departments, school jurisdictions, teachers, and teacher preparation personnel have worked toward the identification of a variety of models to facilitate the delivery of effective and efficient services to all students. It is towards this goal of service delivery that the model below is directed.

A number of previous authors have attempted to describe the contribution factors that facilitate effective and efficient program and service delivery systems. For example, Karnes and Lee (1977) and Bryan and Bryan (1979) both focussed on teaching techniques of modelling (observational learning) to encourage more appropriate learning behaviours with students having mental handicaps. Yoshida and Gottlieb (1977) have also studied the individualized program planning process, often touted as an effective means of ensuring adequate school experiences for exceptional students. Maher (1980) examined models for evaluating organizational effectiveness, and found no generally accepted conceptualization that would assist in evaluating special educational services.

Conceptually and pragmatically, the most fundamental belief of education involves the child as the *raison d'être* for all educational programs and services, including those for students with special needs. Given this child-centred focus, the principle of natural justice becomes the major overarching principle in the provision of education to children with special needs. Section 7 of the Charter of Rights and Freedoms uses the phrase "fundamental principles of justice" with its intent appearing to equate these principles with natural justice and "procedural requirements of fairness."

While some doubt exists regarding the exact definition and meaning of natural justice, section 7 supports an existing *right* to schooling and introduces the issue of procedural fairness. It may be that the most direct application of this section is in the areas of suspension and expulsion. However, the areas of program planning and placement, particularly the classroom placement of students with special needs, may well hold equal or greater application.

Program planning and placement decisions appear to require a set of safeguards, so that decisions are not only followed but are perceived to have been derived from a clear, reasoned, objective, and well-explained process that evolved from the informed participation of the persons affected by the educational decision (e.g., parents, students, teachers, etc.). Indeed, students, particularly past the age of twelve, should be partners in the educational decision-making process themselves. Thus the notion of the right to education as embodied in the Charter would appear to require the involvement of students in decisions that affect them.

Another fundamental principle at the centre of the service delivery model includes identifying the ethical considerations in the decision-making process, relevant to the practice of teaching and the practice of school psychology. For example, many provincial psychology statutes describe, in the code of ethics attendant to the act, the ethical stance required to assist the psychologist in the designation of the client. While this process may be clear in the case of a private practitioner dealing with an adult client, the situation is more complicated for a school psychologist employed by a local school jurisdiction involved with clients legally considered "minors." Conflicting views of appropriate professional behaviour are possible, both in the determination of who the actual client is (e.g., the school, the parent, or the child) as well as in the determination of what information should be considered confidential. Kimmins, Hunter, and Mackay (1985) have referred to this dilemma in their review of provincial legislation and litigation regarding the practice of school psychology in Canada.

Other principles forming the philosophical basis of any service provision model include the following areas: teacher preparation and qualifications; the provision of due process for review of placement decisions (i.e., an appeal procedure for parents or advocates); administrative, fiscal, and governance support to school systems in the provision of special educational programs (Kysela & French, 1983). With regard to teacher preparation and standards of qualification, personnel involved with students having special needs should possess the requisite skills and knowledge in order to meet the students' special needs, whether in the areas of assessment, program planning, or program provision. They are:

- Skills in reflection and self-evaluation of teaching practice
- Group problem solving, sharing program responsibility, co-operative teaching methodology, establishing interdisciplinary working relationships
- Methods for working with heterogeneous groupings of students including curricular adaptations
- Rationale for mainstreaming, general preparation, inclusive education strategies
- Familiarity with consultation and collaboration models of service provision
- Uses of in-class lesson modelling for immediate feedback on instructional strategies
- Methods in generic and specific content area teaching
- Using co-operative learning models, peer coaching, behaviour management techniques.

These teacher competencies are felt to be crucial for teachers when dealing with students' special needs (Chomicki & Kysela, 1992). This requirement extends from infancy and early childhood through the developmental stages to early adulthood and the transition into community living. This principle and its attendant policy require attention by almost all jurisdictions in Canada, as the foregoing review of legislation indicated.

The provision of due process or appeal procedures by independent persons for the parent, child, or advocate, ensures their access to the decision-making process. In this way, an attempt is made to maintain the notion of natural justice (vis-à-vis the child's peers and accepted social standards) regarding placement and program decisions. Some may argue that this is unnecessary in

Canada, but the very fact that persons with handicaps have continued to experience inequitable treatment, and that provinces vary regarding statutory provisions, *requires* the provision of these safeguards for the student. Finally, the provision of administrative, fiscal, and governance support for special programs provides the vehicles for actually ensuring the provision of services to all students within a jurisdiction. At both the legislative and the policy levels, these provisions will assist school jurisdictions in identifying the means by which to provide special education for students with special needs.

By way of summary, then, the fundamental principles of natural justice, ethical considerations, teacher preparation, provision of an appeal process, and administrative and fiscal support are interconnected with federal and provincial legislation, regulation, and policy. Each of these provisions in turn has an impact upon the design, delivery, and evaluation of special education programs and services. Further, these principles and policies influence the roles and responsibilities held by and/or assigned to the partners in the educational decision-making process.

• • •

PROGRAM DEVELOPMENT AND
IMPLEMENTATION ISSUES

The design, delivery, and evaluation of special education programs can be examined from a molecular viewpoint pertaining to program planning for the child, or as a molar issue pertaining to the provision of programs throughout a school system. Within either analysis, however, a set of hierarchical activities exists in a sequence. These activities move from information gathering and assessment regarding the student and the services available, through information synthesis and program planning to the identification and assignment of resources, followed by program placement and implementation monitoring, and evaluation (Kysela, Barros, Grigg, & Kanee, 1985). The process provides for feedback, in that the monitoring and evaluation functions lead back to more information gathering and subsequent possible program modifications and changes in placement. For each of these four stages, overarching principles or policies exist that guide actions and determine specific roles and responsibilities of the various partners.

The program-planning approach removes the necessity of using labels to describe student needs. Rather, each student is viewed as an individual with particular strengths and needs requiring attention in program selection and implementation.

Freeze, Bravi, and Rampaul (1989) have developed a school-based model for service delivery to children with special needs. Theirs is a consultative-collaborative model, which not only avoids the need to label a child, but also supports the position that all children can be successfully educated in the regular classroom. The approach is non-categorical, based on indirect service to children with special needs through direct resource support to classroom teachers. Assessment and intervention is ecological in nature, focussing on a match between student characteristics and the learning environment. The process is a decision-making one, and involves continual hypothesis testing and reformation, as well as the exploration of many systemic intervention options.

Professional development is a major component in the consultative-collaborative model developed by Freeze et al. (1989). Improved professional competence is targeted through the previously mentioned indirect service approach. The model progresses through six levels of service delivery, beginning with the classroom teacher, and involving teacher teams, the resource teacher, the in-school and divisional support services teams, and ancillary services.

The advantage to such a model, as suggested by Freeze and colleagues, is that it emphasizes and encourages the professional consultation, collaboration, and professional development necessary for improved service delivery not only to children with special needs, but also to all children, within the context of the regular classroom.

A brief consideration of each of these four planning phases will now be pursued, including a description of policy issues associated with each step of the process.

Assessment and Information Gathering

At the system or school jurisdiction level, the decision-making process involves setting policies, guidelines, and procedures to ensure early referral for concerns regarding student progress. Such procedures have been perceived by local school jurisdictions as their responsibility, backed up by provincial support (Kysela & French, 1983). Further, it is proposed that such procedures are more effective when supported by specific referral instruments that document, clarify, and operationalize the reason for referral.

A second systems-level priority involves the provision of specific screening procedures facilitating early detection of hidden disabilities, an important component of an effective and efficient system of special education services. Such procedures should be viewed as general indicators to be supported by individualized follow-up diagnosis. In a review of court decisions in the United States, relative to assessment practices, Baker (1982) identified a number of specific assessment practices that school jurisdictions should consider as standard policy:

1. The language of assessment should reflect the dominant language of the child.
2. Assessment of students from diverse ethnic backgrounds should reflect the cultural standards of the childrens' specific group.
3. Placement and program decisions should use a variety of sources of data rather than a single measure of potential and/or actual achievement.
4. The competence of those individuals responsible for assessment should reflect professional practice competencies set out by appropriate professional groups.
5. Parental permission and active involvement relative to assessment, including screening and subsequent placement and program decisions, should be guaranteed.

Since the major reason for screening and referral is to ensure the accurate identification of student needs, reports should convey accurate and educationally relevant information that can lead to any one of an array of programs and services. Several models have been advocated to provide a continuum of services to all students (Freeze et al, 1989). Recent models suggest that all students can be accommodated in the child's age-appropriate regular classroom (Gartner & Lipski, 1987; Stainback, Stainback, & Jackson, 1992).

The specific components of the assessment/information-gathering phase of the decision-making model include the use of a functional skills assessment across a variety of learning environments, developmental assessment including several developmental domains, and multidisciplinary assessments addressing areas such as medical, academic, speech, and vocational competencies and family priorities. Information gathered in this phase provides data to collate and interpret into an educational plan.

Information Synthesis

Several responsibilities exist within the phase of information synthesis. As well, a number of critical decision points exist in this phase. For example, it is the responsibility of the school administrator to ensure that the synthesis and planning process is undertaken. The teacher has the responsibility to focus upon instructional strategies that have been effectively used with the student or to modify those that have been ineffective.

Parents have the responsibility and should in all cases have the right to participate in the discussions. Such involvement allows them to seek clarification of information that is not clearly understood, to outline their perceptions of the goals they have for their child, and to provide specific input relative to program planning, particularly any placements available to their child, both within and outside the system. The school psychologist has the responsibility for ensuring the breadth and depth of educationally relevant data presented regarding the educational, personal/social, and career development needs of the student. Students also have a right to be involved in the educational decision-making process. Given that programs and services are for students' special needs, their perspective and input are essential both to the process and outcomes of the planning process.

Individual educational plans or programs (IEPs) resulting from this process serve both a process and a product in identifying, documenting, and synthesizing information about student needs, ensuring the implementation of the selected program, and evaluating its effectiveness. While mandatory in only one province (Ontario), the IEP has been the focus of special education during the past fifteen years.

In considering the role of the IEP, Morgan (1977) has identified six key functions: a written commitment of resources; a program-compliance monitoring document; a communication device between home and school; a management tool to ensure that each student receives the special programs and services necessary; and an evaluation device for determining the extent of student benefit and progress. The highlight of the IEP as a process should be on its communicative function.

In surveying teachers' attitudes towards the IEP, Hayes and Higgens (1978) found that many feared the document and its process as an accountability measure. This concern existed despite the stated intent of Public Law 94-142 regarding IEPs, which indicates that the use of IEPs does not guarantee student progress. In fact, educators may wish to use the IEP in advocating for specific programs and services. The alternative viewpoint is that the IEP states what the partners have agreed upon, a reasonable approach for dealing with the student's learning problems, subject to further modification through ongoing monitoring, data collection, synthesis, and further program alternations.

Program Implementation

School administrators are responsible for securing sufficient funds to operate the variety of programs necessary for the students in their district. As well, a range of facilities and materials, professional development programs for all staff, and the provision of student transportation require support and maintenance by the administrative personnel. The important issue is that these principles and policies should be implemented with regard to the notion of natural justice and fairness to the student as the client.

During this program-implementation phase, the above policies support a number of specific activities carried out by the significant partners in the provision of educational service. Long- and short-term goals are specified, teaching strategies are defined, and materials are located and obtained. Peer, student, and family involvement in the student's program are also specified and planned. Finally, some mechanism of ongoing monitoring of the student's progress is put in place to aid in the feedback process for program revisions.

Program Evaluation

The program evaluation process may result in immediate, specific program modifications or in reconsideration of both short-term and long-range goals. As well, some evaluative data may indicate that re-assessment and information gathering are necessary, prior to revisions to IEPs. Thus, both formative evaluations that impact upon specific program characteristics and summative evaluations, often employed to make larger, system-wide decisions regarding program or staff adequacy, require some policy support.

At the systems level, Mollenkopf (1982) suggested that evaluation may include the determination of program effectiveness, provide a basis for a public relations program regarding educational provisions, and assist in the development of more systematic approaches in future program development and service provision. In this same context, Mollenkopf described a discrepancy model for evaluation that examined programs in a constructive manner. Comparisons between what is found and what should be are made in this approach; if a difference or discrepancy is obtained, further evaluation is carried out to determine whether the discrepancy involves positive or negative features and what further actions may be required.

Finally, plans for transitional experiences to the potential sources for advanced education and community living should be developed, so that this process begins long before the student's last year in secondary school. Table 1 summarizes the various policy areas discussed under each of the four phases of information gathering, synthesis, program implementation, and program evaluation. These policy areas will require school jurisdictions and provincial governmental personnel to examine their legislation and regulations to ensure an equitable experience for those students within their realm of responsibility who have special needs or handicapping conditions.

TABLE I
Referral/Assessment/Program Development Issues

Information Gathering	Information Synthesis	Program Implementation	Program Evaluation
	Development of IEP	Refining Individual Programs	Formative Evaluations
Referral	Parental Reporting	Placement Options/ Decisions	Summative Evaluations
Screening	Responsibilities of Professionals	Physical Facilities	
Reporting	Student Participation	Planning Transitions/ Transportation	

• • •

NEW DIRECTIONS

The interrelated nature of legislative reform and new, appropriate policy development illustrated in this chapter sets the stage for specific implications of these legislative and policy mandates. The "new directions" postulated in this discussion are centred around the need for teachers to become competent in specific instructional domains to promote effective education for childrens' special needs. Specific areas of teacher competency, emphasized by legislation and policies aimed at providing a better education for the handicapped, will now be described.

One domain characterizing the beginning point in the educational enterprise is that of assessment. In order for adequate and appropriate program planning to take place, teachers are required to have competencies in the assessment of the children they teach. Unlike the typical child for whom curriculum guides provide a framework for instruction, each student's unique capabilities and needs must be identified to design appropriate instruction. Such a task requires that the teacher be able to accurately identify the various strengths and needs of each student.

Closely associated with this set of skills, teacher preparation programs will have to prepare educators in the area of program planning. Skills in this domain address not only identification of appropriate objectives for each student, but also prepare the teacher with a sufficient repertoire of methods to achieve those objectives.

Given that a wide variety of professionals from diverse disciplines, and a variety of paraprofessionals, are typically involved in the provision of an appropriate education for each student with special needs, teachers in the field will have to develop skills to work with persons in these diverse roles. Because such a range of professionals is in contact with the child, it is essential that the professionals communicate well with each other. Working effectively with paraprofessionals within the classroom will also require teachers to manage and plan for others besides themselves within an instructional framework. These aspects necessitate skills, strategies, and competencies in communication and consultation.

A final area of teacher preparation concerns equipping teachers with specific teaching strategies and techniques so that they are able to employ those best suited to their students. Such approaches include teaching the general case as incorporated into a variety of "mastery learning curricula" and instructing students how and when to apply a variety of "cognitive strategies" to learning material and situations. In both instances, the emphasis is on teaching general learning, thinking, and problem-solving strategies that the learner can apply in a variety of situations, not just those situations within the classroom (Thousand & Villa, 1990).

Similarly, transition into the community will be aided if students are taught to generalize the skills and knowledge learned in the classroom and apply them to other environments. Therefore, in view of education's ultimate goal, that of successful integration of students with special needs into the community where they can maximize their involvement with society, teachers must develop special teaching strategies that can be applied in more than one setting. These strategies are not only helpful for students with special needs but enhance the effectiveness of learning for all children.

• • •

IMPLICATIONS AND CHALLENGES

There are numerous implications and challenges arising from our overview of the Constitution, provincial legislative practices, and policy/program development. Rather than comment on the whole range, there are a few issues that warrant particular attention at this time: the process of restructuring that is taking place in education, multiculturalism, regular classroom placement, and program planning.

Skrtic (1991) has proposed an alternative approach to the structure and organization of schools that he refers to as "adhocracy." When compared to the non-adaptability of the existing professional bureaucracy in schools, adhocracy is based "on the principle of innovation rather than standardization" (Skrtic, 1991, p. 170), emphasizing problem solving, collaboration, and mutual adjustment. Information communication among school team members leads to co-ordination in inventing solutions to problems on an ad hoc basis, emphasizing creativity in the problem-solving, collaborative process. Suggested as well by Skrtic is the resultant achievement of increased accountability among professionals when principles of adhocracy are followed.

There is growing activity addressing the involvement of all children in the regular classroom. However, two areas of concern are the lack of strategies that teachers have in their repertoire and the general lack of understanding of the issue.

The more serious concern is the fact that teachers may not develop the skills needed to work with students with a wider range of needs in their classroom. Most teacher education programs require at the most one half unit in the study of special needs. This half unit tends to be a survey course covering the range of exceptionalities rather than an in-depth analysis of how to meaningfully teach students with special needs.

With regard to teacher development programs, the situation is perhaps more serious. With the exception of certain school districts and provinces that have made a concerted effort to upgrade the knowledge base of their teachers, many current teachers graduated from teacher education facilities at a time when not even one unit of study of special needs was required.

Two examples of the many areas that have attempted to respond to the needs of teachers have existed in Newfoundland and in Metro Nova Scotia. In Newfoundland, the Government in co-operation with four pilot local school districts provided an overview of policy development and implementation relative to meeting the needs of students with exceptionalities. These pilot districts were intended to serve as lighthouses for surrounding districts to avail of similar policy development and implementation programs. While it is not known how well the program has worked, initial study by Trimm-Daye (1988) suggested that the four pilot districts in effect did not have any better policy development than many of the other districts in the province. However, this study took place earlier in the process and a specific examination of changes in the pilot district approach was not undertaken. The long-term impact of the process has not yet been widely examined by the Newfoundland government.

Another example of responding to the needs of teachers relative to meeting a wider range of needs within the classroom took place in Halifax. Three school districts and a university formed a consortium to develop and deliver a series of mini-institutes with teachers and principals addressing the issue of integration and a range of strategies to respond to the strengths and needs of persons with special needs. Participating districts selected a principal and three or four teachers from each school to attend the institute as a team. An emphasis was placed on program planning, team building, and collaborative agenda setting. Following the institute, the school team would return to their school with an action plan and begin work with their colleagues in refining the initial action plan. Teachers could serve as mentors for other teachers in the same school and principals could mentor other principals in nearby schools. A follow-up institute was held with the same team reporting on the effectiveness of planning and addressing further needs.

Implications for administrators and teacher educators are many, but revolve around the need to provide enhanced coverage on the nature of students' special needs. The celebration of differences and similarities of all children as persons also requires emphasis. The real challenge, however, continues to be in helping teachers work in meaningful, effective, and caring ways with all children in their classrooms.

A final challenge resides in the realm of multiculturalism. What does our legislation and policy do to protect and enrich the rights of the culturally different? There is disproportionate representation of children from different cultural backgrounds in certain programs such as "basic," "vocational," "special," and "alternate." This has been documented by Myles and Ratslaff (1988) and Cummins (1984). The idea that children from different cultural backgrounds are seen as being handicapped is serious and continues the marginalization of whole groups of people within the educational system. The challenge that lies ahead is in finding ways to respond more appropriately to our culturally diverse society without continuing the process of marginalization.

• • •

REFERENCES

Baker, L.E. (1982). *Assessment issues in special education: Dissemination packet.* Monroe Courts, IN: Joint Special Education Co-operative.

Baldwin, R.S. (1991). The legal dimensions of parental control in special education. *Education and the Law, 3.*

Barnsley, R., & French, F. (1988). Special education in Nova Scotia: The emergence of appeals. *Nova Scotia Journal of Education.*

Bryan, J.H., & Bryan, T.H. (1979). *Exceptional children.* Sherman Oaks, CA: Alfred Publishing.

Chomicki, S., & Kysela, G.M. (1992). *Teacher attitudes towards mainstreaming: What do they think and what do they need? A literature review.* Department of

Educational Psychology, University of Alberta.

Cummins, J. (1984). *Bilingualism and special education: Issues in assessment and pedagogy.* San Diego: College Hill Press.

Dickinson, G.M., & Mackay, A.W. (1989). *Rights, freedoms and the education system in Canada.* Toronto: Emond Montgomery.

Freeze, D.R., Bravi, G., & Rampaul, W.E. (1989). Special education in Manitoba: A consultative-collaborative services delivery model. In M. Csapo & L. Goguen (Eds.), *Special education across Canada: Issues and concerns for the 90's.* Vancouver: Centre for Human Development and Research.

Gartner, A., & Lipski, D.K. (1987). Beyond special education: Toward a quality system for all students. *Harvard Educational Review, 57,* 367–395.

Hayes, J., & Higgens, L.F. (1978). Issues regarding the I.E.P: Teacher on the front line. *Exceptional Children, 46,* 44.

Karnes, M.B., & Lee, R.C. (1977). *Mainstreaming in the preschool.* Washington: Institute of Education.

Kimmins, R., Hunter, W.J., & Mackay, A.W. (1985). Educational legislation and litigation pertaining to the practice of school psychology in Canada. *Canadian Journal of School Psychology, 1,* 1–16.

Kirk, S.A. (1979). Educating exceptional children. In M.S. Lily (Ed.), *Children with exceptional needs.* New York: Holt, Rinehart and Winston.

Kysela, G.M., Barros, S., Grigg, N.C., & Kanee, M. (1985). The integration of exceptional children within preschool environments: A decision-making model. In R.J. McMahon & R.D. Peters (Eds.), *Childhood disorders: Behavioral developmental approaches.* New York: Brunner, Mazel.

Kysela, G.M., & French, F. (1983). *Special educational administrative policies in Alberta and Newfoundland during 1982: Implications for policy development and service delivery.*

Unpublished manuscript, Department of Educational Psychology, University of Alberta.

Maher, C.A. (1980). Evaluating organizational effectiveness of special services departments: Comparison of two models. *School Psychology Review, 9,* 259–266.

Mollenkopf, D.A. (1982). *Program evaluation: Information dissemination packet.* Hamilton, ID: Special Education Co-operative.

Morgan, D.P. (1977). *A primer on individualized education programs for exceptional children.* Reston, VA: Council for Exceptional Children.

Myles, D.W., & Ratslaff, H.C. (1988). Teachers bias towards visible ethnic minority groups in special education referrals. *BC Journal of Special Education, 12,* 19–28.

Reynolds, M.C., Maynard, C., & Birch, J.W. (1977). *Teaching exceptional children in all America's schools.* Reston, VA: Council for Exceptional Children.

Skrtic, T.M. (1991). The special education paradox: Equity as the way to excellence. *Harvard Educational Review, 61,* 148–206.

Stainback, S., Stainback, W., & Jackson, H. (1992). Toward inclusive classrooms. In S. Stainback & W. Stainback (Eds.), *Curriculum considerations in inclusive classrooms: Facilitating learning for all students.* Baltimore: Paul H. Brooks.

Thousand, J.S., & Villa, R.A. (1990). Strategies for educating learning with severe disabilities within their local home schools and communities. *Focus on Exceptional Children, 23,* 1–24.

Trimm-Daye, F. (1988). *Special educational administrative policies in Newfoundland: Implications for practice and for school psychology.* Unpublished master's thesis. Halifax: Mount Saint Vincent University.

Yoshida, R.K., & Gottlieb, J. (1977). A model of parental participation in the pupil planning process. *Mental Retardation, 27,* 206–211.

Special Needs Pupils and their Educational Rights:

An Analysis of Major Contemporary Developments

...

R . S .   G a l l

INTRODUCTION

*T*he approach of this article will be to review a variety of developments
that are unique to the Canadian special education enterprise and briefly
contrast these to the American example. A sample of the education statutes in
several provinces will be evaluated on the basis of how they "educate" exceptional children. The Canadian Charter of Rights and Freedoms will be examined
to identify in what manner the rights and responsibilities of Canadian school
authorities to special needs children are actualized. Finally, I will offer some
suggestions for improvements to the present conditions given the rapidly evolving political situation in Canada during the constitutional crisis of the 1990s.

The terminology in this field is often value-laden and subjectively loaded.
Therefore several terms should be defined.

Special students, special needs students, exceptional students, and *disabled students* are
terms used interchangeably to identify those pupils who experience persistent
difficulty in academic learning or social adjustment. Their (in)ability to perform
in school according to formally established criterion levels of competence is the
single most significant factor in their formal label and in the school system's
reactions to them.

Generally, such students do not benefit from rigid adherence to expectations
regarding achievement levels held for their age peers. Therefore, they need "special" or "exceptional" services beyond those normally provided, including:

- the skilled intervention available from trained professionals and paraprofessionals;
- the use of curriculum adaptations; and, where appropriate,

- the use of adapted equipment (e.g. computer-based adaptive peripheral devices), or the application of special equipment (e.g. the use of special sensory-enhancing devices such as hearing aids or Braille devices).

Special Education is a term that refers to that sector of public education that attempts to accommodate the students defined above. *Special Education Services* includes all of the activities that provide for the individualization of education such students require. Most commonly this includes special placements (such as resource rooms), human and material resource allocation, and specialized curricula.

Inclusive Education is a concept which holds that the statutory and moral right of special needs students to attend publicly supported schools, and to access qualitative supports therein, is unchallengeable. Therefore, "inclusive educators" are those educators who reject the administratively popular "mainstreaming" philosophy based on the "Cascade Service Delivery" model—these practices are seen to encourage some degree of exclusion. All pupils, regardless of (dis)ability, are seen to benefit from the "liberating" environment that the neighbourhood school represents—siblings and friends interact more vigorously in such settings. According to this perspective, any form of educational segregation (special classes, special schools, and special institutions) is extremely discriminatory.

In advocating for the implementation of a full inclusion policy, the author is fully aware that this is a very complex process that demands intensive planning and implementation strategies and requires:

- the unprecedented collaboration of the educational and legal professions in an examination of the concept of "rights";
- the reallocation of present resources by administrators and legislators;
- the development and filed implementation of innovative teaching strategies by educators in the school and university sectors.

Further, this discussion of inclusive education occurs in an environment where the debate is accelerated by the growing impatience of parents who are not willing to remain passive on this issue. There is a growing insistence that provincial governments and the national/provincial courts must change the existing legal framework to accommodate their demands.

This chapter is restricted to a consideration of the educational rights of special needs "school-age" students in the public education system. A small number of principles based on the guarantee of the provision of equality rights for all students will be advanced. Several historical and contemporary sociocultural developments related to special education issues will be examined, but the focus will be more on the role of the federal and provincial courts and their regulatory agencies. This is done to accommodate the larger base of jurisprudence literature that is now available to call upon.

Our limited examination of service delivery factors (i.e. the "quantitative" issue of school access and the service system that results) will reveal that the real or implied threat of legal action spurred by litigation and legislation (e.g. the Canadian Charter of Rights and Freedoms) has had limited impact to date. Equally there is little evidence that the quality of educational services for special needs pupils has substantially improved in Canada. Unfortunately, these generalizations cannot be defended finitely within the context of this paper.

• • •

AN OVERVIEW OF THE CANADIAN
DISABILITY ENVIRONMENT

The present review of Canadian legislation and related case law appears to suggest an expanding national vision of equality rights for the handicapped. In general, it could be said that there is a greater acceptance of the diversity of the human condition as reflected by the noticeable physical presence of "non-normal" citizens on our streets and in our workplaces. To some extent, this could be interpreted broadly as an indication of increasing respect for individual differences in Canadian society at large. However, the supportive evidence for such a trend is difficult to find, and representatives of the electoral and judicial system often do not reflect this humanistic ideal.

To illustrate, in the fall of 1992, the *Globe and Mail* reported that the rights of the handicapped were jeopardized by the revised Constitutional Agreement ("Accord puts," 1992). Specifically, a clause to protect the disabled was "mysteriously dropped" from the final version of the accord, creating a hierarchy of rights in which it appeared that the handicapped would have fewer rights than women or racial minorities. Incredibly, the Canada clause that listed the fundamental characteristics of Canadian society, totally ignored the rights of the handicapped.

The principles of equality and equal opportunity, as concepts, are elusive ideals in Canada—nonetheless, they are fundamental precepts that impact all of our social values and the service systems designed to activate those values.

Achieving recognition for equality is especially important for handicapped individuals as they have long been the targets of discrimination—direct and indirect, purposive and unintended. The burdens and disadvantages faced by the handicapped are the result of their reduced social and economic status in Canada.

• • •

THE CANADIAN SPECIAL
EDUCATION ENVIRONMENT

Internal and external criticism has been persistently directed at the special education service system in Canada. Two decades ago, Perkins (1974) suggested that, as a "have" country, Canada required a comprehensive special education delivery system that removed geopolitical inequities.

In 1975, the International Organization for Economic Co-operation and Development investigated Canadian education structures at all levels and concluded that special education services in this country were comparatively impoverished (OECD, 1976).

Major unrest and debate continue to characterize the special education sector in Canada. The Canadian special education environment has been described as an "intricate patchwork quilt of political accident, professional ambition, and pedagogical oversight loosely bound together with provincial permissive or mandatory red tape and federal neglect" (Csapo & Goguen, 1980, p. 215).

While a trend toward the physical integration of special needs students in Canadian schools can be noted today, the question of the quality of their schooling is largely avoided. It is to be recalled that special education options in Canada, as elsewhere, were largely developed to accommodate those students who were unable or unwilling to respond to the standardized curriculums and traditional strategies of public education. It is unclear whether Canadian segregated classes continue to be established to serve and protect special needs children from the harsh world, or rather to insulate the larger Canadian society from incursion by those who are different.

As a minimum, the Cascade service model and its correlate principle of the "least restrictive environment" (which appears to be as popular in Canada as in the United States) must be challenged, given that it forces "those who ascend . . . (to) do so one step at a time; some will ascend more steps than others and some may never ascend at all" (Smith, 1992).

Consider the following statement by the Canadian Association for Community Living (1985) as an alternative:

> children with handicaps and children without handicaps learn best and
> prepare for adult life best when they learn and prepare together in the

same schools and classrooms. We know that education is most effective when it starts early, involves the family, and is directed toward acquiring skills, information, and experiences that are essential to social and economic participation.

Yet the vast majority of children and handicaps are isolated in segregated schools and classrooms, and are not being given the opportunity to learn those things that will foster the levels of independence and participation of which they are capable.

To further indicate the domination that outdated service models have over the special education profession, the International Council for Exceptional Children, (which has several thousand Canadian members) in mid-1992 published its commitment to a spectrum of administrative placements for special needs pupils in a document entitled *Educational Environments for Exceptional Students*. Recommended placement options included removal from regular classrooms, and if necessary from homes and communities.

As could be expected, this stance has drawn extensive criticism:

> (this) position has long been a frustration to the many . . . who have demonstrated the damaging impact of labels and segregation and who have developed and pioneered strategies to make regular education a successful experience for students who have been previously served in special education settings. (TASH, 1992)

By contrast, it is interesting to note that the Association for Supervision and Curriculum Development, an influential North American regular education advocacy organization, recently presented its 1992 resolutions. The full inclusion of "special programs" was identified as a focus area for action.

We have, therefore, some evidence that the North American special education community is retrenching toward the traditional service model that preserves a continuum of special education placements, including the most restrictive.

• • •

SPECIAL EDUCATION SYSTEMS—CANADA VERSUS THE UNITED STATES

Perhaps the most noteworthy disparities between US and Canadian cultures are the two governments' basic commitments: to life, liberty, and the pursuit of happiness in the United States; and peace, order, and good government in Canada." (Lethwaite, 1980)

American interpretations of individual rights are essentially guaranteed by the Constitution. There exists in the US a strong historical commitment to the right of the aggrieved individual to employ litigation and court intervention to verify individual rights. Court-imposed standards for special education service delivery (such as the Individual Educational Plan) are seen as a natural outcome of this commitment. Accordingly, equitable service standards are systematically monitored by individual parents, government officials, and advocacy groups with a vigorous spirit of advocacy that is not matched in Canada.

Practical problems, attitudinal barriers, and administrative resistance characterize an often hostile environment for special needs children and their parents in Canada. It appears that developmental and preventive measures (such as the provision of early intervention programs, early childhood education, respite care parent support, and improved professional and paraprofessional training), are not implemented systematically and universally by the federal government. Simply put, "special education" is not a national issue in Canada.

There is some evidence that on a provincial level, positive gains toward the creation of inclusive school communities is occurring. Some of the impetus for this can be credited to the pressure for change demanded in American legislative statutes. The most important document in this regard was the Education for All Handicapped Children Act passed in 1975 (commonly known as PL 94-142). This national statute demonstrated to Canadians that legislative will at the most senior levels can lead to positive change and action at the local school level. Several provisions of PL 94-142 appeared to create models for Canadian legislators and educators to follow. These include:

- the Least Restrictive Environment principle;
- the provision of "appropriate" education;
- the Individualized Education Plan; and
- the guarantee of procedural due process.

At one point, PL 94-142 was regarded by many Canadian educators as the exemplary legislative standard. Subsequent evaluation of the long-term impact of PL 94-142 has not reduced that observation, although it is apparent that Canadian laws must also reflect Canadian social traditions and therefore modifications are necessary in the regulatory components.

Canadians generally see themselves as less litigious than Americans, perhaps because the temperament of the country does not encourage court resolution of personal disputes. Canadian and US legal traditions have evolved different roles for the legislative, administrative, and executive officers in each country. Roles specified by the Constitutional documents and their regulatory mechanisms, as well as the activity of the judiciary in enforcing them, differ in each country.

While the entrenchment of the Charter of Rights and Freedoms into the Canadian legal environment might provide ultimately for the provision of educational opportunity for the handicapped, at the time of writing not a single special needs education case has advanced to the Supreme Court for adjudication based on the Charter. Accordingly, those who argue that the Charter will profoundly alter the provision of educational rights in Canada must await further action to prove their point.

In summary, Americans presently appear to be testing the limits of special education service provision by intensifying the monitoring process at the local school level. Canadians, by contrast, seem unable to achieve consensus regarding a viable political process that would facilitate the achievement of qualitative special educational services. Major inconsistencies in special education policies are the norm in Canada: "In many districts the goals of special education are still shrouded in mystery, stated in purposefully vague, diffuse, and politically non-offensive terms to satisfy the imagination of every potential adversary group" (Csapo & Goguen, 1980).

There is undoubtedly general agreement that each citizen has the right to participate in the mainstream of Canadian society—the key to that participation is the right to education. Canadians must act expeditiously to remove special needs children from the political buffer zone that presently exists between federal and provincial levels of government.

· · ·

ESSENTIAL PRINCIPLES

The following principles should be understood by readers at the outset of the present analysis:

Principle 1. The individual is the most important entity in the Canadian interpretation of the democratic society. Further, special needs individuals have unique value that should act to guarantee their equitable treatment within Canadian society.

Rationale:

As members of society, each of us is influenced by these cultural beliefs . . . and cultural stereotypes [which] are translated into group and individual behavior that constitutes exclusion, institutionalization, and abuse. True integration can occur only when dehumanizing attitudes are replaced with attitudes that promote the common human experiences of all people. (Lusthaus, 1991, p. 28)

This principle is advanced to counteract the unjust and corrosive effects of prejudice and discrimination against the special needs pupil. It is apparent that such individuals must be both respected and valued if the overt and covert discrimination against them is to end. Since discrimination is dependent on the context in which it occurs (in this case the school system) and the value systems of the parties involved (in this case the educators, parents, and the pupils themselves) there is every reason to target the educational systems of Canada for vigorous anti-discriminatory action. Further, it is obvious that discriminatory acts are themselves being re-examined in Canadian society, as is seen most overtly in the recent discussions regarding feminist rights and gender equality. This re-examination process should be extended to the issue of educational equity as well.

To illustrate, traditionally identified on the basis of their alleged deficiencies, special needs pupils have been exposed to systematic and pernicious processes of (de)classification. The most pervasive of these practices remains the wholesale misuse of norm-based "intelligence testing" procedures, which most commonly results in long-term placement in a variety of segregated services where genetically restricted abilities will be further restricted by environmental repression.

To the extent that special needs children have different learning styles and less effective learning strategies than their age peers, they can be expected to demonstrate major educational problems when they interact with the traditional curricula, pedagogical methodology, and administrative organizations found in the regular schools.

The special needs group most prejudiced against in this sense is undoubtedly the one labelled "mentally retarded" or "developmentally delayed." In the light of contemporary social concepts, what is to be served by continuing to focus on the limitations implied by their labels? The same intelligence testing movement that decades ago labelled them "idiots," "imbeciles," and "morons" today employs the terms "trainable" and "educable" as a reflection of their "intellectual ceilings." Pervasive negative connotations toward these individuals persist, and our system of identifying such individuals for service contributes to this.

Within this population, there are at least two subcategories. In the first are the quantifiably handicapped—essentially those moderately and severely retarded individuals who are relatively easy to identify due to persistent learning difficulties and associated physical anomalies. In the second are the non-quantifiably handicapped—essentially the mildly retarded who are better described as educationally disordered. Smith and Greenburg (1975) coined the phrase "six-hour retardate" to describe the environmentally competent child forced to appear defective in the school setting by inappropriate exposure to ineffective curriculum and pedagogy.

It is important to keep this distinction in mind, given that services for the quantifiably handicapped have indeed increased during this past decade in response to government action at the federal and provincial levels. By contrast, services for the non-quantifiably handicapped appear to be more difficult to obtain and sustain because the degree of deviation from normal behaviour that such individuals demonstrate is less severe. It is all too easy to label such individuals as disruptive or socially destructive, and therefore policies of exclusion can be more readily enacted against them. More external pressure can be, and should be, brought upon Canadian school systems by concerned citizens who are unwilling to accept school authorities as society's screening agents. Developmentally delayed students must be made welcome in the educational system.

Principle 2. Education is a basic inalienable right of all citizens of Canada; that right must be extended equitably to all.

Rationale:

I lay it down as a prime condition of sane society . . . that in any decent community, children should find in every part of their native country, food, clothing, lodging, instruction, and parental kindness for the asking . . . The children must have them as if by magic, with nothing to do but rub the lamp, like Aladdin, and have their needs satisfied. (Shaw, 1914)

It is argued that the education of any society's youth, to the fullest extent possible given the resources of that society, is a reflection of investment in the long-term economic, moral, and social well-being of that society. During the 1960s, a near-universal renaissance of attitude and cognition occurred in North America that exposed many traditional practices in special education to critical review and challenge. Johnson (1962) suggested that adequate objective evidence to support the effectiveness of special classes was difficult to obtain. Dunn (1968) also called for a moratorium on the placement of mildly handicapped students in segregated settings.

For the past two decades the focus of special educational intervention shifted to the modifications required in the educational system and large community environment. Service models were developed that emphasized accountability and the monitoring of service provision, and the concept of "zero reject" became an acceptable philosophical principle. As was noted with regard to the developmentally delayed:

> These striking changes in social responsiveness to mentally retarded people have been paralleled by a steady increase in knowledge concerning prevention, detection, learning, adjustment, and treatment of retarded development. Despite these important improvements, the agenda of needed research, undelivered services, ineffective practices, and unfulfilled promises is still extensive! (Cegelka & Prehm, 1982)

Principle 3.   The neighbourhood school is the most logical setting for the formal education of all citizens.

> Rationale:
>
> The evidence is clear and damning. Segregation does not work. Children in segregated settings do not do well in gaining academic skills and do not get the chance to learn social skills. They do not learn to live in the real world. Likewise, the real world does not learn to include and value persons with a mental handicap.

The neighbourhood school, as a microcosm of society, offers an opportunity to address the equitable distribution of the resources and aspirations of the larger society. It can be the primary environment where all children can gain access to society's pool of knowledge and skills, learn to socialize, and eventually fulfill their roles as contributing and participating citizens. To deny any child access to full inclusion in this citizenship training process is to deny the most fundamental right.

Principle 4.   Canadian governments at the national and provincial levels must legally mandate the universal right to education, and subsequently strengthen the supportive regulations and the bureaucratic infrastructure to guarantee those rights.

> Rationale:
>
> To facilitate understanding of this principle, the Canadian legislative framework must be explained to some extent. The original Constitution Act of 1867 restricted the national government's authority over education to residents of the Yukon and Northwest territories. The specified exceptions—educational services to military bases, Indian reserves, and federal penal institutions—remain a federal responsibility even to this day.[1]

Provincial legislative bodies were thereby granted exclusive authority to legislate in the field of education, subject only to restrictions that prevent provincial abrogation of the rights or privileges pertaining to denominational schools guaranteed at the time of entry into the Canadian family. Therefore, for over a century, constitutional questions regarding educational matters were restricted to denominational rights.

In 1982, this situation changed dramatically, with the constitutional entrenchment of the Charter of Rights and Freedoms in the Constitution Act and the declaration of the supremacy of the Constitution. In effect, any law at the national or provincial level that was inconsistent with it was ruled invalid (section 52.1). Further, while the prevailing opinion indicates that private schools are not affected, it is apparent that "public school boards are bound by the Charter and an analysis of recent decisions of the Supreme Court of Canada . . . supports this view" (Smith, 1992).

The Canadian Charter of Rights and Freedoms has several critical elements that are of importance to this discussion. These include: section 1 which guarantees that the "rights and freedoms set out in it are subject only to such reasonable limits prescribed by law as can be demonstrably justified in a free and democratic society"; and section 15 (1) which indicates that "every individual is equal before and under the law and has a right to the equal protection and equal benefit of the law without discrimination and, in particular, without discrimination based on race, national or ethnic origin, colour, religion, sex, age or mental or physical disability." Unfortunately, it also appears that the equality rights provided for in section 15 are subject to two constraints: "reasonable limits" and the "override" section introduced into the Charter as a political compromise to the provinces.

In spite of this, it is generally agreed that the Charter ushered in a new era for the protection of equality rights in Canada, because the Supreme Court of Canada has stated on more than one occasion that the interpretation of the Charter should be "a generous rather than a legalistic one, aimed at fulfilling the purpose of the guarantee and securing for individuals the full benefit of the Charter's protection" (Smith, 1992).

Further modifications beyond those presently enacted, to both the Canadian Constitution and the Charter of Rights and Freedoms, must be processed without delay in order to redress the historical and contemporary discrimination against special needs individuals in Canadian society.

Principle 5.   Educational practice at the local school level must reflect a genuine commitment to special needs pupils as reflected through their full placement in community schools. Concurrently, professional educators must implement and monitor individualized instructional processes that more accurately reflect the individual's ability to learn and the teaching profession's ability to teach.

Rationale:

Once children with disabilities have a right to enter the front door of the school, . . . and presuming that they are not ushered out the back door, the second phase of inclusion begins. On a broad basis, this phase can be considered as the beginning of the right to education—as opposed to a right to schooling. (Smith, 1992)

Pupils with special needs must not only have access to the full facilities and services within the school, they must as well have an appropriate placement guaranteed. This requires that thorough planning processes are initiated and facilitated by educators. They must involve as well the parents as full partners given that the most beneficial long-term learning will occur when full co-operation is achieved between the home and the school. Finally, the assistance of academics from university and community college settings will be required on site to insure that research findings are implemented into the daily practices of the teacher.

Principle 6. Parents have a right to full involvement in planning for the education of their children towards the positive end of individualizing and maximizing their educational outcomes.

Rationale:

parents have little, if any, legal means to influence the delivery of the special education services that their children receive. This is irrespective of the elaborateness of the provinces' education legislation. Nor is it likely that human rights legislation or the Canadian Charter of Rights and Freedoms will assist parents in advancing their cause. (Baldwin, 1991)

In making this statement, Baldwin identified that the courts are unlikely to interfere with the discretion of school authorities given that: the special education enterprise is imprecise and defies monitoring; parents of special needs children lack appropriate political impact; many special interest groups do not reflect the specific concerns of individual parents. "Canadians appear to be in large measure content with their public education system. Perhaps it is this contentedness that has contributed to the insidious decay of parental involvement in education . . . evident in the lack of authority that individual parents have to direct the schooling of their children" (Baldwin, 1991).

Educational standards and control of the resources for education are now exclusively the responsibility of the provincial government. In reality, members of the provincial Legislative Assemblies are closer to the citizens they represent than are the members of the House of Commons. While some power over decision making is delegated to regional or local school authorities, it is still at the provincial level that the most critical educational decisions are made. To that extent, planning for special education services at the provincial levels must directly involve the creation of input mechanisms so that the views of the parents of special students can be implemented.

The progress of parents, acting individually and collectively on behalf of their children, has been documented in numerous sources. It has been noted that American parents have been more vigorous in pressing for legislative change to benefit their children.

· · ·

ANALYSIS OF SPECIAL EDUCATION DEVELOPMENTS IN SEVERAL CANADIAN PROVINCES

The permission granted to Canadian special needs pupils to attend school stands on a fragile base indeed, for as all provinces guarantee the right to education, none appear to have gone as far as the American system in providing for the ongoing monitoring of those qualitative factors that would facilitate persistent educational gains. Further, as will be shown, the Canadian system appears to strengthen and reify control by school authorities; bureaucratic safeguards are in place to protect administrators at all levels.

It is the principle of "appropriate education" that marks the key distinction between the American and Canadian systems: the specific requirements of Public Law 94-142 encourages the external adjudication of educational effectiveness by both the professional and the lay publics. In Canada, however, while most provinces provide universal access to school, there is limited opportunity for those external to the educational system to investigate and evaluate the adequacy of school programs.

To review, Canadian bureaucrats at all levels are overprotected and overpowered; teachers are largely unorganized on this issue, and therefore unprepared to press collectively for special education change; parents are just beginning to recognize that they have power but have not organized that power collectively. Unless provincial and federal legislation begin to incorporate regulatory measures that provide for accountability, the rights of special needs children will remain elusive and inconsistently applied. A more detailed analysis of this situation in representative provinces in Canada follows.

British Columbia

A brief review of historical factors leading to the provision of special education services in B.C. is appropriate at this point. During the 1968-69 school year, the Department of Education created the Special Education Division, thereby giving central co-ordination and beginning the transition of special services in the province (Csapo & Goguen, 1980).

In the 1970s the name change of the "Special Education Division" to "Integrated and Supportive Services" reflected the willingness of local and provincial authorities to accept the emerging ethic supporting at least partial integration. Pupils are considered of school age between the ages of five to nineteen years. All children are entitled to educational services and basic educational programming. However, it is still the case that special education services are non-prescriptive and inconsistently applied, with program developments reflecting local conditions and circumstances (Csapo & Goguen, 1980).

During the 1980s, provincial authorities improved funding and established a monitoring system that incorporated parental review, and the development of individual educational plan guidelines. Nonetheless, problems persisted: "If we could start with nothing we could probably develop a rational, comprehensive and coordinated system . . . We cannot, without great difficulty however, divest ourselves of our past. We therefore live with a system that is somewhat short of being ideal" (Leslie & Goguen, 1984).

BALES VERSUS CENTRAL OKANAGAN (SCHOOL DISTRICT 23) (1984)

In 1984, the most discussed case on school integration in Canada involved action taken on behalf of Arron Bales of Kelowna, B.C. who was ten years of age at the time. His parents alleged that placement in a segregated school had harmed him, and that the harm ought to have been foreseen by the school board. There was evidence that Arron had lost skills acquired during two previous school years when he was in an integrated class. However, Mr. Justice Taylor said it had not been established that this harm was caused by the segregated placement. An ancillary argument presented was that Arron's right to liberty was denied when he was barred from attending the neighbourhood school. Justice Taylor again refused to state that the board's action was unreasonable.

The final outcome of this case seems to have been influenced by evidence that the Board was actively considering a recommendation to close the segregated school. In fact they did so at the end of the 1983-84 school year, and Arron was then placed in a partially integrated setting. As was later noted:

> It was held that . . . policy supported mainstreaming, among other place-
> ment alternatives, but did not impose any such obligation upon school
> boards . . . It was held that the board had acted reasonably in placing
> Arron in the segregated facility, which was deemed appropriate for such
> children . . . the most important aspect of the decision is its characteriza-
> tion of segregated education as non-discriminatory because it is intended
> to provide handicapped students with "the special treatment they require."

Accordingly, special education could be considered, on the basis of this view, as affirmative action (Smith, 1992).

Alberta

An examination of developments in the province of Alberta can be used to illustrate the major differences that exist in Canada regarding philosophies held by those responsible for special needs education.

The Alberta School Act (1980, section 33) called for pupils between six and sixteen years to attend school, but refuted that requirement in section 134 by allowing school jurisdictions to exclude special education youngsters from attendance.

> A board may temporarily excuse from attendance in a regular classroom
> any pupil whose special educational needs in the opinion of an inspector or
> superintendent are of such a nature that regular classroom experience is not
> productive or is detrimental to the pupil or to the school.

CARRIERE VERSUS COUNTY OF LAMONT #30 (1978)

Shelley Carriere was eleven years old when her mother applied to the Supreme Court of Alberta for an order requiring the Lamont County School Board to accept her as a pupil or to purchase educational services for her from another board. The school board had "excused" Shelley from attending school because she had cerebral palsy.

Mr. Justice O'Byrne directed the board to either accept Shelley as a pupil or to make arrangements for her to attend a school in another district. He stressed that he did not have the authority to force the board to comply. The school board chose to admit Shelley to the school nearest to her home, but made no attempt to design a program appropriate to her needs.

Unbelievable in today's context, an informal agreement was made between several teachers to take turns having her in class for half-hour periods. Mrs. Carriere had to threaten further legal action before the board agreed to provide transportation to and from school (Endicott, 1988).

YARMOLOY V. BANFF SCHOOL DISTRICT # 102 (1985)

In June of 1984, Nicole Yarmoloy was thirteen years old and completing her sixth year in a special education program in a Banff elementary school. A report to the Banff School Board recommended that she be sent to a school in Calgary (135 kilometres away) for the continuation of her schooling. Without notifying the parents in advance, the board implemented the report and informed them that Nicole would be best placed in Calgary.

The policies of the Ministry of Education provided for a two-stage appeal process for such decisions. The first was appearance before a local appeal board. If that was inconclusive, a Provincial Appeal Board would be established. The Yarmoloys asked for an appeal, but the school board asked the Minister to direct the case to the Provincial Appeal Board. The Minister agreed, but when the Provincial Appeal Board convened (nearly a year later, during which time Nicole was kept at home) the members decided that they had no jurisdiction to hear the appeal on the grounds that the local appeal board had been by-passed. The family then sought an order in the Court of Queen's Bench. The Court found that it could not direct the board to make a particular placement, but ordered the board to carry out its discretionary role for Nicole's placement in accordance with the principles of procedural fairness. No determination could be made as to Nicole's school placement without granting notice and a hearing to her parents. The school board chose not to contest the matter. Nicole has attended the local Banff school since September 1985.

These decisions clearly reflect the complex problems that ensue when mandatory legislation and supportive regulations are absent in a province. Further, they indicate the protracted and often volatile process that is undertaken in such cases. It appears that special needs children can be served through the application of local pressure and without the security of mandatory legislation— However, that seems entirely inappropriate if the larger moral responsibilities of society were to prevail. The Alberta situation clearly presents the relative impotence of parental authority and the persistence of entrenched attitudes among the judiciary and the bureaucracy.

Ontario

Ontario's system has undergone major revisions during the past two decades. As recently as 1974, the Ontario School Act provided no legal right to education; typically, local boards were encouraged, but not forced to adopt special provisions.

In 1978, regulations were introduced to force boards to establish placement and review committees regarding individual programs. The 1980 Education Amendment Act brought mandatory legislation, primarily the result of unrelenting pressure by several parent advocacy groups. With the passage of Bill 82 in 1980, the principles of universal access, public financial support, appeal procedures, appropriate program monitoring, and a child review process were established—on paper at least.

MURRAY V. BRANT COUNTY BOARD OF EDUCATION (1986)

The Murrays had legal custody of a foster child, Mathew Gallagher. They wanted the Special Education Tribunal to order that he be placed in a regular Grade 8 class in their neighbourhood school with an individually adapted curriculum and the support of a teacher's aide. Alternatively, they were prepared to accept placement in a TMR class in a regular public school where he could experience some "meaningful integration." The earlier tribunals had recommended placement in a segregated school. The tribunal ruled that Mathew lacked the communication skills that would be required for placement in a regular class, but accepted the Murrays' alternative position and ordered that he be placed in a class for trainable retarded pupils in a regular public school.

The Murrays moved to St. Marys', and subsequently learned that the rulings of provincially constituted Special Education Tribunals are not transferable to other provincial school districts.

ROWETT V. YORK REGION BOARD OF EDUCATION (1986)

The Rowetts challenged the decision of the York Region Board of Education to place their daughter, Jaclyn, in a segregated class. They wanted her to attend a regular class with appropriate supports in their home community.

The Tribunal ruled that the placement in the segregated class was appropriate. They refused to consider any possible implications of the Charter of Rights and Freedoms. Several challenges have exhausted the appeal provisions in the Education Act and Regulations, including the Special Education Tribunal. The

Rowetts were denied the right to advance evidence as to the detrimental effects of a segregated placement for Jaclyn or to support their contention that integration would be in Jaclyn's best interests.

Many of the sections of the Ontario Education Act dealing with special education originated with Bill 82. These special provisions are generally aimed at "exceptional" pupils. However, it appears that Bill 82 allows for the separation of such pupils from those considered to be uneducable; the latter "hard-to-serve" pupils can be excluded. Another exclusionary policy allows school boards to excuse students from compulsory attendance on certain specified grounds.

In making general comments on the Ontario cases, one legal analyst indicated that they were suggestive of other trends in Canada as well. Specifically:

> The motivation of parties to settle a dispute are more complex than the simple fear that they will lose . . . so do considerations of adverse publicity and the impact of a judgment in place of a settlement. . . . It is often considered more expedient to accommodate one aggressive set of parents and let the status quo prevail for the rest. (Smith, 1992)

Nova Scotia

In 1969 only one province, Nova Scotia, had developed mandatory legislation. This was formally confirmed and strengthened with the passage of the Education Act of 1973 and the special Mandate of Regulation that required school jurisdictions to provide for all students, including the handicapped.

ELWOOD VERSUS HALIFAX COUNTY/BEDFORD DISTRICT SCHOOL BOARD (1987)

In September, 1986 after he had spent two years in a segregated special class in a school far from his home, Luke Elwood was enrolled in a regular Grade 3 class in his neighbourhood school. Officials of the School Board informed the school principal that Luke was to be returned to the school he had attended before. Luke's parents were determined to prevent his placement back into the segregated setting, and their lawyers applied for and obtained an interim injunction ordering that he remain in the neighbourhood school, with appropriate supports and services, pending the trial of his educational rights pursuant to the Charter of Rights and Freedoms. The main action was framed in terms of Luke's right to be educated in the least restrictive environment and in terms of his right to equal benefit of the education law of the province without discrimination based on mental disability.

Just before the action was to be tried, the parents and the board entered into a Settlement Agreement that guaranteed Luke significant integration and a process for mutual input into his individual education plan for his entire school career. The Settlement Agreement was endorsed by the Supreme Court of Nova Scotia.

• • •

CONCLUSION WITH RECOMMENDATIONS FOR ACTION

It has been shown that the Canadian special education sector imposes real hardship upon many Canadian children and their families in both a *de jure* (legal) and *de facto* (real) sense. Canadian special needs pupils require constant and unwavering advocacy, at the local, provincial, and national levels. That advocacy must be demonstrated by parents, professionals in both the legal and educational fields, members of the judiciary, and those elected to represent the citizenry at all levels.

Recommendations Regarding Legislative Action

Canadian legislators at the national and provincial levels are currently working to enact appropriate legislative and regulatory modifications necessary to support appropriate special needs education. The national government could seize control of education policy at the provincial and local levels by indirect means, including the following:

Firstly, a reduction of unconditional grants to the provinces could be imposed, replacing them with direct grants that mandate the national right to education for all as a precondition.

Parliament could argue that the universally accepted principle of the right to education for all, coupled with Canada's historical tradition of neglecting special needs children, merits this direct control and central co-ordination.

As in the U.S. (the example being Public Law 94-142) provinces would be forced to conform or lose significant grants provided for the support of other components of education as well as general public works. In the present political environment, this move would generate intense debate and litigative action from both the provincial and local authorities.

Secondly, regulatory monitoring processes could be adopted on a voluntary but universal basis, allowing the status quo to prevail with provinces retaining exclusive control of education.

Leadership would be required by the Council of Ministers of Education acting in the national interest. They have already demonstrated that they can reach consensus on matters related to national qualifying examinations—why not in the special education area as well? It is the author's opinion that this solution will not receive attention in light of the other demands made upon bureaucrats regarding their responsibilities arising out of the Constitutional debate presently raging in the country.

Thirdly, legislators at the national and provincial levels could simply act as individual advocates to raise the issue of education for special needs pupils to a "priority" status through the creation of a national Office of Special Education. This office could be administered through the Secretary of State, and act to coordinate the present Council of Ministers of Education. National–provincial cost sharing arrangements beneficial to all parties could be implemented through this office to provide equity of service across geopolitical boundaries. The office could further provide a forum for the resolution of inequities and the establishment of new funding formulas that could strengthen provincial power while still recognizing federal involvement through central co-ordination and financial support. Once again, in the face of the present Constitutional debate, this option is also considered highly improbable.

Recommendations Regarding Academic Advocacy

Expressed simply, the special education/regular education "debate" balances these opposing opinions. On one side are those who assert that separate special classes are necessary, and only a minority of special needs students with disabilities can be integrated; on the opposing side are those who assert that separate special education classes are unnecessary, except in transition, and that all children can be integrated. Since this debate has become highly polarized, improved policy research and a more dispassionate analysis of the issues is required in Canada.

Academics wishing to provide a more balanced perspective could do so by:

- undertaking a comprehensive review of the professional literature;
- examining the legislative framework for human rights and education (not only in Canada but as well in those western countries that might serve as exemplars);
- participating in a multi-disciplinary analysis of these issues with their colleagues in the legal profession.

Recommendations Regarding Parental Initiatives in Litigation

Earlier in this paper, the grievances held by parents of special needs pupils were briefly treated. In summary of that position, it appears that Canadian school authorities need only provide some form of accommodation for these pupils to fulfill their legal commitment under the present legislative structure. It also appears unlikely that this will change in the immediate future, parents should be encouraged to take their grievances to the courts for adjudication of issues at the local level. This suggestion is in line with the following position statement:

> First, parents should have access to the courts to challenge the discretion of school boards. This challenge must occur outside of a hierarchy where administrative values and school board practices are automatically given greater importance than the educational objectives of the parents. . . . Secondly, teachers and school authorities should be open to liability like other professionals.

Recommendations Regarding National Action by the Canadian Association for Community Living

As noted earlier, the parents and professionals who advocate for their cause have come to be described as the "inclusive education" movement. In Canada, that movement is most clearly expressed in the activities of the Canadian Association for Community Living, its provincial affiliates, and its technical-professional arm, the Roehrer National Institute. Given that the author agrees that the overwhelming discretionary power that school officials have over pupils and their parents must be balanced by legally enforceable accountability procedures, a challenge is issued to this national advocacy group to press for vigorous educational standards for special needs pupils.

• • •

A FINAL WORD

In closing, it has been the author's intention to raise several fundamental issues in this paper. At stake here is the evolution of the Canadian school system either in harmony or in contention with the value system of the larger society. An examination of our collective and personal belief systems are at the core of this discussion.

Canadians must continue to ask the "administrative" questions:

1. What are the most appropriate modes of service delivery for meeting the needs of all students?

2. How can we change administrative systems to better meet the challenges created by special needs students?
3. How could scarce resources be better managed?
4. What are the key policy issues to be addressed to make the system more responsive to its mandate?

Canadians must continue to ask the pedagogical questions regarding the circumstances whereby some curricula and teaching strategies are more effective with special needs pupils. Finally, Canadians must ask the moral and ethical questions regarding the fundamental rights and duties to be guaranteed to students with special needs. Toward that end, we must:

- implement fully the ideal of "zero reject";
- re-examine our assessment and placement practices;
- provide individualized and appropriate education;
- guarantee equitable court procedures to students and parents; and most importantly
- develop effective procedures that incorporate parents and guardians into the process of educational decision making at the local and provincial levels.

· · ·

NOTE

1. Erosion of this traditional federal power to control Indian education is underway in Canada as Native communities assume local control of education. The best example of this transition process can be found with the Peigan Nation of Southern Alberta, which is establishing innovative non-traditional services for special needs students as a priority.

· · ·

REFERENCES

Accord puts handicapped in jeopardy, coalition says. (1992, September 4). *The Globe and Mail*.

Association for Persons with Severe Handicaps. (1992, July 2). CEC Slips Back; ASCD Steps Forward. *TASH Newsletter*, (18).

Baldwin, R.S. (1991). The legal dimensions of parental control in special education. *Education and Law Journals, 3*, 217–261.

Canadian Association for the Mentally Retarded. (1985). *A statement of principles*.

Csapo, M. & Goguen, L. (Eds.). (1980). *Special education across Canada: Issues and concerns for the '80s*. Vancouver: Centre for Human Development and Research.

Cegelka, P., & Prehm, H. (1982). *Mental retardation: From categories to people*. Columbus, OH: Charles E. Merrill.

Dunn, L.M. (1968). Special education for the mentally retarded—Is much of it justifiable? *Exceptional Children, 35*, 5–22.

Endicott, O. (1988). *Canadian special education cases.* Unpublished manuscript. Toronto: G.A. Roehrer National Institute.

Johnson, G.O. (1962). Special education for the mentally retarded—A paradox. *Exceptional Children, 29*, 62–69.

Lethwaite, G. (1980, March 5). So many differences, so much in common. *Vancouver Sun*, p. 6.

Lusthaus, E. (1991). Drastic actions: The results of viewing people as less than human. *Developmental Disabilities Bulletin, 19*, p. 28.

Leslie, P.T., & Goguen, L. (1984). British Columbia's educational policies: A retrospective examination. *Special Education in Canada, 58*(2), 47–49.

Organization for Economic Development and Cooperation. (1976). *Review of national policies for education: Canada.* Paris: OECD.

Perkins, S. (1974). *Shortcomings in the delivery of special education services in Canada.* Paper presented at the meeting of the Council for Exceptional Children, New York.

Shaw, G.B. (1914). *Parents and children.*

Smith, I.L., & Greenburg, S. (1975). Teacher attitudes and labelling processes. *Exceptional Children, 41*, 315–324.

Smith, W.J. (1992). *Inclusive education and the law in the special-regular education debate.* Unpublished manuscript. Learning Centre of Quebec, Montreal.

ISSUES RELATED TO THE
INTEGRATION OF CHILDREN
WITH SPECIAL NEEDS

...

Lorraine Wilgosh

The accelerating movement toward integration of children with disabilities into regular classrooms has arisen largely from the concerns of their parents. These parents want their children to have individually planned programs, with families having easy access to the school and related services to facilitate parent involvement. Parents of children with disabilities want their children to have opportunities for making neighbourhood friendships, enhanced by attendance at the local school and to be prepared for living and working in society as adults. However, the integration movement is not without debate. This chapter will focus on issues of direct relevance to classroom teachers.

• • •

DEFINITIONS OF INTEGRATION

Numerous definitions of integration exist.[1] For some, integration means "full inclusion," and, as Bunch (1991) states, calls for "nothing less than a redefinition of what education is and of what a student is. Advocates of full inclusion argue that education must never separate learners no matter whether the focus of learning is to be social or academic or both" (p. 83).

For other advocates, integration has meant that children with disabilities should attend their neighbourhood (home) schools, with varying levels of additional support. To educate students with severe intellectual disabilities, Brown et al. (1991) state, "However, a regular classroom base in a home school is a necessary, but not sufficient, condition for minimally acceptable education. These students should spend some of their time elsewhere" (p. 39). "Elsewhere" may be a special class or another school or community setting, because "some educational services that are different from those offered nondisabled peers must be provided" (Brown et al., 1991, p. 39). The second of these positions appears clearer in recognizing and specifying the needs of each individual student and in categorizing integration as a process as well as a philosophy.

Brown et al. (1989) have presented an excellent discussion of issues associated with home–school placement of children with disabilities. Whether a regular classroom base for students with disabilities will affect nondisabled students is an issue of some concern. Dissenters predict that nondisabled students will receive less instructional time and be distracted by the presence of children with disabilities. Those who argue the affirmative viewpoint propose that, with appropriate resources and services, all difficulties can be resolved in ways that do not affect the nondisabled students. "If professionals with reasonable experience, expertise, and resources are unable to address effectively . . . interfering actions, the classroom may not be the most appropriate environment at certain times of the day" (Brown et al., 1989, p. 10).

Furthermore, the home–school classroom base raises administrative issues with no clear answers: "How much will it cost? What kind of pre-service and in-service training is needed? What kind of changes in regular education curricula, organization, and management are appropriate? How must teacher–student ratios, licensing, and certifications change?" (Brown et al., 1991, p. 46).

Winzer (1990) has presented a very comprehensive discussion of general principles of integration. She noted that the philosophical belief of *normalization* supports provision of an educational and living environment as normal as possible for all individuals, regardless of their levels or types of disability. An outgrowth of that philosophical position has been the process of *de-institutionalization*, the movement of individuals from institutional living into community-based living arrangements. In the educational context, normalization has translated into *mainstreaming*, the philosophy of educational integration. The primary goal of the integration process is the "provision of free, appropriate education in the most suitable setting for all youngsters" (Winzer, 1990, p. 84). Winzer specified that children with mild disabilities may be fully integrated in the regular classroom, with additional help in resource rooms or from other educational specialists, but cautioned that, "if children are to be integrated into regular classrooms this requires that they be members of the class not just physically but also intellectually, socially and emotionally" (p. 84).

Winzer (1990) also considered that research and practice lag behind the philosophical commitment toward mainstreaming:

While educators, legislators, parents and others advance the notion, the manner in which the process will work most successfully has not yet been clearly delineated. There is not yet a quantitative measure of how great a handicap must be for special services to be offered, nor are there definite numbers or combinations of characteristics that must be identified before a pupil is diagnosed as exceptional. Because of these inherent difficulties, no other concept in today's educational system seems so fraught with confusion and misconceptions. (p. 85)

To facilitate discussion of the issues, Winzer (1990) also provided an outline of what integration is and is not. For Winzer, integration involves:

1. placing the child with special needs with peers as much as possible,
2. allowing for special help as needed while the child is enrolled in a regular class,
3. collaboration of professionals in program development and curriculum modification,
4. the provision of educational options, and
5. adaptability to a variety of settings such as regular class and resource room.

Integration is not the elimination of all special education classes, support services, and teachers, while indiscriminantly dumping children with special needs into regular classrooms without support services. Integration provides for equal opportunities for all children by uniting the skills of regular educators and their collaborating special educators.

Thus, to equate the terms mainstreaming and integration with full integration into regular classrooms is to represent only one option. Therefore, families, professionals in schools, government and teacher education settings must take care to define the terms clearly and discuss fully the variables and the range of services that may be involved in making decisions about integration.

Osborne (1992) examined the legal issues for education of American children with disabilities. The majority of U.S. court decisions have held that "an appropriate education" means less than providing the best possible program but more than simple access to programs. The courts have not entered debates on "best methodology," but have recognized that the mainstream setting is not appropriate for all students with special needs, and that education encompasses instruction in basic life skills. Furthermore there must be meaningful gains from education: (a) for those with moderate disabilities, passing grades, and grade advancement; (b) for those with severe disabilities, progress toward greater self-sufficiency and independence. In Canada, O'Reilly (1991) noted that while section 15 of the Canadian Charter of Rights and Freedoms prohibits exclusion from school of children with disabilities, the question arises whether education in a non-segregated setting is an option or a right? The U.S. courts are bound by a federal statute requiring delivery of special education services in the least restrictive environment, whereas in Canada there is no similar provision for the least restrictive environment. The Canadian "courts seem to be reluctant to examine either the content or the quality of educational decision-making" (p. 18). There is evidence that the courts will favour the least segregated option that provides educational progress; however, no one is entitled to "best possible service" (p. 19).

Inherent in the definitional discussion are a number of concerns that directly impact on the classroom teacher. What means are available to determine the needs of children with disabilities and the best setting and learning strategies? What teacher education preparation is needed to teach children with disabilities in regular classrooms and other settings? What amounts and types of additional supports are necessary and available to the classroom teacher? What placement options in other classrooms, schools, or the community are available? What are the priorities of parents and of the school? What are the procedures and practices for parent–teacher consultation and collaboration, and for collaboration between professionals? These concerns are not unlike those raised by today's students in faculties of education who are approaching the end of their preparation for entry into the teaching profession.

• • •

PERSPECTIVES OF EDUCATION STUDENTS
AND EDUCATORS

Because the province of Alberta is moving toward the regular classroom as the option of first choice for children with disabilities (Wilgosh, 1992), I probed the attitudes and concerns of my fourth year students in the "Basic Issues in Contemporary Education" course prior to writing this chapter. Most of my students have had no background in special education during their B Ed program, although a small number had taken a minor or a single course in special education. The following views came from these students, who generally claimed to feel unprepared to begin teaching in regular classrooms that might include several children with moderate to severe disabilities. To facilitate this possibility, education students want:

1. assurance that there will be support systems in place to provide them with assistance in locating resources;

2. the opportunity to discuss children's needs and problems with knowledge-able persons, before a regular class placement is made;

3. practicum experience with children who have special needs; hands-on experience can dispell fears;

4. information on developing individual educational programs, classroom management, and assessment/evaluation of children with special needs;

5. specific training, e.g., for working with medically fragile children, and for working with teacher aides and other support personnel, as well as for communicating with parents and families.

These students also noted the importance of having the right attitude, and recognizing the individuality of children, some of whom will have special needs. Further confirmation of these concerns was provided from two student projects (Forwick & Waggoner, personal communication, May 28, 1992; Noseworthy, personal communication, June 4, 1992).

These student perceptions are consistent with the literature on teacher percep-tions and concerns about integration of students with special needs. For exam-ple, Semmel, Abernathy, Butera, and Lesar (1991) surveyed a large number of U.S. regular and special educators in the United States to assess views on main-streaming (the Regular Education Initiative or REI).[2] The vast majority of respondents were of the view that regular education teachers do not have the skills and ability to provide one-to-one and small group instruction. With less than one-third of the sample supporting the regular classroom as the best place-ment for students with mild disabilities, such placements may not result in favorable outcomes, especially if teachers' expectations are negative. Nesbit (1991) has warned that integrated children whose teachers have not been prop-erly trained and have negative attitudes run the risk of emotional abuse.

In Alberta (Alberta Education Response Centre [AERC], 1992b), a teacher survey indicated that pre-service and in-service teacher education is inadequate for preparing teachers to integrate students with special needs. While the regu-lar class has social benefits for the child with special needs, almost half of the respondents felt that regular class placement does not meet the needs of stu-dents with special needs, and reduces the time spent by teachers with regular students due to lack of adequate instructional time, program materials and resources, and inadequate training and supports.

Yellowhead School Division in Alberta, a rural system, was the first in the province to adopt a full-integration policy. A five-year review (AERC, 1992a) provides an excellent overview of the issues involved in adoption of such a pol-icy. A majority of surveyed school staff indicated dissatisfaction with the amount of input they had into the integration decision and process. A large majority felt that they did not have adequate training at the outset and were not given adequate ongoing training. As well, available resources were seen as inadequate. Teachers recommended the need for training and in-service, particularly in the assessment of student needs and the management of behaviour problems, and for open communication and feedback. They urged proceeding more slowly in implementing integration policies. Parents indicated wanting more involvement with the planning and process of integration and wanted more resources, particularly in aide time, for individualizing assistance. They also recommended a slower approach to integration, and some preferred a partially integrated or segregated setting for their children with special needs. From the Yellowhead report (AERC, 1992a), it is clear that administrators play a vital role in integration. They must initiate effective change plans and be actively involved in the development of integration programs. Regular education and special education teachers must be integrated into a unified group, working together to implement the integration programs.

A number of individual Canadian schools and school divisions are reporting successful integration programs (e.g., Alberta Education, 1992; Jarrell, 1992; Davidson & Wiener, 1991). Common to these programs are strong administrative support; strong parent–professional relationships; and flexible, committed teachers with sharp observational and assessment skills, and skills in management and individualizing programs.

. . .

PREPARING TO TEACH CHILDREN
WITH SPECIAL NEEDS

Having identified the knowledge, skills, and attitudes that teachers require to facilitate integration of children with special needs, some discussion is warranted on teacher preparation. We must be cautious not to seek simplistic solutions to teacher preparation; the following comments are intended to provoke further discussion and development of teacher pre-service and in-service programs.

Assessment Issues

Ysseldyke, Algozzine, and Thurlow (1992) critiqued the use of categories and labels for children with disabilities. Furthermore, they suggested that, "The search for universal and specific features of various conditions is dependent on the nature of measurement instruments used to identify them and society's need to deal with what it sees as problems" (p. 111), rather than on deficits inherent within children. Ysseldyke et al. urged that tests and other assessment instruments be given and interpreted only by people who have the necessary competence, and urged that assessment must be directly linked with instruction.

There are vast numbers of assessment instruments available for assessing student skills and abilities, classroom and teacher variables, and many other dimensions of the learning environment. Ysseldyke and Christenson (1987) commented upon the many different uses of such instruments, particularly upon using assessment information to plan intervention, evaluate pupil progress, and evaluate effectiveness of programs of instruction. They noted that the dominant approach to planning has been the use of norm-referenced tests to identify students' strengths and weaknesses, an approach of "limited efficacy" (p. 17). Indeed, Yellowhead School Division (AERC, 1992a) reported that, when student achievement was assessed, there was overlap, "with a portion of special needs students apparently functioning better than control group students. This finding raises questions about how students with special needs were identified" (p. 187). Also of limited use, according to Ysseldyke and Christenson (1987), have been task-analysis approaches designed to match instruction to the learner's developmental level. Therefore, Ysseldyke and Christenson (1987) have argued for the necessity of examining the instructional environment as well as student and curricular/instructional variables in individualizing instructional programs for students with special needs.

In addition to skills and knowledge in administering and interpreting assessment instruments, teachers need to be able to evaluate critically the quality and usability of instruments and to select from the vast array of instruments those suitable to their individual classroom needs.

Behaviour Management Issues

Yellowhead School Division (AERC, 1992a) reported that children with special needs had more behaviour problems than did other children. "About 40% of the special needs population *did* have behavior problems severe enough to be considered in the clinical range" (p. 187). For the teachers, "the generally increasing prevalence of behavior problems was a significant unresolved issue" (p. 211). Furthermore, teachers felt that there were few strategies available to help them in managing behaviour problems. Ysseldyke et al. (1992) reported that, "Most teachers express a reluctance to teach students with behavior disorders" (p. 228). The difficulty is not a lack of behaviour management models, but the proliferation of models offered to the teacher with little published research demonstrating efficacy, and teachers with little training in selecting and implementing appropriate strategies (Goldberg & Wilgosh, 1990).

Goldberg and Wilgosh (1990) developed a checklist, based on teacher-identified components of effective behaviour management models. This checklist allows teachers to select from the array of available models, one that is most congruent with their personal and classroom instructional needs. According to Goldberg and Wilgosh, a model of behaviour management should match the school philosophy, while also meeting the teacher's professional needs. It should emphasize the importance of a positive pupil-teacher relationship, while promoting on-task behaviour. The model should provide a range of strategies and apply to a range of situations and inappropriate student behaviours. The Goldberg-Wilgosh checklist was provided as an alternative to having teachers uncritically accept the claims made by writers and workshop organizers, without research support. Clearly, preparation in behaviour management strategies is essential for all teachers.

Instructional Planning and Intervention

As for assessment and management strategies, teachers must make critical, appropriate choices of instructional strategies for individualizing instruction of children with special needs. Ysseldyke et al. (1992) reported the willingness of classroom teachers to educate students with special needs if they did not have to make major modifications to their lessons, did not have to design individual instructional programs, and if someone else did the teaching for those children. "Assumption of responsibility for instructing students is clearly the critical issue in teaching students with disabilities, but a close second place goes to the demand among educators for instant, simple, easy-to-implement solutions to incredibly complex instructional problems" (Ysseldyke et al., 1992, p. 229). Ysseldyke et al. provided criteria for consideration in selecting methods and curricula, warning that no evidence of universal effectiveness of curricula and methods exists. Interventions must be designed for individuals and monitored frequently. Likely some of these concerns would be alleviated by sound preparation in individualized planning and instruction for all teachers.

Facilitating Communication and Collaboration

Finally, teachers must be prepared to communicate with parents and children, with educators and other professionals. At least some of the motivation lies in the noted concerns with assessment, management, and instructional planning— complex dimensions of education that frustrate teachers working in isolation. To illustrate, Jenkins and Leicester (1992) found that regular class teachers had considerable difficulty in implementing intervention programs for children with special needs in their regular classrooms. This supports the need for collaborative or expert consultation in planning and implementing such programs in regular classrooms for teachers with no special education training. In Yellowhead School Division (AERC, 1992a), "Regular classroom teachers are given the final responsibility for preparation of IEPs (individual educational plans) for children with special needs, although they consult with a variety of others including the classroom support teacher, the principal, the counsellor, the aides and the parents" (p. 216). As integration becomes more prevalent, ways to facilitate teacher collaboration must be explored. Part of the solution lies with comprehensive teacher preparation in communication and collaboration.

• • •

ESSENTIAL CONSIDERATIONS

Clearly, a primary consideration involves defining the term integration for each jurisdiction and specifying the range of program offerings which will be considered within "integrated" settings, e.g., in home schools. A common understanding, by all local stakeholders, on the definition and scope of the integration process will allow meaningful discussion, planning, and implementation.

Each child has individual educational needs and these needs are greater for children with disabilities. We should be examining what the best possible setting and program would be, to maximize both academic and social gains and to allow each child to function effectively within mainstream society. There must be strategies in place to assess the needs of each child as well as the specific program considerations. Better integration policies and practices develop only through study of well-designed, carefully implemented programs that have demonstrated success through long-term follow-up with meaningful outcome measures.

With the objective of individualized programs and differentiated curricula, consideration must be given to teacher support and preparation. School personnel must have the understanding, knowledge, skills, and attitudes required to meet the needs of all students. As can be seen from the complexity of issues related to each of the dimensions of teacher preparation discussed above, there are no easy solutions. Sound preparation for all teachers, covering all of these dimensions, as well as ongoing research on the efficacy of assessment, management, collaborative planning, and instructional models are necessary so that educators can best meet the needs of individual children in classrooms.

• • •

NOTES

1. A portion of the section on definitional issues has been adapted from Wilgosh (1992), and is reprinted with permission from *The Canadian Administrator.*

2. The reader is referred to Wilgosh (1992) for a discussion of issues related to the U.S. Regular Education Initiative (REI).

• • •

REFERENCES

Alberta Education. (1992). Integration at Warburg Elementary School–An old theme in a new way. *in-fo-cus, 4*(3), 4.

Alberta Education Response Centre. (1992a). *Integrated services review. Yellowhead School Division No. 12.* Edmonton, AB: Alberta Education.

Alberta Education Response Centre. (1992b). *Survey on integration of special needs or exceptional students into the regular classroom. Executive summary.* Edmonton, AB: Alberta Education.

Brown, L., Long, E., Udvari-Solner, A., Schwarz, P.,VanDeventer, P., Ahlgren, C., Johnson, F., Gruenewald, L., & Jorgensen, J. (1989). Should students with severe intellectual disabilities be based in regular or in special education classrooms in home schools? *Journal of the Association for Persons with Severe Handicaps, 14*(1), 8–12.

Brown, L., Schwarz, P., Udvari-Solner, A., Kampschroer, E., Johnson, F., Jorgensen, J., & Gruenewald, L. (1991). How much time should students with severe intellectual disabilities spend in regular classrooms and elsewhere? *Journal of the Association for Persons with Severe Handicaps, 16*(1), 39–47.

Bunch, G. (1991). Full inclusion: Parent and educator objective for students with challenging needs. *Developmental Disabilities Bulletin, 19*(1), 80–101.

Davidson, I., & Wiener, J. (1991). Creating educational change: The in-school team. *Exceptionality Education Canada, 1*(2), 25–44.

Goldberg, J., & Wilgosh, L. (1990). A strategy for comparing and evaluating classroom discipline models. *Education Canada, 30*(2), 36–42.

Jarrell, J. (1992). Providing integration alternatives. *The ATA Magazine, 72*(3), 23–26.

Jenkins, J., & Leicester, N. (1992). Specialized instruction within general education: A case study of one elementary school. *Exceptional Children, 58*(6), 555–562.

Nesbit, W. (1991). Emotional abuse: Vulnerability and developmental delay. *Developmental Disabilities Bulletin, 19*(2), 66–80.

O'Reilly, R. (1991). The role of the courts in placement decisions. *Exceptionality Education Canada, 1*(2), 1–23.

Osborne, A. (1992). Legal standards for an appropriate education in the Post-Rowley Era. *Exceptional Children, 58*(6), 488–494.

Semmel, M., Abernathy, T., Butera, G., & Lesar, S. (1991). Teacher perceptions of the Regular Education Initiative. *Exceptional Children, 58,* 9–24.

Wilgosh, L. (1992). Integration of children with special needs. *The Canadian Administrator, 31*(4), 1–9.

Wilgosh, L. (in press). High achievement in a cross-national context. *Education Canada.*

Winzer, M. (1990). *Children with exceptionalities: A Canadian perspective* (2nd ed.). Scarborough, ON: Prentice-Hall.

Ysseldyke, J., Algozzine, B., & Thurlow, M. (1992). *Critical issues in special education* (2nd ed.). Toronto: Houghton Mifflin.

Ysseldyke, J., & Christenson, S. (1987). Evaluating students' instructional environments. *Remedial and Special Education, 8*(3), 17–24.

THE EDUCATION OF THE INTELLECTUALLY GIFTED STUDENT

...

G . P a t r i c k O ' N e i l l

R o b i n P . N o r r i s

INTRODUCTION

*T*he education of intellectually (academically) gifted children in Canada, until the last decade, was largely the responsibility of the regular classroom teacher. The results, however, have been disastrous in light of the fact that nearly 20 percent of the high school dropouts in North America have been gifted/talented students (Marquis Academic Media, 1977; Rice, 1980; Zorn, 1983). Obviously, this tragedy is a sad reflection on the school systems of both Canada and the United States.

The first program for the gifted in Canada dates back to 1928 (Kahanoff, 1979). There were sporadic movements in the 1950s and 1960s, but it was not until the mid-1970s that the impetus gained momentum. Ontario has led the way (Dennis, 1981; Kahanoff, 1979), although according to a survey (Borthwick, Dow, Levesque, & Banks, 1980), no province can afford to rest on its laurels. In essence, the study found that: departments or ministries of education did not make special financial provisions for the gifted, school boards generally reported difficulty in finding extra funds for the gifted, gifted education was not a priority among faculties of education, and with the exception of Ontario, none of the provinces required special certification for teachers of the gifted.

No doubt these conditions have improved somewhat since this first major survey was conducted (McLeod & Kluckman, 1985). Lobbying by parents for special funding, schools, and programs (Dennis, 1981) has prompted the formation of task forces (Alberta Education, Planning Services, 1983) and in some cases concrete legislation (Ontario Ministry of Education, 1980). Regardless, many school systems are still struggling with the establishment, or maintenance, of special facilities for the gifted (Adamson, 1983). It is in this context that the following article is written. The article provides direction and guidance for those interested in planning, organizing, implementing, and/or refining programs for the academically gifted student. The corpus is divided into four major areas, namely, defining giftedness, identification, implementation, and programming.

$$\bullet \ \bullet \ \bullet$$

DEFINING GIFTEDNESS

The term giftedness has a wide range of applications. Indeed, one could get lost readily in all the jumble and jargon. For example, Levin (1981) found that

> There is considerable controversy in the literature regarding a cut-off IQ score for giftedness. Some researchers maintain that only those in the upper 1% of measured IQ (around 137+) should be called gifted while others feel that all those within the top 10% of measured IQ (around 120+) should be included. Some view giftedness in terms of a "superior" IQ range (around 116–124+), a "gifted" range (about 132–140+), and an "extremely gifted" range (172–180+). (p. 1)

Others have attempted to make distinctions between the moderately gifted and the highly gifted (Powell & Haden, 1984; Roedell, 1984). Once again, though, divisions are not clear-cut as "some researchers cite IQs above 145 as indicating highly gifted abilities, while others reserve the label for children whose IQs exceed 165 or even 180" (Roedell, 1984, p. 127). Clearly, then, there are great variations in terminology. What is deemed gifted in one jurisdiction may be high ability, average gifted, or superior in another jurisdiction.

For purposes of this article, the term intellectually gifted will be defined as that two to three percent of the school-age population that have IQ scores in the 130-plus range (Hewett & Forness, 1977; Patchett & Gauthier, 1991). This definition is considered to be functional, pragmatic, and utilitarian as it represents a compromise between practical and philosophical considerations. That is, most boards could not cope with the larger numbers of an expanded definition, that included for example the superior child (IQ 116–124+). If, on the other hand, the definition was restricted to only students with IQs above 140, the numbers would be so low (about two in an average school of four hundred) that it would likewise be difficult to operate a successful program (Vernon, Adamson, & Vernon, 1977). Hence, the *modus operandi* of most school boards is the 130-plus IQ range (Adamson, 1983).

...

IDENTIFICATION

Of course, no operational definition of academic giftedness should be based solely on measures of cognitive ability, rather giftedness should be viewed as a composite of many factors. Hard-line cognitive test scores are extremely important, yet other auxiliary factors such as overall school achievement (grade-point average), biographical data, and performance in specially designed problem-solving situations (Kirschenbaum, 1983) should also be considered. Thus, identification strategies should hinge on multiple sources of information (Feldhusen, Asher, & Hoover, 1984; Kirschenbaum, 1983; Swassing, 1984). The options are many, but most school boards rely on a combination of behavioural procedures such as student interviews, rating scales, and checklists of various sorts (Yarborough & Johnson, 1983). However, rating scales and checklists are regularly discounted as dependable sources because most lack validity and reliability information (Feldhusen et al., 1984). Still, there are some supposedly promising instruments on the market, mainly, among others, the GIFT rating scales (Male & Perrone, 1979a, b, 1980), the Multi-Dimensional Screening Device (Krantz, 1978) and the Scales for Rating the Behavioural Characteristics of Superior Students (Renzulli, Smith, White, Callahan, & Hartman, 1976). Interviews are usually employed to help confirm or negate a child's score on a test or series of tests (Lewis, 1984). As with checklists, though, interviews are prone to subjectivity and biased reporting. Perhaps this is one of the reasons why interviews are rarely used (Yarborough & Johnson, 1983).

A more attractive alternative, and one that is commonly utilized, is that of parent or teacher nominations, or both. Nominations are based, for the most part, on informal observations. Interestingly, parent nominations, as a rule, correlate more closely with success in gifted programs than do teacher nominations (Clark, 1979; Kahanoff, 1979; Roedell, 1980; Strom, 1983). Teachers often confuse compliance and diligence with giftedness (Kirk, 1966; Pegnato & Birch, 1959) when, in fact, such attributes are not necessarily signs of being gifted. Plainly,

> Gifted children are frequently not "good" students. Good students sit in the seat, get out the book and work on an assignment, or stand in line until it's time to play the game, just like they are told. Gifted children often don't. (Tingey-Michaelis, 1984, p. 64)

For the gifted, "getting ahead, pleasing and meeting the expectations of society are of secondary importance. When required to learn things they consider meaningless, they resist, ignore or give token acquiesence" (Yatvin, 1984, p. 15). Hence, many high-ability youngsters perform poorly in terms of conventional norms.

Teachers unaware of the characteristics of giftedness might label such children hyperactive, socially immature, or emotionally disturbed. Indeed, evidence suggests that untrained teachers tend to be inaccurate "spotters" (Gear, 1976). Whitemore (1980), for instance, tells of Bobby (IQ 153) who spent a second year in the first grade because of his disruptive behaviour and his failure to complete daily classroom assignments. It is therefore imperative that teachers, as principle nominators, be cognizant of the traits customarily associated with giftedness.

What attributes then separate the gifted child from the average learner? First, and perhaps foremost, the gifted are seen as being extremely independent (Powell & Haden, 1984; Ricca, 1984; Stewart, 1981; Vail, 1979) because they have an internally structured locus of control (Dunn & Price, 1980; Powell & Haden, 1984; Stewart, 1981). Often, they cannot identify with the society-at-large and as a result retreat into, "a personal, secret world in which imagination becomes the only reality" (Tingey-Michaelis, 1984, p. 65). Withdrawal is due in part to both peer pressures to conform and to insensitive, ambivalent parents. If the gifted are consistently labelled "different and strange" by their playmates, they may internalize this designation and become eccentric social isolates (Roedell, 1984). Parents have also been known to confuse a child who is not a replica of either the mother or the father. On the one hand, the parents may take pride in the child's outstanding achievements, but on the other, fear that special treatment

> will adversely modify relations within the family or shorten the period of parental influence. Others believe that labelling will cause their child to develop an inflated self-image that can interfere with personal relationships throughout life. Some mothers and fathers want their children to be well thought of and believe that gifted classes may take away from time with age mates, the proper group with whom children should first learn to relate. (Strom, 1983, p. 296)

This inconsistent feedback confuses the child to the point of not knowing whether it is "good" or "bad" to be highly intelligent (Powell & Haden, 1984). As a result, the child may conclude it is not smart to be smart and decides therefore to either "hide" his or her ability in an effort to be accepted (Feldman, 1984), or the child may simply withdraw into a make-believe world.

Their independence is also reflected in their thinking styles. Rather than reason in a sequential manner, that is, step-by-step, they frequently "skip-think" (Powell & Haden, 1984). Translated, they solve complex problems without going through the so-called normal channels. Consequently, their work is very imaginative (Strom, 1983) and distinctly original (Tingey-Michaelis, 1984). As well, they are able to concentrate for extended periods of time (Strom, 1983; Vail, 1979), they exhibit unusual levels of task persistence (Dunn & Price, 1980; Griggs & Price, 1980; Strom, 1983) and they generally prefer solitary activities (Griggs & Price, 1980; Price, Dunn, Dunn, & Griggs, 1981; Strom, 1983), activities in which lecture and discussion are kept to a minimum.

In addition, the gifted are self-motivated (Dunn & Price, 1980; Griggs & Price, 1980; Vail, 1979), very creative (Levin, 1981), although not always in a conventional fashion (Vail, 1979), and they are extremely perceptive (Dunn & Price, 1980; Griggs & Price, 1980; Perry, 1988; Vail, 1979). Perceptive in the sense that they are, "alert, keen, observant and respond quickly" (Tingey-Michealis, 1984, p. 64) to the demands of the situation. In other words, they are the first to notice patterns, trends, and special relationships in seemingly disappropriate subjects and, as a consequence, new material may seem more recognized than learnt.

Other traits commonly associated with giftedness include abounding curiosity, physical and psychological stamina, better memory although not necessarily more accurate memory, and heightened sensitivity (Perry, 1988; Vail, 1979). The gifted have often been described as "having 'one skin less' than other children; with their above average sensitivities and concerns for problems of society" (Shiner, 1980, p. 8). The tendency, though, to be offended easily or to respond quickly to criticism can lead to feelings of rejection and despair. The gifted, for example, may be ridiculed for overreacting, thereby increasing their feelings of being "odd" (Roedell, 1984). Meanwhile, their acute awareness of society's injustices and mammoth hypocrisies can compound their feelings of scepticism (Jones, 1983) and cynicism (Roedell, 1984). Hence, the gifted need a "warm and safe psychological base from which to explore" (Khatena, 1978, p. 93), and they need understanding and support in their pursuit of excellence. Without this extra support, their curiosity is often suppressed and this, in turn, can lead to serious behavioural problems (Khatena, 1978).

In summary, identification procedures should depend on more than one source of information. Although individual and group intelligence tests are the most widely employed screening devices (Mitchell, 1984; Yarborough & Johnson, 1983), they are not without problems. Truly, many tests ignore cultural idiosyncrasies and environmental factors (Hewett & Forness, 1977) and individual tests, in particular, are expensive to administer (Kahanoff, 1979; Payne, 1974). Still, a high IQ score

> is a sufficient indicator that a type of giftedness exists. Moreover, an unusually high test score ought to alert us to the possibility that we are in the presence of one of those rare individuals who can make a momentous impact on human thought and civilization. (Brown, 1984, p. 126)

At the same time, a multidimensional approach can help clarify the type of giftedness and confirm the need for a specific type of facility. Thus, identification strategies

> should be started early in the school life of children and be continued. Progress should be continually monitored and procedures should be established for withdrawing those who do not show promise. Withdrawal should not be seen as a punishment, but rather as lack of congruence between the program's objectives and the child's specific needs. When many students are not performing well, however, the program should be reassessed and modified accordingly. (O'Neill & Scollay, 1983, p. 12)

• • •

IMPLEMENTATION

The development and successful implementation of programs for the gifted depend on a number of factors; most notably, funding, space allocation, staffing, and administrative and community support. The process will also depend on whether the impetus is grassroots or board mandated. Summy (1983, pp. 45–46) offers a list of ten practical suggestions to help teachers, and other interested parties, launch a grassroots movement. The proposals are aimed at overcoming institutional obstacles, financial barriers, suspicious colleagues, and reluctant administrators. Abbreviated, the list is outlined as follows:

1. Make a commitment
2. Be enthusiastic. A positive thinker is a goal achiever.
3. Research G/T (gifted/talented) theory and programs, thoroughly. Begin by reading books and articles.
4. Formulate a G/T program that fits the needs of your students, school, and community.
5. Set short and long range goals. Be realistic about the goals and the time sequence in which the goals are achieved.

6. Write your proposal and document it with the research sources you used. Make sure the proposal is consistent with the goals and curriculum of your school.

7. Present the proposal to your immediate supervisor. Be prepared to answer tough questions and do not become defensive; it will only work against you.

8. Do not take it personally if you are not sucessful in the beginning with your supervisor.

9. Do not ask for money. Design the program so that initial funding is not needed.

10. Be flexible. Change the program if there is need. Summy (1983) concludes his article with some sound advice. Specifically,

> What you are about to embark upon is a commitment to do more than you are doing now. It will take more time, planning, risk taking, energy and work. Regular duties will have to be performed, and you will still receive the same pay. Don't start any project unless you are willing to sacrifice! (p. 46)

Regardless of the impetus, there are two cardinal rules to the successful implementation of a gifted program. The first involves public awareness and the second concerns tailoring activities to the individual needs of a particular school and community. All those involved in the program should have a thorough understanding of what the organizers are trying to accomplish. Newsletters, introductions at PTA meetings, and mailed requests for volunteers can help increase community awareness and support (Zorn, 1983). Orientation sessions might even include movies or slide/tape presentations that have been developed by both staff and students (Reis & Renzulli, 1984). Whatever route is taken, it is imperative that all participants, students included, have a clear understanding of the selection strategies, the models of instruction, the goals, the teaching methods, the resource materials, and the evaluation techniques. Further, the participants must be provided continually with up-to-date feedback. Correspondence in the form of progress reports, bulletins, and periodic invitations to visit the school can help maintain high-interest levels.

Faculty can be best briefed through a formal series of in-service workshops, seminars, or colloquia. According to Reis and Renzulli (1984), a minimum of three in-service sessions should be scheduled and each should address a separate topic.

> Sequential subjects to be covered include a detailed structural overview of the entire system; a definition of giftedness and resulting identification

procedures; the specific roles and responsibilities of classroom and resource teachers; and, finally, an indepth session on compacting or streaming the regular curriculum to ensure that students have an adequate challenge in the regular classroom as well as time to participate in the gifted program. (Reis & Renzulli, 1984, p. 31)

The second cardinal rule stated simply is: build-in flexibility and maintain program uniqueness. Every gifted facility should be carefully planned with a specific school and community in mind (Reis & Renzulli, 1984; Summy, 1983). In other words, the planners should never fall into the trap of copying a model designed for another school. Each district's local administrative priorities, scheduling practices and budgetary constraints must be fully weighed before a program is launched. Organizers should feel free to borrow ideas but not exact blueprints.

· · ·

PROGRAMMING

Programming can be divided into four complementary areas, namely, goals or objectives, structural design, models of instruction, and program evaluation. Naturally, the goals should correspond closely to the design and models of instruction. As well, the goals should be listed in sequential, hierarchical, and developmental terms. In the case of the Purdue Three-Stage Model, for instance, the goals are differentiated explicitly by levels of performance. In short, the goals include "the development of basic creative thinking and problem solving abilities; the development of higher level thinking skills, independent study, and research skills; and the development and maintenance of positive self-concepts through interaction with other gifted students" (Kolloff & Feldhusen, 1984, p. 53).

There are several structural designs, but most fall within the domain of either acceleration or enrichment (Cannon, 1989). Acceleration involves administratively moving youngsters through regular programs at a faster rate. Such an approach could include early admission to kindergarten or Grade 1, collapsing grades (three grades in two years), enrolment in extra classes to earn advance credit(s), and advanced placement in some subject(s) (Southern & Jones, 1992; Vernon et al., 1977).

Acceleration has several financial and administrative advantages. Once implemented, for example, there is no need for additional space, materials, or teachers as students can be readily accommodated within the boundaries of existing structures. Acceleration, then, only requires ingenuity and flexibility on the part of the administration, the staff, and the students.

However, a potential problem with acceleration is that of excessive repetition (Feldman, 1984). Elaborated, schools must guard against merely doing more of the "same" old things. As Renzulli (1976, p. 316) warns, "the word 'course' automatically implies a certain amount of structure and uniformity," which, in turn, often means fixed time allocations, prescribed textbooks, and limited choices. In such circumstances, there is a danger that quantity, rather than quality, could become the guiding principle.

At present, most programs fall within the domain of enrichment practices (Jones, 1983). Strictly speaking, there are two levels of enrichment, mainly, horizontal and vertical (Banks, Bélanger, Bettiol, Borthwick, Donnelly, & Smith, 1978; Payne, 1974; Vernon et al., 1977). Horizontal enrichment refers to the provision of a wider range of experiences at the same level of difficulty, whereas vertical enrichment pertains to higher level activities of increasing complexity (Payne, 1974).

Enrichment programs can be orchestrated on an individual basis within the confines of the regular classroom or outside on a daily or weekly basis depending on space allocations and availability of support staff. Full-time classes can also be arranged when resources and numbers permit.

At the elementary level, the pull-out program is the most frequently employed alternative (Cox & Daniel, 1984). The term

> describes an administrative arrangement that places gifted students in a heterogeneous classroom for most of their instruction and "pulls them out" to study with other bright youngsters in special classes and a special setting for a portion of the school week. The special classes may meet in the student's home, school or the students may be bused to another school or designated center. Time spent in pull-out classes varies from less than an hour a week to a full day per week or more. (p. 55)

Pull-out programs should either supplement what the children are learning in their regular classes or they should be directly related to the standard curriculum. Teachers must be careful not to fall into the "brain exercises" trap (Mirsky, 1984). Problem-solving games, puzzles, and brainstorming sessions are fun, but unless they have continuity and enduring value, they are of little worth.

Pull-out programs allow children the opportunity to socialize and interact with peers like themselves. This opportunity can be a refreshing experience especially if they feel alienated by their classmates. Indeed, evidence suggests that grouping can enhance both their social and emotional development (Newland, 1976; Speed, 1978; Woodliffe, 1977). At the same time, though, pull-out practices can be a disruptive force. Many teachers oppose such programs because they further fragment the school day (Cox & Daniel, 1984; Mirsky, 1984). There is also the danger of "affective dislocation" (Cox & Daniel, 1984). Translated, participants may physically feel their difference when they "get up" and go to a gifted class. Their peers can be cruel and resentment, expressed or otherwise, can compound their feelings of being different. One solution to both problems, of course, is to schedule pull-out classes for a full day rather than for part of a day.

Another more attractive option is to establish full-time gifted classes. Self-contained facilities have several advantages over pull-out programs. First, there is no disruption and no fragmentation of other classrooms. Second, the teacher can incorporate a wider range of activities that cater specifically to each student's individual skills, talents, and abilities. Third, a permanent family grouping can create a safe environment in which the child can explore freely without the fear of having to constantly defend his or her eccentricity. This freedom can have a profound positive influence on student morale. Truly, there can be

> an openness and excitement about culture and the humanities that would quickly be forced underground in a heterogeneous class. Having taught the entire educational spectrum, I can safely say I have seen intellectual curiosity buried for fear of scorn. (Mirsky, 1984, p. 26)

Cries of elitism are regularly levelled at full-time gifted programs (Plaisance, 1988). Such criticism can be softened somewhat by building in a "pull-in" component (Mirsky, 1984). That is, students from other classes can be invited to participate in some field trips, projects, and in special presentations. Students can also be invited "in" for a game of checkers, chess, or Scrabble, and there can be a sharing of some weekly activities with other classes.

> By opening up certain enrichment sessions and inviting as many students as possible to listen to a lecture or to participate in a workshop on creative dramatics, all children benefit at certain times from the special program. Program ownership is thus extended to students outside the talent pool, and everyone has a better appreciation of and a more positive attitude toward its very existence. (Reis & Renzulli, 1984, p. 33)

The Enrichment Triad Model (Renzulli, 1977) is the most widely used instructional paradigm in America (Mitchell, 1982). There are other models of instruction, but due to space limitations, this discussion will be confined to the Enrichment Triad Model. The model is divided into three types of activities. The first type deals with general exploration, the second with group training, and the third with individual and small group investigation.

Type I activities should be deliberately designed to generate areas of personal interest. The teacher should expose students to a wide variety of topics from which they can select problems for independent study. Throughout this stage, the teacher should be actively involved, providing information, provoking curiosity, and encouraging further study. Interest centres, resource personnel, and field trips can help facilitate the process.

Type II activities are concerned with the development of high-level thinking and feeling abilities, critical, divergent, reflective and creative thinking, problem-solving skills, inquiry methods, awareness development, and sensitivity training. Certain taxonomies, such as those proposed by Bloom (1977), Krathwohl, Bloom, & Masia (1974), and Guilford (1967), can be used to help classify these cognitive and affective behaviours in a progressive pattern. It should be remembered that this stage is devoted primarily to the development and expansion of thinking skills, not the teaching of specific content. Students may acquire factual knowledge as a by-product of the process, but the focus should be procedural, not informational.

Type III activities should be directed toward solving "real" problems. According to Renzulli (1983), a real problem has four characteristics.

1. A real problem must have a personal frame of reference, since it involves an emotional or affective component as well as an intellectual cognitive one.

2. A real problem does not have an existing or unique solution.

3. Calling something a problem does not necessarily make it a real problem for a given person or group.

4. The purpose of pursuing a real problem is to bring about some form of change and/or to contribute something new to the sciences, the arts, or the humanities. (pp. 49–50)

A real problem, then, is genuine when it has meaning for the young investigator. Problems prescribed, presented, and predetermined by the teacher are not real problems. Teachers can focus, suggest, direct, and guide, but they should not structure the learning experience. Although there is nothing wrong with looking up information and summarizing existing facts and figures from encyclopedias and other reference books, such activities are classified as reporting, not researching. Researching involves real problems, problems that go beyond existing knowledge to create new constructs, concepts, or theories based on a synthesis of past research. In a real problem situation students assume the role of a first-hand inquirer.

> They may pursue these roles at less complex levels than adult researchers, artists and other creative producers, but the main point is that they go about their work thinking, feeling and doing like the practicing professional. The end product of their efforts is not merely learning about existing knowledge. Rather, the major purpose is to use existing knowledge and methodology to create something that is new. (Renzulli, 1983, p. 50)

Once a problem has been researched, the results should be presented to an appropriate audience or published in a newspaper or magazine. Dissemination will depend largely on the format of the final product and on the grade level of the student. With the younger students, it is sometimes best to limit the audience to classmates, parents, and teachers. Type III activities should consume approximately one half of the time students spend in enrichment classes. In addition, they can, and should, be employed with all gifted students, from preschool (Sloan & Stedtnitz, 1984) to senior high school (Zorn, 1983).

Program evaluation should provide feedback as to the success or failure of the instructional model. The process, however developed, should be closely linked to the goals of the program. In other words, the evaluator(s) should continually monitor the original goals to see if they are being achieved, and if so, to what extent.

Reis and Renzulli (1984) developed a software package that contains structured forms to monitor program activities, questionnaires for those with vested interests in the program and instruments designed to assess cognitive and affective growth. The items are intended as a set of "friendly enforcers" that help pinpoint areas of deficiency. Another equally attractive alternative was developed by Morris & Fitz-Gibbon (1978). Their book entitled the *Evaluator's Handbook* describes how to conduct a systematic formative evaluation of a gifted program. The book is divided into a series of four consecutive steps commencing with setting the boundaries for the evaluation and terminating with reporting procedures.

Whatever approach is selected, it is important not to rely entirely on standardized achievement tests. Administering pre- and post-tests can present a distorted picture because most gifted students would be performing initially at the 95th percentile. In fact, post-test scores may show decreased performance due largely to the phenomenon known as regression toward the mean.

• • •

CONCLUSION

This article has looked at the education of the intellectually gifted student. The text defines the term gifted, offers guidelines for identification of members, and provides information on the implementation and operationalization of programs for the group.

In the United States, public support of gifted education has been rapidly increasing to the point where, in 1980, their school systems were, "in the midst of enjoying the strongest amount of acceptance and public support that has ever been accorded to the gifted child movement in America" (Renzulli, 1980, p. 3). Moreover, there is every indication that the movement has and will continue to "thrive" and "flourish" (Mitchell, 1984).

In Canada, gifted education has progressed more slowly than in the United States. As late as 1980, for instance, there was little public support of facilities for the gifted (Borthwick et al., 1980). In the interval, the movement has been gaining force. Canadian educators are becoming involved and they are starting to provide special services for the gifted (McLeod & Kluckman, 1985).

Ultimately, special programs for the gifted should be part of every school system in Canada, no matter how big or small. At the moment, this challenge may be somewhat idealistic, but remember, in the end, it is the gifted who will brave the unknown and bridge the universe. Let us not forget, therefore, that the more we deny them, the more we deny ourselves!

• • •

ADDENDUM

The above article was written in 1986. Recent references have since been added to the text, although the text itself has not been altered significantly. It was written at a time when gifted education was gaining momentum. In the interval, there have been advancements, but not as many as initially anticipated. On the one hand, for example, there have been many excellent conferences and symposia on giftedness in both Canada and the United States of which one in particular is worthy of note. In May 1988, the second Canadian symposium on the future education of gifted learners was held in Regina, Saskatchewan. As a result of the proceedings, a document entitled *Canadian Guidelines: Preferable Future Practices in Programming for Gifted Learners* (Lipp & Casswell, 1990) was published. The guidelines can be used to implement new programs or to evaluate existing programs regardless of level, that is, classroom, school board, or ministry (department) of education.

On the other hand, governments have been slow to react to demands for gifted programs. Of the ten provinces and two territories, for instance, four still have no specific laws or policies on gifted education, namely, Manitoba, Newfoundland, Prince Edward Island, and the Yukon (Goguen, 1989). Five other provinces and one territory (Alberta, British Columbia, New Brunswick, Nova Scotia, Quebec, and the Northwest Territories) have specific Ministerial policy statements, but no legislation. This leaves only Ontario and Saskatchewan with specific legislative provision for the education of the gifted. And, this is a potential problem because policies can change with governments.

What then does the future hold? Will the 1990s be the reverse of the 1980s? Will all that has been gained be lost? At this stage, it is too early to predict, but the recession is playing havoc with gifted education programs in the United States (Cohen, Jeffcott, & Swartz, 1991). As the coffers dry up, so too have the programs.

Likewise, in Canada, it is expected that gifted programs will be targeted early because, for the most part, they are not supported by the public. For example, in Ontario, Grayson and Hall (1992) found that only thirteen percent gave unqualified support to gifted education programs. Another sixty-three percent gave support provided it did not take resources away from the regular classroom. Nineteen percent offered no support.

No doubt, governments are aware of this indifference and will act accordingly, especially at election time. Of course, political short-term gains at the expense of the gifted is, in our view, scandalous. The solution to our present crisis is not to cancel programs for the gifted, but rather to expand them. It is time for Western societies to stop denying giftedness and start rewarding it. Otherwise, we will slip further and further behind countries like Japan where giftedness is treated with reverence (Plaisance, 1988). Already, their commitment is showing. Indeed,

> Japan now produces almost twice the number of scientists and engineers per 10,000 people as the U.S. . . . the Japanese are now playing a leading role in fashion design, the arts, and almost all other areas of industrial, commercial, and domestic design. . . . Japan's annual share of American patents grew over the last 15 years from 4% to 19%, while our own share dropped 20% over the same period. . . . Average Japanese students achieved higher than the top 5% of the U.S. students in college preparatory mathematics. (Renzulli & Reis, 1991, p. 27)

There is presently a shadow of uncertainty cast over the future of gifted education in Canada. We are, so to speak, at a crossroads. Will we go forward or will we go backward? The latter is unthinkable, but, at the same time, we must brace ourselves for the worst scenario. Of course, if we go backward, ultimately no one will escape. To sustain a high standard of living, we must nurture our most precious resource. The sooner we face this fact, the sooner we will begin to secure our future.

• • •

REFERENCES

Adamson, G. (1983). Giftedness/creativity: The coin with more than two sides. *ATA Magazine, 63*, 28–29.

Alberta Education, Planning Services Branch. (1983). *Educating gifted and talented pupils in Alberta.* Report of the Minister's Task Force on Gifted and Talented Pupils. Edmonton: Alberta Education.

Banks, R., Bélanger, B., Bettiol, I., Borthwick, B., Donnelly, B., & Smith, A. (1978). *Gifted/talented children.* Toronto: Ontario Ministry of Education.

Bloom, B. (Ed.). (1977). *Taxonomy on educational objectives. The classification of educational goals handbook I: Cognitive domain.* New York: Longman.

Borthwick, B., Dow, I., Levesque, D., & Banks, R. (Eds.). (1980). *The gifted and talented students in Canada: Results of a CEA survey.* Toronto: The Canadian Education Association.

Brown, M. M. (1984). The needs and potential of the highly gifted: Toward a model of responsiveness. *Roeper Review, 6,* 123–127.

Cannon, N. (1989). Special education for the gifted. *Education Canada, 29,* 26–29.

Clark, B. (1979). *Growing up gifted: Developing the potential of children at home and at school.* Columbus, OH: Charles E. Merrill.

Cohen, L. M., Jeffcott, G., & Swartz, E. (1991). Recent trends in gifted education. *Gifted International, 7,* 13–29.

Cox, J., & Daniel, N. (1984). The pull-out model. *G/C/T, 34,* 55–60.

Dennis, W. (1981, October 19). Charting a brighter course for genius. *Maclean's Magazine, 94,* 53–54.

Dunn, R., & Price, G. (1980). The learning style characteristics of gifted children. *Gifted Child Quarterly, 24,* 33–36.

Feldhusen, J. F., Asher, J. W., & Hoover, S. M. (1984). Problems in the identification of giftedness, talent, or ability. *Gifted Child Quarterly, 28,* 149–151.

Feldman, R. D. (1984). Helping the gifted grow up. *Instructor, 94,* 92–94.

Gear, G. H. (1976). Accuracy of teacher judgement in identifying intellectually gifted children: A review of the literature. *Gifted Child Quarterly, 20,* 478–489.

Goguen, L. (1989). The education of gifted children in Canadian law and ministerial policy. *Canadian Journal of Education, 14,* 18–30.

Grayson, J. P., & Hall, M. H. (1992). Education for the gifted: What does the public think? *Education Today, 4,* 25.

Griggs, S., & Price, G. (1980). A comparison between the learning styles of gifted versus average suburban junior high school students. *Roeper Review, 3,* 7–9.

Guilford, J. P. (1967). *The nature of human intelligence.* New York: McGraw-Hill.

Hewett, F. M., & Forness, S. R. (1977). *Education of exceptional learners.* Boston, MA: Allyn and Bacon.

Jones, V. (1983). Current trends in classroom management: Implications for gifted students. *Roeper Review, 6,* 26–30.

Kahanoff, A. (1979). Educating Canada's gifted. *ATA Magazine, 60,* 27–29.

Khatena, J. (1978). *The creatively gifted child: Suggestions for parents and teachers.* New York: Vantage Press.

Kirk, W. D. (1966). A tentative screening procedure for selecting bright and slow children in kindergarten. *Exceptional Children, 33,* 235–241.

Kirschenbaum, R. J. (1983). Flexible methods for identifying the gifted. *Education Digest, 49,* 58–60.

Kolloff, P. B., & Feldhusen, J. F. (1984). The effects of enrichment on self-concept and creative thinking. *Gifted Child Quarterly, 28,* 53–57.

Krantz, B. (1978). *Multi-dimensional screening device for the identification of gifted talented children.* Grand Fork, ND: Bureau of Educational Research, University of North Dakota.

Krathwohl, D. R., Bloom, B. S., & Masia, B. B. (1974). *Taxonomy of educational objectives. The classification of educational goals handbook II: Affective domain.* New York: David McKay.

Levin, B. (1981). Identification of intellectually gifted students. 1: Overview of issues. *Research Peel Board of Education Bulletin, 3,* 1.

Lewis, G. (1984). Alternatives to acceleration for the highly gifted child. *Roeper Review, 6,* 133–136.

Lipp, M., & Casswell, C. (1990). Canadian guidelines: Preferable future practices in programming for gifted learners. *Canadian Journal of Special Education, 6,* 79–87.

Male, R. A., & Perrone, P. (1979a). Identifying talent and giftedness: Part I. *Roeper Review, 2,* 5–7.

Male, R. A., & Perrone, P. (1979b). Identifying talent and giftedness: Part II. *Roeper Review, 2,* 5–8.

Male, R. A., & Perrone, P. (1980). Identifying talent and giftedness: Part III. *Roeper Review, 2,* 9–11.

Marquis Academic Media. (1977). Gifted and talented. In *Yearbook of special education 1977–1978* (pp. 531–533). Chicago, IL: Marquis Who's Who.

McLeod, L., & Kluckman, J. (1985). *A trans-Canada survey of special programming for gifted children, preliminary report.* Saskatoon, SK: University of Saskatchewan.

Mirsky, N. (1984). Starting an interage full time gifted class. *G/C/T, 33,* 24–26.

Mitchell, B. M. (1982). An update on the state of gifted/talented education in the U.S. *Phi Delta Kappan, 63,* 357–358.

Mitchell, B. M. (1984). An update on gifted/talented education in the U.S. *Roeper Review, 6,* 161–163.

Morris, L. L., & Fitz-Gibbon, C. T. (1978). *Evaluator's handbook.* Beverly Hills, CA: Sage Publications.

Newland, T. E. (1976). *The gifted in socio-educational perspective.* Englewood Cliffs, NJ: Prentice-Hall.

O'Neill, G. P., & Scollay, B. M. (1983). The education of intellectually gifted children: A challenge for the 1980's and beyond. *Comment on Education, 13,* 11–16.

Ontario Ministry of Education. (1980). *Bill 82–An act to amend the education act, 1974.* Toronto, ON: Author.

Patchett, R. F., & Gauthier, Y. (1991). Parent and teacher perceptions of giftedness and a program for the gifted. *B. C. Journal of Special Education, 15,* 25–37.

Payne, J. (1974). The gifted. In N. G. Harding (Ed.), *Behavior of exceptional children–An introduction to special education* (pp. 189–214). Columbus, OH: Charles E. Merrill.

Pegnato, C. W., & Birch, J. W. (1959). Locating gifted children in junior high schools: A comparison of methods. *Exceptional Children, 25,* 300–304.

Perry, M. (1988, December). *The influence of conventional and enriched curricular programs on gifted students.* Paper presented at the Ontario Educational Research Council, Toronto, ON.

Plaisance, S. (1988). Negative attitudes toward gifted education. *McGill Journal of Education, 23,* 50–57.

Powell, P. M., & Haden, T. (1984). The intellectual and psychosocial nature of extreme giftedness. *Roeper Review, 6,* 131–133.

Price, G., Dunn, K., Dunn, R., & Griggs, S. (1981). Studies in students' learning styles. *Roeper Review, 4,* 38–40.

Reis, S. M., & Renzulli, J. S. (1984). Key features of successful programs for the gifted and talented. *Educational Leadership, 41,* 28–34.

Renzulli, J. S. (1976). The Enrichment Triad Model: A guide for developing defensible programs for the gifted and talented. *Gifted Child Quarterly, 20,* 303–326.

Renzulli, J. S. (1977). *The Enrichment Triad Model: A guide for developing defensible programs for the gifted and talented.* Mansfield Center, CT: Creative Learning Press.

Renzulli, J. S. (1980). Will the gifted movement be alive and well in 1990? *Gifted Child Quarterly, 24,* 3–9.

Renzulli, J. S. (1983). Guiding the gifted in the pursuit of real problems: The transformed role of the teacher. *Journal of Creative Behavior, 17,* 49–59.

Renzulli, J. S., & Reis, S. M. (1991). The reform movement and the quiet crisis in gifted education. *Gifted Child Quarterly, 35,* 26–35.

Renzulli, J. S., Smith, L. H., White, A. J., Callahan, C. M., & Hartman, C. M. (1976). *Scales for rating the behavioral characteristics of superior students.* Wethersfield, CT: Creative Learning Press.

Ricca, J. (1984). Learning styles and preferred instructional strategies of gifted students. *Gifted Child Quarterly, 28,* 121–126.

Rice, B. (1980, February). Going for the gifted gold. *Psychology Today, 13,* 55–67.

Roedell, W. C. (1984). Vulnerabilities of highly gifted children. *Roeper Review, 6,* 127–130.

Roedell, W. C., Jackson, N. E., & Robinson, H. B. (1980). *Gifted young children.* New York: Teachers College Press.

Shiner, S. M. (1980). Challenge and commitment for the gifted: A task for the 80's. *Orbit, 11,* 6–8.

Sloan, C., & Stedtnitz, U. (1984). The Enrichment Triad Model for the very young gifted. *Roeper Review, 6,* 204–206.

Southern, W. T., & Jones, E. D. (1992). The real problems with academic acceleration. *G/C/T, 15,* 34–38.

Speed, F. (1978). Teaching the bright child. *Orbit, 9,* 6–11.

Stewart, E. E. (1981). Learning styles among gifted/talented students: Instructional technique preferences. *Exceptional Children, 42,* 134–138.

Strom, R. D. (1983). Expectations for educating the gifted and talented. *Educational Forum, 47,* 279–303.

Summy, J. (1983). Gifted and talented program development: The teacher as a change-agent. *Education, 104,* 44–46.

Swassing, R. (1984). The multiple component alternative for gifted education. *G/C/T, 33,* 10–11.

Tingey-Michealis, C. (1984). Gifted kids are not all gift wrapped. *Early Years, 14,* 64–65.

Vail, P. L. (1979). *The world of the gifted child.* New York: Walker.

Vernon, P. E., Adamson, G., & Vernon, D. F. (1977). *The psychology and education of gifted children.* London, England: Methuen.

Yarborough, B. H., & Johnson, R. A. (1983). Identifying the gifted: A theory-practice gap. *Gifted Child Quarterly, 27,* 135–138.

Yatvin, J. (1984). Gifted or bright? *Principal, 63,* 14–16.

Whitmore, J. R. (1980). *Giftedness, conflict, and underachievement.* Boston, MA: Allyn and Bacon.

Woodliffe, H. M. (1977). *Teaching gifted learners—A handbook for teachers.* Toronto, ON: The Ontario Institute for Studies in Education.

Zorn, R. L. (1983). A comprehensive program for the gifted/talented pupils in grades 1 through 12. *Education, 103,* 310–315.

TEACHER TRAINING
AND CURRICULUM
DEVELOPMENT

...

Educators have been under attack from critics who charge that teachers being trained today are inadequately prepared to assist our youth in coping with the complexities of a society in transition, or perhaps more properly, a society in a continuous process of transformation. Some lament the erosion of traditional educational values; others stress the need for change in educational goals and assumptions. The authors in this section identify several of the issues facing those involved in teacher training and curriculum development in Canada today and offer possible directions for the future.

To Birch and Elliott, "the paramount issue in teacher education is the formulation of a conception of teacher education of sufficient scope to accommodate the full reality of the task." In discussing this theme, they concentrate on issues surrounding the selection of candidates for teacher training, the appropriate subject-matter preparation for elementary and secondary school teachers, the necessity of adequately linking theory and practice in teacher preparation programs, and the conceptualization of teacher education as being an integral endeavour carried on throughout teachers' careers.

Difficult economic times create pressures for schools to improve their efficiency. Bezeau discusses two types of efficiency, technical and allocative, in the context of optimizing the achievement of the objectives that our society has for the school system. Allocative efficiency refers to choosing the combination of resource inputs in a manner that maximizes the output of schools. Technical efficiency refers to procedures within schools that combine the available resources in the most effective manner.

The "socio-political tasks of genuine affirmation of historical realities," the "sensitive management of tensions between groups," and the "productive management of change" are the challenges that, according to Westwood, face the modern day counsellor-educator. As Canadian society becomes more culturally complex, the practice of counselling will also have to become more complex. Westwood points out that the models of intervention currently in use will have to begin to incorporate, and be sensitive to, the wide array of practices and values that are part and parcel of our everyday society. In order to facilitate this, Westwood proposes a five-stage developmental model for training "multiculturally-skilled counsellors," which will allow the counsellor-educator to adequately work within an everchanging counselling profession.

Pratt discusses how the curriculum planner can help teachers and students with the recognition, construction, and integration of public, interpersonal, and personal meaning. Public meaning refers to the areas of knowledge and technical competence that can be realistically communicated in verbal and numerical forms. Interpersonal meanings refer to meanings that can only be understood and shared by those in some sort of relationship. Personal meanings are essentially intuitive and can only be fully comprehended by the person who experiences them. Through this context, Pratt raises many extremely relevant and thought-provoking questions that merit serious consideration by educators at all levels if we are to effectively prepare young Canadians for life in the twenty-first century.

Towards a New Conception
of Teacher Education

...

Daniel R. Birch

Murray Elliott

How is teacher education to be conceived? While it has not always been recognized as a crucial issue, how teacher education has been conceived—by those preparing to become teachers, by those providing preparation programs, and by the profession generally—has had major implications for the quality of teacher preparation and ultimately for the quality of teaching in society's schools.

Our contention is that teacher education has often been conceived much too narrowly. University students and faculty members alike often refer to the teacher preparation program as the "fifth year"—the one year that graduates spend in a faculty of education between a degree program and a teaching position. Those in concurrent teacher education programs frequently separate in their minds the pedagogical courses and student teaching experiences from the liberal arts and science components of their programs; they regard the pedagogical courses and student teaching as the *professional* part of their degree program—as their *teacher* preparation proper—and the non-pedagogical components as something of an irrelevant intrusion into their teacher education.

Whether concurrent or consecutive, a teacher education program culminates in the award of a teaching certificate or licence—culminates and, in many minds, terminates. The teaching certificate marks the attainment of the status of a fully qualified teacher and the end of an individual's teacher education.

In our view these positions represent serious distortions of how teacher education should be conceived and of how it must be developed if teachers are to be adequately prepared for the complex challenges facing them, both as individuals and as a profession, in the 1990s and beyond. In this paper we will address selected aspects of this theme. In particular, we will focus attention on:

1. the selection of teacher candidates;
2. the subject-matter preparation of teachers;
3. bridging theory and practice in teacher preparation; and
4. teacher education as a career-long endeavour.

• • •

THE SELECTION OF TEACHER CANDIDATES

We regard teaching as fundamentally an intellectual and moral activity. A free and democratic society depends on its citizens' ability to exercise the right and responsibility of making informed choices. Schools and teachers have a substantial role in enabling children and young people to develop the understanding, the critical thinking skills, and the attitudes and values essential to exercising that responsibility. We regard teacher education as the process of enabling teachers to gain the necessary knowledge, understanding, skills, and inclinations to carry out this intellectually and morally demanding role.

We are conscious that the challenge of teaching effectively is great and we will consider below several aspects of what a teacher must know and be able to do. It would seem self-evident that the teaching profession should be populated by the brightest and the best. We have to ask, then, what could make the selection of teacher candidates an issue. First, it is widely perceived that those who enter teaching are not the brightest and the best, and we will explore that perception. Second, in addition to their manifest educational tasks, schools play a part in social role selection. If recruiting members of certain minority groups can mitigate the systematic de-selection of group members for higher status roles in society, that has implications for practice. Third, it may be desirable to increase diversity among teachers merely to increase the richness of the learning resources represented by teachers collectively.

Meet the average Canadian teacher. In 1979–80, she was thirty-seven years old, a woman, held a bachelor's degree, and had ten years' experience working under the supervision of a male principal in a school with a pupil/teacher ratio of 19:1. In the intervening years, decreased mobility in teaching and fewer openings for new teachers mean that today's average teacher is over forty years old, and still female, in all Canadian provinces. Increased awareness of the folly of overlooking talented women is slowly reducing the percentage of male principals.

And is this "average teacher" perceived by the Canadian public as the brightest and the best? Polls show the public perception of Canadian teachers to be quite positive and markedly more so for respondents with current or recent school contact. Of all public institutions, schools head the list in degree of public confidence followed in order by local government, the church, and the courts.

Teachers are generally seen as performing well in a salient role. Nevertheless, one frequently encounters in the press or among members of the public indications of a belief that those who choose teaching are somehow less able than others. Indeed, Shaw's dictum that, "he who can, does; he who cannot, teaches," is widely quoted, not infrequently with the tag, "and he who cannot teach, teaches teachers."

What causes people simultaneously to hold the views that schools and teachers are doing a good job, that teachers are less intelligent than other university graduates, and that teacher education is less effective than other programs? People rate local schools better than schools in general and rate them even more highly if they have their own children in them. Thus, it appears that many share a vague, general impression that is less positive than local impressions, especially those based on direct experience. But there is more than a grain of truth underlying common views of selection for teacher education.

• • •

SELECTION

When compared with other professions, teaching has traditionally been characterized by a relative lack of selectivity.

A major factor is the sheer size of the teaching profession. The number of teachers in Canada's elementary and secondary schools is well over one-quarter of a million (compared to 6500 doctors and fewer than 50 000 lawyers). At the peak of teacher demand in the mid-1970s, almost fourteen percent of the university undergraduate enrolment in Canada was in education (compared to 2.7 percent in each of medicine and law). Thus, whatever the aspirations of the profession, it would be impossible for faculties of education to insist that all students be drawn from the top fifteen or twenty percent of all university students. Relative size alone, apart from status—and the two are not completely independent—has made it impossible for teacher education programs to be as selective as those in medicine or law. Nevertheless, virtually all teacher education programs have minimum standards for admission and retention well above those in arts or science (including particularly standards for achievement in arts and science courses). In addition, most programs experience demand exceeding capacity and many have several qualified candidates for every opening.

Probably the majority of candidates for teaching in Canadian teacher education programs are A or B students, with quite a number of C+ students in some institutions. Assuming that society also wants bright and committed engineers, lawyers, physicians, and scientists, we might ask what is a reasonable proportion of the most outstanding students that can be attracted into teacher education. Our view is that the demands of teaching, properly understood, are almost overwhelming. The potential for teacher education, properly defined, to challenge students intellectually and to stretch them also in terms of performance skills is enormous. Consequently, there should be room for the most intelligent and no room for the unintelligent.

It may be true that programs attract the students they deserve. If so, as teacher education becomes more rigorous and more effective itself in providing students with the conceptual tools and the skills needed for effective teaching, it will generate greater demand for admission. As it becomes known for practitioners capable of analyzing their experience, of taking a reflective stance, it will prove more attractive to those able and willing to move beyond a superficial, merely technical training. This entails not only intellectual, but above all moral development: the ability to identify with the moral purposes of education and to act autonomously on the basis of considered principles.

Whatever the particular teaching strategy adopted for specific purposes, the effective teacher is fundamentally a communicator, and communication skills are, therefore, an appropriate basis for selection. We propose that, at several points in the formal preparation program, admission or continuation be contingent on achieving a specified level of competence in speech and writing in the language of instruction.

Past behaviour is frequently one indicator of future interest and activity. It is, therefore, sensible to seek in prospective candidates for teaching some evidence of previous interest in teacher-like roles and activities. We, therefore, would ask candidates to provide statements of prior experience and would look for indications that opportunities for relevant experience had been sought out and that some success had been experienced, whether in clubs, youth work, playground supervising, tutoring, or camp leadership.

As we enter the 1990s, competition for places in teacher education programs has increased. Grades on previous courses continue to be used for admissions decisions, but most faculties of education across the country have explored means whereby "biographical data" (such as experience profiles, motivation statements, and letters of reference) can be combined with course grades in selecting applicants for admission. Some faculties have interviewed selected applicants. Even so, most faculties have experienced an increase in the academic average as high as that required for admission to such traditionally selective programs as law, medicine, commerce, and dentistry.

This is an area in which further research is needed. With some faculties reporting as many as ten qualified applicants for every place in their programs, it becomes a matter of urgent institutional policy whether the required academic average should continue to rise into the 80 and 90 percent range as competition dictates, or whether data other than grades can fairly and validly form part of the basis for initial selection.

Perhaps the most important aspect of selection is that it is a continuous or repeated process over an extended period of time. There are many appropriate points for review, selection, testing, and affirmation of achievement. More serious attention to selection is an important element in promoting identification with the profession.

Affirmative Action for First Nations Teachers

Schools function implicitly to sort young people for various roles in life, most often in such a way that their status approximates that of their parents. To recognize this is not to make it a goal of schooling or even to condone it. But deploring this latent function of schools will not change its effects one iota. Any change is likely to require significant social interventions. Such interventions have taken place in the development of teacher education programs with, by, and for First Nations people. The inclusion of First Nations people as home/school co-ordinators and as resource people for First Nations language and culture was an effort to enhance the relevance of the school to First Nations children. Their inclusion represented important steps toward enhancing the participation and success of these children in public schools. Nevertheless, they were typically restricted to marginal and precarious roles. Recruiting and training First Nations teachers would not only reduce the distance between their cultural groups and the schools but would also provide First Nations children and young people with influential role models.

In the past fifteen years many programs have been established to prepare First Nations teachers. The best have entailed co-determination in the selection of students and staff, substantial cultural content, and extensive tutoring and counselling support. First Nations people are well represented on staff and serve as administrators. Perhaps the most important single factor is that, although some affirmative action may be necessary at the time of initial selection and admission, no adjustment of standards or expectations takes place at the time of completion and graduation.

Programs for First Nations teachers have multiplied many times over the representation of First Nations people in the profession. In addition some have moved through teacher education and into other fields, particularly law, and graduate programs are now emerging for administrators and leaders. Young people faced with role models and psychological support are staying in secondary school to graduation.

Diversity in the Teaching Profession

In today's urban schools in Toronto, Montreal, or Vancouver—the major recipients of recent immigrants—the student population is very diverse in cultural and ethnic origin. The students and their families are thus a rich source of multicultural knowledge and experience. The teaching staff, on the other hand, is substantially less diverse. If the school is at once to reinforce the values of unity and diversity in Canada, diversity in the ethno-cultural background of teachers is desirable. Representation of ethnic minorities in the ranks of the teaching progression makes a teaching staff a potentially richer resource and serves to reinforce the identity of students with various ethnic backgrounds. Recruiting a culturally diverse student body in teacher education may be a reasonable end to pursue, quite independent of any need for affirmative action.

. . .

THE SUBJECT-MATTER
PREPARATION OF TEACHERS

Contrary to what is sometimes maintained, we do not accept that studies in the liberal arts and sciences are irrelevant intrusions into a teacher education program. On the contrary, such studies are as essential to the professional preparation of teachers as are studies in the various aspects of pedagogy.

The liberal arts and sciences cover a wide range of human knowledge, and universities generally include in their curricula both courses of a general survey character and courses narrowly focussed on relatively obscure or highly technical areas of the disciplines. Some of these courses may be designed primarily with the interests of prospective researchers in mind and it is understandable that prospective teachers might find them ill-suited to their objectives. Nor are all subjects offered in a large "multi-versity" equally important areas of study from the perspective of prospective teachers. There are, however, certain disciplines, and within these, certain courses and types of courses that are essential components of the preparation of professional teachers.

The Liberally Educated Teacher

We want first to argue for the importance of every teacher achieving a sound liberal education incorporating studies from the major areas of human intellectual and cultural achievement (Phenix, 1964; Hirst, 1974; Bailey, 1984). This is as important for the kindergarten and first grade teacher as for the junior- or senior-secondary teacher. It is equally important for those who will serve as generalist teachers as for those who will specialize in teaching but a single subject.

Education is, fundamentally, an intellectual and moral enterprise (Peters, 1966, 1967). It is concerned at root with introducing people to their intellectual heritage; with helping them learn how to make valid discriminations within different dimensions of their experience of the natural and interpersonal worlds; and with helping them to master the concepts, the procedures, and the sensitivities necessary for creating and refining meaningful and valid expressions of the longings and achievements of the human spirit. Education is concerned with enabling people to understand their world; to accept, respect, and rejoice in their world; and to interact with and control that world both effectively and responsibly.

If teachers are to be equipped to structure and facilitate young people's education, conceived in these broad terms, they must themselves have the breadth of understanding and perspective represented by the liberally educated person. If they are to assist young people in differentiating and enhancing their various abilities and sensitivities, teachers must themselves have sympathies and achievements in these same areas. Teachers must have developed aesthetic sensitivities as well as the ability to make and build upon reliable empirical discriminations; they must have some substantial awareness and respect for alternative ways and styles of life and of living; and they must acknowledge the importance of moral demands in human interactions.

How are these important understandings, sensitivities, appreciations, abilities, and achievements acquired? In one sense these are the achievements of living and maturing as a person. But these specific human achievements are also the focus of systematic and sustained attention in the academic disciplines that constitute the curriculum of the liberal arts and science faculties of a university: such studies as history; the visual, performing, and literary arts; philosophy, ethics, and theology; the physical, life, and social sciences; and language, logic, and mathematics.

The achievement of a liberal or general education incorporating some or all of these studies has frequently been advanced as an important value, but one different from the demands of professional or vocational education. In the case of the preparation of a teacher, we maintain, this distinction between liberal and professional education breaks down. Given the distinctive task of the teacher, liberal education has not only the importance it has generally for all persons; it has in addition a distinctive professional urgency. Given that educating young people is what teaching is about, acquiring the achievement of a liberal education is, for the prospective teacher, a part of professional education.

The general argument in favour of liberal education as essential for the professional preparation of teachers may be particularized differently depending on the level and specialization aspirations of the prospective teacher. The generalist primary teacher will assume responsibility for assisting children to differentiate and develop the full range of human sensitivities, capacities, dispositions, and understandings. In order to discharge this broad responsibility, a teacher must have a broad range of developed achievements. Granted, children's target capacities, sensitivities, and understandings will not be developed to a highly sophisticated level in a kindergarten or first grade setting; it is, however, essential that sound foundations be laid there as a basis for more advanced work at a later stage. If children's scientific understanding, aesthetic appreciation, or moral attitudes are distorted or thwarted in the first grade, later recovery and rebuilding is rendered more complicated and less probable. In order to guide and facilitate this learning, the first grade teacher must have a sound, even if limited, grasp of the structure and procedures of the forms of human inquiry being taught.

Senior secondary teachers typically teach only a single subject or perhaps two related subjects. This notwithstanding, we submit, it is still essential for them to have a comprehensive understanding and appreciation of the different forms of human inquiry and of their potential for enriching human understanding and illuminating the fullness of human experience. With the rapid increase in human knowledge and with the greater complexity of many fields of professional practice, university and other post-secondary programs have become more highly specialized and more narrowly focussed. One result of this has been that the breadth of understanding across the full range of human achievements has become increasingly difficult to embrace as an objective of such programs.

Moreover, as such programs have become more sharply focussed, the admissions requirements have become more narrowly defined. The justification for this streaming is to enable students in such programs to attain a higher level of knowledge and skill in their chosen field by the completion of their post-secondary program. An unfortunate consequence of such streaming, however, is that the number and range of elective courses that can be accommodated within either the post-secondary or the preparatory secondary program is limited. Accordingly, students risk having only narrow bands of their total human capacities developed.

In the extreme, when an individual aspires to a program that requires secondary preparatory studies narrowly and exclusively composed of work in, say, mathematics and the sciences, the development of the student's broader capacities and sensitivities depends crucially on the teacher's sensitivities, sympathies, and accomplishments in the arts, humanities, and other areas. The breadth of such students' liberal education is dependent on the abilities of these teachers to present their subjects within a clear context of the total domain of human inquiry and achievement. Similarly, when a student is for one reason or another restricting formal studies to the humanities or the arts, that student's possibilities for achieving broadly based understanding of the full range of human possibilities depends on teachers of these subjects communicating their subjects within the broader context of forms of human inquiry, including the mathematical and scientific.

Breadth of educational achievements of the sort usually referred to as liberal education must thus be a part of the professional requirements of all teachers.

Subject-Matter Studies

Studies in subject fields in arts or science faculties, as well as certain other areas are also essential to teachers' professional preparation in that it is precisely these studies that provide the substance of what the teacher will teach.

Clearly, not everything that the teacher attempts to teach and that the student is to learn, is knowledge. But much of it typically is and much of the remainder, though not knowledge itself, is knowledge-related—such things as concepts, investigative procedures, the criteria and procedures for assessing factual discoveries and explanatory theories, and such inquiry-related dispositions as inquisitiveness, intellectual honesty, and the propensity to actually test conclusions against the relevant evidential experience or canons of reasoning.

To acquire a base of information and understanding of the content and procedures of the subjects to be taught is one essential objective of including subject-matter studies in the curriculum of prospective elementary and secondary teachers.

It has long been accepted that secondary teachers require substantial studies in the subjects they propose to teach. However, there has not always been full agreement about the proper amount or the ideal nature of such studies. Common consensus frequently favours the equivalent of at least one full year of post-secondary studies per teaching field, spread over several academic years; some maintain that considerably more subject-matter study (i.e. study to the master's level) is essential for those who would teach at the senior-secondary level, particularly for students planning to specialize in that subject later.

The question of the nature and amount of subject-matter study necessary for elementary teachers has not, in our view, been well addressed. This is understandable, for the elementary teacher typically serves as a generalist teacher with responsibility for the full range of subjects in the prescribed curriculum— language, the arts, mathematics, social studies, science, music, physical education, and drama, with subjects like a second language, religion, and/or computer studies added as well. The scope of the elementary teacher's subject-matter responsibility is really quite overwhelming!

Until recently, conventional wisdom tolerated elementary teachers having no post-secondary studies in some or even all of their teaching subjects. Recent research has documented this unfortunate lack of subject-matter preparation in both mathematics (Robitaille, 1981) and science (Orpwood & Alam, 1984; Taylor, 1982). The situation is probably similar in other fields. After all, it was argued, the content of the elementary school curriculum is not all that difficult, and any person with secondary school graduation and some pedagogical training is sufficiently beyond the achievement levels of the children to be able to teach. The challenges of elementary teaching are not content challenges, but pedagogical ones.

Precisely such an argument has had the effect of condoning the teaching of distorted and erroneous subject-matter in elementary schools: bad mathematics, bad science, bad art, bad history, bad physical education, etc. In some subjects such as mathematics or science, bad subject-matter has led to confusion, error, or incoherence; in others such as the arts, bad content has resulted in a hardening of human sensitivities and a withering of the creative imagination; in still others such as physical education, bad and ill-selected activities have proven physically damaging to individual students.

In our view, the subject-matter preparation of elementary teachers is at least as demanding as that of secondary teachers, indeed more so because of the greater number of subjects in which detailed preparation is required. With the mushrooming of knowledge in all fields, it is questionable whether the ideal of the elementary generalist teacher is still defensible (Elliott, 1985).

We must not be misled by the apparent lesser sophistication of the treatment of content in elementary than in secondary classrooms. There is a fundamental continuity of the intellectual content of education at all levels. The primary teacher is as much concerned with teaching, within the level of students' capabilities, fundamental concepts, procedures, and skills of inquiry in science, art, or literature as is the university graduate instructor.

Clearly, the primary teacher does not require the same detailed mastery of the advanced content of subjects that is essential to the professor or even to the secondary teacher. The primary teacher can function effectively with a lesser *quantity* of subject-matter mastery than is needed by teachers of older and more accomplished students. But the *quality* of that understanding is no less important. If the primary teacher is to teach faithfully what differentiates the arts, that teacher must have achieved a sound understanding of the nature of the different approaches to exploring human experience and consciousness; such a teacher must appreciate the scientific, the aesthetic, and the ethical approaches to conceptualizing the relevant dimensions of human experience and to expressing and testing those conceptualizations.

It is trite but true that sound understandings of the content, structures, and procedures of types of inquiry are acquired through the systematic study of these disciplines. Such study must be from both within and without. That is, the subject-matter preparation of teachers must include studies of both these disciplines themselves (science, art, history, etc.) and also systematic accounts of the nature and structure of the disciplines (history and philosophy of science, aesthetic criticism, historiography, etc.).

Admittedly this is a tall order for the adequate preparation of teachers, especially elementary generalists. The foundations of systematic human inquiry are laid in the elementary school, however, and it is important that they be laid well by people who appreciate fully what they are teaching.

Pedagogical Foundations

The systematic study of certain disciplines in the liberal arts and sciences makes a further important contribution to the professional preparation of teachers. It undergirds the study of pedagogical theory and practice.

Teaching, as we have already said, is fundamentally an intellectual and moral enterprise (Gideonse, 1982). It is an enterprise teachers engage in deliberately and in which they make choices both about procedures to bring about specified ends and also about appropriate ends themselves. These choices are not, for the professional teacher, arbitrary choices. They are made on the basis of the results of accumulated professional experience and of systematic pedagogical research.

Pedagogical research is not *sui generis*; it is grounded in certain basic disciplines. Research on the effectiveness of particular instructional strategies generally builds on and applies the investigative procedures and strategies of various of the social sciences: developmental and social psychology, sociology, cultural anthropology, and others. Similarly, debate on fundamental policy questions and on questions of objectives in and for education is grounded in the same sorts of basic disciplines on which systematic discussion on other questions of social policy is grounded: political, social, economic, and ethical concerns, as well as factual material from other pertinent fields.

Accordingly, studies in several disciplines within the liberal arts and sciences, notably, anthropology, economics, philosophy, political science, psychology, and sociology, provide the academic foundation for an understanding of pedagogical research and theory. Such studies are thus, in an important sense, likewise components of the professional preparation of teachers.

Summary

In this section we have not attempted to rank particular studies or to make an "absolute" case for the inclusion of specific studies in preference to others within limited programs of teacher education. We have rather been intent on making the case for a broader conception of professional teacher education than has sometimes prevailed, a conception that incorporates, rather than contrasts with, studies in the liberal arts and sciences.

Nothing that has been said is intended to diminish the importance of pedagogical studies or school experience in the total preparation of elementary or secondary teachers, but to complement those aspects. We now turn to address a major issue about this important dimension of teacher education.

• • •

BRIDGING THE GAP BETWEEN THEORY AND PRACTICE

From the time we are born into a society, we experience the process of socialization. Through interaction with those around us we transact meanings, attitudes, values, and role relationships. We experience sanctions and internalize norms. The entire complex of shared meanings and values constitutes our culture, and socialization is the label we give to the processes by which the social and cultural molding takes place. Much of the curriculum of socialization is hidden, in the sense that it is invisible to the participants. They are not aware that they are making choices or frequently that there are even choices to be made. This is not to suggest that all socialization is unconscious behaviour but that we are frequently unaware and uncritical in taking on the modes of belief common to our culture.

Socialization always involves a particular group of people to whose world view and life ways the individual is adjusting. Professional socialization entails internalizing the shared meanings and values, the common role expectations and patterns of belief and behaviour of teachers, or at least of teachers in those institutions the neophyte has experienced. Without rigorously limiting our definition of teacher socialization, we take it to be the product of the whole complex of interpersonal processes and institutional influences that shape the ideas, attitudes, and behaviour of the teacher. Unconscious modelling and conscious emulation, reinforcement of behaviour elicited by pupil actions, communication of parental expectations, approval and disapproval of supervisors are among the elements that combine to ensure that the shared culture of teachers is reflected in those inducted into the profession.

The formal schooling required of prospective teachers is extensive, but the period of general education is much longer than the period of specialized professional preparation. The period of general education, usually fifteen or sixteen years, is longer than that associated with most occupations. Indeed, it is equivalent to the general education requirements of divinity, law, and medicine. It is unique to teaching, however, that the entire period of general education constitutes a potent element in occupational socialization. In the course of fifteen years the prospective teacher has transacted numerous student-teacher role relationships. Although socialization has been in the student role, transacting role relationships requires development of at least a modicum of empathic understanding of the complementary role (i.e. teacher). Every school day, year in and year out, teachers have played out their roles under very close scrutiny of their students and those students have internalized operational norms and expectations for teacher behaviour, however partial and imperfect. From the time the individual begins to entertain the possibility of entering the teaching profession, all of the outcomes of this prior experience become part of that individual's anticipatory socialization. In its contribution to preparation for the teacher role, this necessarily extensive prior experience can be more of a bane than a blessing.

Our view of teacher education as a process designed to increase the teacher's ability to make rational choices about the ends and means of education requires the teacher educator to ensure that the process of socialization is understood by the prospective teacher. We would go further and say that teacher education should enable candidates to become active agents in their own development rather than passive recipients of the forces and effects of socialization. Central to this requirement are the analytical skills and reflective inclinations essential to achieving understanding of the teaching and learning process as it is experienced, and insight into the potential effect of alternative choices and courses of action.

One factor affecting the completeness of socialization is the sense of "shared ordeal" of candidates who are selected and who complete extensive and rigorous formal preparation. A second is the sense of induction into the otherwise mysterious complexity of skills and knowledge essential to members of the guild. We have noted that the teaching profession is necessarily less selective than law or medicine, for example. That portion of the formal preparation usually labelled professional is shorter and less arduous. The skills and knowledge seem less mysterious by virtue of being exhibited to the constant scrutiny of the society's entire youth population. To all these characteristics is added an exposure to professional skills that fails to reveal the systematic patterns in their complexity. And the knowledge presented is inappropriate or insufficient to promote an understanding of professional practice or insight into the prospective teacher's own interaction with subject matter and pupils.

The power of socio-cultural molding and the stability of established patterns of behavior have led Cogan (1975) to put forward what he terms a heretical proposal. His heresy is to propose that pre-service education include no less than three full years of rigorous professional study, supervised practice, and "closely and systematically supervised internship" (p. 212). His contention is that in teacher education we grossly underestimate both the quantity and the quality of instructional and psychological inputs required.

Joyce (1975) has pointed out that existing teacher education programs have worked to maintain the status quo. Student teaching serves essentially as an apprentice system socializing the neophyte to the norms and practices of the established teacher. Methods courses are designed to deal with current trends in traditional curriculum fields. Separation of methods courses from student teaching minimizes the influence of the methods instructor, particularly if there is a gap between school practice and methods instruction. The foundations courses and subject-matter courses in teaching fields are not even expected to meet the criteria of pragmatism implicit in the methods courses. The very structure of the program and organization of the curriculum, with the apparent separation of theory and practice, encourage the student teacher to dismiss radical ideas as mere theory. Joyce's characterization presents teacher education as ideally structured to allow education professors to present whatever they want to present without any great risk that it will affect practice in any way at all. Many professors who consider themselves agents of change may well be merely agents of the rhetoric of change.

In considering the theory/practice gap we must avoid the trap of seeing professional education as consisting ideally of theories to be learned and applied. Theory and practice are not connected in a one-way relationship with the flow always from concepts to skills. The relationship is much more dynamic than that, and the effective teacher's concepts are fashioned from the stuff of actual classroom practice. The challenge of teacher education is to bring within the student teacher's field of perception the relevant samples of practice from which to form concepts and theories in action. In so doing, we will be helping the teacher acquire the tools for interpreting practice and, in turn, guiding further action.

A core issue in teacher education is the need to ground skill development conceptually and to develop practices for doing so, not merely potentially but effectively. Thus teacher training must be integrated with teacher education. Otherwise the actual practice of teaching will be picked up happenstance without conceptual referents other than the folk wisdom of the teaching craft. Equally pointlessly, educational theories will be picked up without referents and will be no more than excess baggage.

The centrality of a body of theory on which to base practice and the process of developing theory out of practice are among the elements that distinguish a profession from a craft. Members of a profession develop theories in action (Argyris & Schön, 1974; Schön, 1987) that guide professional practice and theories of action that guide professional education. An important criterion of professionalism is the ability to select and use skills on a rational basis to achieve desired ends. This entails both a rich resource of ideas and concepts and an appropriate repertoire of skills. Indeed, if rational decision making is an integral characteristic of the professional teacher, then the use of particular skills to achieve particular ends must be grounded in a set of concepts. In the capacity for reflection lies the potential for a communicative relationship between concepts and skills.

Promising Strategies

Fragmented teacher education programs that rely on lectures, seminars, and student teaching, organized in courses and practice have been unable to guarantee bridge-building between clear concepts and productive skills. Can we, then, identify promising alternative strategies with a greater probability of achieving our goal of the reflective teacher able to marshal appropriate skills in effective strategies to appropriate goals? If so, what are the characteristics of tactics and strategies for effective teacher education? We present several strategies and approaches followed by some general observations about them.

MICROTEACHING

A product of Stanford in the 1960s, microteaching is a strategy designed to focus attention on a limited number of skills at any given time and to provide the opportunity to concentrate on developing them under conditions designed to limit distraction (Alen & Ryan, 1969). With advance agreement on the one skill or cluster of skills to be practiced, a student teacher teaches a mini-lesson to a small group of real pupils in a campus clinic. The lesson is videotaped and subsequently analyzed by student teacher and supervisor together, with particular attention to the agreed-upon skill(s). Goals are then formulated for the next lesson and the cycle is repeated, with the same lesson being taught (sometimes immediately) to a different group of pupils.

Examples of skills emphasized in microteaching are presenting, questioning, and responding to pupils. Microteaching is designed to enhance skill learning by allowing for focussed practice in a non-threatening environment with immediate feedback. Its critics point to weaknesses in the research base establishing links between particular teacher skills and student outcomes. Advocates and critics respectively emphasize the similarity and contrast to the regular classroom when predicting the effectiveness of transfer of training. Microteaching has repeatedly been shown to enhance the initial acquisition of particular technical skills, but evidence of transfer to the classroom in the form of increased use of those skills is less clear.

MINICOURSES

The minicourse approach was developed in California's Far West Laboratory for Educational Research and Development. Microteaching is incorporated into a complete package that includes description and analysis of the skill(s) to be learned and videotapes of actual classrooms with teachers modelling the skills. Although the minicourses are used in pre-service teacher education, their application is not limited to neophytes. Experienced teachers using minicourses use their own pupils and classrooms as the clinical context for skill development. In these applications, unlike most pre-service applications studied, the minicourse has proven effective not only for the initial learning of specific technical skills but also in extending the range of technical skills used in the actual classroom after the program is completed.

The most obvious explanation of the enhanced transfer of training is the similarity of the training context and the transfer setting (the teacher's own classroom in each case). However, considering the classroom as an ecological system suggests a further explanation. The experienced teacher using a minicourse and practicing the skills in the classroom will have induced the pupils to exhibit the expected reciprocal behaviours. As the teacher has practised certain behaviours so have pupils, and these behaviours are mutually reinforcing. In this context the specific skills learned in the minicourse are more likely to persevere.

PROTOCOL MATERIALS

Demonstration and observation have been traditional means of giving student teachers a sense of the reality of teaching and the nature of particular practices, whether classroom management or teaching strategies. The quality of the demonstration and the effectiveness of the observation vary greatly. A very large number of variables interact in a classroom at any given time, and perception is structured by the concepts available to the observer as well as attitudes and expectations. Moreover, the action is ephemeral and, once past, cannot be recaptured. Protocol materials are written records and audio- or videotape recordings of actual classroom episodes illustrative of specific concepts. The advantage of protocol materials over unstructured observation is that they are selected from a larger corpus of recordings, edited, analyzed, and highlighted to focus observation on particular, significant behaviours and interactions. The record can be re-examined as often as the observer wishes. As with microteaching and minicourses, the use of protocol materials has been shown to contribute to skill development, but as yet little evidence has been obtained about the frequency with which teachers use the skills thus developed or the extent to which the skills are maintained over time.

These strategies incorporate some or all of the following. They focus perception on specific teacher behaviours and their effects on student behaviours. In addition to modelling particular skills for student teachers (or experienced teachers), they provide concepts for understanding those skills in action and relating them to one another and to pupil learning. They provide the opportunity to emulate the particular skills and to practice them in an interactive context, to obtain analytical feedback about that practice, skills, and strategies described by clear concepts, detailed planning, guided practice, explicit feedback, and re-teaching are practices that hold promise for bridging theory and practice.

MODELS OF TEACHING

In their book *Models of Teaching*, Joyce and Weil (1972) present sixteen models in four families. A set of concepts is used to analyze and describe each model in terms of its characteristic learning environment. These concepts include the orientation or focus of the model, its syntax or phasing, principles guiding the teacher's reaction to student activity, the social system characteristic of the model, support systems required, the actual classroom implementation (including transcripts or anecdotal descriptions and analysis), and finally the concept of the general applicability of the model.

Including an interaction analysis schema developed for use with the models, this represented a thorough-going attempt by Joyce and his colleagues at Columbia University Teachers College to overcome the kind of fragmentation they had observed to be so characteristic of teacher education. Exploration of a particular model of teaching appeared at first to give student teachers a recipe for action but its effect is to provide a conceptually structured way into discovering layers of meaning in the rich fabric of classroom interaction.

Although it is one of the most ambitious and one of the most coherent, the models of teaching approach is but one of hundreds of alternatives to emerge in the late 1960s and early 1970s. Many new programs developed in response to a continent-wide call for reform in teacher education. Virtually every faculty and college of education in Canada provided prospective teachers with a choice among programs. These programs had several characteristics in common. They were almost always small, and had a distinctive focus reflecting a shared commitment of the staff members working in them. The staff constituted a team and the major teaching assignment of each team member was in the program. In many cases the team included both university faculty and co-operating teachers and not infrequently the program was field-based. Staff and students shared a common location in space dedicated to the program.

In general, it can be said of alternative programs that a distinctive focus contributes to faculty and student identification with the program. This may be enhanced by a shared ideology and shared educational and social commitments, particularly where the students have chosen the program and have the sense of having been selected. A common language of discourse contributes greatly to the level and quality of professional dialogue. When the major teaching commitment of the staff is in the program, their accessibility to students and students' perceptions of their helpfulness are enhanced. The reduced fragmentation in such programs and closer contact make it more difficult for instructors to ignore problems of practice or to avoid responsibility for responding to the student teacher's concerns. Of course, these characteristics in themselves cannot guarantee effective bridging of the theory/practice gap.

STUDENT TEACHING

Most efforts to integrate theory and practice have focussed on student teaching as the means to that end. As Gaskell noted (1984), Dewey addressed the issue directly.

> On the one hand we may carry on the practical work with the objective of giving teachers in training working command of the necessary tools of their profession: control of the technique of class instruction and management, skill and proficiency in the work of teaching. With this aim in view, practice work is, as far as it goes, of the nature of apprenticeship. On the other hand we may propose to use practice work as an instrument in making real and vital theoretical instruction, the knowledge of subject matter and of principles of education. This is the laboratory point of view. (p. 51)

In Dewey's terms, the key lies in transforming practical experience from an apprenticeship into a laboratory for testing hypotheses based on existing theory and generating new knowledge and insight to contribute to the elaboration of theory.

Evidence is overwhelming that the student teaching experience serves primarily as an apprenticeship. A "group management" orientation rather than an "intellectual leadership" orientation appear to be fostered by extensive field experience. In contrast to other professions that are practiced on individual adults, teaching entails working with large groups of children, frequently with different needs, interests, aptitudes, and cultural backgrounds. The sheer press of events works directly against the ideal of responding to children as individuals. Under such circumstances it is not strange that the neophyte's survival need is to develop skill in maintaining order and managing the flow of events. However, essential though management may be, it can only be considered unfortunate when the concern for management supersedes concern for learning.

The laboratory point of view advocated by Dewey would make school experience an opportunity to examine ethical issues, to reflect on the theories implicit in teacher actions observed and experienced, to consider the decisions made or avoided in curriculum development and materials selection, to study how children think and feel. But in the competition with the practical and the technical, intellectual and ethical concerns are almost always relegated to second place. The *immediate* and the *urgent* drive out the *important*, thereby minimizing the potential for developing the concepts and habits of thought essential to the reflective practitioner capable of independent development and renewal throughout a professional career.

It has been suggested that student teaching experience negates the more liberal effects of university teacher education, but closer examination reveals that university and school influences combine in exerting a common pressure on student teachers to conform uncritically to the expectations of the co-operating teacher and the routine of the school.

On the basis of his study of student teachers in a special summer enrichment program, Gaskell (1984) describes several conditions that facilitate the development of an analytic perspective: "responsibility for teaching accompanied by frequent, focussed, visible interaction with co-operating teachers who assumed responsibility for a rational analysis of teaching." These conditions are difficult to achieve in student teaching during the regular school term. He concludes that the quality of supervision is of central importance and that the training of co-operative teachers as clinical supervisors could not only enhance the quality of the student teaching experience but also, in the words of Lortie, encourage "a tilt towards pedagogical inquiry" within a school staff. Time for reflection, opportunities for peer observations, and encouragement of experimentation do not normally characterize the school.

CLINICAL SUPERVISION

Enhancing student learning by improving the teacher's classroom behaviour is the goal of clinical supervision. Continued growth is inherent in the overriding purpose of achieving "the development of a professionally responsible teacher who is analytical of his own performance, open to help from others, and withal self-directing" (Cogan, 1973, p. 12). These goals are to be achieved through first-hand observation of actual teaching events, data analysis in a face-to-face context, consideration of the meaning of the data and of their implications for student learning, and agreement on goals for both long-term development and also further teaching and supervision. Ideally, the teacher is an active agent and the supervisor is a "colleague" providing skilled feedback and psychological support for behavioural change in directions desired by the teacher. Clinical supervision is explicitly formative in its goals and will be of only transitory value unless provision is made for successive cycles of supervised teaching and systematic, preferably non-directive, feedback.

One of the more helpful metaphors to appear in the dialogue about teacher education is the notion of coaching. The performance of complex skills by an athlete of national calibre is not the product of a few lectures and seminars. Nor is it the product of occasional demonstration and observation. It is unlikely that it has developed solely while serving as equipment manager for the team although an "apprenticeship of observation" is not irrelevant either. An outstanding performance normally follows years of focussed observation and endless practice of bits of the complex sequence of skills involved. It follows analysis and feedback, enhanced today by videotape and even computer graphics, tools to stop the action, to extend perception, to heighten awareness. The effective coach becomes virtually an alter ego, challenging and supporting, ultimately enabling the athlete to achieve performance far beyond previous levels. In the process, the athlete has achieved skills and understandings and the ability to relate each to the other in action—a process of empowerment.

• • •

TEACHER EDUCATION AS A CAREER-LONG ENDEAVOUR

One further persistent misconceptualization of teacher education has been the tendency to conceive of it as those studies leading to and *concluding with* the award of a teaching certificate. In our view this is the fallacy of mistaking the part for the whole.

In all professional areas, there is a level of knowledge and skill that is essential before an individual is judged competent to practice that profession independently. But it is a mistake to regard this initial preparation for professional practice as sufficient to inform and sustain a full career in that profession. Initial professional preparation prepares people only to begin practicing the profession; it is important that professionals progress beyond this level of competence and that, throughout their careers, they incorporate into their repertoire of professional knowledge and skill new advances in their field. Initial professional education must be supplemented with continuing professional education.

We will address this issue in two parts: first, the experienced teacher's ongoing needs for continuing professional education and, second, the special needs of new teachers for further professional education during their induction year—that first year of teaching following completion of a program of initial teacher education.

Continuing Teacher Education

The tragedy of continuing teacher education has been its haphazardness. Left at times entirely to the whim of those interested in taking courses, and the happy correspondence of their desires with the offerings of those interested in providing such courses, there has been only fortuitous matching of the work being done with the projected staffing needs of schools.

We must recognize that in our schools our most valuable resource is the competence of experienced teachers and that this resource needs to be managed with foresight and imagination. Management, in this context, involves not only deploying particular personnel where their special strengths can be used most effectively; it involves planning carefully to ensure that all teachers receive periodic enrichment and renewal in both pedagogical and subject-matter areas and also that appropriate persons acquire new or special competence for which a need can be projected. Continuing or in-service teacher education needs to be planned both in relation to the priorities and requirements of the school or school system and also in relation to reasonable career priorities of and for individual teachers.

Teachers, school administrators, and society generally all must recognize that continuing teacher education can not be only an option for the professional teacher. It is not something that some may take and others may leave: it is essential for all. Moreover, this work must be recognized as part of the proper work of teachers, just as is daily lesson preparation and delivery.

Continuing education must not be viewed as something teachers are expected to do in evenings in addition to their daily marking and preparation. Nor must it be done solely by a few dedicated teachers as a sort of seasonal sandwich compressed between two school years and the annual family vacation. Continuing teacher education must be provided for deliberately in our overall educational planning, as a matter of both right and obligation.

An expectation of regular periods of sustained in-service study for all teachers is required. One- or two-day professional development events, evening study groups, and short courses are all important in in-service education. For extensive enrichment or renewal of subject-matter or pedagogical knowledge and skills, especially before major changes of teaching assignments, teachers should expect to be sent for extended periods of personal study, perhaps as long as a year or more depending on the nature of the task. Such study must not be regarded as "time off" from a teacher's regular duties, but as an essential part of those duties. Nor should such study be undertaken solely on the teacher's own time or at the teacher's own expense. It is in society's interest that children be given the best possible education, and society must ensure that teachers are enabled to provide this.

Consistent with points made earlier, a teacher's personal program of continuing professional education must include a judicious balance of pedagogical and subject-matter components. We would not wish to specify in advance what this proper balance should be; clearly it will vary from teacher to teacher and from situation to situation depending on the specific achievements of the individual teacher and on the current strengths and projected needs of the school or school district. We must note, however, that significant increases in the rate of knowledge-production in all disciplines and substantial changes in school curricula to reflect achievements in human inquiry conspire to make a strong *prima facie* case for subject-matter studies figuring more prominently in the continuing education of teachers than has been so in the past (Lynch & Burns, 1984).

Planning for the continuing professional education of teachers must not stop with the design of the content of such work. Thought must also be given to appropriate scheduling, to effective means of program delivery, and to the most suitable "packaging" of the needed studies.

The Induction Year

It is widely recognized that the new teacher's first year in the classroom is crucial in shaping professional style and behaviour patterns and in determining whether the person remains in the profession. A teacher's first year is a "make or break" year. Many teachers retain fond memories of supportive colleagues who helped them through their first year when the sharp shock of classroom reality often seemed more than they could bear. Others, without such collegial support, marvel at how they ever made it. Still others did not make it.

In times of a teacher surplus, the system can perhaps allow some people who complete programs of initial teacher education to drop out of the profession during or after their first year of teaching: "they were not really cut out for teaching," we say to ourselves. Now that a serious teacher shortage once again looms on the horizon, we can ill afford such waste. We must do a better job of inducting teachers into the profession, of supporting them during that crucial first year so that they emerge from it with increased professional competence and commitment.

This problem needs to be addressed on three interrelated fronts. First, and most important, is the matter of human support for the first-year teacher. Teaching is a lonely occupation. For five hours per day the teacher works behind a closed door with little adult contact. Such contact that does occur is too frequently of a non-professional "coffee break" character; it too rarely includes a sufficiently close association that presents the new teacher with either a vivid and forceful role model or a clear message that the work being done is noticed and valued by colleagues who care about the new teacher, the pupils, and their individual and collective accomplishments.

It is ideal when human and professional support systems develop spontaneously. In organizations and institutions they do not, however, always develop by themselves: they need to be managed. Those responsible for managing schools—principals, department heads, and district personnel—must design into schools both personal and professional support for new teachers. The designation of an appropriately experienced and specially prepared teacher to serve as a mentor for each beginning teacher, with sufficient protected time for both mentor and protégé to ensure that the relationship has existence in fact as well as on paper, is one possible structure for facilitating the effective induction of new teachers.

For a mentor-protégé arrangement to be effective, the relationship must be carefully conceived and clearly articulated. Of paramount importance is the recognition that whether or not the two individuals might be personal friends, the relationship of mentor to protégé is a professional one. As such, the responsibilities and duties of both roles should be recognized within the professional assignments of both teachers. This assignment should include provision for assessing the success of both mentor and protégé.

A second and more powerful possibility for the effective induction of new teachers into the profession is through an internship program. We must make clear that, as we understand internship, it is not a component within an initial teacher education program, such as an extended practicum, nor is it an alternative to a carefully designed and delivered program of initial teacher education, such as an apprenticeship. Teacher interns are neither student teachers nor apprentices: they are qualified professional teachers, albeit qualified teachers who are just beginning to practice their profession. As qualified professionals, they have all the rights and responsibilities of other members of the profession: they have teaching credentials, they exercise professional judgment, and they are recompensed on the same basis as others in relation to the magnitude of their assignment.

An internship, as we conceive it, incorporates but is not limited to the features of the mentor-protégé relationship sketched above. In addition, it includes a carefully planned experiential orientation to the full range of activities and services of the school and the community, scheduled opportunities to observe and analyze the work of the teaching mentor and others, and a gradually increasing amount and complexity of instructional responsibilities over the year.

There have in recent years been a number of attempts to develop so-called internship programs. Many of these are, in our view, useful and effective for what they are but misdirected and only partially effective in relation to the conception of internship presented here. Some have been designed fundamentally to solve the social problem of unemployment, not the problem of teacher induction. Some have been designed not to induct qualified teachers into the profession, but to give a greater sense of reality to student teaching programs within initial teacher education. And some have been designed to solve the problem of teacher shortage in certain high-demand secondary subject fields by minimizing or by-passing the period of teacher education prior to the assignment of full classroom responsibility.

Not all of these are totally incompatible with the ideal of internship we have presented. What is crucial is the degree to which in the design of the program the paramount consideration is support for and continuing professional development of a newly qualified teacher. It is encouraging to note that beginning in 1991–92, the B.C. Ministry of Education has made available to school districts a number of matching grants of up to $15 000 to support induction programs for new teachers. Although these small grants do not make possible full internships as we have characterized them, the initiative is a step in the right direction. Also of note is the work of the Learning Consortium involving Michael Fullan and colleagues at the University of Toronto in co-operation with school personnel in the Toronto region. One of the thrusts of this venture has been facilitating the new teacher's transition from pre-service teacher education to the initial teaching appointment (Fullan, Bennett, & Rolheiser-Bennett, 1990).

A third area that deserves special reflection and planning in relation to the induction of new teachers is their continuing professional education. Ideally, an internship program should encompass for all new teachers carefully selected opportunities and requirements for continuing professional education. As for all teachers, this must go beyond the few designated but disconnected days set aside for professional development. And, as for all teachers, continuing education for new teachers must address subject-matter as well as pedagogical concerns. New teachers need to relate their general pedagogical knowledge to their particular instructional situation and they need to attend to gaps in their subject-matter background (Department of Education and Science, 1982).

For new teachers, there is a special concern to be addressed, namely the *establishment* of the basic expectations for a career-long approach to continuing professional education. Appropriate professional attitudes, behaviours, and habits need to be nurtured early in the new teacher's career. Responsibility for inducting a new teacher into the profession includes responsibility for helping that teacher develop appropriate patterns and activities for professional enrichment and renewal.

...

CONCLUSION

In this article we have been concerned with developing a conception of teacher education that transcends some of the traditionally assumed or ascribed limitations.

If, as we maintain, teaching is fundamentally an intellectual and moral enterprise, then an adequate conception of teacher education must transcend narrow behavioural limitations and prepare professionals who are sensitive, compassionate, deliberative, and reflective. If, as we maintain, studies in the liberal and fine arts, in mathematics and the sciences, and in other areas of human inquiry are essential components in the preparation of teachers, then an adequate conception of teacher education must encompass more than what is narrowly pedagogical. If, as we maintain, there are important personal qualities that contribute to teacher effectiveness, then an adequate conception of teacher education must not be indifferent to the means whereby these qualities are developed in prospective teachers. If, as we maintain, teacher education cannot be confined to a single "professional" year, or even to a full undergraduate degree program, but is a career-long endeavour, then an adequate conception of teacher education must encompass programs of both initial and continuing teacher education.

The paramount issue in teacher education is the formulation of a conception of teacher education of sufficient scope to accommodate the full reality of the task. This article has been directed to that objective. In the course of our reflections, we have indicated implications of such an expanded conception for the practice of teacher education. On this, of course, much more needs to be said as the general conception is translated into detailed policies, programs, and syllabi for particular teachers in particular situations.

...

REFERENCES

Allen, D. W., & Ryan, K.A. (1969). *Microteaching*. Reading, MA: Addison-Wesley.

Argyris, C., & Schön, D.A. (1974). *Theory in practice: Increasing professional effectiveness*. San Francisco: Jossey-Bass.

Bailey, C. (1984). *Beyond the present and the particular: A theory of liberal education*. London: Routledge and Kegan Paul.

Cogan, M.L. (1973). *Clinical supervision*. Boston: Houghton Mifflin.

Cogan, M.L. (1975). Current issues in the education of teachers. In K. Ryan (Ed.), *Teacher education, 74th yearbook of the National Society for the Study of Education, Part II*. Chicago: University of Chicago Press.

Department of Education and Science. (1982). *The new teacher in schools: A report by Her*

Majesty's inspectors. HMI Series: Matters for discussion 15. London: Author.

Dewey, J. (1965). The relation of theory to practice in education. In M.L. Borrowman (Ed.), *Teacher education in America: A documentary history*. New York: Teachers' College Press.

Elliott, M. (1985). Can primary teachers still be subject generalists? *Teaching and Teacher Education, 1*.

Fullan, M.G., Bennett, B., & Rolheiser-Bennett, C. (1990). Linking classroom and school improvement. *Educational Leadership, 47*, 8.

Gaskell, J.J. (1984). Developing an analytic perspective during student teaching: A case study. In M. Arlin (Ed.), *Research on teaching and the supervision of teaching: Four Canadian studies*. Vancouver: Centre for Study of Teacher Education.

Gideonse, H.D. (1982). The necessary revolution in teacher education. *Phi Delta Kappan, 64*.

Hirst, P.H. (1974). *Knowledge and curriculum: A collection of philosophical papers*. London: Routledge and Kegan Paul.

Joyce, B. (1975). Conceptions of man and their implications for teacher education. In K. Ryan (Ed.), *Teacher education, 74th yearbook of the National Society for the Study of Education, Part II*. Chicago: University of Chicago Press.

Joyce, B.R., Weil, M., & Wald, R. (1972). *Basic teaching skills*. Chicago: Science Research Associates.

Lynch, J., & Burns, B. (1984). Non-attenders at INSET functions: Some comparisons with attenders. *Journal of Education for Teaching, 10*.

Orpwood, G.W.F., & Alam, I. (1984). Science education in Canadian schools. *Statistical Database for Canadian Science Education, Background Study 52*. Ottawa: Science Council of Canada.

Peters, R.S. (1966). *Ethics and education*. London: Allen and Unwin.

Peters, R.S. (1967). What is an educational process? In R.S. Peters (Ed.), *The concept of education*. London: Routledge and Kegan Paul.

Phenix, P.H. (1964). *Realms of meaning*. New York: McGraw-Hill.

Robitaille, D.F. (1981). *The 1981 B.C. mathematics assessment: General report*. Victoria: Ministry of Education.

Schön, D.A. (1987). *Educating the reflective practitioner: Toward a new design for teaching and learning in the professions*. San Francisco: Jossey-Bass.

Taylor, H. (Ed.). (1982). *British Columbia Science Assessment: Summary Report*. Victoria: Ministry of Education.

EFFICIENCY IN EDUCATION

...

Lawrence M. Bezeau

In times of economic difficulties, politicians look to public services such as health and education for possible budget cuts but are reluctant to accept that lower expenditures may lead to reduced service levels. Public education is especially vulnerable to expectations of even higher service levels at times of financial constraints. Difficult economic times have invariably been accompanied by high unemployment rates for which education is seen as the cure. Politicians, noting that high unemployment among the poorly educated co-exists with productivity-sapping shortages of technically educated labour, urge schools to retain more students in school longer and teach them more while they are there. And all of this is to be done with less money.

Doing more and doing it better with less money means doing it more efficiently. But efficiency in education has always been an elusive goal partly because we are unsure of which way to go to achieve it and, in fact, are not even certain that we would recognize efficiency if we did achieve it. As a corollary to this we can say that we do not know what levels of efficiency characterize education today or what the potential is for improvement. Nevertheless, the popular press and the political milieu abound with talk of solutions including a longer school year, reduced dropout rate, larger schools and school districts, and that perennial favourite, back to the basics.

Professional educators tend to express contempt for these suggestions but, when asked for alternatives, are hard pressed to come up with anything that does not cost more money. More money may not be such a bad idea but it's a zero-sum game out there, at least in the short run. In other words, more money for education means less money for something else. Unlike educators, politicians cannot ignore the other side of the equation, who gets less? Should more resources be channelled to education at the expense of health, social services, the environment, or all of the above? Or should the fiscal system be juggled to reduce expenditures on essentially private goods such as food, clothing, shelter, and personal transportation? Maybe greater efficiency isn't such a bad idea after all.

• • •

EFFICIENCY DEFINED

Efficiency is easy enough to define in the abstract in terms of benefit-cost analysis. An efficient education system produces the maximum possible output at the minimum possible cost. To achieve efficiency, education systems must maximize output per unit of cost. But what is this output that must be maximized? The output of education can be assessed only in terms of the achievement of the objectives that societies have for education. Educational objectives like educational systems are provincial but a rough consensus exists across provinces on broadly defined objectives. British Columbia, for example, in its *Year 2000* initiative, summarizes all objectives in a one sentence mission statement (British Columbia Ministry of Education, n.d.). "The purpose of the British Columbia school system is to enable learners to develop their individual potential and to acquire the knowledge, skills, and attitudes needed to contribute to a healthy society and a prosperous and sustainable economy" (p. 3). Further clarification is provided by a list of the goals of education in three categories: intellectual, human and social, and career. Statements from other provinces differ. Some want to do more than just sustain the economy, but few would consider the British Columbia statement to be unreasonable. Vague as these objectives are, they do provide educators with considerable guidance in determining specific instructional goals and curricular content. They also provide a rough framework for the evaluation of output and the assessment of efficiency.

The rough consensus on broadly defined objectives disappears on closer inspection of either the consensus or the objectives. Alesch and Dougharty (1971a) in studying efficiency in public services at the local level describe the problem.

> While it may be possible to settle somewhat amicably on the chemical and biological standards for our sewage treatment plants, it is more difficult to find agreement on what our children should be like. And even were such agreement reached, it would take a long time before the results come in. If society must wait twenty years before a proper evaluation can be made, the spectre of what could happen in the meantime is so evident as to need no elaboration. (p. 38)

Information on the achievement of the ultimate objectives of education comes in so slowly that educators rely on short-run, day-to-day operating objectives that do not conform closely to long-run objectives and that have an uncertain relationship with them.

Statements of objectives rarely contain any indication of the relative weights to be given to different objectives. In the presence of multiple objectives, weighting is essential to measuring output and to showing school systems what direction to take in maximizing that output. Take AIDS education as a recent well-publicized example. Schools across Canada at all levels have been thrust into the front line of battle against this terrible disease that was unknown to doctors as recently as the 1970s. And why not? AIDS education achieves important public health objectives at a small fraction of the cost of caring for AIDS victims. But AIDS education consumes instructional time that must be taken from other school subjects. How much time should it be given? What other objectives are to be compromised to achieve this important goal? Should more time be spent on health at the expense of mathematics for example? Perhaps another health-related area could absorb the time penalty. Should it be nutrition education? A back-to-the-basics philosophy might dictate the elimination of leisure-related subjects such as art or music in favour of AIDS education and an even stricter interpretation of this philosophy could avoid the problem altogether by rejecting the whole notion of AIDS education.

Educators in school systems operate in terms of costs and short-run objectives. Although conceptual difficulties and measurement problems abound in cost analysis, these problems pale in comparison to those encountered in examining the output of educational institutions. Thus at the school and classroom level, efficiency is dealt with mainly in terms of cost savings, that is, of maintaining the quantity and quality of output while reducing costs.

The costs we are concerned with are primarily differential costs based on alternative uses of resources. Changes in school organization or resource inputs result in costs that are compared with those incurred before or without the changes. In determining costs, any use of resources must be compared with alternative uses. Resources without alternative uses are economically free or costless. The time of elementary school children provides an example of an educational input with no apparent alternative use and therefore no cost. Teacher time is another story; paying for this produces the largest single school board expenditure. Teacher salaries are invariably more than fifty percent of total board expenditure. Thus the efficient use of teacher time makes an important contribution to the overall efficiency of schools.

Time spent by teachers doing things that do not contribute to educational objectives is time used inefficiently. The travelling time of an itinerant teacher does not directly achieve educational objectives; hence, the cost of such a teacher must be justified entirely in terms of instruction actually offered. The travel time of school district central office personnel visiting schools in their districts is dead time.

Time that teachers use that does contribute to educational objectives but at a greater cost than is necessary also contributes to inefficiency. Teachers who spend time balancing attendance registers achieve educational objectives at a much higher cost than those whose boards have arranged to have this done by computers. Some school boards hire paraprofessionals or use volunteers to supervise playgrounds at a lower cost per person-hour than is the case when teachers perform this function. Parent volunteers are sometimes used to release teacher time for the performance of tasks with high educational value added.

It has already been noted that the time of elementary school students is costless. In fact, one of the incidental benefits of schools at lower grade levels is the supervisory or custodial service performed by teachers in caring for children. Without this service, working parents would be forced to spend additional money on day care and non-working parents would have less leisure time. Somewhere beyond the elementary school, students become capable of caring for themselves and become potentially productive in an economic sense. At these higher levels, student time becomes an economic cost of education, but not one borne by actual expenditures. High school students have job opportunities that they must forgo to attend school. The lost income of these students represents lost production opportunities and therefore a real economic cost for society.

At the point that students become potentially productive, their time becomes valuable. Cohn and Geske (1990) estimate that the forgone earnings of students account for twenty-eight percent of the total cost of education at all levels. The percentage is zero at the elementary level, higher at the secondary level, and higher still at the post-secondary level. The clear implication is that to be efficient, schools must use student time efficiently. The emphasis placed on time on task by proponents of the effective schools movement illustrates a recognition of the importance of dedicating high percentages of both student time and teacher time to the achievement of educational objectives.

We can all think of unproductive uses of time in school systems, some avoidable, some not. Students spend educationally unproductive time on buses, some of which is avoidable. Unfortunately, decisions on school size and location are often made without reference to either the direct costs of busing or the cost of student time spent on buses. These decisions then have an important and often negative impact on efficiency over a long period of time.

Assessing the efficiency of time use within schools raises more questions than a quick glance might suggest. Efficiency of time use can be judged only in terms of the contribution of time to the achievement of educational objectives. Not all educational objectives are strictly academic and it therefore follows that non-academic time is not necessarily wasted time. And time used for academic purposes can be misused. But activities do occur in schools that no unbiased observer could ascribe to the achievement of any educational objective. These, of course, should be minimized and it behooves teachers to clearly relate all school activities for which they are responsible to the achievement of educational objectives.

Efficiency as discussed up to this point is often referred to as technical efficiency. It deals with ways of making the best use of the resources of time and materials that we have in our schools. Another type of efficiency, allocative efficiency, deals with the selection of these resources.

• • •

ALLOCATIVE EFFICIENCY

The term allocative efficiency refers to the types and proportions of inputs, called factors of production, used in producing a good such as education. Assessing allocative efficiency involves looking at schools as productive units like factories that take in raw materials and produce output. The raw materials, less-educated pupils, are taken into the school and worked on by the factors of production to produce the output, more-educated pupils. Schools, like factories, must add value to the raw materials in producing output. The value added by schools, which is often substantial, can be crudely estimated by economic benefit studies. Haveman and Wolfe (1984) have reviewed more than one hundred of these. The emphasis here must be on the word "crudely" since educational value added must incorporate all the educational objectives of the school system appropriately weighted, and these studies only measure some rather narrowly defined economic objectives.

Economists often classify the factors of production as capital and labour, but for teachers to make judgments on allocative efficiency in schools a much more detailed classification is required. Certainly there is capital in the form of land, building, furniture, and equipment. There is labour, primarily teachers, but also teacher assistants, attendants, librarians, custodians, bus drivers, secretaries, counsellors, administrators, and a variety of central office staff at the school board level. Other inputs can usefully be considered factors of production including books, pens, pencils, paper, computer programs, gasoline for school buses, and many others, compiling a bewildering array of inputs often called expendable supplies.

In a simple world where all-knowing teachers control education and everything is understood, all the teacher has to do to optimize allocative efficiency is to purchase inputs such that each additional unit of input employed is that input which makes the maximum contribution to the output value-added relative to the cost of the unit of input. This is sometimes referred to as getting the most scholar for the dollar or the greatest bang for the buck. To be technically correct, it should be phrased as the greatest marginal bang for the marginal buck. In theory, the teacher with a dollar to spend on inputs looks at all possible inputs and divides the output value-added for a unit of each input by the cost of that unit and chooses the input with the highest value-added per dollar. Allocation decisions are marginal in that additional input resources are added to existing inputs to produce more or better output. Small decisions are made on the margin of the existing mix of inputs.

An important principle in determining the appropriate balance of inputs is that of the diminishing marginal product of each input. The marginal product of an input is the contribution to the output value-added of one additional unit of that input. The principle of diminishing marginal product dictates that the contribution of one additional unit of any input to the output must decrease as the number of units of that input increases. If this were not so, then we would not use a mixture of inputs to produce goods and services. If we determined, in building an automobile for example, that the highest output value-added per dollar of input was obtained by adding steel and if this ratio did not diminish as we added more and more steel, then the car would end up being made entirely of steel. Both the manufacturer and the consumer who was foolish enough to purchase this automobile would be in for a rough ride. In reality, the more of one input we use, the more optimal it becomes to use other inputs. We would never attempt to educate children in schools without teachers nor would we employ teachers to teach in schools without books. Or at least, if we did, it would not be allocatively efficient.

At a more practical level, we can apply these principles to the decision to be made by a teacher, who has received a grant of money for computer software, to purchase certain programs and not to purchase others. In theory, the teacher needs only two pieces of information about each available program, its price and the amount of educational value it will add to the pupils, that is, its marginal product. After purchasing one copy of the program with the highest value-added per dollar of cost, the additional value-added from a second copy of the same program will be less than it was for the first, according to the principle of diminishing marginal product. The teacher will purchase a second copy only if the marginal-product price ratio for that particular program is still the highest. If the ratio has dropped below that of another program, a copy of that other one will be purchased instead. This process continues until the teacher has exhausted the grant. Although the teacher needs only two pieces of information to make the correct decision, the situation is not as simple as it might appear to be at first glance. Prices are straightforward enough but the additional value-added or marginal product of the new programs will depend, not only on those programs themselves, but also on what programs and other resources the teacher already has. And of course, the marginal products must be derived from the educational objectives of the school and will depend on the characteristics of the pupils, among other things.

The importance of input prices on allocative efficiency has not always been appreciated. As the price of an input goes down, the marginal-product price ratio goes up and it becomes more efficient to employ that resource. Comparing today's elementary schools with those of the 1950s, we note that the number of books per pupil has greatly increased over the past four decades. But a much higher percentage of these books are poorly bound paperbacks that are less expensive relative to other inputs, such as teachers, than the hardcover books available in the 1950s. Books are no more important to education now than they were forty years ago but they are cheaper now relative to other inputs than they used to be so it is optimal to purchase more of them. The increased availability of books in schools is a pure price phenomenon.

The optimal mix of inputs may vary from school to school because of different prices. It is well known that teachers in Canada generally prefer to teach in urban areas than to teach in remote isolated areas. These preferences can be equalized by paying higher salaries in the least preferred areas and, as such, these differing preferences can be interpreted as input price differentials for teachers at given quality levels. This shifts the optimal input mix in remote areas away from teachers toward other inputs. As a consequence those teachers who do teach in remote areas often find that they are well supplied with equipment and expendable materials. They may also find that the school board will supply them with housing. In remote areas it is often relatively inexpensive for the board to construct housing for teachers but very difficult for teachers moving into the community to obtain housing on their own. For some remote boards, constructing housing for teachers improves allocative efficiency whereas the same allocation of resources by an urban school board would be a complete waste of money. Unfortunately, highly centralized education systems tend to overlook these very important differences among boards.

Achieving allocative efficiency clearly requires that those responsible for allocating resources make informed and intelligent choices. Part of the answer lies in ensuring that each decision is made at the level in the organization where the relevant information is most likely to be available. Teachers, for example, are often the only decision makers familiar with individual pupils and are therefore in the best position to make allocation decisions that directly affect the instruction of individuals.

Considerations of efficiency often figure into the assessment of school and school district size. Average school size and average district size have increased enormously since the turn of the century and the trend continues today with some provinces consolidating school districts and schools and others considering it. This leads to a discussion of economies of scale.

• • •

ECONOMIES OF SCALE

The term "economies of scale" refers to the effect of the size of an enterprise on its efficiency. In education, economy of scale studies have concentrated on school size and school district size. These studies attempt to determine whether students can be educated more efficiently in large or small schools or districts. The possible results include economies of scale, diseconomies of scale, and constant returns to scale. A finding of economies of scale suggests that bigger is better, whereas diseconomies of scale implies that small schools and districts can produce the same output at lower cost. In the presence of constant returns to scale, size makes no difference to cost or output.

Although the vocabulary is the same for scale economies at both the school level and district level, results based on studies at one level do not apply to the other level. Alesch and Dougharty in their analyses of economies of scale in public services illustrate this in the education sector (1971a, p. 4).

> It is possible to analyze economies of scale either in terms of individual facilities or in terms of jurisdictions that might have encompassed several facilities. There may be economies of scale for a single facility, but not for a jurisdiction encompassing many such facilities. For example, large schools may be efficient, but not large school districts. On the other hand, large

> school districts may be efficient, but not large schools. It is possible, of course, that there are economies or diseconomies of scale for both large facilities and large jurisdictions.

This distinction disappears with those very small school districts that have only one school.

Since research on scale economies depends on notions of efficiency and relationships between inputs and outputs, none of which are very well defined or understood in education, the results of such studies are often equivocal. Alesch and Dougharty (1971b, p. 14) classify public services into three categories according to whether the assessment of scale economies is "relatively simple," "relatively complex," or "complex and difficult." Needless to say, education has been placed in the complex and difficult category. Economies of scale are easier to assess where input and output are standardized, where adequate measures of output quantity and quality exist, and where the relationships between input and output are well understood. Education satisfies none of these criteria.

These problems are well reflected in the available research. Fox (1981) reviewed the existing studies at both school and district levels. After rejecting a large number of studies because of inappropriate methodology, he was left with thirty-four from which it was impossible to draw any clear conclusions. Many studies found economies of scale, some found none, and a few found diseconomies of scale. Those that found economies of scale generally proposed a U-shaped curve when graphing school or district size measured in numbers of pupils against cost per pupil. The number of pupils at which the bottom of the curve occurs on the cost axis represents the point of minimum cost per pupil. As school or district size increases, per pupil cost declines up to the minimum point and then begins to increase as the enrolment goes up even further. Among the studies that found economies of scale, there was considerable variation in this minimum cost enrolment for which schools and districts should strive to become efficient. Some of the more useful studies used a disaggregated approach and concluded that gymnasiums (King & Wall, 1977) and pupil-teacher ratios (Michelson, 1972) were important factors contributing to economies of scale. Since capital outlays are rarely included in studies of scale economies, findings about physical plant components such as gymnasiums are unusual. The following review of some Canadian studies provides support for the conclusion that pupil-teacher ratios impact importantly on economies of scale.

Examining only studies done in Canada reduces their number to a manageable figure and permits a look at several important elements of these studies. To begin with, we can classify the studies into those that simply look at sources of per-pupil cost variation among schools or districts and those that actually attempt to demonstrate economies of scale. The latter type of study requires some control for the achievement of objectives by the school or district to distinguish between true economies and simple failure to achieve objectives.

Wales (1973) studied variations in per pupil costs in British Columbia using disaggregated costs. He concluded that the major factor in determining cost per pupil was the pupil-teacher ratio, which tended to be lower in smaller boards and schools. At the district level he found small economies of scale in administrative costs up to a board size of about 3000 pupils.

Ratsoy and Bumbarger (1976) in reviewing a number of Alberta studies found that very small schools were more expensive than large ones but also noted that many of the small schools are necessarily small for reasons of low urbanization, or population, density or geographical isolation caused by natural or artificial barriers. Isolation may also occur for linguistic or denominational reasons where separate schools are available for minorities.

Coleman and LaRocque (1984) did a micro-level study of cost variations in British Columbia. They found the major sources of differences in per pupil costs to be teacher salaries and pupil-teacher ratios. Those districts with high per pupil costs had high-cost necessarily small schools. They concluded that school district consolidation would not reduce average per-pupil costs but would conceal high-cost districts by averaging their costs into those of low-cost districts. They noted economies of scale in administration but saw little value in consolidating to reduce such costs.

> Although it is true that unit costs for administration are relatively high in small districts, and that administrative costs are strongly associated with gross operating costs, independently of other variables, they are such a small proportion of the total, even in small districts, that amalgamation to reduce administrative costs seems unjustified. Hence, it is concluded that focussing on small districts, and eliminating them through amalgamation, is not likely to have any useful impact on gross operating costs in the province. (Coleman & LaRoque, 1984, p. 32)

Coleman and LaRocque acknowledged the higher cost of small schools and districts but concluded that the higher per pupil costs that existed were either trivial in magnitude or largely unavoidable.

Dawson and Dancey (1974) completed a true economies of scale study for Ontario using standardized test scores to control for achievement of objectives. They considered district economies separately for the elementary and secondary levels and found no economies of scale at the elementary level and some economies at the secondary level for which the minimum cost point was 4000 pupils. They also found pupil-teacher ratios to be the major determinant of cost variation.

We can conclude that there are not large economies of scale for schools or school districts and that those economies of scale that do exist are exhausted at relatively small school and district sizes. Teacher salaries and pupil-teacher ratios cause most of the variation in per-pupil cost but these are not always easy to control.

Nevertheless, some education sector activities are known to be characterized by major economies of scale because they incorporate large up-front fixed costs. Curriculum development provides an important example. Development costs which are often very high, must be borne before the curriculum is used in the classroom on a large scale. The unit cost or cost per pupil of the curriculum depends heavily on how many pupils use it. As a consequence, many curricular innovations originate in urban school systems, provinces, and states that are able to spread their fixed costs over large numbers of pupils. In contrast, many observers have been disappointed at the lack of curricular innovativeness that characterizes private schools (Bibeau, 1973). But private schools are much too small to capture the economies of scale inherent in most curriculum development work.

Educational technology provides another important example of scale economies in education. This includes film and television instruction and more recently computerized and multi-media instruction.

Public television stations learned long ago that they must co-operate nationally and internationally to provide quality programming. Each station produces very few programs because of the cost but shares programs with many other stations. On the other hand, community television channels, at least in Canada, have been an embarrassing disappointment. In the absence of significant numbers of viewers, they have not generated the revenue necessary to produce quality programming or, in some cases, any programming. On a different scale, an educational children's television series such as *Sesame Street* has very low unit costs, measured as dollars per child-hour of viewing. This is not because *Sesame Street* is cheap, it's not; but because it is viewed by tens of millions of children every day.

Scale economy problems have arisen in computerized and multi-media instruction as well. It has been difficult for developers of educational computer programs or software to invest the large up-front sums of money necessary to develop high-quality instructional software without any assurance that the software will be widely enough adopted to permit a reasonable return on this investment. Consequently, quality has been low; educators have been disappointed in much, if not most, educational software; and computers have not yet made large inroads into instruction in schools.

Contrary to what many would think, the economies of scale in both educational television and computerized instruction are not primarily a function of hardware costs. Computer hardware becomes cheaper by the week but this has not been paralleled by major improvements in instructional programs for computers. In producing quality television programs, the cost of the camera, recording, and broadcasting equipment is small relative to production costs. Scale economies in educational technology are little different than those in curriculum development.

• • •

CONCLUSION

Those readers who have come this far may be disappointed at the absence of any ready formulas for increasing the efficiency of education. Unfortunately, the easy fixes have already been implemented and we are left to struggle with making small changes here and there to gain small improvements. Many of the proposed methods of improving efficiency such as school and district consolidation, if attempted, are unlikely to achieve success. Other attempts to improve efficiency do reduce costs but also compromise the achievement of objectives. The result is a reduction in both the cost and the effectiveness of education without any increase in efficiency. Nevertheless, educators who are diligent may be able to find and exploit novel techniques for increasing efficiency. There is still room for improvement.

• • •

REFERENCES

Alesch, D.J., & Dougharty, L.A. (1971a). *Economies-of-scale analysis in state and local government* (report R-748-CIR). Santa Monica, CA: Rand Corporation.

Alesch, D.J., & Dougharty, L.A. (1971b). *The feasibility of economies-of-scale analysis of public services* (report R-739-CIR). Santa Monica, CA: Rand Corporation.

Bibeau, G. (1973). Causerie. *Biboie.* 2.

British Columbia Ministry of Education. (n.d., circa 1990). *Year 2000: A framework for learning.* Victoria: Province of British Columbia.

Cohn, E., & Geske, T.G. (1990). *Economics of education* (3rd ed.). Toronto: Pergamon Press.

Coleman, P., & LaRocque, L. (1984 Summer). Economies of scale revisited: School district operating costs in British Columbia, 1972–82. *Journal of Education Finance, 10*.

Dawson, D.A., & Dancey, K.J. (1974). Economies of scale in the Ontario public school sectors. *The Alberta Journal of Educational Research, 20*(2), 186–197.

Fox, W.F. (1981 Winter). Reviewing economies of size in education. *Journal of Education Finance, 6*.

Haveman, R.H., & Wolfe, B.L. (1984). Schooling and economic well-being: The role of non-market effects. *The Journal of Human Resources, 19*, 3.

King, R., & Wall, B. (1977). Estimation of cost-quality-quantity relationships. *National Conference on Nonmetropolitan Community Services Research*. Washington, DC: Senate Committee on Agriculture, Nutrition, and Forestry (95th Congress, 1st Session).

Michelson, S. (1972). Equal school resource allocation. *The Journal of Human Resources, 7*.

Ratsoy, E.W., & Bumbarger, C.S. (1976). School size and quality. *The Canadian Administrator, 15*, 5.

Wales, T.J. (1973). The effect of school and district size on education costs in British Columbia. *International Economic Review, 14*, 3.

COUNSELLORS IN A CHANGING SOCIAL-CULTURAL CONTEXT

...

Marvin J. Westwood

INTRODUCTION

oday's Canada faces the challenge of affirming the distinctive heritages and legitimate aspirations of three historically significant groups: Anglo-Canadians, French-Canadians, and Native Canadians. Canada must also conceive ways in which these groups may live harmoniously together and gain fair access to the wealth and privileges of Canadian society. One of the greatest challenges facing Canada will be that posed by a realignment of the relationship between Anglo- and Francophone communities due to a redefined Canadian Constitution along with more definition of our relationships to the First Nations People. At the same time, changes in immigration patterns that are currently occurring will mean that many other culturally distinct groups are being recognized within the Canadian context for the distinctive contribution they can make to Canada's future development.

In addition to these social factors, economic factors will have a strong bearing on Canada's future. Economic growth predicated on protectionism and environmental plunder cannot be sustained, and high unemployment, especially among the young, is threatening to become endemic in Canadian society. The future, once imagined to be a smooth upward path towards greater wealth and happiness, is no longer clear, nor is there consensus on how to construct it. These socio-economic changes and the challenges facing Canada will have definite impacts on the practice of educational counselling and on the training of counsellors for the future (Nevison, 1987).

As well, these socio-political tasks of genuine affirmation of historical realities, sensitive management of tensions between groups, and the productive management of change parallel the challenges faced by counsellors and counsellor-educators as we enter the twenty-first century.

• • •

THE CHANGING FACE OF CANADA

Since World War II, three countries have accounted for the bulk of permanent immigration; Australia, the United States, and Canada; three large, resource rich, and relatively less densely populated countries. These three countries have also shared similar immigration admission policies characterized by early blatant racism in some cases through the 1940s and 1950s, though this appears to have changed in the early 1960s to an emphasis on such factors as education, training, and skills rather than country of origin and race. These changes have led to a rapid expansion in the number of countries providing immigrants and a shift in the focus of which countries are the primary contributors to immigration. These changes are likely to continue. As a result there is an increase in ethnic diversity in each of these countries. It is estimated that Canada will need to admit 250 000 immigrants per year by the year 2000 in order to keep the Canadian population at relatively stable levels. The official policy of Canada is now described as "multiculturalism within a bilingual framework" and this type of government endorsement is one indicator of commitment to changing demographics in the foreseeable future.

The effect of the rapid change in the cultural mix of a population is felt at many levels. Schools are faced with the problems of accommodating students from a range of cultural backgrounds with varying levels of facility in the language of instruction. Teachers, as one of the key contact groups will need to possess intercultural competencies as part of their professional formation in order to maintain their effectiveness. Social welfare agencies are being asked to provide services to a much more multicultural society. Counselling services are challenged to find relevant ways of helping client groups whose experiences and expectations of the helping process may be radically different from the dominant modes in Canadian society.

• • •

COUNSELLING AMID SOCIAL CHANGE

Counselling is a culturally embedded activity and the history of counselling development in English-speaking countries is one of competition for dominance between a few models (Westwood & Ishiyama, 1990). For the most part, theories and therapies that tended to emphasize individualism and hedonism predominated and most either ignored cultural differences or assumed cultural homogeneity (Sue & Sue, 1990). As Canadian society becomes more culturally complex, the practice of counselling will also have to become more complex. Within this practice, a wider range of practices must be valued and an emphasis must be put on continuing change and development, especially in terms of models of intervention that incorporate factors of race and culture (Pedersen, 1990).

A major change in the lives of people occurs when people move to a new country. There is an inevitable sense of loss and cultural disorientation and people may have adjustment difficulties that interfere with normal daily life (Taft, 1977). Ishiyama (1989) refers to the need for validation of the personal and cultural histories of people in transition. He refers to individuals' needs for security, comfort, and support; self-worth and self-acceptance; competence and autonomy; identity and belonging; and love, fulfillment, and meaning in life (see figure 1). Failure to affirm one's cultural identity is a common experience among new immigrants and can lead to feelings of isolation, incompetence, insecurity, meaningless, and loss of self-esteem.

A dramatic description of loss of cultural identity has been given by Natallia Semyenova (1992) in a keynote address to the International Conference on Intercultural Counselling and Therapy at the University of British Columbia, in which she described the current situation in Russia. People in Russia have lived under a totalitarian regime for seventy years, during which time their cultural and spiritual identity was suppressed. At the present time, following the breakdown of Soviet Russia, much of the population is disoriented, confused, and lost as to who they are, principally due to having lost contact with their cultures of origin.

As modern Canada has been established by immigration, one could expect that appreciation for the immigrant experience would form part of the collective Canadian consciousness. Is this so, or have earlier Canadians denied these experiences in the face of the need to survive in a harsh environment? It is notable that the three migrant-receiving countries referred to earlier emphasize individual responsibility for one's life. All have an image of themselves as resourceful and self-reliant, and place emphasis on success in the face of adversity rather than struggle. For immigrants to adjust and flourish in a new country, it is necessary to help them to acknowledge the losses of loved ones, ties to place, and connections to former cultural practices. Too often, help is given only with language training and assistance with finding work. We fail to facilitate clients' achievement of the necessary psychological reorganization required on entering a new culture (Ishiyama & Westwood, 1992).

FIGURE I

Psychological Themes and Components of Self-Validation

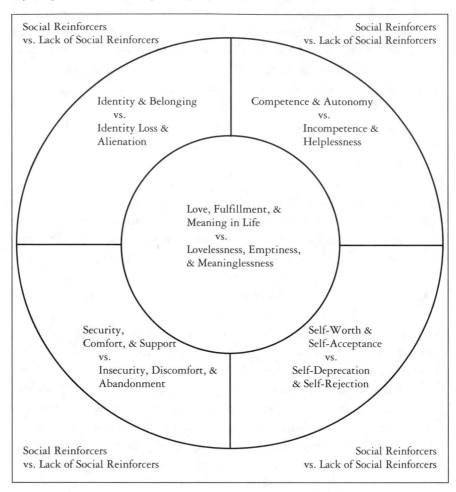

Social Reinforcers
vs. Lack of Social Reinforcers

Social Reinforcers
vs. Lack of Social Reinforcers

Identity & Belonging
vs.
Identity Loss &
Alienation

Competence & Autonomy
vs.
Incompetence &
Helplessness

Love, Fulfillment, &
Meaning in Life
vs.
Lovelessness, Emptiness,
& Meaninglessness

Security,
Comfort, & Support
vs.
Insecurity, Discomfort, &
Abandonment

Self-Worth &
Self-Acceptance
vs.
Self-Deprecation
& Self-Rejection

Social Reinforcers
vs. Lack of Social Reinforcers

Social Reinforcers
vs. Lack of Social Reinforcers

· · ·

THE FUTURE FOR COUNSELLING
AND COUNSELLOR PREPARATION

Human beings are thinking, feeling, acting, meaning-making individuals who, with knowledge of their individual and collective socio-cultural histories, live in an adaptive relationship with their environments.

Theories of human behaviour and of counselling need to reflect this understanding and are evolving to include the concept of multicultural competence (Ponterotto & Casas, 1987). Sue, Arredondo, and McDavis (1992) have called for competence in multicultural counselling to be seen as a crucial element of counsellor competence and they suggest three counsellor characteristics and three dimensions that describe nine counsellor competencies. The three counsellor characteristics are (1) counsellor awareness of their own assumptions, values, and biases, (2) an understanding of the world view of the culturally different client, and (3) the ability to develop appropriate intervention strategies and techniques. The three dimensions that produce the nine competencies matrix are beliefs and attitudes, knowledge, and skills. Wehrly (1991), drawing on work by Carney and Kahn (1984) and Sabnani, Ponterotto, and Borodovsky (1991), outlines a five-stage developmental model for the preparation of multiculturally skilled counsellors. This model aims to move trainees from an ethnocentric perspective in which the approaches and goals of counselling reflect the trainees' own world views rather than the clients' needs and views, through to a position of competence whereby counsellors see themselves as multicultural change agents, continually learning and adapting in a multicultural context.

The practice of counselling will need to continue to develop in imaginative ways to include the following six areas.

1. *A balance between individual counselling interventions and interventions within the systems of families, schools, businesses, and community groups.* Although individual counselling will continue to form an important part of professional activity, the skilled counsellor of the future will need to have acquired the ability to work with groups and in teams, and be ready to move into different modes of assisting others. This is more culturally appropriate, because a group or collective approach to helping is for many cultures a preferred mode to the one-to-one approach. The realities of scarce resources will also require counsellors to question carefully the efficient use of their time. Psychotherapies predicated on long-term interventions will need to be justified and counsellors will need to have an openness to alternative intervention strategies.

2. *A balance between the preventive and therapeutic functions of a counsellor.* This matter has been and will remain one of the essential tensions in the allocation of funds. Administrators of counselling services will be charged with the task of achieving a dynamic balance between programs that seek to intervene in problem situations and programs that are based on an understanding of how people adjust and adapt in new situations.

    Group programs that seek to teach culturally effective strategies and skills are preferred as one way to prepare clients to lead effective lives. If developmental programs of this type are not provided, many clients will have to be seen in crisis or remedial situations—resulting in personal costs to the individual and economic costs to the society.

3. *Career counselling and the immigrant client.* Immigrants have special challenges in finding and keeping a job. The special needs for the immigrant group must be understood by the counsellor if clients are to become productive and satisfied citizens in the new country. Westwood and Ishiyama (1991) describe the common barriers to employment for immigrants and suggest some specific ways that the counsellor can help the immigrant client overcome these barriers.

4. *Greater co-operation between counsellors and other professional workers.* The delivery of counselling services that incorporate a mutual honouring of the contribution of other groups will need to be a prevalent feature in the future. The need for co-operation also becomes salient in the multicultural context as many cultures will have evolved different ways of helping and healing that may not sit easily with current counsellor training programs.

   One example is the need to work co-operatively with teachers of English as a second language as they are often the first to come in contact with newly arriving immigrant students. Another is the need to be in contact with and working directly with key members of the community who are identified by their communities as "leaders," "healers," and "guides." An example of this in the Canadian context, is the need to integrate into our professional work, culturally distinct approaches such as the "sweat lodge" or the "medicine wheel" in meeting the counselling needs of certain First Nation clients.

5. *A continuing critical evaluation of the cultural validity of psychological tests and counselling interventions and a willingness to be professionally adaptive in their application.* Much has been written about the validity of the degree to which psychological tests are culture-bound. The correction of this will finally be the responsibility of researchers (Sue & Sue, 1990). However, counsellors who are working with client groups will need to have considerable sensitivity to the ways tests may produce inaccurate pictures of culturally different clients and to feed these perceptions back to test developers and researchers. This activity assumes that counsellors will have been given basic training in test construction as well as interpretation and have a good

level of cross-cultural sensitivity that will alert them to the inappropriate use of language and concepts.

6. *The preparation of counsellors to be competent in working across cultures.* Given the time constraints for assisting clients, along with the value of providing skills for achievement, it is imperative that counsellors working with culturally diverse clients be both comfortable and confident in cross-cultural settings.

In order to be skilled and effective, counsellors working within a rapidly evolving multicultural society will require:

- a firm core understanding of theory and practice that enables them to be genuinely and appropriately eclectic in their practice and protects them from an uncritical relativism, blown aimlessly about by the winds of change;
- training in generic models of counselling that allow for adaptation and flexibility and which include culturally-specific components and yet retain a primary focus on the universal aspects of all humans;
- the development of links with multicultural workers in the community;
- experience during their training in a wide range of settings with people from varied backgrounds;
- a level of comfort with their own personal and collective histories so that they can work respectfully and sensitively with people from a wide range of cultural backgrounds; and
- a commitment to what Nevinson (1987) has called "a lifelong combination of work and study." She writes that "schools will be judged excellent only if all those leaving them want to continue to learn" (p. 305). Similarly, counsellors also will only be judged to be excellent if they exhibit such a desire.

The profession of counselling itself will also face the need to manage its own internal tensions as the profession begins to reflect the nature of the society in which it is embedded. The arrival of immigrants from a broad range of countries means that counsellors trained in models other than the dominant North American models will seek entrance to the profession. Such contact can only enrich the counselling profession because it will bring with it the inevitable discomfort of having familiar ways of thinking and acting challenged. This will require a maturity of the profession that prepares counsellors to listen attentively to many voices and enter into assertive and respectful dialogue with them.

. . .

CONCLUSION

A number of factors and issues facing counsellors have been examined. Counsellors and the counselling profession are now challenged, just as their clients are. How does one cope with change and meet these challenges successfully? A number of suggestions were considered in order that counsellors and other allied professionals, such as teachers, can begin to meet the changing needs of individuals living in the changing Canadian milieu.

. . .

REFERENCES

Carney, C.G., & Kahn, K.B. (1984). Building competencies for effective cross-cultural counseling: A developmental view. *Counseling Psychologist, 12*(1), 111–119.

Ishiyama, F. I. (1989). Understanding foreign adolescents' difficulties in cross-cultural adjustment: A self-validation model. *Canadian Journal of School Psychology, 5*(1), 41–56.

Ishiyama, I., & Westwood, M.J. (1992). Enhancing client-validating communication: Helping discouraged clients in cross-cultural adjustment. *Journal of Multicultural Counseling and Development, 20,* 50–63.

Nevinson, M. B. (1987). Counselling in a society in transition. In L. Stewin and S. McCann (Eds.), *Contemporary Educational Issues: The Canadian Mosaic.* Toronto: Copp Clark Pitman.

Pedersen, P. (1991). Multiculturalism as a generic approach to counseling. *Journal of Counseling and Development, 70,* 6–12.

Ponterotto, J.G., & Casas, J.M. (1987). In search of multicultural competence within counselor education programs. *Journal of Counseling and Development, 65,* 430–434.

Sabnani, H.B., Ponterotto, J.G., & Borodovsky, J.G. (1991). White racial identity development and cross-cultural counselor training: A stage model. *Counseling Psychologist, 19,* 76–102.

Semyenova, N. (1992). *Psychotherapy under acute social turmoil in Russia.* Address to the International Conference on Intercultural Counselling and Therapy. University of British Columbia, Vancouver. July 1992.

Sue, D.W., Arredondo, P., & McDavis, R.J. (1992). Multicultural counseling competencies and standards: A call to the profession. *Journal of Counseling and Development, 70,* 477–486.

Sue, D., & Sue, D. (1990). *Counselling the culturally different: Theory and practice.* New York: John Wiley and Sons.

Taft, R. (1977). Coping with unfamiliar cultures. In N. Warren (Ed.), *Studies in cross-cultural psychology.* London: Academic Press.

Wehrly, B. (1991). Preparing multicultural counselors. *Counseling and Human Development Monograph, 24*(3), 1–24.

Westwood, M.J., & Ishiyama, I. (1990). *The communication process as a critical intervention for client change in crosscultural counseling, 18,* 163–171.

Westwood, M.J., & Ishiyama, I. (1991). Challenges in counseling immigrant clients: Understanding intercultural barriers to career adjustment. *Journal of Employment Counselling, 28,* 130–143.

THE OWL, THE ROSE, AND THE BIG BANG:

CURRICULUM OPTIONS FOR THE TWENTY-FIRST CENTURY

· · ·

David Pratt

MEANING AND CURRICULUM

There is an Eastern story of a certain Seeker after Truth. As a young man, he abandoned his wealthy family in Baghdad and left the city to wander wild and barren places in search of enlightenment. After some years of travel, he heard of a Holy Man who had helped many pilgrims in their quest. This Holy Man lived deep in the desert of An Nafūd, and could be reached only by the most determined. The Seeker after Truth, after many days of heat and thirst, reached the cave where the Holy Man lived. He poured out the story of his years of poverty and hardship in search of enlightenment. The Holy Man listened patiently and then said, "Walk five days toward the rising sun. You will come to a village. At the crossroads you will find what you are seeking." And the Holy Man retired to his cave. The Seeker after Truth followed the instructions, and coming on the fifth day to a small village at the edge of the desert, he eagerly made his way to the crossroads. But nothing was to be seen there but three small, mean shops. One sold wood of every kind. One sold wire of various strengths and calibre. And the third sold ivory in all shapes and sizes. The Seeker after Truth was overcome with anger and disappointment that he had been sent on this meaningless mission. He left the village and continued his solitary wanderings. It was many years later, when he was an old man, that he was resting one evening at an oasis in the Wadi Araba, when the sound came to him of the most beautiful and enchanting music he had ever heard. As he listened, it seemed that the music reconciled and resolved the meanings he had been seeking, harmonizing them in a way that could not be expressed in words. He rose and moved through the dusk toward the music, and found the musician sitting under a date palm.

And in a moment of immense enlightenment, he saw that he was playing a sitar constructed of wood, and of wires, and of pieces of ivory.

The world of the curriculum planner is a world of meanings. I take it as axiomatic that the primary responsibility of the curriculum worker is to assist teachers and students with the recognition, construction, and integration of different kinds of meaning. In discussing curriculum options for the twenty-first century, I shall organize my remarks about three broad classes of meaning: public meaning, interpersonal meaning, and personal meaning. In the first of these domains, that of public meaning, Canadian schools discharge their responsibilities relatively effectively. Recent breakthroughs in instructional science give us the capability of working even more effectively in this area. That has been the great achievement of educational research in the last two decades. But it has not been matched by advances in the personal and interpersonal domains, which are being largely ignored by educators. I shall argue that this imbalance rests on a deficient concept of what it is to be a human being, and that this deficiency renders our schools increasingly anachronistic as we approach the twenty-first century.

. . .

THE OWL

Public Meaning

It has become a truism that the post-industrial society is an information society, a society in which information, its acquisition and use, are the primary routes to wealth and power. Conversely, those who lack information or the ability to acquire and use it will face in the next century lives of increasing poverty and powerlessness. I would like first to look at the challenges that confront us in this area, the area of knowledge and technical competence, which I refer to as the domain of public meaning. This domain embraces those areas of human experience that can be communicated and understood by people in common ways. "3 + 3 = 6," for example, means much the same to everybody; so does "Paris is the capital of France"; and so do most basic skills, whether of reading or using a computer. It is a characteristic of public meanings that they can be readily expressed in words or numbers. The conventional academic disciplines lie within this area of meaning, and it is the function of the disciplines to express areas of human experience in terms of public meanings. Such knowledge and skills are relatively straightforward to teach, to learn, and to evaluate, and schools traditionally spend most of their time and energy on such learnings.

A Revolution in Instructional Theory

In this area, the domain of basic knowledge and skills, a quantum leap has been made over the past ten or fifteen years. Twenty years ago, the curriculum field, by then about fifty years old, had virtually nothing to say to school practitioners that merited their attention. Faced with their failure to discover manipulable determinants of school achievement, many educational theorists sought comfort in sociological determinism. Aided by simplistic interpretations of such studies as the Coleman Report (1966), and by vaguely articulated notions of class, educators concluded that school achievement was fixed at birth by family background and social-economic status. Like many other myths in education, this one has taken a long time dying. As Enrico Fermi pointed out, the only way you can overcome opposition to a new idea is to wait for the opponents to die out.

The fact is that we are now aware of many variables that are under the control of the school and that can affect school achievement much more decisively than does social class. Indeed, a strong relationship between children's social class and success in school could now be taken as prima facie evidence of a malfunctioning school system.

The first major breakthrough was made with Benjamin Bloom's concept of mastery learning. Bloom (1968) hypothesized that almost all students could master most conventional learning very well if provided with certain conditions. In some ways, this was not a novel perception. Take driving a car—that requires a very high level of skills of observation, reaction, co-ordination, computation, and compensation. Yet almost everyone who attempts to learn to drive succeeds, and succeeds in doing so very well. This makes one suspect that when we say that certain students cannot learn well, we are commenting not on lack of student aptitude but on our own failure to find appropriate strategies of motivation and instruction. The conditions that Bloom identified as necessary for mastery learning included provision of cognitive prerequisites, high but realistic expectations, and rapid correction of error. Bloom's hypotheses were subsequently supported by thousands of experimental studies in almost all disciplines, age groups, and cultures (Kulik, Kulik, & Bangert-Drowns, 1990).

No sooner had Bloom's concept of mastery learning taken hold than a second research theme—school and classroom effectiveness—began to yield results. Statewide testing in the United States made it possible to examine in detail and in naturalistic settings, while controlling for such factors as social class, those schools that were at the high and low extreme in terms of their production of student learning. As a consequence, researchers were able to identify the unique characteristics of effective and ineffective schools and classrooms. The characteristics that were typical of effective instructional settings included such factors as a positive, orderly atmosphere; a clear academic focus; high expectations; collegial planning of curriculum; active student involvement in learning; high student time-on-task; and appropriate difficulty of instruction (Kulik & Kulik, 1989).

And then emerged a third type of research, meta-analysis, which triangulated and complemented the findings of mastery learning and school effectiveness. Meta-analysis is a statistical procedure that allows the integration of findings from many experiments into a single statistic representing the net effect of a particular treatment. In an integrative study using data from over 3000 experiments, Walberg (1984) was able to show that such factors as socio-economic status, peer group influence, tracking, and class size had relatively little effect on achievement. Effects more than twice as great could be achieved by such practices as graded homework, peer tutoring, co-operative learning, and reinforcement. Many of these findings will not surprise practising teachers, but rather will reinforce their intuition. But some findings are more surprising. Research syntheses have shown clearly that acceleration—often frowned on by teachers and administrators—is highly effective in enhancing the achievement of faster learners (Kulik & Kulik, 1984). It has also shown that retention in a grade—a practice that costs Canadian taxpayers several hundred million dollars a year—results in lowering the achievement and attitudes of most retained pupils significantly in the following year and for the rest of their school career (Holmes, 1989).

It is true that these findings have not yet penetrated very far into the schools, and that classroom learning in Canada today closely resembles that of twenty or even fifty years ago. But considerable progress is being made, often spearheaded by teachers' organizations rather than by faculties of education. One can be reasonably optimistic that research in instruction will gradually begin to inform instuctional practice, with a consequent improvement in student learning.

Meaning and Boredom

We are now in the happy position of knowing how to teach amost all students most of the things that teachers and parents have traditionally considered important. Does this mean that the curriculum issues for the next few decades amount to gradual implementation of research in cognitive learning? I think not. In fact, implementing the technology of instruction may actually distract us from the more significant and urgent agenda of curriculum planning. That agenda was proposed in 1860 by Herbert Spencer in his essay "What

Knowledge Is of Most Worth?" For evidence that we have not addressed that question, we need only to look so far as the surveys of Ontario students, conducted by Michael Fullan (1981) that asked students to respond to the statement "Most of my classes are boring." Twenty-nine percent of elementary students and fifty percent of secondary students responded in the affirmative. We are bored by what we find meaningless. And who would not find meaningless some of the knowledge taught in schools—the system of land tenure in New France; the solution of square roots by the formal method; the topography of Peru; the identification of predicate modifiers; the dates of birth and death of the major composers. This is a version of Trivial Pursuit. It is not the way to fill a mind; it is the way to fill a wastepaper basket.

I think we need a more creative approach to student boredom than to blame the victim. We are engaged in a dubious morality if we require students to commit their most precious resource, their time, to activities they find meaningless. In his recent memoir, Irving Layton writes that "people doing things to which they do not bring their whole selves—a job, a marriage, an affair, even a friendship—provides the real meaning of inauthenticity" (1985, p. 256). He is in good company. Pope John Paul II has written: "Nonfulfilment of a self in the performance of an act is a moral evil" (Wojtyler, 1981, p. 34).

The Politics of Curriculum

Teaching and curriculum planning are intrinsically moral activities. One reason why our curriculum is out of step with our needs is that this moral activity has, in this country, become almost entirely a political activity. Not only are we not addressing the question of students' needs for the twenty-first century, we cannot properly address this question, given our present modes of curriculum decision making in this country.

Curriculum change in Canada comes about largely by accretion, and through a process that is primarily political. Unfortunately, political solutions will not always solve non-political problems (the citizens of Indiana learned this quite early when, in 1897, the General Assembly of Indiana passed a bill ruling that the value of pi was four: this ensured that all mathematical and engineering calculations in the state would be wrong), but it is inevitable that, as new areas of intellectual activity develop, they build constituencies that press for their inclusion in the school curriculum. Those constituencies that use the political process most effectively will be most influential in affecting the curriculum. However, all areas currently represented in the school curriculum have constituencies of their own. They have teachers who have invested ego, time, energy, and training. This can be called "career justification bias." And they have graduates whose status or self-concept may rest in part on continuing recognition of the importance of their academic background—"initiation justification bias." Jurisdictions that choose to eliminate existing areas of the curriculum face a kind of wrath well known to newspapers that omit the horoscope or television networks that preempt the daily soap opera. Consequently, new curricula tend to be added, with existing curricula allowed to jostle for the diminishing proportion of student time and public resources. Eventually, established curricula will stage a comeback, as English has done recently in many provinces. One faculty of education in Ontario went even further in 1986, signalling its bold march into the future by reinstating Latin as a teaching option.

That this is a political process operating in a democracy, does not make it a democratic process. Indeed, it can be seen as the reverse. Those who are close to educational decision making in the provinces of Canada know how political, idiosyncratic, and often bizarre are the factors that influence curriculum decisions at the highest levels. But there are alternative models. Sweden and New Zealand have based major curriculum reforms on wide-ranging needs assessments and surveys of public opinion. The committees that draft curriculum documents in Canada are almost entirely composed of professional educators (Pratt, 1989). Some of the committees working on curriculum for native students are an honourable exception to this rule. Usually, the clients of the schools, that is, students, parents, graduates, and taxpayers, are treated as people whose opinions do not matter. Yet Gallup polls in Canada, as in the United States, show that the general public is interested in schools, concerned about the quality of schooling, supportive of educational efforts, and, at least when asked intelligent questions, manifestly sophisticated in its educational thinking.

What Is Significant?

It is not my intention to abuse the Canadian educational system. On the basis of my experience in several English-speaking countries, I am convinced that we have in Canada the best educational system in the English-speaking world. So long as we compare ourselves with Britain and the United States (rather than Japan or the USSR), we can draw considerable comfort from the comparison. My purpose, however, is to talk about curriculum options for the twenty-first century, and, in this regard, I would say that Canadian schools are currently doing a commendable job of preparing their students for life in the 1960s— that is, for a world sufficiently rich and complacent that it can afford significant waste and inefficiency in its schooling. Student boredom is one symptom of this waste, resulting from a failure to determine and teach what is significant. And what is significant at this point in history, if not solving square roots by hand and learning about predicate modifiers?

It is the extinction of one animal species from the world every day that is significant. It's the destruction of eleven million hectares of forest each year. It's the native languages of Canada dying out at the rate of one a year. It's the ten thousand homeless families in Toronto. It's the one thousand girls in this country aged fifteen or younger who will have babies this year. It's the six thousand Canadians who will find existence so miserable or meaningless that they will take their own lives. It's the fact that, in the age of computer data banks, personal privacy has now ceased to exist. It's the fact that organized crime in North America is now virtually beyond control of government. It's the routine use of torture in police stations, prisons, and military barracks in scores of countries around the world. It's the trade union official in El Salvador whose mutilated body is found by the roadside, her dead baby lying beside her with its fingernails torn out. It's the fact that half of the world's scientists are engaged in the development of weapons. It's the two billion dollars the world spends on armaments every day, which makes paupers of half the world and may make corpses of us all.

And then again, it's the vast outpouring of generosity toward the starving people of Ethiopia. It's the heroic work of organizations like OXFAM, Amnesty International, and Médecins Sans Frontières. It's the retired clergyman in Ontario who said recently on his one hundredth birthday, "I feel as though I'd drunk fully from the cup of life, and all the sweetness is in the bottom of the cup." It's the flowering of the arts that we can see in many parts of Canada today. It's the moral stature of individuals like Mother Teresa, Aung San Suu Ryii, Jean Vanier, Martin Luther King, and Terry Fox.

Technical Developments

If we are to develop a curriculum that is viable for students who will live most of their lives in the twenty-first century, then we must turn from tradition as a criterion of significance. Consider this question: What will be the significant events and discoveries of the next forty years? Pessimists tend to respond with such suggestions as world starvation or nuclear war. Optimists say world government or a cure for cancer. One of my more optimistic graduate students suggested that by the year 2000 a woman would be elected pope and that computers would be sold with comprehensible manuals. Some developments that might be anticipated over the next forty years are: controlled nuclear fusion; weather control; a science of parapsychological healing; organ and limb regeneration; successful brain transplants in humans; true artificial intelligence; and control of ageing.

The last of these is the most intriguing. Longevity cannot be much increased by control of disease, because the normal life span of the members of any species is determined genetically. Successive transplants of organs, including the brain, could extend life only in the same fashion as an Ottawa Valley woodsman proudly showing off his axe, who said to an acquaintance of mine, "I've had this axe since 1946; it's had two new heads and three new handles." The most interesting developments lie in the area of genetic engineering and recombinant DNA. Suppose the microbiologists discovered the exact structure of the molecules in the DNA that control ageing. They take this genetic material from a long-lived species such as a redwood fir tree, inject it into the nucleus of a newly fertilized human egg, and transplant the reconstructed egg into a human foster-mother. Nine months later, you are born human in all respects except for your life span, which is 700 years (you might also be very tall). Suppose this kind of development takes place thirty years from now. Scientists and technicians will not be the only people concerned. Legislators, lawyers, judges, editors, and clergy will also be involved. So will academics, for, as is well known, there is no crisis to which academics will not respond with a seminar. Most of these people are presently students in our schools. The understandings they will need are primarily philosophical and moral understandings, and now is the time for them to receive the necessary grounding. Valiant work is being done by values education and moral education specialists, but schools still pay little attention to a deliberate study of ethics, moral decision making, logic, critical thinking, or other branches of philosophy. The consequences of such neglect are already apparent in the moral chaos that surrounds many recent medical advances. It is this chaos that has resulted in many valuable medical developments, such as chemotherapy, the respirator, and the venous drip, today being widely used not to save lives or alleviate suffering, but to artificially prolong the dying process, and hence to add to the sum of pain and suffering in the world.

Significant Learnings

It does not take enormous prescience to suggest some other areas that will become increasingly critical as we approach the year 2000. The major cause of death in Canada prior to the age of forty-five is traffic accidents. More than ninety percent of traffic accidents are caused by human error. Yet, in no

Canadian province is driver education a credit subject in secondary school. A second major cause of death among the young is suicide. You will peruse Canadian curricula in vain for evidence that this tragic fact is taken seriously by educators. The most significant social role that the majority of our current students will play in the next century will be as parents. In the age of the single-parent family, many people are learning that parenting is a skill they will have to perform twice as well. We are a long way from recognizing parenting skills as core curriculum. Finally, take the most central, the most crucial task of the school, now and in the future—teaching people how to learn. Yet we do not even teach our students how to study, let alone how to learn. Some students will pick up such skills from parents or siblings. These students are mostly middle-class, and will be selected for advanced education. Working-class students, less likely to have parents able to provide models or advice on study skills, will tend to be discarded by the school. By deliberately withholding critical skills from their pupils (and ultimately we have to say it is deliberate), schools play into the hands of those Marxists who charge that the mission of the schools is to perpetuate class distinctions and class privileges.

Many teachers will immediately point out that they do indeed touch on some of the topics I have just mentioned. But, if there is one thing I am reasonably sure of after twenty years in the curriculum field, it is that "touching on" a subject is as good as useless. If we want to achieve something in education, we have to target it exactly, plan it systematically, and teach it wholeheartedly.

Cognitive Reductionism

In the area of information and technical competence, the domain of public meaning, we have a long way to go in this country in terms of developing a curriculum that is valuable (not relevant, or useful, but in the widest sense valuable), either in the present or the future. But there is a more basic reservation about a curriculum that concentrates exclusively on public meaning. The owl has for centuries been the symbol of wisdom. Its hunched posture and binocular eyes surrounded by radiating feathers gave it an air of studious and bemused intelligence. But is it owls that we want our schools to produce? Several years ago, the British philosopher Paul Hirst proposed that all areas of human experience were reducible to seven forms of knowledge, each consisting of a class of publicly testable propositions (Hirst, 1974). What was extraordinary was not Hirst's fantasy that an area like music could be reduced to publicly testable propositions, but the large following he achieved among curriculum specialists, particularly in Britain, where his seven forms of knowledge just happened to correspond to the academic organization of the British grammar schools. Hirst's philosophy can now be seen as a relic of logical positivism, purveyed to educators long after it had lost its credibility among most philosophers. I am not sure that this approach will even produce owls, in the sense that the owl is the symbol of wisdom, not merely of accumulated knowledge. There is more to wisdom than knowledge, and there is more to living than wisdom. The sole object of education is all too often construed as the mind—a mind conceptualized as distinct from the hand, the heart, the emotions, the will, the body, and the spirit.

It is some of these other areas of human experience I now want to explore. The domain of public meaning is important, indeed critical, for the future, but it is not sufficient. If people become happy by accumulating knowledge, then happiness could be purchased for the price of an encyclopedia. A central question educators must address is, what makes people happy?

• • •

THE ROSE

Interpersonal Meaning

I suggest a simple answer: people make people happy. For most of us, our relationships with other people are the primary ingredient of our happiness and our unhappiness. "To be human," says Paulo Freire, "is to engage in relationships with others and with the world" (1976, p. 3). At this point, we enter the domain of interpersonal meaning. Unlike public meanings, which are accessible to everyone, interpersonal meanings are shared only among the parties to a relationship. A friendship, a family, a task force, a theatre company, a team, a community, are all replete with meanings that can be fully understood only by the participants.

Isolation

Such meanings cannot be taught like knowledge. But they can be facilitated. Schools can teach certain social skills and provide certain social experiences. Teachers in Canada generally take a commendable interest in the social experiences of their students. But not all children develop the capacity for rewarding human relationships. Some twenty percent remain isolates—these are the children you can spot in the schoolyard at recess who seem to ignore their peers and are ignored by them. Isolation is not a benign condition: it is predictive of probable social and psychological difficulties throughout life. Yet the condition is easily diagnosed, and can be considerably ameliorated by knowledgeable and skillful teachers. Essentially, we are talking about shyness, a condition that probably affects four million Canadians mildly, and four million severely. Philip Zimbardo (1977) describes shyness as the fastest-growing and most crippling social disease in North America. Shy people fear social rejection, believe others are rejecting them, but constantly send out messages to others to keep away. Shy people are often intensely lonely, but they are experts at rationalizing their loneliness, often in terms of "I don't need" kinds of statement. Many intelligent people are shy; the philosopher Immanuel Kant was such a person. It took him a long time before he finally plucked up courage to call on a lady to propose marriage, only to find that she had left the district twenty years before. Shyness is not unknown among teachers. Despite the social nature of teaching, teachers are often lonely people who lack deep relationships with their colleagues. Two questions might be asked of every teacher: whom do you nurture? And, who nurtures you? Many teachers who are themselves very nurturing of their pupils pay insufficient attention to their own needs for nurturance, affiliation, and friendship.

But how true is Francis Bacon's assertion of three hundred years ago:

> It is a meere and miserable Solitude to want true Frends, without which the World is but a wilderness . . . No Receipt openeth the Heart, but a true Frend; To whom you may impart, Griefs, Joyes, Feares, Hopes, Suspicions, Counsels, and whatsoever lieth upon the Heart, to oppresse it. (Bacon, 1985, p. 81)

A contemporary writer, Maurice Friedman (1985), puts it this way:

> Mutual confirmation is essential to becoming a self. . . . We do not exist as self-sufficient monads, . . . we exist as persons who need to be confirmed in our uniqueness by persons essentially other than ourselves. (p. 14)

One recognizes here the influence of Martin Buber: "Spirit is not in the I, but between I and Thou (1970, p. 39)."

Friends are not a luxury, but a necessity for human health. They are particularly necessary in times of stress, and, whatever the future holds, we can be sure it will bring its share of stress. Part of this stress is the burden of choice. There are no longer ready-made roles awaiting the young. Not in employment, and not in lifestyle. The life stages of the 1950s, viewed with the simplification of retrospect, appear to have consisted of two: childhood and marriage, separated by a short period of drive-in movies. People can now choose, with remarkably little social pressure, to live in nuclear or communal families, childbearing or childless marriage, heterosexual or monosexual unions, monogamous or polygamous relationships, and married or single lifestyles. These choices are themselves stressful, but additional stress is placed on relationships by the apparently long-term prospect of dwindling economic resources. As resources decline, competition intensifies; as competition increases, relationships deteriorate. The next century will be a hard time for those who cannot build supportive relationships.

Classroom Structures

We need, therefore, to pay serious attention to the way in which our schools help students to construct interpersonal meanings. As a case study of our current approach to this issue, we might examine the seating pattern that prevails in most classrooms after about Grade 5. Many educators think of classroom layout as a relatively trivial and insignificant subject. I would maintain that it is neither trivial nor insignificant, but is highly revealing of teachers' beliefs about society and the world. In most classrooms you will find rows of desks all facing in the same direction, each isolated as far as possible from its neighbour. In such classrooms, what students learn best is the shape of the back of the head of the student sitting in front. The only legitimate social contact in such classrooms is that of the teacher with individual students, not a relationship of equality but of subordination. This social microcosm is a model of society of authority, fragmentaion, isolation, focus, and task orientation—in a word, a masculine model. It does not reflect qualities of collaboration, diffusion, integration, process-orientation, and caring, which can be viewed as more feminine qualities. One of the obstacles faced by women seeking career advancement in education is that they work in institutions where not only are authority structures masculinized, but masculinization affects the very physical organization of space in the buildings where they work. Is this model, in which people are objects rather than subjects and in which social interaction and co-operation are defined as disciplinary infractions, the model of society that we want to inculcate in the young?

I doubt very much that this mode of spatial organization reflects our own personal experience of learning. If we were to ask a random sample of adults to recall the three most significant learnings in their life, I would predict that the great majority of these learnings would have been acquired in the context of some significant relationship. As it happens, we are now in a much stronger position than a decade ago to draw conclusions about the effects of different kinds of relationships in classrooms. This is largely because of the outstanding work on co-operative learning by such scholars as Robert Slavin at Princeton, and Roger and David Johnson at the University of Minnesota. Their work is as important a breakthrough as mastery learning or meta-analysis. What is shows is that co-operative classroom structures have an enormously beneficial impact on learning. Syntheses of research show that introducing co-operative learning strategies can improve student achievement by twenty to thirty percentile points. This increase in achievement is paralleled by increases in student attitudes towards learning, the teachers, the grading system, and one another. These results hold for all levels, subject areas, and types of learning task. Increases in achievement are supplemented by affective changes. Students who experience co-operative learning like the teachers more; regard the grading system as fairer; trust, communicate with, and share resources more with their peers; develop higher motivation and less fear of failure; become more divergent and risk-taking in their thinking; and are more inclined to believe that they are liked, supported, and accepted by other students (Johnson, 1981). To use only individualistic and competitive structures in the classroom can now be seen not only as socially dysfunctional but also as pedagogically unsound.

Future Needs

In *Megatrends*, John Naisbitt (1984) claimed that "we are shifting from a managerial society to an entrepreneurial society" (p. 165). He points out that, in the United States, most of the new jobs created in the past decade have been in small businesses, the number of which is increasing exponentially. We might conclude from this that education for entrepreneurism should be considered core curriculum. But we do not need to conclude that this means fostering in schools competition and rugged individualism. The key qualities of the entrepreneur, in addition to creativity and drive, may well be the ability to co-operate, to listen, to trust, to delegate, to learn together, and to build small dynamic groups. Even for more conventional employment, social skills are at least as important as technical skills. The major reason for job termination, accounting for sixty-six percent of all firings, is a breakdown in human relations (Frost, 1974). Attitudes and skills of co-operative work are probably the most relevant skills for employment, as for life itself.

We have to recognize that we are living through an age that militates against these principles. In some Western countries, public callousness towards poor people and poor nations has not only become respectable, but an integral part of government policy. My own reading of history is that callousness, whether it appears in the form of conquest, persecution, colonialism, oppression, or patriarchy, rarely goes unpunished in the long run. Even in the short run the costs are high to the uncaring, as to the uncared-for. It is therefore reassuring to see indications of another kind of trend, represented by the publication of such books as Nel Noddings' (1984) *Caring: A Feminine Approach to Ethics and Moral Education* or John Miller's *The Compassionate Teacher*; by the increasing emphasis on personal qualities in the selection of applicants for teacher education (Pratt, 1987); and by the success of such organizations as CUSO, Canadian Crossroads International, and Canada World Youth that provide young Canadians with work experience in developing countries. We have another symbol to place beside the owl, and that is the rose. I have in mind the dictum of Baha'u'llah: "In the garden of your heart, plant but the rose of love."

. . .

THE BIG BANG

Personal Meaning

The third kind of meaning, personal meaning, is the most difficult to describe, because personal meanings can be fully understood only by the individual who experiences them. They are not propositional, but essentially intuitive, what Polanyi (1966) calls "tacit knowing." Our reaction to a work of art is to a great extent personal and incommunicable. As Kenneth Clark puts it, "It is extremely rare for anyone who is capable of the intense and dreamlike joy, which we call aesthetic emotion, to do more than utter cries of satisfaction." Our self-concept, our tastes, our physical being, our gender identity, cannot be fully understood by any other person. Most irreducibly subjective of all areas is the spiritual, the means by which we "transcend the limitations and conflicts of lived experience" (Webster, n.d.). Such areas cannot be fully captured or communicated by words. As the Taoist saying has it, "The Way that can be spoken of is not the eternal Way." Despite this difficulty, some of the personal areas to which future-oriented curriculum planners might pay attention can be mentioned briefly.

Physical Integrity

The coming decades are going to be stressful for most of us. If there is one thing we can be sure people will need, it is good physical health. Schools do not currently appear to be addressing this issue adequately. As long as curriculum thinks of people as disembodied intellects, it cannot do justice to the need for physical integrity. People's health and their sense of physical well-being are of the utmost importance to them. They are particularly important to adolescents, many of whom do not feel good about their physical appearance (King, Robertson, & Warren, 1986). But this is an area of personal meaning and, as such, does not fit readily within the prevailing cognitive model of curriculum. There is no school of curriculum thought that recognizes the legitimacy of somatic objectives— outcomes having to do with the physiological status of students.

What is the consequence of this? From numerous studies we know that Canadian children are at their healthiest and fittest the day before they enter school. They deteriorate on almost every aspect of health and fitness until the day they leave—in their flexibility, body/fat ratio, aerobic fitness, eyesight, hearing, teeth, posture, and nutrition (Bailey, 1973). And how could it be otherwise? Cramped into standard and ill-fitting furniture, our children are surrounded with a hot, dry, ion-depleted, and chemically polluted atmosphere. We provide them with junk food from coin machines and school cafeterias. A national study conducted in 1973 by the Department of Health and Welfare showed that the overwhelming majority of Canadian teenagers are suffering from severe malnutrition (Nutrition Canada, 1973). And we systematically deprive them of exercise and sunshine at an age when the young of every species most require them. Whenever I visit a kindergarten, I almost invariably see a group of children sitting on the floor around a teacher, and the teacher will say something like, "I like the way Jennifer is sitting up so straight and still. Wouldn't it be nice if all the rest of us could sit as straight and still as Jennifer?" Unfortunately, I have doubts as to whether it is appropriate for a five- or six-year-old to be sitting indoors, straight and still, at all.

The Arts

I would like to think that, in the twenty-first century, people will be able to achieve fulfillment more from being and doing than from getting and having. One of the implications of this would be much greater attention to the arts. At present, across North America, music and the visual arts receive less than five percent of curriculum time in schools. Surveys show that most parents and teachers consider this about right. The arts simply do not seem to fit the prevailing norms of public meaning. In some ways the situation is better in elementary than in secondary schools, because many elementary school teachers, despite considerable difficulty, attempt to integrate the arts into their daily work. I was recently in a school where the popular principal was about to leave, and, in one of the Grade 4 classes I visited, each student had produced some work of art to give him. One child had written this poem: "Roses are red/Violets are blue/You're the best principal/We ever had." Another painted a picture of a man standing in a field. The caption said, "This is a picture of Mr. Pritchard milking his cows. The cows have all gone to the barn. I can't draw cows."

In secondary schools, even mainstream arts like literature appear to be experiencing heavy doses of instrumentalism. In many secondary curricula, literature has been downgraded to nothing more than a mode of communication, to be analysed, understood, and emulated in students' own writing. This seems to me almost entirely to miss the point. People do not read novels or see plays or watch movies or go to poetry readings in order to study or perfect their communication skills. They engage in these activities as ends, not as means, because these are aesthetic and vicarious experiences. Two or more people who have read the same novel share not so much a body of knowledge as a body of vicarious experiences. Here is a passage from Gabriel García Márquez's remarkable novel *One Hundred Years of Solitude:*

> When it was opened by the giant, the chest gave off a glacial exhalation. Inside there was only an enormous, transparent block with infinite internal needles in which the light of the sunset was broken up into colored stars. Disconcerted, knowing that the children were waiting for an immediate explanation, José Arcadio Buendia ventured a murmur:
> "It's the largest diamond in the world."
> "No," the gypsy countered. "It's ice."
> José Arcadio Buendia . . . put his hand on the ice and held it there for several minutes as his heart filled with fear and jubilation at the contact with mystery. . . . With his hand on the cake, as if giving testimony on the holy scriptures, he exclaimed:
> "This is the great invention of our time." (Márquez, 1970, pp. 25–26)

What results from contact with works such as this is not factual information but vicarious experiences realized by an access of imagination. And this is a crucial difference between private and public meaning. Public meaning is essentially cognitive; personal meaning is essentially experiential.

Experiences

Several years ago, Benjamin Bloom conducted a study of one hundred college students. The question he asked them was to recall a "peak learning experience" that took place during their formal education: any classroom experience that was totally absorbing, interesting, stimulating, memorable. From the one million hours of schooling undergone by his sample of students, he obtained reports of a total of only sixty such experiences (Bloom, 1981).

Here I think is an illustration of the extent to which schooling has become instrumental. Curriculum, it is assumed, must be a means to an end, and cannot be an end in itself. We cannot take a class to see a live Shakespeare production as an aesthetic experience, unless on their return they write an essay or a test to prove some accretion of knowledge. It has come to the point illustrated in a *New Yorker* cartoon. Two kindergarten children are looking at a rabbit on the teacher's desk, and one says to the other, "Don't touch the rabbit, or Teacher will make you write a report on it." In other words, nothing in schools is to be done for fun. People must not do things for fun. There is no reference to fun in any of the provincial curriculum guidelines.

But this is a perverted philosophy. All philosophies of life ultimately come down to personal fulfillment, for oneself or for others, in this life or in some other existence. An instrumental education is at variance with every philosophy. It makes everything an instrument, including people. A cognitively oriented curriculum makes people objects; experience-oriented education makes people subjects. When we look back on our lives, what we see is not increments of knowledge, but key experiences like milestones along our path. Our personal identity is not cognitive, but experiential and historical.

The Big Bang

We are the products of experiences going back to our birth. But, for the historically enlightened, events before our birth are also part of our consciousness, determining the conditions within which we live and act. The study of history will take us back a few centuries, a few millenia at most, a tiny slice of the human experience on earth. To go back before the invention of writing we must turn to the work that anthropologists have done in cultures resembling those in which our forebears lived for hundreds of thousands of years. The work of anthropologists helps us to understand our roots back for two million years, and then we must rely on the ethologists, whose studies of animal behaviour provide the closest clues to the lives of our ancestors in the pre-human era. This takes us back some twenty million years, at which point we have to turn to the palaeontologists, and then to the geologists. The geologists' writ runs back to the formation of the earth. Beyond that, we are in the realm of cosmology and physics.

It is at this point that I part company with those who claim that modern science has deprived people of the sense of wonder, because the more I learn of the origin of the universe, the more my sense of wonder increases. It is astonishing to consider that our sun is one of more than one hundred billion such stars in the Milky Way galaxy, which is one of tens of billions of similar galaxies in the universe. These galaxies are speeding outwards through space at an enormous speed: in the case of our solar system, at thirty kilometres per second. Run the film backwards in time, and the galaxies recede toward a central point. All the matter we can perceive in the universe and in our world was present at that point in a different form. Every human cell comes from that original source: every atom in our bodies was once part of a star. We are, literally, star children. As we go back further in time, temperature increases, matter has not yet condensed into galaxies. Further back, and it is too hot for the existence of the heavy elements; only the lighter gases can exist. Further back, and it is too hot for the existence of atoms; the density of the universe is enormous. And further back, back to the first billionth of a second after the Big Bang, and the universe had infinite density: the entire observable universe "was compressed within a sphere of radius equal to one thousandth of a centimetre, the size of the point of a needle" (Silk, 1980, p. 104). And before that, there was no matter at all, nor was there space or time, there was only energy. We are all products of that primal energy. I do not claim to understand this. I do not know whether it is, in any ordinary sense, understandable. If we wish to stay in school curriculum with what is readily understandable, we will avoid this area. One can only echo Einstein: "The most beautiful thing we can experience is the mysterious. It is the source of all art and science" (Einstein, 1934). School curricula have profited from the doctrine of learning for mastery. I would like to see educators begin to pay attention to learning for mystery.

Choices

If curricula in the Western world have a common characteristic, it is their restricted character. Narrow perceptions of mind and of human existence have led to narrow prescriptions for education. These prescriptions in turn limit the choices of the next generation. Those graduates of our schools whose social and personal capacities are underdeveloped are deprived of choices in significant areas. As we approach the twenty-first century, such deprivation becomes more damaging, more impoverishing, and more dangerous. And what is education if not the process of widening people's freedom of choice in all areas of their lives? I once asked Marilyn Ferguson, author of *The Aquarian Conspiracy* (1980) what the major thing was that adults could do for the young. She replied, to set the example of living a happy and joyful life. The agenda that the future sets for present-day curriculum planners is to find the means to develop in learners the public, personal, and interpersonal capacities that will enable them freely to choose lives that are happy and joyful.

• • •

REFERENCES

Bacon, F. (1985). *The essayes or counsels, civill and morall*. Cambridge, MA: Harvard University Press.

Bailey, D.A. (1973, Sept./Oct.). Exercise, fitness and physical education for the growing child. *Canadian Journal of Public Health, 64*, 421–30.

Bloom, B.S. (1968). *Learning for mastery*. UCLA Evaluation Comment, *1*(3), 1–12.

Bloom, B.S. (1981). *All our children learning*. New York: Harper and Row.

Buber, M. (1970). *I and thou* (2nd ed.). New York: Scribner.

Coleman, J.S. (1966). *Equality of educational opportunity*. Washington: U.S. Office of Education.

Einstein, A. (1934). *Essays in science*. New York: Philosophical Library.

Eisner, E.W. (1984). *The art of educational evaluation: A personal view*. London: The Palmer Press.

Feng, G., & English, J. (1972). *Tao Te Ching*. New York: Knopf.

Ferguson, M. (1980). *The aquarian conspiracy: Personal and social transformation in the 1980s*. Los Angeles: Tarcher.

Freire, P. (1976). *The practice of freedom*. London: Writers and Readers Publishing Cooperative.

Friedman, M. (1985). *The healing dialogue in psychotherapy*. New York: Jason Aronson.

Frost, K. (1974). Why 4000 people were fired. *Administrative Management, 35*(2), 54–55.

Fullan, M.G. (1991). *The new meaning of educational change*. New York: Teachers College Press.

Hirst, P. (1974). *Knowledge and the curriculum*. London: Routledge and Kegan Paul.

Holmes, C.T. (1989). Grade-level retention effects: A meta-analysis of research studies.

In L.A. Shepard & M.L. Smith (Eds.), *Flunking grades: Research and policies on retention*. London: Falmer Press.

Johnson, D.W., & Johnson, R.T. (1990). Cooperative learning and achievement. In S. Sharan (Ed.), *Cooperative learning: Theory and research* (pp. 23–37). New York: Praeger.

King, A.J.C., Robertson, A., & Warren, W.K. (1986). *Canada health attitudes and behaviours survey: 9, 12 and 15 year olds, 1984–1985, Summary Report by Queen's University Social Program Evaluation Group*. Ottawa: National Health and Welfare.

Kulik, C.C., Kulik, J.A., & Bangert-Drowns, R.L. (1990). Effectiveness of mastery learning programs: A meta-analysis. *Review of Educational Research, 60*(2), 265–299.

Kulik, J.A., & Kulik, C-L.D. (1984). Effects of accelerated instruction on students. *Review of Educational Research, 54*, 225–236.

Kulik, J.A., & Kulik, C-L.C. (1989). Meta-analysis in education. *International Journal of Educational Research, 13*, 221–340.

Layton, I. (1985). *Waiting for the Messiah: A memoir*. Toronto: McClelland and Stewart.

Márquez, G.G. (1970). *One hundred years of solitude* (G. Rabassa, Trans.). New York: Harper and Row.

Miller, J. (1981). *The compassionate teacher: How to learn and teach with your whole self*. Engelwood Cliffs, NJ: Prentice-Hall.

Naisbitt, J. (1984). *Megatrends: Ten new directions transforming our lives*. New York: Warner Books.

Noddings, N. (1984). *Caring: A feminine approach to ethics and moral education*. Berkeley, CA: University of California Press.

Nutrition Canada. (1973). *Nutrition: A national priority*. Ottawa: Information Canada.

Polyani, M. (1966). *The tacit dimension*. New York: Doubleday.

Pratt, D. (1987). Predicting career success in teaching. *Action in Teacher Education, 8*(4), 25–34.

Pratt, D. (1989). Characteristics of Canadian curricula. *Canadian Journal of Education, 14*, 295–310.

Silk, J. (1980). *The Big Bang: The creation and evolution of the universe.* New York: Freeman.

Spencer, H. (1911). *Essays on education.* London: Dent.

Walberg, H.J. (1984, May). Improving the productivity of America's schools. *Educational Leadership, 42*, 19–30.

Webster, A. (n.d.). *The educative process.* Unpublished manuscript, Massey University, Palmerston North, New Zealand.

Wojtyler, K. (1981). *Toward a philosophy of praxis.* New York: Crossroad.

Zimbardo, P. (1977). *Shyness.* New York: Harcourt Brace Jovanovich.

Section Seven

TRENDS AND CONTROVERSIES, TODAY AND TOMORROW

...

Canadian education at all levels is undergoing change. The process of evaluation and redirection appears to be fostered by many factors including governmental priorities and conflicts, financial restraint, the development of alternative educational settings and delivery systems, technological changes, unemployment and under-employment, the challenge of the global market, and pressing demands for new curricular approaches to prepare citizens more readily for a society in flux. The authors in this section examine current developments that have impact for the future of education in Canada and also speculate on possible scenarios so that we may be somewhat more able to better direct our educational endeavours in the next century.

Computer technology has the demonstrated capacity to revolutionize most aspects of our society, including education. Compared to the impact of computers on other areas such as communication, transportation, manufacturing, and business, however, the widespread impact on education perhaps still remains more of a potential than a realization. Olson and Sullivan present a guarded and pessimistic view of the future of computers in Canadian education. Will the computer simplify and accentuate power inequalities within our society? Will the computer separate students according to class structure? Will the computer create a new division between those who are "skilled" and those who are "deskilled"? Will the computer serve to centralize or decentralize education? According to Olson and Sullivan, these and other related questions have not met with close enough scrutiny. Given the promotional campaigns of computer companies, the proper perspective for guiding educational computer use may be missed. Olson and Sullivan stress the need for a critical evaluation of our educational needs and how the computer may be of service in meeting these needs. Howard and Kysela review the computer evolution, explore its influence on educational practice and research, identify new developments and emerging fields of inquiry in education linked to computer advancements, and discuss important implications for educators stemming from these influences and developments.

Focussing on the critical questions that surround research on education via a second language and Canadian French immersion programs, Carey provides a critical appraisal of the political and societal prejudices underlying the assumptions of research on bilingualism, as well as the willingness of developing countries to base their language poicy for schooling on the results obtained by North American researchers in the area of bilingualism.

One of the major findings involved, and on which much policy turns, is that "attitudes within the family, school and society may be very powerful predictors of the students attainment of proficiency in that language." This result has, through political and societal pressure in the guise of the inherent value of bilingualism, been used to further implement and entrench French immersion programs in Canada. These findings, however, are to some extent unique to Canada and generalization from one country to another must proceed cautiously, because of the differing political and societal pressures involved. The implications and differences between the findings of (ESL) programs and immersion programs in the North American context are examined, which leads Carey to give a brief analysis of the possible unifying aspect of language within a society. Carey goes on to conclude that in the future our teachers will need to be educated in teaching a second language so as to keep up with the reality of a multilingual society.

Standards and standardized testing continue to spark hot and contentious debate. As educators, we are constantly under attack from some quarters for perceived declines in academic standards and for our use of what are seen as unrealistic or inappropriate methods of assessment. Within academic circles, too, there is considerable disagreement about the longitudinal stability of standards and the merits of standardized testing. There are those who would move to abolish all forms of standardized assessment in the school setting because they are viewed as perpetuating discrimination and inequality of opportunity. On the other hand, there are those who would argue that promising advancements in test construction and administration techniques may overcome several of the previously perceived inadequacies and shortcomings. Palmer and Brackenbury outline the rationale for measures of the performance of our educational system and describe the Canadian approach to developing an innovative and educationally valid system of indicators. The focus in this chapter is on national achievement tests of reading, writing, and mathematical content and problem solving.

Canada is recognized as being a leader in the implementation of whole language principles at both the classroom and the governmental policy level. McKay deals with the hotly debated but often little understood controversy surrounding the "whole language" teaching approach. To McKay, "it is critical to see that the beliefs underlying whole language are part of a large and interconnected body of thought on how the world works, on how we think about the world in general, and how we think about education. While people may choose to take opposing views to those underlying this view, or paradigm, it is important to understand that whole language is not an isolated phenomenon nor a peculiar educational bandwagon, but is part of a powerful paradigm or view that is influencing the sciences and the humanities and places emphasis on understanding our world from an organic and process oriented position. When seen as part of a powerful philosophy and system of beliefs, whole language cannot be as easily dismissed as when it is seen at the level of just another fad or method to teach reading and writing."

BEYOND THE MANIA:
CRITICAL APPROACHES TO COMPUTERS IN EDUCATION

...

C . Paul Olson

E . V . Sullivan

he past few years in education have witnessed a mania sparked by computers. The flurry of activity and speculation is everywhere. The January 1983 cover of *Time* magazine gives a glimpse of the cultural ebullience of the topic. The issue is normally devoted to the "man of the year" and features a person on the cover but, in this issue, there is no man on the cover; in his place, there is a plaster model sitting on a chair, looking at a computer. Instead of the 1983 award going to the "man of the year," it is presented to the computer. The title of the cover story is "The Machine of the Year: The Computer Moves In." The view that the computer is the wave of the future remains today and is widely shared in the popular culture.

In Canada there were also great expectations for the computer. Much of the emphasis lay in a belief of the innate capacity of the machine itself. In September, 1984, there were approximately 27 000 computers in Canadian schools or a student pupil ratio of about 1 to 200 students. These numbers themselves created a "politics of scarcity" around computers that itself limited what could be done with computers based upon logistics alone. In classroom practice, it also meant, of virtual necessity, that the majority of teachers were left out of functional classroom computing. As our own studies of Ontario schools showed (Sullivan, Logan, & Olson, 1986) in school settings, computing was handled primarily by a select set of teachers with special interests or mandates to implement computing. The overwhelming empirical data was that for all the rhetoric, computers were not used by the majority of the teachers in most curricular settings but that important localized use of computers was found.

The belief in computers as a panacea remained strong, and much of the strategies of educational ministries across Canada focussed on the issues of hardware and software acquisition themselves. Most ministries developed strategies in the mid-1980s to dramatically increase the number of computers in classrooms. These were often augmented by schemes that placed the issues of software and hardware configurations squarely at the centre of policy strategy. Perhaps the most notorious (or noble—depending on one's perspective) of these attempts was carried out by the Ontario Ministry of Education that as a policy offered boards to subsidize seventy-five percent of the cost of the Ontario-based ICON system. The Ministry also backed this strategy by undertaking software development and support. This focus on hardware, as we shall argue later, led to a variety of problems. Nonetheless, it is true that the number of computers increased in classrooms during the 1980s but not as much as one might believe from the rhetoric. There remains in most Canadian schools little more than one to two computers per classroom on average and there usage remains spotted.

The general interest in educational computing mirrors a wider transformation within society itself. Canadians seem to share an enthusiasm for computers in many areas of life. In a report by the Canadian Department of Labour (1982), the computer is pictured as a "triggering technology." A "triggering technology," according to the report, is an industry that will improve economic growth by utilizing or developing computers and "high" technology. The report advocates supporting further development of micro-electronics because of the supposed benefits of technological innovation. Questions about computer deployment are proposed in this light as essentially technical ones; that is, as a matter of developing adequate hardware and software to get on with the job of delivering the new order. Questions of implementation, the delivery of the fullest social benefit, and the impact of the new millenium are seen as primarily technical, even if pressing, issues.

There is an underside, or alternative view, of educational computing that relates to a blindness within educational theorizing; this is the tendency to underplay or to ignore the fundamental issue of power distribution. There is every indication in the history of technological innovation in the twentieth century, that innovations become a means of control and have differential results for different classes, racial groups, gender divisions, and so on. There is also sound historical evidence that schooling serves the needs of dominant groups within the work world. Thus, the computer, as well as other information technologies, may possibly accentuate and amplify power inequalities within our society. The whole issue of how "computer literacy" will affect job and status opportunities is an open one at this point, but there is every reason to believe that new status divisions in the labour force, created by changes in production facilitated by computers, will create power differentials in society itself, acting to "skill" some workers (thereby giving them more power) while "deskilling" others (thereby lessening their power).

Michael Apple's work on the effects of computer-assisted instruction in the United States shows that standardized computer-based programs often act to deskill teachers by "modularizing" the curriculum and thereby effectively limiting what an individual teacher may undertake (Apple, 1979; 1984). Even more powerful is the potential impact of such standardized curricula on the presentation of particular points of view. In the Canadian textbook industry, for instance, the selection of texts can be influenced by decisions made in a few U.S. states, particularly California and Texas. The decision to follow the standards set by these states is not a pedagogical or educational one but, instead, an economic one. If a text is approved in Texas or California or, better, in both (together they have a population greater than all of Canada), then it is virtually assured success. If a text fails to make the approval lists in Texas and/or California, it is open to question how successful it will be. This essentially means that a full range of views, including views held by many Canadians, is not presented. The reason is that such views may prove offensive to particular constituencies of Americans. The most notorious example of this kind of information control occurred at Ginn Publishing when that U.S. company summarily fired its entire textbook staff for failing to get Ginn textbooks approved on the Texas state curriculum (Apple, 1984). This incident may seem irrelevant to our concerns about educational computing in Canada, but we would like to suggest that it provides a lesson.

While computing may seem to be a general, technical skill, the content of computer programs is highly susceptible, in much the same way as textbooks, to social pressures that determine and stratify the educational curriculum. Such seemingly remote social processes have effects ranging from the banal to the profound. Thomas Malone's review of children's preferences and motivations in the use of computer games, for instance, shows that sensationalism and sensory stimulation were chief components in determining children's interest levels (Malone, 1981). From a content level, the most popular games featured hangings and explosion—games that presented the joys of domination. Listed at the bottom of the preference list were programs that aimed to be educational. The microchips for many of the "invader" games, which were very popular with school-aged, computer-oriented boys, were originally developed, not coincidentally, by the U.S. military. While we are not suggesting that computing promotes militarism or anti-social behaviour, there is little evidence indicating that the content or medium of computing has inherently superior pedagogical, never mind moral, properties for teaching children. Harold Innis and Marshall McLuhan were instrumental in pointing out that particular forms of communication convey biases, and that changing the form, or power structure, of the media changes how information is processed (Innis, 1951; McLuhan, 1969).

The computer is individually operated by the child. In this respect, it is a "personal" medium. The machine requires an initial level of competency to master, which is also engaging for the child. This initial interest quickly becomes routinized. The act of having to interface with a machine that also "responds," and is thereby interactive, leads analysts such as Turkel (1984) to posit that the "personal" form also provides a projective medium to establish a reflection of oneself. Yet, as a medium for this type of analysis, the computer has a rather limited range of sensory feedback that it can furnish. What the child watches, after all, is a flashing dot screen. Various media analysts have argued that vitacon-based media such as television often function as passive media. Because the initial stimulation of the feedback of the medium is quickly routinized, lessons rapidly become boring unless they are structured to have an interest that involves the child cognitively in ways that go beyond the innate qualities of the medium. Otherwise, if the medium is used in a passive manner (where one effectively watches rather than mentally participates), higher and higher levels of stimulation are needed to maintain full interest. Boys who are games enthusiasts, for example, seek models that are increasingly violent and reflect a world view that is desensitized to possible consequences for others. Computers as a medium are surely not alone in conveying this idea, but the form of the medium is quite well suited to expressing this type of message. The "innate" utility of the computer as tutor can only be judged as it is used in particular applications.

In evaluating the impact of computers as a medium, there is a question of the ways computers interact with established trends in school in terms of social variation and a variety of implementation issues. For instance, a number of historical reviews of schooling and the curriculum document how social sorting in schools, on the basis of class, gender, and ethnicity, results in differential access to society's opportunity structure. Although computers are nominally classless and sexless, their use-patterns are filtered through institutions, like the school, that have, as part of their *de facto* work, the perpetuation of dominant systems of thought and language, leading to class, gender, and racial inequalities in schooling. It is not hard to imagine how such divisions will occur again with computers. The reciprocal relationship between schooling and technology is well established. It seems most probable that the level of skill training in high technologies will increase. The pattern for market demand seems to be well established; for example, the Economic Council of Canada, in "Jobs for the Eighties" reports that high technology is a key area of vocational growth in Canada. Similarly, the national assessment of education in the U.S. suggests that, "The gap between the number of highly skilled workers needed and the number of students prepared for high-level jobs is widening. Clearly we are not cultivating the raw material, our future workers, who will be vital for both economic progress and ultimately for economic survival" (U.S. Department of Education, n.d.). This view has been eagerly taken up by a variety of key Canadian educational leaders. The former Ontario Minister of Education, Bette Stephenson, for example, was quoted as saying, "As this specialized edition of *Education Ontario* will demonstrate, education will have an even more important role in shaping the computer age we are entering. Our technological future can be what philosophers have dreamed of for centuries . . . or it can be a nightmare of mechanization. Schools will have strong influence in which future awaits us" (Ontario Ministry of Education, 1982, p. 1).

With the dawning of the "age of the chip'" much was expected for computers and schooling. In part, some of this has transpired. In our own work (Sullivan, Logan, & Olson, 1986) we found effective use of computers in remedial education, drill and practice exercises, as aids in giving additional labour support to teachers, and in teaching the gifted. Similar studies have been reported across Canada in mathematics learning (Pereira-Mendoza, 1989) and in other areas (Hawes, 1988). The patterns of computer usage nonetheless remain spotted. Ognibene and Skeels' (1990) review of the literature in the United States reports that computer usage is actually down in schools and that patterns of under-use and misuse of computers are common.

Indeed, the assessments of the exact nature of the computers' impact on schooling are filled with contradictions at this early juncture. We are, for instance, assured by one group of notable scholars that the *medium* of technology will revolutionize the forms of learning (Jamison, Bangert, & Williams, 1974). With this bit of hopeful wisdom in hand, we proceed toward our next socio-educational insight. Quickly, however, we are greeted with the sobering news from equally eminent researchers that, when controls are made for exogenous factors (e.g., Hawthorne effect, variances in the method of instruction, quality of teachers, etc.), there are no long-term benefits provided by computers or other slick-trick educational innovations (Kulik, Bangert, & Williams, 1983; Kulik, 1983). First we go east; then we go west.

Inconsistent conclusions abound with respect to the most interesting issues raised by the social impact of computers on schooling. Some examples are listed below.

1. Do schools "skill" or "deskill" (Apple, 1979)? Canadian data seem to suggest that they do both. Jane Gaskell's work at the University of British Columbia shows how girls' education varies radically depending on whether one is taking computing in the business stream or in the academic stream (Gaskell, 1981; 1984). The contrasts are revealing. Within the business stream, for instance, there is repeated emphasis upon *mechanical* and *routinized* tasks to *service* the machine. There is very little learning of general skills (e.g., underlying logics, programming skills, symbolic codes, etc.) that might later be translated to another context. The girls interviewed by Gaskell were aware that mechanical skills would not lead to high-level careers. Nonetheless, they felt that, in relation to other studies, the business stream was "the most practical." This pattern contrasts dramatically with programming in the academic stream. Here the emphasis is on *general* and *symbolic* processes that lead to long-term *control*, regardless of the systems that may evolve. The emphasis is on high-level programs and forms of technical knowledge that give this control. What we are witnessing, in effect, is the use of computers to stratify knowledge, hence establishing a new entrance gate for "achievers" and a new barrier for those destined to less desirable fates.

   Yet, it is true that computers are used to improve reading and whole learning as supplements to programs for learning reading, such as those used by Donald Graves. It is certainly the case that in many schools in all Canadian provinces, individual teachers are using computers in a variety of subject areas (Olson, 1991). Many individual boards have also experimented with specialized schools or classrooms for learning and these dedicated situations have made some significant learning gains. The question, as we shall argue below, remains as to the sole etiology of these gains: that is, are the gains attributable to the computers, to well laid plans executed by competent teachers, or both?

2. Do computers reduce or increase differences in class-based learning? In our own studies, we tentatively have found on a limited sample that middle-class

children have more frequent access than working-class children to advanced computers in both home and community situations (Sullivan, Olson, & Logan, 1986). Since we know that such non-school settings have a powerful impact on how children perform within schools, there is every reason to believe that this will also influence the level, availability, and ultimate uses of knowledge, based along class lines. Since this knowledge, even more than conventional education, is capital intensive (you need an expensive computer, peripherals, software, training books, etc.), it leads to a possible powerful basis for further class division between those who can pay and those who cannot. Pat Campbell, in an overview article of U.S. results, found that in 1983, sixty-seven percent of wealthier U.S. school boards had computers while only forty-one percent of poor schools had microcomputers; that one study of schools in New Jersey found gaps in programming usage between white and black schools by margins of 3 to 1; that richer suburban boards teach programming skills while poorer schools use CAI. Campbell's survey also reviewed learning gaps between poorer and richer blacks and whites in computer usage such as those found in curricular areas. A study comparing Newark, New Jersey, city children to their suburban counterparts found differences in availability of both hardware and software. The same study also found that, even the best Newark inner-city children tended to be two years behind their suburban counterparts in computer-use ability.

A number of efforts to use computers to address equity issues have taken place, notably in handling issues of special education (Galloway, 1990) and in matters of gender and racial equity (Fredman, 1990). However, again the results of these studies are spotty and left largely to local action and individual projects or initiatives.

3. Will computers centralize or decentralize education as a source of knowledge? Again, the speculation in the area is highly divided. In Canada, our colleague, Robert Logan (1982), working from the McLuhan and futurist perspectives, argues the common position that computers offer us unlimited potential for highly individualized instruction and for making knowledge more available. However, another colleague, Ted Humphries (1980), argues that computers create powerful databases capable of invading privacy and automating the workplace, thus representing a fundamental erosion of individuality (and privacy).

4. Does the implementation of computers assist the curriculum, and the development of individual autonomy, or does it lead to greater dependence

on rigid learning packages and rote form? Our own work in the area suggests that the answer is highly dependent on how the program itself is *implemented* and that *teaching* is an influential determinant of computing outcomes (Fullan, 1982). How computer use is integrated with the curriculum also appears to be an influential factor in this area. Nonetheless, there is no single, clear answer provided by the literature.

The list goes on. At any turn, if you name your preference, you can readily garner evidence that you are headed in the right direction. It is plain that a new day is upon us. But where we are going is in question.

The central issues in why computers have or have not performed in classrooms is far less a function of the innate abilities of computers themselves than it is a matter of the ways in which computers have been taken up by teachers and the *planning* and *training* that have accompanied them. In this respect the empirical data has been overwhelming from across a variety of industrial societies including Canada. Overwhelmingly computers, for all the rhetoric, have been implemented with inadequate teacher training or argumentation for why these constitute a superior curricular tool. The result is that while many children can compute, much of this skilling, particularly among middle-class children, has come in the home and is often of mixed quality. A variety of trans-national studies (Brummelhuis & Plomp, 1991; Jarlaluddin, 1990; Prokasy, 1991; Druget, 1990; Boyd-Barnett, 1990; Eraut, 1989; Hawkridge, 1990) all make essential the same points: it is the quality of training, curricular planning and support, organization, and attention to context that differentiates successful computer learning from that which is not. This sensitivity to the relationships of implementation to practice have many levels and concrete consequences.

Israel Scheffler (1991) argues that computer learning, like all learning, is a cognitive activity and therefore issues of emotion and the importance of relation to context remain as strong in technologies learning as in any other learning. In this important respect, computer learning is little different from other learning. Hugh Mehan (1989) argues this point further by stating that computer learning has less to do with the medium itself than it does with the social practices around computing. "Social practices" can mean a variety of things that may be positive or negative. In planning for computers, for instance, it is clear that far too much emphasis has been placed on hardware versus training and curriculum planning. The effect is that teachers have not taken up computers on mass because the relationship to the curriculum has often been vague, except to a few who use them.

Computers can be a useful complement to a host of teaching activities. In our own studies of classroom computing for instance, computers were used effectively to teach co-operation, supplement geography, produce newspapers, teach poetry, and a host of other beneficial activities. In all cases where this occurred, however, there was considerable planning and artful construction by the teacher to achieve these ends. To understand why this may be so, it is useful to recall Philip Jackson's classical 1968 study of life in classrooms. Jackson noted that in any given day in an elementary classroom, there were more than 1500 exchanges or transfers of attention a teacher must attend to. Teaching and learning, in short, are highly complex sets of interactive exchanges that vary regularly with context. In learning computers, this is no less true, and in practice the computer may in fact distract from ordinary teaching or classroom activities (Olson, 1988). Some students may dominate, patterns of teacher-student knowledge may vary (children often know more about computers than do their teachers), and a constellation of changes may take place. There are ways to overcome this and to turn the computer to an advantage. Many of these involve organization practices such as using other students as mentors both to involve children more intimately in the learning and as an auxiliary teaching/labour force: developing groups to individualize levels of instruction and so on. None of this happens automatically and virtually all of it requires some level of planning and thinking out and execution of the relationship of practice to curriculum.

What happens in most schools is that "training" takes place after school, on lunch breaks, or during weekends. Training typically constitutes learning to access the machine (although it is not uncommon for teachers to have no actual hands-on use in such sessions), and to run a few basic programs such as Logo or other word processing packages. How these rudimentary lessons are to be used cognitively is left up to teachers. Motivation and use are left largely to faith, imagination, and a few examples. This can be little motivation for most but even when particular uses are constructed by interested teachers, obstacles often remain: computers can fail or be sabotaged; interesting databases turn out to be unavailable; available software is only partially compatible with the curriculum, and so on. Our own survey of teachers who did not use computers in our "model" schools (the overwhelming majority) were by and large hardly Luddites. One teacher's statement epitomized many. She told us:

> I know computers are important, and [the computer consultant] is great,
> he'll take his own time to help you with anything. But it's one more thing
> to learn in my spare time. In this board they always add on things you are

supposed to know and never take any off. What do I not do if I'm learning computers? I worry that what I will not be doing is teaching my kids.

These patterns of implementation as a key variable are hardly unique to computers in education, they touch virtually all innovations (Fullan, 1990). What differentiates computers in classrooms from other innovations is that the expectations for computers have been so high while the on-line support has been so checkered or misdirected. Ontario's decision to opt for the ICON may be argued to be just such a choice. When the decision was made to subsidize the ICON, two principle rationales were given: first, the support of technology would keep Ontario and Canada first in technology, and second, that the ICON would be supported by the ministry to ensure that the most advanced software available was always in place. Note that the emphasis in both instances is upon the technology; where technology is a metaphor for hardware and software and where these, in turn, are images (icons) for technological and industrial (knowledge) supremacy. This latter point is important since it was this fear of *not* being pre-eminent that was the motivation for action. The response was geared not out of empirical studies of what facilitated learning but instead out of a kind of moral panic that a government would fail its people, leading them into what has been called "techno-peasantry" if action was not taken—and taken pre-emptively.

Action was taken to subsidize the ICON and few of the results have been especially sanguine. First, most teachers who actually had taken the time to involve themselves in writing curricular programs for computers had done so on the IBM, Apple, Commodore, or clones of these machines. This meant the most dedicated cadre of teachers actually involved in educational computing was now outside the dominant technology favoured by the ministry. This exclusion was compounded by the fact that ICON's programs were written in "C," a technically superior computing language to the BASIC computer language used by most teachers, but also one most teachers did not know.

The impact continued. Many boards were either unwilling to implement what they saw as expensive new machines or did not trust the ministry's belief that the ICON could compete against the largest international computer players, where forces of pre-eminent technology were global. [The ICON itself had originally been produced in Ontario, one reason for its choice as technology, but subsequently moved production to South Korea for economic reasons.] Worse yet, many boards hedged their bets. Either wishing to take advantage of the ministry's subsidy or not wishing to appear unpatriotic (for not buying Canadian), many boards split their computer budgets. In practice, this meant duplication, incompatibility, and that at the user level there was one more daunting level of knowledge to penetrate before one could actually use computers in classrooms.

Perhaps more importantly, placing such a heavy emphasis on hardware and software diverted funds that could have been used for training and to have curricular adaptation into what will probably be comparatively vestigial technology in short order. Planning began as if the technology were an answer per se not a part of a far more complex learning process and environment. Empirically, computing in classrooms, like much other learning, has been at its best when these contextual issues have been thoughtfully and directly addressed. Computing has also been at its worst when these were not, and too often computing in classrooms has been left to a happenstance that mitigates a situation where negative, or more frequently, non-use of computers has remained the rule.

· · ·

THE COMPUTER AS SINNER OR SAINT

If the computer has failed to fire us with unified resolve about its effects, it has certainly not failed to spark our passion and our imagination. There is a plethora of technical material about the computer, but there is little that is without bias. Almost none of this material is without an opinion on where computers can (and should) take us. And, again, sharp division exists about effects.

The views, again, tend to be organized around sharp polarities: one extreme is protechnological or *millenialist*, while the other is anti-technological or *cataclysmic*, seeing such technological innovations as hyper-extensions of the state's bureaucratic and mechanized control (Sullivan, 1983). Within these conflicting archetypes, there is considerable variability in the form of argumentation and the sophistication of proponents. Nonetheless, there are those favouring such technology who argue that computer-based learning will lead to greater individualized freedom and to the breakdown of authoritarianism and standardized classroom forms and mentalities (Papert, 1980; Martin, 1981). Again, they see the use of computers as resulting in an expansion of literacy, economic opportunity, and generalized decentralization of social control. Various theorists within the pro-technological camp draw upon McLuhan's work to argue the decentralizing nature of the medium, comparing its impact to that of the alphabet in extending individual knowledge and control (Logan, 1982). Opponents of the new technologies argue that the use of computers to "deskill" work represents an extension of technical control (Noble, 1977). They link the technology to an increase in the gap of wealth and power between classes and between nations—between industrialized countries, like Canada, and Third World countries. Others in this camp emphasize the disastrous effects on dislocated workers, particularly the historically disadvantaged such as minorities and women (Dept. of Labour, 1982; Bluestone & Harrison, 1982), and/or fundamental civil liberties such as the protection of privacy (Humphries, 1980). What we are witnessing in the research on the impact of computers on schooling is the emergence of a discourse based less on overt facts about the computer's *technical* effects than on covert treatises about what schools can and should do. In essence, in the guise of a *research* debate is a *moral* debate (Wootton, 1975; Sullivan, 1984). This discourse is akin to a theological debate between the believers in the computer and the heretics (Sullivan, 1983).

· · ·

THE POLITICS OF LITERACY

Schooling itself has always been promoted for the sake of a people's future, social, moral, and technical development. That it has in fact been a contested terrain for competing ideologies is plain in schooling's history (Apple & Weiss, 1983; Archer, 1979; Bernstein, 1979; Bourdieu & Passeron, 1977; Harp & Hofley, 1980; Livingstone, 1983; Prentice, 1977; Whitty & Young, 1977). The current debates on computing and schooling also mirror the older ideological debates on schooling. The arguments used in these debates conform even more closely, however, to futurist debate on the general social effects of computers. It is within the arena of combative ideologies that we must understand *Time's* choice of the computer as "Man of the Year," and, conversely, the thesis that the "Third Wave"—the vision put forward by futurologist Alvin Toffler that the industrial era has come to an end and been replaced by a "post-industrial" or communications-based society—should be greeted apprehensively, since such an era will see increasing bureaucratic control of liberty and imagination by technical domination (Ellul, 1964; Grant, 1967; Schiller, 1983).

We submit that, in order to comprehend both the plurality of effects attributed to the computer and the moral tone of discussion, it is vital to examine how the so-called consequences of computer implementation affect different individuals and serve different social interests. It is also useful to examine how individual or group intentions, which computers should serve, come to represent explicitly or to establish differential relationships of utility for different persons in critical interactions such as those among schools, technology, and homes. The issues here range from career patterns and marketing strategies to micro-social issues (such as teacher/student interactions) to the ways in which computers have radically re-ordered market possibilities. What we are arguing is that a historical and contextual approach is needed. We are not denying that the debate around computing is (and should be) a moral one, but that assessment of trends needs to be grounded in particular understandings of how different aspects of computer use affect various groups.

The computer has become in our own lives, a metaphor for using ideas of social living. Part of this metaphor is placed in the material realm of reorganized productive relations. Another part of the computer metaphor draws substance from our fantasy and projects about this device. Sherry Turkel, in her widely quoted book, *The Second Self*, raises the issue of how "artificial intelligence," as symbolized by the computer, brings into question what is fundamental to our humanness (Turkel, 1984). This type of reflection is in part a basis for our sense of computers.

But part of our relationship lies in material reality. And still another part is given to us in images about the computer. These latter images about computer capabilities are important to our understanding of computers (and their metaphoric use) because they are constructed "for us." Computer companies, for instance, have a vested interest in "portraying" computers as solely positive factors or necessities in schooling. The trade-off in terms of the costs of the machines, the time they divert from other activities, the appropriateness of procedures for integrating their use with curriculum and other studies are seldom discussed. The drawbacks of the vulnerability of hardware, the limits of number of machines available, and their relative non-interactiveness are not discussed in glowing advertisements. These are very real issues. In one school in Ontario, the principal had to choose to increase the number of computers in the school by three (at a cost of several thousand dollars) or to fund a music program to an adequate level to support a group large enough to constitute a band. In tight economic times for education, even a small computer purchase can expend as much as ten to twenty percent of a school's discretionary funds. What we see in both corporate advertising and in ministries of education releases is only the glowing side to computers. Ministries of education, like corporations, "sell" themselves by trying to show their relevance and awareness. Claiming that computers are fully integrated into schools often placates media, even where software, hardware, support instruction, and/or appropriate usage frequently does not exist in anywhere near the form claimed by ministries' optimistic portrayals when one looks closely at the local classroom level. Yet, even more than these distortions, discussion of computers is done a disservice by the relative absence of questioning of how computers come to be controlled by human agency.

The debate suffers from lapses within educational research, which, in the last five decades, has been dominated by a liberal or universalist model portraying schooling as equal and occurring by consensus. Whatever may be its other advantages, steadfastly holding to this position tends to downplay or ignore the existence of very real structural, cultural, and other power relationship conflicts within schools and society (Giroux, 1983). But this consensus by these oversights also eclipses the role of "intentional agency" as a part of the educational planning process. Such eclipses, Sullivan says, are tantamount to tunnel vision (Sullivan, 1983); but a discourse that assumes technology such as computers could be introduced "neutrally" or in an "objective" fashion without reference to the larger context of who benefits and also who suffers from such change ignores the social context and thereby reflects an inherent bias that favours *technical* solutions and efficiency models. These positions, while appearing technical, can become implicit value positions and can, for instance, lead to a view that technology of touchtones is good for society (Feinberg & Rosemont, 1975). This is why *Time* can centrestage the computer to the exclusion of all forms of personal agency, be they male or female. This is one reason why we are presently looking to solve problems by the use of machines as if there were no trade-off. The digital computer, with its incredible capacity for speed and memory, out-performs the computational paces obtainable by humans. Our romance with speed, once vested in the automobile, was enhanced with the advent of the computer.

• • •

THE MATERIAL AND THE SPIRITUAL REMADE

In order to understand computers and information technologies, we must understand what they are and what they can do. What they are, very plainly and simply, are efficient *tools* for information processing. This statement is simple enough on the surface; yet, as we are continuously rediscovering in a host of diverse settings, the full range of the impact of the computer as a tool is complex. Knowledge of how and where computers can be efficiently used will doubtless remain an ongoing discovery. But technical understanding of possible usages is not enough. No tool autonomously organizes and employs itself alone from *tabula rasa* to the operational program. Tools are used by people for particular ends (good and bad). Understanding who uses them, how, and for whose benefits—the structure of intentional action—is necessary if we are to assess how computers are likely to be actually employed. Computers announce a remarkable technical advance because they facilitate the rapid execution of a multiplicity of work processes. The introduction of computer technology alters the parameters (and the cost) of executing work and in some cases, is necessary if work is to be undertaken at all. The level of technology theoretically limits productive capacities such as work loads, but what work is to be done, by whom, and for whose benefits—questions of distribution and processes of production—cannot be given by technology alone. Understanding how computers affect schools, labour markets, and models of social organization, therefore, requires that we look at the various interests that are served and the organizational as well as purely technical decisions. This is a most appropriate project if we are to adequately evaluate the effects of computer implementations since the computer as a tool does fundamentally reorganize material relationships and organizations of production.

Because the computer directly affects so many of the most important areas of human activity—the organization of information, processes of production, our psychological sense of the possible, and so on—it also potentially changes relationships of social power. Many of these are structural relationships, for example, changes in how work gets done (essays are now word processed, math drills in schools are computer assisted, tickets are booked globally by computers). Who controls such information very much affects one's level of power within society, one's ability to get a job, and even how much of some kinds of knowledge one may obtain. Industrial societies count on computers for the "competitive edge." Yet all these structural changes are ultimately made by people. Not everyone's interest is the same. Understanding this is massively helpful to separating authentic educational benefits of computers from vested claims. When we move beyond the mania of hopes and fears that cloud our perceptions about computers in education to a critical evaluation of how they work in practice, we will best be able to use the potential computers hold for schools.

We must take a hard look at the applied uses of computer technology and ask ourselves if these methods are authentically better ways of doing work. We must calculate the effects of deskilling, the depersonalization of learning, and the areas where computers are pedagogically helpful. We must be practical in our assessment of whether they are more or less expensive (and fashionable) toys. At the same time, we should explore ways to use the computer to assist us in education. If some drill is better done on a computer than at a desk, then we should do the work in this manner. Where computers free us from drudgery or open new avenues of art, science, printing, and the like, we should foster their growth. What is most essential, however, is that we consciously understand what is happening in practice, how it is happening, and who it serves. Ultimately, it is we as conscious actors who must generate the metaphors about computers, and control the practical uses of computers. The principle of critically evaluating what our education is about is equally applicable to computerized and non-computerized learning. The computer simply re-opens old questions about technology, equality, and whose school interests should be served.

It can be concluded for now that the effects of computers are mixed. We must be both empirical and critical in our claims about their impact. Dreams and fears are part of being human. But if we are to use computers as tools, tutors, and machines to serve our students, we must examine the full range of their actual use and, in conducting our examination, be resolved to keep control and have this new cultural invention serve democratic ends. Democratic ends, not fashion, not technical analysis, not market forces, should control the use of computers. Knowledge ought to bring us greater flexibility and freedom, not new forms of subordination.

• • •

REFERENCES

Acher, M. (1979). *Social origins of educational systems*. London: Sage Publications.

Apple, M. (1979). *Ideology and curriculum*. London: Routledge and Kegan Paul.

Apple, M. (1984). The political economy of text publishing. *Excellence, reform and equality in education: An international perspective*. Buffalo and Toronto: SUNY Buffalo and OISE.

Apple, M., & Weis, L. (Eds.). (1983). *Ideology and practice in schooling*. Philadelphia: Temple University Press.

Bernstein, B. (1979). *Class, codes and control: Towards a theory of educational transmission, Vol. 2* (2nd ed.). London: Routledge and Kegan Paul.

Bluestone, B., & Harrison, B. (1982). *The deindustrialization of America*. New York: Basic Books.

Bourdieu, P., & Passeron, J. (1977). *Reproduction in education, society, and culture* (Trans R. Nice.). London: Sage Publications.

Boyd-Barnett, O. (1990). School computing policy as state-directed innovation. *Educational Studies, 16*(2), 169–185.

Braverman, H. (1974). *Labor and monopoly capital: The degradation of work in the twentieth century*. New York: Monthly Review Press.

Campbell, P. (1983). *Computers in education: A question of access*. Paper presented to the Annual Meeting of the American Educational Research Association, Montreal.

Connell, R.W. (1982). *Teachers' work*. Sydney: Allen and Unwin.

Department of Labour. (1982). *In the chips: Opportunity, people, partnerships*. Report of Labour Canada Task Force on Microelectronics & Employment. Ottawa: Queen's Printer.

Duguet, P. (1990). Computers in schools: National strategies and their extension to the international level. *Prospects, 20*(2), 165–172.

Economic Council of Canada. (1982). *In short supply: Jobs and skills in the 1980s*. Ottawa: Supply and Services Canada.

Ellul, J. (1964). *The technological society.* Toronto: Vintage Books.

Eraut, M. (1989). *The information society—A challenge for education policies? Policy options and implementation strategies.* Strasbourg, France: Council of Europe.

Feinberg, W., & Rosemont, K. (1975). *Technology and education: Dissertation essays on the intellectual foundations of American education.* Urbana, IL: University of Illinois Press.

Fredman, A. (Ed.). (1990). *Yes I can: Action project to resolve equity issues in education.* Cleveland, OH: International Society for Technology in Education.

Fullan, M. (1982). *The meaning of educational change.* Toronto: OISE Press.

Fullan, M., & Steilbaur, S. (1991). *The new meaning of educational change* (2nd ed.). Toronto: OISE Press, Teachers College Press.

Galloway, J. (1990). Policy issues for learning disabled computer integration. *Journal of Learning Disabilities, 23*(6), 331–334.

Gaskell, J. (1981). Sex inequalities in education for work. *Canadian Journal of Education, 6,* 54–72.

Gaskell, J. (1984). Gender and course choice: The orientations of male and female students. *Journal of Education, 166*(1), 89–102.

Giroux, H. (1983). *Theory and resistance in education: A pedagogy for the opposition.* South Hadley, MA: Bergin and Garvey.

Grant, G. (1967). *Technology and empire.* Toronto: Anansi Press.

Harp, J., & Hofley, J. (Eds.). *Structural inequality in Canada.* Scarborough, ON: Prentice-Hall.

Hawes, D. (1988). *Schools, computers and learning project. Interim report #1 from the Kingston Regional Pilot Test Centre: A description of the research setting.* Toronto: Ministry of Education.

Hawkridge, D. (1990). Who needs computers in schools, and why? *Computers and Education, 15,* 1–3.

Humphries, E. (1980). *Privacy in jeopardy: Student records in Canada.* Toronto: OISE Press.

Innis, H.A. (1951). *The bias of communication.* Toronto: University of Toronto Press.

Jalabuddim, A.K. (1990). Educational applications of computers for lifelong learning. *Prospects, 20,* 2.

Jamison, D., Suppes, P., & Wells, S. (1974). Effectiveness of alternative instructional media: A survey. *Review of Educational Research, 44.*

Kulik, J. (1983). Synthesis of research on computer-based instruction. *Educational Leadership, 41.*

Kulik, J., Bangert, R., & Williams, G. (1983). Effects of computer-based teaching on secondary students. *Journal of Educational Psychology, 75.*

Logan, R. (1982). *The axiomatics of the Innis-McLuhan school of communications.* Unpublished paper presented to the Culture and Technology Seminar, University of Toronto.

Malone, T. (1981). Towards a theory of intrinsically motivating instruction. *Cognitive Science, 5,* 333–370.

Martin, J. (1981). *Telematic society: A challenge for tomorrow.* Englewood Cliffs, NJ: Prentice-Hall.

McLuhan, M. (1969). *The Gutenberg galaxy: The making of typographic man.* New York: New American Library.

McLuhan, M. (n.d.). *Explorations: Studies in culture and communications, Nos. 1–9, 1953–1959.* Toronto: University of Toronto Press.

Mehan, H. (1989). Microcomputers in classrooms: Educational technology or social practice. *Anthropology and Education Quarterly, 20,* 4–22.

Noble, D. (1977). *America by design: Science, technology, and the rise of corporate capitalism.* New York: Knopf.

Ognibene, R., & Skeels, R. (1990). Computers and the school: Unused and misused. *Action in Teacher Education, 12,* 2.

Olson, C.P. (1988). Computing environments in elementary classrooms. *Children's Environmental Quarterly, 5*(4).

Olson, C.P. (1991). Teaching equality: Using computers to popular ends. In C. Julie, A.

Manie, D. Meerkotter, R. Prodgar, & D. Reeler (Eds.), *Computers for transformation in education*. Capetown, South Africa: Wyvern Press.

Ontario Ministry of Education. (1982). *Educational Ontario: The computer age and education*. Toronto: Author.

Papert, S. (1980). *Mindstorms: Children, computers, and powerful ideas*. New York: Basic Books.

Pereira-Mendoza, L. (Ed.). (1989). Conference Proceedings of the Canadian Mathematics Educational Study Group. Annual meeting, Winnipeg.

Prentice, A. (1977). *The school promoters: Education and social class in mid-nineteenth century Upper Canada*. Toronto: McClelland and Stewart.

Prokasy, W. (1991). The new pedagogy: An essay on policy and procedural implementations. *Innovation Higher Education, 15*, 2.

Scheffler, I. (1991). *In praise of the cognitive emotions, and other essays in the philosophy of education*. New York: Routledge, Chapman, and Hall.

Schiller, H. (1983). *The world crisis and new information technologies: A way out or deeper in?* Unpublished paper, University of San Diego.

Sullivan, E. (1983). Computers, culture, and educational futures: A critical appraisal. *Interchange, 14*, 3.

Sullivan, E. (1984). *Critical psychology: Psychology as interpretation of the personal world*. New York: Plenum.

Sullivan, E., Olson, C.P., & Logan, R. (1986). *The development of policy and research projections for computers in education: A comparative ethnography*. Ottawa: Social Science and Humanities Research Council of Canada.

Turkel, S. (1984). *The second self*. New York: Simon and Schuster.

United States National Commission on Excellence in Education. *A nation at risk: The imperative for education reform. A report to the nation and the secretary of education*. Washington: U.S. Dept. of Education.

Wootton, A. (1975). *Dilemmas in discourse: Controversies about the sociological interpretation of language*. London: Allen and Unwin.

COMPUTER USE IN EDUCATION:
CURRENT STATUS AND EMERGING ISSUES IN RESEARCH AND PRACTICE

. . .

Dale C. Howard

G . M . Kysela

he advent of computers and computer technology has quickened the pace of development and change in many disciplines, but no more so than in education and educational research. Since the discipline of education actually synthesizes and combines knowledge and strategies of research from many fields of practice, the potential contribution of advanced technological influences upon education is vast. We will explore the range of these influences as well as identify new developments and emerging fields of inquiry in education. Finally we will touch on some important implications for educators stemming from these influences and developments.

. . .

COMPUTER APPLICATIONS IN THE CLASSROOM

Computer Literacy

Shortly after the introduction of the microcomputer in the late seventies, public interest in computers skyrocketed. Concerns were expressed over what some perceived as a national computer literacy "crisis" (Luehrmann, 1980; Molnar, 1978). In response to these perceptions and a rapidly growing dependency on computer technology in business and industry, learning how to use the computer became part of many public educational curricula.

PROGRAMMING AND PROBLEM SOLVING

Initially, computer programming was the focus in most computer-literacy classes. Although it is evident that most students do not require programming skills to effectively use a computer, practitioners continued to introduce programming as one aspect of computer literacy. Computer programming continues to be a controversial area in computers in education.

The majority of the polemic has centred around whether or not computer programming fosters problem-solving skills. Some reports recommend caution concerning the claims that computer programming and other computer activities have significant effects on students' ability to solve problems (Khayrallah & van den Meiraker, 1987; Krasnor & Mitterer, 1984). Others suggest most criticism does not take into account differences in pedagogy nor the philosophical presuppositions underlying many of the studies (Burnett, 1988; Emihovich & Miller, 1988; Papert, 1987). More specific studies report improvements in visual-spatial skills, identification of multiple variables, inductive discovery, and general technical-scientific thinking after exposure to computer games (Greenfield, 1987). Computer programming has also been found to enhance some specific cognitive skills such as procedure comprehension and problem translation (Mayer, Bayman, & Dych, 1987).

Whether or not computers or computer programs can be directly associated with an increase in problem-solving skill or changes in thinking is still open to debate. However, more and more evidence suggests that computers and computer activities do contribute to changes in students' views of themselves as learners and that the future of computers in the schools should be viewed as a bright one (Burns & Hagerman, 1989; Laboratory of Comparative Human Cognition, 1989; Weir, 1989).

APPLICATION SOFTWARE

Most students will need to know how to use the computer rather than train to be computer specialists. For this reason, schools often emphasize computer applications rather than computer programming in their computer curricula. The most common student application is word processing. A recent and comprehensive review of word processing in schools (Cochran-Smith, 1991) indicates that word processing:

1. encourages collaborative classroom environments thereby positively influencing the social organization of a classroom;
2. improves the composing process through easier facilitation of revision;
3. increases the quantity and quality of student writing;
4. promotes a positive attitude toward word processing; and
5. improves keyboarding skills.

The learning of word processing, spreadsheets, and databases is often accompanied by the introduction to more specialized productivity software, such as grammar and style checkers, electronic dictionaries, and presentation managers, or, in some instances, students become familiar with cognitive enhancers, such as idea generators, report outliners, biofeedback machines, and artificially intelligent problem-solving systems.

TECHNOLOGICAL AND INFORMATION LITERACY

Although some kind of computer experience by young adults is nearly universal, computer literacy still remains, in many respects, only computer awareness (Adams, 1989). In response to a growing concern that computer literacy has not fulfilled its mandate, attempts are being made to include computers in a broader context, referred to as technology education (Lauda, 1989). Computer literacy may only be the beginning of a broader, more general technological and information literacy associated with a continued perception that a technological society will have to be competent in both the use and language of technology. Knowing a language is arguably the most important component of any culture. Being literate means to understand the cultural significance of the communication. Technological and information literacy, then, means to be informed and able to understand, appreciate, and critique technology and information systems. It is to be better able to participate in an electronically connected technological culture, to share rights and privileges, and to shoulder responsibility for a technological society.

Instruction

Currently, research suggests that computer-mediated instruction compares favourably with conventional instruction (Kulik & Kulik, 1987) and appears to be particularly effective with special learners, either those experiencing difficulty or those who are highly independent. Most often this is discussed as computer-based instruction (CBI) or computer-based training (CBT).

Numerous programs are available to assist teachers in presenting material across most standard curricula such as mathematics, reading and language arts, science, and social studies (Bullough & Beatty, 1991). Other software is available to teach foreign languages, critical thinking, art, and physical education. For the most part, many of these programs are designed to fix concepts and facts, already learned, in the minds of learners. These programs are often described as drill and practice programs. Other computer programs assume the role of the teacher and determine previous knowledge, present material, and test for retention. These are called tutorials.

Computers are also being used to assist in cognitive tasks. Examples range from the medical student using an expert system to diagnose different cancers to the physics student examining randomly changing patterns on a computer screen in an investigation of chaos theory. Other cognitive enhancers include such devices as outliners to assist in the generation and organization of ideas, biofeedback machines that allow reading-disabled students to observe and control brain wave patterns in certain parts of the brain, and artificially intelligent coaching systems that assist an economics student in identifying the variables most likely to determine the need for a price increase of "widgets."

Materials Development

The variety of authoring languages used to create CBI is staggering, ranging from low level programming languages such as PASCAL, C, and BASIC, to high level dedicated CBI languages such as Authorware Professional. Further to authoring languages are authoring systems. High level authoring systems offer some obvious advantages. They are often easy to learn and many have "built in" instructional design features to help guide the author in lesson development. Others come with libraries and tutorials.

However, the more dedicated the system is to particular assumptions about learning, the more restrictive the system may be. The less dedicated, the more difficult a system is to learn by inexperienced course developers who have limited or no computer programming expertise.

When choosing an authoring system or language, there are some some factors one may want to consider before selecting the system or language, such as: built-in instructional design principles; access to outside programs or libraries; initial costs of program purchase; training and support costs; and royalties.

Equipment selection is determined by the sophistication of the materials one wants to develop. Multimedia productions could require several thousands of dollars in capital equipment, not to mention the student platform needed to receive such material. A great deal of quality programming can be developed and delivered on mid-range microcomputers. Every year, the power and speed of microcomputers goes up and the costs come down.

The development of print-based courses is a good foundation for the development of computer-based courses. Many similar techniques and instructional design principles apply across mediums. However, the computer medium is different than print-based medium. For example, CBI authors have to acquire some ability to design computer screens, create efficient menus, and incorporate graphics and sound appropriately. Because "flipping" from place to place in a computer program is less efficient than movement within a print-based medium, lesson flow and continuity is a priority in CBI. It is very easy for a student to get "lost" in a poorly designed lesson. Besides, well-designed CBI does not rely on human tutorial backup; thus, more emphasis must be placed on analysis and preparation of student responses and potential student difficulties with the material. CBE requires, at least, minimal piloting.

Administration

Managing the planning, implementation, and evaluation of instruction can be very time consuming. Word processors, spreadsheets, and databases are often used by practitioners to record student performance data, design schedules, and to track inventory. More dedicated computer programs are also available such as electronic gradebooks, test generators, and attendance software (Bullough & Beatty, 1991). In some instances, desktop publishing programs are used to create newsletters, announcements, flyers, and brochures.

Computer-managed instruction (CMI) or computer-managed learning (CML) systems are computer programs especially developed to assist practitioners in planning, implementing, and evaluating student educational experiences. Although interest in these systems has waned somewhat, they have proven efficient and valuable in instances where accountability has been a major priority. Special education, with its unique student population, has utilized CML more extensively than other areas of education (Kolich, 1985). The emphasis on individualization and a real need for accurate record keeping (Morgan & Rhode, 1983) has literally forced special educators into investigating the possible labour saving advantages of implementing a computer-managed learning system.

Selection of a CML system usually depends upon need and budget. However, a system should be easy to use, have good editing features, be expandable, have adequate sorting and indexing power, and format and generate comprehensive reports. If given the choice, selecting the hardware around the CML package is superior to selecting software that does not meet one's needs because of the limited capabilities of the hardware.

• • •

NEW DEVELOPMENTS AND EMERGING FIELDS
Electronic Dissemination of Research

A growing number of researchers are beginning to use the worldwide computer networks and conferencing systems to publish their research (Quarterman, 1990). The formality of the publications distributed electronically varies from newsletter and listserver bulletins such as the Information System for Advanced Academic Computing (ISAAC) out of the University of Washington, and the Distance Education Online Symposium (DEOSNEWS) at Pennsylvania State University, to reviewed journals such as Interpersonal Computing and Technology (IPCT) at Georgetown University. It is very likely in the near future that some commercial publishers will also begin to distribute their academic and professional journals electronically.

Computer-based Learning Environments

Computer-based learning environments serve in this chapter as a catch-all for computer-assisted instruction (CAI), computer-managed instruction (CMI), and computer-based instruction (CBI). This field, for the most part, is a continuation of the precepts of Programmed Learning (PL), initiated by Sidney L. Pressey (from Hergenhahn, 1988). Although Pressey's ideas were not popular at the time, several years later they were adopted by B. F. Skinner (1958). Skinner believed that by presenting a learning task in small steps, in a way that would produce overt responses that could be immediately reinforced through feedback, learning could be significantly accelerated.

Programmed learning was further extended by Fred Keller (1968) in what is called the Personalized System of Instruction (PSI). Key elements of PSI centre around defining, organizing, and categorizing specific subjects or topics into segments. Criteria are also developed to measure mastery of each segment. More importantly, students are allowed to move through segments at their own pace, thereby eliminating many of the factors that cause variations in student mastery and, therefore, test score distributions. In the PSI system, then, tests are more likely to be taken when the learner is most prepared to take them.

Further support for programmed instruction was garnered through the development of task analysis, behavioural objectives, criterion-referenced testing, systems approach models of instructional design, and formative evaluation (Reiser, 1987).

Although not prevalent, computer-based instruction (CBI) is becoming more common and a body of research has been accumulating which indicates that CBI is modestly more effective and substantially more efficient than conventional instructional delivery systems (Kulik & Kulik, 1987). However, Ross and Morrison (1989) suggested that better research design is necessary before much optimism can be expressed concerning the potential effectiveness of CBI. These authors cite external validity, media replication, and learner control as issues to be addressed.

Bresler and Walker (1990) cautioned that there is some inherent complexity in determining the effects of CBI on achievement. These researchers suggest, "Factors such as teachers' and students' attitudes, extent of integration into the curriculum, and user interface with hardware and software, determine the impact of technology on achievement no less than the technology itself" (p. 66).

The use of computers means that education can be delivered taking advantage of all the effective developments in instructional design and development. Student achievement can be monitored electronically and content can be modified to suit the needs of individual students. Technology in this context means more expedient and efficient training. For some, this may influence the meaning they have of education in general. However, there is a more subtle meaning associated with computer use in the classroom. The computer means order, sequence, and procedure. The computer serves as a metaphor for appropriate instruction and for procedural thinking by both the teacher and the student.

Valid as these criticisms are, exciting new advances continue to stimulate the imaginations of educational researchers and practitioners. The most promising area of educational computer technology deals with those technologies that allow for student interaction with the study materials or allow the learner to explore new ways of study and understanding. Within this realm, the most spectacular are simulations, multimedia materials, hypermedia and hypertext, information technology, and alternate delivery strategies.

SIMULATIONS

Simulations provide students or trainees with the opportunity to experience the "real thing" without the associated dangers, costs, and time inconveniences. They help young scientists to safely manipulate variables in a chemical experiment or enable animal dissections without loss of life, or endure the smell of formaldehyde. They give student pilots a chance to fly a 747 without leaving the ground, a neophyte oil well firefighter the thrill of capping a well without using an asbestos suit, the budding geologist an opportunity to visit the inside of a volcano, and the aspiring marriage counsellor a setting to experiment with broken relationships. Yes, there are even social dynamics simulators, such as the curiously titled Marriage Contract Game (Joyce, 1988).

MULTIMEDIA, HYPERMEDIA, AND HYPERTEXT

Multimedia and hypertext represent an exciting area for educational technology. They provide the learner with opportunities to explore multiple levels of the learning material without extensive research and auxiliary resources. Imagine for a moment the proverbial springtime slough study, sloshing around in the creek looking for all kinds of wonderful insects, exotic plant life, and hard-to-find animals. This experience can be had through the use of integrating graphics, audio, video, and text into one elaborate and sophisticated computer program. With the simple click of a "mouse," a blade of grass is identified and described. A blackbird's wing can be magnified to full screen, displayed in splendid detail, and labelled from the upper wing coverts to the primaries and secondaries. If a caterpillar is selected, instantly the student begins to witness the miracle of metamorphosis as the little creature transforms into a beautiful butterfly. The only thing missing is the "sloshing," and that too, with advances in computer graphics, and "virtual reality," may soon be included.

INFORMATION TECHNOLOGY

Anyone with a computer and minimal communications hardware and software can become, as the saying goes, "connected." This means having access to several large private and commercial databases. To the student, being connected allows a Grade 4 student in Alberta to exchange an essay with a classmate in California or Peru. It means going to the library and signing on to CD ROM or an on-line database at the local museum and finding out everything there is to know about dinosaurs. Information technology allows teachers to deliver lectures to students at a distance, through teleconferencing and computer conferencing. It helps educators, anywhere in the world, to share ideas with colleagues and to collaborate on projects.

However, this is only the tip of the iceberg. Through the use of two-way video and audio transmission, and the ability to exchange data, satellite information technology has all but provided for the "virtual classroom." In the near future, students will experience desktop video conferencing that will have all the characteristics of *Hollywood Squares*. Cordless communication will allow instructors to grade assignments, announce course updates, tutor students, and prepare next week's notes, all while waiting for the foursome ahead to get off the next green.

ALTERNATE DELIVERY STRATEGIES

Most instruction is modelled after the conventional lecture. An authority in a particular subject area usually stands at the front of the class and imparts knowledge to the receptive minds in the room. However, with the rate of increase we currently are witnessing in published knowledge, few if any individuals, can be considered the sole authority in their field. Couple this with changing demographics in students attending post-secondary institutions as older more experienced individuals, there is little wonder that conventional educational institutions are experiencing difficulty meeting the demands for accessibility and flexibility. Therefore, it is encouraging to see newer perceptions of education (Cross, 1988; Knowles, 1984) that recognize learners as increasingly capable of self-direction and self-learning and able to access information by themselves.

Many requests for training and retraining can be met efficiently or expediently by utilizing alternative instructional techniques and delivery strategies—strategies to meet the learner where the learner is, physically and intellectually. Asynchronous instruction involves the delivery of materials and instruction anywhere anytime. The learner in this environment may take a course without the restriction of time and place. Athabasca University in Alberta for instance, primarily operates within an asynchronous environment. In a similar fashion, the University of Phoenix offers an entire MBA program on-line. Other institutions send itinerant teachers to remote locations, delivering the program, as it were, on alternate weekends. On the corporate side, more companies offer upgrading, retraining, and further education while the employee is on the job. The use of electronically mediated instruction and information technology have removed the walls of the classroom. In many instances we are not likely to see them raised again.

Alternate delivery strategies and new educational tools have allowed for diversity in curricula presentation and student demonstration of learning. Many educators would subscribe to a theory of multiple intelligences. Students display numerous talents and abilities that are not easily measurable using conventional intelligence and aptitude tests. Through recognizing divergences and accommodating differences in learning style and cognition, new computer technologies can broaden the range of alternatives for content delivery and student assessment. An automotive technician may learn about customer relations through a role-play exercise presented through interactive video. A junior high school student may demonstrate an understanding of the difficulties in achieving Canadian confederation while playing a computer game designed to simulate nineteenth-century railway transportation. A music student may take ear training through computer-synthesized sound.

The issue in using alternate teaching techniques and delivery strategies is not to make learning "fun," although that may happen, but to present alternatives that may use other talents and abilities of the student to support learning.

Information is often confused with knowledge. Alternate teaching and delivery strategies are attempts to transform information into knowledge, to make information meaningful. In many instances, the computer can help.

Artificial Intelligence

Only a few years ago, artificial intelligence was restricted to mainframe computers. However, like most computer applications, artificial intelligence has become the domain of the microcomputer as well. Artificial intelligence (AI) is defined as programming computers to carry out tasks that would require human intelligence. Tasks might include the activity of learning or remembering from experience, the actions needed to acquire and retain knowledge and the problem-solving routines seemingly similar to human's solving of problems. Essentially, artificial intelligence is the computer emulating human decision making (Colantonio, 1989).

Humans have a couple of abilities, however, that are difficult for computers to emulate. Humans effectively and efficiently recognize patterns, by using visual, auditory, and tactile senses. As well, they are able to solve problems using a form of logical processing. Although we may categorize these intellectual abilities quite differently, they both share the unique characteristic of imagination. The brain is able to form meaningful concepts, it can deal with varying levels of abstraction, and at times goes beyond the facts, into the realm of creativity. The brain is able to transform information into knowledge. Rarely does a human require all the parts to recognize the whole. Computers do not function very well without the whole program. It is in pattern recognition and knowledge processing that artificial intelligence research is the most active.

Pattern Recognition

VISION

What the eye does is difficult to duplicate electronically. For instance, the sources of variability in recognizing printed text are astounding and when multiple type styles are used, the variability is increased still further. Yet, AI has made tremendous strides in pattern recognition. Optical character recognition (OCR) devices read books to the blind, the Finger Print Identification System (AFIS) assists law enforcement agencies, and the analysis of blood-cell images has provided more efficient and expedient recognition of cancer (Kurzweil, 1990).

HEARING, TOUCH, AND SMELL

We may not think of computers as having the ability to hear, but advances in digitized sound have made it possible for machines to compare one sound pattern with another. The applications vary from education to security systems. By far the most work has been done in automatic speech recognition (ASR), with some systems capable of recognizing upwards of 10 000 words or more (Kurzweil, 1990). The problem still remains, however, to develop ASR systems that recognize large vocabularies from multiple speakers, a human quality that is often taken for granted. Chemical analysis systems and tactile sensors have been developed to recognize patterns of odor and the sense of touch (Kurzweil, 1990). The next decade should see robots that see, talk, smell, and feel.

Knowledge Processing

EXPERT SYSTEMS

An expert system is a computer program designed to collect, crystallize, and disseminate expertise in a specific knowledge domain (Hofmeister, 1988). Potentially, expert systems can be employed in any area where a reasonably stable knowledge base exists, where rules have been established to manipulate knowledge, and where problems have established solutions (Lubke, 1988). The major difference between an expert system and a conventional computer program rests in the expert system's abilities as an interpreter or a control strategy rather than a fixed control of data structures. This interpreter is referred to as an inference engine.

An expert system has certain advantages over human expertise as well as particular disadvantages. Computer expertise is nonperishable, easy to transfer, easy to document, consistent, and affordable. On the other hand, expert systems are not intuitive, adaptive, perceptive to sensory experience, broadly focussed, and are not endowed with common sense knowledge (Waterman, 1986). Several examples of expert systems are described in Table 1.

The use of expert systems in education has been somewhat limited, largely because educational knowledge is often not stable. However, some areas of education lend themselves to this technology, such as the area of Intelligent Tutoring Systems (ITS). These systems are often used for knowledge assessment and are capable in some manner of emulating the interactive nature of teaching (Frasson & Gauthier, 1990; Wenger, 1987). Many of these systems adjust to the knowledge of the student and teach from domain specific information, for example SCHOLAR. Others include a particular pedagogical perspective, as in the

TABLE I
Types of Expert Systems

TYPE	EXPERT SYSTEM	DESCRIPTION
Interpretation	PUFF	Diagnoses lung disease by interpreting data from pulmonary function tests.
Prediction	I &W	Helps predict when and where a major armed conflict will next occur.
Diagnosis	PROSPECTOR	Helps geologists evaluate the mineral potential of a region.
Design	ACES	Performs the cartographer's job of map labelling.
Monitoring	ANNA	Helps administer digitalis to patients with heart problems.
Debugging	DELTA	Helps identify and correct malfunctions in locomotives.
Repair	TQMSTUNE	Fine tunes a triple quadruple mass spectrometer.
Instruction	STEAMER	Teaches the operation of a steam propulsion plant.
Control	PTRANS	Helps manage manufacture and distribution of DEC computer systems.

Source: Waterman, 1986, pp. 42–48.

case of QUADRATIC (Wenger, 1987). The Minnesota Adaptive Instructional System (MAIS) is an example of a system that has a macro-component that establishes the conditions for learning and a micro-component that adjusts to moment-to-moment individual learning needs (Tennyson & Park, 1987). Other educational expert systems serve as educational consultants. For example, CLASS.LD2 goes beyond instruction and helps classify learning disabled students (Hofmeister, 1988).

NATURAL LANGUAGE PROCESSING

Natural language processing employs the same strategies and techniques as the expert systems previously described. Processing language is more than speech recognition. It is the understanding of all the ambiguities, idiomatic expressions, and intonations of human language: ambiguities such as "to be or not to be"; idiomatic expressions like "go play in the street"; and intonations such as "really?" What is easy for a small child to do will require far more AI innovation before machines can be considered competent in the nuances of language. Nevertheless, systems have been devised to translate one language into another. In a few years, the field of natural language processing is expected to generate an industry worth over $300 million (Kurzweil, 1990).

ROBOTICS

Robotics is the field of AI where pattern recognition and knowledge processing come together. The science fiction literature has often portrayed robots as perceptual, thinking, and at times emotional machines. First generation robots, in the 1970s, were able to grasp and move objects from one place to another. By the 1980s, a second generation machine was capable of more delicate and refined movement. These robots were employed to do welding and spray painting in such industrial settings as automobile assembly plants. During the mid-1980s, third generation robots were equipped with visual and tactile sensory systems, and became capable of complex assembly tasks. Currently, they are being used to sheer sheep, disarm mines, and to perform delicate experiments in bioengineering laboratories (Kurzweil, 1990). Wabot-2, a third-generation robot, reads sheet music, plays the organ, can trace the pitch of a human singer and adjust its playing tempo accordingly, and is capable of engaging in a simple conversation (Roads, 1986).

• • •

SUMMARY

Ethics

With new ideas come new responsibility. Although there are several ethical issues associated with the increasing use of computers in various societies, some are more pertinent to the educational researcher than others.

COPYRIGHT

Making an unauthorized copy of software is often referred to as pirating. Once a particular program is purchased, a user is allowed to make one copy of the software for archival (backup) purposes. More copies are considered illegal. The sale of pirated software is frowned upon even more. It takes time and effort to produce quality software. Software authors need to be encouraged, not turned away because the market is poor due to an illegal proliferation of their products. However, besides the obvious moral and legal issues associated with the breaking of copyright law, the spread of "infected" disks is becoming a major problem. Computer viruses account for much of the computer crime that sabotages or destroys computer files. A computer virus is a small computer program, written by malicious individuals, and placed on a computer disk. It is designed to alter or damage other computer files on the disk or the internal hard disk of a computer. The primary source of virus contact is the sharing of computer disks by unsuspecting users, such as the exchange of software. Viruses are often very difficult to detect until they have caused damage. However, many virus protection programs are currently available, often for free.

ACCURACY

The sheer speed at which data can be generated, analyzed, and shared makes researchers even more obligated to ensure that their research is scholarly and accurate. Because of the enormous quantity of writing, brought about through word processing, the normal safe guards of traditional publishing may be weakened or be rendered inoperative (Heim, 1987). We may become less thorough, critical, and reflective.

PEDAGOGIC RESPONSIBILITY

Through the use of graphics, sound, animation, and the like, computer programs can be truly entertaining. As well, the power and convenience afforded by administrative tools can be very appealing. Educators should be careful to scrutinize the educational merit of the programs they employ as instructional aids and guard against unquestioned reliance on electronic information systems. Too much emphasis could be placed on the theatrics of some educational software or the data generated by powerful utilities. Not enough emphasis may be placed on instruction.

When we use any tool, that instrument mediates our experience (Ihde, 1990). Therefore computers have an effect on our lives. Critics of technology warn of the dangers of "technological thinking" (Barrett, 1979; Leiss, 1990; Mumford, 1967). They are often cautious, even pessimistic, about a technological future. It is the responsibility of educators to be sensitive to the experiences students have in the presence of computers. They should become familiar with the theories of human–computer interaction. As they teach students to use technology to transcend the human condition, they must balance their enthusiasm by informing students of the technological condition, instilling in their students a responsibility toward informed and prudent use of these powerful technologies.

EQUITY

There is evidence to support that computer technology has created inequities. Cole and Griffin's national survey of American schools (cited in Cochran-Smith, 1991) found that middle- and upper-class children have more access to computers than do poor children, poor children are more likely to be instructed with drill-and-practice rather than more enrichment software, and regardless of ethnic origin or class, girls are less involved with computers in school than boys are.

The computer as a tool for students means higher production, higher quality, and more fun, but the other side of the coin suggests that computer technology also may mean greater gender and socio-economic discrimination.

• • •

CONCLUSION

Computer technology has evolved quickly and educational research and practice has reaped many of the benefits. Small desktop machines are able to collect, store, and analyze data efficiently and expediently. The carrying out of research projects, the writing of research documents, and the daily management duties of instruction and learning has become far less difficult through the assistance of word processor, spreadsheet, database, and specialized productivity software. Statistics and text coding programs are serving the needs of both quantitative and qualitative researchers, allowing both more time to interpret data. Information technology enables researchers and teachers around the globe to communicate and collaborate as they become "connected" through such electronic networks as the *Internet*. As well, the information disseminated by the entire scientific and educational communities is readily available through both on-line and off-line databases. New developments in educational computer technology offer practitioners more opportunities to share with their students exciting interactive materials and alternate delivery strategies. Moreover, the future holds many new promises of new research fields for educators as investigations and developments of artificial intelligence theories and applications produce more insight into human learning and understanding.

• • •

REFERENCES

Adams, R. S. (1989). Computers in school: What's the real use? *Issues 89, 6*, 26–31.

Barrett, W. (1979). *The illusion of technique.* New York: Anchor Books.

Bresler, L., & Walker, D. (1990). Implementation of computer-based innovation: A case study. *Journal of Computer-Based Instruction, 17*(2), 66–72.

Bullough, R. V., & Beatty, L. F. (1991). *Classroom applications of microcomputers.* Toronto: Collier Macmillan Canada.

Burnett, D. (1988). The spirit of logo. Proceedings of the Sixth Annual Conference of the ATA Computer Council. Calgary, Alberta.

Burns, B., & Hagerman, A. (1989). Computer experience, self-concept and problem-solving: The effect of logo on children's idea of themselves as learners. *Journal of Educational Computing Research, 5*(2), 199–212.

Cochran-Smith, M. (1991). Word processing and writing in elementary classrooms: A critical review of related literature. *Review of Educational Research, 61*(1), 107–155.

Colantonio, E. (1989). *Microcomputers and applications.* Toronto: D.C. Heath.

Cross, K. P. (1988). *Adults as learners.* San Francisco: Jossey-Bass Publishers.

Emihovich, C., & Miller, G. (1988). Effects of logo and CAI on black first graders' achievement, reflectivity, and self-esteem. *The Elementary School Journal, 88*(5), 473–487.

Frasson, C., & Gauthier, G. (1990). *Intelligent tutoring systems: At the crossroads of artificial intelligence and education.* New Jersey: Ablex.

Greenfield, P. M. (1987). Electronic technologies, education, and cognitive development. In D. Berger, K. Pezdek, & W. Banks (Eds.), *Applications of cognitive psychology: Problem solving education, and computing* (pp. 17–32). Hillsdale, NJ: Lawrence Erlbaum.

Heim, M. (1987). *Electric language: A philosophical study of word processing.* New Haven, CT: Yale University Press.

Hergenhahn, B. R. (1988). *An introduction to theories of learning* (3rd ed.). Englewood Cliffs, NJ: Prentice-Hall.

Hofmeister, A. (1988). *Expert systems and decision support in special education: Results and promises. A technical paper.* Logan, UT: Utah State University.

Ihde, D. (1990). *Technology and the lifeworld.* Indianapolis, IN: Indiana University Press.

Joyce, C. (1988). This machine wants to help you. *Psychology Today, 22*(2), 44–50.

Keller, F. S. (1968). Good-bye teacher. *Journal of Applied Behavior Analysis, 1,* 69–89.

Khayrallah, M., & van den Meiraker, M. (1987). Logo programming and the acquisition of cognitive skills. *Journal of Computer-Based Instruction, 14*(4), 133–137.

Knowles, M. (1984). *The adult learner: A neglected species.* Houston: Gulf Publishing.

Kolich, E. M. (1985). Microcomputer technology with the learning disabled: A review of the literature. *Journal of Learning Disabilities, 18*(7), 428–431.

Krasnor, L., & Mitterer, J. (1984). Logo and the development of general problem-solving skills. *Alberta Journal of Educational Research, 30*(2), 133–144.

Kulik, J., & Kulik, C. (1987). *Computer-based instruction: What 200 evaluations say.* Paper presented at the Annual Convention of the Association for Educational Communications and Technology, Atlanta, GA. (ERIC Document Reproduction Service No. ED 285 521).

Kurzweil, R. (1990). *The age of intelligent machines.* Cambridge, MA: Massachusetts Institute of Technology Press.

Laboratory of Comparative Human Cognition. (1989). Kids and computers: A positive vision of the future. *Harvard Educational Review, 59*(1), 73–86.

Lauda, D. P. (1989). Technology education: Its place in the secondary school. *NASSP Bulletin, 73*(519), 1–3.

Leiss, W. (1990). *Under technology's thumb.* Montreal: McGill-Queen's University Press.

Lubke, M. (1988). *Expert systems: Where do you start.* Paper presented at CEC/TAM Conference on Special Education and Technology, Reno, NV.

Luehrmann, A. (1980). Computer, illiteracy: A national crisis and a solution. *Byte, 5*(7), 98–102.

Mayer, R. E., Bayman, P., & Dyck, J. L. (1987). Learning programming languages: Research and application. In D. Berger, K. Pezdek, & W. Banks (Eds.), *Applications of cognitive psychology: Problem solving education, and computing* (pp. 17–32). Hillsdale, NJ: Lawrence Erlbaum.

Molnar, A. (1978, July–August). The next great crisis in American education: Computer literacy. *The Journal, Technological Horizons in Education.*

Morgan, D. P., & Rhode, G. (1983). Teachers' attitudes toward IEPS: A two-year follow-up. *Exceptional Children, 50*(1), 64–67.

Mumford, L. (1967). *Technics and human development: The myth of the new machine.* New York: Harcourt Brace Jovanovich.

Papert, S. (1987). Computer criticism vs. technocentric thinking. *Educational Researcher, 16*(1), 22–30.

Quarterman, J. (1990). *The matrix.* Austin, TX: Digital Press.

Reiser, R. A. (1987). Instructional technology: A history. In R. M. Gagne (Ed.), *Instructional technology: Foundations* (pp. 11–48). Hillsdale, NJ: Lawrence Erlbaum.

Roads, C. (Summer, 1986). The tsukuba music robot. *Computer Music Journal, 10*(2), 39–43.

Ross, S. M., & Morrison, G. R. (1989). In search of a happy medium in instructional technology research: Issues concerning external validity, media replications, and learner control. *Educational Technology Research and Development, 37*(1), 19–33.

Skinner, B. F. (1958). Teaching machines. *Science, 128*, 969–977.

Tennyson, R. D., & Park, O. C. (1987). Artificial intelligence and computer-based learning. In R. M. Gagne (Ed.), *Instructional technology: Foundations* (pp. 319–342). Hillsdale, NJ: Lawrence Erlbaum.

Waterman, D. A. (1986). *A guide to expert systems.* Don Mills, ON: Addison-Wesley.

Weir, S. (1989). The computer in schools: Machine as humanizer. *Harvard Educational Review, 59*(1), 61–73.

Wenger, E. (1987). *Artificial intelligence and tutoring systems: Computational and cognitive approaches to the communication of knowledge.* Los Altos, CA: Morgan Kaufmann Publishers.

ONLY IN CANADA YOU SAY—PITY!:

ON THE GENERALIZABILITY OF FRENCH IMMERSION RESULTS TO ENGLISH IMMERSION AND OTHER COUNTRIES

...

Stephen Carey

One of the critical questions surrounding education via a second language in general and Canadian French immersion programs in particular concerns the capability of these programs to produce students who can successfully compete academically in these second languages. The question is an important one globally since presently more than half of the world's students are receiving their education through the medium of a second language. Consequently, an increased understanding of the particular language and comprehension competencies that education via a second language such as French immersion can produce may be used not only to improve immersion programs but also to improve academic programs in second languages elsewhere in the world. There has been a massive amount of research on bilingualism both in Canada, due to the implementation of official bilingualism, and in the U.S.A., due to the debates on the optimal weighting and sequencing of languages in transitional bilingual schooling for immigrant populations. The results from research on bilingual schooling in North America are frequently referred to by other countries that are in the process of language planning for schools.

In addition, due to the globally prevalent realignment of old national boundaries or the creation of new countries and language borders there are a large number of countries that are in the process of changing their national language(s) policy and in particular their language policy for schooling. While these evolving language policies may entrench the linguistic rights of the constituent ethnic groups on the one hand, there is a new fervour to also produce a policy for schooling that will provide students with the competitive edge to compete in the rapidly expanding and increasingly competitive global economy.

This factor of competitiveness in an increasingly tight global economy casts existing language policy in a new role in many countries that have thrown off their colonial languages after gaining their independence. For example, some African countries discontinued the language policy of schooling their children in the colonial language and eagerly embraced schooling in a black language as part of their expression of a post-colonial black nationalism. These countries now find themselves expressing a need to re-implement that colonial language as the language of schooling in order to produce graduates that compete effectively in the global academic market as well as in the global economy. In many respects, this choice reflects the maturity and self-confidence of these countries that may have gained this self-assurance from having developed their educational system in a black language and then subsequently developed a language policy that reflected their political and economic reality. Such countries as Namibia, Tanzania, and South Africa look to the research results on immersion programs and bilingual education in Canada to inform their discussions and deliberations on language policy. Consequently, the choice of the particular language for schooling may be the same language as the original colonial language. However, it is not perceived as such because this language has been chosen by the populace as an extension of their development beyond their indigenous languages, rather than being perceived as a language imposed by a colonial power. For example, in South Africa there is a strong demand by the black population for access to education in English rather than in their indigenous black languages. This is because they regard English as the vehicle to political and economic power and black language education is viewed as limiting their future development. Moreover, the results from Canadian immersion programs and programs elsewhere are cited as evidence that students can be educated via a second language at no cost to their first language or to academic mastery.

Those who make these generalizations may fail to realize that the level of literacy developed by students prior to their enrolment in Canadian French immersion schools is quite different than that of black students in South Africa. Nevertheless, the motivation and positive attitudes among some black students towards learning English as a second language (ESL) may be so powerful as to overcome this difference in emergent literacy between black students and typical Canadian immersion students.

This point is critical since it has become perhaps the best known and universal finding from research on second language acquisition, namely, that the attitudes within the family, school, and society may be very powerful predictors of the students' attainment of proficiency in that language. Thus differing attitudes towards a language may reflect the communicative capital or utility of the language (Bourdieu, 1980), or the status of the language group with which the language is associated (Lambert, 1974). These differing attitudinal factors may also explain many of the apparent discrepancies between research findings or educational outcomes from various bilingual and immersion programs.

The power of attitudes toward and status of the second language in influencing that language's acquisition has been extremely well documented in the research on immersion programs and was an important component in the implementation of these programs as amply demonstrated in the research by Wallace Lambert and Robert Gardner. For example, in order to improve the marketability of French immersion programs in Canada, it was important to associate them with a new methodology of "l'approche communicative" and a certain bilingual elite who were of upper socio-economic status and who would have access to improved educational, employment, and political opportunities in a new bilingual Canada. Similarly it was essential to distance this form of learning French from that old drill method of learning French by the "j'entre dans la salle de classe" method, that in some parts of western Canada was as renowned for its inability to produce communicative French as it was for producing a dislike for the French language. Consequently, in the initial promotion and lobbying for French immersion programs, which were seen as essential for the promotion of the new bilingual policy in Canada, it was imperative that these programs be perceived as successful since they were, for many people, the flagship of the new bilingual policy for education in a bilingual country.

Thus, consultants to the government and ministries insisted on the necessity for these programs to be perceived in a very positive light. The programs had to be presented as highly successful and capable of producing a high degree of competence in French. It was even suggested that these enriched programs would possibly lead to some cognitive advantages, giving rise to an even higher academic achievement than was likely for someone who enrolled in a regular unilingual program. One researcher went so far as to claim that parents who didn't enrol their children in these new cognitively enriching programs that produced "cognitive flexibility" should be liable to be charged with child neglect. Of course "cognitive flexibility" was often not well defined or was defined in a rather circular way such that someone who spent more time on symbol manipulation would be better at symbol manipulation, which was then defined as cognitive flexibility. Such circumlocutions, however, were nevertheless acceptable to those who were more than a little "cognitively flexible" (even loose) themselves.

However, these new French programs have been instrumental in promoting a new sense of promise and purpose to official bilingualism that led to even greater promotion by the federal government. What is critical to realize is that if the acquisition of a second language has status, if it can be perceived as representing access to power and prestige, and if it can be viewed as being essential to employment and political office, then the acquisition of that language, like the acquisition of any other form of social behaviour, should be more easily attainable. Furthermore, if researchers were able to find all sorts of "cognitive advantages" to these politically motivated programs, there could be no harm in providing government subsidies for journals to promote these findings and for funding of centres that would do action research that promoted the benefits of bilingualism. These are standard procedures in language planning and policy for those countries that have the human and financial resources to do so. Canadian French immersion programs are widely recognized as one example of successful official bilingual language planning in Canada. However, although the promotion of bilingualism is central to the mission of the federal government and it was appropriate to provide funding to ensure the success and perceived success of these programs, it is important when attempting to generalize these findings to other countries to bear in mind that Canada had the human and financial resources to dedicate to this national challenge. Consequently, it is important to recognize the difficulty of generalizing these results to other educational situations. Indeed, the results from immersion studies in Canada are often used inappropriately to argue against other language programs in other settings both nationally and internationally where the financial and human resources for teacher training programs, curriculum development, and implementation do not enjoy the same national commitment.

• • •

SOME IMPLICATIONS OF IMMERSION FINDINGS

It is often claimed that English-speaking students, who enrol in Canadian early French immersion programs starting with day care, kindergarten or Grade 1 and continue their schooling in French, have no loss in academic achievement or in their mother tongue of English. This claim has several implications, interpretations, and misinterpretations.

First, if English-speaking students can be immersed in second language French schooling, then some would argue it should follow that non-English-speaking students can be immersed in regular English-speaking programs with no need for special mother tongue education prior to English as a Second Language (ESL) programs for immigrant children who wish to be educated in English. Consequently, some would argue that there should be no need for special transitional bilingual programs in California for hispanics since these individuals should be able to be immersed in English from Grade 1 just as English-speaking children are immersed in French from Grade 1. Similarly, some would claim that in many countries throughout the world, such as in Namibia, Tanzania, or South Africa, that non-English-speaking students could be successfully immersed in English with no loss to academic or mother tongue achievement. Let us consider each of these claims individually.

ESL in Canada

Since ESL students in cities such as Vancouver, Toronto, or even San Francisco are truly immersed in an English environment in which English has high status and is readily accessible for all aspects of living it is possible to say that this is a total immersion experience. However, there are several problems with this orientation. First, there is the danger that this could be a "submersion" experience. If only a few ESL students are placed in a class or school where the remainder of the students are anglophones, consequently the ESL student is placed in a language environment that is simply overwhelming. The student will comprehend little of the social interchange that will lead to feelings of frustration and alienation. While this may be unlikely in Vancouver, since more than fifty percent of students in Vancouver are ESL students and there are many classes and schools where ESL students comprise the majority of students, there are settings throughout North America where this does occur. Furthermore, in many schools and classes the unilingual anglophone is the minority child who is to some degree immersed in a multilingual social setting of other ESL students. However, this is a distinctly different classroom from some of the traditional French immersion programs that in the past often consisted of classes where the majority of anglophone children came from unilingual backgrounds. Consequently, we have to be careful in generalizing from French immersion programs to ESL programs.

A second difference between French immersion schooling and ESL programs is that traditionally, French immersion students were schooled in French for a few hours each day and then lived in an English environment for the remainder of the time. Because French immersion students did not use their French outside the classroom, much to the disappointment of many French immersion teachers, there was little danger of their losing their fluency in their mother tongue. It is a very different situation for ESL students who may not have sufficient opportunity to maintain their mother tongue. Consequently, their first language may fall into disuse or if they are second generation immigrants, the initial acquisition of their first language may be incomplete and the language will be even more rapidly lost. Finally, French immersion teachers ideally had special training programs to qualify them as second language teachers. Unfortunately, this is not always the case for all ESL teachers. In many cities, every teacher is an ESL teacher and there is an increasing need for all teacher preparation programs to incorporate second language teaching courses. This trend will only increase in the future as the unilingual child becomes more and more a minority person in many cities and therefore all teachers will require second language immersion teacher training.

With regards to generalizing French immersion results to situations in African countries, it is important to consider the specifics of each situation. For diverse reasons, many groups are demanding access to English education and claiming that denial to English education is denying them access to the international language of commerce and academia. In Namibia for example where English has recently been adopted as an official language, there are neither sufficient trained teachers nor books nor the budget to remedy the situation and it is problematic to attempt to generalize the results from Canadian immersion studies to such a situation. First, one must consider Namibia's motivation for choosing English as the official language when the language is spoken by few Namibians but is regarded by many Namibians as a neutral language that has the potential for giving the country a window on the economic and academic world. To compare this situation with Canada's necessity to promote bilingualism is strained but also instructive. Because countries like Namibia have several local language groups that compete with each other, one way to unite the country is to have an official language that favours none of the competing groups thus eliminating the friction between the rival parties. In this way the goal of unity of the country is promoted just as unity is promoted in Canada through the promotion of bilingualism. The difference is that these countries lack the resources, both human and financial, to implement a policy of English as the language of education. In Canada, one of the major difficulties in promoting immersion programs has been to train a sufficient number of French immersion teachers who are competent in both French and English languages. The problem is compounded in countries like Namibia, Tanzania, or South Africa by the low level of literacy, the lack of teacher training programs, the general low level of education of the populace, the lack of an educational infrastructure, and the lack of a budget with which to rectify the situation. Moreover, the low participation rate of students is accompanied by a high dropout rate.

While some of these factors would make the challenge seem insurmountable, programs like Canadian French immersion give room for hope in some of these countries where it is difficult to imagine the English school language being used outside the school in the first years of schooling, just as French is not used by Canadian French immersion students outside the school. Since French immersion programs produce communicative competence even though the students do not typically use this language outside the school, there is some hope in Namibia that a level of communicative competence could be reasonably expected even though it is unlikely the students could use the language in the first years of their schooling in socio-linguistic settings outside the class, such as the home or town.

Similarly, in South Africa, there is growing pressure by the black communities in their demand for access to English instruction as the route to political, economic, and academic power. The strong desire on the part of these communities to demand an English education for their children will be their strongest ally. As stated above, for those students who identify the acquisition of a second language as essential for access to power, social status, and economic well-being, the possibilities for language acquisition even in positions of minimal infrastructure, teacher training, and resource materials can be encouraging. In this sense, language planners and policy makers do not have to market ESL in South Africa in the same way that bilingualism was promoted in Canada; nevertheless the task is daunting. French immersion programs in Canada still only comprise a small percentage of the total school population after a truly heroic effort on the federal government's part to promote them. In South Africa, an English immersion program would be needed for over ninety percent of the population with few resources and a limited government budget to implement such a massive initiative. The enormity of the undertaking is apparent.

Bilingual Transitional Programs for Minorities in the U.S.

The success of education through a second language as demonstrated by Canadian French immersion programs is frequently used as an argument to deride the necessity for bilingual transitional programs for minorities. Since anglophones can be placed in a total French immersion program, why cannot immigrant and hispanic populations in the U.S. be placed in total mainstream

English classes? The traditional argument has been that such students would be submerged in an English class that was simply over their heads leading to frustration and academic loss. More recently, it has become evident in places like California and British Columbia that the majority of the student population will be ESL and even elsewhere in North America where we have a reversal of roles between majority and minority language roles. In most classes in Los Angeles, San Francisco, or Vancouver the majority of the students are ESL and traditional arguments that ESL students will be submerged or placed in a class where the level of language usage is over their heads is rapidly becoming an anachronism.

• • •

CONCLUSION

Thus in many areas of North America the growth of cosmopolitan cities will necessitate teacher preparation programs that will require all teachers to be schooled in teaching in a second language. The important lessons that we have learned from Canadian French immersion programs, which in themselves had a methodology based on much that was learned from ESL, now have contributed to second language learning situations throughout the world and have both informed and been informed by those second language educational situations.

• • •

REFERENCES

Bourdieu, P. (1980). *La distinction*. Paris: Editions de Minuit.

Gardner, R. (1985). *Social psychology and second language learning: The role of attitudes and motivation*. London: Edward Arnold.

Lambert, W.E. (1974). The St. Lambert project. In S.T. Carey (Ed.), *Bilingualism, biculturalism and education*. Edmonton: University of Alberta Press.

NATIONAL TESTING IN CANADA

...

Roger Palmer

Jim Brackenbury

INTRODUCTION

At their 1991 meeting in Whistler, B.C., the Canadian premiers directed the Council of Ministers of Education, Canada (CMEC) to continue its efforts to "put in place effective mechanisms for appropriate evaluation and improved accountability in provincial and territorial education systems. These mechanisms should be developed with teachers, parents, trustees and other interest groups. The objectives to be addressed are high standards of numeracy and literacy, and the development of a true lifelong learning culture." For Canada, this was an unprecedented commitment to a national education initiative.

The idea of a national test was raised at a June 1988 meeting of provincial educational officials in Edmonton in the aftermath of the publication of the Southam News 1987 study of literacy in Canada, and as a follow-up to a CMEC 1987 study of student and system evaluation across Canada. A national assessment of student achievement had been considered impossible because education in Canada is a provincial responsibility. A national testing program was seen as an infringement on the autonomy of the provincial education systems. However, Southam had provided a national measure of our performance—or at least that was how it was being portrayed in the press. The educational system was being judged on the basis of this test, and whether the educational community thought it a reasonable basis for judgment or not, the public and our politicians took it very seriously indeed. The educational system had been judged and had been found wanting.

• • •

THE NEED FOR A VERY
DIFFERENT EDUCATION SYSTEM

Education is at the top of the political agenda. The federal government's prosperity initiative (1991) has focussed on education and training as critical to our economic future and almost every province has an educational reform program. The premise is simple: global developments are making us truly one world, and as we evolve to post-industrial, knowledge-based societies, our economies will depend on the intellectual and creative skills of the citizens to a much greater extent than ever before.

If such an evolution is possible, success will depend on our ability to create an educational system that is very much more powerful than the one we have now. An industrialized economy had jobs for relatively unskilled workers. Dropping out of school was unfortunate but was not a disaster. The post-industrial society will have much more limited room for such people. North American economists project that new jobs created over the next decade will require much higher levels of education. The proportion of jobs that will be available to young people with less than Grade 12 will be much lower. Most new jobs will require post-secondary training and that training will become outdated more quickly. It is no good to counter the demands for lower dropout rates by pointing out that our current rate is the lowest in history. The skills and knowledge we now expect of our high school graduates must be expected of all our students, and we need to raise the expected level of skills for our academically talented students to much higher levels.

Whether we accept this as a plausible scenario or not, the important consequence is the remarkable coincidence of objectives of the educational community and the political agenda. While the attention directed at the university-bound student has been a point of friction between the educational and business communities, teachers care about all students. Educators have been trying to increase the emphasis on communication skills and problem solving for years. The educational system now envisaged by the business leaders has the same goals. The potential for synergy is enormous.

Time For "Show Me"

Fortunately, the politicians in Canada have not followed the lead of those in many parts of the United States. There, the political solutions have tended towards minimum competency tests and increased course requirements. So far, our leaders seem more willing to accept the professional responsibility of educators to decide how the system should change. What they are demanding is evidence of change. As the minister of education for Alberta said to a meeting of school trustees, we've passed time for "believe me," it is time for "show me."

This demand for accountability is not a uniquely Canadian phenomenon. Many industrialized nations are trying to define educational performance measures. The Organization for Economic Co-operation and Development (OECD) has made education its top priority and is developing a system of international educational indicators: England has introduced a National Curriculum and a system of Standardized Assessment Tests; Australia and New Zealand are redesigning their curricula and assessment systems; and the United States is moving towards national testing. In each case there is a similar political and economic rationale.

The Southam News literacy study (1987) is significant because it gave politicians and business leaders a simple measure of our overall performance in one key area. Educators know that it was a simplistic measure that said very little about the current situation in our schools but, in the absence of anything better, it will remain a basis for judging the system. Our task is to provide a valid measure of the performance of the educational system while providing the evidence that the public demands, in a form that looks simple.

Teachers have resisted the introduction of external measures of educational performance for good reason. Test results have sometimes been misused in the past and any system of measures can narrow the curriculum. Measuring the right skills in the right way is critical. The November 1991 issue of *Kappan* provides a very good summary of the pitfalls of high-risk large scale testing. These problems are well known and we must do our best to address them. But the educational systems will be judged. We can provide valid data for an informed judgment or we can leave it to non-educators to provide the picture they wish to present. It is up to us to decide.

• • •

SAIP: NOT A MINIMUM COMPETENCY TEST

A central assumption of the CMEC School Achievement Indicators Program (SAIP) is that there are a few key elements that can be measured that provide a good proxy of the overall health of the system. Carefully selected statistical information can be a reliable measure of how the systems are doing. The key indicators chosen were student participation rates, graduation rates, and student achievement in the areas of reading, writing, mathematical content, and mathematical problem solving.

This article will not deal with the technical concerns of achieving consistent measures of participation and graduation. CMEC, in co-operation with Statistics Canada, has developed definitions that can be applied by the provinces to obtain comparable data in these areas. Clearly, it is important to have this type of information if we are committed to a philosophy of education for all students. A focus on participation rates also helps to avoid the potential for manipulation of achievement information.

Representatives from the provincial ministries of education were charged with the task of designing the guiding principles for the achievement testing program. The design accepted by the ministers through their 1988, 1989, and 1990 meetings had the following features:

- The test would be low risk. The program would be a measure of the performance of the provincial educational system, not of individual students. A matrix sampling technique would be used that guaranteed the anonymity of the students involved. It was agreed that the lowest level of reporting would be the province, not the school district, not the school, and not the classroom.
- The assessment instruments were to be criterion-based, designed from criteria for reading, writing, and mathematics that were agreed upon by representatives from ministries and departments of education across Canada. While the existing provincial curricula would be respected, the assessment would not be narrowly linked to the curriculum of any particular province.
- The results would report the profile of achievement in each province and Canada-wide, not an average or any other single number. To achieve this, criteria would be developed that describe five levels of achievement in each of the target areas that would span the full range of achievement that might be expected among the students in school.
- The changes in achievement over time are as important as the absolute results. The assessment should be designed to facilitate longitudinal comparisons.
- Students aged thirteen and sixteen would be involved in the assessment. Ages rather than grades were used to define the population because of the different streaming practices among the provinces; we wanted a measure that was not contaminated by different definitions of the target populations. Sixteen was easily agreed to because it is the end of compulsory

schooling in most of Canada—the oldest group where the vast majority are still in school. There was considerable debate about the choice of thirteen. In the end it was a compromise that would allow some opportunity to show growth but still be close enough to sixteen so that the same test could be used with both ages to provide comparability.

- The minimum sample of students would be involved in the test that would still be fully representative of the provincial populations. (Later the provision for individual provinces to select from other large sub-populations within their province was incorporated into the plan.)
- The assessment would be designed with the largest possible participation of teachers and ministry officials from all the provinces, and from other stakeholder groups, to help screen the instrument for quality and validation considerations, including cultural and social bias.

Stating the principles this way does not reflect the way that the project evolved. Throughout its four-year history, the project has been revised and reconfirmed many times. As the participants changed, parts of the plan were reworded to meet the political needs of the ministers. The development process was not smooth. However, the plan is much the same as that originally accepted by the ministers at their Regina meeting in 1988. That is not to diminish the political importance of the changes of nuance the ministers required along the way.

The five-level structure scheme was chosen as a way of making a clear break with any perception that this would be a minimum competency assessment. This structure is not based on formal stage theory. Level five has been defined with the expectation that very few students can demonstrate that level of knowledge and understanding. However, some students will have reached this level, allowing us to display our high expectations for the academically talented and put to rest the widely held view that schools are not challenging. We hope to show that more and more students are reaching level five at each subsequent administration of the assessment. Similarly, nearly all students should be at or beyond level one by age thirteen. In future, we will be able to provide evidence of improvement by pointing to a decline in the proportion of students at level one. It is anticipated that this will provide a framework for teachers to work towards growth with every child, according to ability and background without the unrealistic implication that each student should be achieving at some fixed national standard.

A 1989 CMEC study found that no existing test or set of tests could meet these requirements. Therefore the ministers established a consortium of the

CMEC Secretariat, Alberta Education, le Ministère de l'Éducation du Québec, and, since January, 1992, the Ontario Ministry of Education, to develop the test instruments. The work of the consortium has been directed by a "Request for Proposals (1990)," prepared by the Ad Hoc Test Development Group and approved by the Deputy Ministers Steering Committee in December, 1989. The workplan was further modified by a "Memorandum of Understanding (1991)," agreed to at the 60th CMEC meeting and by a "Letter of Agreement (1992)" agreed to by the CMEC Secretariat, Alberta, Quebec, and Ontario.

• • •

THE DEVELOPMENT OF THE SCHOOL ACHIEVEMENT INDICATORS PROGRAM

Stage One: Development of the Criteria

The consortium started its work on student achievement indicators in the fall of 1990. The first stage involved the development of criteria describing student performance across five broad levels of achievement in reading, writing, and mathematics.

Ministries of education named key contact people to work with the consortium team. The key contact people responded to various drafts of criteria and related documents and met in January, 1991, to endorse the preliminary criteria as the basis for consultation meetings in each province and territory. The extent and nature of consultation on the preliminary criteria varied significantly across the country. In some instances, discussions were limited to departmental staff, in other instances to subject advisory committees and specialist teacher councils, and in other instances to regional meetings involving a wide cross section of education and community groups and organizations.

CMEC held a national meeting of more than twenty non-governmental organizations in Toronto on 5 June 1991. Materials prepared by the project team were distributed to participants prior to the meeting; revised drafts were distributed at the meeting. Project team members served as small group consultants. Participants reviewed materials in small groups and provided reactions and recommendations to the project team.

Meetings of "independent consultants" were held the next two days at the CMEC office in Toronto. These independent consultants were selected from across the country by the CMEC Secretariat in consultation with the project teams. They represented a variety of academic interests in reading, writing, and mathematics. Most were from university faculties. They reviewed all materials and provided reactions and recommendations to the project team.

Revised criteria and related materials were sent to ministries in preparation for an interprovincial/territorial meeting in Toronto on 20–21 June. At that meeting, the criteria for numeracy, reading, and writing were endorsed as the basis for assessment instrument development. Specific conditions were attached, including the limitation that the criteria not be regarded as "final," but would continue to evolve throughout the project as a result of additional consultation and field testing.

These recommendations were endorsed at the August, 1991, meeting of the Advisory Committee of Deputy Ministers of Education (ACDME) and at the September meeting of the Ministers of Education, Canada (CMEC). This successfully concluded the first stage of the project.

The most significant caveat to this apparent success was the "observer status" role announced by the Honourable Marion Boyd, Minister of Education, on behalf of the government of Ontario. Although Ontario officials received all draft materials during this period, and had an "observer" present at each of the meetings of key contacts, no input was received from Ontario officials on the various drafts of the criteria and related materials. Notwithstanding this important limitation, the project team was authorized to proceed with the second stage of the project, the development of assessment instruments based on the criteria.

Stage Two: Development of the Assessment Instruments

The major emphasis in this stage was on the development of alternative forms of assessment instruments in reading, writing, mathematical content, and mathematical problem solving for thirteen- and sixteen-year-old students.

Textual material for the reading assessment was solicited from ministries in the spring of 1991. Through consultation with individual ministries, it was generally agreed that available assessment instruments and activities were unlikely to match the particular needs of the CMEC assessment, given the criterion-referenced descriptions that had been developed in stage one of the project. Ministries were invited to send teacher participants to the summer work sessions as an alternative. This option was exercised in Halifax, where teachers from Nova Scotia, New Brunswick, Prince Edward Island, and Newfoundland and Labrador participated.

Teacher committees met during the summer of 1991 in Halifax, Quebec City, Edmonton, and Calgary to develop assessment activities and instruments. Members of the Quebec and Alberta project team participated in each of these work sessions. The Halifax work sessions were organized co-operatively by the

Atlantic provinces, with members of the project team in attendance. Considerable follow-up work was done by team members, both individually and through joint meetings.

The project team prepared initial field trial materials that were tested out in Alberta, Quebec, and New Brunswick schools in October, 1991. Results of these preliminary trials were used to revise, re-develop, and reject various assessment activities. In addition, questionnaires were developed to collect information from students about background and their related interests and activities.

The project team met on a number of occasions to ensure parallel assessment instrument forms and questionnaires for field testing. It has been particularly challenging to ensure that the assessment instruments being developed are parallel in both languages, an issue still not fully resolved as this is written.

Sampling design and placement procedures for field-testing were completed by the project team in March, 1992. All provinces and territories except Saskatchewan identified specific schools and target groups for the May, 1992 field tests. Field tests and questionnaires were finalized for Canada-wide field testing in May and June, 1992.

Development work on stage two was significantly affected by the December, 1991 Memorandum of Understanding (MOU), which served as the basis for Ontario's re-entry to the program. This MOU outlined the objectives for the program as well as a number of conditions to be met in the development of the program. The MOU included provision for the active participation of all provinces and territories in all phases of the program. It included a commitment to ensure that the assessment techniques respond to current pedagogical practice. It included the requirement of a process to ensure that the assessment instruments are as much as possible in keeping with the curriculum requirements and orientations of the provinces and territories. It outlined procedures to ensure that the assessment instruments are free from cultural and gender bias and stereotyping so that all sectors of the population are fairly treated. It included a provision for Ontario to participate in the consortium. Other provisions related to sampling, report development, budget, scheduling, and communication strategies.

Following the MOU, officials from Ontario, Quebec, Alberta, and the Secretariat negotiated a Letter of Agreement in January, 1992. This letter outlined the specific provisions regarding Ontario's involvement as a member of the consortium. One consequence was the need for significantly more direct meetings of the project team than had originally been planned.

Ministries provided extraordinary co-operation in providing timely feedback on bias reviews and sample selection. Summaries of feedback received on bias reviews were prepared and distributed to ministry officials. The feedback was valuable in preparing materials to the field test stage. The field test stage provided another significant opportunity for ministries to provide comprehensive feedback to the project team.

The CMEC Secretariat provided national non-governmental organizations with bulletins and background papers regarding the progress of the project to date. A detailed response to a brief from the Canadian School Boards Association was prepared jointly by the Secretariat and the project team, and distributed widely.

Members of the project team met with representatives of the Report Development Group in February, 1992, and reached agreement on a number of recommendations regarding the reporting of results.

Instrument Design

MATHEMATICS

The idea of using two separate instruments to measure content and problem solving was endorsed at the June, 1991 meeting of key ministry contacts. For the content component, the assessment will be divided into five parts, one part per level. A placement test will determine the student's entry level. Each student will be required to do at least two levels in order to show what he or she can do. For the problem-solving component, the students will be given a number of problems that will elicit student performance at more than one level. Some problems are intended to facilitate the demonstation of performance at all five levels described by the criteria. All students will be given a student questionnaire on their school, language, and mathematics background.

In order to specify the content of the assessment in relationship to the criteria, a definition of domains complemented by a table of specifications was established and presented in the 17 June 1991 document entitled "Considerations for Instrument Design." That document specified the assessment domains concerning the evaluation of conceptual knowledge and understanding, procedural knowledge, and the ability to use and solve problems. It also presented the distribution of items by mathematical ability and by strand and level.

In July and August of 1991, over 650 items were developed in item-building activities that involved fifty teachers from Alberta, Quebec, and the Atlantic provinces. Because of the high costs and the complexity of building appropriate problems for the problem solving component, approximately thirty problems were built by experts in the field. All questions and problems were field-tested on a small scale in Alberta and Quebec in the fall and were revised extensively by the work teams and committees of teachers from Quebec, Alberta, and Ontario before the general field-testing stage.

READING

The final reading assessment instrument is expected to comprise three forms that will be assigned to students according to a multiple matrix sampling model. Although the individual student will only be exposed to four texts, this model allows for more diversity in the overall choice of types and contents of texts. Each form is expected to contain four texts and between forty and fifty accompanying questions of various types (selected response and constructed response). The texts on each form will be of varying degrees of difficulty. The nature and content of texts selected for the assessment greatly influence the questions or tasks to be developed. Item development schemes were modified for some texts because all pieces of literature do not lend themselves to the same development pattern.

The questions on each form are intended to cover the full range of levels described by the criteria and students will be asked to do as many as they can.

The definition of domain, developed from the criteria, is based on a concept of the reading process that supposes that students reconstruct meaning from a text by drawing on prior knowledge and experience, integrating a variety of complementary reading skills, and exploring and extending the ideas and knowledge in personally relevant ways. The instrument will assess interpretation of explicit meaning, interpretation of implicit meaning, the synthesis of elements to interpret overall focus and impact of text, the evaluation and justification of interpretation of text, and the adaptation of text by extending information.

Across Canada, there are different approaches that are used in assessing reading. The project team undertook to create an instrument that reflected a balance between different views. Every attempt to specify the design of the instrument was therefore tested for feedback. The team was committed to acknowledging the different critical views while still carrying out the mandate of developing valid and reliable assessment instruments.

Selection of texts was revised by item builders from Alberta, Quebec, and the four Atlantic provinces. Item development activities on the texts retained took place in Alberta, Quebec, and Nova Scotia over the summer of 1991 and involved about fifty teachers. Preliminary field-testing took place in the fall in

Alberta, Quebec, and New Brunswick. Extensive revision and rebuilding of items was done by the project team to address ongoing developments in the specifications of the assessment design.

Nine texts with two sets of questions were field-tested in the spring of 1992. Several more texts were field-tested in the fall. The reading assessment design has brought about new workplan and budget requirements as about fifty percent of the questions will be of a constructed response type. Such questions need to be marked by teachers according to individual scoring grids for each. A student questionnaire gathering information on each student's school, language, and reading background is included in the design.

WRITING

The original draft of a design for the writing assessment instrument was developed in June and September of 1991. One or two writing tasks were to be assigned within a two and a half hour period. A proposal was also endorsed in June to collect a sub-sample of students' best pieces of writing as one way of addressing concerns expressed about "one-shot" writing assessments.

During the summer of 1991 item-building sessions for reading, feedback was obtained from participating provinces on topics, writing tasks, and procedures. In October and November, some topics were field-tested on a small scale in Quebec and New Brunswick.

Observations gathered from the field test, discussions with English and Language Arts teacher associations, and discussions related to the MOU confirmed the need for the introduction of innovative elements in the design. As a result, pre-writing activities aimed at stimulating thoughts and collaborative work on the pre-writing activities and on the task itself were included. A student questionnaire intended to collect information on each student's school, language and writing background is part of the writing assessment material.

CONCLUSION OF STAGE TWO

An emerging issue, as of mid-summer 1992, was that of the comparability of the English and French versions of the test forms, particularly for the reading assessment.

Since the project team (Quebec and Alberta) began its work in the fall of 1990, we have attempted to achieve comparable sets in the French and English versions of all assessment materials. Materials, other than reading texts, have been translated and both versions exchanged between team members, with ongoing efforts to achieve comparable sets. An important guideline in the selection of texts for the reading assessment was that the texts be authored by Canadians and published in both official languages. This has limited the pool of potential texts that might meet other selection criteria.

We have interpreted the term "comparable sets" as meaning "parallel" in the two languages primarily from the student's point of view. For example, are the demands on the student (vocabulary, context, cognitive level, sequence) reasonably equal between the forms in both languages? The issue, in the context of the SAIP, is, "will a level 2 performance in one language be reasonably equal or parallel to a level 2 performance in the other language?"

The project team, which includes Ontario, feels confident that comparable sets in the math assessment have been achieved. Minor differences in field-test materials have been identified and will be corrected prior to the development of final materials. We are confident that the criteria and the scoring guides for mathematics are comparable in both languages.

The materials produced to date in reading and writing are also comparable. The criteria are essentially the same. The spring 1992 field test texts and the questions were identical in both languages. There is still some fine-tuning to be done on precise points of translation.

The effort to develop comparable materials for the language part of the SAIP assessment has proven considerably more difficult than for the mathematics section. There remain differences deemed to be reflective of different rhetorical traditions in Canada. One tradition appears to place more explicit emphasis on matters of detail and linguistic precision, and emphasizes a detailed analytical approach in scoring. Another language tradition places more emphasis on overall communication, with a combination of holistic and analytic approaches to scoring.

Our efforts to achieve parallelism in the reading and writing have led to questions concerning the extent to which comparability of French and English forms should be an overriding consideration. Translations of text are generally considered to be problematic. This issue is relatively minor at the lower levels of text complexity, but becomes more of a problem with more complex and literary texts. Some people in our consultations have expressed surprise, and disagreement, that we are even attempting to assess in a parallel way in the two languages.

Stage Three: Validation of the Assessment Instruments

The third stage of the project involves the validation of the assessment instruments and preparation of final forms. Validation includes ministry reviews for curriculum consistency and bias, teacher reviews for quality, and field-testing

with students across Canada. Bias reviews have been conducted by all participating ministries, using their normal provincial/territorial policies and procedures to examine the assessment materials. Feedback received was used by the
project team to revise the materials.

The project team prepared a large set of field test assessment instruments and
related materials for Canada-wide field-testing scheduled from 18 May to 12
June, 1992. School sets of materials were distributed to provincial/territorial
field test co-ordinators between 11 May and 19 May, 1992. Participating
schools had been selected by each province and territory in accord with guidelines provided by the project team in February and March, 1992.

The field-test materials prepared for each school included documents for
teacher validation of the levels and the assessment instruments. Teachers were
asked to assign their students to levels based on the criteria provided. These
teacher judgments were used as the anchor against which the field-test results
were compared. Teacher comments on the actual assessment instruments were
collated along with all other feedback received.

Standardized administration manuals were provided to each provincial/territor-
ial co-ordinator, each school co-ordinator, each field test administrator, and teachers involved in assigning students to levels and validating the assessment
instruments. Guidelines were also provided to each province and territory for conducting reviews of the SAIP field test materials for bias and curricular consistency.

Field-testing of the assessment instruments was conducted across Canada in
late May and early June. Saskatchewan was the only province that did not participate in the field testing. The Minister of Education had announced in
January that Saskatchewan was adopting observer status on the project.

Scoring of the field tests took place over the summer. The reading field tests
were scored in Edmonton in early July; the writing field tests were scored in
Montreal in late July; the mathematics field tests were scored in Quebec City in
August. Additional forms of the reading field test were field-tested in the fall.
The Edmonton marking session included teachers from Alberta, Yukon,
Ontario, Quebec, Prince Edward Island, and Newfoundland and Labrador. The
marking sessions in Montreal and Quebec City will also include a number of
out-of-province teachers, particularly from the Atlantic provinces.

The major problem with the spring field-testing was its timing, leading to
fewer participating schools than had been anticipated. In many cases, schools
were unable to conduct the field test because of the lateness in the year and the
year-end pressures associated with final exams, particularly for students in their
final year of secondary schooling. Provincial/territorial field test co-ordinators

have recommended that the full 1993 administration be scheduled for late April rather than late May.

Feedback from the teachers involved in marking the reading field tests was enthusiastic. They were impressed with the innovative assessment design, with the involvement of teachers in the scoring, and with the efforts to achieve comparability between the French and English forms of the materials. The Alberta project team compiled all feedback from students, teachers, and administrators, along with actual field test results and questionnaire responses to inform the development of fall field tests in reading and final forms.

The Quebec project team compiled student questionnaires and all other feedback from students, teachers, and administrators for the writing and mathematics field tests. The Ontario project team is developing scoring grids for writing and developed new reading material of French language origin for the fall field testing. All three project teams prepared for the marking of the mathematics field tests.

The issue of the comparability of the French and English forms for the reading assessment is currently under review by members of the consortium team, who remain committed to the principle of comparability, but are exploring alternative means of achieving that principle.[1] The project team expects to hand over the validated instruments to the CMEC in December, 1992. The CMEC is responsible for the full administration of the assessment which is scheduled for the spring of 1993 for mathematics and the spring of 1994 for the reading and writing assessment.

• • •

CONCLUSION

The November 1991 *Kappan* criticized the high-risk testing program proposed for the United States. We have tried to demonstrate that the Canadian plan is very different. The members of the consortium believe that we are very close to achieving the goals we set for ourselves. We will be able to provide the politicians with a valid measure of the performance of the provincial educational systems. Our measures will support good instructional practices and the results will be reported in a way that will minimize the chance for misuse. In addition, the criteria developed to describe the five levels of performance will provide a basis for informed debate about the expectations we hold for our schools.

• • •

NOTE

1. As this paper goes to press, the consortium team has recommended that one reading form be common to both languages, and that the other two forms in each language be assembled according to a common framework and include one common text on one and two common texts on the other. Guidelines have also been developed to ensure comparability in scoring procedures.

• • •

REFERENCES

Creative Research Group. (1987). *Literacy in Canada: A research report prepared for Southam News, Ottawa, Canada*. Toronto: Creative Research Group.

Gough, P. B. (Ed.). (1991). National testing: A *Kappan* special section. *Kappan, 73*(3), 219–251.

Government of Canada. (1991). *Prosperity through competitiveness: Draft discussion paper for pre-consultation meetings*. Ottawa: Government of Canada.

WHOLE LANGUAGE:
DEFINING OUR BELIEFS, EXAMINING OUR PRACTICES

...

Roberta McKay

INTRODUCTION

The term "whole language" is currently used in much of Canada and the United States in relation to the teaching and learning of reading and writing in schools. The various meanings associated with the term are causing controversy and lively, sometimes bitter, debate in the educational community and in the public at large. Articles appear in educational journals with titles such as "Filling the Hole in Whole Language" (Heymsfeld, 1989), followed immediately by "Whole Language *Is* Whole: A Response to Heymsfeld" (Goodman, 1989). Parents, concerned about how their children are being taught to read and write, have formed groups such as The Reading and Literacy Institute of Alberta, which has as its mission to be a resource to parents who are dissatisfied with a whole-language approach and who support intensive explicit phonics instruction. Some school districts and provincial departments of education have mandated whole language, while others may frown upon use of the term. These are examples of the type of controversy, debate, and positions "whole language" has provoked.

This article will address some of what I see as the major areas of controversy and debate surrounding whole language. This will include a discussion of these issues in a broad educational and philosophical context, and commentary related to specific issues including whole language in the Canadian context.

...

DEFINITIONS OF WHOLE LANGUAGE

A discussion of whole language must begin with some definition of the term, for the term itself has become problematic due to its many definitions and meanings.

Some define whole language as certain instructional methods and materials, while others define it as a philosophy, a set of beliefs, an attitude, or a perspective on language and language learning. Controversy arises when whole language is defined in an adversarial relationship to phonics, spelling, and grammar, implying that these are not part of whole language beliefs and practices. Weaver (1990) suggests that as the term becomes more widely used, it becomes less clearly understood, and Newman (1985) suggests that there is no simple definition of whole language because the term encompasses notions related to many aspects of teaching and learning, not just those related to language.

While acknowledging the complexities of defining whole language and the misunderstandings of the term that do exist, I believe that experts in the field generally operate from the basic position that whole language is a melding of a series of beliefs about learning, language, teaching, and curriculum (Altwerger, Edelsky, & Flores, 1987; Goodman, 1986a; Smith, 1992; Weaver, 1990). There also seems to be general agreement that methods, materials, and techniques do not sufficiently define the essence of whole language.

Altwerger, Edelsky, and Flores (1987) state that equating whole language with a method is an error in level of abstraction. Like Weaver (1990), they suggest that some practices are more reflective of whole language beliefs than others, but that "there are no essential component practices for a Whole Language viewpoint" (1987, p. 148). These scholars in the area of whole language, along with others such as Goodman, Smith, Harste et al., argue that the essentials of whole language operate at the level of component principles or beliefs. The essential question in relationship to practices in whole language then becomes, "Do my practices reflect my beliefs?" or stated another way, "Do my beliefs shape my practices?" Understanding whole language in this way enables us to see that whole language cannot be equated with the whole word approach or the language experience approach (see Altwerger, Edelsky, & Flores, 1987 for a complete discussion), but rather is a term that operates at the level of the theoretical viewpoints underlying such approaches or methods.

In this article, I will define whole language as a philosophy, inclusive of a set of beliefs about language, learning, and the relationships between and among children and adults, including teachers. These beliefs are rooted in current thought and research in a variety of disciplines including philosophy, education, linguistics, psychology, psycholinguistics, sociology, and anthropology. Perhaps most importantly, unlike many educational reforms, whole language is grounded in the beliefs and practices of teachers as they live together with children in classrooms. It is the stories of teachers and children using language that embody whole language and characterize its uniqueness and power. It is in the classroom stories that whole language beliefs about language learning and being with children come to have life. It is for this reason that most scholars in the area of whole language work with teachers and children in classrooms, co-author with teachers, and encourage teachers to write their own stories. Perhaps it is for this reason as well that Jerome Harste calls whole language "practical theory."

· · ·

BELIEFS UNDERLYING WHOLE LANGUAGE

I have argued for a definition of whole language as a philosophy, inclusive of beliefs about language, learning, and the nature of relationships between and among children and adults. The purpose of this section is to summarize what those beliefs are. Following this will be a review of the sources of these beliefs in various contributing disciplines.

Beliefs About Learning

- Learning begins in, and is nurtured through human relationships.
- Human beings learn all the time. It is not a specialized type of behaviour—it is a condition of being human.
- Learning is an active meaning making process. The learner is actively engaged with what is being learned.
- Learning is personal, social, and cultural.
- Everyone knows something.
- All learning has a past and a future.
- We learn from the demonstrations around us.
- Learning involves time, choice, response, responsibility, and risk-taking.

The danger in producing such a list is that the concepts may seem simplistic and general, easy to agree with and dismiss. Educators who shape their practices around beliefs about learning such as these realize the power embedded in the concepts and also realize that this is a view of learning that may be very different from the implicit or explicit beliefs about learning held by many educators. Behind these beliefs is a view of learning in a broader context than what happens in school September to June, Monday to Friday, 8:30 a.m. to 3:30 p.m., starting when a child is about five-years-old. If we hold beliefs such as those listed above, we recognize that a child is learning continuously, twenty-four hours a day, seven days a week, throughout life. We acknowledge the tremendous amount of understanding and skill the child brings to school and view school learning as a continuation and contribution to the life learning process, not as a beginning and ending in and of itself. We understand that learning is the product of an active reaching out on the part of a child in order to make sense of the world of people and things. Because a child is seen as an actively involved agent in the learning process, choice and risk-taking become important elements of learning. Support, encouragement, and love from other people are essential responses to foster learning. Other people are the reason for reaching out and taking risks in the first place, as a child strives to connect with those around himself or herself and ultimately be like them, specifically as well as culturally. In this way, the social and cultural context is learned by a child. This learning does not have to be rigidly controlled by others because a child wants to be like the people around her or him.

Beliefs About Language and Language Learning

- Language begins in, and is nurtured through human relationships.
- Language is our major symbol system for individual meaning making and negotiating meaning with others.
- Language is inclusive and indivisible—the whole is always greater than the sum of its parts.
- Language always occurs in context—meanings are based on interpretation of the context.
- Language is learned through use.
- Language and thought are interwoven.
- Language is personal, social, and cultural.
- Oral and written language are parallel modes; both are dynamic, constructive processes.
- Language is a rule-governed system where the subsystems (phonological, graphophonic, syntactic, semantic, pragmatic) are simultaneously present and interacting when language is used.

These beliefs about language are nested within the beliefs about learning. Language is viewed in a broad social and cultural context. It is seen as being motivated by our human relationships and enabled by the capacity of the human mind to use symbol systems to create and express meaning. Meaning is central to language and while there are subskills involved, language is learned through using it wholistically in the context of creating and expressing meaning with others. These characteristics apply to written as well as oral language.

Learning to read and write in this view are not only individual accomplishments, nor only the business of schooling, but are social and cultural, connected to the home, society, and culture of the child.

Beliefs About Teaching and Curriculum

- Teaching begins in, and is nurtured through human relationships.
- Teaching is based on well-understood and articulated beliefs about learning and language learning.
- Teaching is a process of guiding, supporting, monitoring, encouraging, and facilitating learning, not controlling it.
- The classroom and school are a community of learners.
- Teaching is geared toward individual growth.
- Teaching is based upon respect for the learner and the teacher.
- Curriculum and language processes are integrated. Language is used to learn.
- Curriculum is related to what the child experiences and knows outside of school.

These beliefs about teaching and curriculum support the beliefs about learning and language. What happens in school is viewed as building upon what a child already knows and can do with language and must connect with what she or he already knows about the world in general. Children are respected as capable and knowledgeable and not viewed as blank slates or empty vessels. Teaching is modelled more on how children learn outside of school and school learning is viewed as one part of a child's learning. The beliefs about learning and language are seen to apply to adults as well, therefore teachers are viewed as capable and able to make decisions and choices based on the needs of the particular children in their care.

Summary

The above listing of beliefs is a synthesis from many sources including Goodman, Smith, Weaver, Newman, Graves, Hansen, Altwerger, Edelsky, and Flores. The latter state that:

> the key theoretical premise for Whole Language is that, the world over, babies acquire a language through actually using it, not through practicing its separate parts until some later date when the parts are assembled and the totality is finally used. The major assumption is that the model of

acquisition through real use (not through practice exercises) is the best model for thinking about and helping with the learning of reading and writing and learning in general. (1987, p. 145)

Weaver summarizes her response to the question of beliefs underlying whole language by characterizing what she sees as "whole" in whole language. This includes language kept whole rather than fragmented into skills; literacy skills and strategies developed in the context of whole, authentic literacy events; reading and writing experiences permeating the whole curriculum; and learning within the classroom integrated with the whole life of the child. Thus, according to Weaver, "a whole language philosophy may also be referred to as a *whole or authentic literacy* philosophy, which promotes whole learning throughout students' whole lives" (1990, p. 6).

In my opinion, the key belief underlying whole language philosophy is that learning, language, and teaching begin with and are nurtured by caring, supportive human relationships. As Frank Smith so rightly points out, "methods can never ensure that children learn to read. Children must learn from people" (1992, p. 440).

• • •

WHERE DID WHOLE LANGUAGE BELIEFS COME FROM?: INSIGHTS AND IDEAS CONVERGE

The beliefs underlying whole language are a convergence of insights and ideas from many disciplines. While this is not intended to be a comprehensive review of thought and research from all contributing disciplines, I have selected work that I believe has provided fundamental underpinnings for whole language.

Whole-language philosophy is one manifestation of a much broader educational stance. This broader educational stance is based on a conception of the learner as an active constructor of meaning rather than as a passive recipient of information. The educational philosopher, John Dewey (1963), called for education to be based on an acknowledgement of the child's experience, and on the notion that what is known is inextricably connected to the knower. Weaver (1990) terms this view of learning, as an active meaning-making process, transactional, in contrast to a transmission view, where learning is characterized as passive. Others such as Barnes (1985), label these contrasting views as interpretive and transmission. Crucial to the distinction regardless of the label, is the notion of learning as an active meaning-making process in which the learner is actively engaged. Meaning, process, and human relationships are central tenets.

The transmission view of education has been influenced by the behaviourist tradition. In this tradition, the language learner is seen as passive. Noam Chomsky (1965), was one of the first linguists to suggest that rather than passively awaiting external reinforcement, children were actively attempting to understand the language around them. The work of the linguist Michael Halliday (1975, 1978) has been influential in contributing to whole language. Halliday's basic premise is that language is learned through use. From his research, Halliday postulated seven functions of language, suggesting that the child learns how to mean as he or she uses language for these functions. Halliday's theories not only stress a functional view of language, but also suggest that language and meaning are social processes. Halliday proposes a functional view of language, where language is viewed as the major symbol system through which the social system is created and expressed. The child learns the social system of the culture by using language.

Cognitive and developmental psychologists, also moving away from work done in the behaviourist tradition, have contributed to our understandings of the child as an active meaning maker. Piaget enabled us to view the child as a developing, mentally active participant in making sense of his or her experience. His work shifted our focus from product to process and the cognitive operations involved. While current work such as that of Margaret Donaldson (1978) and Jerome Bruner (1986) is reassessing some of Piaget's interpretations regarding the relationship of language and thought, his contributions cannot be minimized.

The work of Lev Vygotsky is highly significant in helping us to think about the relationship of language and thought and about how children learn and learn language. Vygotsky's work, conducted in the 1930s, was not translated from the Russian for over thirty years. His research posited that language and learning are social—that every function in the child's cultural development appears first between people (interpsychological) and then inside the child (intrapsychological). "All the higher functions originate as actual relations between human individuals" (1978, p. 57). These higher functions include language and thought. Vygotsky asserts that thought development is determined by language, that is, language (the interpsychological) leads thought (the intrapsychological). This would imply that human relationships are critical to the development of individual language and thought.

Vygotsky also has contributed to our view of learning. He recognizes, along with Dewey, that learning grows out of experience and that learning and development are interrelated from the child's first day of life. He goes on to suggest that "human learning presupposes a specific social nature and a process by which children grow into the intellectual life of those around them" (1978, p. 88). Vygotsky hypothesizes that "developmental processes do not coincide with learning processes"; rather "the developmental process lags behind the learning process," resulting in what he terms, "zones of proximal development" (1978, p. 90). The zone of proximal development is actually the zone of learning; it is where the child or learner can engage with experience with the guidance or collaborative assistance of adults or more capable peers. With the notion of the zone of proximal development, Vygotsky is suggesting that learning leads development—what a child can do today with help (learning), she can do by herself tomorrow (development). These views on language, thought, and learning, contrast to those of Piaget, who while conceiving of the child as an active meaning maker, suggested that thought leads language, and development leads learning. Piaget's views place emphasis on language, thought, and learning as moving from the individual out to the social relationships. Vygotsky places emphasis on the social relationships as the generator of individual language, thought, and learning.

Jerome Bruner's work (1986) has also contributed to our growing understanding of language and learning. Bruner states "that learning how to use language involves both learning the culture and learning how to express intentions in congruence with the culture" (1986, p. 65). For Bruner, language is the major symbolic form through which we negotiate and renegotiate meaning, and culture is the forum in which this meaning making takes place. Education, says Bruner "should also partake of the spirit of a forum, of negotiation, of the recreating of meaning" (1986, p. 123).

From this constructivist stance, Bruner emphasizes learning as a communal activity, a sharing of the culture. He states that he has reconstrued his constructs about discovery learning:

> My model of the child in those days was very much in the tradition of the solo child mastering the world by representing it to himself in his own terms. In the intervening years I have come increasingly to recognize that most learning in most settings is a communal activity, a sharing of the culture. It is not just that the child must make his knowledge his own, but that he must make it his own in a community of those who share his sense of belonging to a culture. (1986, p.127)

Educators and educational researchers looking for a research paradigm more consistent with a philosophical stance emphasizing people as active meaning makers began looking away from statistical-experimental research to disciplines such as anthropology where researchers would spend years living as part of a culture to learn about it. Such an approach falls under the broad category of human science research, defined by Van Manen as "a name that collects a variety of approaches and orientations to research in education" (1990, p. 181). These human science orientations include ethnography, ethnomethodology, symbolic interactionism, critical theory, semiotics, hermeneutics, and phenomenology (see Van Manen for a description of each). What these approaches all have in common is a focus on *meaning* and a methodical approach that uses *descriptive, interpretive*, and *critical* devices. For example, central to ethnographic research engaged in by anthropologists is direct examination of the context through participant observation, interviews of key informants of the culture, and extensive written documentation of observations, through keeping of field notes. This is done over long periods of time. Such research, termed naturalistic and contextual, was seen to be consistent with the type of beliefs underlying whole language. Harste, Woodward, and Burke argue that an experimental research approach "assumes that the world is made up of identifiable variables which interact to form a language event," whereas as an ethnographic research approach "embodies an alternative world view [where] there are no such things as variables" (1984, p. 52). Their position is that the subcomponents of a language event cannot be removed from the whole without distorting it, so the event must be observed in its entirety. Ethnographic research enables such observation of language events in context. This type of research is important for teachers to know about. Whole language philosophy blurs the distinction between teachers and researchers. All are seen as learners in the classroom context. What teachers and children know and can do is valued. The classroom site and the relationships there are seen as central to understanding teaching and learning. This research often is written up as stories of life in classrooms and has great meaning for teachers as they see other teachers and children engaged in language and learning in the context of real classrooms.

Moving to such a research paradigm or model, educators and educational researchers began to spend time with teachers in classrooms observing children as they actually engaged in language and learning. Other researchers, such as Wells, Clay, Holdaway, and Heath, began observing the language development and interactions of children in their home environments. Weaver (1985) states "it is predominantly naturalistic research that has provided the theoretical basis for a whole language philosophy." Such research "stems from observation and analysis of how children learn language and develop an increasingly sophisticated understanding of their world, how they learn to read and write in relatively natural settings, and how readers process text to construct meaning" (1990, p. 127).

Across such research and thought, language learning is viewed in broader more inclusive, interconnected contexts. What happens in school is seen as part of a larger cultural context, with a major premise being that reading and writing are not only individual achievements and not only the business of formal schooling but are part of the broader context of real life literacy.

This paradigm or view of language and learning emerging from the convergence of insights and ideas from many disciplines is being paralleled in sciences such as quantum physics, chemistry, and biology. Weaver (1985), in a brilliant article illuminating some of the parallels between new paradigms in science, reading, and literary theory, states that an emphasis on organicism and process are basic to both. She sees this organic view as being in sharp contrast to the mechanistic model that has been so widely accepted in the sciences and which has also been highly influential in reading and literary theory. Weaver outlines four major "revolutionary" concepts that are common to the emerging paradigms in both the sciences, in reading, and literary theory:

1. Reality is fundamentally an organic process.

2. There is no sharp separation between observer and observed, reader and text, reader/text and context.

3. The whole (universe, sentence, text, etc.) is not merely the sum of parts which can be separately identified.

4. Meaning is determined through transactions (between observer and observed, reader and text, reader/text and context, and among textual elements on and across various levels). (pp. 312–313)

Summary: Insights and Ideas Converge

I have taken considerable space nesting whole language in a philosophical and educational context broader than the teaching of reading and writing in school because I believe an understanding of these contexts is crucial to understanding whole language. It is critical to see that the beliefs underlying whole language are part of a large and interconnected body of thought on how the world works, on how we think about the world in general, and how we think about education. While people may choose to take opposing views to those underlying this view, or paradigm, it is important to understand that whole language is not an isolated phenomenon nor a peculiar educational bandwagon, but is part of a powerful paradigm or view that is influencing the sciences and the humanities and places emphasis on understanding our world from an organic and process-oriented position. When seen as part of a powerful philosophy and system of beliefs, whole language cannot be as easily dismissed as when it is seen at the level of just another fad or method to teach reading and writing.

Questions and issues related to whole language then are not only questions at the level of teaching methods but are questions and issues at a broader level of belief system; how we view the world and ourselves in relation to it; questions of the relationships between the whole and the parts at the level of the universe.

. . .

THE EDUCATIONAL CONTEXT

Educators, both teachers and researchers, began to think about the implications of the research and thought described above for language learning and teaching. Britton (1970, 1992) focussed on the importance of talk in school for developing thinking. The role of talk between and among students was emphasized. Goodman (1967) proposed a psycholinguistic model of reading that recognized the presence of the cuing systems of graphophonics, syntax, semantics, and pragmatics in the reading process. Reading began to be viewed as not just a "one way street" of getting meaning from the page, but as an interactive process whereby the reader actively constructs meaning, based on what he or she brings to the page. Viewing reading as a meaning-making process in which the reader is actively engaged meant a focus first on whole text.

Understanding reading in a broader context of society and culture, suggested a move away from the concept of reading readiness, with a focus on particular skills prerequisite to reading, to a focus on emergent literacy, where learning to read was viewed as a continuous process over time influenced by the child's total experience with reading and writing events in the context of daily living.

Writing, too, began to be viewed as a process, as teachers and researchers spent time observing what adult writers and child writers actually do when they write (Britton, Emig, Murray, Graves). Based on the kind of beliefs about language learning outlined previously, teachers and researchers working together began to ask how teaching practices needed to change to reflect their beliefs about language and learning. Whole language became a reform movement in North American education, characterized by classroom teachers making changes to their practice based on their meaning-focussed, process-oriented beliefs about language, learning, and teaching. Altwerger, Edelsky, and Flores state that the overriding consideration for classroom practice in relation to reading and writing is "that these be real reading and writing, not exercises in reading and writing" (1987, p. 145). They further characterize classroom practices consistent with whole language beliefs as consisting of a print-rich environment including literature and environmental print, writing for a variety of purposes, focus on curriculum topics as the context for much of the real reading and writing, and a focus on assessment as observation and documentation of children's growth in their actual work.

• • •

POLARIZATION: WHOLE LANGUAGE VERSUS PHONICS, SPELLING, GRAMMAR, BASALS

Underlying much of the controversy surrounding whole language is a polarization of the concept with more traditional approaches to teaching language arts, particularly beginning reading. Whole language has been drawn into the "Great Debate" (Chall, 1967, 1983, 1989; Carbo, 1988) of whether phonics or whole-word approaches are the most effective way to help children learn to read. As discussed earlier, equating whole language with an approach is an error in level of abstraction but there are other issues as well. Research done by Clay (1975, 1976) and others such as Harste (1984) and Holdaway (1979) has helped us to realize that early reading and writing are part of a child's "growing into" the literacy of the society and culture surrounding him or her. As Smith argues, children learn to read more from "the company they keep" (1988, 1992) than anything else. Learning to read must be seen in a far broader context than whether or not phonics is emphasized in primary school years.

Another issue is the way in which whole language is placed in an adversarial position to phonics; the debate becomes phonics versus whole language, implying that the two are mutually exclusive. This is incorrect. In the psycholinguistic model of reading, Goodman outlines the major "cuing" systems that interact simultaneously to give the reader language cues as he or she constructs meaning. These include the pragmatic system (situational context, intent, and expectations), the graphophonic system (letter-sound correspondence), the syntactic system (grammatical framework), and the semantic system (meaning brought to language by reader, writer, listener, speaker). All of these systems of language are always present and working together simultaneously as a reader constructs meaning. For this reason, when children come to words they do not know when reading, they need to be able to draw on many strategies including a process of asking questions: what is this story about; what do I know about this topic, about this type of story that will help me think about what words would make sense (pragmatics, semantics); what do I know about the type of word that would make sense in this place in a sentence (syntax); and what do I know about the sounds these letters and combinations of letters make that can help me know what word this is (graphophonics). To suggest that phonics is not considered part of whole language is simply incorrect. The disagreement comes again at the level of beliefs—do we teach/learn from whole to part or part to whole?

Dorothy Watson (1989) states that isolated phonics lessons fragment language and are not consistent with whole language beliefs. However, she says that using graphophonic information as a confirming strategy in combination with the other language cuing systems would be consistent.

Similar issues are involved in controversies regarding the teaching of spelling and grammar. Writing process research (Graves, Calkins) like reading process research, focusses on meaning and process, but not to the exclusion of skills and products. The issues again are confused when areas like spelling and grammar are seen to be excluded from writing practices consistent with whole language beliefs. Just as phonics are part of reading in whole language, spelling and grammar are part of writing in whole language. The issues are the same—do we teach/learn from whole to part or part to whole? Whole language proponents would argue that spelling strategies and grammatical correctness are taught/learned within the context of the writing process rather than as isolated skills, fragmented from their usefulness in assisting communication of written meaning as a finished public product.

In my work with pre-service teachers, I have found that while these teacher novices may agree with the philosophical stance and beliefs about language and learning inherent in whole language, unless they have specific alternatives for how to work with children in the context of the whole in the areas of phonics, spelling, and grammar, they revert to practices that focus on these as isolated skills. This is understandable and underscores the importance of viewing whole language as beliefs that are the basis for our practice. We need the interplay of both. Beliefs without consistent practices do not become realized in action. Practices without articulated beliefs behind them become merely activities, methods, and materials that are ends in themselves, rather than means to an end. When we run out of the activities and materials, we don't know what to do next because we don't know why we were doing them in the first place. We have no context for our practice. We need to know *what* to do and *why* we are doing it. Beliefs provide the continuous threads that weave practices into a meaningful fabric of learning.

The controversy of basals versus literature is also complex. Basal readers have traditionally been written for the purpose of teaching reading. As such, older basal series had controlled vocabulary and skills sequences built into stories written for the sole purpose of teaching reading. The basal approach involved all children, or groups of children sorted by ability, reading the same story at the same time and being taught the same specified decoding and comprehension skills through prepackaged teacher guide material and student workbooks.

Whole language beliefs would not be reflected in either the practice of writing stories for the sole purpose of teaching reading nor with the practice of having all children read the same story all the time and be taught the same skills. Whole language advocates suggest that real literature should be the basis for reading. Other issues revolve around who controls the learning/teaching, when basal series are utilized. Certainly, teachers and children do not have ownership or choice and both can be disempowered when such programs are followed prescriptively. Since whole language with its focus on real books and literature has become an educational movement, publishing companies have rushed in to produce "whole language" series. These series, while many utilize real stories and literature, continue to raise the same issues from the whole language point of view as the older basal series. These include issues of control of teaching and learning, and issues of "basalizing" whole language processes by such practices as having all children go through a certain series of "steps" each time they write, in the name of the writing process or replacing contrived stories with literature to teach reading, but not changing anything else. Graves says "the enemy is orthodoxy" (1984, p. 184). Replacing old orthodoxies or maxims for teaching with new ones does nothing to change learning and teaching. Graves argues that to guard against this, it is critical to listen to and observe children and take our cues about what to do next from them, not from any step by step, inflexible program or set of teaching orthodoxies.

This again points out the problems of defining whole language only as methods and materials and of changing practices without defining and articulating beliefs. Malicky (1991) suggests that while whole language philosophy may have the potential to place power and control in the hands of teachers and children, many of the practices being done in the name of whole language do very little, if anything, to realize such emancipatory goals of literacy. She argues that "whole language has been essentially basalized in Canada" and that this, "in combination with the adoption of commercial series by provincial governments has removed control and power from children and teachers and placed it in the hands of publishers and editors" (1991, p. 344).

The pitting of whole language against phonics, spelling, grammar and basals, while erroneous to begin with, engenders an "either-or" stance that prevents examination of the beliefs we hold about language, learning, and teaching and how these shape our practice. The "either-or" stance separates and fragments, forces us to take one position and exclude or dismiss the other.

. . .

UNDERSTANDING THE CONCEPT OF DEMONSTRATIONS: WHOLE LANGUAGE IS NATURAL LEARNING

Another area provoking controversy occurs when whole language proponents argue that learning to read and write is natural and easy and that children will learn how to do these things without isolating skills and instructing in fragmented ways. Two areas of controversy emerge from these statements, one concerning what we mean by learning "naturally" and the second, related issue, that teachers are somehow abdicating their responsibilities if they are not "teaching" these skills—the issue is what we mean by "teaching."

Many whole language advocates such as Ken Goodman and Frank Smith operate from the belief that learning is natural. As discussed previously, learning from this stance is seen not as a specialized type of behaviour, but as a condition of being human. As such, it is "continuous, spontaneous, and effortless, requiring no particular attention, conscious motivation, or specific reinforcement; learning occurs in all kinds of situations and is not subject to forgetting" (Smith, 1992, p. 432). Smith goes on to state that learning is social and that in combination with being natural, learning, in this view, can be summarized in these words: "we learn from the company we keep" (1992, p. 432).

It is at this point that an understanding of Smith's notion of learning from the demonstrations around us becomes critical. He suggests that the young want to become like those around them, they want to become "members of the club." In the broadest sense, this means they want to be human in the way they see those around them being human. Children learn quite effortlessly and spontaneously what is demonstrated to them by those around them. But what does this mean? An example often cited is that children learn to walk naturally. But natural does not mean that they are left on their own and that suddenly one day the child walks, as a single "now you have it, now you don't" event. Everyone around the child walks. This is a demonstration to the child—it is not done to teach the child to walk; it is done because this is part of being human. In addition to this powerful demonstration by all those around them, the child's caregivers facilitate learning to walk. They often provide toys and devices that stimulate the child to move. They care for the child so his or her body grows and develops physically. They celebrate the first day the child flips over, crawls, walks with help, takes a step alone. They encourage, support, and assist. They teach the child to walk in this way. So while this may be said to be a natural process, it would not occur without the demonstrations of walking by those the child wants to be like and the other "teaching" that the people around the child do over a lengthy period of time.

I believe that lack of understanding and explicit explanation of what we mean by learning as "natural" has led some people to believe that advocates of whole language believe "anything goes" and that teachers won't be teaching the children anything. Demonstrations and teaching of the kind I have described in learning to walk are essential to whole language beliefs and practices. Children must see the people around them, whom they want to be like, demonstrating literacy as a meaningful activity in and out of school, and they must be nurtured and supported in a learning environment that is structured so learning and teaching can occur "naturally."

Part of the reason that public focus on whole language tends to be at the level of teaching methods, is that we in the teaching profession have not articulated well what the underlying beliefs of whole language are. When we as teachers say such things as "I teach whole language so I don't teach phonics, grammar, and spelling because the children will learn them naturally," it is understandable that the public might interpret this to mean that we are abdicating our teaching responsibilities and taking an "anything goes" attitude. We must articulate our beliefs about language and learning to parents, treat their questions seriously, and specifically be able to discuss with them the practices we are using as their children are learning to read and write.

Smith believes that large numbers of teachers regard whole language as a method and "do not trust children to learn unless their attention is controlled and their 'progress' monitored and evaluated" (1992, p. 440). This raises issues of how or if staff development related to whole language has taken place. To be effective, our staff development practices must also reflect whole language philosophy and beliefs about language and learning. Staff development that demonstrates a transmission view of teaching and learning cannot successfully enable teachers to examine whole language beliefs and practices. Teachers must be involved in staff development practices that are like the practices reflecting whole language beliefs that we want to encourage with their students. This means acknowledging teachers as active constructors of meaning, as individuals who know something, and as people who use language to learn.

This issue of making our beliefs explicit and examining our practices in light of our beliefs is critical, regardless of whether the source of our beliefs is in a transmission or transactional, interpretive view of education. Smith suggests that the great debate about learning to read perhaps should never end and he argues, "the most productive way to deal with fundamental educational controversies might be to take them into every school and every community where they can be dissected, discussed, and honestly argued (1992, p. 441). And I would argue that the debate should be raised beyond the level of arguments over how and when to teach phonics, spelling, and grammar, whether to use literature or basals, portfolios or standardized tests, to the level of the underlying beliefs about language and learning that guide each of these practices, whether or not we are explicitly aware of it.

• • •

WHOLE LANGUAGE IN CANADA

The issues related to whole language are similar in Canada to those in the United States. Most of the public controversy focusses not on issues of philosophical stance and what we believe about language, learning, and human relationships, but on issues of teaching practices related to phonics, spelling, grammar, use of basal readers, and assessment.

While much of the early research related to whole language philosophy and specific work related to oral language, reading, and writing has come from the United States and Great Britain, Canada is recognized as being on the forefront of implementing whole language beliefs, not only at the classroom level but at the level of policy documents issued from ministries and departments of education. Weaver states, "Canada is significantly ahead of the United States in moving toward a transactional model of education, as reflected particularly in a whole language philosophy" (1990, p. 63). She suggests that for several years now, provinces such as Alberta, British Columbia, Quebec, and Nova Scotia have had models of education more reflective of a transactional than a transmission model of education. Goodman (1986a) notes that "whole language views are represented in official documents and innovative practices all across Canada (1986a, p. 63).

As an example, Alberta Education has recently implemented a *Language Learning Program of Studies* (1991) that replaces the previous language arts curriculum guide. The new document is built around seven fundamental principles about language learning and the conditions that support it. Although these principles are reflective of whole language philosophy, the term "whole language" does not appear anywhere in the document. While whole language philosophy and beliefs have been sanctioned in Alberta as good language learning pedagogy, the term has been avoided, likely due to the controversies and misunderstandings surrounding it. While taking this stance on the one hand, Alberta Education has also listed for approved use several prepackaged "whole language" series. For some teachers, this may prove problematic, if they do not have well-defined beliefs about language, learning, and teaching to guide the use of such materials.

In Alberta, not only does the *Language Learning Program of Studies* (1991) reflect a transactional or interpretive view of learning and teaching, but this is also being utilized in provincial program development in mathematics and science. A learning model is being used in all three areas that focusses on meaning as a process of exploring, constructing, and communicating. This seems to add considerable support to the idea that whole language is neither a bandwagon nor a fad approach to teaching reading but rather is based on a philosophy and beliefs with broad educational and societal implications.

While whole language philosophy and beliefs are only recently becoming influential in formalized curriculum, an important feature of whole language in Canada for many years has been the grassroots support of whole language beliefs through the networking of teachers. For example, in Winnipeg, Halifax, and Edmonton, as well as many other areas across Canada, there have been support groups formed of teachers who share whole language beliefs and meet regularly to discuss how these beliefs can shape their practice.

For several years, during the mid- to late-1980s, the *Whole Language Newsletter* was distributed across Canada by Scholastic-TAB Publications Ltd. It was originally free of charge and was published as a service to classroom teachers and consultants. The newsletter addressed concerns of teachers who were interested in whole language and its implementation and offered support through editorials related to philosophy and beliefs, and through articles, written by teachers and consultants, related to their classroom practice. Although the newsletter is no longer published, it served as a network for Canadian teachers interested in whole language—a Canada-wide support group.

Mary Clare Courtland, at Lakehead University in Ontario, agrees that whole language is garnering much interest and support across Canada but suggests that implementation is not without its concerns and that there are issues to be addressed. As discussed previously, the essential components of whole language are beliefs about language and learning, not specific activities and materials. For this reason, research cited by Courtland (1990) on implementation of whole language in Canada suggests that a basic problem is teachers' lack of a strong theoretical base upon which to anchor their practice.

Some teachers implement in a way consistent with whole language philosophy; others are implementing one or more elements of whole language such as journals or writing folders and labelling the combination whole language. There appears to be confusion about the role of the teacher, the use of appropriate strategies for teaching spelling and language usage, the correction of student's errors and grading practices.

Courtland points out that Canadian faculties of education are also experiencing confusion over the meanings of the term whole language and that the range of meanings to which pre-service teachers are exposed varies across classes and student teaching experiences.

Courtland suggests that we must pay attention to the questions and issues raised by parents, teachers, and teacher educators. If whole language is to permanently change language teaching and learning which Courtland argues it has the potential to do, it must survive its current "bandwagon" appeal and the predictable fate of most educational bandwagons.

• • •

CONCLUSION

Whole language philosophy has the potential to change dramatically what is happening in schools, not only with respect to teaching reading and writing, but in a much more pervasive and profound sense as we act on associated beliefs about the nature of teaching and learning. Yet, despite the fact that the research and thinking for over more than twenty years has been generating a re-examination of traditional ways of viewing language learning in schools, it seems that there is much misunderstanding, suspicion, and perhaps little that has changed. Malicky suggests that despite three decades of debate, "the bottom line has changed very little. There are still significant numbers of children being labelled as failures in reading and writing in our schools" (1991, p. 333). She makes the observation that "most children, particularly those from middle-class families, will learn to read no matter whether we use a phonics approach or a whole language approach because they have been read to many thousands of hours before they arrive at school and hence can make sense of phonics instruction" (1991, p. 343). She points out that it is poor and minority children who often do not come to school with this advantage and that more of these children "fail to learn to read than those from middle-class backgrounds no matter what approach is used" (1991, p. 343).

This is why it is so crucial that whole language be understood *first* as a philosophy consisting of interrelated beliefs, not just about language, but also about learning and the nature of the relationships between and among children and their teachers. As long as whole language is viewed at the level of methods, activities, and materials, its potential to change schooling and thus society will not be reached. For emancipatory goals of literacy to be realized, we must examine the issues on the level of what we believe about language, learning, and children in our society and culture and ask questions about how our beliefs shape our practice. It seems relatively easy to echo belief statements about active meaning-making, choice, faith in the learner, the importance of a sense of community to language and learning, and that language is learned as it is used in the dealings of our daily lives. The difficult part is to examine our practices for their congruence to our beliefs. If whole language is not making much difference in the teaching of reading and writing and other teaching/learning practices, either our current practices are incongruent with our beliefs, or we do not really believe what we say we do—we hold other beliefs that are guiding our practice.

This is not an issue of which set of beliefs is right or wrong, but rather an issue of being up front and explicit about what these beliefs are—making those beliefs public, open to examination and debate. Dewey states that "any theory or set of practices is dogmatic which is not based upon critical examination of its own underlying principles" (1963, p. 22). This is what Graves is warning us against when he says to beware of the orthodoxies—beware of turning whole language beliefs and practices into "the truth."

Sharon Rich, a former editor of *The Whole Language Newsletter* says "we must be careful not to insist that everyone accept our beliefs and practices without question. If we do that, we have simply exchanged one type of authoritarian system for another" (1985a, 1985b).

Weaver (1985) suggests that the organic paradigm of how the world works must transcend dichotomies of "either-or" and suggests that it must be inclusive to avoid becoming a prison that prevents us from understanding other aspects of our world.

We must define our beliefs about language, learning, and teaching in terms of what we want for our society and culture. When we do this we raise issues of power and control; of politics. Those who view whole language at the level of a philosophy and belief system realize that whole language is about power and control at many levels. Is the power and control of learning/teaching with children and teachers in any given classroom, or is it with the prepackaged publishers' materials, the provincial programs of study, and the school district and provincial testing programs? And what do the answers to these questions suggest about issues of power and control in our society and culture? Rich says "teaching is a political act to the extent that it has the power to either free or enslave minds" (1985). The whole language "debate" or "controversy" must rise above the level of polarization, "either-or," and address the critical issues of what we really believe about language, learning, and teaching and the potential of those beliefs to either free or enslave minds.

• • •

REFERENCES

Alberta Education. (1991). *Language learning program of studies*. Edmonton: Author.

Altwerger, B., Edelsky, C., & Flores, B.M. (1987 November). Whole language: What's new? *The Reading Teacher, 41*, 144–154.

Barnes, D. (1985). *From communication to curriculum*. Harmondsworth: Penguin.

Britton, J. (1970). *Language and learning*. London: Alen Lane, Penguin Press.

Britton, J. (1992). *Language and learning* (rev. ed.). London: Penguin.

Britton, J., Burgess, T., Martin, N., McLeod, A., & Rosen, H. (1975). *The development of writing abilities* (11–18). Urbana, IL: NCTE.

Bruner, J. (1986). *Actual minds, possible worlds*. Cambridge, MA: Harvard University Press.

Calkins, L.M. (1980 May). When children want to punctuate. Basic skills belong in context. *Language Arts, 57*, 567–573. In R.D. Walshe (Ed.), *"Children want to write . . .": Donald Graves in Australia* (pp. 89–96). Portsmouth, NH: Heinemann.

Calkins, L.M. (1983). *Lessons from a child*. Portsmouth, NH: Heinemann.

Calkins, L.M. (1986). *The art of teaching*. Portsmouth, NH: Heinemann.

Cameron, I., & Mickelson, N. (1989). Whole language and basal readers. *Reading-Canada-Lecture, 7*(3), 267–271.

Carbo, M. (1981). *Case study of Jimmy*. Roslyn Heights, NY: Reading Styles Inservice Notebook.

Carbo, M. (1984 May). Why most reading tests aren't fair. *Early Years K-8*, 73–75.

Carbo, M. (1987 February). Reading style research: "What works" isn't always phonics. *Phi Delta Kappan, 68*, 431–435.

Carbo, M. (1987 March). Ten myths about teaching reading. *Teaching K-8, 17*, 77–80.

Carbo, M. (1987 November). Deprogramming reading failure: Giving unequal learners an equal chance. *Phi Delta Kappan, 69*, 197–202.

Carbo, M. (1988 October). What reading achievement tests should measure to increase literacy in the U.S. *Phi Delta Kappa Research Bulletin*, No. 7.

Carbo, M. (1988 November). Debunking the great phonics myth. *Phi Delta Kappan, 70*, 226–240.

Chall, J. (1967). *Learning to read: The great debate*. New York: McGraw-Hill.

Chall, J. (1983). *Learning to read: The great debate* (rev. ed.). New York: McGraw-Hill.

Chall, J. (1989 March). Learning to read: The great debate 20 years later—A response to "Debunking the great phonics myth." *Phi Delta Kappan, 70*, 521–538.

Clay, M. (1975). *What did I write?* Portsmouth, NH: Heinemann.

Clay, M. (1976). *Young fluent readers*. London: Heinemann.

Clay, M. (1986 February). *Why reading recovery is the way it is*. Paper presented at the Reading Recovery Conference, Ohio Department of Education, Columbus, Ohio.

Clay, M. (1987). *Writing begins at home.* Portsmouth, NH: Heinemann.

Clay, M. (1988). *The early detection of reading difficulties* (4th ed.). Portsmouth, NH: Heinemann.

Courtland, M.C. (1990). Reflections on whole language. *L.A.R.C. Newsletter, 1*(2). Canadian Society for the Study of Education.

Dewey, J. (1963). *Experience and education.* New York: Collier.

Donaldson, M. (1979). *Children's minds.* New York: W. W. Norton.

Emig, J. (1971). *The composing process of twelfth graders.* Urbana, IL: NCTE.

Emig, J. (1983). *The web of meaning: Essays on writing, teaching, learning, and thinking.* Portsmouth, NH: Boynton/Cook.

Froese, V. (Ed.). (1990). *Whole language: Practice and theory.* Scarborough, ON: Prentice-Hall.

Goodman, K. (1965). A linguistic study of cues and miscues in reading. *Elementary English, 42,* 639–643.

Goodman, K. (1967). Reading: A psycholinguistic guessing game. *Journal of the Reading Specialist, 6,* 126–135.

Goodman, K. (1973). *Theoretically-based studies of patterns of miscues in oral reading performance.* Detroit: Wayne State University. Educational Resources Information Center. ED079708.

Goodman, K. (1986a). Basal readers: A call for action. *Language Arts, 63,* 358–363.

Goodman, K. (1986b). *What's whole in whole language?* Richmond Hill, ON: Scholastic-TAB. Available in the U.S. from Heinemann, Portsmouth, NH.

Goodman, K. (1989). "Whole language is whole: A response to Heymsfeld." *Educational Leadership,* 69–70.

Goodman, K. S., & Goodman, Y.M. (1979). Learning to read is natural. In L.B. Resnick & P.A. Weaver (Eds.), *Theory and practice of early reading, Vol. 1* (pp. 137–154). Hillsdale, NJ: Erlbaum.

Graves, D. (1983). *Writing: Teachers and children at work.* Portsmouth, NH: Heinemann.

Graves, D. (1984). *A researcher learns to write.* Exeter, NH: Heinemann.

Gunderson, L., & Shapiro, J. (1987 Spring). Some findings on whole language instruction. *Reading-Canada-Lecture, 5*(1), 22–26.

Halliday, M. A. K. (1975). *Learning how to mean: Explorations in the development of language.* London: Edward Arnold.

Halliday, M. A. K. (1978). *Language as social semiotic.* London: Edward Arnold.

Hansen, J. (1987). *When writers read.* Portsmouth, NH: Heinemann.

Hansen, J. (1989). Anna evaluates herself. In J. Allen & J.M. Mason (Eds.), *Risk makers, risk takers, risk breakers* (pp. 19–29). Portsmouth, NH: Heinemann.

Hansen, J., Newkirk, T., & Graves, D.M. (Eds.). (1985). *Breaking ground: Teachers relate reading and writing in the elementary school.* Portsmouth, NH: Heinemann.

Harste, J.C. (1984). *Language stories and literacy lessons.* Portsmouth, NH: Heinemann.

Harste, J.C., Woodward, V.A., & Burke, C.L. (1984). Examining our assumptions: A transactional view of literacy and learning. *Research in the teaching of English, 18,* 84–108.

Heath, S.B. (1983). *Ways with words: Language, life, and work in communities and classrooms.* Cambridge: Cambridge University Press.

Heymsfeld, C.R. (1989). "Filling the hole in whole language." *Educational Leadership,* 65–68.

Holdaway, D. (1979). *The foundations of literacy.* Sydney, Australia: Ashton-Scholastic. Available in the U.S. from Heinemann.

Holdaway, D. (1984). *Stability and change in literacy learning.* London, ON: University of Western Ontario. Available in the U.S. from Heinemann.

Holdaway, D. (1986). The structure of natural learning as a basis for literacy instruction. In M.R. Sampson (Ed.), *The pursuit of literacy.* Dubuque, IA: Kendall Hunt.

Malicky, G. V. (1991). Myths and assumptions of literacy education. *The Alberta Journal of Educational Research, 37*(4), 333–347.

Manning, G., & Manning, M. (Eds.). (1989). *Whole language: Beliefs and practices, K-8.* Washington, DC: National Education Association.

Newman, J. (1984). *The craft of children's writing.* Richmond Hill, ON: Scholastic-TAB. Available in the U.S. from Heinemann, Portsmouth, NH.

Newman, J. (1985). Insights from recent reading and writing research and their implications for developing whole language curriculum. In J.M. Newman (Ed.), *Whole language: Theory in use* (pp. 1–36). Portsmouth, NH: Heinemann.

Newman, J.M., & Church, S.M. (1990). Myths of whole language. *The Reading Teacher, 44,* 20–26.

Rich, S.J. (1985a). Restoring power to teachers: The impact of "whole language." *Language Arts, 62,* 717–724.

Rich, S.J. (1985b). The politics of teaching. *The Whole Language Newsletter, 3*(2). Richmond Hill, ON: Scholastic-TAB.

Smith, F. (1971, 1978, 1982, 1988). *Understanding reading.* Hillsdale, NJ: Erlbaum.

Smith, F. (1979, 1985). *Reading without nonsense.* New York: Teachers College Press.

Smith, F. (1981 January). Demonstrations, engagement, and sensitivity: A revised approach to language learning. *Language Arts, 58,* 103–112.

Smith, F. (1981 September). Demonstrations, engagement, and sensitivity: The choice between people and programs. *Language Arts, 58,* 634–642.

Smith, F. (1983). *Essays into literacy.* Portsmouth, NH: Heinemann.

Smith, F. (1988a). *Insult to intelligence: The bureaucratic invasion of our classrooms.* Portsmouth, NH: Heinemann.

Smith, F. (1988b). *Joining the literacy club: Further essays into education.* Portsmouth, NH: Heinemann.

Smith, F. (1989 January). Overselling literacy. *Phi Delta Kappan, 70,* 352–359.

Smith, F. (1992). Learning to read: The never-ending debate. *Phi Delta Kappan,* 432–441.

Vacca, R. T., & Rasinski, T. V. (1992). *Case studies in whole language.* Orlando, FL: Harcourt Brace Jovanovich.

Van Manen, M. (1990). *Researching lived experience.* London, ON: The Althouse Press.

Vygotsky, L.S. (1978). *Mind in society: The development of higher psychological processes.* Ed. M. Cole, V. John-Steiner, S. Scribner, and E. Sopuberman. Cambridge, MA: Harvard University Press.

Vygotsky, L.S. (1982). *Thought and language* (E. Hanfmann & G. Vakar Trans.) Cambridge, MA: MIT Press.

Watson, D. (1989). Defining and describing whole language. *The Elementary School Journal, 90,* 129–141.

Weaver, C. (1985). Parallels between new paradigms in science and in reading and literary theories: An essay review. *Research in the Teaching of English, 19,* 298–316.

Weaver, C. (1990). *Understanding whole language: From principles to practices.* Toronto: Irwin Publishing.

Wells, G. (1986). *The meaning makers: Children learning language and using language to learn.* Portsmouth, NH: Heinemann.

Derek J. Allison, Ph.D., is an associate professor in the Division of Educational Policy Studies in the Faculty of Education at the University of Western Ontario. His research and writing centre on theories of organization, administration, and leadership with specific reference to the development and current operation of schools and state schooling systems. He is presently involved in studies of problem solving in the principalship of school systems and the structure of cognitive theories used in adminstrative behaviour.

Lawrence Manning Bezeau, Ph.D., is an associate professor in the New Brunswick Centre for Educational Administration in the Faculty of Education at the University of New Brunswick. His research and writing interests lie in the areas of school law, education finance and planning, research methodology, and computer applications to social science research.

Daniel R. Birch, Ph.D., is a professor of education and vice-president (academic) at the University of British Columbia. His research and writing focus on teacher education and on social studies and cross-cultural understanding.

James Brackenbury, M.A., is the director of the Alberta team for the development of the Council of Ministers of Education, Canada, School Achievement Indicators Program. He has been a teacher in the Alberta school system, a regional consultant, and an assistant director of curriculum with Alberta Education.

S. Brenton-Haden, M.Ed., is a lecturer in the Department of Educational Psychology at the University of Alberta. Her research and writing interests are in metacognition, teacher training, and special needs children.

Donald A. Burgess, Ph.D., is an associate professor in the Department of Administration and Policy Studies in Education in the Faculty of Education at McGill University. His research and writing interests include Quebec education and education and the law.

Stephen Thomas Carey, Ph.D., is Director of Modern Languages Education at the University of British Columbia, Vancouver. His research focusses on bilingualism, academic achievement, minority language policy, and international education.

Larry Eberlein, Ph.D., is a professor in the Department of Educational Psychology at the University of Alberta. His research and writing are concerned with the implications of law and ethics in the fields of education and psychology.

Murray Elliott, Ph.D., is an associate professor teaching philosophy of education in the Department of Social and Educational Studies at the University of British Columbia. He is also the associate dean (teacher education). His research and writing interests centre on teacher education and moral and religious education.

William T. Fagan, Ph.D., is a professor in the Department of Elementary Education at the University of Alberta. His research and writing interests focus on language arts, the cognitive and linguistic processes underlying reading, methodology for assessing reading and cognitive behaviour, effective strategies for teaching reading, and the philosophies of reading and their relationships to the effective teaching of reading.

Frederick Frank French, Ph.D., is an associate professor and the co-ordinator of the graduate program in school psychology at Mount Saint Vincent University. His research and writing focus on cognitive processing in children and adolescents, cognitive instructional models for use in schools, special education administrative policies in Canada, and career development models as a part of the academic, personal/social, and career needs of youth.

John D. Friesen, Ph.D., is a professor in the Department of Counselling Psychology at the University of British Columbia. His research and writing focus on the family and the socialization of children, the interface between the school and the family, career development, parenting, marriage preparation, and marriage and family therapy.

John W. Friesen, Ph.D., is a professor in the Department of Educational Policy and Administrative Studies at the University of Calgary. His research and writing interests are in multicultural education, Native education, anthropology in relation to minority groups, language and culture, and teaching as a profession.

Robert Stephen Gall, Ph.D., is a professor in the Department of Educational Psychology at the University of Lethbridge. He is also an associate of the National Institute of Mental Retardation and co-ordinator of communications with the Alberta Education Response Centre Project. His interests are in rural special education, microcomputer applications to special education, microcomputer telecommunications in special education, and rights/equity issues in special needs education.

Jane Gaskell, Ph.D., is a professor in the Department of Social and Educational Studies at the University of British Columbia. Her research and writing interests are in the sociology of education, schooling and work, women's experience in education, and social science research and public policy.

William J. Hague, Ph.D., is a professor in the Department of Educational Psychology at the University of Alberta. His research and writing interests are in the psychology of religious and moral development and in counselling psychology.

Edward Stephen Herold, Ph.D., is a professor in the Department of Family Studies at the University of Guelph. His research and writing interests focus on the sexual and contraceptive behaviour of Canadian youth.

Gretchen C. Hess, Ph.D., is an associate professor in the Department of Educational Psychology at the University of Alberta. Her research and writing interests centre on learning and development, adolescence, school health and guidance curricula, sex education, student teaching practica, and professional communication among educators and health professionals.

Dale C. Howard, Ph.D., is an assistant professor in instructional psychology at the Centre for Research in Distance Education at Athabasca University. His research and writing focus on human and computer interactions and on the transition from secondary school to university-level studies.

David Jenkinson, Ph.D., teaches in the Department of Curriculum: Humanities and Social Sciences at the University of Manitoba. His research and writing interests are in children's and adolescent literature and school librarianship.

Gerard Martin Kysela, Ph.D., is a professor in the Department of Educational Psychology at the University of Alberta. Dr. Kysela's research and writing interests are in early intervention with families and younger children who exhibit exceptional conditions or handicaps, in policy development in the field of educating exceptional children, in early childhood intervention, and in transitional experiences for youth and young adults from secondary school to vocational life situations.

Romulo F. Magsino, Ph.D., is a professor and head in the Department of Educational Administration and Foundations at the University of Manitoba. Dr. Magsino's research and writing interests lie in the areas of multicultural education; the rights of students, parents, teachers, and school boards; moral education; and teacher education.

Stewart J.H. McCann, Ph.D., is an associate professor in the Department of Psychology at the University College of Cape Breton. His research and writing interests are in the interactions of student characteristics and teaching strategies; individual differences and academic achievement; the effects of social, political, and economic threats and stressors on various aspects of society and education; worry; and political leadership.

Roberta McKay, Ph.D., is an assistant professor in the Department of Elementary Education at the University of Alberta. Her research and writing interests include language learning, constructivism, children's writing, language, and thinking, teacher education, journal writing, classroom research, social studies education, and integration of curriculum.

Robin P. Norris, M.Ed., is a professor in the School of Nursing at Ryerson Polytechnical Institute. Her research and writing interests are in special education, nursing education, and higher education.

C. Paul Olson, M.A., is an associate professor in the Department of Sociology in Education at the Ontario Institute for Studies in Education. His research and writing interests are in the areas of inequality and social reproduction; the politics of bilingualism, particularly in regard to the introduction of French immersion into the school system; and computer usage in the schools.

G. Patrick O'Neill, Ph.D., is a professor in the Graduate Department of the Faculty of Education at Brock University. His research and writing interests are in special education, teacher education, and higher education.

Louis A. Pagliaro, Pharm.D., Ph.D., is a professor in the Department of Educational Psychology at the University of Alberta. His research and writing interests are in the areas of substance abuse education and treatment, computer-assisted instruction, intravenous drug use and AIDS, and pharmacopsychology.

Roger Palmer, Ph.D., is an Assistant Deputy Minister of Education in Alberta and chairs a project team established by the Council of Ministers of Education, Canada, to lead the development of the School Achievement Indicators Program. He has taught in England and has been a teacher and administrator with Edmonton Public Schools.

Alan R. Pence, Ph.D., is a professor in the School of Child and Youth Care at the University of Victoria. He is interested in historical and ecological perspectives and research approaches to early childhood care and working parents.

David Pratt, Ph.D., is a professor of education at Queen's University. He has also been a high school teacher in Ontario and in England. His research and writing interests are in curriculum planning, history teaching, selection and education of teachers, and technical and humanistic orientations to education.

Douglas William Ray, Ph.D., is a professor of educational policy studies in the Faculty of Education at the University of Western Ontario. His interests include human rights in education, multiculturalism, international understanding, international development, the development of human rights curriculum materials for elementary education, and international curriculum development projects.

Leonard L. Stewin, Ph.D., is a professor and chair in the Department of Educational Psychology at the University of Alberta. His research and writing interests focus on the developmental aspects of concept formation, information processing and its applications in learning, and the social psychology of the classroom.

Edmund V. Sullivan, Ph.D., is joint professor of applied psychology and history and philosophy in education at the Ontario Institute for Studies in Education. His research and writing focus on various religious and educational topics and issues.

Carl Urion, Ph.D., is a professor in the Department of Educational Foundations at the University of Alberta. His research and writing interests focus on anthropology and education, education of Amerindians, anthropology linguistics, ethnographic methodology, applied anthropology, and education in development in North America.

Marvin J. Westwood, Ph.D., is an associate professor in the Department of Counselling Psychology in the Faculty of Education at the University of British Columbia. His research and writing interests are in the areas of group and inter-cultural counselling.

Lorraine Wilgosh, Ph.D., is a professor in the Department of Educational Psychology at the University of Alberta. Her research and writing interests focus on vocational/career education for individuals with disabilities, and adjustment and coping of families of children with disabilities.

John Rowland Young, M.Ed., is an associate professor in the Department of Educational Foundations and the Department of Sociology at the University of Alberta. His interests are in social theory, multiculturalism, and the socio-historical analysis of Canadian education.